LET ME
BE MELTED
IN THY
DIVINE OCEAN
AS A PEARL
IN WINE.

VADAN

A Pearl in Wine

A Pearl in Wine

Essays on the Life, Music and Sufism of Hazrat Inayat Khan

Edited by
Pirzade Zia Inayat Khan

Omega Publications
New Lebanon

The material contained in *A Pearl in Wine* is original work with the exception of Raden Ayou Jodjana's article, which appears here by permission of the C.W. Daniel Co.; and Jerome Clinton's article, parts of which appeared elsewhere in different form as noted in his article. Except as noted, translations in the articles have been provided by the author of the article.

Cover design by Nikitas Kavoukles.
Book design by Abi'l-Khayr.

Published June, 2001
Cloth 0-930872-69-X
Paper 0-930872-70-3

Omega Publications
256 Darrow Road
New Lebanon NY 12125-2615
goodbooks@omegapub.com

The publisher invites you to explore other materials drawn from the Sufi tradition at www.wisdomschild.com.

Contents

I. LIFE

II. MUSIC

III. SUFISM

IV. MEMOIRS

Illustrations

Color Plate Section Following Page 48

Sangītratna Mawlābakhsh
Murtażā Khān
Ḥaydar 'Alī
Ṭīpū Sulṭān
Zanāna in 1896, photo by 'Usmān Khān
Murtażā Khān and Sardār Bī, with servant children
'Alā al-Dīn Khān (Dr. A.M. Paṭhān) and Chānd Bī
Allāhdād Khān and Mehr al-Nisā'
Prof. Inayat Khan Rahmat Khan Pathan
Hazrat Inayat Khan
Portrait of Hazrat Inayat Khan by M.H. Thurburn, 1913
Hazrat Inayat Khan playing the *vīṇā*
Hazrat Inayat Khan, Amina Begum and family
Children of Hazrat Inayat Khan and Amina Begum
The Royal Musicians of Hindustan
Maheboob Khan
Musharaff Khan
Muhammad Ali Khan

Color Plate Section Following Page 304

Dargāh of Ḥażrat Khwāja Mu'īn al-Dīn Chishtī
Dargāh of Ḥażrat Khwāja Quṭb al-Dīn Bakhtiyār Kākī
Ḥażrat Khwāja Farīd al-Dīn Mas'ūd Ganj-i Shakkar
Dargāh of Ḥażrat Khwāja Farīd al-Dīn Mas'ūd Ganj-i Shakkar
Dargāh of Ḥażrat Khwāja Niẓām al-Dīn Awliyā'
Khānqāh of Ḥażrat Khwāja Niẓām al-Dīn Awliyā'
Dargāh of Khwāja Naṣīr al-Dīn Maḥmūd Chirāgh-I Dihlī
Dargāh of Ḥażrat Shaykh Kamāl al-Dīn 'Allāma
Dargāh of Ḥażrat Shaykh Sirāj al-Dīn, Ḥażrat Shaykh 'Ilm al-Dīn, and Ḥażrat Shaykh Maḥmūd Rājan
Dargāh of Ḥażrat Shaykh Jamāl al-Dīn Jamman
Dargāh of Ḥażrat Shaykh Ḥasan Muḥammad and Ḥażrat Shaykh Muḥammad Chishtī
Masjid of Ḥażrat Shaykh Ḥasan Muḥammad

Dargāh of Ḥażrat Shaykh Shāh Kalīm Allāh Jahānābādī
Dargāh of Ḥażrat Shaykh Shāh Niẓām al-Dīn Awrangābādī
Dargāh of Ḥażrat Shaykh Mawlānā Fakhr al-Dīn
Dargāh of Ḥażrat Shaykh Ghulām Quṭb al-Dīn
Dargāh of Ḥażrat Shaykh Ghulām Naṣīr al-Dīn Kāle Miyān
Dargāh of Ḥażrat Shaykh Muḥammad Ḥasan Jīlī Kalīmī
Dargāh of Ḥażrat Shaykh Abū Hāshim Madanī
Dargāh of Hazrat Pir-o-Murshid Inayat Khan

Images Included in the Text

Diagrams

A glossary of foreign terms not explained in the text of chapter one appears on pages 59–60, courtesy of Shaikh al-Mashaik Mahmood Khan; a separate glossary of foreign musical terms used in the *Music* section appears at the end of that section, on pages 204–205, courtesy of Prof. Allyn Miner.

Introduction

Nearly a century has passed since Hazrat Inayat Khan introduced the practice of Sufism to Europe and North America, a century that has witnessed the appearance of numerous varieties of Sufism in these regions. Indeed, Western Sufism already has a rich and complex history. Until very recently however this history has gone almost entirely unnoticed in academic publications. And even now, scholars known for their insightful readings of premodern Sufi texts almost never maintain similar standards of research and analysis when discussing modern Western developments. The implicit assumption is that Western Sufism is merely a pale imitation, or worse a corruption, of "classical" models.

It is as a challenge to this assumption that this volume presents itself. The view is taken here that Western Sufism represents a historically significant phenomenon in its own right, deserving of close examination and thoughtful interpretation in its many facets. Inasmuch as Hazrat Inayat Khan laid the groundwork for those that came after him, conditioning the discourse of his followers and critics alike, his biography and body of work are prime material for such a project.

The thirteen essays in this volume collectively bring to the fore Hazrat Inayat Khan's remarkable multidimensionality. The figure that emerges eludes easy categorization. We are confronted with a paragon of high Mughal culture who was equally a forerunner of postnationalist cosmopolitanism; a performer of sacred music and a sage with a musical message; a tradition-sanctioned Chishtī initiator inspired with an urgent transcendental vision of radical ecumenism and global spiritual renewal.

The opening section, focusing on Hazrat Inayat Khan's biography, begins with a pair of essays by Shaikh al-Mashaik Mahmood Khan. Shaikh al-Mashaik's survey of Hazrat Inayat Khan's genealogy is informed by oral traditions that have until now remained the exclusive preserve of the Mawlābakhsh family, to which the author belongs. His second essay offers a critical review of the available biographical material. The next essay, by Donald Sharif Graham, views Hazrat Inayat Khan as an institution builder. Drawing on legal documents and unpublished papers, among other sources, Prof. Graham traces the early development of the organizations he founded, the Sufi Order and the Sufi Movement.

The two essays that make up the next section, on music, examine Hazrat Inayat Khan's Hindi and Urdu musicological writings and gramophone recordings. Prof. R.C. Mehta evokes the artistic milieu of turn-of-the-century Baroda. Dr. Allyn Miner guides us through Hazrat Inayat Khan's Urdu masterpiece, *Minqār-i mūsīqār* ("The Beak of the Musiqar"), written in Hyderabad. Both essays offer insights into the interplay between mysticism and music.

The third section considers the literature and institutions of Sufism in the premodern and modern periods. In Dr. Jerome W. Clinton's essay, Hazrat Inayat Khan's well-known sexual egalitarianism prompts a finely nuanced rereading of a classic Sufi fable. Dr. Omid Safi finds echoes of the Persian Sufi "Path of Love," pre-eminently represented by Aḥmad Ghazālī and 'Ayn al-Qużat Hamadānī, in Hazrat Inayat Khan's message of Love, Harmony and Beauty. Hazrat Inayat Khan's *silsila* (initiatic genealogy) is traced from Khwāja Mu'īn al-Dīn Chishtī to Sayyid Abū Hāshim Madanī, with synopses of the lives and teachings of each of the successive lineage-holders, in the editor's essay. In Dr. Marcia Hermansen's contribution, Hazrat Inayat Khan's brief but fateful contact with Khwāja Ḥasan Niẓāmī is recalled. In comparing the two figures, Dr. Hermansen shows how impulses common to both took divergent channels due to the differing cultural contexts of their respective careers. The section closes with Pir Vilayat Inayat Khan's analysis of some of the most original aspects of his father's teaching.

The volume concludes on an informal note, with three memoirs. The first, excerpted from *A Book of Self Re-education* by Raden Ayou Jodjana, offers first-hand reflections on the personalities of Hazrat Inayat Khan, his family, and early disciples. In the memoir which follows, Murshid Wali Ali Meyer draws upon official esoteric archives, recorded interviews, and his own memory to recreate important moments in the history of Sufism on the North American West Coast. Finally, Peter Lamborn Wilson presents a lively account of his experiences of the Chishtī Order in India in the

1960s and '70s. Through a bricolage of observations and anecdotes Wilson artfully evokes the unique *zawq* ("savor") of the Chishtiyya.

In addition to the authors, several individuals brought great energy and dedication to the preparation of this volume. Abi'l-Khayr, Publisher of Omega Publications, offered immense support at every stage, and also compiled the index and bibliography. Saniya Ammerlaan assisted in the technical preparation of Shaikh al-Mashaik Mahmood Khan's articles and created the accompanying charts. Hafizullah extended crucial technical assistance and provided the calligraphic flying heart *nishān*. Moineddin Kavoukles designed the cover and retouched all illustrations. Shaikh al-Mashaik Mahmood Khan attentively read the manuscript and offered numerous improvements. Dr. Allyn Miner provided the definitions and appropriate transliterations of Sanskrit terms (any remaining errors are solely the responsibility of the editor). Hayat Ruh helped greatly in innumerable ways. Dervish Sirri drew the borders featured on the cover and epigraph. The volume was generously supported by grants from The Sufi Order International, North America, and Richard M. Glantz. Each has my deep gratitude.

Zia Inayat Khan

Hazrat Inayat Khan

Life

Mawlābakhshī Rājkufū A'lākhāndān: The Mawlābakhsh Dynastic Lineage, 1833–1972

SHAIKH AL-MASHAIK MAHMOOD KHAN

The biography of Hazrat Inayat Khan, poet-philosopher and musician-mystic, is best studied against its most authentic background: the era of the Mawlābakhshī *a'lākhāndān*. Brief but brilliant, that may be said to run from the birth of Sho'le Khān Mawlābakhsh in 1833 to the death of his sole grandson in line male, Allāhdād Khān-i Mawlābakhsh (A.M. Paṭhān the younger) early in 1972.[1] After him, the Mawlābakhshī *a'lākhāndān* as a kinship, occupational, status and cultural unit evaporated, due to a conjunction of both exterior and internal causes. Amongst the latter, the major factor clearly has been the unforeseen permanence of the "saint-musician" Hazrat Inayat Khan's absence (until autumn 1926) and that of his brothers' (until 1967) in the West. Few things can have been as unintended by them, and so ultimately ruinous to all (in that it destroyed all members' natural home base, with the fatal weakness that entailed), as the decay of their *ashraf rājkufū pavitra a'lākhāndān-i Mawlābakhsh* (or *-i Mawlābakhshī*).[2] Yet how important Mawlābakhsh, the "prince-musician," and his life's work forever remained to them is illustrated by the fact that not even the shortest biographical note on any of them omits mention of him, their maternal grandfather.

Before 1833 begins the field of oral prehistory, to which future examination of extant records in time may provide some corroboration or correction. As will be the case with outstanding

---

[1] A genealogical diagram of family members mentioned in the text is on page 61.

[2] For definitions of Arabic, Persian, Urdu, and Sanskrit terms, see the glossary at the end of this article, pages 59–60.

personalities, the life stories of both Mawlābakhsh and Hazrat Inayat Khan have sprouted outgrowths of popular embellishment—interpretative, fanciful or indeed (in the former case), adverse. Moreover, in Mawlābakhsh's case, the kind of popular stories always floating about in the Indian public domain occasionally have attached themselves to his colorful personality as to so many others. Indeed, the seniormost authority on the Mawlābakhshī musical tradition today, the eminent musicologist Prof. R.C. Mehta, of Baroda, has grown so skeptical of all such mythology as to prefer discarding even such reasonably reliable biodata as to how Sho'le Khān turned into Mawlābakhsh or became a pupil of Ghasīṭ-khwān. It is true of course that even such events remain marginal to his outstanding accomplishments in the theory and practice, composition and scholarship of Indian music. Three brief but useful biographies of Mawlābakhsh are available to us today. Hazrat Inayat Khan's own 1915 article strikingly sums up Mawlābakhsh's musical activities and ideals.[3] Those are elaborated further in the uncharacteristically competent entry on him in the *Biography of Pir-o-Murshid Inayat Khan*, a selective secretarial compilation of anecdotes and memoirs as eloquent in its omissions as its contents.[4] Building upon and expanding from those data through tireless journalistic enquiry, Van Beek offers an informative all-round image that includes Mawlābakhsh's two sons and three daughters as well.[5] Many useful remarks are found in Musharaff Khan[6] and Dr. E. de Jong-Keesing,[7] as well as in the early T'Serclaes,[8] Bloch[9] and more recent

---

[3] Inayat Khan, "Moula Bux," *The Sufi Quarterly* 1, no. 3 (1915): 47–55.

[4] *Biography of Pir-o-Murshid Inayat Khan*, ed. Nekbakht Foundation (London: East-West Publications, 1979).

[5] Wil van Beek, Hazrat Inayat Khan: Master of Life, Modern Sufi Mystic (New York: Vantage Press, 1984).

[6] Musharaff Moulamia Khan, *Pages in the Life of a Sufi* (London: Rider, 1932; reprint, Wassenaar, Holland: Mirananda, 1982).

[7] Elisabeth E. de Jong-Keesing, *Inayat Khan, a Biography* (London and the Hague: East-West Publications, 1974; revised edition, New Delhi: Munshiram Publishers, 1981).

[8] Rycklof-Michael Cunningham baron de T'Serclaes de Kessel, "Biography of the Author," introduction to *A Sufi Message of Spiritual Liberty* (London: The Theosophical Publishing Society, 1914).

[9] Regina Miriam Bloch, *The Confessions of Inayat Khan* (London: The Sufi Publishing Society, 1915).

Pallandt[10] introductions of Inayat Khan to his Western audiences and readers.[11] Jean Overton Fuller's well-known best-seller *Madeleine*, a masterpiece of careful investigation and striking description, was republished in an expanded version as *Noor-un-nisa Inayat Khan*, which includes almost an overdose of historical fragments cited as once current in Sufi adherents' circles, so by now largely antiquated but in view of their pioneering character and the book's deservedly widespread readership, well worth drawing into the discussion of certain biographical details.[12] Some significant new data recently have been included in Prof. Allyn Miner's fascinating research work on *sitar* and *sarod* history.[13] Her introduction to *Minqār-i-mūsīqār*, providing new data and insights, is indispensable to all students of the life and work of both Mawlābakhsh and Hazrat Inayat Khan.[14]

Hazrat Inayat Khan's valuable 1915 article was not his first endeavor of the kind. During his "ladhood," as *Biography* has it (i.e. from the ages of seven to ten according to its very first editor, Alim Almgren), he already drew up a sketch of Mawlābakhsh's life that was published in the Gujarati journal *Mahajan Mandal* later, in 1896, the year of Mawlābakhsh's death. At the time of that early effort, to young Inayat, musicianship ranked only and uniquely with sainthood and nobility. Subsequently disenchantment with less-than-holy or -aristocratic musicians not only shocked him but quite clearly has provided one early incentive to his consistent spiritualization of music and nobility in later life. Indeed, it would

---

[10] Floris baron van Pallandt, "Hazrat Inayat Khan's Life and Work," in *The Sufi Message and the Sufi Movement*, introductory booklet to *The Sufi Message of Hazrat Inayat Khan*, 12 vols. (London: Barrie and Rockliff, 1964).

[11] To readers of Dutch, Theo van Hoorn's Herinneringen aan Inayat Khan en het Westers Soefisme (Memoirs of Inayat Khan and Western Sufism) (The Hague: East-West Publications, 1981) cannot too strongly be recommended for his recollections of the Suresnes Summer Schools and its highly cultured, idealistically Romantic participants, colorfully reviving a vanished era. The omission in that context of the notable, early Sufi philosopher Louis Hoyack (mentioned in the next article) should be rectified by consulting van Beek and Biography.

[12] Jean Overton Fuller, *Madeleine* (London: Gollancz, 1952); revised edition, *Born for Sacrifice* (London: Pan Books, 1957); revised edition, *Noor-un-Nisa Inayat Khan* (Rotterdam and London, East-West Publications and Barrie & Jenkins, 1971).

[13] Allyn Miner, *Sitar and Sarod in the 18th and 19th Centuries* (Wilhelmshaven: Florian Noetzel Verlag, 1993; reprint, Delhi: Motilal Banarsidas Publishers, 1997).

[14] Allyn Miner, introduction to *Minqar-i musiqar* (forthcoming).

not be surprising in the least if more advanced research than has long been possible, should here find the reply to his particular version of the *dos pou sto* query. That is to say, his specific firm ground from which to move the world, rather than from some spot of messianic religious reform of a kind often so imaginatively imputed to him by his following in the as yet headily Romantic second and third decades of the twentieth century. However, the above ladhood sentiment (which in a sense never left him or his brothers), explains the charming but curious initial line on Mawlābakhsh's origins that precedes a life story with which, even as the "lad" he then was, Inayat of course could be familiar himself. His opening statement proudly proclaims that Mawlābakhsh was descended of "a caste of Muslim musicians," a claim genealogically sufficiently puzzling to provoke a corresponding rejoinder. They were not a caste, not Muslims, and not musicians. That is to say, strictly, they no longer were a caste group but not quite fully yet a *khāṣṣat* one; that in turn due to the fact that rather than Muslims they were as yet *musalims*, recent converts to whom the three-generation rule of social convention was not yet entirely applicable; whilst even as musicians they were no genuine professionals at all, but at best talented dilettanti, music having filled their leisurely land-owning days alongside an (inevitably mystical) religion and the (obligatorily mounted) martial arts—that holy trinity of traditional Indian gentry (in so far as not rather addicted to the unholy triad of game, drink and women).

This is no mere genealogical hair-splitting. It is this set of circumstances that helps to solve a highly pertinent question posed by Professor Mehta, as upon further consideration he was then able to confirm. The problem is that Mawlābakhsh's musical pedigree cannot be traced, either by descent or transmission, to any of the known *gharānās* or *khāndāns* of what Professor Miner so aptly defines as the "lineage musicians," the established court professionals so largely, if not exclusively, responsible for the cultivation and development of classical Indian music throughout the ages. How then could he, as an upstart musician suddenly arising from nowhere, as a single individual in a collectively ordered society, in the cultural context of his day, have secured such wide recognition and acclaim? Had not his importance in and for

Indian music more or less been overrated by posterity? In other words, were not on the one hand his social pre-eminence and on the other the dissemination of his fame even unto the West by his admiring grandson Inayat, reflected in the posthumous estimates of his music and musical scholarship? (Where and when, for instance, would he himself ever have staked a claim to be the "Founder" or "Inventor" of Indian musical notation—apparently a non-problem under recent discussion in India?)

There were two considerations that persuaded Professor Mehta that questions like those mentioned above (and quite apart from what later adulation might have attributed to him without further investigation) could be decided safely in favor of Mawlābakhsh's genuine musical quality. The above genealogical one will be illustrated further in what follows. A purely musical consideration regarded as very convincing by Professor Mehta, was Mawlābakhsh's long and close association with the greatest *pakhāvaj*-player of his time, the well-established and universally celebrated Naṣīr Khān. That he should have associated himself above all with Mawlābakhsh when all the subcontinent's greatest soloists would eagerly have sought his collaboration, constituted in Professor Mehta's view indubitable evidence of Mawlābakhsh's exceptional musical stature. *Biography* mentions Naṣīr Khān as his lifelong friend. Hazrat Inayat Khan's brothers recalled Naṣīr Khān's striking remark on Mawlābakhsh's death: "Now, my art has become as a widow"; a photograph of his remained one of their cherished mementos. A fuller description is given in Musharaff Khan.[15]

Now to return to the question of origins. To a popular or religious, i.e. a "public" musical performer, it would have been next to impossible to enter the secluded "private" world of musical *khāndān*s and *gharānā*s dominating the world of classical music from the courts, to say nothing of the Brahmanical music of the South. In the absence of copyright security, musical as so many other skills were strictly guarded and handed down only within the tight loyalty bonds of kinship and "initiatic" linkage (the latter the cultural counterpart of feudal vassalage). On the other hand, however, transition from a cultured *zamīndārī* level to courtly circles or feudal magnates could come naturally whenever need

---

[15] Musharaff Khan, *Pages*, 81–82.

arose. Professionalization of leisure proficiencies cannot always have been easy psychologically, but if accepted could turn out admirably. Success at the courts could lead to renewed acquisition of *zamīns* and/or *jāgīrs*, allodial and feudal estates, and to the return to a *rentier* lifestyle now enhanced by proven talents and courtly honors.

Thus, leisured cultural proficiency meant gentry security. And there was a need for such insurance. In matters of property and inheritance, the Hindu joint family, rather like the British strict settlement or the European fideicommis, was perfectly adjusted to landed or urban real estate, securing its continuance for generations without recurrent subdivisions. Exactly the opposite, however, was true of Islamic canon law, laying down division of property amongst numerous categories of heirs. That had nothing to do, as is sometimes asserted, with proto-democratic or crypto-socialist tendencies, but simply reflected the Arab realities of the earliest Islamic times. As the ancient Arabs were socially organized in tribes and clans, such property divisions mainly amounted to redistribution within the group itself, in any case responsible for the wellbeing of all its members. Since, moreover, the principal wealth of those early Arabs consisted of herds and flocks, then extending to merchandise and such urban bounties, rather than large landed estates or investment properties (prior, that is, to Islamic imperial expansion), division between multiple heirs was fair enough. In predominantly agricultural societies, it was little less than disastrous. Reliance on local *'ādat* rather than on *sharī'at* provisions continued to be a recurrent preoccupation amongst Muslim landowners, presupposing, of course, family members' loyalty to their *khāndān* as such, beyond whatever personal relations might be (cf. Khadīja Bī's remarks on her paternal inheritance[16]). But where family relations became strained, or the younger generation sought to strike out on its own, tensions could naturally run high. In Muslim societies, it would appear, mechanisms and conventions of reconciliation always have been rather superior to those of conflict avoidance or containment; at least in India, however, the base line remained that, above all, any such tensions if occurring must not percolate onwards to still

---

[16] Nekbakht Foundation, *Biography*, 33.

younger generations of descendants. What all that amounts to is that where amongst Indian Muslim landowners *sharī'at* (Islamic canon law) property divisions did prevail, descendants in time might find themselves left with precious little or no land. And like British younger sons and continental cadets, they might well go off seeking fortune elsewhere from whatever skills family culture might have imparted to them as the more valuable bequest—a point tellingly made by Khadīja Bī.

Now, literature and poetry, the religious sciences and such artistic or scholarly concerns were essentially urban accomplishments—lengthy, costly, calling for introductions and intermediaries to be cultivated not only for their own sake, but profitably practiced in society; much the same applied to an adequate military position. But that highest and most distinctive of Indian arts and sciences, music, despite all its courtly glamour, yet also had always retained something of its earliest Brahmanical, ascetic, world-renouncing associations. That is, as we would say: quite private and personal associations; in highly gregarious non-Western societies, privacy becomes like, and is perceived as, some kind of renunciation! (cf. Hazrat Inayat Khan's *Moral Culture*, lectures in which renunciation becomes the spiritualization of privacy or individualism). A talented young man lacking inheritance but adequately cultured, could honorably renounce his home society and seek musical training from some such kind of individual preceptor, whether ascetic or otherwise. The musical student years of both Mawlābakhsh and Mashaykh Raḥmat Khān provide a good example of such "renouncing" training.

Culturally close as India's peoples generally are, yet, given the kinship unit's being the basis of society and the highly distinctive character of each religious faith and law, conversion to another religious system is bound to be a radical step. Without going that far, indeed, even a girl's marriage into a caste-wise acceptable but otherwise unrelated family is regarded almost as we would regard naturalization into another land. The same applies where, conversely and much more exceptionally, a bridegroom is taken on into his bride's family as *dāmād-i ghar*, mostly for particular reasons in special circumstances. That being so, the impact of the much more radical step of conversion, rather than one into another kinship group, may well be imagined: not just a change of citizenship, but of national consciousness and socio-cultural identity. But beyond that, it also involves an absolute change of legal status. In both Hindu and Islamic law, all kinship relationships, family ties and everything those entail, become null and void by conversion and its consequent transition to another legal system. Even where Hindus or Muslims live under alien, secular legal systems, those standards continue to be observed (beyond the barest legal inevitabilities the system of their adopted domicile involves) in every moral and social sense and with all possible emphasis—a change of identity all concerned will have to acknowledge as such. Much the same applies, of course, in case of marriage between incompatible caste groups with Hindus and such Muslims as seek and manage to dodge the egalitarian and not confessionally exclusive provisions of *sharī'at* law. Needless to say, therefore, that in such conversion cases all rights of ritual or ceremonial, and inheritance participation, or succession, lapse automatically, and that by universal Indian consent: the consequences of a change of identity have to be absolute, or else the very security of identity provided by the caste and community systems would be in serious peril. And from that point of view, the anonymous mass individualism of the present-day West is seen as an awful instance of human insecurity, ultimately benefiting only those latter-day high priests, the psychiatrists.

A new lineage

The oral tradition is secretive but specific as to how the Mawlābakhshī family originated. The decisive step, transition from Hinduism to Islam, was taken by the scion of a *zamīndār* family supposedly in the fourth ascendant generation from Mawlābakhsh, that is, by his great-grandfather. He is said to have been of a Brāhman group, his name being given as Vyās or Byāsjī. Here the questions begin. "Brāhman," in older usage, might refer not only to one caste and its several ramifications, but to the religious community in its entirety, that is, as synonymous with "Hindu." Van Beek notes that the name in question might equally well be a caste sub-group's as a personal one. The variant form, Byāsjī, does make a personal name much more likely. That still leaves his caste category unaccounted for. In general, only Rājpūts or singularly aspiring Kśatriyas would have felt free, upon islamization, in a society functioning under tight social control, to assume or claim authorization to adopt the title or caste designation of *khān*. Brāhman or other "twice-born" Hindu converts would rather adopt that of *shaykh*. But then, again, as *zamīndārs*, landed gentry, convert members of any such Hindu category *would* have been able to turn into Khāns, then rather in the sense of "gent." or "esq."

In any case, Vyas/Byāsjī as a convert of whatever caste category, must have taken a Muslim *ism-laqab* (suffixed name); this has not been transmitted. Inevitably, that raises the question whether Mawlābakhsh's great-grandfather or, rather, his grandfather, was the *musalim* who turned from Vyas into, supposedly, Anvar Khān. The latter identity, however, raises questions of its own, for the same name has been attributed in some early notes to Mawlābakhsh's maternal uncle and his first music teacher, which then found their way into Western biographical descriptions of comparably happy-go-lucky character. A clear confusion of identities, of course, since in the case of two or more close associates of similar *ism-laqab*, some distinguishing term would have been added to either. This threefold Anvar-khānlical riddle now seems definitely solved thanks to Prof. R.C. Mehta's quite recent unearthing of an early Gujarati work which, though including some inaccuracies of its own, equally clearly offers details indubitably correct. This recently discovered work states that it was Mawlābakhsh's maternal grandfather, Anvar Khān, who was his earliest music teacher.

In Indian terminology, maternal and paternal relations are, of course, too clearly distinguished to leave room for any confusion. In *Biography*'s English, it is said that Mawlābakhsh's "grandfather Anvar Khān had been a successful singer."[17] It must have been its earliest editor, Almgren (first also to venture a clarifying "family-tree"), who understood that to mean what any Western reader would suppose, i.e. a reference to the paternal lineage. It could not pass altogether unnoticed that this grandfather Anvar Khān then also forms the first of the "five generations of musicians" that in early printed materials had to compensate for the fact that Mawlābakhsh and Hazrat Inayat Khan did not

[17] Nekbakht Foundation, *Biography*, 19.

descend from any long-established musical *khāndān* or *gharānā*. If that were the intended emphasis, it would provide another good illustration of how among them the matrilineal line continued to be as genealogically weighty as the paternal one.

The early reference to a maternal uncle rather than grandfather is very probably an easy confusion in orally transmitted and vaguely-remembered recollections. In the Mawlābakhsh family and their social environment, there had always been a certain emphasis on the maternal uncle, "*māmūṅ*"—that is, however, the one of Ṭīpū Sulṭān, Qāsim Bī's direct ancestor. Even more decisively, however, it was his maternal uncle (hence, Anvar Khān's son or son-in-law) who accompanied young Mawlābakhsh on his early journeys, first to Ratlam and Tonk State, and, after his stay at Baroda, to Bombay and onwards.

Quite clearly, then, the reference was to Mawlābakhsh's maternal grandfather, Anvar Khān, who taught the young Mawlābakhsh for the three years or so following upon his meeting with the Chishtī dervish, and then encouraged him to travel in search of "a real master." This remark might well suggest that Anvar Khān would have been a talented dilettante. Had he been a genuine professional, it is hard to imagine he would have encouraged Mawlābakhsh to seek a change of masters, and a really competent one, and then have accompanied him in doing so. Here again, the initiatic rather than businesslike nature of the master-disciple linkage should be borne in mind—the sacred, unchanging, indissoluble bond of a teaching and occupational relationship: the *gurū*, the "inspiring teacher," fulfils, in his transmission of knowledge and abilities, the divine function in human life that culminates in the "illuminated soul" of mystical spirituality.

There is no divergence in the oral tradition, however, as to the reason for Byāsjī's islamization: his daughter's marriage to a "Mughal." Of course, some of the more remote oral sources had to assert matrimony into the imperial dynasty or even to the sovereign himself—all that obviously preposterous. "Mughal" simply is one of the four categories that make up the immigrant *ashrāf* (nobles') group of Indian *khāṣṣa* (or *khāṣṣat*) Muslims, the others being the Sayyids, the Paṭhāns and the Shaykhs, according to most authoritative accounts (and discarding the gradual but steady upward movement into most of them). The usual inference is, however, that his arrangement of that clearly prestigious marriage caused such dismay amongst his own joint-family group that he took the further step of islamization (if we follow on what all reports agree). However, for ages, Indian Muslims—immigrants *and* converts—have been marrying Hindu wives, who by and large remained free, especially in the higher and highest social strata, to continue with their own religion, as were Christian and Jewish wives further West. To this day, in such cases it is said "she accepted *nikāḥ*," i.e. Islamic law marriage (and normally, a Muslima name); whether that implies religious acceptance as well, or continuance with her own *dharma*, or some kind of mix of both, is nobody's business. The blind bigotry that would seek to compare aspects of Hinduism with pre-Islamic Arab polytheism is laughed off by most Indian Muslims (and not merely the educated ones) as a rather ridiculous form of insanity. And they have history on their side, for the first Arab invaders in India (from C.E. 711) were given specific orders to discard any such analogy. In other words, there would have been no need for Vyās' daughter, let alone for himself, to decide on religious conversion. But on the other hand, in an orthodox Hindu view, he had rendered his own child casteless—an insult to the purity of the caste shared by all its members. This, incidentally, would seem to make it likely that they indeed were of some Brāhman caste group, and so particularly meticulous about their ritual condition. Yet again, this conversion in itself also illustrates how the *zamīndār* landowners as a group had in fact grown together in the social and cultural sense. Only religion distinguished the Hindu, Sikh and Muslim amongst them. And precisely because of this, within the kinship group itself, that distinguishing element might well be all the more stressed, particularly in devout families. Nevertheless, transition still remained one within the larger socio-cultural framework and outlook shared by all, and from that angle Vyās' islamization remained a relatively minor step and certainly a rather easy one in the personal sense. He did, of course, have to relinquish his caste and joint-family circle, along with the livelihood it secured. This he would have known, and so been able to afford, from the outset. The Islamically anonymous convert forefather, despite his son's equal namelessness, yet has always been understood to be Mawlābakhsh's great-grandfather. That also was the view of "Ammā-ḥużūr," the Nepalese wife of Dr. A.M. Paṭhān, who counted six generations from Byāsjī to Allāhdād Khān. Dr. Paṭhān, Mawlābakhsh's younger son of a Mahratti mother, was the only family descendant willing openly to mention the Vyās conversion and descendance—a testimony to his secular sympathies and his unimpeachable social position.

Finally, the question must be raised whether, given the close affinities of the *zamīndār* class, Vyās might not rather have become Muslim either from cultural assimilation, religious conviction, or social aspiration. In that case, his daughter's Mughal marriage would simply have been a logical consequence, but one sufficiently spectacular later to have come to be regarded as the main feature of the Vyās conversion itself. Given the general nature and character of Indian traditions, this view is the one that most recommends itself to the present writer, but cannot of course be more than a theory.

Be that as it may, Vyās the *musalim* and his family—who *Biography* notes generally had "an inclination towards music"—remained prosperous enough to continue a leisured lifestyle and secure it for his two sons. It seems he had been fortunate in acquiring well-watered lands, including a high-grade freshwater well, apparently much in demand in the neighborhood (and so possibly an additional source of income). For his son and two grandsons, Gīsū Khān (after the mystic Gīsū-darāz) and Imām Khān, there were no marital problems: they all married in the Mughal or Paṭhān groups, generally regarded as the Muslim martial counterparts of the Rājpūts and Kśatriyas, the castes of warriors, knights and rulers. The Paṭhān connection was to become of some particular significance to Mawlābakhsh and Hazrat Inayat Khan as well as Dr. A.M. Paṭhān.[18]

Main data

Events dealt with more fully elsewhere need be but briefly recalled here. Mawlābakhsh was born as Sho'le Khān, son of Gīsū Khān, in 1833 at Chither, near Revari (Bhivani); orphaned early, he was brought up by his uncle Imām Khān and his wife,

---

[18] For the latter, cf. Van Beek, *Hazrat Inayat Khan*, 17–18

fondly remembered as "Bīmā Bī" (or: "-Bībī") who survived in Mawlābakhsh House until well after Hazrat Inayat Khan's departure for the West. Sho'le Khān grew up expecting to live a *zamīndār's* heir's life; when about fifteen, a Chishtī dervish encouraged him to sing for him, which he did but shyly, saying he was quite unskilled. Impressed by an as yet untutored, potential talent, the dervish gave him the new name of Mawlābakhsh (God's gift, hence God-gifted). Such a change of name would normally be an optional extra upon initiation into mysticism, and in general was nothing unusual in colorful societies like the Indian or Indonesian, where names and appellations might keep changing to accord with age, attainments, conditions of life, place within the kinship group or in society, social or moral stature, etc. The hesitant young Sho'le is unlikely to have sung a highly demanding, classical composition to the dervish; rather, probably, a religious or devotional song (one would hope, at least, no popular *qawwālī* or debased *ghazal*!), so as to comply with the dervish's "soul's longing." The dervish might have hoped to stimulate a future lyrics recitalist in order to meet his Chishtiyya Order's need for vocal talent. If so, he overshot his mark by the widest possible margin!

From the first, Mawlābakhsh aimed at the classical repertoire (if not, his search "for a real teacher" would have been quite pointless). It was some three years later that Mawlābakhsh decided to take up music in earnest, during which time he benefited from the amateur skills of Anvar Khān, his "maternal-uncle"—which may also have meant a cousin in any degree of his mother's generation and family group. According to *Biography*, he set out to travel, in search of professional instruction, "with his uncle's consent" (i.e. Imām Khān's). An Indian oral source, however (again Chānd Bībī, "Ammā-ḥużūr"), instead told of an estrangement between them, with young Mawlābakhsh's Islamic-law share in the family land inheritance at issue, and which he failed to obtain (applying to the *qāżī* law-court was, of course, "not done"). Imām Khān and Bīmā Bī were childless; at least, no children survived. As Mawlābakhsh was travelling through India some years later, Bīmā Bī, by then a childless widow, already had become the much-respected elder lady of her nephew's household, thus continuing in her earlier maternal function towards him and his family members. Clearly, any property dispute between uncle-proprietor and nephew-heir cannot have been very decisive; there also has been no suggestion anywhere of any kind of economic or financial crisis (which in that case would have made Mawlābakhsh's career that much more spectacularly heroic—almost self-sacrificial), or of any other issue bringing matters to a head. That leads to the interesting question as to why Mawlābakhsh made up his mind to take up music full-time? Did he idealize the dervish's pronouncements, feeling it to be a spiritual injunction or initiatic guidance? Was he keen on exploration, adventure, achievement in the world beyond his uncle's leisured but maybe to him uneventful, and perhaps authoritarian, lifestyle? It has always been affirmed that Hazrat Inayat Khan's character and personality resembled Mawlābakhsh's most closely. It might therefore be worth looking up what *Biography* has to say on a somewhat comparable phase in his case, even though in all its briefness already reflecting the "excusez du peu" style of that ruthlessly devotional tome.[19] After returning from a first successful trip to Madras and Mysore: "Inayat acted as the foremost worker in the State Musical Department, although his two uncles" (i.e. Mawlābakhsh's two sons) "were the figureheads"; yet even so, "there was no scope for him in Baroda State, since the best positions in music were occupied by his two uncles. He began to feel uncomfortable at the lack of opportunity to exercise his ability and he therefore left Baroda." Whether or not this suggests valid analogy, it is easy to see that any such venture by Mawlābakhsh (then younger and much less experienced than was Inayat Khan in 1903: twenty-one and quite exceptionally well-qualified) would have been firmly opposed on the part of Imām Khān—whose sole heir he by then might well have been; and that he would not have been prepared to underwrite such an uncertain proposition quite outside his control by granting his nephew his paternal inheritance share. He must have considered that the dervish had merely been seeking to turn a Khān into a *khwān* (recitalist); that, established as comfortable independent landowners, their position should not again be put in jeopardy by needless personal careerism. Professor Mehta's comments about

[19] Nekbakht Foundation, *Biography*, 65–66.

Mawlābakhsh's simply not belonging to any established *khāndān* of musical courtiers, "lineage musicians" as such guarding the treasures of classical music, and so how could he really have gained his supposed achievements at all?—this query probably already worried Imām Khān, albeit in the future rather than in the past tense, he being evidently more interested in their own *zamīndārī* than in other people's courts. It is characteristic of Mawlābakhsh, as it was to be on several occasions of Inayat Khan, that he set out anyway, without the comforting support of some private income or others' moral encouragement.

He was apparently accompanied, however, by his young sister as well as his maternal uncle, and so, doubtless, by some other relations or retainers as well. For another source states that during Mawlābakhsh's stay at Ratlam, his sister, known as Bībehin Bī (or: "-Bībī"), i.e. "her ladyship sister," was married to her Paṭhān husband Aḥmad Khān Ṭopezāi. Their grandson and selected heir-*jāgīrdār*, Muhammad Ali Khan (1881–1958), was to be Hazrat Inayat Khan's cousin-brother and lifelong companion, joining him from his first departure to the West in 1910, later famous as a masterful practicing Sufi mystic, inspiring singer and astonishingly successful spiritual healer, in all respects the third greatest figure of Hazrat Inayat Khan's Sufism in the West.[20]

Musical achievement

Mawlābakhsh was thoroughly trained in Hindustani music in "Gujarat" (i.e. Baroda) by the then famous Ghasīṭ-Khwān and later in Malabar received an equally intensive education in the theory and practice of Karnatak music from "Subramani Ayar, the most honored musician among the Brahmins of his time."[21] Mastery in both of these very distinct musical traditions was a

---

[20] Musharaff Khan, *Pages*, 89–90, 91; Van Beek, *Hazrat Inayat Khan*, 223–229, Van Hoorn, *Herinneringen*, 56, 62. Cf. also Sophia Saintsbury-Green, *The Wings of the World or The Sufi Message as I See It* (Deventer, Holland: E. Kluwer, 1934), 27–9; *The Sufi Quarterly* 1, no. 2 (1933): 103–6, 2, no. 2 (1936): 51–8; *The Sufi Record* (1960): 34–52; *Toward the One: A Journal of Unity* 1, no. 1 (spring 2000): 42–44.

[21] Curiously, *Biography* applies the same name to "a great musician of Carnatic" who visited the Gāyanshālā and was impressed by Inayat Khan's extraordinary musical talents as a boy. Nekbakht Foundation, *Biography*, 51.

unique feature in his time and remains exceptional even today. Two great musical conventions took place, one in Mysore, focusing on Karnatak music, and later one at Baroda, where Hindustani music was represented by its specialists. Though independent of one another, both assumed the character of a competition between India's most celebrated musicians. On each occasion, Mawlābakhsh was ultimately acknowledged as the greatest, most proficient, all-round and scholarly musician, technically as well as artistically, and from then on was regarded as India's leading musical genius. In some striking compositions of his own, as well as in the variations elaborating other great vocal music, Mawlābakhsh succeeded in combining some of the most aesthetically satisfying features of the Hindustani and Karnatak styles—Northern subtlety of ornamentation and lyrical expression, vocal yet "absolute" music, and the extraordinary Southern command of thematic development and rhythmic elaboration. His elder son and heir, Murṭażā Khān, continued and was imitated along those lines—so much so that years after, in the late nineteen-thirties, when Hazrat Inayat Khan's brothers received some gramophone records from India, whilst listening to Khānṣāhab 'Abd al-Karīm Khān they were touched and amused to recognize exactly Murtażā Khān's style of *sargam* variations in time-honored Karnatak tradition.

National relevance

Mawlābakhsh thus was well placed to represent the two different styles of Indian music as one united-Indian musical culture—a contribution to a united India in a to Indians all-important, creatively artistic sphere, emphasizing an overall unity of the Mughal and Dravidian forms of Indian culture and civilization generally. He was particularly pleased to represent that united Indian musical culture *vis-à-vis* the British, and had an exceptional opportunity of doing so when invited to the Vice-regal Durbar at Delhi in 1877 on the occasion of the proclamation of the Empire of India. To this day, Mawlābakhsh continues to be honored both as the acknowledged greatest all-round musician of his time, and as personifying, as such, at the highest—that is to say, musical—level of India's aesthetic identity, the Subcontinent's essential unity beyond the differences and distinctions of Aryan and Dravidian, Hindu and Muslim, states and systems.

It is easy to see how these ideals, of harmonizing unity beyond enriching diversity, provided a model and mould to Hazrat Inayat Khan's later ideals of mystical unity and the contemplative cultivation of musical beauty, the highest of all aesthetic or conceptual perceptions as being the most abstract one. What has caused Mawlābakhsh to remain lively remembered as well, are two related achievements that caught people's imagination: his foundation and direction of the Gāyanshālā Academy of Music at Baroda, and his development of a system of Indian musical notation and the publication of a number of music textbooks applying it practically, written by himself, Dr. Paṭhān and Inayat Khan. Professor Miner records that his musical notation was in Gujarati script, and that it "followed upon that of Ksetra Mohan Gosvami" in Bengal, the promotion of whose notation there was supported by Mawlābakhsh.[22] The 1915 article and *Biography* also do not assert Mawlābakhsh to have been the original "founder" of Indian musical notation, although the former has some veiled criticism obviously of the Bombay musicologist Bhāṭkhaṇḍe and some rivaling Hindustani musicians in Baroda itself, claiming priority in relation to those. What both publications rather emphasize is Mawlābakhsh's aim of forming "a special method by combining Southern with Northern music and theory with practice. He went to Calcutta with his new system."[23] Neither article is altogether clear on the subject, though *Biography* seems to connect his notation with the Calcutta visit. Possibly a distinction may have to be drawn between Mawlābakhsh's aims of combining the Hindustani and Karnatak musical techniques into one musical system, and that of evolving a notation method. In any case, the Mawlābakhshī musical tradition still remains a promising field for further research. The fact remains that the joint effect of a music academy open to all and a notation system making music available in print to everyone, was perceived as altogether revolutionary, signaling, in both principle and practice, a break with the traditional

---

[22] Miner, *Sitar and Sarod*, 151, 155.

[23] Inayat Khan, "Moula Bux"; notation is mentioned only after the foundation of the Gāyanshālā.

monopoly of the *khāndān-gharānā* transmission of music hereditarily or through initiatic affiliation, only.

Detractors and devotees

Of course Mawlābakhsh had his rivals and detractors, though never at his own level of competence—which did not help to mitigate such jealousies! Representatives of a Northern, Hindustani style of music settled in Baroda, criticized almost everything he did whilst trying to copy him, even going so far as to assert that as a proper Muslim he ought not to propagate the Hindu music and culture of the Dravidians. Such attitudes were countered with contempt, but did introduce a jarring note occasionally making itself felt. This in turn led Mawlābakhsh and his sons to a more critically selective approach as to whom was to be admitted to court and specialist musical circles in so far as such admission was in their gift. As noted above, it clearly was to counter imitations from those rivaling Northerners in Gujarat, that emphasis came to be laid on the priority and original character of Mawlābakhsh's notation system and its all-Indian relevance. A generalized extrapolation of that argument cannot really have been intended and, in any case, where direct polemics should not be the purpose, sweeping statements of the kind have to be understood as poetic exclamations rather than as musicological statements.

Aside from family members and some further relations, most of Mawlābakhsh's personal pupils were Brāhmans, men of immense commitment and devotion.[24] But after Mawlābakhsh's own lifetime they, like his elder son, heir and successor Murtażā Khān-i Mawlābakhsh, represented an ageing generation. His younger son 'Alā al-Din Khān (Dr. A.M. Paṭhān) and Murṭażā's son Allāhdād Khān (A.M. Paṭhān the younger) spent the decisive years of their lives in Nepal. Hazrat Inayat Khan and his brothers, by far the most promising quartet of potential perpetuators, had come to settle in Europe, where Allāhdād Khān narrowly missed joining them, to everybody's subsequent regret, and whence the third generation of "Inayatides" (*Inayatzādagān*) eventually fanned out to Britain and the United States.

[24] A number of them have been mentioned in the concluding paragraph of Inayat Khan, "Moula Bux." Cf. Musharaff Khan, *Pages*, 92–93.

In that unforeseen way, the Mawlābakhshī music tradition, for all its grandeur, was sacrificed and vanished even well before the collapse of the *a'lākhāndān* itself—even though still very much alive in textbooks and documents. In a real sense, Hazrat Inayat Khan's Sufism is the direct heir of Mawlābakhsh's music—indeed a successor at its expense. Precisely therefore, a singularly rich heritage still remains to be acknowledged, to the indubitable advantage of both!

Security of identity

Social and psychological security of the kinship group, its identity and values is, of course, the whole point of the caste system and its *dharma*. Other such ancient units, like tribal, clan, or nobility structures, all in principle clearly represent, albeit more fragmentarily, similar universal human needs and aspirations. The issue of security of identity in the lineage from Vyās and Wyaspur to Mawlābakhsh had to face up to two considerable challenges: convert status, and music as a Muslim and performing art. In the first place, the Indo-Islamic *khāṣṣa* (upper class) was, in theory at least, made up of immigrants into India, the *ashrāf*, except for a relatively small number of islamized Rājpūts maintaining their caste identities. Such immigrant precedence is a well-known phenomenon everywhere, as in India in the case of the conquering Aryans and the British in their own time. In this case, however, the standard again had been set in early Arab times, when upon the occupation of areas outside Arabia proper—from Syria to the Atlantic and from Iraq to Transoxania and the Indus—the Arabs settled there as a privileged ruling class. Eventually, they were replaced everywhere either by other conquering elites, like the Turks and Circassians, or by talented subjects, like the Iranians, or by the two jointly, as in Spain by the Berbers, Slavs (i.e. all islamized outside Europeans) and Andalusians (Muslim Spaniards).

But as their culture continued, so did their social conventions, as, again, is usual in such cases; and so, the theory of immigrant pre-eminence. For Indian converts of the higher social strata islamization therefore implied a search of identification with a certain immigrant group (again excepting the Rājpūts), this being all the more desirable as they had had to give up their original caste capacity and the security of identity it could offer. Consistent intermarriage into an immigrant group would lead to ever-increasing assimilation; non-immigrant origins meanwhile had better be concealed or forgotten. Technically moreover, converts commenced a new family lineage when changing from one religio-legal system into another, as pointed out earlier. There could be no genealogical or biographical continuity in any case. Thus, also, upward movement into *ashrāf* categories became an obvious, soon inflationary, pattern. It needs to be emphasized that it was the interest of former twice-born-caste members in seeking a new social circle and security in a new identity, that induced secretiveness as to convert origins, and not religious prejudice towards the former faith, conversion often simply a matter of "pour changer réligion, il faut être très religieux." This secretive mentality may now be changing, with an authoritative example to follow. The eminent poet-philosopher Sir Muhammad Iqbal Shaikh, the supposed ideologue of Pakistan (though he doubtless would have deplored the eventual partition and its human, sociological and cultural consequences) publicly proclaimed his pride in his Brāhman (Sapru) descent.

For people like Byāsjī and Anvar Khān, the *zamīndārī* system naturally offered a ready-made environment. But that meant its conditions, and the land supporting it, had to be maintained emphatically in whatever circumstances, as we saw with Imām Khān. Anyway, once a human environment of acceptable level could be found or maintained, much of this issue could be left to theory or sentiment, even if conversion origins continued very largely unmentioned. It was only with regard to the issue of finding appropriate marriage partners that a question of *musalim* or *nau-musalmān* status became of any practical interest, and there were both more material and more romantic means of overcoming that one.

The second challenge was of much more practical significance, and played a decisive part in the lives and moods of the Mawlābakhshīs, including Hazrat Inayat Khan himself. In India, as Hazrat Inayat Khan always reminds us, music is the most divine art and science, intimately linked to spiritual wisdom and mystical realization. Most Indians would doubtless agree on music being their master art: that of the gods and Rishīs of old, of saints and Brāhmans ever since, at its worldliest of princes and performers at all times. Amongst Muslims, however, again old Arab times might intervene. Initial Arab music had largely consisted of love and war songs. Only later, Andalusia provided classical Arabian music, philosophers developed the musical sciences as integral to their discipline, and the building of ever better instruments continued apace. While all that was going on, the doctors of religious law still only knew about the love and war items, decided they were unfit for Paradise, and introduced anti-music pronouncements into the law. This only impressed the puritans, the ignorant, and the fanatics in search of a cause.

Otherwise, the people happily continued with love and war, the educated and the courts with ever more refined "Andalusian" art music, a process continued on their own by Persians, Turks, Javanese and virtually all other civilized Muslim peoples. Today, the doctors of Islamic law will agree that all the "Prophetic traditions" pronouncing against music are so-called "weak" ones, that is, tendentious forgeries. At an earlier time, anti-music puritanism might still impress. In India, the Chishtīs in particular developed devotional singing. Classical Hindustani music was immensely enriched by Indo-Islamic contributions; the majority of star musicians and musical professionals were Muslims. Those found all prestige protection from orthodox prejudice at India's many royal and princely courts; from the *Mahābhārata* onwards, musicians had been inviolable. In this way came into existence the *khāndān*s and *gharānā*s of "lineage musicians." As courtiers, playing only at *darbārs* or private circles of music lovers and specialists, they also were to a significant extent protected from another stigma: that of being professional performers. Yet that was as far as they could normally rise: at best, a protected group of service-nobility, courtiers in attendance on a ruler—recalling medieval Europe's knightly troubadours and more generally what Carl Burckhardt has called untranslatably: "the noble commonalty of ministerials and minstrels."[25] *Biography* records Mawlābakhsh's

[25] Carl Burckhardt, *Kultur der Renaissance in Italien*, ed. Kaegi (Bern: Hallwag, n.d. [1944 ?]), 17: "die Ritter, ... das dienende und singende Adelsvolk", lit.: "the knights (and) the serving and singing noble folk", which apart from

deep dismay at Wājid ʻAlī Shāh of Lucknow's having called his company of musicians "*arbāb-i nashāṭ*," "masters of pleasure."[26] By contrast, in Southern Karnatak music, musicians were Brāhmans, men of learning, of religion and mysticism: they sang and played to God, rather than to any prince—the greatest of them all named Tyāgarāja: "he who renounced the princes." With them, no stigma of being performers or religious libertines: they were the saints of sound, and as such deeply revered.

Mawlābakhsh developed both as a composer and musical scholar and as an unusually proficient singer and *vīnā* player. Yet his landed background gave him and all his family and descendants a particular sensitivity with regard to either prejudice, that is, music necessarily divided them from the *mullās* and the masses; and, professionalization must not affect their leisured-class social stature. Being a professionalized *zamīndār* was fine for a while, but should not put one's background permanently at risk, especially if one's ancestry was left suspended in mid-air just four generations previously. So meticulousness remained paramount. Mawlābakhsh, his sons and grandsons became expert musicians, but forever continued to maintain the distinction between the professional recitalist-musician and the gentleman-musician—between the *khwān* and the Khān. *Khānṣāḥabī gānā*, singing in the noble style, with no popular concession, its subtlety only fully followed by the few, always remained their ideal standard—it also remained their highest praise for a truly magnificent rendering by whatever artist. Grants and purchases of land in time made them affluent beyond whatever Imām Khān's concerns might have ultimately yielded. And real estate probably explains why Mawlābakhsh kept coming back to Baroda despite his conflicts with two Maharajas in succession. However, his discovery of the Dravidian South still was to him his life's decisive experience in every respect, comparable with the elation of Westerners discovering an oriental civilization in that Romantic period of exotic exploration. He was to become the expert exponent of Karnatak music in the North, that is, India

---

referring to the medieval courtiers mentioned in the text above, might almost as well render "the Rājpūts and Kśatriyas" or, for that matter, "the Khāns and the *khwāns*"!

[26] Nekbakht Foundation, *Biography*, 26.

beyond the Deccan. He came to know at least the most euphonious and musical Dravidian language, Telegu, well. He loved the country, the culture, its ideals and values. He became a vegetarian (beef, of course, was refused by most Mawlābakhshīs at all times, in deference to Hindu feelings). Extant paintings depict him with a Southern-style turban. Above all, to the South, the State of Mysore, he owed the gain of a security of identity to an altogether exceptional extent. In one move, it raised him and his succeeding heirs beyond any further concerns as to *zamīndār* or court lineage social positions—an independence of status of which landowners or courtly musicians could hardly have dreamt. That move was the elevation by the Maharaja of Mysore, of Mawlābakhsh, the Northern country gentleman become an aristocratic musical courtier, to the "high" nobility of his State and thereby in India generally. In the eighteen-nineties, a disastrous palace fire unfortunately destroyed all relevant court records, but this singular honor continued to be used and recognized during and after Mawlābakhsh's own lifetime.[27]

It remains to be added that in Dravidian India the principle of compatibility of rank and social status between marriage partners (*kufū*) always had been rigorously observed. In Islamic societies, despite *khāṣṣa-'āmma* distinctions, that was only the case to a much less extent. This was due to a genuine religious-egalitarian feeling grown out of tribal roots, as well as by the legal regulation of marriage, including of such special niceties as polygamy and concubinage (these two roughly corresponding to the *khāṣṣa-'āmma* distinction). Those, in combination, soon cancelled out early Arab

[27] Cf. Nekbakht Foundation, *Biography*, 22–23; Van Beek, *Hazrat Inayat* Khan, 9–23. Nobility honors for musicians were known in Europe as well, witness the marquisate accepted by Corelli but refused by Verdi, the papal knighthood brandished by Gluck but discarded by Mozart, the ennoblements lavished on the Couperins, Dittersdorf and Weber but denied to, of all people, Johann Strauss; the practice is continued to this day in Belgium, but in the sole Dutch case, King Willem III's offer of a barony was declined by his court pianist, Buziau. Above all, there is the recent, unique British peerage for that truly noblest of modern musicians, Yehudi Menuhin, who for so long has embodied all the musical and human virtues and characteristics Hazrat Inayat Khan is so fond of attributing to genuinely great musicians (apart altogether from the curious fact that his Khazar ethnic strain so closely matches the Central Asian one in Hazrat Inayat Khan, that in certain modes of speech and facial expression he and Inayat's elder son, Pir Vilayat, may be observed to display a wholly exceptional likeness of type and style!).

pretensions as to the ranking precedence of inter-Arab matrimony. Like in Europe and Java, among Rājpūts and Dravidians, "high" nobility implied the right and duty of marriage amongst princely houses or noble ones of the same category. Mawlābakhsh gained the opportunity of such a *kufū* marriage with a daughter of the Mysorean branch of the Ṭīpū Sulṭān dynastic lineage. He further expressed his newly acquired high-nobility rank in the prerogative of ennobling his wife's vassals by the title of *khān-i sharīf*. Later, in Baroda, he was to organize his family along explicitly dynastic lines, again applying Southern ideas. It is his elevation itself, and his marriage, that call for further consideration.

The literature mentions three grounds for Mawlābakhsh's "high" ennoblement: to enable him, having become her equal in rank, to marry the Ṭīpū Sulṭān daughter; because of personal friendship with the Maharaja; and because after the Mysore musical convention and competition he was acknowledged as incomparable, as the champion of Karnatak music, so to speak. The first proposition[28] may be rejected out of hand; it seems impossible that he should first have established marriage negotiating contacts and then sought and obtained his elevation for that reason. Conversely, his elevation enabled his marriage. As for the third view, it is true that the rank was only granted him, and the accompanying ceremonial carried out, after his acknowledgement as the supreme Karnatak musician. But *Biography* equally states that it was well before, and not in consequence of any contest that the Maharaja "wished to bestow upon him the highest marks of honour it is possible to give in India"—whereupon "the Brahmins" protested and organized the ten-month musical contest.[29] Why should the Maharaja have wished to honor the stranger from the North to that extent beyond his own Brāhmans, who might well be sensitive about it? Naturally, it was gratifying that an outsider should have become so enthusiastically committed to their Karnatak music and culture; but that cannot of course be the whole answer. The 1915 article records that earlier, during Mawlābakhsh's first stay at Mysore, the Maharaja already had been intending to reward him richly when suddenly he left the Court and State of Mysore, feeling vexed and saddened. That was

---

[28] As suggested in Fuller, *Noor-un-Nisa Inayat Khan (Madeleine)* (Rotterdam and London: East-West Publications and Barrie and Jenkins, Ltd., 1971), 20.

[29] Nekbakht Foundation, *Biography*, 22.

because a learned leading expert on Karnatak music, daughter of a senior court official, had flatly refused to instruct him in it. She told him that "her art belonged to the Brahmins alone," "as sacred to them as their religion": "learn when you are born as Brahmin"! (One really wonders whether Mawlābakhsh, a deeply religious practicing Muslim of a very liberal-mystical Sufi persuasion, stopped to weigh the irony of his own Brāhman great-grandfather Vyās becoming a Muslim with notable advantage to his daughter, though not to his son and now to the detriment of his great-grandson!).

The Maharaja was well aware that the distinguished stranger had left his court feeling insulted and humiliated and must have been gratified by his return, as promised, if and after he would have mastered the art elsewhere. He, too, could not turn Mawlābakhsh into a Brāhman. But he did have it in his gift to ennoble him, and did so in the highest possible degree—a truly royal gesture, gracious as a compensation for the past, a reward for both the past and present, and an honor for the present and all future. The later clash it caused at Baroda only served to confirm Mawlābakhsh's stature the more widely.[30] He was accepted as such at the vice-regal Durbar and all the princely courts he chose to visit; Jaipur an especially well remembered one,[31] with contacts that were to continue later also with Inayat Khan. And subsequently at Baroda, the famous Mahārāja Sayājī Rāo Gāekwāṛ granted him an honor somewhat matching the Mysorean one, by including Mawlābakhsh amongst his *Nauratan*, the "Nine Jewels of State."

Mawlābakhsh's Mysorean rank often has been described as "princely." Assuming that such comparisons are at all valid, that would call for some more careful consideration. The technicalities involved are beyond the scope of the present paper. For our present purposes it remains to be noted, that of some such kind of princely rank, also Hazrat Inayat Khan and his three brothers preserved a very clear image and explanation—reflecting both their Indian experience and knowledge and their remarkable insight in European social hierarchies and their standards, due to their musical and Sufi experience with them. However, Hazrat Inayat Khan himself was

---

30 Cf. Inayat Khan, "Moula Bux," 51–2; Nekbakht Foundation, *Biography*, 23–24.
31 Cf. Van Beek, *Hazrat Inayat Khan*, 12.

much more interested in Mawlābakhsh's wife's Ṭīpū Sulṭān ancestry and background,[32] clearly because that was felt to be truly within the Mughal tradition—and, maybe, because it was not also shared by Dr. A.M. Paṭhān, who was nonetheless to inherit the family honors, lands and properties in succession to his elder brother Murtażā Khān.

Hazrat Inayat Khan's brother "Pyārū Mīr" Maheboob Khan was most concerned with their paternal immigrant *mashaykhān* tradition. Thus often it remained for the eldest amongst them, their "cousin-brother" Muhammad Ali Khan as grandson of Mawlābakhsh's sister, in the best of Dravidian matrilineal traditions, to continue principal emphasis on the central significance to them all, of the Mawlābakhsh *rājkufū* nobility in itself.

True enough, whatever the dissimilarities, feudal societies in whichever civilization do demonstrate striking resemblances in one way or another, as well.

Nonetheless, Mawlābakhsh's grandiose attainment did present new and perplexing challenges to his family's younger descendants; along with the entire range of his music, those were to shape the destinies of 'Alā al-Dīn Khān (Dr. Paṭhān) and Hazrat Inayat Khan in particular. Here reference to Van Beek's remarks thereon will have to suffice.[33]

Qāsim Bī

Biography describes Qāsim Bī almost as a Byzantine "grande dame" reigning from her gynaikion, rather than as an Indian princess shining from her *zanāna*: she "maintained the strictest seclusion," "held herself aloof even from visits of the ladies of Baroda"; "her ancestry was never referred to in words"; the grandchildren, unhelpfully, "never heard the full story of her life."[34] "Mawlā Miyāṅ" Musharaff Khan related that she felt it to be her joint mission in life, her *dharma* so to speak, to live her religious faith, and to live and represent, and so perpetuate, her ancestral standards and values—those of Ṭīpū Sulṭān of Mysore, his father Ḥaydar 'Alī, and his family group. Housekeeping and the practice of

---

[32] There is a good example in Fuller, *Noor-un-nisa Inayat Khan*, 40.
[33] Van Beek, Hazrat Inayat Khan, 18.
[34] Nekbakht Foundation, *Biography*, 22–23.

family management were to be left to a secondary wife. The brief *Biography* account of her is heavy with tragedy, without at all explaining anything about it. It could be that the British slaughter of Mughal princes in Delhi after the 1857 Mutiny had struck terror all around. But the sons and descendants of Ṭīpū Sulṭān in the far South, though exiled to Bengal, were living as comfortable lives on British pensions and personal holdings, as did Shāmil's of Caucasia in Russia.

Qāsim Bī's particular line of descent is known only in the most general terms. Dravidian India was the homeland of the estimable matrilineal family system, once described by the Austrian anthropologist (and Sufi mureed) Umar von Ehrenfels as the most "democratic" because most "consultative" type of kinship structure. Under North Indian influence, that time-honored system now is disappearing fast, precisely when all the world is screaming about women's rights! But, as Indians invariably will say: "That's India!" However, from the matrilineal point of view, it was natural for the Maharaja of Mysore, since Ṭīpū Sulṭān's own descendants had been exiled by the British, collaterally instead to install Ṭīpū Sulṭān's maternal uncle and his descendants in their place, as premier Muslim nobles of his State. During Ṭīpū's regime, which had briefly superseded the Wadyār Maharajas' dynasty and then again had been replaced by it, Mysore had been expanded into a mighty and famous kingdom with important international connections, and it since has continued as India's largest and most prestigious Hindu State, second only to Mughal Hyderabad. Allāhdād Khān-i Mawlābakhsh (A.M. Paṭhān the younger), fourth holder, as heir and successor after his father and uncle, of the Mawlābakhshī family honors and lands, as well as his four cousins in the West, all used to affirm that Qāsim Bī descended from the lineage of Ṭīpū Sulṭān's *māmūṅ-ḥużūr*, maternal uncle—the eldest representative of the lineage continuing to bear the same titular name, colloquially also varied as "Ṭīpū-ṣāḥab" to avoid confusion with the original Ṭīpū. Now this line of Ṭīpū Sulṭāns and their families, by the eighteen-sixties had been living, for several generations already, in ease and honor in a pretty Mysorean palace built for them by the Maharaja (today become a school building). So what is all the drama and danger about, reflected in so much of the available literature? The most extensive picture is painted in Fuller's

Noor-un-nisa Inayat Khan, the bestseller on Hazrat Inayat Khan's elder daughter, the wartime heroine Noorunnisa code-named Madeleine. This book might reflect impressions picked up by Hazrat Inayat Khan's young children when visiting Baroda in 1928-29. Similar information, however, had already found its way in the *Biography*.[35] On the other hand, at least Hazrat Inayat Khan's brothers never mentioned anything of such suggested dramatic events, fond as they always remained of remembering their family's elder generations—indeed, those were hardly ever absent from their daily conversations.

But there is a curious twist. In a Hindi textbook used in Baroda (Gujarati) schools for decades, one story closely resembles what is being evoked in *Biography* and Fuller. A young girl descendant of Ṭīpū Sulṭān lives in hiding in a jungle at the fringe of a city in which an old mysterious retainer regularly appears for shopping. Intrigued, the story's writer contrives to follow him into the jungle and there discovers the girl and the awful events of her life, and so forth. Ṭīpū Sulṭān fell in 1799, the only warlike activity remotely and unlikely connected with rumored descendants of his, was some trouble at Vellore in 1806. The story thus could only have been set about 1800–1810 at latest. The Mutiny in the North in 1857 had, of course, inflamed imaginations and may have led to novels or children's textbook tales along such lines. Given the fact that so little information on Qāsim Bī was available (and vulgarizing bio-data on a high-born lady, of course, simply was "not done"), imaginative and credulous minds around, or even in, Mawlābakhsh House, innocently or deliberately, have met the need of the curious with hearsay deriving from that story (maybe children in surrounding houses or living quarters telling all that they had learnt at school, were believed). *Biography's* first part is formally attributed to Mawlavī Mehr-bakhshe-yi Ja'far Khān, cousin and brother-in-law of Hazrat Inayat Khan and Maheboob Khan; the earlier, very limited Almgren edition captions the entire Part 1 (on Hazrat Inayat Khan's life in India) with: "narrated by Moulavi Mehr Bakhsh" (sic).[36] Since it is likely that Hazrat Inayat Khan

---

[35] Ibid.

[36] "*Mehr*," transmitted orally into Gujarati and Urdu transcription, may represent Persian "*mihr*": 'sun', 'love'; or, etymologically more likely, Arabic "*māhir*":

in this way sought to draw the eldest "brother"[37] of their generation a little more to the attention and recollection of his readers, it could seem pedantry on the part of the 1979 editors to have dropped that specific mention altogether. Actually, he may have sent information or recollections then included in the text of that editorially doubtful collection. Mehr-bakhshe was from Punjab, did not attend school in Baroda, a scholarly, stern and upright man, a bit *khushk* ("dry") by Baroda standards. He would never knowingly have transmitted doubtful materials, but how was he to know about Hindi schoolbooks? It cannot besides be at all certain that it was he who contributed such dramatic if vague evocations.

If the brothers in the West, or their brother-in-law, could not themselves have been primary sources of those dramatic suggestions, then where did they originate, to whom are they to be attributed? With reference to Qāsim Bī, the *Biography* text speaks of the woes of: "the terrible political situation," "the tragedy in the fate of her house," the "mystery and tragedy that surrounded her," and so on.

It is worth turning back for a moment at this point. The 1915 article with all its careful musical detail, is not void of colorful description either. Thus, on Mawlābakhsh's first disenchanted departure from Mysore, it says: "He felt so humiliated that he left Mysore, avoiding the acceptance of the royal prize which was ready for him. He left word behind that he would only visit Mysore when he had thoroughly mastered the Brahmanic Science. If not, he would never show himself there again. On hearing this message all his admirers, from Rajah to servant, became very sad." Despite that vivacity, it is quite bland however, on the *rājkufū* marriage, stating merely: "He then married a lady of an ancient Royal House. This period of prosperity caused his fame to ring throughout India." In *Biography*, the catalogue of woes frames the phrase: "This girl had been protected by two devoted adherents to her house, with whom Mawlābakhsh became acquainted and after his marriage he took these two loyal and devoted guardians as part of his household, and even after their death their families lived under his roof." And again: "No doubt, the presence of the two guardians, who knew her

---

'able', 'capable', 'ingenious'. On "*bakhshe*," see below, note 71.

[37] Cf. Musharaff Khan, *Pages*, 55.

history, heightened the atmosphere of mystery and tragedy that surrounded her.[38] Fuller's report carries this on to a totally baffling extent. At first is stated, soundly objectively: "[Noorunnisa Inayat Khan 'Madeleine's'] brother Vilayat made it very clear to me that they held no documentary proof of their descent from Tipu, and that he could tell me only what he had understood from his father, as his father had understood it from the older generations; the uncles of Noor-un-nisa and Vilayat" (i.e. at the time, Muhammad Ali Khan [Ṭopezāi] and Mawlā Miyāṅ Musharaff Khan [Paṭhān]) "also laid stress upon this lack of anything which could be shown as evidence, and made the point that they were not claiming anything, only repeating what had been passed down to them, believing it to be true." But then, having cleared the decks with simple sobriety, the narrative continues, astonishingly:

> One of the sons of Tipu, who was known as Tipu II, participated in the Indian Mutiny of 1857, and died in the fighting ... and it was his orphaned daughter, a girl of about fourteen named Casime-bi who was stolen to safety by two faithful servants of her father's. ... The assumption of responsibility for Casime-bi placed them in considerable danger, both from the British ... and even from the males of the Tipu dynasty who might be still at large, since they might not view in the best light the action of the two faithful servants in taking care of a lady of their house. ... They conducted her secretly to Mysore, and after hiding her there for a while, took the step of making their presence known to a young Muslim nobleman, Moula Bakhsh.[39]

That absurd caricature does not even merit serious rebuttal, but its following after the reference to Hazrat Inayat Khan's brothers, implicitly suggesting they might in any way share responsibility for this muddled nonsense, calls for strong reproof. In reality, they always affirmed, as did their cousin-brother the male-line heir at Baroda, Allāhdād Khān-i Mawlābakhsh, that Qāsim Bī, as said before was a descendant of Ṭīpū Sulṭān's *māmūṅ-ḥużūr* (maternal uncle) at Mysore. Doubly absurd that a girl from that line should have been spirited from Delhi all the way to that city of the Ṭīpūs, if those guardians feared their wrath as much as the British! In the Mutiny no Ṭīpūs fought and were killed in Delhi

---

[38] Nekbakht Foundation, *Biography*, 22–23.
[39] Fuller, *Noor-un-Nisa*, 19–20.

(let alone any "Ṭīpū II"!), but Ṭopezāis fought at Gwalior: four brothers (two parental, two cousinly) of genuine (frontier) Paṭhān stock, escaped with others to Tonk, Rajasthan. As he used to tell almost a century later, Muhammad Ali Khan as a young boy and grandparental heir at Tonk, was admonished by Bībehin Bī's family there, forever to remember, never ever to forget, that they were the Ṭopezāis.

"A girl of about fourteen": that was not Qāsim Bī, but Khadīja Bī when she married Mashaykh Raḥmat [-Allāh] Khān after the death of his first wife, her elder sister Fāṭima Bī, when she also took over the care of her sister's young daughter, Jena (Zayna) Bī.

Suggestions in subsequent passages are equally groundless: "She could only be married to a royal Prince" does reflect something of the strictness of marriage compatibility observance in the Dravidian South, but in such an interpretation has little validity.[40] Whereas the final paragraphs' view—that the Maharaja might have had some policy motivation in facilitating the match by Mawlābakhsh's elevation—again amounts to pure fantasy. He did have a motivation *vis-à-vis* Mawlābakhsh, however, as has been discussed earlier.

It cannot escape notice that all that drama and danger around Qāsim Bī puts at center stage as the real dramatis personae, the: "two devoted adherents," "loyal guardians,"[41] "two faithful servants."[42] Indeed, the latter's passages include their correct names, lending an air of veracity to the romantically fantastic report of confused misunderstandings. For indeed, these men were perfectly well known. As *Biography* rightly relates, Pīr Khān-i Sharīf and Sulṭān Khān-i Sharīf continued to live at Mawlābakhsh House and so did their families.[43] Sulṭān Khān had a son 'Usmān Khān, Pīr Khān[44] one called Shāhbāz Khān,[45] who in turn had a son Shamshīr

---

[40] Unless "royal" is meant to convey "*rājkufū*," i.e. "of equal marriage status with princes"—the less cumbrous German "Ebenbürtigkeitswürde." The point is that Mawlābakhsh's rank, though certainly a princely, was not thereby also a royal one, although intermarriable with such houses.

[41] Nekbakht Foundation, *Biography*, 22.

[42] Fuller, Noor-un-nisa Inayat Khan, 19.

[43] Nekbakht Foundation, *Biography*, 22.

[44] On him, cf. Musharaff Khan, *Pages*, 50–51, 75.

[45] Cf. Musharaff Khan, *Pages*, 22, 50, 93.

Khān, whose children dispersed into the unknown but for a daughter, Afżāl, regarded as the last representative of that Khān-i Sharīf family. ʻUsmān, who remained childless, and Shāhbāz were rather older than Hazrat Inayat Khan. Mawlābakhsh saw to it that they received a good education. The bright and smart ʻUsmān Khān did particularly well, acquired a sound knowledge of the new art of photography, and benefited from the British-modernizing influences brought home from Europe by Dr. Paṭhān. He was, naturally, in the rather awkward position of an educated son of serving, "vassal," parents. That may have made him somewhat ambitious, assertive, perceived as hard to gauge and in all, a somewhat doubtful character. In prominent Houses like that of Mawlābakhsh, it happened frequently (and more emphatically, or insidiously, than in the case of the above-mentioned) that unrelated vassal or retainers' families came to identify with, or tried to pass themselves or their forebears off as real members of, the family in question. Traditions of tribal affiliation, and conversion by patriarchal leaders or order shaykhs, tended to facilitate such genealogically fallacious identifications, known in Europe as well from Poland to Spain. Without, maybe, going quite that far, ʻUsmān Khān ("Paṭhān," of course) was exactly the kind of person wishing to impress others with the significance of his father and uncle to the Mawlābakhsh family. ʻUsmān Khān and Shāhbāz Khān figured frequently in the memories of Hazrat Inayat Khan's brothers, mostly in some connection with Dr. ʻAlā al-Din Khān Paṭhān. ʻUsmān Khān was on amicable terms with Mehr-bakhshe; from a very young age, Inayat, who so loved romantic stories of the Indian past, must have gained impressions from him. Maheboob Khan, much younger, genealogically precise, seems always to have kept a certain distance from him; Muhammad Ali Khan only returned to Baroda at fifteen, past the age of such stories of old, and himself a mine of authentic information on family members. We, therefore, have: the Khān-i Sharīf family and their younger generation with ʻUsmān Khān most articulate, all doubtless happy, if not eager, to emphasize their role in the Qāsim Bī-Mawlābakhsh matchmaking; the environment responding to, forgetting, fragmentarily or faultily recalling, such old stories: servants, hangers-on in and around the House, the neighbourhood and the entire Yakūtpūrā quarter, as it had gradually sprung up around Mawlābakhsh House—most early inhabitants in some kind of serving, delivering or employment relationship to it; equally important, the distant military and police lines, where lived the military bandsmen under the immediate command of Dr. Paṭhān. Here stories and rumors multiplied in profuse confusion. And precisely because one could never take a great lady's name in any personal sense, it was her vassals who were central to all the storytelling.

Then there was the Hindi schoolbook story, the single old man, who was easily multiplied into two vassal retainers. The Ṭīpū wars before 1800 had long been forgotten amongst all that ignorant if admiring folk; but all knew the name of Ṭīpū Sulṭān, and the 1857 Mutiny in the North was a living memory: again, the association was easily made. Even after World War II, it was asserted of Shamshīr Khān that, after all, "he" had only come in after the Delhi *barwa* (Mutiny)! Currents from all these sources must have reached Mehr-bakhshe, young Inayat Khan, and his own young children in 1928. And so found their way, not only in the *Biography*, but in the most widely read book on any member of the family, as already mentioned in the foregoing, rightly celebrated for its painstaking research and vivid description, that is, J. Overton Fuller's *Noor-un-nisa Inayat Khan.*

In fairness to the Khān-i Sharīf family and the *evolué* 'Usmān, with their extraordinarily successful, if deceptively one-sided, ever further confusedly elaborated contribution to our Sufi-biographical literature, some points remain to be made. Their version of events may have been self-interested or self-centered, but India's is not a historically-minded culture, as is that of Islam or the West; in compensation it possesses a uniquely rich mythology. Then, for many people everywhere it is hard to relate events that impressed them without centering on themselves and reaching out from there. Witness the numerous recorded memoirs of Hazrat Inayat Khan in the "I and my Master" style. Again, as pointed out repeatedly, discussing women, and especially high-born ladies, with others, was disrespectful and so, offensive: Bīmā Bī and Bībehin Bī could only be referred to thus, and above all not by their personal names, which to all Indians was really improper. Divulging one's actual name, rather than one's alias, degree or title for public purposes was shocking, breaching accepted conventions. Even the deliberate shortening of names out of reverence, although grammatically faulty—such as Inayat Khan for Inayat Allah Khan—contained something of that dissimulation of the "real" name. Besides all such generalities some further justification, at least explanation, of the vassal retainers' one-sidedness might be found, not in menaces of physical violence, but in the rapidly changing conditions and moods in those eventful times—threatening enough to the older order in their own way.

Even though the inferences drawn can only be conjectural, a likely other side of the story must not be wholly lost sight of. It has been reported, and to all appearances reliably so, that Qāsim Bī's mother was one of those delicately beautiful women only produced by that swathe of territory running from Ethiopia and Somalia down the East African coast into somewhere in the indeterminate south. To the ancient Greeks, those Africans were the finest human specimens on earth, and the Arabs followed them up, not only in written word,[46] but in doubtful deed. Some decades after our period, that is, in the late nineteenth century, "'Abd al-Ghaffar" Snouck Hurgronje in his book on Mecca notes that whilst well-to-do Arabs there carefully considered their wives, their real enthusiasm was reserved for their Ethiopian slave girls. Their predilection was followed all over the Islamic world (and not necessarily confined to East African women only, witness the famous Hausas from the West or Omar Vrioni's African settlement at Ulcinj (Dulcigno), then in fully European-Muslim territory). Dr. De Jong-Keesing refers to Ethiopians settled in Hyderabad, "whose daughters were much in demand as brides." It seems unlikely that Qāsim Bī's mother originated there, however, since a Hyderabadi background, with its prestigious associations of high Mughal culture, would hardly have gone entirely unmentioned. Naturally, the more beautiful the girls, the more expensive to obtain them; and the more the slave trade was at long last being suppressed, the higher the price of those deviously smuggled in anyway. In other words, those girls fast and

---

[46] Cf. Nekbakht Foundation, *Biography*, 116–117, for Hazrat Inayat Khan's own remarkable contrasting of Afro-Americans with colonized, outworn Asians: "to me it seems the coming race will be the race of Negroes; they are showing it from now," "conscious of all prejudice, the Negro does not allow his ego to be affected by it," "he stands upright with a marvelous spirit."

increasingly became status symbols as well, affordable only by the affluent.[47] Correspondingly, children whose looks reflected their mother's origin, testified thereby to their belonging to a great house at first glance.

Apart from the very earliest, "provincially" inward-looking Arab times and some churlish individuals in later centuries, it has well been said of Muslims generally that they wouldn't know how properly to discriminate, racially or color-wise, if they wanted to. The difference of hues and colors in the Qur'ān being regarded as from amongst the beneficent "signs of God," and Islamic universalism with its pride in mixed descents (very much shared by the Mawlābakhshīs) also contributed to such an open-minded attitude. By contrast, both the Hindus and the British had strong feelings on race and color. And as Muslim power and social attitudes had to give way to imperial British force and modernizing Hindu self-confidence, a new public mood forced itself upon them. However good their looks, Muslim Afro-Indian children, rather than aristocrats, now tended to become witnesses to the slave trade and antiquated human standards. Where such acquired girls were combined with wives from earlier arranged (hence hardly personally-selected) marriages and when relationships then really soured seriously enough, the Indian wives, always smart since self-centered family fixers, might easily outmaneuver the African favorites on the ancient Sara-Hagar principle. Nevertheless, under Islamic law concubines still retained a more secure position than wives; that is, once become "mother of a child" (*umm-walad*) their contracts could not be undone, they were undivorceable, in contrast to wives—reason for them often to refuse matrimony to amorous masters. In the most outstanding Islamic sovereign houses—the later Umayyad, then the 'Abbāsid Caliphs, the Ottomans, etc.—most if not all rulers were sons of slave mothers held on concubinage terms, a matter of policy as much as freedom of

---

[47] In Europe, the Ethiopian beauty fashion was followed by Fürst Pückler, whose famous ice cream doubtless testifies to his good tastes, and this despite his marriage to the daughter of Prussian State chancellor Prince Hardenberg - that much for Germanic racial prejudice, in fact more a South German-Austrian and, as always everywhere, plebeian phenomenon rather than one of the oft-reviled *Junker* Prussians, their very name Balto-Slav rather than Germanic!

choice. In caste-conscious India, of course, such standards could not apply. The Mughals' policy of reconciliation involved marriage with Rājpūt princesses, though again, those had to be offset by Muslim marriages to take account of the powerful Islamic aristocracy. Given that position in the North, in the Dravidian regions of South India, distinctions in status of marriage versus concubinage arrangements, clearly would be regarded even more as making some real sense or other, never mind beauty or other desirable personal qualities. In the great houses, of course, slave or other girls coming in on legal concubinage terms, would be given, in accordance with the promise they appeared to hold, a careful training in aristocratic standards of culture and behavior, the system thus turning out ladies, as British public schools gentlemen, these systems very much being thought of in similar terms; also, *zanāna* ladies were apt to make a hobby out of educating children or young girls come in from outside in whatever way. Having regard to all this, it might just be thinkable that in this instance of the Ṭīpū Sulṭān family, some such events took place. That is, that British and Hindu fashionable moods had come into play, alongside the ever-present, strict caste compatibility standards, all such currents acting on the *zanāna*—with the possible result of Qāsim Bī's mother being more or less plucked, if not dropped, from the family tree in the sense of being relegated to a secondary station, one giving a more marked responsibility to a service staff of which these two retainers were part; although, of course, Qāsim Bī's marriage still would have been primarily a matter for her father or the eldest male relative in his place. Some experience of that kind might have conditioned a tragic life-sense in Qāsim Bī (supposing that were not merely evoked by the retainers, paraphrasing the entire Ṭīpū history of rise and fall in constant battles, and in that way enhancing their own significance: cf. *Biography*'s quotation given earlier, as to their presence emphasizing the "atmosphere of tragedy"[48]). But again, all this is theory. A much simpler likely role for the retainers is described below, but cannot account for the tragedy bits—unless the retainers or their descendants were really determined to interpose themselves at the cost of Qāsim Bī's Ṭīpū blood relations altogether.

---

[48] Nekbakht Foundation, *Biography*, 123.

Most of the visiting Barodan ladies would have been Hindus or Muslimas who, in Sir Muhammad Iqbal's phrase, had "out-Hindued the Hindus"; and who therefore might have reacted race-consciously to African, or for that matter, Dravidian, features. And that might explain Qāsim Bī's reluctance, rather than any further "sense of tragedy," to receive them.[49]

All in all, however, it is perfectly clear that the retainers' self-important stories have dramatized her personality and course of life to an untenable extent. All that somber stuff, whilst the family in question, including Qāsim Bī's parents, their names stubbornly withheld, for over half a century and several generations, had been living safe and sound and doubtless happily, in their dainty Mysore palace![50] And again, is it really to be believed that Mawlābakhsh, repeatedly living at the Mysore court, going through a ten-month musical contest, being given princely honors celebrated by ceremonial and a public procession—that with all that he would not have been acquainted with and known to, and probably in close contact with, the premier Muslim nobles of State?

True, the retainers may well have acted as go-betweens, once marriage orientations were being launched. Those could not have been initiated by Mawlābakhsh, for how was he to know of any marriageable daughters in the famous family and even if so, he, a stranger from far away, could not have begun any such action on his own. Traveling as yet alone or at least without female family members, who could have established contacts with the Ṭīpū ladies, or with whom could those ladies have sought contact? Conversely, the Ṭīpū Sulṭāns themselves could not have taken any open, formal initiative personally: any marriage proposal, as obviously in India as in Europe, would have to come from the prospective bridegroom's side. So the only remaining possibility obviously would have been mediation: a discrete, confidential, wholly informal dispatch of some trusted retainers, acting as if quite on their own, to find out

---

[49] Ibid, 22.

[50] Actually, Māmūṅ-ḥużūr and descendants, far from sharing Ṭīpū Sulṭān's and his lineal descendants' fates, had done very well indeed out of a timely protection of their own feudal interests, regarded as a perfectly legitimate priority in times when nationalist allegiances or sacrifice for abstract purposes was regarded as senseless or irresponsible. No tragedy anywhere in their ascent into the Ṭīpū Sulṭān succession at all!

whether or not Mawlābakhsh was married already, whether he would be free and interested in a Ṭīpū match at all, what the conditions of such an arrangement were to be, how the wedding celebration was to take place. Plenty of work and worry for diligent retainers, therefore!

Once a "high" noble, Mawlābakhsh's attractiveness as a possible match for any of their daughters or nieces must have been great indeed to the Ṭīpū Sulṭāns. Yet nothing of all that has transpired in the available texts. The above for the moment cannot therefore mean more than the most likely substance of a working hypothesis. But what may be said is that some Indo-African ethnic and aesthetic characteristics have continued, however disparate, further to enhance the notably good looks of Mawlābakhshīs for three to five generations now, and at least in one case have produced some exquisite female beauty that would appear to owe almost everything to Qāsim Bī's African heritage.

Baroda scene

Baroda State had a Gujarati majority. By far the most advanced Gujarati-speaking element were the immigrant, strongly anglicized Parsis. The Gāekwāṛ Maharajas and the Hindu ruling class were Mahrattas. Talented and well-qualified Muslims drawn into State service from elsewhere were joined to the ruling class as the "Sardārīs." Amongst the Gujaratis, about ten percent were Muslims including mercantile convert castes like the Bohrās. Apart from such special groups, the *mullā*-led Muslim generality tended to be very orthodox, and all too clearly there was no love lost between them and the residents of Naulākha—later Mawlābakhsh House or Mawlābakhsh Pavitravilās before becoming Moula Bux Building—today an unromantic unstately ruin,[51] close to the equally decayed old Sarkarwada Palace of the Gāekwāṛs on Mandvi Road. Although a minority, Baroda Muslims not only

[51] Pictures in "The Golden Jubilee of the Sufi Message" (1960), 10, and in Dr. H.J. Witteveen, *Universal Sufism* (Shaftesbury, England: Element Books, 1997) (photograph no. 5), reproducing Reinder Visscher's sketch of the house with its summarily repaired roof as it stood abandoned along an as yet un-overpopulated Yakutpura Main Road, Champaner Gate. For description cf. the first and final chapters of De Jong Keesing, *Inayat Khan*, both entitled: "The House of Moula Bux."

never felt discriminated in any way, but right up to the end of Gāekwāṛ rule on the contrary were convinced that theirs' was a privileged position. That might be no more than a tribute to the even-handed equity and sympathy of the Maharajas, but an excellent conviction to hold for any minority anywhere! Much beyond that general population and chief amongst Muslim groups was the "feudal" land-owning element, including Nawābs and a family of "Mīrs" (Amīrs), living in large town establishments and owning important estates. The seniormost Nawāb in those days used to receive from the State an income of four lacs of rupees (i.e. four hundred thousand). When he was to attend State functions or Court ceremonies at the Palace's Durbar Hall but arrived late, not an unusual Indian predicament, the custom was for the Maharaja himself to receive him at the entry door in welcome. In this well-ordered Baroda State society, Mawlābakhsh, with all his name and fame, and his family-members were newcomers; their position had to be carefully balanced. As incoming Sardārīs, in their capacity of gentleman-musicians they had to be attached to and protected by, but not become wholly dependent on, the Gāekwāṛ court; independent livelihood and landed property and status had to be emphatically upheld, to say nothing of the Mysorean high-nobility rank. Social relations with Gujaratis other than the Parsis, was, therefore, "not done." In any case, puritan-orthodox rejection of music prevented much Muslim fellow-feeling. The fact that the Gāyanshālā Academy and musical introduction books and courses made music available to non-professionals, with private instruction even open to girls, instead of music remaining confined to some courtier coteries, made matters even worse to the orthodox multitude. Such antagonism as there was met with condescension on the Mawlābakhshī side, and if that did not suffice in that strongly stratified society, with downright contempt. Thus Hazrat Inayat Khan grew up in an environment intensely committed to a mystically conceived but punctiliously observed Islam; intensely proud of Muslim civilization and culture generally and of the specifically Indo-Islamic and Mughal variety in particular, that is, with an admiring sympathy for the Hindu world and values as well; with receptive open-mindedness towards the nascent notions of both Ottoman panislamism and European modernism; and alongside all that, with a feeling of the local Muslim masses largely being little better than barbarians, *mullā* knowledge senselessly elementary. As classical and creative musicians and landowners they could not help being the aristocrats they so happily were; the Mysore elevation gave that attitude a veritable *dharma* quality. Though it never extended to the view of the Muslim world's tribal egalitarianism as a whole, yet this dual sense of distance of the local community, regarded as benighted because of their attitude to music (or, rather more perhaps, towards musicians as such) and socially more in general, as primitive commoners, undoubtedly has colored, possibly also in some ways conditioned, Hazrat Inayat Khan's views of things communally Islamic or democratically (rather than religiously or personally) egalitarian.

But that did not mean, of course, that the Nawāb nobility for its part did not regard the *rājkufū* musician with *à priori* reserve. In their circle, unrelated newcomers were uncalled for, and Mawlābakhsh's commanding presence and defiant retort to Mahārājā Khaṇḍe Rāo had not been forgotten amongst them. Had he not implicitly, as "*vidvān*" (genius, knower), claimed a "kingdom" beyond political monarchy? The "knowers" were the Brāhmans, as such ranking beyond princes and kings, like them entitled to be honored as "*mahārāj*" (so that worldly rulers gladly switched to the Mughal "*ḥużūr*," approximately "Your Highness," with the additional advantage of having, in Urdu at least, a separate variant for more spiritual respectability, i.e. "*ḥażrat*"). Given that royal respect towards *vidvāns* and their kind, it was hard even for Muslim Nawābs to think of an appropriate retort restoring the balance. So Nawābs and Mawlābakhshīs kept aloof from each other as well, for a long while. Until, again, in the third generation almost a century later, one of the Nawābs took the initiative of proposing two simultaneous marriage arrangements between his children and those of the Mawlābakhsh-Paṭhān family then returned from Nepal. The Mawlābakhshī parents, fourth in holding their Mysorean family honors, were naturally pleased to comply. But their children in question had received a modern English education and refused, insisting on remaining free so as to make their own personal choices. That was the watershed between feudal and contemporary standards, and the *a'lākhāndān* never recovered. Its decline has since been speedy and steep.

It is to be remembered that in the late nineteenth century, still the golden age of the Indian princes under the pax brittanica, in sheltered and prosperous Baroda State neither religion nor social structure was felt to be in any kind of danger, much rather the opposite; so that group solidarity for the sake of all, whatever any personal divergences, was not yet an issue in the least. Much later only, after the "watershed" crisis, the younger generations bridged the gap with the Muslim community as a whole in an inflationary current in which the kinship group identity was finally dissolved. The feudal and allodial groups, as a distinct comprehensive category simply were no longer in the field after the States' absorption into independent India.[52] It was amongst the Sardārī and Marhaṭṭā groups, along with the Parsis, that the three generations of Mawlābakhshīs enjoyed most of their social relationships, i.e. with the Shī'ī Tayyabjīs, judiciary officials, the Gāekwāṛ brothers of the ruler, with the Powār *zamīndārs*, above all with a large number of Brāhman scholars and devotees. The saintly Narsinghjī Mahārāj was prominent amongst them, Mawlābakhsh composing music to his poems:

> *Suniyo re suno na re bacana koi, Hariras nirmala hai anantko*
> *Bhāgya bina nahīn pāye, yeh to bhāgya binā nahīn pāye*
> *Guru krupā binā pāye nahīn re, upāya kariyo hazār, bacana koi.*

> (Whether you listen or do not listen, whatever the words [it makes no difference but] the serenity of feeling God, Who draws all towards Himself, is forever. Without a blessed destiny it cannot be attained, this indeed, without a blessed destiny it cannot be attained. Without the Guru's mercy that [blessed destiny] cannot be obtained. Even if you attempt a thousand solutions, whatever the words ... [i.e. conceptions and arguments cannot take the place of live experience, which once attained, is forever].)

Despite all that, essentially the Mawlābakhshīs throughout their "era," were very much a world unto themselves. As Prof. Allyn Miner has very rightly observed: "Mawlābakhsh maintained a

[52] A view explicitly if regretfully held by Maharaja Fatehsingh Rao Gaekwar, who succeeded to his ancestral *gādī* (throne) in a personal, social and honorary capacity after Baroda State's political annexation to the Indian republic.

strongly self-contained household."[53] In his multi-layered music, he was a man with a message, and all his ideals and enthusiasms were involved in that contribution to the revival of a national all-inclusive all-Indian perspective.

Ideals of consolidation

The *a'lākhāndān's* comparative aloofness was, therefore, impelled by a positive intent. In Mawlābakhsh's life, events had moved with unusual swiftness and intensity (reminiscent of Hazrat Inayat Khan's later life in both India and the West). Consolidation became a real necessity if continuity, and crystallization from the inside outwards, were to be provided for. And that in first instance called for privacy rather than the public eye or image. Here Mawlābakhsh and his descendants were so successful that despite later challenges and tensions and a falling apart of the original tightly joint entity, essentially the spirit, the style and as it were the ideology of the Mawlābakhsh lineage was maintained throughout three generations in greatly changing circumstances, ending only with his grandson. Whilst in Hazrat Inayat Khan and his brothers' life and work in the West, the same impulse and outlook survived within the alien cultural environment, even if more abstract and diffuse, as lacking the material home base and its presuppositions. Yet in ideal, dynamism, self-confidence and conviction, they continued Mawlābakhsh's brilliance in spirit and practice, their mysticism the lineal descendant of his music, their idea of living and transmitting something of essential value to their fellow-men and humanity generally, a continuation of his.

The main lines along which the Mawlābakhshī life-sense proceeded and to which the young were attuned, could be categorized as those of Dravidian culture (with music, of course, as its central theme[54]), *a'lākhāndān* principles (taking into account both the musical *zamīndārī* past and the fresh perspective of the Mysorean *rājkufū* nobility), and what can best

[53] Introduction to *Minqar-i-musiqar* (forthcoming), 2.

[54] Whilst women were not supposed to enter the male (hence potentially occupational) field of music, the matrilineal emphasis *and* recognition of the all-important role of all females in the kinship structure and its relationships, compensated them and their status twice over for their abstention from active musical participation.

be rendered as the Mughal (Indo-Islamic) values in their widest sense.[55] Good impressions of these may be gleaned from *Biography* and Van Beek.[56]

All that was of course a largely verbal, almost "atmospheric" mode of awareness and cultivation, no written set of ideas or directions. Analysis of family members' song verses and poems, as of Hazrat Inayat Khan's teaching, will probably be helpful in approximating those perspectives rather more closely, but must once again be left to future investigation. There is, however, one area in which all those three categories found concrete and, to the kinship group, vitally significant expression. Both as a matter of affectionate family ideal and in order to extend, strengthen, and so secure their *a'lākhāndān*, new and as yet lacking collateral branches, Mawlābakhsh and Qāsim Bī were insistent that their daughters upon marriage, with their husband and children, remain members of their lineage and resident at their House. That involved an absolute requirement of their husbands to accept the quality of *dāmād-i ghar*, consorts to their wives within the *a'lākhāndān*, instead of the reverse taking place as usual. The practice was not of course unknown in Northern India, for example to enable one girl of a family without sons or close nephews, to remain home and represent the younger generation of her parents' family. But the insistence that all girls as a matter of high principle remain part of their parental lineage, would seem to owe everything to the example of Dravidian matrilinealism. Not of course, that in this Hindustani Muslim case, the daughters' lines were to be primary descendants instead of the sons'. Both were to continue alongside one another, as a truly dynastic arrangement. It was applied successfully in the cases of Fāṭima Bī's and Khadīja Bī's marriage to Mashaykh Raḥmat Khān. Fāṭima's daughter Jena Bī, and as last and final case, the latter's daughter Panāh Bī, still were accounted full members of the *a'lākhāndān*. However, the practice was stopped and the principle abrogated as from her, Panāh Bī, Jena Bī's and her cousin-husband Mehr-bakhshe's child, herself married "outside." In Khadīja Bī's case, her sons "Chhoṭā Miyāṅ" Inayat, "Pyārū Miyāṅ"

[55] Here not meant, of course, in the *ashrāf*-group sense!

[56] Nekbakht Foundation, *Biography*, 28, 41, 55–6, 78–9, etc.; Van Beek, *Hazrat Inayat Khan*, 14, 32, 38, etc.

("Pyārū Mīr") Maheboob, and "Mawlā Miyāṅ" Musharaff Khan in a very real sense *were* the Mawlābakhshī *a'lākhāndān*, alongside the sole male-line succeeding heir, their cousin-brother Allāhdād Khān-i Mawlābakhsh. In addition, that is, to their second-degree cousin-brother Muhammad Ali Khan who, giving up the lands and properties that were his, as his maternal grandparent's heir, for the benefit of his numerous fellow-descendants, joined the Mawlābakhsh family. He thus filled the void left by Karāmat Khān,[57] Inayat and Maheboob's younger brother, who died at eight and always remained remembered as having had a character, a sense of adventure, courage and enterprise, that matched that of Hazrat Inayat Khan himself. Muhammad Ali Khan, in effect, took over the third place in his stead. Really this "matrilineal" principle had been conceived as applicable only to the three Mawlābakhsh-Qāsim Bī daughters themselves and not beyond their generation, notwithstanding the later extension in favor of Jena Bī, Panāh Bī and Muhammad Ali Khan. In the original daughters' generation it ended, moreover, on a note of such tragedy that any feeling for continuing with it withered away altogether, even though still embodied and for their lifetime carried on by Bībehin Bī's, Fāṭima Bī's, and Khadīja Bī's three (grand-) children.

Inayatayn heritage: Bī into Khān

Fāṭima's and Khadīja's younger sister was to be married to another Tonk cousin, who as such had a priority claim in the matchmaking. Mawlābakhsh remained very close to his sister and brother-in-law, the latter well remembered from his Baroda visits. The couple itself had four daughters, amongst whom Ashraf Bī and her husband, the Baroda officer Aḥmad 'Alī Khān, were the parents of Muhammad Ali Khan, who, after their early deaths, was taken to his grandparental home in Tonk, Rajasthan, educated by his aunts and selected as family heir by his grandparents. But the grandfather's Ṭopezāi brother and cousins had numerous sons, of whom one, Ghulām Muḥammad, was selected as prospective bridegroom for his Baroda cousin. However, he refused integration

[57] On him, see Musharaff Khan, *Pages*, 7, 10. He continued to be vividly remembered by Maheboob Khan as well.

into and settlement with, the Mawlābakhsh-Qāsim Bī family on the *dāmād-i ghar* principle, probably from a mixture of personal pride and concern for his landed interests in Tonk—*jāgīrs* (fiefs) the State might resume if not adequately represented at court. She, on her part, steadfastly refused all pressure to abandon her own house and lineage: loyalty to her parental principles, the Mawlābakhshī ideals and perspectives, came first. She swore that she would rather die than give up the environment and lineage of which she, too, was a trustee. Tragically, the crisis broke her heart and she died, the youngest of all Mawlābakhshī children. And yet, this proud and modest girl bequeathed to the *a'lākhāndān* and wide circles beyond it, an heirloom of resounding value and repute. As she lay dying, her elder surviving sister's son was born and she in her agony blessed him with her own name, that he might uphold and extend the ideals that had inspired her and she so cherished.

Mureeds and admirers of Sufism might well occasionally spare a thought for that 'Ināyat Bī whose nephew carried, along with those ideals, her name wherever he went, into whatever he achieved, and for whatever time his life's work will be returned to by that unknown quantity, the future. And not only for her most poignant case: all those benefiting from Sufism are heirs to all family females' enabling attitudes as well! Of the ladies of the Mawlābakhshī lineage, it has somewhere been said, rather ponderously: "Those ladies knew their responsibilities and duties." They have also known how to die sacrificially: 'Ināyat Bī by setting their values beyond life, Khadīja Bī spurning life over the loss of Karāmat Khān, Jena Bī at Panāh Bī's birth, newly-wed Ṣabīra Bī over the four-year long separation from her husband (Maheboob Khan), Noorunnisa in translating her father's teachings on spiritual liberty and divine self-sacrifice into altogether extraordinary, deeply idealistic, wartime courage for the sake of future human freedom.

In the history of the three generations, Mawlābakhsh to Allāhdād Khān, and the biography of the five brothers, Hazrat Inayat to Allāhdād Khān, those female five, and not exclusive of the others in the modest background, deserve the recognition of remembrance whenever the names and themes of this impressive human and cultural tradition are fondly and profitably recalled.[58]

Within a mere few years' time (about 1880–1882), Mawlābakhsh had lost two of his three daughters, Fāṭima Bī and 'Ināyat Bī. It remained recollected how the old patriarch used to mourn and remember them, seeking comfort from an unbearable pain in his own way, taking his *vīṇā*, reclining, singing, tears flowing, his own poem and song in Pīlū *rāga*, devoted to their memory, in a prayer begging forgiveness for the frailty of his human grief, not meant as a fatherly outcry against what was ordained for the best by the Most Merciful:

> *Hamāre sarva gupta bāten āpko vidita hain*
> *Tum kṣamā karo krupānidhāna, yeh pratīta hai*
> *Hamāre namra prārthanā krupākārī svīkārnā*
> *Dayānidhāna deve doṣa ko nivārnā.*
>
> (Our all hidden secrets [pains] are known to Thee alone; Thou wilt grant forgiveness, O Gracious One, this [alone] is clear. Our humble prayer in Thy loving kindness do accept; Compassionate One, O God! Do Thou remove our faults of limitation!)

Richness of emotion, too, may be a consolidation spanning the generations.

Well over sixty years later, in the depths of the Second World War's miseries, dangers and deprivation, when "from every side came only messages of weeping voices," Shaikh-ul-Mashaik Maheboob Khan used to sing and teach this song, and composed it to Western harmony with some Indian-style variations. His mystic's inwardness and ever-veiled sensitivity, covered by his proud Anglo-Mughal sense of reserve, never admitting of any complaint whatever life's fate, must clearly have found comfort in the piercing magic of that divine incantation, as had Mawlābakhsh in his day.

At the time of 'Ināyat Bī's death and Inayat Khan's birth, her elder sister and his mother, Khadīja Bī may have been only sixteen years old, possibly still fifteen.[59] How young then must 'Ināyat Bī

---

[58] In the half-century and more since World War II, of all Inayat-Khans, Noorunnisa has become the most famous one by far in the world at large; in Sufi circles, often probably still one of the least-known ones. The elder Indian generation's wholly natural embarrassment about the name and the person of a girl from their lineage becoming "public," "going into the public domain," can be respected without being artificially copied.

[59] In the oral tradition, Khadīja's age at the birth of Inayat used to be given

Above:
Sangītratna Mawlābakhsh

Left:
Murtażā Khān

Right:
Ḥaydar ʻAlī

Below:
Ṭīpū Sulṭān

Above:
Zanāna photo taken in 1896 by 'Usmān Khān. First row from left: Sārā Bī (third wife of Murtażā Khān), Jenā Bī (daughter of Raḥmat Khān and Fāṭima Bī, wife of Mawlavī Mehr-bakhshe), Awliyā Bī (daughter of Mawlābakhsh's sister, wife of 'Alā al-Dīn Khān, mother of Ulmā Bī), Umrāo Bī (second wife of Murtażā Khān), Hindu neighbor; second row: Khadīja Bī (second wife of Raḥmat Khān, mother of Hazrat Inayat Khan), Amīr Bī (second wife of Mawlābakhsh, mother of 'Alā al-Dīn Khān), Bīmā Bī (wife of Imām Khān), two Hindu neighbors; third row: Fāṭima Bī (aunt of Muhammad Ali Khan) with Ulmā Bī, Sakīna Bī (sister of 'Usmān Khān), Begum Mā (aunt of Muhammad Ali Khan)

Left:
Murtażā Khān and Sardār Bī, with servant children

Above:
'Alā al-Dīn Khān (Dr. A.M. Paṭhan) and Chānd Bī

Right:
Allāhdād Khān and Mehr al-Nisā'

Above:
Prof. Inayat Khan Rahmat Khan Pathan

Left:
Hazrat Inayat Khan

Above:
Portrait of Hazrat Inayat Khan, painted by M. H. Thurburn, Paris 1913

Left:
An Indian portrait of Hazrat Inayat Khan

Above:
Seated: Hazrat Inayat Khan and Amina Begum. Standing: Maheboob Khan and Musharaff Khan. Children, left to right: Noorunnisa, Khairunnisa, Hidayat, Vilayat
Below:
Noorunnisa, Hidayat, Khairunnisa, Vilayat

Above:
The Royal Musicians of Hindustan

Right:
Maheboob Khan

Below, right:
Musharaff Khan

Below, left:
Muhammad Ali Khan

have been at the time of her death, and what can have been those ideals of hers *Biography* speaks of in such grandiosely empty terms?[60] And she must have been the youngest of the three sisters, or else, rather than the elder two, would have had priority in marrying Mashaykh Raḥmat Khān. Theoretically, of course, she might have been the middle daughter, by her own intended engagement no longer available when Raḥmat Khān lost Fāṭima Bī. But oral reference to 'Ināyat Bī always has been as to the youngest girl. It might also be that hers was a (cousinly) child marriage, on Hindu lines, or almost so, meaning no more than a girl's passage (in principle) into her in-laws' home for further education in that family's *dharma* and standards.[61] It is equally possible that the two younger daughters' marriages were put forward due to the preceding death of their own mother Qāsim Bī, of which no year has been related. In those days, of course, parents were regarded as offensively negligent in having at home young marriageable daughters for whom no wedding had yet been arranged. Whatever was the case, it is easy to understand 'Ināyat Bī's extreme reluctance to being hauled off to faraway Tonk; even apart altogether from any Mawlābakhshī "semi-matrilineal" ideology, such must have struck her as a veritable banishment at the best of times. Still, their shared kinship values were very real, at a genuinely idealistic level. Again, then, which could have been 'Ināyat Bī's ideals, of whatever age she may have been? From the key-phrase well remembered but unmentioned in *Biography*: that she would die if forced to leave Mawlābakhsh House, it at least is clear enough that the threefold values mentioned in the foregoing as the ideals of consolidation,

---

variously as "about" fourteen or fifteen; her age difference with Raḥmat Khān, however, was twenty-three years. As Raḥmat Khān's year of birth is given as 1843, that would make Khadīja sixteen at the time of birth, possibly just still fifteen. It seems obvious that Khadīja's age of marriage and at her son's birth have tended to become confused. Close enquiry about a woman, again, was held to be disrespectful. That might give one reason amongst others for considering the parental age difference datum, of greater curiosity value in any case, the more reliable one: it was often mentioned, as a matter of entire certainty.

[60] Nekbakht Foundation, *Biography*, 35.

[61] Analogously, Muhammad Ali Khan, orphaned in Baroda, was brought to Tonk, prosperous Baroda with its brilliant Gāekwāṛ court being seen by his grandparents as a far too worldy, materialist city for their heir, intended to become a courtly and leisured-class *mullā*.

into which she was born and bred, would have come naturally to her as to all family members. If Hazrat Inayat Khan had returned to Baroda with his brothers, as quite clearly he was still intending to do during his World War I residence in London, those shared aims would have been updated and reinforced into permanent survival. But granted the significance of those ideals of consolidation to family members, what wider interest could they possibly have had? Here we come to the third, most diffuse category of "Mughal values." The consolidation of the *a'lākhāndān* itself, if intended for the biographical unit and its individual members, was not merely genticentric. It also was meant to fulfil something of a lighthouse function, flashing its beams all around and lighting up the enduring values of Mughal civilization and culture. That seen as including an appreciative understanding and experience of all Indian cultural currents, integrating new hopes and visions coming in from the West, open-mindedness combined with firmness of conviction in embodying and representing what was felt to be the highest, most humane mode and standard of life ("*insāniyat*," humane-ness, humanity, was a key word). In short, modernizing maintenance and development of the Mughal way and outlook of life as being the highest, richest, most all-inclusive Indian way of life attainable, and in which all communities always had participated (whatever the political relationships). And to this idealist vision, the Ṭīpū Sulṭān descent, the *rājkufū* nobility, the courtly and gentlemanly musicianship, however of value in the personal sense within the *a'lākhāndān*, in the wider sense were ways and means, instruments through which the intended music might adequately find expression. That vision, however conceptualized, permeated and inspired all family members from Mawlābakhsh to his grandsons, very much including the ladies of the House of all generations. The Mughal Empire had given way to the British Raj—as a cultural concept and attitude it lived on, perpetuated and reinvigorated at the level of committed, appropriately-bred kinship units, those basic units of human society: a service to all India and a signal to all the West that here was a unique heritage of meaningful human existence. In this sense it was, if an aristocratic, yet equally a universalist set of ideas and attitudes.

Hazrat Inayat Khan's later Sufi teachings, even the structure his work then assumed in the West, are unthinkable without the dynamic and aspiration shaped by that nourishing vision. To that extent, he straddles the boundary between a recent and rich Mughal Indian past and today's challenging world of practical and ideological modernism. Whilst this much can be confidently affirmed, a full discussion of the impact of Mawlābakhsh's person and practice on Hazrat Inayat Khan and his musico-mystical work will still call for much detailed study. That will doubtless underline that Mawlābakhsh's modernizing development of music became a similar development of mysticism in Hazrat Inayat Khan; his all-Indian orientation became universalism in his grandson. Mawlābakhsh reached the highest level of human attainment in the world of his time and society: the *rājkufū* rank, the equal of princes of the realm; Hazrat Inayat Khan, the highest level of spiritual life attainable in all human existence, that of "the God-realized mystic." What further expansion and fulfilment could Mawlābakhsh have hoped for?

That attainment too, was Hazrat Inayat Khan's inimitable reply to the question confronting the younger descendants of the House of Mawlābakhsh, above all its two brilliant young men, himself and 'Alā al-Dīn Khān. How were *they* to perpetuate, fulfil, enhance, the legacy of Mawlābakhsh? That was no problem for the elder Mawlābakhsh son, Murṭażā Khān; for he became his father's heir and successor, representing his person and position, music and style, family honors and landed interests in all the plenitude of his substantial, hugely impressive self. It was up to the two younger protagonists, *wājib* (morally obligatory) on them, to fulfil their ancestral *dharma* in their own way. 'Alā al-Dīn modernized; Inayat Khan spiritualized; their parallel courses faced in different directions. To 'Alā al-Dīn, transformed into Dr. Paṭhān, the course seemed clear: modernization, secularization, Anglicization. The British country squire, with his townhouse and his country estate, became his ideal model, realized to a considerable extent. He became a nationalist, but still on the British country gentleman's and Indian musical courtier's terms,[62] for which India's emergent

---

62 With estates as far apart as Nepal and Bangalore, a senior military rank in Nepal (as director of music), enjoying the rank of a royal courtier and on terms of

political groupings felt no need whatever, a sentiment heartily reciprocated by him, realizing they spelt the end of the States and estates system. Though no Qāsim Bī descendant, he arranged with his elder brother, Murṭażā Khān, to become his primary heir of family properties and income as well as the family honors, with which Murṭażā was glad to comply. Upon Dr. Paṭhān's return from Nepal in the nineteen-thirties, he gave the reconstructed Mawlābakhsh House its last period of brilliant cultural and social life, lasting until his death in 1949. Murṭażā's only son, the single male-line heir, Allāhdād Khān, took over from him, but in the disastrous circumstances after Independence (1947) and the usurpation of Baroda State by an India republican and socialist with a vengeance, he could do little more than maintain a prestigious personal representation, in which he continued to excel to the extent his indifferent health—having been poisoned in childhood—permitted. As dignified as he was amicable, he matched his far-off cousin-brothers in the West to an altogether extraordinary degree, in physical appearance as in general manner, style and mentality. Consolingly so whilst he lived, and monumentally so in comprehensive biographical perspective, Allāhdād Khān, the last of the three Mawlābakhshī-era generations and of the five cousin-brotherly grandsons, set the seal on a socio-cultural family tradition of unusually rich fascination.

Hazrat Inayat Khan's paternal background

This cursory survey of Hazrat Inayat Khan's biographical background and the questions raised both in historical perspective and in relation to his own life's work, inevitably has concentrated on the Mawlābakhshī family history. However, something at least needs to be said of his paternal lineage. For although its last three survivors all married into the *a'lākhāndān*, it represents a family tradition with a character all of its own—if only because it included the notion of there being at least one mystic in each of its generations (of which Inayat, Maheboob, Karāmat and Musharaff Khan are stated to have been the sixteenth).

---

close personal friendship with the ruling (Vice-regal) Rana dynasty.

It might be said that consideration of Hazrat Inayat Khan's paternal family really fits more appropriately in a life story of his brother, Shaikh-ul-Mashaik (Mīr Pyārū Miyāṅ) Maheboob Khan, whose personality represents that ancestry, as Hazrat Inayat Khan does Mawlābakhsh's. In any case, few hasty indications will have to suffice here.

It is to be noted that their personal names always omitted the divine name that ought to complete it, as we saw earlier. These formally ought therefore, to be read as: 'Ināyat Allāh, Maḥbūb Ilāhī, Raḥmat Allāh, Karāmat Allāh, Ni'mat Allāh. Out of respect for his elder brother, the saintly poet, musician and mystic Ja'far Khān, Raḥmat Khān modestly avoided using their principal caste (*khāṣṣat*) title of *mashaykh*; there is no reason why we should not now give Hazrat Inayat Khan's father his due. The juniormost form of that caste designation was *mashaykhzāda*, later transformed by Pir-o-Murshid Hazrat Inayat Khan into "Pirzade" and "Murshidzade" for, respectively, his elder (Noorunnisa, Vilayat) and younger (Hidayat, Khairunnisa) son and daughter[63] and their descendants insofar as continuing observance of relevant *khāṣṣat* and *taṣdīq* standards (these, the counterpart of Hindu caste *dharma*, adherence to which constituted the criterion of recognized kinship). Three separate investigations, carried out for Murtażā Khān around 1900, by Hazrat Inayat Khan himself from Lahore in late 1926, and again in the mid-fifties on behalf of Pir-o-Murshid Muhammad Ali Khan, all confirmed the family had become totally extinct in its original (immigrant) homeland of Punjab. This despite the fact that the veteran Sir Muhammad Zafrulla Khan, first Foreign Minister of Pakistan then judge in the International Court of Justice, repeatedly affirmed that in his early childhood days, the Jum'ashāh Mashaykhs family was still being remembered.[64]

The last known members of that family all three entered the Mawlābakhshī *a'lākhāndān*. Mashaykh Raḥmat Khān and Mawlavī

---

[63] Cf. Fuller, *Noor-un-nisa*, 38.

[64] In their young days, Mashaykh Raḥmat Khān once took Inayat and Maheboob to Punjab for the *qadam-bosī* (veneration, lit. "foot-kiss": cf. Musharaff Khan, *Pages*, 99) of his last surviving male relation in the elder generation: his uncle Day 'Umar-bakhshe. The girl mentioned by Musharaff Khan, *Pages*, 6–7, in all likelihood would have been in some way related, or a clan member, as well—her sense of honor, an honor to all their *khāndān*: one instance of Rājpūt standards of honor immigrant Khāns were so eager to emulate.

Mehr-bakhshe-yi Ja'far Khān both as *dāmād-i ghar*, Sardār Begum as wife of Murtażā Khān (of whose earlier three notably beautiful wives no children survived), then mother of Allāhdād Khān. As Mashaykh-related girl she was only traced after considerable effort and at the insistence of Khadīja Bī, hoping that in future male-line Mawlābakhshīs should equally descend from the Jum'ashāh Mashaykhs as the Mashaykhs did in the female line, from Mawlābakhsh. Their entrance into the *a'lākhāndān* as the last of their line, also involved their contribution to it of the *ashrāf* quality, one of their epithets (*laqabs*) having been *ashrāf-i atrāk*, Turkestani *khawāṣṣ* migrants. The *ashrāf*'s was, of course, precisely the category aspired to by Indian convert families, and so the *a'lākhāndān* in addition to *rājkufū* and *pavitra*, henceforth could hold itself to be entitled to the quality of *ashrāf*—"upward movement" in action!

A measure in the same vein that however in time proved itself the opposite of an "upward movement" was experimented with by Hazrat Inayat Khan. Having set up his Sufi Movement in the West, with the initiatic Sufi Order as the central component within it, the initiatic degree of "Murshid" was established in it, coupled to the function of "senior representative" of the Head of the Order, the Pir-o-Murshid. After the death of his elder *mashaykh*-line cousin Mehr-bakhshe in 1924, the Pir-o-Murshid Hazrat Inayat Khan introduced their senior caste rank of "Mashaik" in the Order structure. It was set at the level and as an equivalent in principle, of the Murshid's rank—with, however, a more "exoteric" in addition to "esoteric" semantic association. As a caste (*khāṣṣat*) title, after all, it faced both ways. But the new arrangement was no success. Recipients of the new degree felt they were merely handed a consolation prize, having been judged not good enough to be initiated as Murshids, so that it meant no more than a badge of failure. (One recipient even returned the acknowledgement form along with his signature, with the remark: "for one year"!) Conversely, family members were apt to feel somewhat unhappy about their caste characteristic being inflated by but mildly meritorious outsiders. The arrangement unraveled and was again annulled in later years, with the initiatic order ranks and the caste designations each again going their separate ways—an advance in sobriety and a relief to everybody.

Three curious questions in conclusion.

Mashaykh Raḥmat Allāh's biodates are usually given as 1843–1910. The *Biography's* pretentiously fussy 1979 edition notes however that, "according to an old MS probably by a member of the family, he died aged 80"[65]—hence was born in 1830. Indeed, in Baroda a story has long continued as well saying he was older than Mawlābakhsh himself (his father-in-law, born 1833). Unless the manuscript could be proven to be of Mehr-bakhshe, immensely devoted to his uncle,[66] as was often attested to by the brothers orally as well, that assertion must be regarded as quite untrue. No mention of such a remarkably high age was ever made by his sons or by the genealogically notably well-versed Muhammad Ali Khan. It would have made him sixty-six at least, when making the arduous trans-Himalayan trek to Nepal and back, and five to ten years older still, when Hazrat Inayat Khan's Hyderabadi friend 'Abd al-Majīd met him as a teacher at the Gāyanshālā Academy, seated on a garden bench at the end of day. He would have married Khadīja Bī at fifty-one when she might have been anything between sixteen and fourteen. And while that would not have been altogether unthinkable at the time, if imperative family policy so necessitated, yet an age difference of thirty-seven years might have rendered the marriage, for all mutual marital devotion, into a somewhat formal, hierarchical affair. On the contrary, their marriage by all accounts was known to be a particularly happy and personally close one, a point illustrated by several touching stories. And, in view of the father's life expectancy in those days, their four children might not have been quite so widely and carefully spaced (1882, 1887, 1892, 1895). The popular rumor, doubtless inspired by Raḥmat Khān's patriarchal, not to say authoritarian style, contrasting with Mawlābakhsh's and his two sons' more easy-going ways, cannot possibly therefore be regarded as likely.[67]

---

65 Nekbakht Foundation, *Biography*, 30, note 31.

66 Cf. Musharaff Khan, *Pages*, 54–55

67 De Jong-Keesing's comments (*Biography*, 57) of his having been a "somewhat lonely man" who "had been overshadowed by his father-in-law" is unconvincing in view of what is known about him otherwise. There may have

Mashaykh Raḥmat Khān's grandfather, Mashaykh Ni'mat Allāh Khān, is said rather vaguely to have been "a musician." In view of Ja'far and Raḥmat Khāns' later vocation, that would seem likely enough. The latter's father, however, has always been described as a military (or martial) man as well as some kind of community head or village chieftain (as reported by Musharaff Khan). It need only therefore to be noted in passing that the "five generations of musicians" of Hazrat Inayat Khan's ascendants, as mentioned in early printed materials, can only be arrived at by zigzagging between the paternal and maternal lines, with Ni'mat Khān coming in handy between Mawlābakhsh and Anvar Khān.

Finally, a curious point recalling the Qāsim Bī confusions. The earliest biographical note on Hazrat Inayat Khan in English (as well as French and Russian), drawn up or compiled by a Belgian living in London, Ryckloff T'Serclaes de Kessel as an introduction to *A Sufi Message of Spiritual Liberty*, states that "Professor Inayat Khan comes from the Mashayakh (Saints) family of Punjab where one of his ancestors, Jumasha, was canonised. Many still go to visit his tomb." One wonders through what (probably transatlantic?) mists the good baron obtained his information. The latter phrase, of course, is standard with Hazrat Inayat Khan when speaking of Khwaja Mu'īn al-Dīn Chishtī of Ajmer. Mercifully, the Punjab has always lacked a pope of any description, sanctifying ascetics' excesses into canonization. And Sufi saints are *walīs* (*awliyā'*, pl.) rather than *mashā'ikh* (an irregular alternative plural to *shuyūkh: shaykhs*).

In Punjab, there is an important tradition of Sufi saints, such as Angārā Shāh, Lāl Shāh, and indeed also including a Jum'a Shāh, to whom various anecdotes are supposed to refer. Confusion may have arisen between him and Raḥmat Khān's ascetic music teacher, engagingly called "Saint Alias" in *Biography*,[68] that is, Sayn Ilyās. T'Serclaes was copied by Bloch, but even the uncritical *Biography* omits mention of "Jumasha," which yet was taken over in several

---

been phases or occasions when there was a certain distance between Raḥmat Khān and his exuberantly gifted hence unruly elder son, and his image in Inayat Khan's view may have been overshadowed by Mawlābakhsh and Abū Hāshim. But that concerns their mutual relationship, not Raḥmat Khān's person on his own, or in relation to others.

[68] Nekbakht Foundation, *Biography*, 30.

subsequent publications from both within and outside Sufi circles[69]; the record therefore, needs to be set straight.[70] That is, a clear distinction here is to be made with the count of sixteen generations over five centuries (or six, dependent obviously on whether the counting started in the 19th or in the 20th century!) of Hazrat Inayat Khan's Jum'ashāhān-Mashaykhān ancestry.[71] A fuller discussion

[69] Including even Musharaff Khan's, the editors of which have allowed in other astounding mistakes, like calling Ja'far "Zafar" and describing Bahādur Khān as a mystic. In general, these colorfully evocative and attractive memoirs bristle with such inaccuracies; their revision is overdue.

[70] Another such story with no apparent foundation is that his mother was somehow related to the ruling house of Khairpur state in Sindh, the Shī'ī Tālpūr family. This is the more preposterous in that not even a reason for such confusion is to be found, giving it the appearance of a pure fabrication. Between his years of musical training with "Saint Alias" and his journey south to Baroda, Raḥmat Khān traveled and worked in Sindh, which included a spell at Khairpur (Musharaff Khan, *Pages*, 32–33). Otherwise, the only connection with Sindh would appear to be the tradition that their standard caste designation of "Mashaykh Jum'a Shāh" was rendered in Sindhi as "Miyāṅ Jem Shāh," this again relevant to insistence that the "*miyāṅ*" attached to their own names (Chhoṭā Miyāṅ, etc) was of Sindhi origin and not Gujarati (considered there to have a more inflated flavor).

[71] Mawlābakhsh and descendants continued exclusively to use the *laqab* of *khān*, acquired / assumed by his *zamīndār* great-grandfather upon islamization. Its value and significance only varying with the position, status or rank any of its members happened to occupy: noble landowner, gentleman-musician, Sardārī courtier, princely aristocrat; or, later, member of the martial (if grossly inflated) Muslim caste category generally equated with the *Indian* (supposedly immigrant) Paṭhāns and the Hindu Rājpūts or Kśatriyas.

By contrast, the honorific and titular lineage *laqabs* of Hazrat Inayat Khan's paternal Yūzkhān *khāṣṣatī*, better known as the Jum'ashāh-Mashaykh *khāndān*, appear to reflect consecutive phases of family history. Alongside the personal names of their three immediately preceding forefathers and the count of generations (since settlement in India), it is those that had to be accounted for by the younger generations for eventual further transmission. Their earliest Turkestani designations, possibly preceding islamization itself, were "*yūzkhān*" ('horde-khān', chieftain of a mounted tribal unit), and "*bakhshī*"/"*bakhshe*," 'patriarch': a literate (elderly?) wise man, writer, cantor, at first doubtless a shaman-like 'medical, musical, mystical' (if not, rather, magical!) practitioner. *Bakhshī* incantations over generations were apt to develop into full musical competence, as did their literacy into learning. With time and migration southward, impelled by upheavals in Central Asia due to Timur Lenk's campaigns, Turki "*yūzkhān*" was expanded and iranized into "*mīr khayl*" ('clan chief'), then indianized into several variants of the (Arabic) j-m-' root, followed by "*shāh.*" These served to connote various functional or honorary capacities—caste membership, community leadership, "free" allodial landownership, captaincy of a mounted unit, etc. As Khāns, Mīrs (Amīrs, Mīrzās) and Shāhān ('free lords'), they could claim to be Muslim counterparts of the Hindu Rājpūt knights and nobles. (Similarly, "*bakhshe*" tended to be equated to such different terms as, e.g., "*beg*" or

thereof must await another occasion. The above notes would seem chiefly relevant to the purposes of the present survey: to set some perspectives for further exploration, in the interest of fuller understanding of Hazrat Inayat Khan's life, work and ideals and their mutual interaction against the historical background out of which they arose.

"*patī*"; though incongruously, "*yūzkhān*" also sprouted that Indian counterpart as "*yudhpati*." Where indianized or native throats elided 'kh', such fanciful or imaginative equations were extended even further to "*bashe*" or "*basha'a*" [both Turki for Persian *sardār*] and an intended "*pāshā*" often rendered as "*bādshā*"!) Their Turkestani Islam strongly imbued with Sufi mysticism, the ancient title of "*bakhshī*" may well have been supplemented with that of "*shaykh*," though of this there is no record or recollection. In India, however, "*shaykh*" became the designation of high-caste Hindu converts (or Europeans like 'Abd al-Ḥāmid and 'Abd al-Ghanī Wilfred-Nation). It therefore could not have distinctive identity value to the Central Asian immigrant *ashrāf-i atrāk*. As done more often in the other Islamic languages, an Arabic plural form was adopted, coming into singular use, instead. In this case one already carrying some castelike spiritual-cum-temporal connotation: "*mashā'ikh*." In an intentional upgrading as from both "*bakhshe*" and "*shaykh*," it then was first contracted into "*mashaykh*," "*maśekh*," also adjusted further into "*mihshaykh*" and "*mahāśekh*," and completed with (Persian) plurals: "*mihshaykhān*," "*mahāśekhān*," as well. At first held by Bakhshe patriarchs, it then came to be regarded as all descendants' caste title, with the seniormost occasionally being marked out as "*malik-maśekh*" or "*mīr-maśekh*." The interest of that designation in those times was, that particularly in its primary form, "*mashaykh*," it could be regarded as counterpart of Hindus' Brāhman castes, whilst in its more secular shapes it could help to reinforce the titles of "*khān*" etc. in their intended equivalence to the second Hindu caste, and to set them off, and secure their erstwhile value, in face of inflationary social movement upwards, as affecting all Hindu and Muslim honorifics, styles and titles. The same applied to aristocratic personal names (styles originally) such as those ending in "al-Dīn," "al-Dawla," "al-Zamān," "al-Nisā" (fem.); as also to female styles or titles, e.g. "*khātūn*," "*khānum*," "*begum*," "*bānū*," "*bībī*." The latter, indeed, became so widespread that the Mawlābakhsh family settled for "*bī*"—regarded less as a contraction than as a variant of "*begum*"/"*begam*," derived from such masculine "*beg*"-versions as "*bey*," "*bī*," "*bik*." In that view "*bībī*" should remain applied only to the Prophet's wife: "Khadīja Bībī," too elevated for popular taint. Application of that form in the case of Hazrat Inayat Khan's mother may have been a negligent breach of that convention, or deliberate, to name her the more emphatically after that Prophetic spouse. In case of the other ladies in *Biography* genealogies, that may be due to the earliest editor, Almgren, or to an Indian informant not resident in the House itself, like Mehr-bakhshe-yi Ja'far Khān, or to anybody's careless imprecision. In any case, the above contention, like so much else, in his young days was instilled into the present writer.

Glossary of words not explained in the text

A=Arabic, P=Persian, U=Urdu, I=Indian languages, H=Hindi, T=Turki

a'lā A – (elative) elevated, serene.

ammā U – mother.

ashraf A – (elative), more- , most high, noble.

ashrāf A – (plur.) "nobles and notables"; leading layers of Muslim migrants into India, its (generally four) categories becoming counterparts of the Hindu Brāhmans and Rājpūts or Kśatriyas.

Chishtī P – member of the Indian Chishtiyya Sufi Order.

dāmād P – son-in-law.

dāmād-i ghar UH – son-in-law "of the house", taken into his wife's family in exceptional cases of special remainder, etc.

darbār P – (princely) court, formal assembly.

dharma I – religion, religious convention or law; the particular religious-canonical duties and customs giving any caste group its specific identity and characteristics, ranging from spiritual observance to diet.

gharānā HI – house, lineage, kinship or family unit.

Ghasīṭ-khwān HP – as a name of honor: the one who is expert in rendering a certain "slide" or "swing" of grace-notes (*gamakas*) in Indian vocal music.

ḥażrat PU (A, *ḥaḍrat*) – your (or his) Eminence, Excellency, "Erlaucht."

ḥużūr PU (A, *ḥuḍūr*) – (plur.) (your, his, her-) presences, highness.

jāgīr P – fief, feudal land.

jāgīrdār P – feudal landholder.

khāndān U (P, *khānadān*) – house, lineage, family unit, of a certain distinction; *a'lākhāndān* – dynasty, pre-eminent lineage.

khāṣṣa A – special, the upper (and educated upper-middle) classes; the aristocracy or élite; the patriciate or gentry.

khāṣṣat PU – variant of the above as applying to a particular group, hence identified with Indian "caste"(-group).

khawāṣ A – (plur.) the "nobles and notables", the élites; "the special" (Sufi teachings).

khwān P – recitalist, singer.

kufū A – compatible, equal; in law, girls must not be given in marriage

---

The editor thanks Shaikh al-Mashaik Mahmood Khan for compiling this glossary of foreign terms used in the preceding chapter.

beneath their own socio-economic status; hence, the first three convert or (tribally, kinshiply or initiatically) affiliated generations must formally prove their ability to maintain a future wife at her own level (or beyond), only then being accepted as her *kufū*. In non-Arabic communities, as among Dravidian or Javanese Muslims, the emphasis is on birth and descent, family status and rank rather than on financial means or economic condition and prospects.

nawāb, *nawwāb* U (A, plur., *nuwwāb*) – "representative" (of a sovereign, ruler or saint), "caretaker...", "vice..."; Indian prince, count, peer-like noble; saint's successor; Muslim counterpart of Hindu Maharaja, Raja or Ṭhākur.

Pārsīs PI – immigrant, indianized Gujarati- and English-speaking Zoroastrians.

pakhāvaj – elongated Indian drum, played with two hands, one either side.

sardār P – headman, chieftain, "baronial" gentleman.

Sardārīs U – Muslim élites settling in a Hindu state in courtly, judicary, public service or academic capacities.

sargam I – notes sung to their "sol-fa" names, instead of poem texts, much used in the variations elaborating a musical theme, practiced with singular mastery in Karnatak music.

sharīf A – singular of *ashrāf*; *khān-i sharīf*: "the noble *khān*" as a personal title beyond that held by origin or descent.

taṣdīq A – selfless attachment, loyalty. In Sufism: inner adherence and commitment. I.e. where Indoislamic caste (*khāṣṣat*) standards are not fully adhered to, (i.e., by incompatible marriage or divergent behaviour), sincere Muslim identification in its religious, legal, or cultural sense, will yet allow a descendant to continue being recognized as a *khāndān* member. Beyond that threshold, all kinship relations cease, being invalidated automatically.

zamīn P – (allodial) land.

zamīndār P – landholder; UI – landed gentleman.

zamīndārī UI – the landed gentry system or property.

zanāna PU – the ladies' quarters of a joint-family house or palace.

Khāṣṣat-i Khawās-i Mashaykhān-i Jum'ashāh
(Figures mentioned in the present volume)

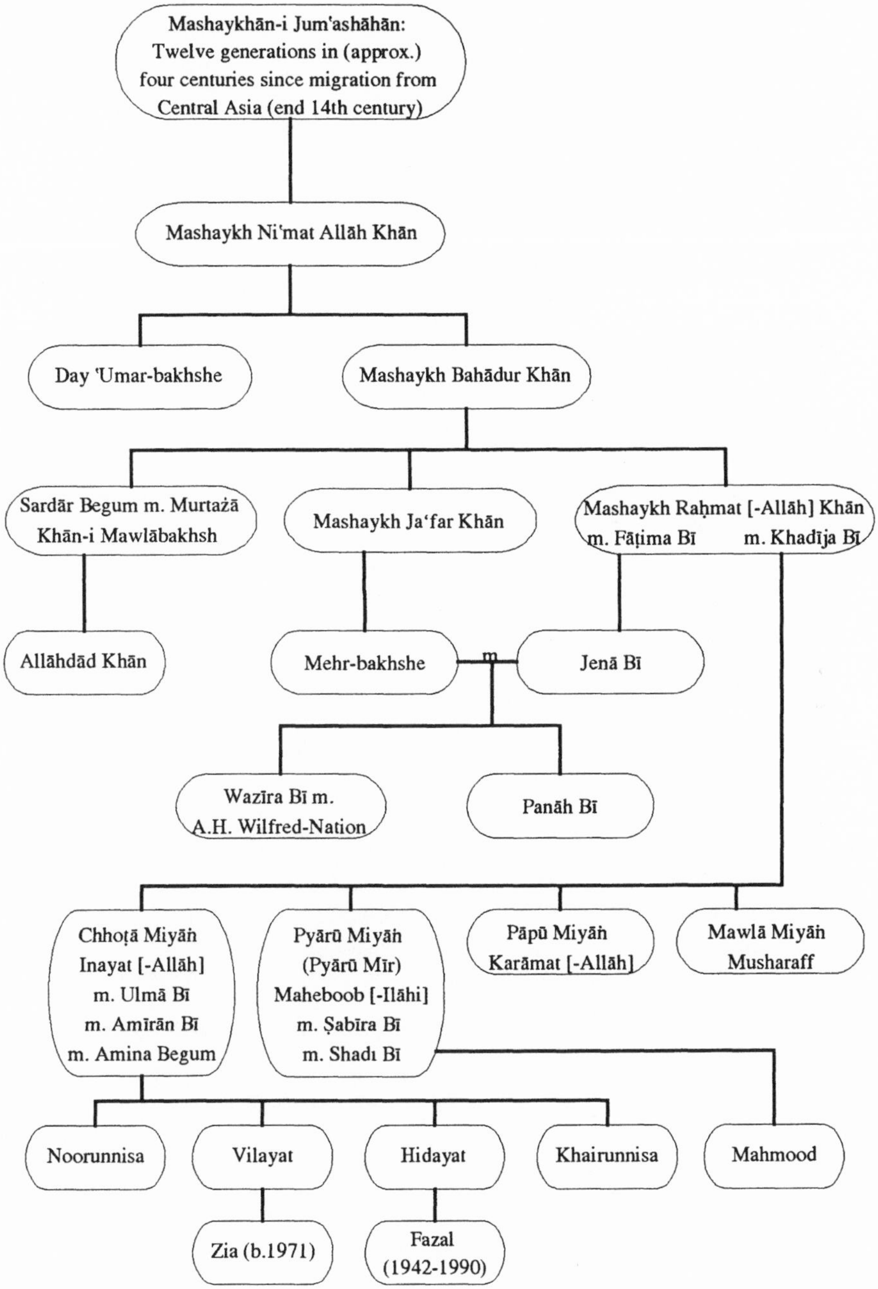

The Mawlabākhshī a'lākhāndān 1833-1972
female line descendants

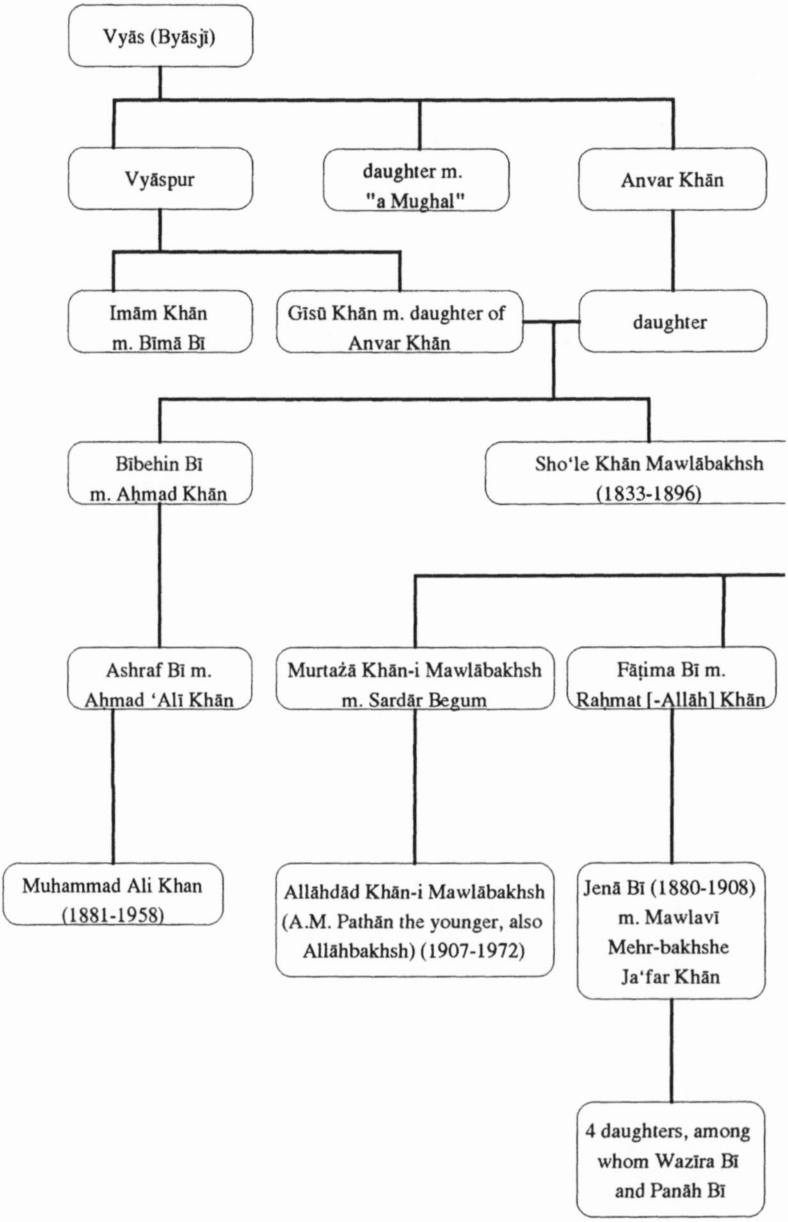

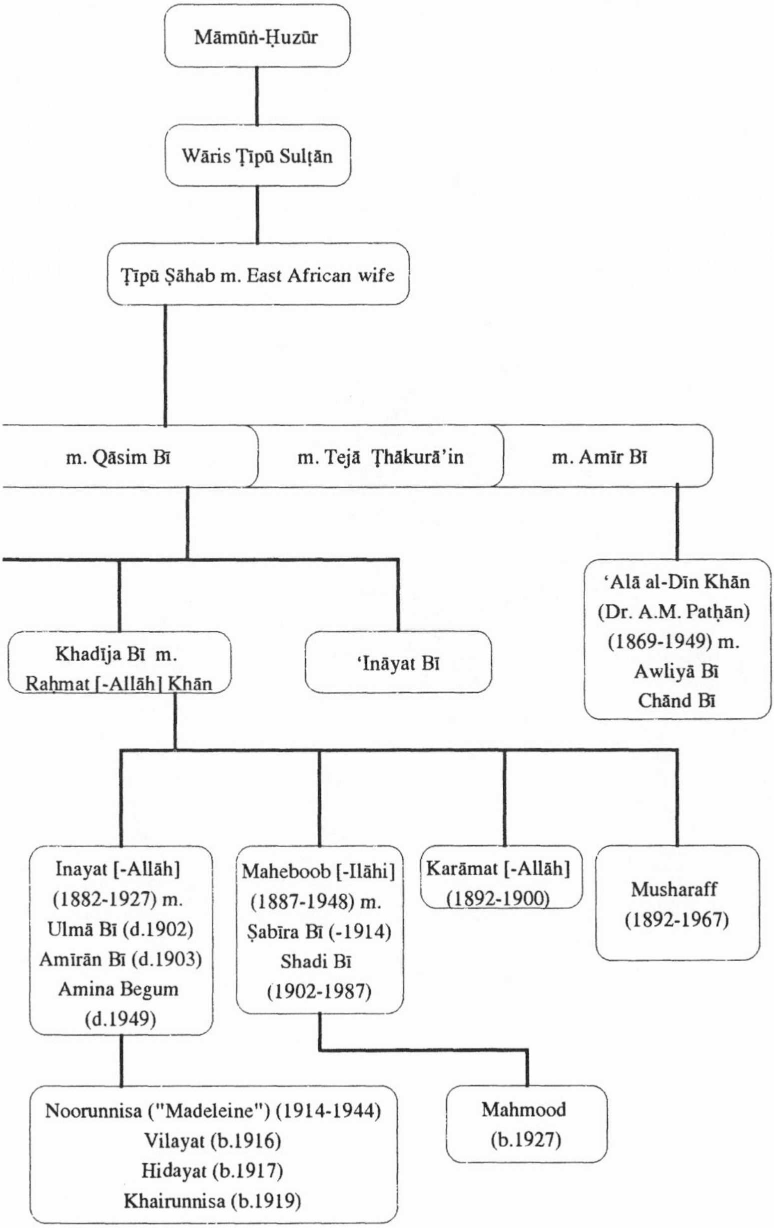
Māmūṅ-Ḥuzūr
Wāris Ṭīpū Sulṭān
Ṭīpū Ṣāhab m. East African wife
m. Qāsim Bī
m. Tejā Ṭhākurā'in
m. Amīr Bī
Khadīja Bī m.
Raḥmat [-Allāh] Khān
'Ināyat Bī
'Alā al-Dīn Khān
(Dr. A.M. Paṭhān)
(1869-1949) m.
Awliyā Bī
Chānd Bī
Inayat [-Allāh]
(1882-1927) m.
Ulmā Bī (d.1902)
Amīrān Bī (d.1903)
Amina Begum
(d.1949)
Maheboob [-Ilāhi]
(1887-1948) m.
Ṣabīra Bī (-1914)
Shadi Bī
(1902-1987)
Karāmat [-Allāh]
(1892-1900)
Musharaff
(1892-1967)
Noorunnisa ("Madeleine") (1914-1944)
Vilayat (b.1916)
Hidayat (b.1917)
Khairunnisa (b.1919)
Mahmood
(b.1927)

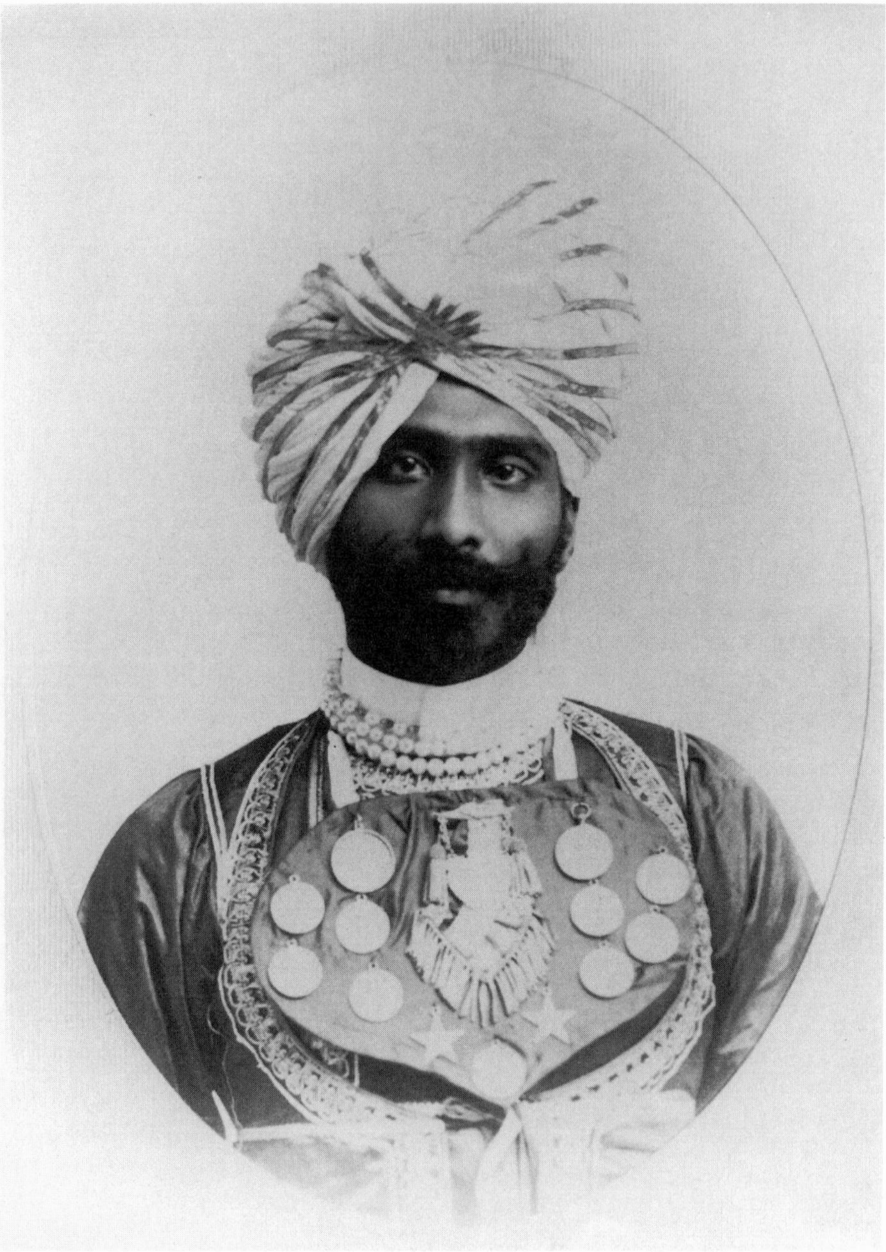

Hazrat Inayat Khan, circa 1910

Hazrat Inayat Khan: A Biographical Perspective

SHAIKH AL-MASHAIK MAHMOOD KHAN

1. INTRODUCTION

1.1. Presentation and studies

Looking back along the twentieth century, it is easy to discern Hazrat Inayat Khan as its most impressive spokesman for Sufi mysticism. There have been other notable practicing, teaching and writing Sufis to whom great credit is due. Modern Orientalism by now also has an outstanding record of research, translation and description, both by Western and Oriental specialists and through ably popularizing publications. The same applies, of course, to other mystical and contemplative philosophical traditions. Nevertheless, for originality and inventive creativity, freshness of approach and aspiration, breadth and depth of perspective and perception, Hazrat Inayat Khan easily stands alone.

To a large extent, however, scholarly acknowledgment of his achievements has been lacking, oddly but unsurprisingly so. On the one hand, Inayat Khan's works offer an attractive and challenging field of studies for an entire range of humanities scholars—philosophers, cultural anthropologists, theologians and phenomenologists,[1] psychologists, musicologists, historians and sociologists—in addition to poets and musicians, of course, and including his early work in Hindi and Urdu. However, in the first place his life's work will have to be comprehensively surveyed and

[1] Followers or keen admirers of Inayatan Sufism have included theologians from Britain, Italy and Tessin, Belgium, Holland and Sweden. One of them, a scholarly parson and later academic was fond of saying that for the one Hazrat Inayat Khan book *The Unity of Religious Ideals*, he would happily give up a bookcase full of theological tomes.

assessed by qualified Orientalists. And this is where the problem lies, since lectures, addresses and teachings in English—even though an old-style colloquial Indian English that, experts assure one, easily reads back into beautiful Urdu prose and "proem"—for them apparently offer too little of a primary linguistic challenge. Language specialists, after all, do want to fuss over linguistic niceties in proving their philological competence. On the other hand, moreover, publication of Hazrat Inayat Khan's works—largely discourses and other oral pronouncements, in addition to numerous aphoristic and poetic notes—mainly has been in the hands of his followers in the West, described by one of the most articulate among them at the time, Hoyack—in an understatement followed by an overstatement—as being mostly: "from the cultured, though not specifically learned, levels of society."[2]

Such publications therefore were, and have since been, largely intended to cater to adherents' tastes and so reflect the interests of the groups into which they have been organized. Editorial policies have accordingly been geared to such in-crowd, often quite fragmentary, requirements. Publicity pamphlets and introductory materials issuing from such quarters pursue other purposes than those of scholarly concern. Admittedly, nevertheless, within wide international Inayatan Sufi circles, there has been a remarkably rich volume of publications from the earliest days onwards (1913/1914), essentially addressed to their members and those sharing their interests and ideals, consisting of books, booklets and brochures, periodicals and translations in numerous languages and versions. More recently, publications by Hazrat Inayat Khan's sons, Vilayat and Hidayat Inayat Khan, understandably have proved both popular and authoritative among them.

Traveling and lecturing throughout his sixteen years in the West, Hazrat Inayat Khan delivered his discourses in widely different contexts, with themes fanning out along a variety of lines and subjects as the occasion might call for. Quite obviously, therefore, to enable advanced study by specialists in so many distinct if interrelating disciplines, there is a real need for complete, systematic, carefully indexed and cross-referenced editions of all his

[2] Louis Hoyack, *Die Botschaft von Inayat Khan* (Zurich: Bollman, n.d.; Dutch original: *De Boodschap van Inayat Khan* Deventer: Kluwer, n.d. [1947?]), 19.

lectures and teachings. Such work, based on the earliest records and transcripts of his discourses and manuscripts, now is in progress (see below); it will be sometime yet before a full text of entire textual and chronological reliability will have become available. However, very much more than ever before can meaningfully be taken up already. If so august a publication as the *Encyclopedia of Islam* can but lamely repeat a popular fallacy in saying, "Inayat Khan ... presented Sufism as a universal religion,"[3] and Leiden academics in their circulated lecture notes stating a similar view, can quote in support an article expounding precisely the opposite, the onus of insouciance, if not mindless neglect, may fairly be deemed to rest as well on the shoulders of the international academic community at large.[4] Even scholars of the standing of Annemarie Schimmel and Jacques Waardenburg appear to base their references to Hazrat Inayat Khan on publicity materials put out by his following or on their activities and comments, rather than on the substance of his own work itself.

A first inventory of Hazrat Inayat Khan's Sufism was attempted by the Dutch-Hungarian philosopher and writer, Louis Hoyack, whose many, often highly original articles on the subject have been supplemented by a full-scale book: *Die Botschaft von Inayat Khan.* Based only upon lectures published before 1940 or those attended by himself in the twenties or thirties, despite all his work's flawless readability it now is somewhat antiquated—besides its occasionally premature conclusions—with a kind of elegantly artistic imprecision, being Hoyackian as much as

---

[3] *Encyclopedia of Islam* II, s.v. "Tasawwuf."

[4] In his work in the West, Hazrat Inayat Khan was simply following up on and extending more consistently, an old Sufi view that initiatic or devotional association to an order of mysticism does not necessarily also call for religious conversion or participation. Cultural and psychological attunement, the love of God, of his creation and of the inner path, are the decisive factors. If the distinction of *sharīʻa* on the one hand, and *ṭarīqa, maʻrifa* and *haqīqa* on the other, is not taken for granted as an absolute principle and all-embracing condition of his life's work, the heavy emphasis of this customary distinction being his mode of 'secularization', any comment on it can only result in sheer nonsense (it often did and does). To Hazrat Inayat Khan, Western secularism and materialism rendered a non-confessionally-bound mode of individually practicable mystical spirituality all the more desirable and relevant. His *Weltanschauung*, philosophy of life, and, *a fortiori*, his contemplative-psychological ('esoteric') method are totally dependent on and derivative of, his central mystical aim and perspective.

Inayatan. And that despite, though possibly because of, Hoyack's being an enthusiastic Sufi mureed (disciple) of the early days.

Half a century later, his example has been followed by Prof. Dr. H.J. Witteveen, whose recent book *Universal Sufism* proved an immediate success, meanwhile translated in over half a dozen languages.[5] It presents a survey of Inayat Khan's main teachings as such, and in relation to both present-day findings or projections and to the forms or derivations in which those teachings took shape in the circles of his immediate disciples and subsequent followers.

Dr. E. de Jong-Keesing, author of the literary-historical *Inayat Khan: A Biography*,[6] subsequently published an anthology with connecting comment and analytic elucidation that consistently repays close study; *Inayat Answers* proves a good deal more substantial than its deliberately popularizing title might suggest.[7] The work is based on the (incomplete) 13-volume collected works edition listed below (cf. 1.3). Equally based on that series as well as on a number of unpublished papers, i.e., mainly the series for candidates and initiates known as the "Gathekas," "Gathas," "Gitas," "Sangathas" and "Sangitas," is Dr. R. Monna's *Dictionary of Foreign Words* (i.e., a bit paradoxically, the oriental terminology in Inayat Khan's lectures), an unequal pioneering work but a useful index to large numbers of relevant passages.[8] A full Index to the 13-volume series, issued by Prof. Donald Graham, provides an indispensable aid to a more incisive perusal of that series.[9]

Dr. K. Jironet's recent thesis in religious sociology, "The Image of Spiritual Liberty," examines the motivations and commitments of a representative cross-section of present-day Occidental mureeds of Inayatan Sufism.[10] It also has the advantage

---

[5] H.J. Witteveen, *Universal Sufism* (Shaftesbury, England: Element, 1997).

[6] Elisabeth de Jong-Keesing, *Inayat Khan: A Biography* (London and The Hague: East-West Publications, 1974); revised edition (New Delhi: Munshiram Publishers, 1981).

[7] Elisabeth de Jong-Keesing, *Inayat Answers* (London and The Hague: Fine Books and East-West Publications, 1977), reprinted as *A Sufi Master Answers* (Delhi: Motilal Banarsidass, 1997).

[8] M.C. Monna, *Short Dictionary of the Foreign Words in Hazrat Inayat Khan's Teachings* (Alkmaar, The Netherlands: Stichting Bewustzijn, 1991).

[9] Sharif Graham, ed., *The Sufi Message: Index to Volumes I-XIII* (Delhi: Motilal Banarsidass, 1990).

[10] K. Jironet, "The Image of Spiritual Liberty" (Ph.D. diss., University of Amsterdam, 1998).

of including, in a brief but competent survey, a useful summary of the *Sufi Message* volumes (c.f. infra ad I.3.1)—an indispensable introduction for scholars in a hurry![11]

Finally, it is worth mentioning three composite works in which the Sufism of Hazrat Inayat Khan has been discussed competently and at length. These offer further insights from authors capable of combining detached scholarly objectivity with some unmistakable admiration.

The most recent of these is that of the Buddhism specialist, Prof. Andrew Rawlinson. His discussion of Sufism in his *Book of Enlightened Masters* in a fresh and authoritative approach highlights the originality of Hazrat Inayat Khan's initiatives. Some of its salient features have been noted below. The earliest of these works is a constructively critical, searching survey of "Spiritual currents in the Christian cultural context" (*Geestelijke Stromingen in het Christelijk cultuurbeeld*) by the Dutch Protestant theologian, Prof. M.C. van Mourik Broekman.[12] Again, it is hard not to feel that his view of Hazrat Inayat Khan is, in the context of his theme, an exceptionally sympathetic one. His single real criticism is directed towards an obsolescent phraseology in one of the three "Objects" of Sufism,[13] which meanwhile had already been revised in both its English and Dutch versions by replacement of the "variety"/"verscheidenheid" "of faiths and beliefs" to be overcome, by the actually intended "bias"/"verdeeldheid." And he then goes on to show that this is what Hazrat Inayat Khan himself in fact meant to convey.

In a similar awareness of the impact of his following upon his teaching, he warns that by over-emphasizing its religious activity, Sufism risked as yet to turn into a religion, "which would be against the Master's own intentions." Praising the beauty of Hazrat Inayat Khan's aphorisms and prayers, discussing the then available literature (notably *The Inner Life*, *Gayan*, *Mysticism of Sound*, the famous opening paragraph of which is quoted in full), he concludes that movements such as

---

[11] Ibid., 84–117.

[12] M.C. van Mourik Broekman, *Geestelijke Stromingen in het Christelijk cultuurbeeld* (Amsterdam: Meulenhoff, 1949).

[13] Cf. De Jong-Keesing, *Inayat Khan*, 147–8, on such texts' doctoring.

Sufism "often are a blessing to those living in the periphery of the Christian life-sense ('levensgevoel'), and this means much." The aim should be that the various faiths and beliefs will come to regard one another in a universal context, as different revelatory expressions ("openbaringsuitingen") of God's reality. It is worth recalling that these enlightened theological views were already written in the nineteen-thirties.

In 1993 was published *Die Mitte der Religionen* by Johann Figl, Professor of Religious Sciences and Director of the Institute for Religious Studies at the Faculty of Catholic Theology at Vienna University.[14] His book reviews the "universalistic" new religious movements of Hindu, Buddhist, and Islamic provenance with notable interest and insight; its second part goes on to discuss "neoreligious universalism beyond the alternatives of secular modernism and traditional religiousness."

The book is full of stimulating perceptions unfortunately impossible to summarize here, since brevity can only do it injustice, all the more so in view of the preciously tiptoeing circumspection in formulation, familiar from Catholic authors in this field (outside, of course, the Dutch and Flemish language area, where they think nothing of calling a spade a cross if they have to). A margin of unintended misrepresentation is thus an almost unavoidable risk of brief description: the book cries out for a full English translation.

Figl *inter alia* discusses themes like "neoreligious movements as alternatives to the established religions," "transcending the alienation between religion and culture," "revival of ecstatic and mystical religious experience," and "mysticism in contemporary conditions." Thus emphasizing the value of mysticism for the renewal of religion, Figl finally deals with the question as to how the (oriental) "non-Christian meditative traditions" could be of service for that purpose: "Here the basic question is, whether meditation practices can at all be extricated from their original religious context, then finding a place in a religion strange to it, in such a reduced shape." The answer is a truly Inayatan one: the "universal religious" aspect of mystical experience is to be kept in

---

[14] Johann Figl, *Die Mitte der Religionen: Idee und Praxis universalreligioser Bewegungen* (Darmstadt: Wissenschaftliche Buchgesellschaft, 1993).

mind. Zen meditation offers the example of having been accepted into Christianity.

In principle, therefore, it is well imaginable that the universal dimension of Sufism be taken over into another religion as well. The monotheistic components here might facilitate such a process, although the pantheistic tendencies and monistic conceptions inherent in Sufism as well, would render the meeting of minds rather more difficult. Hitherto, Sufi elements only have been accepted within Christianity to a very modest extent. In a note, Figl adds that a reason for the almost-entire failure to accept Sufi mysticism (in Christianity) may be the undeniable fact that it is harder theologically to acknowledge a post-Christian religion, since revelation has been terminated with Christ, than a pre-Christian one that may be understood as a preparatory pathway towards the Gospel.

Admittedly, the entire second half of this fascinating book rather recalls the irony of the Poles, who know their stuff, as expressed in their witticism: "Tolerate eatables." Yet this might be unfair to Figl's level of sympathetic sophistication, even if his vision does not attain the level of Mourik Broekman's. His description of the "ideas and practice of universal religious movements" is quite clearly one of scholarly (and personal) interest for its own sake. (Christians, after all, do have a mysticism of sorts of their own to fall back on; from St Augustine to Molinos, even if it means taking in Eckhard and Boehme as well.) And for those concerned with Sufism, his book's part 1 is of particular interest. For having dealt with currents emerging from the Hindu, Buddhist and Shi'i spheres (including *inter alia* Theosophy, Japanese groups, Cao Dai and Bahaism), he devotes almost as much attention and space as to all those jointly, to Sufism, and above all to the Sufism of Hazrat Inayat Khan. Indeed, Figl emphasizes that Inayat Khan's "Neosufism" constitutes the focal point of both the descriptive (part 1) and the theoretic and interpretative (part 2) sections of his book.

As he writes: "An explicit preoccupation with the 'Sufi Movement' and Neosufism also is based on the fact that these quite unjustifiably have been neglected, if not entirely ignored, in descriptions concerning new religious movements published hitherto." (This, clearly, mainly pertinent to the German language area; and even so, Hoyack's Theosophic predilections and personal hobbies in his book on Inayat Khan are sufficiently clearly marked off from his valuable descriptive pages for its oblivion to be inexcusable.)

Space here again prevents the full consideration to which Figl's presentation is entitled. Biographically, while recognizing that it cannot be excluded that Inayat Khan's Sufi work in the West should evince points of contact with his life's earlier phases (in India), he has a healthy warning to offer to readers of the *Biography of Pir-o-Murshid Inayat Khan* and related memorialist publications where he says:

> The purpose of this Movement and its message cannot be understood without knowledge of Hazrat Inayat Khan's biography. The close relationship of work and life should not however seduce one exclusively to read into the biography an anticipation of the future work, so to speak, to go through all the life's phases paying attention only to their significance for the later message, or indeed in all single life stages merely to seek preparatory indications for that later work. Such care is a precondition for all biographical writing, all the more so, however, in the case of a personality of religious importance, with regard to whose achievements one tends to be inclined all the sooner to explain the biography in terms of the subsequent activity.

Professor Figl well knows what he is talking about, as in addition to the authoritative but inevitably not all-inclusive Keesing biography, he has had to rely on mainly antiquated works based on uncritically handled source materials or data. He comes into his own dealing with the substance of Sufism, surveying the literature available and concluding that by it, a thematically relevant discussion of Inayat Khan's ideas has become possible as well, from the point of view of religious scholarship and religious philosophy.

Unsurprisingly (like Professor Smits, referred to under note 1, above) he focuses his discussion mainly on *The Unity of Religious Ideals* (vol. 9, with some earlier materials from vol. 1, of *The Sufi Message of Hazrat Inayat Khan*). Professor Figl's enriching analysis must await further consideration and fruitful discussion. His concluding observation that "Inayat Khan's ... intention also has to be distinguished from missionary movements" is fully corroborated by Hazrat Inayat Khan's own remarks to that effect.[15]

The above-mentioned studies, at least, provide useful and competent entries into the as yet largely uncharted universe of Hazrat Inayat Khan's Sufism.

1.2 Discourse methods and general characteristics

Hazrat Inayat Khan set out as both a poetic and scholarly musical specialist of unusually many-sided (and widely acknowledged) talent before becoming a full mystic and contemplative philosopher. Not only did his Sufi theories and teachings continue to be permeated by musical notions, associations and images. The element of "organic" improvisation, such as is essential to the proper elaboration of all truly classical Indian music, continued to be his preferred method of exposition in his later lectures on Sufism, as well. That, on the one hand, gives his addresses a remarkable liveliness and charm. On the other, of course, improvisation as a method of discourse renders systematization that much more complex.[16]

Hazrat Inayat Khan commenced his career as a professor at the Academy of Music in his hometown, Baroda. A born teacher as much as leader, his lectures in the West almost invariably address the very diverse audiences he spoke to with an aim of providing suitably attuned, if need be adjusted, ideas and ideals. Their overall consistency and integral content cannot, therefore, always be pieced together when approached from the question as to what he had to teach to his pupils or convey to more incidental groups of listeners. It must mainly result from the further search

---

[15] E.g. "Personal Account," in Nekbakht Foundation, *Biography*, 179. Though the term "mission" appears in Bloch's *Confessions*, once realizing its implications, he carefully avoided it except, possibly, for purely poetic or rhetorical purposes (as he does as well, for instance, with the term "illusion").

[16] The excellent remarks on Indian musicianship by Musharaff Khan in his *Pages in the Life of a Sufi* (Wassenaar: Mirananda, 1982), 19–21, may be held to be equally applicable to the psychology, approach and method of Inayat Khan's Sufi discourses. Cf. also the passage: "The Brahmins see in their music the culmination of their science and their civilisation." Karnatak music however was, of course, that of the Dravidian rather than Aryan language regions, i.e., of South India. The above passage denotes another linkage of Mawlābakhshī musical and Inayatan Sufi concepts.

as to what really was his own integral perception and vision of the great themes and subtle details he was seeking to give shape to and develop in generally comprehensible ways. The fact that he was now lecturing in a new medium, English, with differing modes of expression and habits of thought and association, was for him an additional challenge, as well. Yet, in an unfailing, experienced teacher's style, he begins his explanations with the simplest possible instances in seeking to deal with the most abstruse concepts.

Thus, to give one example among many, when discussing the classical Sufi theme of "revelation," from a rationalizing mystic's point of view, he starts with animal instinct and the mental impression made on, or the intuition arising within, any average human being. The related but distinct subject of "impulse" leads further on to profound reflections on the "human and divine" elements within the limitations of manifested life, another theme inviting much further examination. Then again, expressive attitudes often are related to one essential quality from which they are all seen to derive. All positive human feelings, for instance, are subsumed under Hazrat Inayat Khan's concept of love (which, in itself, also translates into the psychological category of the will) in the same way that all negative qualities are subsumed under the concept not of sin, but of "limitation"; which in itself, however, not merely represents a negative condition, but rather one of crystallization, condensation, and therefore clarification in a potentially very positive sense as well. So, for instance, attitudes of respect and devotion, generosity and beneficence, tolerance and forgiveness, etc. all represent certain aspects of the one essential, inborn love quality.

The development and practice of such and similar attitudes then imply not only a personal, mystical and ethical discipline, an inward breeding process, so to speak (reminiscent of the classical Sufi *maqāmāt wa ḥālāt*, "stages and states"): the "training of the ego"; but equally an expansive development of social and cultural awareness with, for all its apparently self-evident simplicity, quite demanding psychological and behavioral implications. Such methods—attunement to listeners; simplification of concepts; reduction to, then expansion from, essentials; and presentation in categories—obviously do lend themselves to easy recollection. They therefore are also well suited to an oral, improvising treatment of elusively subtle subjects yet calling for actual implementation as the means to spiritual realization. The mystic's sense of divine union has to be anticipated by his sense of unity with humankind and all manifestation: realizing the "signs of God," "in the world and within themselves," as Qur'ān 51.21 describes it.

Hazrat Inayat Khan in this way expresses himself in discourses to be perceived poetically before being digested conceptually: to the *aficionado*, either phase holds its particular fascination. Nevertheless, here we have a vast life's work (its full extent still to be established even today), that is disparate in system and method, in circumstances and locations of delivery, in direction and angles of approach (albeit consistent in attunement and tone, hence at once recognizable).

Then again, Hazrat Inayat Khan in the main quite evidently seeks, so to speak, to hide behind his work—not to allow his person to intrude upon the ideas presented and the values underlying them. Adjustment to audiences simultaneous with a search for self-effacement is bound to set very real questions of interpretation. For in time-honored style, imparting instruction, and further development and articulation of ideas and concepts go hand in hand—tuition also being a mode of evolving the latter, not merely an outcome of them. Here again, an essential methodological point often (if not preferably) overlooked by many followers, in search of ready-made statements and solutions rather than processes of conceptual development and expansion.

And it is here that we meet with a paradox, a rather pleasing one. For precisely because of the questions raised by his method and approach, in seeking to study Hazrat Inayat Khan's work in depth as it deserves (and again, i.e. beyond its easy-flowing teaching lines and tone of personal familiarity), what then proves required at almost every point is an examination precisely of the biographical context in which his lectures and teachings were given. The biographical component then of itself connects in turn with the Indian Subcontinental, Hindu-Islamic, Vedantic-classical Sufi, Bhakti-poetic Sufi, musical-mystical home base and background from which Hazrat Inayat Khan set out. In his "new" or "modern"

Sufism "for secular society" as it often is being called, he aimed to speak for and represent, Indian mystical spirituality and contemplative philosophy in its all-embracing entirety, beyond confessional dividing lines or differences of schools and dialectics. That is why his work has justifiably been described as a further, modernizing and above all universalizing development of Sufism.[17]

The primary biographical element of his music, of course, as pointed out earlier, shapes and colors his discourses' form and substance almost throughout. The essential biographical component of Hazrat Inayat Khan's Sufism, naturally, was nothing new to his three brothers Maheboob Khan, Muhammad Ali Khan and Musharaff Khan, who continued to embody and represent his work for a period of forty years after 1927, guaranteeing both its authenticity and the actual implementation of its mystical content, observance and practice.

Indeed, Hazrat Inayat Khan's "cousin-brother" Muhammad Ali Khan was fond of recalling that whenever Pir-o-Murshid Inayat Khan addressed his audiences and, most of all, his mureeds, to those his words were pronouncements of the most abstract truth beyond all else; while to "us," his brothers, his words were the exact picture, the living image of their joint life's experiences and impressions, their shared feelings and reflections. Explicably, perhaps, this was the one comment by that most widely popular as well as most patriarchal of Hazrat Inayat Khan's brothers that never gained favor with his followers. Correspondingly, when the single books, mainly of thematic lecture courses, published before 1940 carried an imprint explaining these to be "extempore discourses," this aroused protest from a leading follower asserting that such was offensive to the element of "inspiration" informing their Pir-o-Murshid's utterances.[18]

---

[17] Witteveen, *Universal Sufism*, passim.

[18] Despite being the Sufi Order chief secretary, the writer of the heavily pontificating note on this forgot or chose to discard the fact that Hazrat Inayat Khan himself quite obviously regarded his lectures as extemporizing improvisations. Such may readily be inferred not only from his conscious continuation of musical modes of elaboration as much as concepts ('rhythm', 'harmony', etc.), but moreover from his explicit advice to his Western co-workers. Thus, he tells them: " ... in improvising, in extemporizing the subject one must always keep (close) to the stem" (Sangatha I, Nasihat: A few remarks on the subject of speaking, privately circulated.). And again:

Such was the late Romantic, idealistically Theosophizing Europe of before World War II—today ages away if not light years! Biographical documentation, then, is a virtually indispensable adjunct to the study of Inayatan Sufism. Published biographical literature listed elsewhere in this volume, here will only be indicated briefly, as far as utilized.

The principal source work by far, magnificently published if doubtfully edited in 1979, is the well-known secretarial concoction somewhat ambitiously entitled *Biography of Pir-o-Murshid Inayat Khan*. Revered by followers, it also has uncharitably been dismissed as "Hazrat's Table Talk"—the Wolfschanze replaced by the lion's den of influential disciples' preferences and prejudices as expressed in scribblings and omissions of all kinds (excluding, for example, the brief but in all its homeliness yet highly instructive note by his wife probably dating back to the early London days[19]). Equally, maybe more equitably, the *Biography* has been characterized as "a mystic's delight, a psychologist's wonder, a historian's despair." Hazrat Inayat Khan's own doubts about it are poignantly expressed in the final paragraph of the 1979 edition's introduction, with an all too clear ring of authenticity: "People do not like it, they find it too simple." By 1979, within the fold such dislike would have come to be regarded as rankly sacrilegious! Still, this is an obviously genuine comment despite its being conveyed by a secretarial assistant whose later pontificating pronouncements normally need to be handled with the utmost care; of the paragraph in question, it may be said that simplification is almost the least of the *Biography's* manifold inadequacies. For all that, this collection of subjectively handled notes and comments remains a reference work of inevitable value, and fortunately is not without its endearing compensations.

In the history of Hazrat Inayat Khan, his life's work and its Occidental consequences, two points need to be taken into account from the start: the originality of his initiatives and the cultural dimensions of his work, the latter also consequent upon the fact

"Keep close to the central theme of the subject. Extemporize on the subject constructively, skillfully, artistically, tactfully ... " (Sangita I, Tasawwuf, privately circulated).

19 The note written by Amina Begum is reproduced in the Epilogue of Prof. Mehta's article in this volume, page 175. *Ed.*

that almost alone among the world's great systems of mystical spirituality, Sufism does not advocate world renunciation as a basic adepts' principle.

Hazrat Inayat Khan's originality and its outcome recently have been exhaustively dealt with, in as far as his work in the West is concerned, by a highly qualified independent observer, Prof. Andrew Rawlinson, in his massive description of spiritual currents in the present-day West, a penetrating study rather than a survey (even though in a vast inventory of this kind, some minor inaccuracies must necessarily be taken for granted).[20] On this subject therefore, Rawlinson's analytic text may be left to speak for itself; here, only a few salient indications need be quoted.

He makes the point that: "Hazrat Inayat Khan was unusual in that his commitment to the West was so full-blooded" (as concrete manifestations thereof he cites his Western marriage, descendants and disciples[21]—his transition to English speech comparatively late in life might still be added). Professor Rawlinson then goes on to emphasize that: "No other Eastern teacher of this time immersed himself in Western life so completely (In fact very few have done so—they usually retain some link with their country of origin)."[22] And again: "... he was unusual for his time—Inayat Khan initiated mureeds/pupils across the international spectrum— ...The Sufi Movement/Order was unique to him: nothing like it existed anywhere else in the world."[23] Those and other conclusions are fully and thought-provokingly substantiated in the body of his work. All this clearly is nourishing biographical fare and henceforth will need to be borne in mind in Inayatan Sufi studies generally.

The cultural dimension as such, also might well be related to Hazrat Inayat's originality as discussed by Professor Rawlinson. As said earlier, Hazrat Inayat Khan above all was a meditatively practicing, rationally modernizing and hence contemplatively universalizing philosopher of Sufi mysticism. In his rich and vast Indian dimensions, in his music and life's ideals, in his travels and (rarer) settlements, in his Summer Schools and institutional

---

[20] Andrew Rawlinson, *The Book of Enlightened Masters* (Chicago: Open Court, 1998).
[21] Ibid., 547
[22] Ibid.
[23] Ibid., 549.

structures, in his personal and public standards and concerns, even in his inevitable concessionary accommodations and compromises with his leading followers (in which, for instance, his breeding as an artist and a courtier, in the rich palette of his personality's characteristics would appear to predominate over the philosopher and the adept he was beyond all else, and hence beyond his pupils' reach)—in all such and similar respects the wide and intense cultural range of his life finds abundant expression, and his work can be enjoyed but not understood without taking due account of it. In that cultural circumference of his mystical value system as well, Sufism and biography of necessity combine and fuse.

1.3. Literature

Text collections

The Sufi Message of Hazrat Inayat Khan, XII vols. 1960–67, vol. XIII 1982. The series includes the single books published 1914–1940, 1955, as well as selections of numerous previously unpublished papers. (London: Barrie and Rockliff/Jenkins).

A Sufi Message of Spiritual Liberty – serial title of the revised, expanded and documented version of the foregoing series (giving lecture dates, including questions and answers pertaining to the lectures concerned, seeking to minimize editing). Serial title after the first short book published 1914, re-introduced at the behest of his sons. (Shaftesbury, England: Element Books, 1991–).

Complete Works of Pir-o-Murshid Hazrat Inayat Khan: Original Texts. The basic publication for research, reference and comparative purposes. Ongoing chronological and verbatim source edition of all records, transcripts, reports, notes, lessons, aphorisms and poems, with relevant references, variants, emendations and summary descriptions. Six volumes hitherto: two of aphorisms and poems, two each covering the years 1922 and 1923. (London/The Hague: East-West Publications, 1988–1990, New Lebanon, NY: Omega Publications, 1996–).

Published biographical works

a. **Biographical introductions or surveys:**

T'Serclaes (1914); Bloch (1915); Pallandt (1964).

b. Published memoirs:

Musharaff Moulamia Khan: *Pages in the Life of a Sufi* (1932/1982);

Th. van Hoorn: *Herinneringen aan Inayat Khan en het Westers Soefisme* (1981).

c. Published source materials:

Nekbakht Foundation ed.: *Biography of Pir-o-Murshid Inayat Khan* (1979).

d. Full-scale biographies:

Dr. E. de Jong-Keesing: *Inayat Khan: a Biography* (1974, revised ed. 1981, second revised ed. forthcoming 2001);

W. van Beek: *Hazrat Inayat Khan: Master of Life, Modern Sufi Mystic*, 1984.

2. Biochronology

2.1. Foreword

The following biochronology is based on *Biography* and De Jong-Keesing unless stated otherwise, with a few minor unspecified adjustments deriving from the oral tradition. Its aim in the present context is to provide main data of a biographical survey in the briefest possible compass, of necessity to be pursued further in the literature readily available today. It is also intended to suggest a preliminary and elementary model for further elaboration in the following sense.

For all the truly timeless value of Hazrat Inayat Khan's mysticism, more advanced substantive study and analytic assessment of the trend and development of his thought and teaching call for a correlation of his work and his biography to quite an exceptional—and exceptionally stimulating—extent. That is so due to the nature of both his discourses and his life's circumstances, as has been argued in the foregoing (1.2). If that view is correct, then appropriate tools will be required for future investigation.

Fortunately, of many of Hazrat Inayat Khan's discourses the exact dates have been recorded; of other and various different materials, times of delivery or notation can be approximated. The invaluable *Complete Works* series mentioned earlier under 1.3.3 thus eventually will provide a full-scale chronological sequence, which in combination with the biographical literature and sources available, in principle will enable much fruitful comparative research.

However, scholars will still need a comprehensive desk reference survey in which the biodata (including where relevant such items as "route sheets" or specific mementos) and the discourses are listed and correlated in columns side by side for ready consultation. It is hoped that the present publication as well may encourage further work to that effect.

2.2. Biochronological surveys

2.2.1 India 1882–1910

1882, July 5, 23.35 hrs.	Inayat [-Allah] Khan born in the house of his maternal grandfather and family patriarch, Mawlābakhsh; his young aunt bequeaths to him her name: "He is born with the ideal for which I am dying."
1887 –	Sent to Mahratti primary school.
1891 –	His rendering of Dīkṣitar's Hamsadhvani hymn to Gaṇeśa at court wins him the prize of a pearl necklace and a scholarship.
1892, 1893, 1899 –	On three occasions: respectively, of his uncle 'Alā al-Dīn Khān's departure for London, Mawlābakhsh's (declined) opportunity to attend the Chicago Universal Exhibition and Parliament of Religions, and the Paris International Exhibition, Chhoṭā Miyāṅ Inayat demonstrates his eager interest in joining in those travels to the West.
1893 –	Visits Patan with his uncle Murtażā Khān, then Idar State (presumably en route or on return from Punjab) with his father and brother Pyārū Miyāṅ.
1894 –	Leaves home in search of *vairāgya*, a life of solitude, contemplation and study, but also aspiring to found another school or music academy on Baroda Gāyanshālā lines. Mashaykh Raḥmat Khān, his father, upon his enforced return teaches him that fulfilling the world's purposes, "in this way living for God and loving God," and this to

	be learnt through family life, is greater than any "solitary and ascetic life." (Musharaff Khan, *Pages,* 77: "about twelve").
1895 –	Inayat's doubts arise as to praying to an unknown, unrevealing God. Mawlābakhsh's and Raḥmat Khān's replies, on the bases of Qur'ān 51.20–21 and 50.16 respectively, subsequently cause him to turn fully and enduringly to immanentism and mystical monism: "This moment to Inayat was his very great initiation."
1896, July 10	Death of Mawlābakhsh, "the very first blow that Inayat received in his early youth," further aggravated by the death of the school-friend who had joined him in his intended *vairāgya*-departure, Sādānand, son of Mawlābakhsh's secretary, Kesarrāo, who thereupon renounced the world to become an ascetic hermit (Musharaff Khan, 77–78).
1896–97	Inayat joins his father on a year-long visit to Nepal, traveling through Gwalior (Tānsen's shrine) and Benares where "he felt exalted ... as though his spirit was going through an initiation; ... it was, to his heart, the first and great pilgrimage of his life"(*Biography,* 58). He becomes enchanted and inspired by the scenic beauty of the Himalayas. Likewise, Inayat receives further lasting impressions of the reigning Maharaja and ruling Rānās, the musicians and saints. Above all, of the ascetic *munī* (silent saint).
1897 –	The return to India of maternal younger uncle 'Alā al-Dīn Khān (Dr. A.M. Pathan) introduces fresh currents of Occidental orientation to the entire younger generation at Mawlābakhsh House. Inayat Khan, Maheboob Khan and Muhammad Ali Khan, as later also Allāhdād Khān, thoroughly familiarize themselves with European music.

1899 – Having from his early college days on his own initiative deputized for its teachers, Inayat Khan now himself becomes a teacher, then professor at Gāyanshālā, the Baroda Academy of Music. From this time onwards, writes a number of musical textbooks, including valuable collections of songs, amongst which one on violin playing.

1900 – Death of his second brother Karāmat [-Allāh] Khān, subsequently entailing: death of Inayat Khan's mother, Khadīja Bī. Followed soon after by the death of his newly-wed cousin-bride, Dr. Paṭhān's only child, Ulmā Bī. Inayat Khan leaves Baroda State for an exploratory tour of Madras and Mysore, thus starting his traveller's career at eighteen.

1901–02 Remarriage at Jaipur, followed that same year by his second wife's death. Prof. Inayat Khan Rahmat Khan Pathan departs from Baroda anew and but for occasional family visits no longer remains in residence there, although "Moula Bux House, Baroda," continues to be given as his "Head Office" address. During brief stay at Bombay (i.e. in "British" rather than "princely" India), thoroughly shocked by music performed at public concerts rather than in private circles, and attendant attitudes towards it: music popularized, commercialized, debased. First impression of the "materialism" and "commercialism" he later was to castigate in life in the West proper.

1903–1907 Prof. Inayat Khan settles in Hyderabad, there writes *Minqār-i mūsīqār*, his Urdu *chef d'oeuvre*. Receives greatest appreciation for his music and contemplative-musical ideals from the Nizam and senior court and state officials, but gaining him the title of Tānsen al-zamān (or: zamān-i ḥāl) rather than a *mansab* (official State position); and on his part gives up his old aspiration of founding a music school or academy there. Above all, Inayat Khan here finds his initiatic teacher in Sufism, Sayyid Abū Hāshim Madanī; as also his academic tutor in Sufism, Professor Hāshimī (whose is the photograph in *Biography*, 406). He now fully devotes his life to music and mysticism, making two family visits to Baroda during this period. Upon the death of Sayyid Abū Hāshim, after three years in his presence, he starts "on a pilgrimage to the holy men of India," commencing with the shrine of Bandanawāz at Gulbarga (i.e. of Sayyid Muḥammad Gīsū-darāz, after whom Mawlābakhsh's father had been named).

1907 – Meeting with Mānik Prabhū "the great Guru of the Brahmins" and his son. In their notable conversation, Inayat Khan touches on several themes later featuring prominently in his discourses in the West; links Sufi unity of being with Vedanta non-duality: "Muslim and Hindu are only outward distinctions, Truth is one. ..." (*Biography*).

1907, June – Return to Baroda, gaining wide recognition, then proceeds to Ujjain to the shrine of Mīrān Dātā[r], place of pilgrimage for the sick and obsessed: "he saw how many illnesses are of the spirit rather than of the mind ... it gave him proof that he who dies before death, and so becomes spiritual, certainly lives after the death of his mortal self." Thence on to Ajmer, gaining lasting impressions of the dervishes he hears and observes there, frequently recalled in later years. But Inayat decides against becoming a dervish or selling "my music for money" (*Biography*, 85, 89).

1907, July 18	Charity concert and lecture for the Parsi community in Bombay, in which Prof. Inayat Khan is joined by Maheboob Khan and Muhammad Ali Khan; after which, Inayat returns to Hyderabad.
1907, November –	Prof. Inayat Khan's visit to Mysore meets with much response. It becomes clear, however, that in changed circumstances emulation of Mawlābakhsh's attainments can no longer be envisaged.
1908 –	Commencing with and from Madras (January–May) Prof. Inayat Khan sets out on a tour of South India, reaching Negapatam and Tanjore in mid- and late July, after further travel arriving at Tuticorin in October; he then proceeds from Tuticorin to Ceylon in November; after a short stay there, sails for Burma "and was most delighted to arrive at Rangoon": "Generous and humble he found them to be, he saw in the life of Burmese his ideal of human brotherhood. For they consider no one, whatever his faith or belief, in any way inferior to themselves … They are over-civilized so the others cannot understand them" (*Biography*, 100).
1909, February 3	Prof. Inayat Khan R. Pathan honored at leave-taking ceremony in Rangoon.
1909–1910	Prof. Inayat Khan settles in Calcutta, "the long-desired place of his destiny." "Though this was against his wishes, yet being advised by his father that he must settle in some place, he stayed there some time" (*Biography*, 103). His permanent address there became 145, Lower Chitpore Road.
1909, February 14	Lecture and concert at the Sangīt Sammilanī (Music Society), Bhowanipore, Calcutta, and (apparently) again on March 15; honored by the Society as "the morning star of Indian Musical Revival."

1909, from April 10 – Series of music lectures arranged at the Calcutta University Institute, with another one at Presidency College. Nevertheless, as in Bombay, popularizing and competitive attitudes make themselves felt in Calcutta as well. Inayat Khan prefers inactivity to conceding to such trends; but even when become well established, the complaint remained "among the professional people" that "Inayat does not associate with the artists of the country" leading to the retort of "those who had known Inayat": "He is not one for you." He lives a life of meditation, attaining the state of *samādhī*: "music was his external garb"(*Biography*, 103, 105, 111).

1909, September 26 and 28 – Recordings made of 31 classical Indian songs by "Professor Inayat Khan Rahmat Khan Pathan Tansen Zamanihal" by the Gramophone Company Ltd., Calcutta.

1909, December 10 Presents a scheme to the government of India supported by Mr. Ross, principal of Madrasa College, for the introduction of "scientific music" into Indian schools; a positive expert advice is submitted to the Director of Public Instruction, Bengal, on March 27, 1910. However "Inayat had not the patience nor the time to stay in one place, so before the answer came, he had already left Calcutta" (*Biography*, 108, 337–339). Retracing his steps from "British India," he resumed his more customary and congenial visits to the States and estates of Bengal, having been encouraged by the response, already in Calcutta itself, of the Maharaja of Natore, the Raja of Rangpur, and Maharaja Tagore.

1910 – Mashaykh Raḥmat [-Allāh] Khān dies during the first quarter of this year.

1910, April 20 Music and lecture at the Maharaja of Darbhanga's bungalow.

1910 –	Visits the states of Lalgola and Cassimbazar.
1910, June –	Stay at Murshidabad State. Thereupon travels to Dacca, where the Nawāb had “invited most of the princes and potentates of Bengal in that occasion.” They are taken aback by Prof. Inayat Khan’s critical comments on their attitude to music as a cultural value; the Maharaja of Dinajpur acknowledges the truth of his observations. From there, he accompanies the Raja of Sylhet to his state in Assam (today Bangladesh).
1910, August –	Prof. Inayat Khan declines the Raja of Sylhet’s offer to settle in his state, with full facility to travel, lecture and practice his music throughout India. This in particular in view of the fact that his long-cherished hope of touring the West was taking shape in a plan for a visit to the United States.
1910, August 31	Prof. Inayat Khan takes leave of Sylhet.
1910, September 13	Inayat Khan, with his parental brother Maheboob Khan and his cousin-brother Muhammad Ali Khan, leaves Baroda late that day for Bombay, there to embark for Naples, thence sailing to New York.

2.2.2. Travels in the West, return to India

1910, autumn –	Hazrat Inayat Khan gives a first lecture and concert at Columbia University. He and his brothers joined by Ramaswami as *tablā*-player.
1911, February–April	Gain opportunity of traveling throughout the United States with Ruth St. Denis; en route, lectures given at Chicago and Denver. They part company with Ruth St. Denis at San Francisco: last joint appearance, April 15.
1911, April 9 and 16	Music and explanations on art and science of Hindu music at The Hindu Temple, San Francisco, gain great appreciation and praise.

1911, April 21	"Presentation in word and song and with instruments" at University of California, Berkeley proves highly successful.
1911, April 27	Lecture on and presentation of Indian music and its ideal at the University of Southern California, Los Angeles; travel to San Diego, then Seattle.
1911 –	Return to New York, lectures at Sanscrit College there. Acquaintance made of Mr. C.H.A. Bjerregaard, librarian of the Astor Library, whose published work since 1912 shows Inayatan influences. He later became an honorary member of the Sufi Order. His book, *Sufism, Omar Khayyam and E. Fitzgerald* was published by the Sufi Publishing Society, London, in 1915.
1911–1912, winter	Continued residence in New York, musical and Sufi activities unfold.
1912, February –	Youngest parental brother Mawlā Miyāṅ Musharaff Khan, who had joined Inayat Khan in Calcutta and continued living there for a time after he left before returning to Baroda, now, at sixteen, rejoins his brothers in New York.
1912 –	Hazrat Inayat Khan with his three brothers and Ramaswami, travel to Britain; many social contacts in London, but little response to Indian music, on which as yet his lectures were fully based and hence dependent.
1912 –	Arrival in Paris; lectures, concerts, cultural and social contacts. "Still, all these years I was learning more than teaching."
1912, October 26	First Indian concert on their own, organized by M. Edmond Bailly with Lady Churchill.
1912, October 9, December 14 –	Accompany Mata Hari, respectively at private performance at her Paris residence and at the Université des Annales.
1913, March 20	Inayat Khan Rahmat Khan Pathan marries as his third wife, Ora Ray Baker at the Registrar's Office of St. Giles, London.

	Upon the *nikāḥ*, Muslim religious ceremony performed in Paris by Muhammad Ali Khan, acting as their *mullā* whenever required, she becomes Pirani Ameena Begum, with the additional Indian *laqab* (alias, nickname) of Sharada (name of the Hindu Goddess of Music, a musical hymn to whom had been one of Inayat Khan's early favorite songs). To the circles of mureeds in later years, she was and remained known exclusively as (the) "Begum," much as Hazrat Inayat Khan came to be addressed and referred to as "Murshid," to this day.
1913, April–May	Contacts with Claude Debussy, the leading French composer.
1913, Summer –	Prof. Inayat Khan and his Begum return to London for some time, his brothers and their accompanist fulfilling his concert engagements in France and Belgium. Intended return to India fails to take place; prospect of Russian tour suggests another return route. *A Sufi Message of Spiritual Liberty* written as an introductory guidebook to Sufism.
1913, June–1914	Visit to Russia most successful period of their early years in the West. "In America the four brothers were coloureds, in England natives, in France aliens, but in Russia, khans" (De Jong-Keesing). Russian version of *A Sufi Message of Spiritual Liberty*, first of Hazrat Inayat Khan's books published in the West. They give up further receipt of remittances from India.
1914, January 1	Birth of Pirzadi Noorunnisa "Bābūlī," the World War II heroine code-named "Madeleine."
1914, May –	Their intended return from Moscow to India via Central Asia is prevented by the Russian authorities due to political disturbances in Turkestan.

1914, late June –	Return to Paris to attend musical congress there.
1914, August –	Hasty return to London after outbreak of World War I; papers and possessions left behind, later prove permanently lost. Take up residence at 100d, Addison Road, Holland Park.
1914 –	*A Sufi Message of Spiritual Liberty* published by the Theosophical Publishing Society.
1915, February –	*The Sufi Quarterly* brought out by Miss R.M. Bloch.
1915 –	Musical lectures at the Royal Asiatic Society. The Sufi Publishing Society brings out its first editions: Bloch's *The Confessions of Inayat Khan* and J. Duncan Westbrook's *The Diwan of Inayat Khan*.
1915, March –	Concert at the Indian General Hospital, Bournemouth.
1915 –	Change of residence to 86, Ladbroke Road, Holland Park.
1915, July –	Charity concert organized by the Islamic Society; improvised nationalist song: "When Rama is performing the adoration (*pūjā*) of Hanuman—then what religion (*dharma*) are you observing?" leads to cancellation of proposed tours to Indian frontline troops and military centers and hospitals.
1915, November 2	"Professor Inayet Ullah Khan and Indian Musicians" play at a Queen's Hall "special Matinee organized by Prince R.E. Singh in aid of wounded Indian soldiers."
1916–1917	First outside Centers formed in Brighton and Harrogate.
1916, June 19	Birth of Pirzade Vilayat Khan "Bhā'ījān."
1915–1919	Emphasis increasingly shifts from public concerts and lectures to privately organized activities. Gradual consolidation and expansion of Sufi work; ever increasing support,

	collaboration and influence of widening circle of initiates.
1917, August 6	Birth of Murshidzade Hidayat Khan "Bhā'īyajān."
1918, October 1	Incorporation of the Sufi Trust Ltd., by which the Sufi Order "was legalized and made official."
1919, June 3	Birth of Murshidzadi Khairunnisa "Māmūlī."
1919–1920	Brief shift to large Gordon Square residence.
1920 –	Hazrat Inayat Khan makes two visits to France during spring, meeting the mureeds there anew, forming a center, giving concerts. With the family, takes up residence in France again later that year, at first at Tremblaye.
1920, November –	First visit to Geneva; lectures at different places in Switzerland and Sufi circle established before return to France by December 1. His proposed further shift of residence to Geneva is, however, resisted by family, hence Hazrat Inayat Khan resolves to settle only his Sufi headquarters there. Change of residence from Tremblaye to Wissous.
1921, March –	Further visit to Switzerland notably successful. First visit to Holland later that spring.
1921, March, May –	Visits to England.
1921 –	Summer School at Wissous, small-scale but international and very successful.
1921, September –	Second visit to Holland, Sufi society and four branches established, first stay at Katwijk and The Hague; followed by the brothers' visit there in November.
1921, spring and autumn –	Visits to Belgium meet with further response.
1921, October –	First visit to Germany.
1922 –	Hazrat Inayat Khan and family take up permanent residence at Fazal Manzil, Val

	d'Or (St. Cloud), area later transferred to the municipality of Suresnes. Commencement of the "classical" Sufi period of three-monthly Summer Schools (June–September, 1922–1926, and continued after Hazrat Inayat Khan's time until 1939).
1922, September –	Fortnightly Summer School at Katwijk where, among others, the *Inner Life* lectures are given. In the dunes there, a small valley, then become known as Murad Hasil, becomes a focal point for meditation to the mureeds.
1923, February 27–June 9	Return to the United States: New York, Boston, Detroit, Chicago, California.
1923, June–September	Summer School. Though it "had no time to be organized as it ought to have been," yet, "the work went well." Commencement of further developments: acquisition of land, purchase of Mureeds' House.
1923, October –	International Movement incorporated for the first time, according to Swiss law; "response as usual" in Geneva to Sufi lectures and work. Visit to Italy: Florence and Rome. Visit to Belgium upon return to Paris.
1924 –	January visit to England. Hazrat Inayat Khan returns to Switzerland and again to Italy; there meeting with Maria Montessori.
1924, June –	Passes through Belgium en route to Holland for a short stay there in early June, to attend with his family his brother Maheboob Khan's marriage at The Hague.
1924, June–September	Summer School. Well-organized, successful. Subsequently, council meetings at Geneva, visit to Swiss centers.
1924, autumn –	Second tour of Germany; then on to Scandinavia, returning through Denmark to Germany, then to Holland, Belgium and on to Suresnes.

1925, January –	Lectures in Paris, i.e. Musée Guimet, Sorbonne. Hazrat Inayat Khan "delighted as ever to visit Switzerland, the land of beauty and charm."
1925, February –	Another visit to Italy, Florence and Rome, return to Paris via Nice.
1925, March –	Lecture tour in Germany: Berlin and Munich; upon return to Paris, Sorbonne lectures.
1925, April –	Visit to England, lectures at Bournemouth and Southampton. Health problems: after repeated pneumonia attacks in the London days, illness at home in winter 1922 and spring 1924, mouth complaint treatment in America in 1923, now severe and painful indisposition in England, still continuing after return to Fazal Manzil.
1925, June–September	Summer School. Notably well organized and successful. Lecture hall on Sufi estate inaugurated.
1925, September –	The annual councils' meetings at Geneva "much more lively than in the previous years": "differences ... gave the meetings a modern tone." Hazrat Inayat Khan dissuaded by Khalif Maheboob Khan from travel to India.
1925, December 6	Third American tour commences at New York, lasts 7 months, itinerary largely similar to previous one, but now again including San Diego as in 1911.
1926, July –	Hazrat Inayat Khan returns to Suresnes, where the Summer School takes place as become usual since 1922.
1926, September 13	Hejirat Day ceremonial in retrospect proves to have been a farewell ceremony, as already feared by some insiders. Procedures preserved on short amateur-film.
1926, September –	Meetings at a farewell visit to Geneva Sufi Headquarters and mureeds there.
1926, September 28	Hazrat Inayat Khan leaves Italy for India.

1926, October – Arrival at Karachi, travel onwards to Lahore. Investigation there confirms extinction of his paternal family line. Journey to Delhi, where Hazrat Inayat Khan rents Tilak Lodge. En route again: Amroha, Lucknow; lectures at Delhi December 15, Lucknow December 22.

1926, December – From Lucknow, Hazrat Inayat Khan travels to Benares, Agra, Sikandra.

1926, December 29 Leaves for Ajmer; falls ill there, indisposed for a week, then travels on to Jaipur.

1927, approx. January 20 – Hazrat Inayat Khan makes his return journey to Baroda. It turns out to be a disappointment. He finds Mawlābakhsh House closed, in a derelict state, a shadow of its former brilliant self. The House's Naulakha area now turned into the Yakutpura residential quarter become increasingly urbanized. Hazrat Inayat Khan then visits Mawlābakhsh's grave and the family cemetery compound surrounding it. He then retires to a hotel, returning to Delhi the next day. There falls critically ill, losing consciousness in the night of February 4 to 5.

1927, February 5, 8.20 a.m. – Hazrat Inayat Khan dies at Tilak Lodge, Delhi and is buried at Nizamuddin. February 5, "Visalat Day" (day of return, reconnection) becomes, for Sufi groups and organizations throughout the West, day of annual commemoration, alongside "Viladat Day," July 5, Hazrat Inayat Khan's birthday, and "Hejirat Day," September 13, the day when Hazrat Inayat Khan and his brothers left from Baroda for the West in 1910 and, in 1926, a ceremonial took place at the end of the Suresnes Sufi Summer School prior to his departure for India via Geneva and Venice.

1988 – Hazrat Inayat Khan's graveyard extended into a large *dargāh* (saint's shrine) with a terraced garden and surrounding structures. The site and its adjoining charitable activities being largely funded by Sufi organizations in the West and their individual members.

1994 – *The Complete Recordings of 1909*, 31 classical Indian songs sung by Hazrat Inayat Khan, following their rediscovery by Michael S. Kinnear and Joep Bor, are re-issued by them as EMI CD. A later Inayat Khan song, a raga melody on Fitzgerald's English rendering of Omar Khayyam's "Awake! For morning in the bowl of the night…", elaborated into a full composition in Western harmony by Hidayat Inayat Khan, was issued on the CD "Sufi Songs" produced by P.B. Schildbach and published for Sufi-Bewegung Berlin, Germany in 1999.[24]

1999 – A large commemorative lecture and concert hall added to the *dargāh* compound. Especially on and around Visalat Day, an elaborate *'urs* (saint's memorial meeting) takes place at the *dargāh*, attended by followers and admirers from all over the world.

3. The Indian years: Baroda to Sylhet

Hazrat Inayat Khan was born and grew up in the *ḥavelī* (large mansion built around a courtyard) of his maternal grandfather. Life in Mawlābakhsh House never has been better characterized than by Musharaff Khan in his *Pages*:

[24] Since his music and songs have become the most neglected part of Hazrat Inayat Khan's legacy, particularly after the death of his brothers by 1967, the issuing of these CDs is of major significance. Precisely for that reason, it may be of interest to rectify a few errors in the text of the accompanying booklets, derived from unverified sources. *Complete Recordings of 1909*, booklet, 10: Mawlābakhsh's Hindustani music teacher "Ghasit Khan" flourished not in Delhi but in Gujarat, i.e. Baroda (cf. Nekbakht Foundation, *Biography*, 19–20, Miner, *Sitar and Sarod*, 155). Ibid.: "Patnam Subrahmanya Ayyar 1845–1902," though doubtless identical with the Subramani Ayar of *Biography*, 51, who was so struck by Inayat Khan's boyhood proficiency, cannot of course have been the Malabar musician given the same name in *Biography*, 21, who trained Mawlābakhsh in Karnatak Music. *Sufi Songs*, booklet, 4, no. 2: Attributions should be amended to read as follows: "Raga-Melody: Hazrat Inayat Khan. Staff-notation, harmonic and stylistic elaboration, composition and arrangement: Hidayat Inayat Khan."

> My grandfather Moula Bakhsh was a happy and commanding personality. In his home ... under his sheltering genius, thirty or forty of his relatives lived at peace together.[25] At his death the family broke up to some extent, to my father's sorrow, the various members each more intent on going his own way. But while my grandfather lived, one kitchen[26] provided food for the whole household ... The place of head of the house was taken by his aunt, and next in authority came his wife, my grandmother, and then my mother. Each member of the household had his or her own obligation and responsibility to the one above in status ... Interest in European education and science was a rising tide, but life in our home remained the traditional life of India. In the house of Moula Bakhsh, as I have said, his many relations lived together in the old patriarchal system. I have heard there is something of this kind still to be seen in certain great houses in Italy. My father refused, it is true, to be dependent on Moula Bakhsh and was always responsible for his share in the household. But Moula Bakhsh never liked the business side of this arrangement. "Are they not my children also?" he would say to my father, when he insisted on providing for his own children. To which I am told my father never made a reply. But in our family, too, the interest in European education was strong ..."[27]

This setting also provided the framework for a rich cultural and spiritual life: "At Moula Bakhsh House were held darbars, meetings of learned men of India, poets, philosophers, musicians, thinkers of all kinds."[28] And as described in *Biography*:

> The house of Maula Bakhsh was practically a temple of talent. All the talented people, musicians, poets, the artistic and literary,

[25] Like with the familiae of ancient Rome, that number at any one time would as well have included (in addition to retainers, servants with their children and incidental guests): relatives from the family in Tonk, Rajasthan, children related to wives married into the family or offered to them by the poor for maintenance and education (examples in Musharaff Khan, 36, 84—the Bābū Rāo who later became Dr. Paṭhān's chauffeur—and 51–52, to which could be added Raḥmat Khān's manservant Khudābakhsh, a cripple useless to his own Bhīl [aboriginal] community); a later relation by marriage as the Irishman A.H. Wilfred-Nation, who in the family's first local venture in Western matrimony married Wazīra Bī, the elder daughter of Inayat and Musharaff Khans' only sister and who, after Wazīra Bī's childless death (cf. Musharaff Khan, *Pages*, 9, 92; "only" should read "eldest") later returned there with his second marriage's children, the eldest son of whom in turn married an adopted Nepalese daughter of Dr. A.M. Paṭhān and forever continued deferentially to refer to their father's previous wife as "my mother"—Wazīra Bī forming their linkage to the family.

[26] Which is said daily to have remained open for twenty-two hours continuously.

[27] Musharaff Khan, *Pages*, 17–19.

[28] Ibid, 8.

> came to him ... Some came to benefit by the opportunity of seeing and hearing many people of great talent. Little Inayat was always to be found sitting quietly in some corner of the room, always wholly attentive to all the conversation and everything that went on. In this way, in his early age, he heard and learned more music, poetry and other arts, than many people could learn in their whole life. The joy of Maula Bakhsh was boundless, seeing that his little grandson was born with the hunger and thirst for knowledge and that he was eagerly ready to learn and practice all that was taught him. He also understood Inayat's great desire to see the mystics and learn about mysticism ... He would sit with his grandfather, who received in his house all those eminent in learning and culture ... His grandfather ... always had Inayat sit on a corner of his own seat ... He exempted Inayat from the obligation in the East, that the young should wait upon the elder in the family and instead of the least place, he was always given the best seat, a thing contrary to the custom of Orientals.[29]

Throughout his time in India, from his earliest years onwards, there were those who felt or discerned the promise that seemed to emanate from him. Brahmin friends would tell his grandfather and father how much was to be expected from him and, as he grew up, revered personalities made clear to himself their regard or expectations for him, a theme too thankfully explored by *Biography* to call for further illustration here.

Alongside the quiet receptivity and reflectiveness, already in young Inayat there was the future leader of men—enterprising, enthusiastic, imaginative, charismatic. In later years in the West, people still used to notice, alongside the depth of spiritual awareness, the enthusiasm, zest for life, inventiveness, that seemed to inform Hazrat Inayat's initiatives great and small.

Many children play soldiers with, or doctor for, others. How many would say they would rather cut off their own head than others', or cause simple servants and maids actually to feel healed of their complaints? The Sufi leader who some decades later had to organize his pupils, laboriously evolve the Sufi Order and Movement, as a boy began life with organizing parades of his toys, turning other children into circus animals to act as he directed—though then again preferring to ride off rather than joining other youngsters in their more inane games and sports

[29] Nekbakht Foundation, *Biography*, 43–44.

(how much of this tendency survived by 1926?—some testimonies would suggest, at least its essentials!). Then again, having been deeply impressed by India's ancient dramatic plays, watching them repeatedly, he tried to enact them at home and, making up plays on his own, would get other children to act; when those forgot their lines and acts, he would stand in for them as well. "So, in reality, the whole play was performed by himself."[30] In later years, it still gave him pleasure to write sketches, rich in caricature, picking mureeds to act in them on a free evening during his Suresnes Summer Schools,[31] one such vividly described by Van Hoorn. In those years of recognition and success, among his ever-increasing following he indeed was everybody's sovereign—though increasingly expected to be a constitutional one: inspiration and vision, like cultural attunement, neatly canalized. But in early untrammeled Baroda days, "In any game or pursuit Inayat always was the leader"; and so: "Inayat was fond of speaking and when eleven years old[32] he formed a children's association and called it '*Bala Sabha*,' he being the youngest of all its members ... Many boys were invited to this sabha from his school, but among them the most willing speaker was Inayat himself."[33] That willingness, fortunately, continued lifelong!

From early ladhood onwards, "Inayat spent his evenings at Gayanshala, the Academy of Music." As a youth attending the Baroda College for Boys (of which the Maharaja's private secretary had become the leading light: the later Shri Aurobindo!), he used to go over and offer teachers to take over their lessons for a while. The

---

[30] Ibid, 41.

[31] Those sketches have been included in the (incomplete) collected-works edition *The Sufi Message of Hazrat Inayat Khan*, vol. 12. Quite inappropriately so; these belong to the biographical and Sufi-historical literature that ought to be issued alongside such series, not as part of it. The same applies to the *Confessions*, also in vol. 12, and the *Voice of Inayat* booklets, later disqualified by him as "very poor," yet now in vol. 5; and indeed, to a certain number of lectures, notably in the "Message"—to "my blessed mureeds"—category.

[32] At eleven, Inayat was taken to Patan by Murtażā Khān, when at their host Bhartijī's residence "sages from different places and of different mystical orders met. And to Inayat this was the most congenial association he ever had in his life. The impression of this meeting always remained with him". The Bālā Sabhā would have been a first outcome of that experience. Nekbakht Foundation, *Biography*, 42.

[33] Ibid, 50.

teachers "were most pleased to let him do it" and "get into the open air, away from that heat … in the class."[34] In all such initiatives and activities, as later in taking music and mysticism to a fascinated if uncomprehending West, he was, naturally enough, not merely teaching others, but learning as well as training himself, developing his own values and perceptions further as he went along. It is precisely this exploratory, almost experimental side of his public activities that gives his lectures such perennial freshness of mood and tone. He was forever seeking to articulate some novel ideas or accents, particularly on such themes as most attracted himself (the *Philosophy, Psychology, Mysticism* series of lectures offer good examples of this). That was not what many of his Western followers saw, or wished to see. They needed to regard him as a Mahatma descended from the highest Himalayas if not from Heaven, to illumine their benighted *belle époque* lives out of the perfection of his unearthly being. It must remain for future research meaningfully to disentangle Hazrat Inayat Khan's own ideas, ideals and contemplative perspectives from the colloquy and role he was cast in, indeed caught in, by his initiatic followers—enthusiastically projecting co-workers—on their own terms. A complex but unusually attractive challenge!

The corollary of play, schooling, was not a duty calculated to make Inayat any happier: "I enjoyed religion, poetry" (and its interpretation, and composition[35]), "morals, logic, and music more than all other learning."[36] Indeed, in mathematics and grammar not only, but as well in geography and history, "Inayat was placed last"[37]: "I preferred punishment to paying attention to subjects wherein I had no interest,"[38] and again, *Biography*: "Inayat … often would be caught drawing pictures on a slate, when everybody was supposed to be learning lessons."[39]

Having himself been sent to school at five, unsurprisingly, in his later courses on education, Hazrat Inayat Khan makes an eloquently persuasive plea for commencing school as from seven.

---

[34] Ibid, p. 57.
[35] Ibid, 40.
[36] Bloch, *Confessions*, 2.
[37] Nekbakht Foundation, *Biography*, 40.
[38] Bloch, *Confessions*, 8–9.
[39] Nekbakht Foundation, *Biography*, 40.

Inayat's parents were modern in the sense that, following Sir Sayyid Aḥmad Khān's appeals to the Indo-Islamic community, they were keen for their sons to receive a modern school education. In Indian caste society at large, a certain sense pervasively persisted that the young were to acquire their various vocations, at whatever social and cultural level, in the kinship and occupational circles of their birth, ideally supplemented from the outside only by *gurū* or *madrasa* (religious teacher or school) tuition. Girls, not intended for public position or employment in any case, were to receive all education at home. Modern schooling and its impact on occupational and/or kinship prerogatives, therefore, aroused mixed feelings if not suspicions. Understandably so—we all know but hate to admit that our quantified, technocratic, collective, general compulsory schooling may turn out duly democratic consumers-taxpayers, but no longer any Mozarts or, for that matter, Menuhins.

Quite clearly, Inayat was affected by that traditional social climate, reinforcing his personal dislikes from primary school onwards; at college, he hardly bothered any longer about meeting formal requirements at all, fully engrossed as he already was in his prospective Gāyanshālā activities. And the European generations to which he spoke still very well understood and sympathized, not just with his boyhood distaste, but his adolescent condescension towards generalist educational standards. In Europe, too, for long you were educated up to academic levels not primarily for gainful professional advantage, but in order to be properly "bred up." Attendance at colleges and universities was not necessarily followed by exams and graduations; a "Ritterakademie" could not reasonably expect much more than cavalier treatment. For the doctor, the notary, the clergyman to be more than village notables what had to be primarily presupposed was not intellect and professional competence, but private means and inherited reputation. The early Inayatan Sufi philosopher, Hoyack, is a good case in point—he studied law, never bothered about a final enabling degree, and spent a lifelong meaningful existence in scholarship and art. Here again, as in several, more decisive respects, one finds a meeting ground, approached from different directions, between Hazrat Inayat Khan and his responsive audiences.

Inayat as well as his brother Maheboob were sent to a Mahratti school; in Gujarati-speaking Baroda, the Mahrattas formed the ruling group headed by the Gāekwāṛ Maharajas. Thus the two brothers grew up trilingually, their home language being Hindustani, allowing them to take Hindi and Urdu in their stride. Young Inayat's fluency in Mahratti became such that by reversing its words and syllables, he invented a secret language of his own shared only with Maheboob, to the amused astonishment of their parents. Of more permanent relevance, the school further stimulated and systematized their familiarity with Hindu poetry and its underlying world-view and ideals. *Biography* provides some welcome details.[40] It also records a first attempt by Inayat at writing an essay of his own beyond a mere school composition, "a dialogue between fate and free-will, picturing them as persons" that gained the approbation of "a great literary man."[41] A Mahratti poet and a scholar further familiarized him with poetry and Sanskrit, respectively.

At a further stage of his boyhood follow Inayat Khan's early but deeply influential religious initiatives: his intended renunciation of worldly life; and his abandonment of prayers to God as He kept failing to grant any revelation. Both events feature prominently in much of the available literature. Musharaff Khan notes that apart from renunciation for the sake of "contemplation, study and solitude"[42] the young Inayat also hoped elsewhere to set up a music school on Gāyanshālā lines, introducing the Mawlābakhsh system of notation, theory, and teaching. Exactly that same intention animated him some ten years or so later, in Hyderabad. His Urdu book, *Minqār-i mūsīqār*, also may have been intended to promote that purpose. A few years later again, in Calcutta 1909–1910, he sought to have the Mawlābakhsh series of music books (and so, its musical system) introduced in schools' music curricula, meeting with some preliminary approval, but not awaiting a definitive result. Nonetheless, here we find first a promising boy, then a widely recognized young professor of music, pursuing an idea, a great ideal, of giving shape to values that had inspired all

---

[40] Ibid, 45.
[41] Ibid, 44-45.
[42] Ibid, 54.

his life, in the footsteps of Mawlābakhsh and as such, as T'Serclaes rightly says: "in the national cause"[43]—a budding genius in search of a message. Equally striking is the young Inayat's turning from transcendentalist religious faith to immanentist mystical comprehension with the single-minded intensity that marked all his novel initiatives or newly discovered fields of interest.[44] His doubts regarding formal religion were allayed and reversed by both (Van Beek) his father (*Biography*) and grandfather (T'Serclaes, Bloch, Keesing) in ways vividly characterizing their own depths of spiritual awareness and mystical perception.

Inayat Khan had just turned fourteen when on 10 July 1896, Mawlābakhsh died, a terrible blow to his devoted grandson. Before long, more tragedy was to follow, and up to 1903, in a purely personal sense, his life seems overcast by continual waves of sorrow. From these, he had to pull himself up by the bootstraps: stern self-discipline, confidence, sense of purpose and great vitality made him overcome them. When later forever he reminded his pupils that "self-pity is the worst poverty," he knew what he was speaking of to the full.

In Mawlābakhsh's stead, Raḥmat Khān, Inayat's father and expert of the classical *dhrupad* style of Hindustani music, was to travel to Nepal for "a great musical assembly called by the Maharaja of Nepal," to which "all the well-known schools of music, which are known as 'Khandan' (families) had been invited." And so: "Providence changed Inayat's environment," for "on Inayat's persistent request to accompany him, his father agreed to his doing so." After that typically *Biography*-style evidence of immanence in action,[45] there are some fine descriptive pages on the impressive if arduous Nepal journey and their year's residence

---

[43] T'Serclaes, "Biography of the Author," 8.

[44] By his own admission: "whatever he took up, he took up whole-heartedly" (Nekbakht Foundation, *Biography*, 63–64), and moreover, "If I wish to accomplish anything in life, I do not fear consequences; I simply go and do it and hold what will be, will be" (*The Sufi Quarterly*, June 1919, quoted in full in De Jong-Keesing, *Inayat Answers*, 10). Inayat Khan's early change or expansion of focus has briefly been commented on by Van Beek (*Hazrat Inayat Khan*, 39), who might have referred to Hoyack's emphasis on their Murshid's "panentheism" rather than the "pantheism" discussed and denied by himself.

[45] Nekbakht Foundation, *Biography*, 58.

there. Two related experiences stand out. Inayat's meetings in the Nepalese mountains with an ascetic who had given up speech, a "silent mystic Muni" as rightly stated by T'Serclaes. *Confessions*[46] and *Biography*,[47] of course, prefer to describe him as a "Mahatma of the Himalayas" in keeping with Theosophic tastes—and as such he became part of the oral mythology cultivated in some Western adherents' quarters. T'Serclaes: [The Muni] "was so pleased with his veena playing that he trained him in the mysticism of sound during the period of one year."[48] *Confessions*: "After I had entertained him with my music he, without seeming to notice, revealed to me the mysticism of Sound and ... the inner mystery of Music."[49] *Biography*: "the light, strength and peace that Inayat received from him designed the career that was destined for him."[50] Dr. De Jong-Keesing rightly comments: "These secrets of sound and silence and the mystical power of music pervade Hazrat Inayat Khan's whole development and later work,"[51] and links Inayat Khan's later words to the Nizam: "What I have brought to you is not only music to entertain, but the appeal of harmony that unites souls in God", to "what he had learned from Maula Bakhsh and had understood from the Muni."[52] And indeed, during the London period, 1914–1920, Hazrat Inayat Khan planned a three-volume magnum opus, its publication announced for years, entitled: "The Mysticism of Sound." It was not to be; after lengthy procrastination, only one slender volume appeared, the early work known under that title and now included in serial volume two. The reasons for this remain to be examined, and should prove instructive. For the original plan again illustrates that Hazrat Inayat Khan regarded his essential teachings as all part of that phenomenon of sound, in which music encountered every other aspect of manifested life—in which tone and rhythm, expansion and contraction, breathing and pulsation, vibration and silence all had their parts to play.[53]

---

[46] Bloch, *Confessions*, 12.
[47] Nekhbakht Foundation, *Biography*, 62.
[48] T'Serclaes, "Biography of the Author," 11.
[49] Bloch, *Confessions*, p. 25.
[50] Nekbakht Foundation, *Biography*, 62–63.
[51] De Jong-Keesing, *Inayat Khan*, revised edition, 17.
[52] Ibid., 29.
[53] Cf. Mahmood Khan, "Music and the Mystic," *Caravanserai* 7 (Dec 1992): 15–18.

In addition to the *munī*, Nepal's other great impression was the beauty and the majesty of nature, and its effect on the mind and spiritual life. That love of nature was to continue with Hazrat Inayat Khan throughout his travels—in Ceylon and California, Italy and Germany, Scandinavia and Switzerland, "the land of beauty and charm" which "I was delighted to visit."[54] And it gave rise not only to many sayings and aphorisms, but in what doubtless will remain one of the finest passages on nature in all mystical literature:

> The secret of happiness is hidden under the veil of spiritual knowledge and ... is nothing but this: that there is a constant longing in the heart of man ... to experience something of its original state ... of peace and joy that has been disturbed ... and can never cease to be sought after until the real source has at length been realized. What was it in the wilderness that gave peace and joy? What was it that came to us in the forest, the solitude? In either case it was nothing else but the depth of our own life, which is silent like the depths of the great sea, so silent and still. ... And this all-pervading, unbroken, inseparable, unlimited, ever-present, omnipotent silence unites with our silence like the meeting of flames. Something goes out from the depths of our being to receive something from there, which comes to meet us; our eyes cannot see and our ears cannot hear and our mind cannot perceive, because it is beyond mind, thought, and comprehension. It is the meeting of the soul and the Spirit.[55]

On two occasions, in the New Forest near Southampton and at Katwijk in Holland during the 1922 two-week Summer School there, accompanying mureeds witnessed Hazrat Inayat Khan's absorption in such "meeting of flames," or rather, the "meeting of the soul and Spirit." The Katwijk dune valley became "Murad Hasil" ("Attainment of Desire"), focus for mureeds' meditation and now the location of the Sufi Movement's annual Summer Schools. In this mystical contemplation of, and absorption in, nature we find the counterpart of Hazrat Inayat Khan's aesthetic contemplation and absorption in and through Indian music—both art and nature to him found their fulfilment, i.e., their meditative culmination, in mystical attainment.

---

[54] Nekbakht Foundation, *Biography*, 202.

[55] Inayat Khan, *In an Eastern Rose Garden*, vol. 7, *The Sufi Message of Hazrat Inayat Khan* (London: Barrie and Rockliff, 1962).

Few apart from his brothers could follow his lead through music; mystical realization through absorption in nature has remained linked to the name of one Western mureed, known as Ekbal Dawla Sahaba-es-Safa.[56]

Upon return from Nepal to Baroda were to follow one huge gain and four further tragedies. Dr. A.M. Paṭhān's return from Europe greatly stimulated interest in the West in every respect; above all, close familiarity with and fondness of European music created a cultural bridge into the heart of Western civilization. "It became difficult for me to uphold the superiority of Indian music any longer, even in my own sight, for comparison became impossible. I found Indian music no doubt much more advanced in some respects, but the Western music seemed to have advanced much further than a musician of India can ever imagine"—Hazrat Inayat Khan's later testimony in his "Journal."[57]

Although much remains unrecorded with regard to Dr. Paṭhān, his influence on his nephews and on Mawlābakhsh House generally, Van Beek's chapter on him provides a fairly all-round view of a personality notably never long absent from Maheboob Khan's conversations with his Brothers.

The deaths of a brother, his mother, and two newlywed brides in succession during the years 1900–1903 created a new crisis in Inayat Khan's life. Asceticism, dervish-life, *vairāgya*, now became his need and mood in a new and adult way. His father excused him from further marriage obligations incumbent on an elder son. The years of travel had begun, no more to cease for his lifetime. Travelling via Bombay on his second departure in 1903, he was horrified by the experience of modern public-performance concerts of Indian music—commercializing and vulgarizing events to the scholarly and courtly musical specialist he had been brought up to be. However, in Hyderabad he again found not only princely, but Mughal India still flourishing fully.

---

[56] I.e. Mme. Ryckloff van Goens-van Beyma, 1880–1972. Mercifully, she never tried to institutionalize her particular Sufi attainments into yet another Sufi "Activity" like several other, mainly English and Dutch, leading luminaries, in whose "Activities" she participated loyally and enthusiastically, but critically, commenting with uncommon perspicacity that: "These (i.e. 'Activities') are not Murshid" (i.e. mere dressed-up fractions of his actual Sufi mysticism).

[57] Nekbakht Foundation, *Biography*, 253.

The triumvirate of Inayat Khan's primary inspirers—Mawlābakhsh, Mashaykh Raḥmat Khān and Dr. Paṭhān—now was supplemented by a second one consisting of the Nizam, the Mawlānā and the Murshid. Understandably, all available literature takes great interest in Prof. Inayat Khan's contacts with the fabulous Nizam of Hyderabad. He met with notable appreciation on the Nizam's part as well, as is evident from the reports of their exchanges. Indeed such was their mutual esteem, that, paradoxically, more concrete steps were discarded on either side. The Nizam did not follow courtiers' suggestions of granting Prof. Inayat Khan a *mansab* (ranking appointment of court and state); Inayat no longer sought to realize his long-held hope of founding another Academy of Music. The ruler would have realized that Inayat was beyond a courtier's role, a genius rather than an official; on his part, having received such exceptional recognition from the greatest of Indian rulers, proudly self-respecting Prof. Inayat Khan can no longer have wished to ask for favors to achieve a purpose inevitably involving state authorization and material support.

On Mawlānā Hāshimī, who taught Inayat classical Sufism, see *Biography*[58]; his photograph is also included, with erroneous ascription.[59] Inayat Khan's initiator, Sayyid Abū Hāshim Madanī, of course stands out, second only to Mawlābakhsh, in all biographical literature. A remarkable analysis of the teaching process and its accompanying conditionings as given in Hazrat Inayat's own lectures is contained in notes 4–8 and 10–11 to chapter 5 of De Jong-Keesing's *Inayat Khan.*[60] Sayyid Abū Hāshim cannot but have noticed Inayat Khan's creative genius, his modernism and longing to go West; he loved to listen to his exceptional *murīd*'s music: "Murshid [Abu Hashim] would be filled with spiritual joy, which is called hal (ecstasy)."[61] On the earliest such occasion, as he first visited his *murshid*, singing a devotional poem to him, Abū Hāshim blessed Inayat saying: "Be thou blessed by the divine light and illuminate the beloved ones of Allah."[62]

---

[58] Ibid., 72.
[59] Ibid., 406.
[60] De Jong-Keesing, *Inayat Khan*, 55–64, 274–5. Cf. also T'Serclaes, "Biography of the Author," 15; Bloch, *Confessions*, 40–41; Khan, *The Sufi Message*, 12:149.
[61] Nekbakht Foundation, *Biography*, 79.
[62] Ibid., 76.

According to T'Serclaes' earliest account: "After the accomplishment of his course in Sufism his Murshid blessed him saying: "Go, my child, into the world, harmonize the East and the West with the harmony of thy music; spread the wisdom of Sufism, for thou art gifted by Allah, the most Merciful and Compassionate."[63] In Bloch, *Confessions*, that becomes: "Fare forth ... spread the wisdom of Sufism abroad, for to this end art thou" etc.[64] This wording then from a blessing becomes an "injunction" in *Biography*,[65] having been, and being, solemnly commemorated as such in innumerable Sufi commemorative meetings and pamphlets, the older meaning of "abroad" ignored and the following interpolation unrecognized: that is how institutionalization works, to say nothing of popularization.

As used in Urdu and other Indian languages, "*dunyā*," "world" also carries the connotation of "the outer life," "the material world"[66]; "to which the word 'Samsara' is equivalent in Hindi."[67] So that "go into the world" also implies "return to life in the outside world." On the other hand, no one has yet been able to come up with the original of "harmony" and "harmonize," a key question in view of the early definition of Sufism as "a religious philosophy of Love, Harmony and Beauty" (also to be glossed psychologically as will, balance and ideal[68]).

In the Subcontinent, of course, a sense of distinction or contradiction might be overcome both through shared perception of music or the impact of inspiring verse sung to it. The extension of perspective to the current great divide, East and West, to his *murshid* could grow naturally out of Inayat's known interests and doubtless intentions. "Harmonizing East and West by music" was what Mawlābakhsh already quite consciously had been attempting in addition to "harmonizing" Northern Hindustani and Southern Karnatak Indian music. Notably so by his attendance at the Viceregal Durbar, presenting his music in his princely apparel, gaining honor and recognition later commented on by the Maharaja

[63] T'Serclaes, "Biography of the Author," 15.
[64] Bloch, *Confessions*, 150.
[65] Nekbakht Foundation, *Biography*, 111.
[66] Bloch, *Confessions*, 44.
[67] Nekbakht Foundation, *Biography*,123
[68] I.e. idealism as mental focus, concentration, absorption.

of Jaipur: "I no longer know how adequately to honor you, seeing that at the Viceroy's Durbar you were seated (in a European armchair) while we all, the ruling princes of the land, were standing!" Mawlābakhsh "had prepared himself for this occasion by diligently studying Western music. He was anxious to prove to the English that the musical art of India was indeed an art; and he felt that the only means of making Eastern art intelligible to an alien ear, was by studying the Western principles."[69] Similarly, in Baroda itself, at a personal level: "the daughter of the British Resident was interested in music and she began to take lessons from Maula Bakhsh, who thus made acquaintance with the Resident, and a friendship sprang up between them. ... In this way, a responsibility of State fell on him," etc.[70] Further, and maybe most significantly, Mawlābakhsh received at Baroda, and explained and exemplified Indian music with particular enthusiasm to, Captain Day, author of the magnificent work: *The Music and Musical Instruments of Southern India and the Deccan.*[71]

"Harmonizing East and West by music," therefore, had its practical precedents with which Sayyid Abū Hāshim would doubtless have been familiar; to Inayat himself, his grandfather's "harmonizing" experience would have held out an apparent promise of Western response to their music and its ideals. His *murshid* reinforced the spiritual dimension, in time become all-important; and his twofold blessing linked Prof. Inayat Khan's classical music,

---

[69] Nekbakht Foundation, *Biography*, 25.

[70] Ibid.

[71] In it, he acknowledged the collaboration of "Maula Bux," of Baroda, among several other "native gentlemen." However, the excellent portrait of "a Binkar" (Northern Indian vina player), which is that of Mawalābakhsh (and a few years ago was subject to much research in India, though inconclusively so), remained anonymous. Captain Day, one of those exploring and reporting, highly cultured British "officers and gentlemen" who contributed so much to a better understanding of India in the nineteenth century, here was properly following the conventions of an earlier age by not in such a way making public the identity of respectable persons: for quite a while longer, personal photographs in newspapers were just "not done," an intolerable breach of privacy and discretion. In their changed times, Mawlābakhsh's grandsons, much photographed and publicized in the West, unaware of the earlier convention (to begin with feeling the West had no etiquette to speak of, anyway) took the omission as a slight. (Which may be why Bloch's mention (*Confessions*, 7) of "Maula Bux ... whose portrait is in the Victoria and Albert Museum" remains without reference to Day or his book in which it is to be found).

steeped in predominantly Hindu Indian divine tradition, to the Sufi cause, in those days assailed by novel orthodox trends, by folkloristic popularization, and by the twin imperial British currents of missionary Christianity and secularizing Anglicization. To that extent, there was no objective need to leave the Subcontinent for "harmonizing" East and West or spreading Sufism.

Sayyid Abū Hāshim's contribution, spiritual and psychological, to Hazrat Inayat Khan's early adult unfoldment has unquestionably been great and valuable. Precisely for that reason, he deserves better than to be mythologized with either sentimentally inaccurate references to "our grandmurshid" or (if less grandpaternally, still grandiloquently in a proselytizing vein quite foreign to both) to an "injunction"—one which would almost be the opposite of a genuine blessing.

Moreover, if the use of that term or the editorial rephrasing of his *murshid*'s blessing were to suggest that but for this spiritual interest, Inayat would never have gone West, that would amount to misreading his entire biography. In addition to Mawlābakhsh's interest in Western cultural contacts, even Hazrat Inayat Khan's father, Mashaykh Raḥmat Khān the conventional patriarch, admired the British rule of law, independence of the judiciary and sense of fair play, and was open to European music. Again, Inayat Khan had been the nephew of Dr. Paṭhān long before he became the *murīd* of Sayyid Abū Hāshim.

Only the earliest source, T'Serclaes, states that Sayyid Abū Hāshim gave Inayat Khan that blessing "after the accomplishment of his course in Sufism"[72]—that is to say, in granting him his *ijāzat*, authorization to teach, in the form of a *shajara*, spiritual "genealogy" of initiators to which his own name had been added: an obvious occasion for a benedictory encouragement highlighting the recipient's proven aptitudes and aspirations. The omission of that matter-of-fact detail in all Sufi biographical literature from Bloch onwards, speaks for itself. Biographically speaking, it is to be borne in mind that until their settlement in Suresnes in 1922, Hazrat Inayat Khan and his brothers' life in the West still retained much of the "Grand Tour," a visit of profound orientation and ever-widening range, but still a visit, from which the return home was self-evidently anticipated.

---

[72] T'Serclaes, "Biography of the Author," 15.

Space forbids discussion of Inayat Khan's renewed travels from 1907 onwards; his conversations with Mānik Prabhū and his son, and his pilgrimage to Ajmer are essential reading to all students of Hazrat Inayat Khan and his Sufism. From February 1909 until early September 1910, Prof. Inayat Khan lived in Calcutta and traveled in Bengal. If not to the same extent as in British Bombay, the social and cultural climate of the then capital of the British imperial Raj seems again for a while to have impelled a certain sense of painful alienation in him. Nevertheless, he acquired good and fruitful contacts as well; moreover, Prof. Inayat Khan in this British India must have gained some novel impressions at first hand unknown to his natural environment, the Subcontinent's one-third that constituted Princely India.

British Bengal was going through a phase of intense political crisis. It had been partitioned into two new provinces by Viceroy George Nathaniel Curzon, to whose name his compatriots appended the rhyme: "I am a most superior person." Due to that engaging trait, in carrying out his efficient administrative reform he overlooked the fact of the Subcontinent's being inhabited by that colorful lot, the Indians, and Bengal indeed by their most excitable variety. Anti-government protest had become regular nationalist practice—a condition unheard of in Princely states: what would be shamefully disloyal there, appeared to be heroically spectacular here: a new way of making yourself heard, of drawing attention to the interests of your supporters, and of securing gains as you went along.

At the other end of the social spectrum Bengal boasted a certain number of Rajas and Maharajas who were no rulers at all, but *zamīndār* landowners whose entitlement had been granted or condoned by the British Raj—the Tagores were a good case in point. Other than their landowning or courtly counterparts in the princely states, they seemed to have no personal overlord above them, to all appearances free masters on their own ground.

That could not fail to be an intriguing curiosity to the grandson of Mawlābakhsh and soon, encouraged by some princes met in the capital, he was on his way once more, visiting rulers and landowners, states and estates, alike. Here was a more familiar atmosphere again; but meanwhile, Prof. Inayat Khan also had grown impatient with some rulers: in Mysore, he had come to realize that Mawlābakhsh's attainment there was no more to be so readily re-enacted; in the notably progressive state of Travancore (now Kerala), the ruler seemed too pre-occupied with novel concerns fully to grasp Prof. Inayat Khan's aims and intentions.

Inayat Khan saw very well that one-sided Anglicization alienated the princes and chiefs from their own civilization and populations, and that this could only lead to their own downfall and the decay of India's cultural values of which their courts had been the customary centers, and of which, to him, music was the highest and most meaningful symbol and expression. Concern at rulers' laxity and alienation, coupled with the new notion of critically confronting authority and Inayat Khan's own fondness of experimentation, now focused on Western ways in view of his intended departure to America, led to his Dacca parting shot at the assembled "princes and potentates" of Bengal—as a further step in British modernity.[73]

The Nawāb of Dacca had invited Prof. Inayat Khan to sing at the festive assembly he was convening, which he accepted on condition that he should first be allowed to speak. To begin with he declined residence as a guest at the Nawāb's Iḥsān Manzil Palace (not "Asan Manzīl" as in *Biography*[74]), only giving in to a repeated invitation at the insistence of his *tablā* accompanist.[75] He evidently sought to avoid incurring an obligation on this occasion, planning to make an up-to-date, Western-style critical speech, berating the assembled princes jointly on their negligence of Indian classical music and their need for, in T'Serclaes'sense, "moralizing" it.[76] So he did and his host, "the experienced Nawab, who was full of goodwill,"[77] as well as the majority of his fellow-princes were clearly taken aback by the young professor's audacity.[78] His music

[73] Nekbakht Foundation, *Biography*, 109.
[74] Ibid.
[75] Musharaff Khan, *Pages*, 65.
[76] T'Serclaes, "Biography of the Author," 9.
[77] Nekbakht Foundation, *Biography*, 109.
[78] It is to be remembered, however, that Professor Inayat Khan R. Pathan's speech was not only a criticism but an appeal. His Bombay experience of music commercialized and going public, had been little short of traumatic: music in its Karnatak and saintly, and in its Hindustani and aristocratic, mode and meaning, seemed under deadly threat from Westernizing modernisms. And if so, so too

thereafter was only given a short hearing. The Maharaja of Dinajpur reacted positively to Inayat Khan's admonitions, but neither from him, nor *à fortiori* from his Dacca host, came the offer of any of the customary farewell testimonials. Genuinely impressed, however, was the Raja of Sylhet, who invited Inayat Khan from there to travel back with him to his state in Assam (now in Bangladesh).

By now, Prof. Inayat Khan's life was changing, not least by the prospect of the American journey. That had become possible by the death of the ailing Mashaykh Raḥmat Khān, probably in the first quarter of 1910. *Biography's* haphazard nonchalance at this point becomes both serious and a caricature, stating that Inayat lived in Calcutta "for several years," "there received news of the death of his beloved father," though "thus his life became free from any duty binding him," then breathlessly adding that "soon another misfortune befell him, namely the loss of his medals."[79] Secretarial blindness to anything but the Master Himself here reaches a peak of obtuse insensitivity, or plain editorial ineptitude. The suggestion that Inayat Khan heard of his father's death already in Calcutta would raise awkward family questions, but is contradicted by the oral tradition, corroborated by Musharaff Khan, who relates the touching story, also involving the noble, though somewhat withdrawn figure of Mehr-bakhshe.[80]

For twenty years now at least, when 'Alā al-Dīn Khān left for Britain to become Dr. Paṭhān, Inayat had been longing to visit the West. The Raja of Sylhet's farewell testimonial, dated 31 August 1910, states of Prof. Inayat Khan R. Pathan that: "He is at present going to America," wishing him success there and all over. The Sylhet episode forms a watershed comparable only to the thwarted

---

would the ways of life of Brahmanical and courtly musicianship, and all that those entailed. How deep-seated a contrast this represented, may well be gauged from his 1915 *The Sufi Quarterly* article on "Maula Bakhsh": "In India, science and art are considered sacred and hereditary possessions … an artist will consider his art in the same light as his family honor … In India, the great artist will not display his talent before large and mixed audiences; he reserves his art for the discriminating few" (9), "her art belonged to the Brahmins alone, sacred to them as their religion" (21). "The music of the South, which has ever been held sacred and as a part of religion..." (24).

[79] Nekbakht Foundation, *Biography*, 107–108.

[80] Musharaff Khan, *Pages*, 54–56.

return to India from Moscow in 1914 and the transfer from Britain to France rather than India in 1920. For the Raja invited him to establish his home-base in his state, with every facility to travel and lecture throughout India.[81]

Few would have declined the generous offer; after all, having secured such an advantageous home-base, an extension of journeys from India to the West could become a self-evident further step, carrying the reputation of the small state of Sylhet, almost unknown elsewhere until 1947, all over the West—as actually happened with Baroda State (which, however, was far more prominent already). Hazrat Inayat Khan had given up residence in Baroda in 1903; in 1914, expecting to return before long, he gave up their remittances, which Mehr-bakhshe had hitherto arranged for them out of their heritage; in London, they decided against any resumption. Reasons of principle apart, what must have played a role as well, was the fact that Dr. Paṭhān's view of Inayat Khan and his brothers' travel to and prolonged absence in the West was very comparable to that of Imām Khān with regard to the young Mawlābakhsh. Dr. Paṭhān knew the West too well to have illusions about any comparative advantages, understanding that too long an absence from one's own environment might lose one one's position, connections and opportunities there, as well—which is exactly what happened. He therefore was eventually proved entirely right, of course; he simply overlooked the elements of quickening intellectual climate, inspiring idealist vision, and profound mystical commitment. Hazrat Inayat Khan's choice not to first establish an independent home base in Sylhet with its own social stability and financial security, before traveling to the West, was therefore a crucial one.

The point is that, in conjunction with his early abandonment of the Barodan, mainly joint-family home-base, with his and his Brothers' persistent renunciation of remittances, and with his unavoidable relegation of music into a purely private background, it determined the course of events in the organization, presentation and shaping of subsequent Sufi work. Music had to be given up not for practical reasons only; more decisively, because the widening circles of Western mureeds could not use it for contemplative and meditative purposes. Even so, it meant another loss of means of

---

[81] Cf. Nekbakht Foundation, *Biography*, 111, and Musharaff Khan, *Pages*, 65.

independent income: once Sufically useless, its maintenance for practical, concert purposes in the circumstances could not be envisaged on any useful scale. The creation of the Sufi Order, then the Sufi Movement and all its institutions meant that, in the replacement of music as a central focus of Sufi cultivation, leading followers' interests and preferences came to play an increasingly decisive part, fully faithfully so, but also fatefully.

This was the issue Hazrat Inayat Khan had to face increasingly, and which he bequeathed to his Brothers once he came to feel that enough had been enough and in that mood left for an increasingly idealized India—alone this time but for a secretary. But in the meanwhile India, too, had changed out of recognition; Mawlābakhsh House was empty and in decay; the tragedy was that Hazrat Inayat Khan's return could only lead to the graveyard township of Nizamuddin, rather than to any background home-base in faraway but evergreen Sylhet.

4. The West

The biography of Hazrat Inayat Khan and his three[82] accompanying brothers, after their departure for the United States, Britain and continental Europe is so inextricably intertwined with the history of his Sufism in the West, that it is impossible to describe the one without the other. Indeed, the Sufi identity literally and formally became their "Race and Caste," under that descriptive entry in British-Indian passports, replacing the "Yuskin" or "Pathan."[83]

---

[82] Out of the five parental—and cousin—brothers of their generation. The eldest, their paternal cousin and brother-in-law Mehr-bakhshe, though greatly considered by them, biographically even if not genealogically rather belongs to the older group of family members. The youngest, "Allāhbakhsh," i.e. Allāhdād Khān-i Mawlābakhsh, born only in 1907, was to have joined them at Suresnes if Hazrat Inayat Khan's death and its consequences had not reversed all further plans. His intended betrothal to Noorunnisa Inayat Khan came to nothing when Dr. Paṭhān's offer, during the family's visit to India in 1928, henceforth to educate the children at his spacious establishment in Nepal, was turned down—he had come to be regarded as too modern and secular on the one hand, and too restrictively joint-family-minded on the other. By that time, he had inherited from his elder brother all the family honors and properties, of which Allāhdād in turn was his heir. After that, only Musharaff Khan maintained the links between the family's "temporal" and "spiritual" branches—i.e., respectively, its Nepalese and European varieties!

[83] Thus, at least, in the case of the last passport issued to Maheboob Khan who, the most formally meticulous of the four brothers, accepted the ascription but

Obviously, that Sufi history is so vast and involved a subject as to exceed by far the scope of the present cursory survey. Brevity, however, yet increases an additional complication. In institutional Sufism, historical analysis and theological, or here rather, Theosophical, synthesis, may well be found to diverge perceptibly, if not glaringly. To some adherents, for all their sophisticated standards, that may seem a sensitive issue. Not all of those really closely committed may relish observation from potentially or pronouncedly contradictory angles. Yet that precisely is the intellectual challenge, the moral discipline and the psychological *finesse* involved in Hazrat Inayat Khan's Sufi teachings: consider for example his "Mental Purification"[84]; "Unlearning"[85]; "Harmony"[86]; and "Balance."[87] In any case, however, here a few brief indications will have to suffice.

Hazrat Inayat Khan's life in the West in retrospect falls naturally into three distinct periods—each transition a veritable watershed. The early period, (September) 1910–(June) 1914, when music mainly determined his and his brothers' social relations and occupational contacts, with travels throughout the West extending from San Diego to Moscow; the London one, World War I and up to 1920 and the return to France, with the emphasis on music gradually receding and that on Sufism extending, which in one of Hazrat Inayat's occasional characterizations might be colorfully described as the "dervish" phase; leading up to the third period culminating in the "classical" Suresnes years 1922–1926, the all too brief "golden era" of Inayatan Sufism.

The course of events during Hazrat Inayat Khan's years in the West (1910–1926) is recounted in the De Jong-Keesing and Van Beek biographies on the basis of *Biography* and other source materials. In May 1914, the Russian government's secret agent and devoted Sufi mureed, Henri Balakin[88] had to convey to the four Khāns the authorities' refusal to allow them to return to

---

hesitantly.

[84] Inayat Khan, *The Sufi Message*, 4:99–107 and passim.

[85] Ibid., 3:108–113, and Graham, *Index to Volumes I–XIII*, 113, s.v. Unlearning.

[86] Inayat Khan, *The Sufi Message*, 2:23–32, and Graham, *Index to Volumes I–XIII*, 41, s.v. Harmony.

[87] Inayat Khan, *The Sufi Message*, 8: 61–67, and Graham. *Index to Volumes I–XIII*, 9, s.v. Balance.

[88] Nekbakht Foundation, *Biography*, 423 (photo 26).

India via Central Asian Turkestan and the emirate of Bukhara. Nominally still independent, its Moscow ambassador had not just invited them, but "urged me very much to go with him to meet the Amir of Bokhara."[89] Precisely such prompting may have aroused Russian suspicions—the newly-published translated version of *A Sufi Message of Spiritual Liberty* emanating from those fellow-Muslims, Yuzkhāns and Bakhshes themselves, might have a less-than-spiritual sequel. Besides, the position of "British Protected Persons, natives of the Indian State of Baroda"[90] might prove a singularly unprotected one in areas where Russo-British rivalries had long been acute.[91] And all the more so if, as Balakin emphasized, a war might break out at any time now.

It would seem the four acquiesced in the enforced U-turn west fairly undejectedly: after their success and recognition in Russia, and by now able as well to build on a reputation and contacts in western Europe, hopes of a corresponding continuance there were, obviously, quite reasonable. However, their Russian experience also had apprised them of the mentality of modern faceless bureaucracies, those worst by-products of the transition from feudal civilization to democratic technocracy, *vis-à-vis* honorable private citizens—so contrary to what one would have expected from the Indian States system such as they knew it, with its careful regard for individual personality. Unsurprisingly, and despite Fox Strangways' earlier advice to focus on France,[92] they made their way to England as the Germans advanced in the French north. Besides, like all Indians for long and to this day, if matters *really* came to a head, they rather trusted the British beyond anyone else—above all beyond nationalist ideological assertiveness from whatever quarter.

Unforeseen problems now emerged. In Moscow, still anticipating an early return to Baroda, they had grandly given up

---

[89] Ibid., 138.

[90] In contrast to British Indian territories under the Governor-General, the Indian Princely states by treaty were protectorates under the imperial Viceroy, their inhabitants hence not British subjects, but under British protection.

[91] An earlier Emir of Bukhara had solicited, and been regretfully refused, annexation to the British empire.

[92] Nekbakht Foundation, *Biography*, 129; De Jong-Keesing, *Inayat Khan*, 108, 110.

their Indian remittances.[93] Now, in wartime London, appropriate maintenance became an unaccustomed challenge, but on no account would they envisage requesting resumption. And facing their prosperous uncles upon a return home from indigence rather than a glorious completion of their "Grand Tour," by now seemed unthinkable altogether. Then, too—was that what Ṣabīra Bī had died for after almost four years of desperate waiting for her husband, household, and, in Indian terms, rehabilitation after an apparently disqualifying neglect of so many years? That priority of the saint over the spouse was indeed a case of what Iqbal was to call Muslims' having "outhindued the Hindus." Not just the House—the entire *maḥalla* (town quarter) would reverberate with rebuke, even more of the saint rather than of the sinner, a devotee after all, himself. Such crosscurrents ran deeper than any outsider could imagine, though are further irrelevant here. In any case, of course, indigence, penance and asceticism fit admirably together.

There now arises that remarkable London condition: Hazrat Inayat Khan and his brothers continued to emphasize the temporariness of their stay in the West as of their current embarrassment; *de facto*, through the gradual expansion and consolidation of Sufism in its novel Inayatan setting, they struck ever firmer roots in Western soil. This London "dervish" phase, at least, suited Hazrat Inayat Khan's long-held ascetic sympathy and practice, as well as his rigorous and very advanced further training in Sufism of his brothers. And it might perhaps be said that a "dervish" period of relative poverty, besides lending itself to followers' subsequent, heroic-sacrificial idealization, may be rendered a little more endurable when accompanied by the realization that a return to the comforts of home is an ultimately non-insuperable matter of swallowing your pride with regard to your *grand-seigneur* uncles.

There were other dilemmas. From his first arrival in Britain from America onwards, Hazrat Inayat Khan became deeply and ever more disappointed with his compatriots in England. With some creditable exceptions, they showed little interest in the ideals of all-inclusive cultural revival and spiritual universalism that inspired his

---

93 That did not signify acceptance of occidentalization in "making their music their merchandise after all" as De Jong-Keesing seems to suppose (*Inayat Khan*, 133)—they simply expected to return home soon, and affluently.

music and lectures. Material and social Anglicization on the one hand, nationalist politics on the other, were their dominant concerns. Religious affiliation for them was not to be deepened in mysticism, but exteriorized into communal, confessionally divisive partisanships, even secularism becoming a contending party ideology decrying others' concrete concerns.

A number of eminent figures did seek spiritual renewal through restatement and elaboration in modern Western terms: Vivekananda and Shri Aurobindo, Tagore and Gandhi, Sir Sayyid Aḥmad and Sir Mohammed Iqbal. Those aimed at an inspiring contemporary revival of time-honored values for their own communities, while simultaneously convincing the West of the abiding greatness or superiority of their religious, philosophical, and mystical systems.

Though of a very high order, of permanent value to humanity as a whole, those impressive intellectual and visionary endeavors also were expressions of the current nationalist mood at a time of imperial expansion. Its authors, each unmatched in their own way, shared the impulses, ideals and aims already cherished by Mawlābakhsh in, and from, music. A stage Hazrat Inayat Khan had started from and left behind. There is no trace of spiritual-nationalist or -expansionist assertion, whether Indian or Islamic, in his life's work. He alone forthrightly faced the challenge that mysticism and contemplative philosophy in the modern world, however deeply indebted to the treasures of the past, would have to strike, then grow and flourish from, its own roots.

Sufism to him was the means thereto, the instrument: it was not an end in itself. That utterly non-propagandistic, non-self-justificatory attitude distinguished him and his mode of seeking and working, from almost all others. This extent of open-mindedness, too, made him a pioneer beyond the ideologies of his day; and, therefore, least understood. But precisely to the continuing need to argue his case and the challenge this implied, we owe some of his finest work.

Even adoringly devoted followers' sanctification could never quite smother his search for ever further experience and expression in the sphere of mankind's ultimate spiritual quest, beyond "the differences and distinctions which divide man." To that extent he was the mystic in both its most authentic and its genuinely universalist sense.

Hazrat Inayat Khan was of course aware of his great fellow-Indians: in Baroda, he knew Aurobindo, his brother a good friend of his own; in London, Gandhi, equally from Gujarat, and Tagore, son of his relations' old family friends. But he saw too well also, that Indian public life was going to be swayed by precisely the sort of educated modern Indians who disappointed him in England. No incentive for developing and carrying on his life's aims in such a context. The older India would not understand, perhaps be in no need, of them; his contemporaries were fully fixed on the excitements of outward life and opportunity, not on inward disciplines and their abiding satisfaction. Spiritual life in a materialist, secular world was not their problem, maybe for long time to come as yet.

It was from among his Western listeners that people came forward who saw the point of his observations, grasped his aims, responded by participation, becoming his admirers and initiates. Intellectual stimulus and idealistic response settled Hazrat Inayat Khan in the West, not any premeditated intention. Naturally, such response came at a price, all the higher as arising out of a very different cultural context and perspective.

The first and heaviest sacrifice was his music. In *Confessions* Hazrat Inayat Khan could still be quoted as saying (upon relating his refusal of support offers to enable him fully to concentrate on Sufism and abandon music): "Music being my very religion, was much more to me than a mere profession, or even than my mission, since I looked upon it as the only gateway to salvation."[94] A touching affirmation of distinctively Indian *dharma*, as any reader of the *Bhagavadgītā* will realize. Yet, by then the gateway soon was all but to close altogether; leading followers' course re-routing to come into full swing; in appearance and presentation, re-adjustment to become increasingly marked. Even so, his Sufism was to blossom out at a variety of spiritual altitudes, (some pretty earthy ones included) and flourish as never before. With indeed, even the mysticism of nature and of music in time "reincarnating" in the spacious Suresnes Sufi grounds and in the brothers' composition and rendering of Hazrat's own English poems.

---

[94] Bloch, *Confessions*, 48.

For long years nevertheless the approach to meditation and mystical realization by means of aesthetic contemplation (i.e. through music above all, but also including poetry or other more concrete expressions of beauty) remained largely relegated to theory. The concept of Beauty itself, from an operative aesthetic concept tended to be understood among the following as a Romantic if not sentimental abstraction, a religious thrill. The methodological void left by the relegation of musical contemplation, became filled up increasingly by mureeds' freshly evolved forms of Sufi presentation, for which Hazrat Inayat Khan's assent and collaboration, hence stamp of authority, were eagerly secured. "Murshid told me," "Murshid wanted me to," became standard expressions among leading Sufi representatives for decades on end. What had been elicited, became understood as having been granted—for preference, confided to privileged recipients. And presentation soon shaded off into interpretation (mainly of Theosophic provenance, but no less Olympian for being Himalayan).

Yet all of this concerned the outward appearance of institutional Sufism, the face it presented to the outside world as done up by the leading followers' cosmetics, and the occasional addresses and pronouncements their Pir-o-Murshid was induced to make in their support. It remained marginal to the actual development of his own Sufi vision and teachings, the substance of his work and the ideals and ideas expressed in it. This is what outside observers and students often fail to take into account. The dual process—Hazrat Inayat Khan's creative elaboration of his Sufi teachings, and mureeds' interpretations and formalized versions of them—continued alongside each other much of the London and all of the Suresnes periods. The latter formed by those "Summer School" years at once stylishly serene and chaotically creative, throughout brimful elation: a sense of attainment and achievement shared by all.

What always will remain striking is the extent to which the person and life's work of Mawlābakhsh constituted too the mould and pattern of Hazrat Inayat Khan's. To begin with, of course, music had been India's noblest art for uncounted generations; only its apogee—mysticism realized through meditative awareness—a yet higher attainment, the very fulfilment of human life itself.

Hazrat Inayat Khan's expansion from music thus was a wholly consistent one: Mawlābakhshī music into Inayatan Sufism. Through his Academy of Music, Mawlābakhsh threw open music teaching and training to all comers, in so doing bypassing and discarding the principle of transmission through affiliation and the monopoly of the privileged courtly *khāndāns*. That was exactly what Hazrat Inayat Khan accomplished in Sufism.

Although Sufi philosophy and poetry always were an integral part of Islamic and Indian scholarship and culture generally, its practice and training long since had been the *raison d'être* of a network of *ṭarīqāt*, orders of mysticism. With those, entire family- or occupational groups for generations might remain associated, in a wide circle around the actual inner one of initiatic adepts and direct disciples. And as Mawlābakhsh did with classical music tuition, so too did Hazrat Inayat Khan emancipate his own Sufi teaching out of such traditional cultural and sociological contexts. In effect, his Sufi institutions also operated as two concentric circles—an inner initiatic one shading off into an outer organizational one—but with the vital distinction of being open to all: universal accessibility as a matter of primary principle; and this was a largely novel initiative.

Gāyanshālā Academy in this way became the conceptual prototype of his Sufi set-up in the West (even if its actual structures closely reflected those of an Indian statelet). That also is illustrated by the title of his first book of aphorisms and poems: *Gayan* (*Notes from the unstruck music from the Gayan manuscript*). Like Mawlābakhsh's in music, this new departure was quite a momentous one.

Sufism had not been confessionally restrictive except in more orthodox orders. What had been obvious but accessory with Rūmī, Ibn al-'Arabī, 'Abd Allāh 'Abdī Būsnavī and the Indian Chishtīs, became a central principle with Hazrat Inayat Khan. He "secularized" Sufi mysticism fully out of communal and confessional contexts, seeking to identify *taṣawwuf* with mysticism *per se*, and ideally identifying it only with *unio mystica,* the ultimate state of mystical attainment: *tawḥīd* in its Sufi acceptance. In his teaching and training, he widely opened up Sufi philosophy and mysticism to all seekers of spiritual insights.

Mawlābakhsh's promotion of musical notation and textbooks with numerous songs in the "Mowlabux Musical Series" made a large amount of music and musical knowledge publicly available. The majority of these books were written by Prof. Inayat Khan Pathan, containing data and collections Prof. R.C. Mehta insists remain of permanent value and interest to Indian musical and musicological work. Sharing out knowledge and experience of one's own cherished fields of study not just with a relatively restricted number of fellow-scholars and specialists, but allowing a wide, anonymous readership of possibly but the slightest competence, to participate in one's particular methods of exposition and development, calls for a very different attitude to life and society than that cultivated in tightly restricted professional in-crowds. Like the other members of their *a'lākhāndān*, Mawlābakhsh and Hazrat Inayat Khan were feudal modernists, with equal enthusiasm convinced of patrician as of professional standards.

It is but natural that Mawlābakhsh and Hazrat Inayat Khan both remained convinced that the truly "greatest"—most classical, intricate and beautiful—music ultimately could only be acquired and transmitted in the time-honored way, from single master to individual advanced pupil. And equally, that music at that level could not be reduced to notation and ought never to: "... in any case, the highest music of India cannot be written ... owing to its fineness and subtlety, and for this reason it must be kept free from all limitations."[95] And likewise, Hazrat Inayat Khan, for all his masterly description, remained convinced that the actual reality of mysticism could never be reduced to intellectual concepts, let alone verbal expression, any more than "the highest music" could be reduced to the "limitations" of notation of whatever kind. Allusive evocation may induce keen inward observation and fragmentary inner experience that, if rightly identified, ultimately may expand to result in *tawḥīd*, "attainment", *ḥaqīqa*, "realization".

The essential message of all Sufism is this: "God constitutes the whole being ... and every soul has the source of the divine message within itself."[96] That realization may be attained through the three

[95] Inayat Khan, "The Music of India" (paper written for the Musical Conference of Baroda), *The Sufi Quarterly* 2, no. 1 (April 1916), 8–18.

[96] Inayat Khan, *The Sufi Message*, 1:33.

stages of *fanā*, "passing from" empirical selfhood at both the physical and psychological level and into full God-consciousness, leading to the lasting state of *baqā*, subsistence in the being of God. Most mureeds, with all their enthusiasm, were only too glad to leave the demanding disciplines underpinning those processes of interiorization to their Pir-o-Murshid.

The very novelty of training Western mureeds, as Dr. De Jong-Keesing has well pointed out, created new problems.[97] To his earliest mureeds, he confided a minimum of two-hour daily meditation training.[98] That soon proved untenable, and gradual reductions ultimately resulted in twenty minutes instead. Meanwhile, many mureeds, fascinated by his teachings as such, were wholly content with those in themselves, alongside some collective meditation sessions and a minimal routine of personal exercises.

In Hazrat Inayat Khan and his brothers' perception, therefore, the practice of Sufism moved from a virtually non-existent circle of full adepts to a far wider one of affiliated adherents: an extending outer circle in which all manner of adventitious elements, products of mureeds' enthusiasms, came into play ever more. But on the other hand, providing remarkably effective platforms and presentations for furthering aspects, however colored or diluted, of essential values of the Sufi cause. Hazrat Inayat Khan, and following him his brothers, were content to leave integral mysticism to be only their personal responsibility—as Mawlābakhsh had done with his own Hindustani-Karnatak compositions.

That kind of two-tier Sufism, like their grandfather's two-tier music, also came natural to their inborn, ineradicable aristocratic persuasion. But more importantly, it induced and enabled Hazrat Inayat Khan vastly to expand the *Weltanschauung* dimension of his Sufism[99]—its philosophy of life, worldview and value system, in the course of time immensely enriched. And the theme of how to live meaningfully in modern secular society, whether as a practicing

---

[97] De Jong-Keesing, *Inayat Khan*, 146.

[98] Cf. Munira Nawn (initiated in September 1911), "An Old Mureed Remembers," *Forty years of Sufism, 1910–1950*, 46–47.

[99] In which the "institutional" lectures, remarks or asides to the "hierarchs" and their pupils are to be distinguished from the general body and trend of his work.

mystic or simply an adherent of an immanentist, "panentheist" (Hoyack) idealism, is one of Hazrat Inayat Khan's most impressive contributions to Sufism, and to spiritual psychology and human thought generally.

At Val d'Or turned Suresnes, the London clouds had dispersed. As the golden Sufi day wore on, it was natural for the shadows to lengthen. Not the body of mureeds at large, but the leading followers and authorized representatives, for all their enthusiastic commitment, were making their weight felt. There was maneuvering for position to be closest to their Pir-o-Murshid, and his ear. The "hierarchs" as they came to be called quite unconstitutionally but very much in Theosophic taste, tended to drift together in two main groups based on the Geneva Headquarters and the Suresnes Summer School management. For them, spreading the Master's work, interpreted in their own terms, took precedence over inward mystical pursuit as such. Their Sufism was being turned inside out: they were, indeed, the ever-widening outside circle.

In that way, to Hazrat Inayat Khan and his brothers, they were close friends, devoted followers, valued supporters, sophisticated collaborators, and as such to be taken very seriously indeed—but not as *mutaṣawwifs*, mureeds "reaching out for Sufism." They were reaching out for their richly charismatic Murshid in the best of Christian-Messianic or Hindu-Theosophic incarnationist traditions, before and beyond anything else—the "*pīrism*" of Oriental folklore Sufism transferred to an elitist level of Occidental society. In the practice of institutional Sufism, that did more good than harm; yet in time, problems were bound to multiply in the confusion of Romantically unbridled idealisms and self-interpretations, enhanced by initiatic and organizational ranks, degrees and functions.

Hazrat Inayat Khan and his brothers reacted in two ways: in the intimacy of their own circle, they preferred to laugh and joke rather than to become frustrated at what they regarded as hierarchs' pretentious antics in the name of Sufi mysticism. Yet Hazrat Inayat Khan the mystic beyond form and concept, realized that he had to approach, sustain and help forward, and, that is, inward, each single mureed on his/her own, and on their very own terms—in modes of comprehension, belief and idealism. That was his task as Pir-o-Murshid, and his artistic attunement helped him to do so creatively.

Yet he began to feel he was making one concession after another without enhanced, genuinely inward commitment from many he so accommodated on his part. Matters came to a head over organizational structure.[100] Hazrat Inayat Khan could let his leading followers direct their "Activities" outwards in their own ways, as long as at the center, inside, he remained responsible and in charge of both mystical and organizational consistency. "Hierarchs'" ambitions of controlling the organization and hence determining their Pir-o-Murshid's mode of work led to considerable disagreement between themselves during the Geneva Sufi Headquarters' council meetings in 1925.[101] Alongside indifferent health, fatigue, disappointment, and a sense that his life's work had reached a certain point of completion, Hazrat Inayat Khan increasingly came to feel he had had enough.

India, meanwhile, to the four brothers had kept looming large.[102] The Sufi constitutional rules of 1917 still contained an introductory paragraph stating: "Khankah, the Headquarters of the Sufi Order

---

[100] The leading followers, deputy initiators themselves, aimed at "hierarchy", i.e. a "theocratic" bureaucracy rising pyramid-like from base to apex, leaving duly spectacular authority at every level and assuring a steady if honorary Sufi career to initiatic élites. Hazrat Inayat Khan and brothers, however, understood leadership as familiar from feudal statelets and clan chieftaincies, i.e., as monarchical, with delegation downwards. A single close personal friend and observer like the younger Pallandt (later editor of the 12-volume *Sufi Message* series (cf. supra under 1.3, 1) remained keenly aware of that "courtly" in contrast to the "episcopal" emphasis within the Sufi organizational structures, but though practical frictions were in due course resolved, the dualism of principle never was. Hazrat Inayat Khan's second successor, his cousin-brother Muhammad Ali Khan, as formidable as warmheartedly mureed-oriented, came close to doing away with the "hierarchy" almost altogether. Municipal expropriation of the Sufi landed property at Suresnes during the mid-fifties, with related troubles and the shockwaves all this sent through the entire International Sufi Movement and Order community, however, caused abandonment of such aspirations.

[101] Cf. References in De Jong-Keesing, *Inayat Khan*, 209–210. "1925" was, of course, the culmination of an element of disenchantment long since making itself felt, but in its attempt to separate the social (organizational) from the spiritual (initiatic) and its insistence on preponderant "hierarchy" rather than "monarchy", it struck at the very roots of their Pir-o-Murshid's own cultural identity—unwittingly but insuperably derogatorily so—the very thing the four brothers had been bred to die for rather than submit to.

[102] Graphically if briefly summarized in De Jong-Keesing, *Inayat Khan*, 216–217.

was, therefore (i.e., as: "the message of the Sufi Order was brought to the West"), for the time being, being removed from India and temporarily established in London. India being, however, the permanent seat of this. It is to be in London until the stay of Inayat Khan, the Pir-o-Murshid and Representative terminates, unless another decision is made in the Executive Council." And in 1918, Hazrat Inayat Khan wrote letters to Baroda aimed at his and his brothers' joint return there.[103]

After the organizational crisis of 1925 he could only with difficulty be persuaded by Maheboob Khan not to leave for India—instead he undertook another lengthy tour of the United States. But in 1926, there was no keeping him back. The Sufism of Hazrat Inayat Khan came full circle at last; his death and its consequences rendered complete the disjunction of the Baroda *khāndān* and the Suresnes-Geneva Khankah, a renewed integration of which had been his life's last ideal aim.

The Sufism of the brothers and the Sufism of the hierarchs henceforth proceeded side by side, the Sufi carriage's two wheels tracing different tracks. But they jointly carried a precious load. For the contribution of the Sufism of Hazrat Inayat Khan to culture "human and divine," to the psychological and spiritual dimensions of consciousness, is bound to remain an abiding, if as yet partly hidden, treasure for as long as civilization will continue to have any meaning in the life of mankind.

---

[103] De Jong-Keesing, *Inayat Khan*, revised edition, 101–102.

Spreading The Wisdom of Sufism: The Career of Pir-o-Murshid Inayat Khan in the West

DONALD A. SHARIF GRAHAM

In 1907, near Hyderabad, India, a very successful young Indian musician received a commission from his *murshid*: "Fare forth into the world, my child, and harmonize the East and the West with the harmony of thy music. Spread the wisdom of Sufism abroad, for to this end thou are gifted by Allah, the most Merciful and Compassionate."[1] The musician was Inayat Khan from Baroda, who subsequently did travel to the West, spent sixteen years in America and Europe, and is still widely published and well-known as Hazrat Inayat Khan. When he returned to India in 1926, and suddenly died there a few months later, he left behind in the West a substantial, vigorous Sufi organization, the Sufi Movement, which continues today in various forms.

The question before us is, how did this Indian Murshid's commission eventually result in the formation of the first Sufi organization in the Western World? In tracing this process, we will

---

[1] Regina Miriam Bloch, *The Confessions of Inayat Khan* (London: The Sufi Publishing Society, 1915). This small book, which of course had to be written in collaboration with Inayat Khan, was assembled in the autumn of 1914, about seven years after the commission itself. At least two other versions of the commission have come down to us. The first, in the biographical section by "Tserclaes" of Inayat Khan, *A Sufi Message of Spiritual Liberty* (London: The Theosophical Publishing Society, 1914), 15, reads: "Go, my child, into the world, harmonize the East and the West with the harmony of thy music; spread the wisdom of Sufism, for thou art gifted by Allah, the most Merciful and Compassionate." Another version, which appears on a publicity flyer from 1914, reads: "Goest thou abroad into the world, harmonize the East and the West with thy music, spread the knowledge of Sufism, for thou art gifted by Allah, the most Merciful and Compassionate." The differences seem slight, and of course all versions were translations from the Urdu, but take on greater significance when thought of in terms of exactly what would be done to carry them out. For example, there could be a great difference between spreading the knowledge of Sufism and spreading the wisdom of Sufism.

be following the method strongly endorsed by Pir-o-Murshid Inayat Khan himself: "In every problem, you must see the lines instead of the points. That is Sufism. There are two points, but one line joins them. If you seek the point you will go to the one or to the other end, but if you hold the line, you understand the whole."[2]

The story is a complex one, and reflects some ambiguities in the commission itself. The Murshid who gave the commission, Abū Hāshim Madanī,[3] was himself of a family from the west (Medina) from the viewpoint of India. He did not explicitly indicate what form this harmonization was to take, nor exactly where it was to occur. All this was for Inayat Khan to discover as he made his way into the world; this voyage of discovery became the central theme of the rest of his life.

In retrospect, considering what actually happened, it seems obvious that Inayat Khan was being sent to the geographical region known as the West, especially Europe and America. However, he did not go there immediately, but stayed in India for three years before traveling to the West. Before leaving India, he first traveled widely to visit many spiritual teachers. He also passed considerable time in the city of Calcutta, where he made plans to set up a music school like the one his grandfather had founded in Baroda, and where he had numerous pupils. A good part of his reluctance to travel farther may have been the fact that his father was elderly and not well. Once his father died, Inayat Khan at once made plans to travel to the other side of the world. On 13 September 1910,[4] accompanied by one of his brothers and a cousin, also musicians, he sailed from Bombay for New York.

It was as a musician that he first presented himself to the New World. This could be seen as attempting to fulfil the first part of his *murshid's* commission. But, we might ask, just how could giving concerts or lecture-demonstrations achieve the goal of harmonizing East and West? And in fact the opportunities even for such presentations proved very limited. It was an entirely different kind of presentation, as musical accompaniment to the famous

---

[2] Munira van Voorst van Beest, ed., *The Complete Works of Pir-o-Murshid Hazrat Inayat Khan*, Sayings II (The Hague: East-West Publications, 1990), 210.

[3] He is referred to in the earliest sources as Murshid Saiyad Mohammed Madani.

[4] This date, remembered as Hejirat Day, has become one of three special dates observed by the mureeds in the line of Inayat Khan.

dancer Ruth St. Denis, which provided "The Royal Musicians of Hindustan," as they called themselves, with the means to live and travel around America. When he could, Inayat Khan arranged for more meaningful presentations, especially in academic settings, where he was introduced as Prof. Inayat Khan. It was a presentation in a Hindu temple in San Francisco in 1911, however, which provided the opening to a different way of working. In the audience was Mrs. Ada Martin, whom he noticed as he was lecturing and as she came up to thank him. A letter from her arrived the next day asking for "further light on the path," which resulted in her becoming his first initiate in the West. It may not have been clear before this that he would even initiate people or create anything like the Sufi orders in the East. Now, having taken this step, he gave Mrs. Martin the name of the great Sufi saint Rabia (Rābiʿa), and trained her intensively (mostly by letter as he continued to travel). By the following year she had advanced so strikingly that he gave her the title Murshida and said that, "the care of a grain of the Message, which was cast in the soil of America, was entrusted to her before I left the United States for Europe."[5] He initiated more people in New York, and, most significantly for his own life, he met a young American who was to become his wife. After nearly two years in America he went to England, and in retrospect he thought there was "not much done" in that time, except that he "began to learn the psychology of the people in the West and the way in which my mission should be set to work."[6]

The word mission suggests that Inayat Khan looked upon himself as a missionary. In a sense this is true, as he certainly knew that he had a mission to fulfil, and that he had been sent to the other side of the world to do so. But he found himself "sharing the missionary's fate, while teaching no particular religion, furthering no special creed."[7] The missionary's fate he refers to is being met with suspicion,[8] as were the

---

[5] Nekbakht Foundation, ed., *Biography of Pir-o-Murshid Inayat Khan* (London-The Hague: East-West Publications, 1979), 126. This was written some years later, and there is no other indication that the term "Message" was in use yet at this early time.

[6] Ibid., 126. This language, of course, comes from later years. There is no indication that Inayat Khan thought of himself as delivering a "Message" in 1910–12.

[7] Ibid., 133.

[8] Suspicion, first of all, of wanting to change people's religion, which was far from his goal, but also of political involvement with anti-colonial groups, which

numerous Christian missionaries in India. But what is interesting here is to note that from the beginning he did not see himself as representing any religion or creed. Within the world of Islam, Sufis, however suspect to the orthodox, have often been seen as playing an important role in spreading the religion. Pir-o-Murshid Inayat Khan was clear from the very beginning that this was not his role. "I have never approved of the idea of mission work, and especially at this period of human evolution, where a new awakening is imminent the world over."[9] If his mission did not involve a religion or creed, then what exactly did it involve? His *murshid* had said "the wisdom of Sufism," and so his task became to give some further definition to that phrase.

His first attempt to do this was in his first book in the West, *A Sufi Message of Spiritual Liberty*. The book was published in England in 1914 by the Theosophical Publishing Society.[10] Even the title strikes a note, and the preface begins "Sufism is a Religious Philosophy of Love, Harmony and Beauty," a phrase which aptly summarizes Inayat Khan's definition of "the wisdom of Sufism." The book proper begins, "Beloved ones of Allah, you may belong to any race, caste, creed, or nation, still you are all impartially beloved of Allah."[11] Later, even Allah was replaced by God,[12] and "Beloved ones of God" became the first thing Pir-o-Murshid Inayat Khan said in each address, echoing the blessing his own *murshid* gave to him: "Be thou blessed by divine light and illuminate the beloved ones of Allah."[13] Even though many parts of the book point to the development toward the universalization of Inayat Khan's Sufi teachings in the following years, it contains much more traditional Sufi material than his later work.

For example, throughout the book appear numerous Sufi terms in Urdu, Persian and Arabic (many are the same in all three

was also not of interest to Inayat Khan (though there are rumors of him and his family being followed by government agents in England and France).

9 Bloch, *Confessions*, 46.

10 He had the manuscript with him when he went from England to France in 1913, and then on to Russia, as the book appeared in French and Russian translation before the English publication.

11 Inayat Khan, *Spiritual Liberty*, 17.

12 Allah being, of course, the word in Arabic for (the) God, used by Arabic-speaking Christians as well as Muslims.

13 Nekbakht Foundation, *Biography*, 14.

languages). These words are translated and explained, and indeed several of them continued to be used; it is just that their density here is much higher than in the later teachings. There are many quotations in the book, mostly from Sufi poets and the Qur'ān, and there are explanations of traditional Sufi practices. In fact, much of the book has the character of an explanation of something exotic and previously unknown by the reader.

From this beginning, Inayat Khan's teaching moved steadily in the direction of basing itself more and more on the life experience of the listeners and readers. A section in the book called "Sufic Training" specifies that "There is no common course of study for mureeds; each receives the special training best adapted to meet his requirements."[14] At this time, the idea of individual spiritual guidance had been all but forgotten among ordinary people in the West. A training course adapted to their lives required knowing all that was involved in those lives, and naturally meant quite a different course from those developed over centuries in India. Inayat Khan had not only to devise appropriate training, but eventually he had to train his Western mureeds to give such guidance to others as well, a large undertaking.

Quite early in the process, the phrase "a Sufi message" in the title of the book underwent the subtle shift to "the Sufi message," and, following the custom of the day, most often Message was capitalized. Delivering the Sufi Message is a somewhat more definite task than spreading the wisdom of Sufism abroad. Naturally, in order to do so, it would be necessary to give some more definite shape to the Sufi Message. This, however, was not easy to do. Anyone who has been involved in any form of Sufism (the word itself a rather unsatisfactory Westernism) will report that one is frequently called upon to say just what that is, and a good reply is very difficult to formulate. The dictionary definition as "the mysticism of Islam" is problematical, and was explicitly rejected by Inayat Khan: "The idea that Sufism sprang from Islam or from any other religion, is not necessarily true; yet it may rightly be called the spirit of Islam, as well as the pure essence of all religions and philosophies."[15] He also said,

---

[14] Inayat Khan, *Spiritual Liberty*, 41.
[15] Ibid., 38

> It is degrading the name of mysticism when people claim to be Christian or Jewish mystics, for mysticism is pure from distinctions and differences. My Pir-o-Murshid once gave me a goblet of wine during a trance, and said, "Be thou intoxicated and come out of the name and shame! Be thou the disciple of love and give up the distinctions of life! Because to a Sufi, 'I am this or that' means nothing."[16]

This extraordinary experience clearly left a radical impression on Inayat Khan, as he was very careful ever after about avoiding distinctions. In fact, a line in his prayer Khatum says, "Raise us above the distinctions and differences which divide men." But how is it possible to define a message without making distinctions and even possibly creating more distinctions? This was exactly the dilemma Pir-o-Murshid Inayat Khan faced in conveying something definite enough to form the basis of his movement, and at the same time avoid all dogma and doctrine, which he clearly saw as the source of the endless bickering which characterizes all religious traditions.

Throughout all of Inayat Khan's teaching, one constantly finds the words "the mission," "the Sufi Message," "the work," "the cause," and it is often very difficult to determine exactly what these are. This is precisely because the Sufism he was teaching did not embrace or include a set of beliefs or doctrines. He described Sufism as "a training of view," "a change of outlook on life," "an attitude toward life." It is far from easy to put this in a way which can be readily understood; in fact, if it could be, it would not require years of training (much of which he called "unlearning"). However, it may be useful here to present one of his clearer statements of what he was undertaking to teach:

> ... The central theme of the Sufi Message is one simple thing, and yet most difficult, and that is to bring about in the world the realization of the divinity of the human soul, which hitherto has been overlooked for the reason that the time had not come. The principal thing that the Message has to accomplish in this era is to create the realization of the divine spark in every soul, that every soul according to its progress may begin to realize for itself the spark of divinity within. That is the task that is before us.[17]

---

[16] Bloch, *Confessions*, 163

[17] Address to Cherags, August 13, 1923 (privately circulated).

This goal was behind all that Inayat Khan was doing, both in his own work and travels and in the institutions he was creating to provide the means for others to join him in this work.

An early publicity flyer from England, probably 1914, begins: "The word Sufi is derived from the Arabic word 'Sufa' or 'Saf', it literally meaning pure (i.e. pure from differences and distinctions)." It goes on to give Inayat Khan's first attempt at definition in the form of seven "Sufi teachings" and five "objects of the Order." Because these were later replaced by the well-known ten Sufi Thoughts and three objects, which we will examine later, this early version is very little known, if at all. Therefore, it bears printing out in full here:

1. To overcome beliefs and disbeliefs by self realization.
2. Never to be enslaved by principles.
3. That the best moral is Love and the most praiseworthy Beauty.
4. To be pure from distinctions and differences by merging into the Oneness.
5. That wisdom is the true religion.
6. That Harmony is in justice, while justice lies in reciprocity.
7. That music is food of the soul and the source of all perfection.

Many aspects of this list are most interesting. In the very first one, it is a telling point that beliefs need to be overcome just as much as, perhaps more than, disbeliefs. There is a story that someone approached Inayat Khan at a gathering and proudly announced, "I do not believe in God." Far from shocked, Inayat Khan replied, "I do not believe in the God you don't believe in either." And the second teaching remained central, as he was constantly trying to free people from their unwittingly voluntary enslavements, and those to principle proved the most insidious. We find the words Love, Beauty and Harmony again prominent here, and they were to take on a special role in the later formulation of the Sufi Invocation. Oneness is of course a central theme and goal for all Sufis, and here is a kind of seed for the reformulation in the following years to the ten Sufi Thoughts.

It is interesting to see music here assigned such a special, central role in the spiritual life, again in line with his *murshid's* commission. This is mentioned again more explicitly in the five objects of the Order which follow:

1. To establish a human brotherhood with no consideration of caste, creed, race, nation or religion, for differences only create a lack of harmony and are the source of all miseries.
2. To spread the wisdom of Sufis, which has been until now a hidden treasure, although it is indeed the property of mankind and has never belonged to any one race or religion.
3. To attain that perfection wherein mysticism is no longer a mystery, but redeems the disbeliever from ignorance and the believer from falling victim to hypocrisy.
4. To harmonize the East and West in music, the universal language, by an exchange of knowledge and a revival of unity.
5. To bring forth Sufi literature which is most beautiful and instructive in all aspects of knowledge.

Here we find again the great place given to music in bringing the world together, and the special role which the wisdom of Sufis and Sufi literature are to play. These last two goals seem to have moved closest to fulfilment in the rest of the century which has just drawn to a close. Indian music has become very well known in the West,[18] as indeed music from all parts of the planet is now quite easily available almost everywhere. Whether or not this has resulted in greater harmony is hard to say, but certainly it has made possible a kind of intuitive understanding of many different cultures. And Sufi literature is now, at the beginning of the next century, becoming much more widely known and appreciated through many new and adventurous translations, particularly of the work of Jalāl al-Dīn Rūmī, but now others as well. Exactly what role the work of Inayat Khan and his Sufi Order played in preparing the ground for this would be difficult to specify, but it cannot be dismissed.[19]

---

[18] How complete this penetration has become was brought home to me recently when I attended a performance of *dhrupad*, an Indian vocal style of which Inayat Khan was a master. The two singers were an Indian and a Frenchman, and it was only with eyes open that a listener could tell which was which. It is one sure sign of the internationalization of music when professional performers can come from quite different cultural backgrounds. Another example would be the composer Philip Glass, who said that in his entire musical education at Juilliard he never heard a single mention of Indian music. He discovered it working on a musical score with Ravi Shankar and other Indian musicians. But of course the harmonization Inayat Khan was instructed to bring about was through *his* music, not through Indian music in general.

[19] In this context it should be noted, as Pir Zia Inayat Khan has pointed out, that two books of poetry prepared by Inayat Khan with the help of an English

The Royal Musicians of Hindustan made just a few presentations in England in 1913, and Inayat Khan again noted, "Very little could I do in the way of my mission at that time."[20] He then went to France, prompted by Mr. Fox Strangways' correct observation that the French would be more interested in his music. The time in France did produce some encouragement. On a chance opportunity, the musical group went on to Russia, where they had their greatest musical recognition. Continuing the trip to India was the original plan, but news of political unrest and the fact that Inayat Khan's wife[21] was in an advanced state of pregnancy, dissuaded them. They left Russia, somewhat reluctantly, a few months after the birth of the child, a daughter, Noorunnisa, and just ahead of the political firestorm which was gathering. As war broke out, they were obliged to go to England, where they had to remain for the next several years. However, he notes, "all these years I was learning more than teaching. I was studying the Western mind, the mentality of the Occidental people, their attitude towards life, religion and God."[22]

His years of intensive observation of Westerners produced an unending flow of profound observations, often embodied in sayings and aphorisms, published in the books *Gayan*, *Vadan* and *Nirtan*. These were mostly observations he wrote down in his small notebooks as he gave personal interviews to his mureeds. Many of the sayings apply to human beings from any part of the planet, but others show deep insight into people as they were in Europe and America. A substantial passage in the *Biography* bears looking at in this context:

> Materialism on one side, commercialism on the other, besides their agitation against the Church, and their interest in the thought of their modern philosophers turned Europeans, if not from God,

---

poet, Jessie Duncan Westbrook, contain the first translations from Urdu poetry to appear in English. *Songs of India* (London: The Sufi Publishing Society, 1915) contains songs from Urdu, Hindi, and Persian, and *Hindustani Lyrics* (London: The Sufi Publishing Society, 1919) is entirely rendered from the Urdu.

[20] Nekbakht Foundation, *Biography,* 129.

[21] Her given name was Ora Ray Baker. Inayat Khan gave her the Sufi name Amina (after the mother of the Prophet Muhammad), but she was known in Sufi circles as the Begum.

[22] Nekbakht Foundation, *Biography,* 129, 133.

> at least from the God of Beni Israel. I found that a man today in the West is agitated, not only against the Church, but also against the autocrat God, Who works without a parliament, and no one before His government has a vote, Who judges people and punishes them for their sin, and before Whom men are supposed to be presented in the hereafter with their lives' record of deeds. The man in the Western world, who cannot stand even a king over his head, naturally rebels against a God to be considered as an Emperor of emperors. The modern man does not want anyone to be superior to himself; a priest, saviour, or God, none of them he cares for. If there is anything that appeals to him it is to know of the divine character to be found in the innermost nature of man. … I had the greatest difficulty to modify my teachings, which are of democratic spirit but of aristocratic form, to those quite opposed to the presentation of the God-ideal in religious form. For me, therefore, there was a ditch on one side and water on the other.[23]

This passage shows many characteristics of Inayat Khan's approach to his task: the wry observation and gentle but telling humour, the understanding of the deep convictions and aspirations of people quite unlike any he had known in the East, and the difficult but necessary adaptation of his work to their needs. The whole thrust of his teaching during the eleven years left to him could be summed up in the phrase "to know the divine character to be found in the innermost nature of man." It is in the context of this insight that we need to try to understand the organization of his work and the institutions he brought into existence.

Once established back in England, the musical group continued to give concerts and performances, but these were not sufficient to provide for the family. They had for some time received money regularly from Baroda, but that now stopped, and a way had to be found for the family to live. In this context, Pir-o-Murshid Inayat Khan began to give lectures and then classes. At first there was very little response. He says, "I cannot forget the time when I spoke for about six months continually to no more than three persons as my audience."[24] It is a recurring theme in the teachings given by Pir-o-Murshid Inayat Khan never to be discouraged by circumstances. Once one is sure of the goal, one is

[23] Ibid., 133.
[24] Ibid., 139.

to pursue it no matter what. He had ample opportunity in this period to practice what he was later to teach. "Yes, with patience and with hope, I carried on my work." In time, support began to appear in the form of mureeds, initiates into an organization yet to be named and defined. The first group began with Zohra Williams, who saw to publications, and included Sherifa Goodenough, who took on many secretarial and organizational duties, and eventually became Pir-o-Murshid Inayat Khan's principal editor. With the inclusion of many talented people, it became possible to organize many more activities. Modest fees charged for some of the lectures and classes began to provide support for the family. One step at a time, but constantly moving forward, the process was set in motion.

The mode in which he was to work now began to be established. It looks as though it took several years for him to discover this way of working. His own view of the matter, however, is strikingly different. The analogy he uses is agricultural: "all that time was given to the tilling of the ground."[25]

The first institution, known as the Sufi Order,[26] was created by Inayat Khan with his small circle of students in the period from 1914 to 1917, when its constitution was duly recorded in London and it became a legal entity. This constitution is a fascinating document which has received very little attention inside or outside Sufi circles.[27] Many drafts are found in the archived

---

[25] Ibid., 147 (referring to 1910–1915).

[26] Sufi Order is a generic name, and as such seems to lack specificity. Traditional Sufi orders generally bear the name of the founder or some central figure in their lineage (as do monastic orders in the Catholic Church). Inayat Khan was initiated into the Chishtī Order in India, but mentions that he was trained in all four of the major Sufi schools (*Spiritual Liberty*, 15). However, he did not choose to include any of these in the name of his order since he knew that he was creating something new. (Although, in the by-laws of the Geneva Constitution, it says: "The later development of the Sufi Order, which was called Chishtia, culminated in the present Order of Sufis, which is established in the West...") There were no other Sufi orders in the Western world at the time he adopted this name. Often it is now referred to as the "Sufi Order of the West," or "in the West," and this is sometimes found even in literature from the time of Inayat Khan, but it has never been an official name. As I have indicated, Inayat Khan did not think of the organization as confined to the Western hemisphere at all. Now that there are many other organizations called Sufi in the Western world, this generic name is sometimes confusing.

[27] The one brief account of it, in Elizabeth de Jong-Keesing's biography *Inayat Khan* (The Hague: East-West, 1974), 159–60, is somewhat dismissive, finding everywhere the hand of formerly Theosophist disciples. While the

papers, some in Inayat Khan's own handwriting, and most in Sherifa Lucy Goodenough's handwriting, undoubtedly working with Inayat Khan. The exact details of how the organization would be set up and run were evidently of great personal interest to the Pir-o-Murshid, and in them we can clearly see his thinking at that time about his great task.

One especially interesting aspect of this is found in the description of Khankah,[28] the name used here for the headquarters of the Order. "Khankah ... was ... for the time being, removed from India and temporarily established in London, India being, however, the permanent seat of this." Clearly, Inayat Khan did not think of his organization as a Western one, but a world-wide one, the eventual center of which would be back in India. This was of course during the First World War, when his activities were temporarily limited to England. Of course the activities did expand greatly after the war, but in the later documents this idea of an Indian headquarters is no longer mentioned. In the lists of the officers of the various parts of the organization, there appear the names of several Indians, mostly family members. Whether or not they participated in any way in the Sufi Order is questionable, but in any case they simply disappear from later lists. The actual work he was able to do was in western Europe and America, though this was certainly never seen as the only sphere of activity, and a vision of much wider reach appears often in his discussions with his workers. An unusual feature of the organizational structure is that the officers are given multiple votes in various councils, the number varying. This may perhaps have been a way of combining hierarchy and democracy.

The Constitution even indicates that various rooms in the headquarters building, which was also the home of the Pir-o-Murshid and his family, were to be used for special purposes and given special names. For example, the library was Kutubkhanah, the Silence Room was Khilvat (the traditional Sufi word for retreat),

---

Theosophist background of several important followers of Inayat Khan is known and no doubt of some significance, giving it such prominence takes away any hope of seeing just what Inayat Khan, who had no Theosophist background, was trying to create in his organization.

[28] The word is a variant spelling of the word *khān[a]qāh*, a Persian word referring to a Sufi center.

and the Place of Worship was Masjid (not then widely known as the Arabic word for what in English is called mosque). A very important division within the organization was called the Propaganda Department, charged with propagating the Sufi message as widely as possible in the world. Evidently, the word propaganda had not yet acquired the negative connotation which prevents its use in any serious context now. This department was charged not only with printing pamphlets for free distribution, but also with arranging lecture tours for the Representative-General (the Pir-o-Murshid), the General Organizer, and their deputies. Its work was supplemented by the Sufi Publishing Society, which was formed as a "business branch," and which began a Sufi magazine in 1915. Publication was always strongly encouraged by Inayat Khan.

The idea of an expanding work pervades this London Constitution. Amidst highly detailed and complicated arrangements about the fees and contributions to be shared among the various parts of the organization appear the "Authorized Sufis," those designated on the basis of their "capability and zeal for the advancement of the Order" to be transferred from place to place and supported, as needed, from the funds of the Order. In other words, he was ready to create a professional class of Sufi teachers from among his Western followers. The Constitution envisions a Society in each country headed by a Murshid, a senior authorized deputy of the Pir-o-Murshid; and Lodges headed by Khalifs, or junior authorized deputies. In addition to the Representative-General—the Pir-o-Murshid himself or some suitable person he may appoint—there was to be a General Organizer, an active vice-president, and National Organizers to travel in the various countries. What all this makes clear is that Inayat Khan envisioned at this early period of the organization a large amount of activity by his dedicated followers, and a rapidly expanding movement over a wide area.

This kind of activity and expansion never happened. At the time the London Constitution was recorded there was only one person of the rank of Murshid, namely Murshida Rabia Martin in California. No other mureeds were given this rank until 1923, and when Pir-o-Murshid Inayat Khan died in 1927, there were four Murshidas and no Murshids. In terms of his vision in the London Constitution, there were not yet workers ready to take up the tasks. However, by that time the structure of the organization had undergone many revisions.

The earliest formulation of the wisdom of Sufism, the seven Sufi teachings which we have already seen, was reworked during the following years, and the result, by 1917, was the ten Sufi Teachings, later renamed the Sufi Thoughts. Perhaps even the word teaching has some hint of doctrine about it, whereas a thought cannot be given so much heaviness. In any case, the form becomes repetitive now:

1. There is One God, the Eternal, the Only Being; none exists save He.
2. There is one Master, the Guiding Spirit of all souls, Who constantly leads His followers toward the light.
3. There is one Holy Book, the sacred manuscript of nature, the only scripture which can enlighten the reader.
4. There is one religion, the unswerving progress in the right direction toward the ideal, which fulfils the life's purpose of every soul.
5. There is one law, the law of reciprocity, which can be observed by a selfless conscience, together with a sense of awakened justice.
6. There is one brotherhood, the human brotherhood, which unites the children of earth indiscriminately in the Fatherhood of God.
7. There is one moral principle,[29] the love which springs from self-denial and blossoms in deeds of beneficence.
8. There is one object of praise, the beauty which uplifts the heart of its worshiper through all aspects, from the seen to the unseen.
9. There is one truth, the true knowledge of our being, within and without, which is the essence of all wisdom.
10. There is one path, the annihilation in the unlimited which raises the mortal to immortality and in which resides all perfection.[30]

---

[29] In later versions, "moral principle" was altered to simply "moral."

[30] It may be worth mentioning that the tenth Thought underwent revision. The early lists of the ten Sufi Teachings or Thoughts, even after the headquarters moved to Geneva in 1920, has the tenth as: "There is one path, the annihilation in the unlimited which raises the mortal to immortality and in which resides all perfection." An early printing from England has the word

The word Sufi does not appear here, nor is music even mentioned. This does not mean that these aspects of the work were abandoned, but that they took on a metaphorical meaning. For example, in the important teachings on health, the ideas of rhythm and tone are central, something quite new in that day.

Naturally, there are parts of these statements which could be objected to and argued over, but really remarkably little. One aspect of Inayat Khan's special genius was his ability to find compelling words for his ideas, and this ability was used to the fullest in formulating these universal thoughts. Those who adhere to a traditional scripture-based religion might find the third Thought challenging. However, considered from the viewpoint of the increasing dialogue between science and religion now, it provides a wonderful opening. This is one of many instances in which Inayat Khan's teachings seem to point to the future, well after his own lifetime. Although some of the Thoughts are revisions of the earlier seven Teachings, others are completely new. Perhaps the number seven, regarded as an esoteric number, is here replaced by the exoteric ten, based on the Ten Commandments.[31] The five objects, on the other hand, were now reduced to three:

1. To realize and spread the knowledge of unity, the religion of love and wisdom, so that the variety of faiths and beliefs may of themselves cease to exist, the human heart may overflow with love and all hatred caused by distinctions and differences may be rooted out.
2. To discover the light and power latent in man, the secret of all religion, the power of mysticism and the essence of philosophy, without interfering with customs or belief.
3. To help bring the world's two opposite poles, East and West,

---

"annihilation" crossed out, and "emerging" written in Sherifa Goodenough's hand, undoubtedly a suggested rewording. The word annihilation is often still disturbing to people, even when it is explained that it is the translation of the traditional Sufi term *fanā*. Oddly, people do not easily warm to the idea of being annihilated, even in the unlimited. In the period from after the Sufi Movement came into official existence in October of 1923, the Thought appears: "There is one path, the annihilation of the false ego in the real, which raises the mortal to immortality and in which resides all perfection." One can only speculate that Inayat Khan was asked about this so many times and saw so much confusion around it that he decided on a new formulation. The idea of the false ego and the real ego became important in his later years.

[31] In fact, a transition from Commandments to Thoughts is very much in line with Inayat Khan's view of the step forward for humanity he was fostering.

> close together by the interchange of thoughts and ideas, that the universal brotherhood may form of itself, and man may meet with man beyond the narrow national and racial boundaries.

Again, no mention of Sufi literature, and no mention of music. Harmonizing East and West is here instead to be brought about by the interchange of thoughts and ideas, very much the work that Inayat Khan was now doing in his classes and lectures. These ten Thoughts and three objects, with only slight revisions, continued to be seen as a useful formulation.[32]

While the Sufi Thoughts give us the ideas behind Inayat Khan's work, and the Constitution gives the structure of the organization, we do not yet have much idea of the actual functioning of this growing movement. Fortunately we can form some picture of this because of a letter Pir-o-Murshid Inayat Khan instructed his Order's Secretary, Sherifa Goodenough, to write to Murshida Martin in California to inform her of the activities of Khankah, the London center. It is dated 20 August 1918. She begins by mentioning that classes run for ten months, from October through July, with a vacation period in August and September. In a variety of subjects, ten lessons are offered in the course of each year, and the classes run for three years. After the completion of the whole course, "some are chosen from the mureeds, such who wish to devote their life to the furtherance of our blessed cause, and are admitted to the Training Circle, and from them Khalif and Murshid are made." There is no indication of exactly what kind of training these chosen mureeds receive, but it is clearly intended to prepare them to give spiritual guidance and to organize the activities of a center or a country. These courses of three years were later formalized, and further classes added. Here we see the beginning of a system.

Sherifa Goodenough describes a Sunday morning "prayer meeting" open to all:

> Murshid holds the service. The order of proceedings is this: First the Secretary reads the teachings and objects of the Sufi Order and

[32] A book assembled from Inayat Khan's teachings by Dr. Grüner, *The Way of Illumination* (London: The Sufi Publishing Society, 1922), contains extensive commentary on the Thoughts.

> announces the subjects of all classes that are held here at Khankah. Then Murshid speaks on some subject for fifteen or twenty minutes. Then passages from the Bible, Qur'an, Qabala, Gita, etc. are read by different members of the Order, after which a hymn is sung. ... This ends the service.

Again here we find the beginnings of what was to become the Universal Worship Service three years later.

In every class, "Murshid dictates the lesson and it is written down by all present." This was apparently a training in paying attention. Later quite the opposite rule was introduced, where only the designated secretaries were permitted to write down what Inayat Khan was saying. He always entertained questions at the end of each class. There was even a class just for questions, where each person wrote down a question in advance, "not with a view of examination or with an intention to dispute, but a question that puzzles him. The question should be so framed as not to be longer than eleven words." Inayat Khan would then read each question, ask each person present to give an answer, and then would give his own answer.

There was a Silence Class where all present held the thought of the unfoldment of the soul. And there was an Initiates Class with the practice of *zikr*, followed by a personal interview of not more than five minutes, during which Inayat Khan gave each person exercises for the week. This was of course only possible because of the small number of mureeds at this early time. By 1925 there were so many mureeds that each person hoped they might be able to have a five minute interview once a year.

On Tuesday and Sunday evenings Pir-o-Murshid Inayat Khan gave public lectures. Sometimes mureeds or invited guests spoke instead. A variety of subjects were addressed in the lectures, and it must have been on these occasions that Inayat Khan's remarkable power as a public speaker became evident. In fact, more and more he became a public speaker in the later years. At the same time that attendance at his lectures was growing, he and his musical group stopped giving performances. Once the war was over, they could easily have resumed where they left off, but they never did. Inayat Khan gave no more musical performances at all. Those in his family remember that he continued to play and sing by himself every day, but never again before others, neither in public performances, nor even in recitals for his own followers. Clearly, he had found another way.

During the time he lived in London during the war, Inayat Khan created one institution which did not last. This was known as the Anjumani Islam, and was dedicated to promoting the understanding of the religion of Islam and to promoting improvement of the social conditions in the Muslim world. Although Inayat Khan never even suggested that his followers should embrace Islam, he of course maintained a personal interest in these matters.[33] However, the institution never really went forward and faced serious opposition even among his own mureeds. The controversy may have had a role in his decision to move from England after the war. In any case, it quietly was left aside and replaced by the new institution of the World Brotherhood, designed to promote understanding among all religions and to participate in the improvement of conditions throughout the world.

In the working documents for revisions of the Constitution, dating probably from about 1920, the following passage is to be found:

> *Sufi Mission.* The main object of the true well-wishers of the Order must be to help and build up the Sufi mission. The first necessity is some mureed to precede Murshid before he goes to new places and arrange lectures at the Societies and drawing rooms and in public halls. The next important thing is for someone to travel with Murshid, to take down the discussions,

---

[33] Inayat Khan was born into a Muslim family, though a very liberal one. He was, for example, sent to the Hindu school in Baroda rather than the Muslim school simply because the Hindu school was better (something that would never happen in India today). He composed poems and songs to Hindu deities, which seem to have caused no consternation. He was naturally taught the practice of his religion as a small boy, and like everyone else did his five daily prayers and practiced all the other observances of Islam. However, once he came West there is no evidence that he continued this observance, and he did not ask his followers to do so (the sole exception was his first Western mureed, Rabia Martin, whom he did ask to learn and practice the Muslim prayers, but not to become a Muslim). Some of the other members of his family continued as observant Muslims even in the West. Inayat Khan, however, did not give his own children any instructions in these matters.

> addresses, and public lectures, and the teaching given in classes, that nothing is left unrecorded. In this way we can preserve for the world, now and in the future, the message which we value most. The worker who undertakes this must be a shorthand stenographer at the same time. Some mureed, if possible, must travel with Murshid, to attend to the financial side of things and to see to the ways and means for our world mission.

In the years which followed, these requirements were to some extent fulfilled.

Several persons undertook the work of preparing for the travel, notably Sirkar van Stolk, who sometimes traveled with Inayat Khan and left behind many stories from his memories.[34] When he returned to America in 1923, van Stolk's sister, Bhakti Eggink, made the arrangements and accompanied Inayat Khan. In England Dr. Grüner, a medical researcher, took down the lectures in shorthand and edited them into a book, *In an Eastern Rose Garden*, published in 1921. Two secretaries were appointed in addition to Sherifa Goodenough, both of whom learned shorthand for the purpose. Sakina Furnée bought a house across the street from the family home (after 1922) in Suresnes, France, and took down very accurately most of the lectures in the Summer School as well as direct dictation. Kismet Stam, her cousin, took down many lectures, and traveled with Inayat Khan to America in 1925–26 and then to India.

The idea that the Pir-o-Murshid's words should be carefully taken down and preserved for the future as "the message" gathered force as he spoke more and more. He presented the idea behind this to the assembly of his mureeds in July of 1919:

> If there is anything I ask of you it is this: you only in the world know the voice that comes to the ears of my heart, for it is the voice which has brought you closer to me, it is the voice which holds you with me. You know whose voice it is, though it is expressed in my words. I wish this voice to reach the end of the world, I wish this voice to spread wide, I wish this voice to become audible to the hearers and visible to the readers who may be ready to hear it and to read it.[35]

---

[34] Sirkar van Stolk with Daphne Dunlop, *Memories of a Sufi Sage* (Wassenaar, Holland: East-West Publications, 1967).

[35] "Pir-o-Murshid's Address," *The Sufi Quarterly* (January, 1920), 4.

Of course, it was not that only he should hear it and speak it. A line in his prayer Khatum says, "Open our hearts that we may hear Thy voice, which constantly cometh from within."

As far as those who were to travel about spreading the Sufi message, only the Pir-o-Murshid himself carried on that work. Once the war was over and he could travel again, he did so very widely. He gave lectures on many topics, many with intriguing titles, such as: "The Alchemy of Happiness," "The Coming World Religion," "The Word that Was Lost," "The Power of Silence," "Life, a Continual Battle," and so on. What is rather surprising is that as he traveled he sometimes gave lectures with the same title in one place one day and then in a different place the next. Looking at the texts one would expect them to be more or less the same. Quite the contrary, they often have virtually nothing in common. He always spoke in English, but there was a simultaneous translation when needed. He never used any notes, and there are even stories that he asked to be reminded of his topic just a few minutes before beginning. Nevertheless, the lectures often have a high degree of formal organization. The language is always very straightforward and simple.

He moved the headquarters of the organization from London to Geneva, where soon afterwards the headquarters of the League of Nations was established.[36] He moved his family to France in 1920 and into a large home in Suresnes, a near suburb of Paris, in 1922. Meanwhile he traveled widely giving lectures most of the year, and giving a long Summer School at his home for which mureeds gathered from many places. He returned to the United States for a lecture tour in 1923, during which he had a long stay at Murshida Martin's center in California. His movements were noted by the

---

[36] A remarkable passage in a later book by Sophia Saintsbury-Green, one of the four Murshidas, indicates this may not have been a coincidence: " ... the Master was ... sitting by the waters of the Lake with one of His disciples. 'How strange,' said the latter, 'how strange, Murshid, that you should have chosen Geneva for the International Headquarters of the Sufi Movement, and that the same place should have been selected by the League of Nations.' The Master turned with a smile. '*Is* it so strange?' he said. 'Perhaps the same place was chosen for these two activities at the same time and by the same thought! When I was here in the Spring of 1914—I have seen them *both* as they would be later, after the War.'" Sophia Saintsbury-Green, *The Wings of the World or The Sufi Message as I See It* (Deventer, Holland: E. Kluwer, 1934), 7–8.

newspapers, and his audiences were large and enthusiastic. He returned again in December of 1925 and traveled widely giving lectures until June, when he went back to Suresnes for what turned out to be the final Summer School, concluded by a grand ceremony on 13 September 1926, the sixteenth anniversary of his departure from India. After that and some meetings in Geneva, he very quietly left for India accompanied only by a secretary. A few months after his arrival there, he most unexpectedly died (he was only forty-four years old).

His travels and work on behalf of the Sufi message were continual, with the help of his several secretaries and organizers. However, no one else had taken up the work in that way. One early mureed, Shabaz Best, had moved to Brazil and did pioneer work in establishing a Sufi organization there and bringing out Inayat Khan's books in Portugese. Several mureeds gave lectures in their own countries about Sufism. However, the Pir-o-Murshid's vision of a highly active group of traveling teachers remained entirely unfulfilled during his lifetime.[37] Of course, for some of his dedicated followers such a life would have been impossible because they would have needed financial support, and the Order never had enough funds to provide it. However, a substantial number of his followers came from the wealthier classes, and needed no support. Just why none of them took up their *murshid's* work in this way is a question I cannot answer, except perhaps to say that they thought Pir-o-Murshid Inayat Khan did the work so well that no one else needed to do it! Inayat Khan himself mentions this viewpoint in his remarkable piece on "Organization"[38]: "Some said, on my requesting them to work for the Cause, 'Murshid, you yourself are your best propaganda,' which did not flatter me, it only showed me that they would rather have me work than trouble themselves." His rather critical tone here, and indeed many places in this piece, quite uncharacteristic of Pir-o-Murshid Inayat Khan, undoubtedly reflects his growing frustration with this aspect of his work.

---

[37] With rare exceptions. For example, Murshida Rabia Martin traveled to India in 1924, where she received a warm welcome and addressed several gatherings, one of more than three thousand, with reportedly great success.

[38] Published in 1979 in Nekbakht Foundation, *Biography*, 234–240. The quotations on the following two pages are all from this sobering discussion.

He begins “Organization” by saying, “There has been no end to my difficulties in the organization.” He goes on to demonstrate this most effectively, describing, without naming any names, the many different people who came to help him in one way or another and in the end made his task more difficult. Pir Vilayat Inayat Khan, his elder son, tells the story that near the end of the last Summer School in 1926, a Universal Worship Service was held in the Sufi Hall which his father did not attend. Vilayat, a boy of ten at the time, sought out his father in the house and said, “Abba, aren’t you going to the Universal Worship?” His father said, “No, it is time for the mureeds to do that themselves.” Then he called over his son and said, “You know, if I had only had to give my teachings, it would have all been so easy. But there was always organization.” Telling the story, Pir Vilayat sometimes adds, “And now, of course, I have experienced that myself.” In the piece on “Organization” Pir-o-Murshid Inayat Khan says:

> … I found that without the organization it was impossible to carry the work through, especially in the West. For in the beginning I had tried to do so, on the same principle as in the East, but could not succeed. Many became interested in the idea, in the Message, most drawn to it, but in the absence of organization there was nothing to keep them together; so, disappointed, many dropped away and become scattered.

Thus the organization was necessary as a kind of container; the Pir-o-Murshid uses an image to convey this: “You cannot collect flowers without a basket.” However, the problems in making the right basket seemed endless, and they were all problems arising from the behaviour of the people who came to help. “Organization” provides a catalogue of various kinds of problems introduced by the more or less willing workers, and is really quite comprehensive. It is a sobering experience to look at this from the viewpoint of the person who put the structure in place and then struggled for many years to make it function in the service of the ideal for which it was formed. Anyone who has ever worked as part of such an organization will recognize him/herself among those described by the Pir-o-Murshid.

First there were those who objected to any organization at all. Despite his sympathy with this viewpoint, Inayat Khan said this is like saying "I like to eat, but I do not think about the kitchen." This visceral dislike of institutions, especially those formed for spiritual purposes, is, if anything, stronger today than in the Pir-o-Murshid's, and is a constant problem. Then there were those who could accept Pir-o-Murshid Inayat Khan, but not any other persons in positions of authority—which would mean that the Pir-o-Murshid would have to do all the work himself! Then there were those who came to help, but did not really assimilate the Pir-o-Murshid's point of view and outlook on life. This meant that at some point they would work at cross-purposes to what he was trying to accomplish. This of course included all sorts of prejudices, racial, national, religious, and so forth. Naturally these were seldom out in the open, so they secretly undermined one aspect or another of the work. There were those who lacked the patience and perseverance necessary in such work, so that when problems and difficulties arose, they disappeared. And then there were those who came to help, but had their own definite ideas of how to work, which sometimes would have required undoing much that had already been done. In many cases this also involved a certain condescension toward the Pir-o-Murshid himself, thinking that as he was from the East he could not really understand how things are done in the West. In fact, he notes that his friends both in the West and in the East tended to speak to him as if he were a child, despite his considerable experience and success. He says it always amused him. But in fact dealing with all these problems was often painful. "On my part a continual consciousness to consider everybody's feeling, and, on the part of some of my co-workers, disregard of this principle, made me at times feel so sensitive as if a peeling had come off from my heart."

And then there was "the financial problem before me to solve, and it still remains unsolved." The organization was of course dependent upon the contributions of its members. None of its activities, including the very important publication of the teachings, produced any substantial income. The Pir-o-Murshid himself and his family were accommodated through the generosity of some of the mureeds, but he often found himself refusing offers of help, sometimes quite large, because of the strings attached. Those who did contribute were often careful to see that their money was used only for those purposes they personally endorsed. This is one of the reasons that the professional group of traveling teachers envisioned in the London Constitution never came into being. The organization, despite having among its members many with considerable means, always operated with a very limited budget and always needed more funds. This was an area in which the Pir-o-Murshid could not very well involve himself directly, and it remained a problem. I have only been able give a representative sample of "Organization" here, but the whole piece is well worth reading.

In 1921 came the inspiration which resulted in the Universal Worship Service. It is a large step from the prayer meeting described earlier. A set of formal prayers, known as Saum, Salat, and Khatum, give the framework of the service. Candles are lit for the major religious traditions, and their scriptures are on the altar together and are read from in turn. Music can be introduced at any point. There is a sermon, and the service ends with a formal blessing. The service was first held in London, and Sophia Saintsbury-Green was ordained as the first Cheraga. This was a part of the vision of the role that the Sufi Message was to play in harmonizing East and West, indeed in harmonizing humanity. Although he lived in a time of great hope for religious understanding, fostered by the nascent ecumenical movement, Pir-o-Murshid Inayat Khan saw that religious differences would be most difficult to overcome, particularly as religion strongly tends to be practiced in a closed community. In this service, originally called Church of All, he provided a setting in which followers of different religions could come together and worship together without being asked or expected to give up their own religion. Once institutionalized in this way, it also provided a definite work for dedicated mureeds to undertake. The ordination as Cherag was viewed as a very sacred trust, but far less inclusive than the total commitment earlier envisioned for the Authorized Sufis. Many mureeds could undertake this work while maintaining their established means of livelihood, and the organization would not need to undertake to support them. In the years which followed, the number of Cherags increased steadily, and the service began to be performed in many places.

Pir-o-Murshid Inayat Khan gave special classes for the Cherags, and in these he often expressed what he was hoping to achieve. For example, in a class from the Summer School of 1923, he says,

> Our sacred task is to awaken among those around us and among those we can reach, in the first place the spirit of tolerance for the religions and scriptures and the ideal of devotion of one another. Our next task is to make man understand people of different nations, races and communities, also of different classes. By this we do not mean to say that all races and nations must become one; only what we have to say is that whatever be our religion, nation, race or class, our most sacred task is to work for one another, in one another's interest, and to consider that as the service of God.[39]

It often seems as though Pir-o-Murshid Inayat Khan's interest in furthering the cause he was serving became all-consuming. Because the focus of the present article is on organizational matters, this tends to be emphasized. However, his work was always centered around working with those who had come to him for guidance, and their welfare was his primary concern. A talk he gave in 1922 discusses the two great duties of mureeds. Showing devotion to the cause is only the second duty. The first duty is to make their lives

> really happy, that others may share [their] happiness. This happiness can be attained by thoroughly studying the nature of happiness, finding out what it is that gives true happiness, for so often in seeking happiness the soul is deceived and deluded and so remains without happiness. The mureeds must take care that their bodies are strong, healthy, vigorous, and ready to work, and their minds are balanced, sound and clear; then they can have happiness and give it to those around them.[40]

Very often in the classes for mureeds he indicates ways of finding out and pursuing what will prove truly fulfilling in life. He always emphasizes the importance of attitude in this pursuit.

The World Brotherhood and the Universal Worship both originally functioned as outreach activities of the Sufi Order, but in 1923 a different way of structuring the activities emerged. When Pir-o-Murshid Inayat Khan decided to relocate the headquarters to

---

[39] Address to Cherags, August 13, 1923 (privately circulated).

[40] Munira van Voorst van Beest and Sharif Graham, eds., *The Complete Works of Pir-o-Murshid Hazrat Inayat Khan*, 1922 II (New Lebanon, N.Y.: Omega Publications, 1996), 128.

Geneva, he also found a new group of mureeds to take the principal offices. He appointed Mr. E. de Cruzat Zanetti, a native Cuban and a Harvard-trained lawyer, as Executive Supervisor, and with his help undertook a thorough revision of the constitution. The result was the creation of the International Headquarters of the Sufi Movement, an umbrella organization which came into official existence in October 1923. In the Articles of Incorporation, the purposes of the Sufi Movement are the same three objects already examined, and the "basis of the Sufi Message" is the ten Sufi Thoughts. The association which is described is a relatively simple one, consisting of an Executive Committee appointed by the Representative General (the Pir-o-Murshid) and an International Council, consisting of the National Representatives from the various countries and the members of the Executive Committee. In all deliberations of the Executive Committee the Representative General has veto power, and in the International Council he has four votes (the Executive Supervisor having three, and the General Secretary and the General Treasurer having two, and the National Representatives one each). Inayat Khan appointed two other relative newcomers, Cuban in origin also, as General Secretary and General Treasurer: Talewar Dussaq and his sister, Countess Pieri. Thus the entire administration in Geneva was made up of people who had come into the Sufi organization after the move from England, making a fresh start. Generally, the Pir-o-Murshid seemed very satisfied with the way things were administered in Geneva, and felt freed from such duties to pursue his extensive lecture tours.[41]

---

[41] However, we must not fail to mention, at least in a note, that he suffered a major disappointment at the meetings of September 1925. A group of members of the International Council wished to challenge the system of multiple votes on the grounds that in administrative matters each person should have one vote, and even argued that the Pir-o-Murshid should be outside voting altogether. This the stronger loyalists rejected entirely. The Pir-o-Murshid was not present for the rather contentious discussion, but voted *in absentia* (his right in the Articles) and the challenge was prevented. Murshida Goodenough famously declared, "When I see that there is one sun in the sky and another sun on the earth, then only shall I be prepared to accept the point of view that a supreme knowledge is incapable in affairs of organization ..." The challenge was taken hard by the Pir-o-Murshid, who wrote to Murshida Rabia Martin, who was not there, that "after the Geneva Council, if it were not for the Cause, I would have left the whole affair and gone to the East ..." He actually experienced a serious illness after the meetings, before he left for America in December.

The Geneva Articles of Incorporation recognize three principal activities of the Sufi Movement: The Esoteric School of Inner Culture named Sufi Order, the religious activity of the Movement named Universal Worship, and the section for social work named World Brotherhood. These activities were now each given a separate structure and administration, which provided yet more opportunities for various mureeds to take on specific tasks. In the years that followed, two other activities were added. The first was the Healing Order, since there was then as now a great interest in spiritual healing. A simple ritual was created by Inayat Khan for group prayer for healing, and some individuals were authorized to conduct this ritual (Conductors) while others could become members of the Healing Order to participate in these circles. Finally, a ritual based on agriculture known as Ziraat began to be developed, although it had not been much elaborated at the time of Pir-o-Murshid Inayat Khan's death in 1927.

This is basically the structure he left in place, and which has continued in various forms since then. The training in the Sufi Order, the Esoteric School, had been elaborated through lessons Inayat Khan dictated from 1920 to 1924, which become known as the Gathas and constituted a series of lessons on seven different subjects. For example, there is a series called *Pasi Anfas* on breath, which approaches the subject from many different viewpoints. Breathing practices were considered fundamental, and were given to all mureeds. These lessons made up an introductory training course of three years. Once these were completed, the courses recorded in the London days were reassigned as Gitas, lessons for the fourth, fifth, and sixth levels (perhaps indicating that Inayat Khan had originally thought his mureeds capable of advancing more rapidly than they actually could; the practices he gave in concentration remain a formidable challenge).

By this time a system of twelve levels of initiation had been introduced, the Pir-o-Murshid being the twelfth. Accordingly, a series of lessons for the sixth through twelfth level were assembled, mostly drawn from material given by Pir-o-Murshid Inayat Khan to restricted classes for the higher initiates at the Summer Schools (but also incorporating material sometimes given even to the public).[42] These are known as Sangathas and Sangitas. The process of compiling this material, one of the many tasks performed by Murshida Sherifa Goodenough, was quite incomplete at the time of Pir-o-Murshid Inayat Khan's death, and had to be continued and finished from already existing material.

This training material became texts for the regularly given classes in all the Sufi centers, and formed the basis for the esoteric training. Each mureed also had a spiritual guide who gave practices, such as the breathing practices, repetition of phrases given by Inayat Khan, one or more of the names of God in Arabic (or sacred phrases in other languages), concentration practices, and so forth. All of this training, however, was aimed not only at personal spiritual development, but also at producing those capable of participating effectively in the spreading of the Sufi Message. No one was urged to undertake any work, but whenever any mureed volunteered, more than enough work was ready at hand. The great need was always for more people who would take up the work.

> I must appeal to the depth of your heart that we sorely need ten thousand good workers to begin our Movement; as long as we have not got this, I do not consider that we have made a beginning. A Cause which is for the whole humanity needs at least the number I have mentioned ...[43]

This shows clearly the very large scale on which he now considered his mission. One of his workers said one day that the great need of the movement was money. This Inayat Khan denied, saying "our greatest need is workers, faithful workers, with balance, with tact, with equilibrium, and with the desire to serve the cause. What I am asking today is ten thousand servers to begin our work."[44] The training in the Esoteric School was designed to produce very balanced human beings. It was just such people who were needed as workers. The other activities were designed to give them some specific work to do.

---

[42] For a fuller account of this process, see the Preface to Munira van Voorst van Beest and Sharif Graham, eds., *The Complete Works of Pir-o-Murshid Inayat Khan*, 1922 I (London-The Hague: East-West Publications, 1990), xvi–xx.

[43] "The Relation in Which Mureeds Stand to Their Murshid," Sangatha I (privately circulated).

[44] "Nasihat," Sangatha III (privately circulated).

In the light of this requirement, it must be said that now, some seventy years later, this many workers have not yet appeared. In fact, the membership rolls of the several Sufi organizations descended from Pir-o-Murshid Inayat Khan probably do not add up to ten thousand, let alone the number of good workers. It is impossible to guess what might have happened had not Inayat Khan died in 1927. In any case, we have had a glimpse of his vision and his hopes. His view of the message that he came to deliver was that it was inevitable:

> If it were a human enterprise there could have been a doubt whether it would be accomplished or not. It must be accomplished and it will be accomplished. Only those of us who are privileged to serve the Cause may just as well find an easier way, a better way, rather than strike a way of difficulty. Greatness is in humility, wisdom is in modesty, success is in sacrifice, truth is in silence. Therefore, the best way of doing the work is to do all we can, do it thoroughly, do it wholeheartedly, and do it quietly.[45]

The line which I have attempted to trace here could be called the emergence of the Sufi message. This emergence came about through the willingness of Pir-o-Murshid Inayat Khan to take on what would seem an impossible task: to introduce the practice of an essentialized Sufism in a part of the world where it was quite unknown, from which it would then spread everywhere.

The determination and confidence with which he approached this task are matched by his creativity. Perhaps it was his long practice as an improvisational musician which prepared him for his task of spreading the wisdom of Sufism abroad. In any case, he adapted his methods to circumstances in a way that really does seem musical. His triumph was in attracting and training a very remarkable group of human beings, and in giving them a set of institutions to work with. The results—what happened once he was gone—are another story, not yet completed.[46] Here we have seen

---

[45] Address to Cherags, August 13, 1923; Munira van Voorst van Beest, ed., *The Complete Works of Pir-o-Murshid Hazrat Inayat Khan*, 1923 II (London-The Hague: East-West Publications, 1988), 359.

[46] The organizational history from 1927 to the present is highly complex, involving not only the Sufi Movement created in 1923, but also the revival in later years of the original Sufi Order (never officially abolished) and the creation of several other organizations. This history

something of how it all began, and that has been the story of what happens when a truly gifted person is given a great task and pursues it single-mindedly.

> If I had no means of help and no helpers standing by my side in my strife, and if the whole world were opposed to me, I should do my work nevertheless. And when I see you, my mureeds, standing by my side in readiness to help, I feel much stronger and I have every hope of furthering our blessed cause by the help of God.[47]

---

merits extensive exploration, especially as only a few of those directly involved are still alive and available for consultation. Pir Vilayat Inayat-Khan, Pir-o-Murshid Inayat Khan's elder son, claims succession from his father, and has worked tirelessly for his father's message throughout his long life. He has an international reputation as a lecturer, and has authored more than ten books. On February 4, 2000, he passed on the succession to his son, Pir Zia Inayat Khan, the editor of the present volume.

[47] "Pir-o-Murshid's Address," *The Sufi Quarterly* (January, 1920), 4.

Hazrat Inayat Khan with *vina*

Music

प्रोफेसर इनायतखां रेहमतखा पठान.

खुदाका शुक्र ेहेसां हे जहां जिसने कियापयदा,
अजब कुदरत ये आलमको कियाहे नूर से शयदा. ॥ १
हवा आतिश आब ओर खाकका जल्वाहे दिखलाया,
बशरेन जिसमे आला सबसे दरजा अक्कल हे पाया. ॥ २
किये हैवां परिंदे ओर चरिंदे इसहिके बसमे,
हुनर इल्मो इबादत हेभरी आदमाकि नसनसमे. ॥ ३ ॥
इलम कैहें अयां लेकिन इल्म मुसकी बडाभारी,
के दरिया बेबहा जिसका जहांमें हे सदाजारी ॥ ४ ॥
अयशो अशरत शहेनशाहत को करते हें निसार इसपर,
इलम मुसकीका इनसांके जो दिलपे होवेपूरा असर. ॥ ५
न सिर्फ इनसान खुश आवाजेसे दिल शाद करते हें,
मगर हेवां भितो कुरबान इसपर जान करतेहें. ॥ ६ ॥
नबत्तर खर से हे मरदूदजो मूसिक नजिस माने,
जमाले नूर नहिं जाने वो रबको केसे पेछाने. ॥ ७ ॥
हे दरिया बेबहा किशती मेरीको दे तिरा खाल्कि,
इनायत तेरि रहेमतकी हो मुजपर हे दोआ मालिक. ॥ ८

Epigraph to *'Ināyat Gīt Ratnāvalī*

Music in the Life of Hazrat Inayat Khan

R.C. MEHTA

> What is wonderful about music is that it helps man to concentrate or meditate independently of thought; and therefore music seems to be the bridge over the gulf between form and the formless. If there is anything intelligent, effective and at the same time formless, it is music. Poetry suggests form, line and color suggest form, but music suggests no form. It creates also that resonance which vibrates through the whole being lifting the thought above the denseness of matter; it almost turns matter into spirit, into its original condition, through the harmony of vibrations touching every atom of one's whole being.[1]
>
> —Hazrat Inayat Khan

Hazrat Inayat Khan's music is a fascinating phenomenon in the history of Indian music. The philosophy of Indian *saṅgīt* (meaning vocal and instrumental music as well as rhythm/dance) has been described in ancient and medieval Sanskrit texts, and this traditional literature has consistently upheld its high ideals. However, in the recent past, there has been no philosopher of music born to the Indian soil comparable in profundity and vision to the Sufi musician Inayat Khan. In the teachings of Inayat Khan the highest ideals of Indian music, found originally in the scriptures, find a new expression and orientation, which is nonetheless in complete harmony with the ancient wisdom and clairvoyance. The insights are profound, and achieve their depth without recourse to pedantry. The philosopher has made his way from seemingly earthly music to the divine, an evolutionary process of ultimate value for the human mind and spirit. This essay is an attempt to know the evolution of Inayat Khan as a musician-philosopher.[2]

---

[1] Inayat Khan, *The Sufi Message of Hazrat Inayat Khan* (London: Barrie and Jenkins, 1973), 2:151–52.

[2] As a preamble, let me make a submission. Fathoming a realized soul is itself an odyssey, a challenging but deeply meaningful journey. Our mind and spirit

In Inayat Khan, music and spiritual philosophy are mutually supportive, nourishing each other and even surrendering their ostensibly distinct identities. The inner growth of the spirit, the spiritual part, is the more elusive and ineffable one owing to its inherently esoteric nature, while the other component, music, is comparatively easier to comprehend on account of its more tangible and less complex nature. It is the latter that has been given special attention by the author of this article, so as to provide some gleanings of the life of the musician, Inayat Khan.

Musical heritage and inheritance

The chroniclers of Inayat Khan's life provide ample evidence to show that Inayat Khan had achieved a high reputation as a musician, earning several gold medals and numerous accolades for his art, including the honor of being dubbed the modern Tānsen[3]—and all of this before he left India in 1910 at the age of 28! The greatness of his achievements prompts one to inquire into his life: his childhood, his mentors, his training, his music, his compositions, etc.

India's musical heritage is linked with the sacred, with gods and goddesses, seers and sages. Brahmā, Viṣṇu, and Śiva (together constituting the Hindu *trimūrti*, or "trinity") are among its spiritual patrons, as is Sarasvati, the Devī-incarnate whose special instruments of divine expression are music and literature. Its historical inception is traced to the Rishis Nārada and Tumburu, and to Bharata Muni,

---

must both be involved; otherwise our findings will remain superficial. Then again, perhaps, both involvement and detachment have to be attempted.

This is how I feel when writing about the Sufi musician Hazrat Inayat Khan. My own life is devoted to music—music in its widest connotation, wherein music and life become ultimately all but identical. This perhaps makes me eligible to contemplate the contributions of a Sufi musician, as an exercise to my own benefit. To my advantage is my early discipleship with the late Khānṣāhab Ustād 'Abd al-Waḥīd Khān (also called Ustād Bahre Waḥīd Khān), who was a Chishtī-Ṣābirī Sufi and who belonged to the Kirānā *gharānā* of *khyāl* music and was famous for his contemplative *ālāp* in a very slow tempo.

If one studies Mīrā Bāī, Kabīr, Swāmī Haridās or Tyāgarāja one notices in their early life a seed that eventually grows and flowers through a variety of experiences. The musician and mystic Inayat Khan grew in a soil and an environment, a tradition and a family conducive to the flowering of a person with unquantifiable propensities. Trying to know the processes of nature is an exercise in awareness and enlightenment.

[3] The musician Tānsen, whose name marks the highest reaches of Hindustani music, was one of the "Nine Jewels" at the court of Akbar (1556–1605).

the legendary sage who codified the celestial arts of music, dance and drama in the inspired book *Bharata Nāṭya Śāstra*.

This spiritual-aesthetic heritage, premised on the unity of music and divinity, spanning thousands of years and flowing incessantly through innumerable generations of artists and connoisseurs of various religious persuasions, expressed itself in its full vitality in the *dhrupad* style of classical music that evolved during the sixteenth century. For the next two centuries *dhrupad*, along with its instrumental counterpart the *vīṇā* (*rudra bīn*), enjoyed recognition as the supreme classical art, in accord with the highest artistic and cultural canons. Mawlābakhsh, Inayat Khan's grandfather, had the great fortune of learning and absorbing the music of this tradition.

Art is everywhere the product of a culture in general, and a community in specific, the heritage of collective as well as individual memory. Thus Inayat Khan's musical inheritance may be said to have both a soil and a house. The first is India, and the second, the House of Mawlābakhsh. What was the particular musical inheritance of Prof. Inayat Khan Rahmat Khan Pathan (to use his full name as printed in his publications)? Who were the *ustāds*, or *gurūs*, of Inayat Khan—that is, from whom did he receive the *mūsīqī ta'līm* (instruction in music)?

Inayat Khan's own elders in the Mawlābakhsh *khāndān* were his *ustāds*. On the whole, Hindustani classical music has been assiduously preserved and orally transmitted through the ages under the traditional system of *gurū-śishya* (*ustād-murīd*, teacher-pupil) *śikshā paramparā* (transmission of instruction). This tradition of *sīna ba-sīna ta'līm*—face to face (lit., breast to breast) instruction—has generally been the exclusive preserve of the male members of musician families. We find the same family tradition in the House of Mawlābakhsh. Thus Inayat Khan studied under his maternal grandfather Mawlābakhsh, his father Raḥmat Khān (a *dhrupad* singer), and his maternal uncles Murtażā Khān (a classical vocalist in both Hindustani and Karnatak styles) and 'Alā al-Dīn Khān (or "Dr. A.M. Paṭhān"; trained in both Hindustani and Western music). He must have studied at home as well as at the Gāyanshālā, the Academy of Music founded by Mawlābakhsh, where he was a student as well as a volunteer teacher.

A northerner who had spent long years studying in the South, Mawlābakhsh enjoyed the rare distinction of fluency in both the styles of Indian classical music, Hindustani and Karnatak. Mawlābakhsh taught Inayat Khan the art of vocal music, in both styles, and the southern (or Sarasvati) *vīṇā*. Mawlābakhsh's biographers tell us that he learned Hindustani vocal music from Ghasīṭ Khān while at Baroda, during the reign of Khaṇḍerāojī Mahārāj (1856–1870). A painting depicting him with a *vīṇā* with large gourds confirms that he had also learnt the *rudra vīṇā*—most likely from the same teacher.[4] *Rudra vīṇā* players played *dhrupad* compositions on the *vīṇā*, so a prerequisite for a good *vīṇā* player was an excellent grounding in *dhrupad*. Inayat Khan seems to have inherited his knowledge of *dhrupad* from Mawlābakhsh, as well as from his father Raḥmat Khān. In the arts of Karnatak vocal and the southern *vīṇā*, Inayat Khan's source of guidance, after Mawlābakhsh himself, was evidently his maternal uncle Murtażā Khān, the elder son and senior heir of Mawlābakhsh, who succeeded his father as Principal of the Gāyanshālā after his passing.

In all respects, Mawlābakhsh wielded a deep influence on the young Inayat Khan—more, perhaps, even than did his father. Widely-traveled throughout the Indian Subcontinent, Mawlābakhsh was a very highly rated musician, respected for his pioneering work in the field of music education for the masses, as the innovator of a

[4] The illustration of a musician—most apparently Mawlābakhsh—wearing courtly attire (*darbārī poshāk*) and playing the large-gourded *rudra vīṇā* (*bīn*) appeared in Captain Day's *The Music and Musical Instruments of Southern India and the Deccan*, and is reproduced in Elisabeth de Jong-Keesing, *Inayat Khan* (The Hague: East-West Publications; London: Luzac & Co., 1974), 13.

In Vibhukumar Desai, *Uttar Hindustani-na Saṅgīt-no Itihās* (Baroda: Pustakalaya Sahayak Sahakari Mandal, 1928), 117, Ghasīt Khān is introduced as a brother of Fayż Muḥammad Khān, an elderly Court musician of the Baroda State. The name Ghasīṭ Khān indicates that he was famous for his ornamentation called *ghasīṭ*, which is possible to play only on plucked string instruments like *vīṇā* and *sitār*.

See also Bālakṛṣnabua Kapileśvari, *Abdul Karīm Khān: Yanche Jīvan Charitra* (Bombay: B. Kapileśvari, 1972). In this 912-page exhaustive biography of the eminent musician Ustād 'Abd al-Karīm Khān, Pandit Kapileśvari recalls a *da'vat* (music-cum-dinner party) in which Mawlābakhsh played *rāga lalit*, on *vīṇā* for half an hour. He was to conclude his session with his vocal classical music, but could not do so, since by that time it was dawn, the assembled musicians having played and sung throughout the night (ibid., 152).

In this same biography, Ustād Fayż Muḥammad Khān is quoted to have said that his brother Ghasīt Khān had tutored Mawlābakhsh in *bīn* (ibid., 101; abridged English translation: Jayantilal S. Jariwala, trans., *Abdul Karim Khan: The Man of the Times* [Bombay: B. Kapileświari, 1973], 61).

system of music notation suitable for wide-spread utilization in India, as an author of compositions for use in the Gāyanshālā and elsewhere, as a writer and publisher of text books on music, and as *gurū/ustād* to his sons, grandsons, and others. Above and beyond the complexities of musical craftsmanship, Mawlābakhsh's instruction fulfilled the highest ethical, aesthetic and artistic goals.

In his youth Mawlābakhsh had received the special blessings of a Sufi saint, and this legacy he passed on to Inayat Khan. Since childhood Inayat Khan was more interested in music than in anything else, and was endowed with a withdrawn temperament suitable for an evolving Sufi. In the best traditions of the Chishtiyya Sufi Order, music is the equipment considered most necessary to stride the path of contemplation, leading to the experiences of mysticism.

What was the musical environment of Inayat Khan's youth in Baroda? In his childhood Inayat Khan may have heard Ghulām Rasūl and Khādim Ḥusayn, who had been in the service of Gāekwāṛ Khaṇḍerāojī Mahārāj. Later he must have been exposed to many of the elder and eminent musicians who were engaged in the state service of Gāekwāṛ Sayājīrāo Mahārāj. Bāī Allāh-rakhī Bāī, Ustād Fidā Ḥusayn Khān, Ustad 'Abd al-Karīm Khān, Ustād Ammu Gammu Khān, Ustād Ghulām 'Abbās Khān, Ustād Fayż Muḥammad Khān, Ustād Dā'ūd Khān, Panḍit Bhaskar Būā, Bīnkār Jamāl al-Dīn Khān, Ustad Naṣīr Khān Pakhāvajī and Ustād Amīr Khān Jaltarang-navāz were in Baroda variously during the period 1890–1910, some continuing in the service, some leaving Baroda for other States or their native place. The art and skills of these musicians must have helped Inayat Khan in the growth of his musicianship.

Considering the nature of the oral transmission of Hindustani music during this period, the question arises: What was Inayat Khan's *gharānā* ("school," musical lineage)? To which *gharānā* did Mawlābakhsh belong? In Hindustani classical music, the *gharānā* system grew much stronger after the decline of the older *dhrupad* style. The *gharānās* where identified with the birthplace or residence of an exemplary musician, often the seat of his patron. This localization helped safeguard the unique characteristics of distinct styles, but also encouraged conservatism and protectiveness, and ultimately led to fossilization. After a good deal of difficulty,

Mawlābakhsh had learned from Ghasīṭ Khān (*dhrupad*/*vīṇā*), who was the brother of Fayż Muḥammad Khān, an elder musician in the Court service at Baroda, who belonged to the Gwalior *gharānā*. Indeed, in his biography of his famous teacher, 'Abd al-Karīm Khān's disciple Kapileśvari cites Mawlābakhsh as belonging to the Gwalior *gharānā*.

But Mawlābakhsh did not cling to this *gharānā*. In the South he had learned from other gurus, and he passed this Karnatak tradition on to his eldest son Murṭażā Khān. Murṭażā Khān demonstrated his mastery of this music when he was interviewed for the principalship of the Gāyanshālā, soon after the demise of his father. Mawlābakhsh's inborn openness and catholic and innovative spirit had helped him avoid the narrowness of the *gharānā* syndrome. The presence of the state Western music band (used for ceremonial purposes) with its completely different musical basis was an eye-opener (and ear-opener!) for Mawlābakhsh, inspiring him to send his son 'Alā al-Dīn to London. 'Alā al-Dīn's achievement of a Doctorate in Music and adoption of modern Western dress and address further enabled Mawlābakhsh to transcend the need to find shelter in the prestige of his *gharānā*. In his writings Inayat Khan never mentions his *gharānā*. When introducing himself to audiences in India, the mention of the House of Mawlābakhsh and its tradition was fully adequate, authentic and appropriate.

The young Inayat Khan appears to have benefited immensely from travel. In 1893, when he was only eleven, he went to Patan, with his elder uncle Murṭażā Khān. At the age of fourteen he and his father visited Nepal, via Gwalior (where they paid respects at the tomb of the legendary Mughal court musician Tānsen), and during their year-long stay he was able to hear some of the most renowned classical artists of the day—and also developed a meaningful connection with a Himalayan saint. Returning to Baroda, he began preparing textbooks in Hindustani, following the advice of his uncle, Dr. A.M. Paṭhān; these texts were published a few years later in 1903. At the age of twenty he traveled to Madras and Mysore on a concert tour, and then to Hyderabad, where he stayed for five or six years. After Hyderabad, between the years of 1908 and 1910, he was on the road again, performing at the cultural centers of southern and eastern India: Madras and Mysore,

Bangalore, Kombakolum and Tanjore (the home of Karnatak Music), Trichinapoli, Madura, Coimbatore, Travancore, Rangoon, Calcutta, and Dacca. Throughout his travels, Inayat Khan's music succeeded well in bringing his audiences near to him and his message. His concerts were often preceded by short introductory lectures, emphasizing the most sacred and divine aspects of Indian music and describing the high ideals of music as found in the ancient literature. Through these concerts and lectures, Inayat Khan was urged toward his life-mission of becoming a messenger of God, by way of a unique path.

We have considered Inayat Khan's background and the contours of his early biography, but the question of his musicianship still remains to be addressed. This calls for some research and exploration.

The composer, poet and performer

There are two valuable sources that provide unquestionable and striking clues to the musicianship of Inayat Khan. First, the books on music authored by him and published in Baroda (and Bombay) in 1903, as well as his comprehensive work *Minqār-i mūsīqār*, published in Allahabad in 1912. And second, the thirty-one classical songs sung by him on 16 gramophone records, recorded on 26 and 28 September 1909, one year before he left India. Both of these collections of source material are extremely important, not only for the light they throw on Inayat Khan's musicianship, but also the information they provide on the musical styles and genres of the contemporary milieu, the aesthetic tastes of the general public, and the musical fare expected of a classical musician. These are helpful in understanding the history of the actual practice of Indian music during this period, for which source data is scant and attempts to provide a historical perspective have been few.

The name Prof. Inayat Khan Rahmat Khan Pathan appears on the title page of four books lithographed in 1903: *Śrī Sayājī garbāvalī*, *Ināyat fiddle śikṣak*, *Ināyat hārmoniyam śikṣak* and *Ināyat gīt ratnāvalī*. The first three are introductory textbooks, while *Inayat gīt ratnāvalī* is a much more ambitious effort meant for use beyond the Gāyanshālā. To know Inayat Khan as a musician, as a theorist, as a composer and as a poet, *Ināyat gīt ratnāvalī* deserves our full attention. Perhaps on account of its being written in Hindustani, and also its unavailability, the book has largely escaped the notice of Inayat Khan's biographers.

What does Inayat Khan's *Gīt ratnāvalī* reveal to us? Printed at two printing presses (Vatsal Press in Baroda and Victor Printing Press in Bombay), it is 24 x 17 cm in size, has 128 pages, and is priced at one rupee. In the preface the author mentions that the book was prepared at the *farmān* (instruction, order) of Dr. ʻAlā al-Dīn Khān Mawlābakhsh Paṭhān, who was then the Baroda State Band Master and Music Superintendent. The preface also expresses the author's gratitude to his maternal uncle, Murtażā Khān, as his teacher in music. The language of the entire text, including that of the songs, is the distinct regional Urdu-Hindi dialect spoken or sung by the practicing musicians and enjoyed by their audiences. The book is clearly meant to serve the general public.

The title of the book, *Ināyat gīt ratnāvalī*, means "a jeweled garland of songs by Inayat." There are seventy-five songs, all with music notation. Out of these, nearly one-third (twenty-four) are the compositions of Inayat Khan himself, in both text and tune, while the rest belong to the popular canon. The author has provided the musical notation for each song in the notational system devised by Mawlābakhsh, the founder of musical notation in India. This part of the job requires excellent grasp of the genre of the song (whether it is a *ṭhumrī*, *ghazal*, *khyāl*, *dādrā*, or *garbī*), a mastery over the notational system employed, and the ability to vocalize the tunes for notational accuracy. All of this points to the author's great involvement and concentration, motivated no doubt by his sense of responsibility toward Mawlābakhsh and toward his patron the Maharaja, as well as toward the larger world of music that had shaped him.

There are a wide variety of songs in this work, representing quite a few genres of music, namely: high classical styles: *dhrupad* and *khyāl*; light classical styles: *ṭhumrī*, and *dādrā*; and poetry-oriented popular styles: *ghazal* (ranging from the simple to the sophisticated), *kaharvā*, *lāvanī*, *garbī*, *marsiyā*, *pad tarāz*, Gujarati *gīt*, Urdu *gīt*. The number of compositions covered in each genre is indicative of the relative popularity of the style in the public. An examination of the contents of the book yields the following information on the types of songs covered in the book:

(A) *dhrupad* – 1	(I) *garbī* – 1	(Q) *riyāżī tarāz* – 1
(B) *khyāl* – 6	(J) English songs – 7	(R) children's song – 1
(C) *ṭhumrī* – 12	(K) *horī* – 1	(S) Hindi *gīt* – 1
(D) *ghazal* – 15	(L) *lāvani* – 4	(T) *mādh* – 1
(E) *dādrā* – 4	(M) Urdu *gīt* – 3	(U) *pad* – 2
(F) *bhajan* – 2	(N) Gujarati *gīt* – 3	(V) Baroda Anthem – 1
(G) *kaharvā* – 1	(O) *marsiyā* – 1	
(H) *garbā* – 1	(P) *masiya* – 1	

By 1903, when the book was published, Inayat Khan was clearly equipped with the forms and styles of several classical and non-classical (i.e., popular) styles and with sufficient literary fluency in Gujarati, Hindustani and Urdu. Not a single song in Mahratti language appears in this collection, which is surprising. It may be that Inayat Khan was primarily interested in reaching the Gujarati residents of Baroda and its outlying townships, where there were State music schools. Hindustani was the most widely understood language in northern India, and one could easily communicate with the majority of Gujaratis in Hindustani.

Nearly everyone musically inclined and eager to learn would be able to find something suited to his or her immediate comprehension and taste in this miscellany, and use it to improve upon his or her own musical repertoire while gaining practical knowledge about other styles and songs, and in so doing, enjoy and enrich himself or herself.

Purely from the literary point of view, most of the songs are devotional and/or romantic songs (*ghazals*) expressing deep love and adoration for the beloved. There are also some seven popular English songs ("Home, home," "Can I forget thee?" "Won't you tell me Mollie darling that you love none else but me?" "There is no place like home," "Gaily the troubadour touched his guitar," etc). There is a song of salutation to the Delhi Durbar, "*Allāh ābād rakh King Edward, Hind ke shāhānshāh-ko*" (May God forever keep King Edward, the Emperor of India, prosperous). Another song, appearing at the end of the book, "Baroda Anthem: God Save the Maharaja," invokes divine blessings for Mahārājā Sayājīrāo—"a king so wise and benevolent." As in the other songs, the final line of the anthem includes the nom de plume of the composer, Inayat.

Primarily, this book is for instruction, hence the music notation, intended to assist teachers and students in the study of the various styles of music. The classical styles of *dhrupad* and the *khyāl* are the most sophisticated Hindustani styles, requiring deep knowledge and discipline in the rendering of the *rāga* and the lyrics. For this reason only one *dhrupad* and six *khyāls* have been given. There are twelve *ṭhumrīs*, a style that usually involves only two lines of text, in Braj Bhasha. The theme expressed in the lyrics is the desire of Rādhā, or the *gopīs*, for their Kanhaiyā (Lord Kṛṣṇa). This style requires a very sweet voice, the elaboration calls for unfolding or projecting various nuances of the meaning of words of the poetry employed, and the style has its own musical demands.

The fifteen *ghazals* annotated in this book follow the familiar form and style of the genre, which was so prevalent in India at the time. The psychology of love, the experience of the *'āshiq* (the lover, the mystic) yearning for the *ma'shūq* (the beloved, God), is expressed in subtle—and indeed often not so subtle—words couched in rhyming verse. Quite a few of the *ghazals* bear Inayat Khan's nom de plume (*takhalluṣ*), Inayat, in the penultimate line, indicating that the author is in this case both the poet and the music composer. That in his younger days in addition to being a musician Inayat Khan was also a poet can be very well seen from these *ghazals* and other poetical compositions. This type of simultaneous involvement with word and sound, apart from its musical value, is suggestive of the evolution of a soul seeking an alchemical marriage between form and the formless.

A musician is often rated on his repertoire of *rāgas*, since it represents the canvas of his skills, the sum of his inheritance and personal acquisition. Even in 1903, when the *Gīt ratnāvalī* was published and when Inayat Khan was only twenty-one, his repertoire was impressive. The classical *rāgas* found in Inayat Khan's 1903 publications are: Kirvāṇi, Jangalā, Kāfi-mādh, Khamāc, Sindh Kāfi Pīlū, Bhairavī, Tilaṅg, Kaharahara Prīyā, Mādh, Manzī, Sindhurā, Pīlū-Zilā, Kalingaḍā, Devgiri Bilāval, Bilāval, Śrīrāga, Soraṭh Malhār, Bihārī, Mālkauṅs, Chāyā Rāmkali, Jhinjhoṭī, Toḍī, Hari Kāmodī, Jhinjhoṭī-Zilā, Bihāg, Miyāṅ kī Malhār, Gārā, Gauḍ Malhār, Māyamālavagauḍ, Kalyāṇ, Āśāvarī, Ānand Bhairavī, Jaṅgalā-Mānjh.

Taking into account the *rāgas* covered in the book and those sung in his recordings, his favorite ones appear to be those parent *rāgas* which permit contemplative exploration as well as artistry, like Bhairav, Rāmkali, Toḍī, Bihāg, Yaman Kalyāṇ, Mālkauṅs, Miyāṅ kī Malhār and Āśāvarī.

The classical artist

To know Inayat as a musician there is no better source than his recordings.[5] What is this music? What does it tell us about the performing artist? What is the quality of his voice? How trained is the voice to meet the demands of the classical style of the *khyāl* and the light-classical styles of *ghazal*, *bhajan*, etc.? How does the singer deal with the lyrics of the *khyāl* compositions? How good is the recording? What does all of this reveal to us about Inayat Khan's later development as a spiritual leader?

As the basis of his upbringing, education, and profession, music was an integral part of Inayat Khan's being. Indeed, music was the medium through which he reached mystical enlightenment. Or, to put it another way, his music—in itself just sound, albeit imbued with hidden nonverbal mystical meaning—expressed its own soul through his gifted and capable personality. This was Inayat Khan's relationship with his music. His message was expressed in the Indian idiom of music, which transcends language. This was of great importance, as his global mission aspired to a transcendent harmony.

In the early twentieth century the Calcutta-based Gramophone Company of India, a British owned firm, made numerous recordings of music on 78-rpm discs. Artists in particular, and the populace in general, responded positively. Naturally, the Gramophone Company's ventures had a commercial interest. The artist had to be a popular one, and the music chosen for recording had to have popular appeal as well. The most popular music was that of *ghazal*, *ṭhumrī*, *dādrā* and *bhajan*.

---

[5] *Inayat Khan: the Complete Recordings of 1909*, EMI CD NF 1 50229–30 (Stereo) Double CD Set (Calcutta: The Gramophone Company of India, 1994). These thirty-one songs were recorded in Calcutta in September 1909 and released on sixteen 78-rpm records in April 1910.

Some of the recorded artists had earned their reputation as classical artists. Classical artists sought recognition and appreciation beyond the ivory tower of private or State patronage, and touring, on the artist's own initiative or by invitation, was very customary. Hence, in addition to the current *khyāl* style, classical vocalists included in their repertoire such lighter genres as *ṭhumrī*, and *dādrā*, and sometimes even *ghazal* and popular folk songs. Inayat Khan wanted to reach a larger public; not merely those cultivated in art music, but also those, including the upper classes, who appreciated the poetry-oriented music of *ṭhumrī*, *ghazal*, etc.

The songs Inayat Khan recorded with the Gramophone Company are classical in the sense that each is based on a *rāga*, and the rendering, even in the *qasīdas* and *ghazals*, involves musical phrases, *tānas* (fast passages) and the ornamentation characteristic of a classical *rāga* presentation. The thirty-one songs (each less than three minutes duration) comprise the following genres: one *dhrupad*, thirteen *khyāls*, two *tarānās*, three *horīs*, four *ghazals* and *qasīdas*, one *bhajan*, one *māṇḍ* (Rajasthani folk song), two "Popetti" songs (Parsi New Year Festival songs), and one Punjabi song. The *rāgas* presented are some of the most popular ones: Yaman Kalyāṇ, Bihāg, Mālkauṅs, Jaunpuri Toḍī, Sahānā, Soraṭh Malhār, Pahāḍī, Jhinjhotī, Sindhurā, Kāfi, Pūrvi, Paraj, Bhairavī, Pīlū-Barva, Sindhu Bhairavī, and Khamāc.

Listening to the recordings, one can easily discern that the singer is highly talented, with a well trained, pleasing voice and wide tonal range. The artist's accomplishment can be discerned from his mastery over complex *tānas* and high tempo "sa-re-ga-ma" (solfaization) ornamentation within the frame of a *rāga*, requiring musical craftsmanship of a high order. This leaves one with the impression of a musician whose artistry is comparable to the luminaries of the present day. Indeed, India lost a great musician when Inayat Khan migrated westward in 1910.

In evaluating Inayat Khan's recorded music, the limitations of the recording technology of his day must be taken into account. Each 78-rpm disc could accommodate a track of no more than three minutes. Unlike the duration-bound compositions of the Occident, Indian *rāgas* unfold free of time considerations. Singing or playing a *rāga* for such a short duration was an impossible proposition, a truncation of the very spirit of the *rāga*, a mutilation. Yet the revolutionary potential of the phonograph was irresistible. So the music had to be reduced to a limited format, allowing only for the presentation of the text of the composition together with a few flourishes of the *rāga*. Inayat Khan's full stature as an artist must not be judged from this dwarfed music, in spite of the fact that we have no other means of knowing the art of Inayat Khan.

Epilogue

Inayat Khan is conjured up in the mind of a spiritually oriented and musically acquainted listener as a Sufi playing a *vīṇā* that vibrates through the totality of being, "lifting the thought above the denseness of matter."[6] His penetrating perception of art is revealed in his explanation of psychometry: "It is learning the language that the objects speak; that apart from the color or form an object has there is something in that object that speaks to you. Either it belongs to that object or it belongs to the one who has used it; but it is in the object."[7]

Inayat Khan's notion of *saṅgīt* was a holistic one, integrating *gāyan* (vocal music), *vādan* (instrumental music) and *ṇritya* (dance). His complex cultural outlook grew out of the transformation of his personal identity, accomplished with full consciousness under the enlightening guidance of his Sufi *murshid*. In this way he gleaned philosophical perspectives and gained, as a kind of gift, mystical insights into the very psyche of the music that he had been privileged to inherit. His music molded his being, shaping it into a sensitive receptacle for "the music of the spheres," *anāhat nād*, unstruck music, the primordial sound from which all words of wisdom flow. Thus, through harmony, accord, rhythm and interplay, he discovered in music the inner balance of the cosmos.

In this context, Inayat Khan's well-known declaration of having given up his music requires re-examination and reinterpretation. To quote Inayat Khan:

> I gave up my music because I had received from it all that I had to receive. To serve God one must sacrifice what is dearest to one;

[6] Inayat Khan, *The Sufi Message of Hazrat Inayat Khan* (London: Barrie & Rockliff/Jenkins, 1960–67), 2: 151–2.
[7] Ibid., 2:207.

> and so I sacrificed my music. I had composed songs, I sang and played the vina; and practicing this music I arrived at a stage where I touched the Music of the Spheres. Then every soul became for me a musical note, and all life became music. Inspired by it I spoke to the people and those who were attracted by my words listened to them instead of listening to my songs. Now, if I do anything, it is to tune souls instead of instruments; to harmonize people instead of notes. If there is anything in my philosophy, it is the law of harmony: that one must put oneself in harmony with oneself and with others. I have found in every word a certain musical value, a melody in every thought, harmony in every feeling; and I have tried to interpret the same thing, with clear and simple words, to those who used to listen to my music. I played the vina until my heart turned into this very instrument: then I offered this instrument to the divine Musician, the only musician existing. Since then I have become his flute; and when He chooses, He plays his music. The people give me credit for this music, which in reality is not due to me but to the Musician who plays on His own instrument.[8]

Was Inayat Khan not perhaps trying to satisfy queries about his ceasing to sing and play, which happened after a period of his life abroad? A musician never ceases to be a musician, even at a stage when he does not sound his music. Once a musician, ever a musician, whether engaged with sound or silence. This view permits one to conclude that Sufi Hazrat Inayat Khan was a musician to the last—a Sufi musician in full accord with the Chishtī tradition of mystical realization through music, a divinely gifted (*mawlā-bakhsh*) illumination on the path of Sufism.

Inayat Khan found himself extremely busy traveling and spreading the Sufi message. Immersion in music always required quiet hours and mental distance from the many chores and demands of daily life. It was a matter of his life's mission, redefined as propagating the divine message of unity[9] as God's chosen instrument (*'ināyat* means divine favor!).

But did he really give up his music: his playing of the *vīṇā* and cultivation of the voice, his use of music as prayer? He may have discontinued the practice of opening his lectures with music, and even ceased entirely to sing and play the *vīṇā* in public. But

---

[8] Ibid., 2:7.
[9] Ibid., 2:263.

consider the brief memoir of his wife Amina Begum, recollecting his daily routine:

> He arises early in the morning, practicing his breathing exercises for three hours steadily, after which he recites *Darood* (his devotional prayer) most heartfully, shedding tears which fill the entire home with an atmosphere of devotion. He usually devotes two and a half hours each day to voice cultivation which is most trying to the neighbors. The remainder of the day is spent with his pupils and visitors. His evenings are usually devoted to music, discussions or lectures on philosophy. During the latter part of the evening he plays the vina and sometimes sings. I dare say his music at home is much more effective than it is outside.[10]

What can be concluded from this description? It may well be supposed that Inayat Khan recited his prayers musically. As for the voice cultivation mentioned here, this most likely refers to the traditional exercises of concentration on the base note for developing steadiness and breath control, and singing ascending and descending scales from slow to fast pace (a practice that *is* liable to disturb neighbors!). Perhaps he left off these exercises during extended periods of travel.

Even while one accepts Sufi Inayat Khan's declaration that he gave up his music as a supreme sacrifice to his mission, the author of this article, as a musician, is not prepared to accept that Inayat Khan left music! It must be remembered that silences are a vital part of great music. Inayat Khan must have continued to enjoy his music in moments of solitude, in a mood of detachment. Music would have always remained, for him, the "meaning of the meaning."

It is best to complete this short essay with Inayat Khan's own words expounding the essence of his philosophy of music:

> The music of the universe is the background of the small picture which we call music. Our sense of music, our attraction to music, shows that there is music in the depth of our being. Music is behind the working of the whole universe.[11]

---

[10] Wil van Beek, *Hazrat Inayat Khan* (New York: Vantage Press, 1983), 104.
[11] Inayat Khan, *The Sufi Message*, 2:79.

Maḥbūb 'Ali Pāshā, Āṣaf Jāh IV, Nizam of Hyderabad r. 1869-1911

The *Minqār-i mūsīqār* and Inayat Khan's Early Career in Music

ALLYN MINER

Introduction

Inayat Khan's profound involvement in music is a well-known aspect of his life, but details about his music and his life as a musician have hardly been explored. He was brought up in a family of accomplished musicians and was a professional performer in India before he left for the West to lead the first Indian ensemble to tour the U.S. and Europe. He later discontinued public performance to devote himself entirely to the Sufi Order, but he made music a central motif in his teaching, developing an inspired philosophy blending musical ideals and universal spirituality. The Hindustani system in which Inayat Khan was immersed thrives today in India and abroad, but recordings from the first decade of the twentieth century are relatively rare, and most admirers of his thinking know little about the music as it was during his time. A set of vocal recordings that he made in Calcutta in 1909 was recently rediscovered and released on CD.[1] The recordings are an exciting find, but they are very different from contemporary Hindustani music. There is much still to know of the music and the individual.

Inayat Khan wrote a manual on the theory and practice of music, the *Minqār-i mūsīqār*, while he was living in Hyderabad from 1903 to 1907. It was meant as an introduction to the art for the educated readers of the day. For modern readers it is a good source of information on the music of the period, and it is of particular interest for its recording of Inayat Khan's thoughts. Much of the book is devoted to technical aspects of theory and

[1] Inayat Khan: Complete Recordings of 1909, EMI CD NF 1 50229–30 (Stereo) Double CD Set (Calcutta: The Gramophone Company of India, 1994).

practice, but introductory sections give us the ideas on the nature of man, music, and the divine that he was developing at the time. The *Minqār-i mūsīqār* has been long out of print. This essay is based on work done in preparing a translation of the book, to be published by the Sangeet Natak Akademi in New Delhi.[2] The essay gives an introduction to the material found in the *Minqār*. To set the context, it begins with an overview of the state of music in North India at the turn of the century.

North Indian music in the late nineteenth and early twentieth centuries

Music and dance, along with formal poetry and the visual arts, had long been supported in the royal courts and wealthy households of North India. At the end of the nineteenth century India was a checkerboard of political entities, with the provinces of British India functioning under British imperial rule, and the Indian states in various arrangements with the crown. New modes of transportation, communication, industrialization, and trade had led to the new growth of some cities and the decay of others. Sources of patronage for many artists were shifting. The most famous musicians had no trouble finding support in the traditional setting of princely courts or landowners' estates, where patrons vied with each other in building elite musical establishments. Lesser singers, dancers, and accompanists found employment in more public urban and court venues. British policy, however, gave little encouragement to Indian music, and in the large cities where the British presence was strongest the growing middle classes came to share a Victorian-inspired disapproval of the profession, associating it with prostitution and immorality. Traditional, and especially professional, musicians became suspect. At the same time, nationalist intellectuals saw in music a symbol of cultural accomplishment and national identity. Intellectuals revived Sanskrit-based music theory, which was seen to exemplify an earlier, more glorious period of history. Educators encouraged amateur and middle class participation in a music cleansed of its corrupt associations. Publications of manuals on

---

[2] I have translated the text with the special collaboration of Zia Inayat Khan. Excerpts appear in this essay. The book is soon to go to press.

learning to sing or play an instrument began to appear all over India in all the regional languages and English. Music societies, schools, and business organizations sponsored recitals, classes, and lectures. The state of music in North India at the turn of the century, therefore, involves a fascinating mix of elite and middle class patrons, reformers and traditionalists, Europeans, princely rulers, hereditary music professionals, and amateurs.

Oral traditions tell us of the great musicians who were prominent in instrumental and vocal music at the end of the nineteenth century. The court at Jaipur is said to have supported 150 musicians who were the leaders in their fields.[3] *Dhrupad* was the oldest and most highly regarded genre of the time, sung by specialists or performed on the marvelous *bīn* or *sursingār*. In Jaipur, *dhrupad* specialists included the great Rajab 'Alī and Musharraf Khān, predecessors of the contemporary *bīn* player Asad Ali Khan. In the princely state of Rampur, Nawāb Kalb-i 'Alī Khān (1864–1887) supported a "golden age" for art and learning. Bahādur Ḥusayn, who played the rare *dhrupad rabāb* and the *sursingār* was the leading musician here. In the court of Indore, Mahārājā Tukojī Rāo Holkar (ruled 1843–86) supported the legendary *bīn* player Banda-i 'Alī Khān (c.1826–1890), who is said to have possessed mystical powers. In Udaipur, were Zakīr al-Dīn (1837–1922) and in Alwar his brother Allāhbanda (1848–1928), ancestors of the famous Dagar family of *dhrupad* singers well known today. *Khyāl* vocal music was the mainstay of North Indian classical music, as it still is today, and masters in different centers were creating the stylistic lineages that would carry through the twentieth century. These lineages, called *gharānās*, "households," were often named after the places in which they were developed. One of the oldest and most prestigious was that of Gwalior. Created by Haḍḍu and Hassu Khān (d. 1875 and 1850 respectively), this *gharānā* was represented in the late century by Haḍḍu Khān's son Raḥmat Khān (1862–1922). His disciple, Bālkṛṣna Bua Icalkarañjikar (1849–1927), would later be the teacher of the great V.D. Paluskar, popularizer of classical music in Maharashtra. Other *gharānā*s thriving at the end of the nineteenth century produced the great vocalists whose *khyāl*

[3] Vilayat Husain Khān, *Fan mūsīqī ke kuc baḍe fankār*. In *Ajkal, mūsīqī ank* (Delhi: Ministry of Information and Broadcasting, 1957), 28–30.

styles subsequently spread all over the country. Allāhdiyā Khān (1855–1946) of the Atrauli *gharānā*; Banda-i 'Alī (1830–1890) and 'Abd al-Karīm Khān (1874–1937) of the Kirānā, and Natthan Khān (1840–1901) and Fayyāż Khān (1886–1950) of the Agra *gharānā* are just a few of the most famous.[4]

Instrumentalists were supported in many of the same centers. By far the most numerous instrumentalists were the *sārangī* and *tablā* players who accompanied all the other musicians and the dancers who performed the ubiquitous but stigmatized nautch, entertainment dance. Delhi and Jaipur supported *sitār* and *sarod* players of the Delhi style of slow-speed composition, while Lucknow, Banaras, and many other courts cultivated the "eastern" style of fast-paced compositions. One of the most influential sitarists was Amṛtsen (1813–1893) of the Jaipur Senia *gharānā* famous for its purity and refinement. The sitarist to have the greatest impact on the early twentieth century was the inventive Imdād Khān (c.1846–1920) who was creating twentieth-century style in Calcutta by adding ideas from a number of genres to his music. Players of the *sarod*, originally localized in the Rampur area but now spread all across North India, were also trading techniques and compositions. The competitive atmosphere and the energy of the time are conveyed in the colorful oral histories of present day performers.[5]

The centers of English education and trade, especially Calcutta and Bombay, were the hubs of intellectual, economic, and political life in North India. Here the Indian intelligentsia initiated an activism that grew out of a complex relationship to Western thought. They embraced social reform and Western-inspired scientific thinking, but were energetically promoting a rediscovery of Indian, especially Hindu, cultural history. These activists founded the first public institutions of music learning and through them began to create a social context for music distinct from the court environment, acceptable to middle class sensibilities and open to

---

[4] Joep Bor and Phillipe Brugiere, *Masters of Raga* (Berlin: Haus der Culturen der Welt, n.d.).

[5] Allyn Miner, *Sitar and Sarod in the 18th and 19th Centuries* (Wilhemshaven, Germany: Florian Noetzel, 1993; Delhi: Motilal Banarsidass, 1997).

amateur participation. They wrote works on history and theory urging a recovery of a glorious musical past.

The most prolific educationist in late nineteenth century Bengal was Sourindro Mohun Tagore (1840–1914). In a lifelong campaign to promote Indian music among the upper and middle classes and defend it against European cynics, he produced books in English, Bengali and Hindi, and in 1871 founded the Bengal Music School, the first institution for music learning in India.[6] It was a place "where vocal music and some of the drawing room instruments began to be taught with the aid of books and according to a system of notation."[7] In the twentieth century Calcutta would continue to be a center for music and literature. Coming from the same family was the Bengali poet-musician Rabindranath Tagore (1861–1941), who would become one of India's first internationally known figures.

Early schools of Indian music appeared in western India as well. The Gāyan Samāj (Music Society) in Pune was founded in 1874 to "revive a taste for our musical science amongst our brethren of the upper class, and to raise it up in their estimation."[8] In the early twentieth century, the new leaders of the music revival movement would be from Maharashtra: Viṣṇu Nārāyaṇ Bhāṭkhaṇḍe (1860–1936) and Viṣṇu Digambar Paluskar (1872–1931). The work of the former in music notation and theory would eventually become standard throughout North India.[9] In Gujarat, several courts were active in their support of music in the late nineteenth century and a number of Gujarati language books on music were published. The most prominent center was Baroda, the home-base of Mawlābakhsh, Inayat

---

[6] For details see the excellent work by Michael Rosse on early institutions of music learning in north India: "The Movement for the Revitalization of 'Hindu' Music in Northern India, 1860–1930: The Role of Associations and Institutions," Ph.D. diss., University of Pennsylvania, 1995.

[7] Sourindro Mohun Tagore, *Universal History of Music* (Varanasi: Chowkhamba Sanskrit Series Office, 1963), 87–88.

[8] From *Hindu Music and the Gayan Samaj* 1887, quoted in Rosse, "Movement for Revitalization," 98.

[9] Vishnu Narayan Bhatkhande's four-volume text on theory is the *Hindustani sangit paddhati* (1909–1932), and the six-volume collection of songs is the *Kramik pustak målikå* (1919–1937).

Khan's grandfather and the most dominant musical presence in the region at the time.

Mawlābakhsh (1833–1896)

The strong personality and ideals of Mawlābakhsh set the model for his family line and clearly affected many of the choices Inayat Khan made in his career. Born as Sho'le Khān, he was the son of Gīsū Khān of a landowning family in Bhivani, near Delhi. He is said to have been given the name Mawlābakhsh, which means "God-given," as a teenager by a Chishtī Sufi ascetic who stimulated his interest in music.

Mawlābakhsh received early training from his uncle, Anvar Khān, an amateur musician, and later sought out and studied with vocalist Ghasīṭ Khān of Gujarat. On a tour to courts around India, he spent time in the south where he studied the Karnatak music system, a difficult task for an outsider and especially a Muslim. He was particularly impressed by the theoretical and devotional leanings of Karnatak musicians.

Mawlābakhsh lived in Mysore for about a year in the 1860s, where he was honored with formal royal insignia, "the Kalaggi or golden circlet, the Sarpanchi, a chaplet of pearls for the turban, the Chatri or gold canopy, which is held over the head by a footservant as the owner walks or rides, the Chamar or stick of honour which the servant carries before, and the Mashal, the torch that is carried before and lighted at night."[10] Here he also married Qāsim Bī, a descendant of the royal lineage of the great Ṭīpū Sulṭān. Mawlābakhsh's royal insignia and his connections with the Mysore court would be a lasting legacy in his household.

Mawlābakhsh came to Baroda as chief court musician at the invitation of the ruler in the mid-nineteenth century and soon established a thriving household. He had two sons, Murtażā Khān (1860–1924) and 'Alā al-Dīn Khān (1869–1948), and three daughters. His daughter Fāṭima Bī, and after her death her younger sister, Khadīja Bī, married Raḥmat Khān (1843–1910), a

---

[10] Nekbakht Foundation, ed., *The Biography of Pir-o-Murshid Inayat Khan* (London/The Hague: East-West Publications, 1979), 22.

dhrupad specialist from Punjab, whom Mawlābakhsh had brought into the household. Inayat Khan was the eldest of Raḥmat Khān's four sons.

In the 1870s Mawlābakhsh left Baroda on a long tour and stayed for about a year in Calcutta, where he was well received by the activist-scholar Sourindro Mohun Tagore and others. While in Calcutta he participated in a number of events and was awarded the title "Professor of Indian Music" by the Governor-General of India, Lord Northbrook.[11] His essay on the principles of Hindustani music and a testimonial to a notational system devised by the scholar K.M. Goswami was signed by twenty-seven contemporary musicians and included by S.M. Tagore in his compilation *Hindu Music from Various Authors*.[12]

Upon his return Mawlābakhsh created a system of notation of his own and founded a school of music. The newly installed Mahārājā Sayājīrāo Gāekwāṛ III (r.1875–1939) was a progressive and reform-minded ruler. In 1882 the Maharaja offered the Mawlābakhsh school state sponsorship. The school was inaugurated in 1886 as the Gāyan Shālā (Academy of Music) and soon became the most prominent school of music in western India. It offered a systematic program of training based on textbooks using Mawlābakhsh's notation. For his accomplishment in promoting notation, Baroda references give Mawlābakhsh the title "Founder of Indian Musical Notation." Mawlābakhsh devoted the last decade of his life to running the school. His sons Murtażā and 'Alā al-Dīn, his son-in-law Raḥmat Khān, and Inayat Khan and his brothers all held positions as teachers and administrators.[13]

---

[11] Rosse, "Movement for Revitalization," 138–40.

[12] Tagore, *Hindu Music from Various Authors* (Varanasi: Chowkhamba Sanskrit Series Office, 1965), 389–97.

[13] "The 'Gayan Shala' of 1886 came to be known later (c. 1936) as the 'Sangit Shala' [Music School], still later (c. 1942) as the 'Bhartiya Sangeet Mahavidyalaya,' with its English translation, The College of Indian Music. With the founding of the Maharaja Sayajirao University in 1949 under the State University Act, all the then existing Colleges and institutions of higher learning or Special Studies, along with the College of Indian Music, became constituents of the University. In addition to the then existing Music Diploma Studies, Degree Courses in music, dance and dramatics were formulated and commenced working from June 1950. In 1953 the institution was renamed as the College of Indian Music, Dance, and Dramatics. In 1984, it was elevated to function

Inayat Khan

Inayat Khan was trained in singing as a child by his grandfather and was exposed to musicians, poets, and spiritual figures in the Baroda court and the Mawlābakhsh household. Dr. R.C. Mehta, in his article in this volume, mentions some of the prominent musicians who were in Baroda at this time. Another important figure whom Inayat Khan might have met was Viṣṇu Digambar Paluskar, who would later become a prominent educator and performer. Stopping in Baroda on a trip North in 1896–97, the young Paluskar received honors from the Maharaja and his mother and stayed for several months. Oral history tells of a concert in which Paluskar agreed to perform after the senior musicians Mawlābakhsh and Fayż Muḥammad, a serious breach of respect.[14]

Inayat was an active student in the Gāyan Shālā where he was thoroughly initiated into Mawlābakhsh's educational ideals. A year spent with his father in Nepal in the 1890s gave him exposure to a large number of lineage professional musicians, and he was not impressed by their behavior. On the way they had stopped in Gwalior where he heard performers representing the famous *gharānā* of that name. In addition to these musical experiences, the European presence was pervasive in Baroda, and Western music had an established presence in the court. Inayat Khan's uncle 'Alā al-Dīn Khān, known as Dr. A.M. Paṭhān, who was sent to London under state sponsorship in 1892–97, returned with degrees in Western music and was put in charge of the state band in the Gāyan Shālā. By all accounts he was an influential source of family impressions about the West.

In 1902, after the death of his mother, Inayat Khan went on his first performance tour to Madras and Mysore at the age of twenty. His grandfather's success in the South must have been a strong initial motivation. A testimonial written there mentions the strengths that were basic to his early musical career: good

---

as a separate faculty—since then re-christened as the Faculty of Performing Arts, offering Diploma and Degree, graduate and post-graduate, doctoral studies in music, dance and theatre arts. The institution is in existence for the last 113 years—the oldest one in India, without any period of discontinuity." R.C. Mehta, private correspondence, July 1999.

[14] Rosse, "Movement for Revitalization," 162–3.

family background, training and performance skills, and an engaging personality:

> Mr. Inayat Khan ... comes of a family of distinguished musicians, his grandfather being the famous Moulabux a distinguished professor of Hindu music and inventor of a system of notation for it as well as the Author of a series of graduated textbooks in music which are in use in the music schools of the Baroda State. He is the nephew of Dr. A.M. Pathan, L.R.A.M., who was educated in England in the European system of music and passed his examinations with high distinction. Mr. Inayat Khan has studied both the Hindu and European systems scientifically and has already acquired great proficiency especially in the former. He has winning manners and the art of rousing the interest and intelligence of his pupils ...[15]

After he returned to Baroda, Inayat Khan wrote instructional books on harmonium and violin for the music school and a collection of seventy-five songs, all of which were published in 1903.[16] Seeing limited scope for his career in Baroda, however, he determined to seek his fortune elsewhere. He left for Hyderabad, the largest and most prosperous of the Indian princely states, in 1903, stopping on the way in Bombay. His Bombay experience confirmed his prior experiences and inheritance from Mawlābakhsh about the degenerate state of professional music. Audiences smoked and conversed during his performances, and musicians he considered inferior challenged his credentials. A brief encounter with V.N. Bhāṭkhaṇḍe, who was becoming the most prominent musicologist of his time, shows little congeniality here. Bhāṭkhaṇḍe is said to have asked the young man on what theoretical basis (*śāstra*) he proved his *rāg*s authentic. Inayat Khan, replying as a practitioner, is said to have responded "according to my shāstra; it is man who has made shāstra, it is not shāstra that has made man."[17] It is clear that the dignified young musician was a performer and an intellectual who allied with neither the lineage professionals nor the musicologists.

---

[15] Nekbakht Foundation, *Biography*, 280.

[16] Khan, Inayat (Professor 'Ināyat-khān Raḥmat-khān Paṭhān), *Ināyat gīt ratnāvalī*; *Inayat hārmoniyam śikṣak pustak pahalā*; *Inayat phiḍal̤ śikṣak* (Baroda and Mumbai: The Auspices of the Government of Sayājīrāo Mahārājā Gāekwāṛ, 1903).

[17] Nekbakht Foundation, *Biography*, 67.

In 1903 Inayat Khan arrived in Hyderabad and took rooms with a Parsi family in the neighboring town of Secunderabad. Hyderabad had long been known for its Urdu language and etiquette, and the Nizam, Mīr Maḥbūb 'Alī Khān, was a generous patron and lover of poetry. After waiting for some months, Inayat had his opportunity to perform for the Nizam, for which he was honored with a generous payment and an emerald ring. After that he had regular access to the Nizam's court. Inayat Khan moved in an atmosphere of educated Muslim high culture in Hyderabad. His writing style in the *Minqār* conveys a dignified formality and reverence for both Islamic tradition and modern thinking. He pays high tribute to his patrons the Nizam and the Prime Minister, Sir Kishan Parshād, and includes in his book several *ghazal* poems which they had composed.

The atmosphere for classical music performance, however, does not seem to have been ideal in Hyderabad. We hear relatively little about performances during this time. Inayat Khan was clearly in search of a higher meaning for his life when he met his spiritual master, Sayyid Muḥammad Abū Hāshim Madanī. Many biographical sources give accounts of the intense period of spiritual training that he underwent under his master. The spiritual path, which took on a dominant importance in his life after this time, gave him a unique angle on his music and new purpose to his musical career.

The *Minqār-i mūsīqār*

Inayat Khan wrote the *Minqār* in 1907 at the age of 25. In the same year, Abū Hāshim Madanī would pass away and Inayat Khan would leave Hyderabad. The book thus encapsulates his thoughts at the end of his stay in Hyderabad. It is written in Urdu in a style that captures the dignity of the atmosphere in which he moved while being lucid and lively. Photographs of the Nizam, the Prime Minister, the author's father and the author himself enliven the book, and the book has a number of charts and hand-drawn illustrations, including the legendary *mūsīqār* bird and twenty dance positions.

Perhaps the most interesting section for many of his contemporary readers would have been the assembly of Persian and Urdu *ghazal*s and the thirty-nine musical notations for singing them. For modern readers, too, the notations are of interest, in particular because six of the songs notated in the *Minqār* are among those he recorded in 1909, to which we now have access. Of interest to historians of North Indian music will be Inayat Khan's notation system and the selection of concepts from Sanskrit theory, especially in relation to those of V.N. Bhāṭkhaṇḍe and V.D. Paluskar. Inayat Khan's ideas and approach to music will be of interest to all readers. The following sections overview the topics covered in the *Minqār,* more or less in the order that they appear in the book.

Principles and ideals

Inayat Khan begins, as is traditional in formal Urdu style, with tributes to God, the Prophet, his *pīr*, his grandfather, the Nizam of Hyderabad and the Prime Minister. He states that his purpose in writing is to restore proper respect to the art of music. The degradation and neglect of the music is to be blamed on the many professional musicians who lack moral integrity and theoretical knowledge. The term *ustād*, expert, is often colloquially understood as denoting lineage professionals.

> It is clear that because of the lack of attention given to it by people these days, this art is becoming uprooted, for what can I say? People who call themselves masters (*ustād*) and experts in this art are revealed upon critical examination to be incompetent. And why? As savants know, this art is of noble pedigree and is more difficult than all others. For all of the fine points and subtleties and movements of this science depend on the mind and intellect, and through it the masters control even desire itself. The complete attainment of this phenomenon depends on tranquility, zeal, peace of mind, and an affectionate, kind, and able teacher, and all of these things must come together at once, without contingencies, except as God may wish.[18]

Contemporary musicians' ignorance of the basic theoretical principles, moreover, has resulted in the inability of listeners to distinguish good music from bad:

[18] Inayat Khan (Professor 'Ināyat Khān R. Paṭhān), *Minqār-i mūsīqār* (Allahabad: Indian Press, 1912), 5.

> Now it is amazing that those who can to some degree perform a particular *rāg* or *tāl* cannot necessarily explain what *tīvra* and *komal* mean and what measure of *tāl* and *mātrā* are being used. To simply sing something one does not have to be conversant with its principles. When artists are of this level, what is to be expected of their listeners and admirers? Facts and principles are eclipsed by pleasure and delight (*zawq-shawq*), but pleasure and delight are contingent upon temperament. Thus the pleasure of a listener will depend on his temperament, and accordingly his exclamations of "*āh, vāh*" may be appropriately timed or misplaced. The whole problem is an ignorance of the art. Unfortunately the temperament is dependent on the spiritual qualities of the listener. Thus on account of ignorance or indiscrimination, music (*rāg*) becomes meaningless. But such people are still our respected companions. It is not for us to make faces at them out of superiority and to receive threatening glances in return. I offer a small example of the difference between temperaments in the experience of pleasure and delight. If several paintings of mixed quality are set up on a single level, the viewers will distinguish beautiful from ugly differently, in accord with their temperaments, and each will be impressed by different paintings. It is the same with the appreciation of eloquence. One person is ardent about the poet Ḥāfiẓ of Shiraz, while another thinks the world of Jān Ṣāḥab Lakhnavī. The intention in my wordiness here is to arouse interest. But to reach the summit of perfection when confronted with a veil of concealment, one needs something else: fortune, ardor, and effort.[19]

Inayat Khan reminds us that the current state of music and musicians should not obscure the fact that music has in the past been held in highest regard. He calls on Islamic literature, no doubt familiar to the Hyderabad readership, for stories of the origin of music. Such stories show that music is not only respectable, but is rooted in the divine. The inspiration of Sufi thought is apparent in the final sentences of the paragraph below.

> Some say that music was named after Ḥażrat Mūsā (Moses)—peace be upon him. Once while in the wilderness, he was passing by a stream whose gentle flow was washing over the pebbles and producing various sounds. He received the revelation "yā Mūsā qe!," that is, "Oh Mūsā, wait!" The word *ṭaharnā,* "wait," means to concentrate, think, or understand. So under the guidance of this

[19] Ibid., 8.

> heavenly or divine communication, Ḥażrat Mūsā drew forth music *(rāg)* from those sounds. If this is indeed true, then by the grace of God this science is divine. How wonderful that it is the very spirit of the soul (*rūḥ kī jān*)! If in this world spiritual, bodily, material, imaginary, and mental phenomena are all manifest on the outer plane, they certainly obtain power from the inner treasury. Thus in every outer form is the disclosure of something inner.[20]

Music is not only of divine origin, Inayat Khan says, but it is universal. Sound (*sur*) and rhythm (*tāl*), are integral features of the world, evidenced in the sound-producing capabilities of objects and the rhythmic character of every human act.

> Now, consider that in your own body the movement of the pulse, the beating of the heart, the passing in and out of breath, and the sensation and movement of all the limbs are never empty of *sur* and *tāl*. Indeed, creation's every activity confirms the validity of my claim. If we cast our eyes upward, there is above all the beguiling charm of the lovely wink of eternity. The original manifestation was that of sound, which is *"Kun"*—"Be!" [21] All things and beings are its manifestation.[22]

Inayat Khan now introduces Sufi concepts explicitly. In a heartfelt verse he makes a reference to his ecstatic plunge into the Sufi path of love:

> The noble Sufis are the swimmers in this ocean of Truth. The sound *"Kun"* still echoes in their ears. They thrash their arms and legs in deep waters, plunge into annihilation (*fanā*), and safely wash up on the shore of immortality (*baqā*).
>
> Marvelous is the state of one intoxicated
> by the sound of pre-eternity
> His milieu is neither land nor sea.
>
> This devotee of *sur* has been, since the day of pre-eternity,
> fallen at the foot of the Beloved.
>
> By practicing godliness, it manifests in the soul,
> whether I find myself in an idol's temple
> or the Ka'ba's precincts.
>
> Inayat has sacrificed his whole being to sound,
> prostrate since pre-eternity at the Beloved's door.

---

[20] Ibid., 6.
[21] The reference is to Qur'ān 36.82.
[22] Inayat Khan, *Minqār-i mūsīqār*, 7.

> All that he requires is mere coarse meal;
> the phenomenal and the Real are inseparably linked.
>
> Inayat, enough of you and this matter,
> the talk of Reality and these circumstances of yours.
>
> The Sun is just a minute particle of God's kindness;
> where there is kindness, hope blossoms forth.[23]

The disapproval of music among orthodox Muslims is a subject that Inayat Khan briefly takes up. He recalls the long history of music in Muslim countries before its fall into disrepute. The true spiritual context of music, he says, is now preserved only among Sufis, but he has hopes that its rehabilitation can come about by educating young people about the real spiritual nature of music.

> Music was a highly approved science near to God, since God gave the gift of his voice to Dā'ūd by way of a miracle. In the next era music became a part of the equipment of battle, as it is today, an important and necessary part. And it was a proud part of the accouterments of the Muslim emperors. Although I am not qualified for formal exegesis, to the extent that a simple Muslim like myself can understand the holy Qur'ān, I have found nothing against music there. The Muslims were not unmindful of the effect that music has on the mind and heart, but it is unfortunate that every art was made into an object of contempt, so that no respectable person paid attention to it. ... Imām Ghazālī—God's mercy be upon him—in his book *Kimiyā-i Sa'āda* presents a discussion about listening to music (*samā'*) saying that it is entirely worthy of respect. Consequently, the dignity of music is strong in the view of many Muslims. Among the noble Sufis to this day, *samā'* is said to be "nourishment for the soul." In fact, its vestiges are preserved only among their orders. It is true that sometimes ill-intentioned people imitate them, but the worth of jewels cannot be affected by external impurities. Our future intellectual and artistic progress is entirely centered on our young students. If a little effort and attention were to be given, then the ugly stain that despicable and ill-mannered people have given to music would quickly be erased. Change in one's attractions and influences comes about through music. When music seems to be merely a stimulation, one should remember that good qualities and education depend on training. People who are well educated and courteous will be engaged to a higher degree than others in the genteel arts.[24]

---

[23] Ibid., 8.
[24] Ibid., 91.

Theory

Inayat Khan's sections on music theory use many of the same terms that were employed by V.N. Bhāṭkhaṇḍe and V.D. Paluskar in their theory texts that became standard in music schools throughout North India. Inayat Khan clearly did not take his ideas from their work. Mawlābakhsh and other scholars had preceded Bhāṭkhaṇḍe and Paluskar, and the work of these early scholars has been under-recognized:

> While the work of Bhatkhande and Vishnu Digambar, carried out in the years between 1901 and 1934, was on a much bigger scale than that of their predecessors, the way had been paved for them by the nineteenth-century societies. ... It was in the interest of Vishnu Digambar, Bhatkhande, and their followers to propagate the impression that it had all begun with them. Within a relatively short time, they succeeded in erasing most memory of their precursors. A 1922 Marathi encyclopedia article on music still mentions the by then deceased S.M. Tagore along with the new stars on the horizon, Vishnu Digambar and Bhatkhande, as the leaders of the music revival. Later on, the names of S.M. Tagore and Maula Bakhsh were remembered only within Bengal and Gujarat, respectively.[25]

The *Minqār* is, in part, testimony to the work of Mawlābakhsh, but Inayat Khan also drew on contemporary sources. He begins his discussion of theory with the scientific definition of sound as vibration carried by airwaves, which he explains in a layperson's terms.

> Sound is produced by the vibration of an object. When a person takes a piece of wood in hand and vibrates it, for example, as many waves as it produces are carried in the air. When the waves pass by the ear a sound is heard. Evidence of the waves is visible if one partially fills a thin glass with water, holds it firmly in the hand, and rubs a finger on it so as to produce a sound. If one observes the water closely one can see it shaking. Touching a metal or gut string of an instrument, one can definitely feel the vibrations. If one strikes the skin of a *ḍhol* or *naqāra* and immediately puts one's hand on it, or puts a hand on the case of a piano or harmonium while it is being played, one will know for sure that it is the vibrations of the objects that are producing the

[25] Rosse, "Movement for Revitalization," 3–4.

sound.[26]

He elaborates on the different speeds of sound through various sound-carrying objects and the dependence of pitch on the wave frequency. A detailed description, complete with English names, of the sound-producing and sound-receiving organs of the human body follows, including the organs of the throat, the mechanism by which they produce sound, the parts of the ear, and the mechanism of hearing. Inayat Khan, in a display of respect for contemporary and practical knowledge, is grounding his study in science. It is clear that for him scientific knowledge and divine presence are perfectly compatible.

His presentation would have been stimulating and informative to an early twentieth century reader. Curiously he does not mention the Indian concept of *nāda*, the "struck" and "unstruck" sound of yogic meditation which are standard to Sanskrit musicological literature. Perhaps the idea of *nāda* was too abstract to be included in this context. Nor does he describe here the Sufi notion of sound. A lecture which he later gave on Hindu and Sufi ideas of abstract sound is to be found, as is a separate talk on sound as physical vibration, reprinted in *The Music of Life*.[27]

The next sections of the book define terms and concepts relating to tone and scale. All of the terms here come from Sanskrit musicological tradition. Some, such as the names of the scale syllables, have been orally carried throughout performance history. Others such as *mūrchanā* and *grām* were revived out of texts, and retained little connection to modern practice. All the terms used in the *Minqār* will be familiar to music students who have had exposure to Bhāṭkhaṇḍe's system. Modern North Indian music theory owes more than is normally attributed to Mawlābakhsh and other nineteenth century predecessors of Bhāṭkhaṇḍe.

The Indian scale has seven main tones, Sā Re Ga Ma Pa Dha Nī, and five flat and sharp varieties, making twelve half steps in the chromatic scale. Inayat Khan gives us charts of the tones and their positions in the scale, and these accord with modern performance practice. He also gives fairly detailed examples of

---

[26] Inayat Khan, *Minqār-i mūsīqār*, 10.

[27] Inayat Khan, *The Music of Life* (New Lebanon, N.Y.: Omega Publications, 1988), chapters 1 and 5.

Western staff notation. Calling on a tradition found in Arabic and medieval Indian sources, he gives us a chart showing associations of the seven Indian tones with a color, planet, season, effect, emotion, place of production in the human body, and animal sound. The section continues with definitions and charts of octave (*saptak*), sharp and flat tones (*sanchārī*), microtones (*shruti*), consonant and predominant notes (*vādī, samvādī*) and the terms *mūrchanā* and *grām*. The mix of European, Arab, and Indian sources in this section is a demonstration of erudition on the part of the author and a show of the rich variety of theoretical traditions available for music.

Rāg is one of the largest topics in Indian practice and theory.[28] *Rāg*, melody type, is the medium for all the improvisations and compositions of the classical repertoire. The detailed melodic characteristics of *rāg*s are carried within performance lineages. In different eras *rāg*s have been classified and categorized in various ways. In the sixteenth to nineteenth centuries, and continuing to some degree into the twentieth century, the imaginative *rāga-rāginī* system designated certain *rāg*s as male (*rāga*), others as their wives (*rāginī*), and sometimes others as sons (*putra*) and daughters (*bhāryā*). In the twentieth century, Bhāṭkhaṇḍe standardized a system of ten scale-types called *thāṭ* into which *rāg*s are placed according to their scale intervals.[29] Bhāṭkhaṇḍe also used a Sanskrit-based tradition in which *rāg*s are typed according to the number of tones in their ascending and descending scale. In the *Minqār* this last type of classification appears to be primary, and it can be assumed that Inayat Khan had learned it from Mawlābakhsh. The five types are 5-tone (*auṛav*), 6-tone (*shārav*), 7-tone (*sampūrn*), mixed (*sankīrn*), and 7-tone crooked (*vakra sampūrn*). Inayat Khan also mentions the

---

28 For more on *rāg*, see Nazir Jairazbhoy, *The Rags of North Indian Music: Their Structure and Evolution* (London: Faber & Faber, 1971) and Walter Kaufmann, *The Rāgas of North India* (Bloomington: Indiana University Press, 1974) and *The Rāgas of South India* (Calcutta/Bombay and New Delhi: Oxford University Press and IBH, 1976).

29 The term *thāṭ* as scale type, from eighteenth-century Sanskrit texts, is found in the writings of S.M. Tagore and other nineteenth century musicologists. Both Tagore and Bhāṭkhaṇḍe seem to credit N.A. Willard with its revival, quoting his comment of 1834: "a thaat comes nearest to what with us is implied by a mode ..." *Bhāṭkhaṇḍe saṅgītśāstra* Part 1 (Hathras: Saṅgīt Kārlaya, 1964), 11. Though considered inadequate by many musicologists and performers, Bhāṭkhaṇḍe's 10-*thāṭ* system is widely taught in music schools today.

now archaic *rāg-rāginī* system and gives us a chart of six male *rāgs* each with six wives, eight sons, and eight daughters.[30]

The largest part of Inayat Khan's chapter on *rāg* consists of a twenty-five page chart of 484 *rāgs* listed by name in Urdu alphabetical order, with the ascending and descending scale for each and a time or seasonal association for some. The list is of little practical use, since phrasings and resting notes are necessary information for even a basic understanding of a *rāg*, but the chart is interesting for several reasons. This is a very large number of *rāgs* for any performance repertoire. Though Inayat Khan does not mention this or distinguish them in any way, the list includes *rāgs* from the South Indian, Karnatak as well as the North Indian, Hindustanī system. Karnatak *rāgs* outnumber the Hindustani. The Mawlābakhsh legacy of training in Karnatak music, Inayat Khan's location in south India, and his desire to present as much material as possible together explain the presence of the Karnatak *rāgs*. One distinguishing factor is that most of those recognizable by name as belonging to the Hindustani repertoire have a time or season noted for them in the chart. Interesting for present day musicians is the difference in some *rāgs*' scales from those of current day practice.[31] Equally interesting, however, is the constancy of most of them since that time. More practical information on the *rāgs* of Inayat Khan's repertoire is to be gleaned from the notations that make up a large part of the second half of the *Minqār*.

The final chapter of the theory section of the *Minqār* deals with rhythm (*tāl*). To convey the power and pervasiveness of rhythm in human life, Inayat Khan describes its effects in a performance of *qawwālī,* the well-known North Indian genre of Sufi music.

> *Tāl* dwells in and is a very great part of every natural thing. *Tāl* is present in every event and action. In the *samā'* gathering, for example, which is often held for the *'urs* at the tomb of the great saints, the gathering is usually graced with noblemen, holy

---

[30] The 6 *rāgs* and 30 *rāginīs* in Inayat Khan's chart are nearly identical to those of the Hanūman system (*mat*) delineated in the sixteenth-century *Saṅgitadāmodara*, a well known text in North India. I have not been able to trace the source for the *putras* and *bhāryās*.

[31] Examples are Bhūpālī which here has *tīvra* M; Bhīmpalās which has *komal* D; and Brindāvanī sārang which has *komal* G.

> persons, learned men and mendicants, and common people as well ... This is called the *maḥfil-i qawwālī*. As soon as a *qawwāl* begins to sing a *ghazal* of the mystical or amorous type or in praise of the Prophet, the *ḍhol* player gives a slap and gradually begins to play the *tāl*. When its intensity reaches a certain level, the beauty of the verses stirs the listener's heart and the *tāl* intensifies the feelings. The *tāl*, called *qawwālī ṭheka*, creates such an effect that the heart of each person, great and humble, begins to tremble in a state of ecstasy. As the pace of the *tāl* grows faster, the heart becomes even more agitated, with each stroke of the *tāl* giving more impetus to the ecstasy and intoxication. And even the motions that are manifested in this state of ecstasy are not empty of *tāl*.[32]

In a section on how to understand *tāl*, Inayat Khan offers an informal explanation of the functions of *sam*, the first beat of a *tāl* cycle, and *khālī*, the midway point:

> In common language *tāl* means the regulation of time. In Indian music there are hundreds of *tāl*s. The junctures of *tāl* are indicated by a motion of the hands, of which there are three types. The first is *sam*, where the *tāl* begins again after each cycle. The significance of *sam* is that the rhythmic cycle and the tune begin again as if anew. If we say, for example, that *sam* is at one o'clock, then after the clock passes two, three, and so on to beyond twelve, *sam* will arrive again. Another example is a woodcutter chopping wood. When he strikes the wood with an ax, it is *sam*. When he raises the ax to strike it a second time it is empty, or *khālī*. The sound emanating from the wood and associated with the *sam* and *khālī* gives comfort to the woodcutter. In fact, he will continue to strike over and over again because he enjoys the sound. The task would be very tedious if *tāl* and *sur* were not there. Similarly, when a bearer lifts a palanquin or when a porter lifts his load, he walks along using a *tāl* and a few words to ease his effort. So also with the goldsmith and the ironsmith, whose hammers mark the junctures of *sam* and *khālī*. All living beings move through *tāl*.[33]

A technical description of the Sanskrit measures of beats (*mātrā*) and their subdivisions (*laghu, drut, guru* etc.) follows, conveying the intricacy and sophistication of the Indian theories of musical time. A large section of the *tāl* chapter consists of a long list

[32] Inayat Khan, *Minqār-i mūsīqār*, 53.
[33] Ibid., 54.

of "current *tāl*s." Here Inayat Khan names 200 *tāl*s and gives for each the Sanskrit-based notations that denote overall length and internal subdivisions. Like the *rāg* chart, this is of little practical use, since *tāl*s in modern practice are largely understood by the drum patterns that express them (*ṭhekā*). The intention here must again be to demonstrate the heritage of the *tāl* tradition. In the later part of the book Inayat Khan gives us the *ṭhekā*s of eighteen *tāl*s, and he makes use of twelve different *tāl*s in the song notations.

Notation

Professional performance is traditionally passed on aurally, and this continues to be true today. The notation of phrases using the syllables of the scale tones, however, appears in Sanskrit texts from the earliest period, and the material has been found to contain a significant amount of practical information.[34] In nineteenth century publications authors used notations of their own designs, giving us many idiosyncratic and inventive styles. The educationists saw the need for a standardized notation, however, and for some decades spirited debate flew over the efficacy of Western staff notation versus several Indian models. A system designed by Mawlābakhsh, usable in both Devanagari and Nastaliq scripts—and so adaptable to Hindi, Gujarati, Marathi, and Urdu—was successful in western India. Bengali notations were used in publications from Calcutta. By the third decade of the twentieth century, the Devanagari notation system designed by V.N. Bhāṭkhaṇḍe, and not very unlike that of Mawlābakhsh, had come to dominate school teaching throughout North India.

The books by Inayat Khan and other followers of the Mawlābakhsh lineage use the latter's notational system. Readers familiar with Bhāṭkhaṇḍe notation will find it easy to follow. In both, the tone syllables (*sargam*) have marks denoting sharp or flat and are laid out in horizontal lines across the page. The text or the instrumental stroke is placed below the corresponding tone. Vertical lines separate the internal divisions of the *tāl*, and specific signs above mark each subdivision. Mawlābakhsh's notation differs from

[34] For a recent study of *rāga* through medieval notations see Richard Widdess, *The Rāgas of Early Indian Music: Modes, Melodies and Musical Notations from the Gupta Period to c.1250* (Oxford: Clarendon Press, 1995).

Bhāṭkhaṇḍe's in using signs beneath the tones to denote durations, where Bhāṭkhaṇḍe joins the tones and uses dashes to denote shorter and longer durations.

In a section of interest to historians of Hindustani music, the *Minqār* includes a thorough description of the Mawlābakhsh system. The idea of notation was still relatively new, and Inayat Khan explains the advantages of having one thus:

> Compositions of the old masters are in current practice today, but they differ in each person's performance. If ten singers were to sing one old composition, each one's song would be different. Because everyone cannot remember a single version correctly, everyone who plays or sings the compositions adds something of one's own to them, so the real form of the old compositions is not to be found. ... [Notation's] real virtue is that, as by learning the alphabet the recipient of a letter comes to know the welfare of the writer, or the reader of a book understands the message of the author, similarly using musical notation one person can write a "letter" to another about his thinking and make it known. A person who knows the system can sing or play whatever is written, and can write for himself whatever style he takes a liking to. It is like a "photo" of music. For the educated person, instead of being difficult and obscure, the art of music becomes very easy to learn through this system.[35]

The nuances of Hindustani music are notoriously resistant to expression in notation, and even today notation is mainly used as a reminder of what has been aurally learned. Still, the notations of the sixty-one songs and forty-seven instrumental compositions in the *Minqār-i mūsīqār* give us some basic information about the music of which Inayat Khan is writing.

Practice

The second half of the *Minqār* is devoted to the practical side of music. Inayat Khan was an educator and speaker, but his retort to Bhāṭkhaṇḍe mentioned above shows that he did not think of himself as a detached musicologist. He clearly considered himself a performer. As a performer, however, he maintained a strict ideological and social distance from professional lineage musicians. In the *Minqār*

---

[35] Ibid., 78.

we recognize the systematic but practical style that differentiated his approach from both types of professionals.

He begins with vocal music and gives an interesting account of the traditional hierarchy of song types and singers. *Ustādī* music is that of the highest level, exemplified by *dhrupad*, with *khyāl* below it, and *atā'ī* music ("self taught," or, in modern terms, light music) below that. Singers used to be categorized according to their expertise in singing, composing and teaching. He comments on what happened in more recent times, and speaks admiringly of educational reforms in Europe:

> In India a fracture occurred in the ranking of these categories when disagreements about the art arose. This happened because the method in each household (*ghar*) diverged and each household had a separate *ustād*. Who would pay attention to the traditional categories when people objected to one another's achievements? The categories began to disappear and everything was heaped together. Not only did the sense of excellence and accomplishment disappear, but whoever managed to produce high and low notes began to consider themselves *ustāds*. But these days improvements in music have been going on in Europe, and universities and degrees there have been put in place in which there are these four highest levels: "Associate of Music," "Licentiate of Music," "Bachelor of Music," and the highest category, "Doctor of Music."[36]

After briefly defining twenty-three song types, covering the modern categories of classical, light classical and regional genres, Inayat Khan begins his long section of notated songs. His first group of notations consists of five *dhrupad*s, five *khyāl*s, five *ṭhumrī*s, two *horī*s, and one *ṭappa, tarānā, tirvat,* and *cok varṇam*. Some of the song texts in this group are by named composers; others are unattributed, and seven are his own, as indicated by the final signature line. Inayat Khan gathers here a variety of song types, a collection in accord with his theme of educating the reader. A very rare source indeed is provided to us in the recorded versions of some of these songs among his recordings of 1909. Six songs notated in the *Minqār* are to be found on the CDs.[37] One of those

---

[36] Ibid., 94.

[37] A *dhrupad* (CD 2:8), *ṭhumrī* (CD1:6), *horī* (CD 2:7), *tarānā* (CD1:13), and two *ghazals* (CD 2:4, 1:10) are found in notation and on the recordings.

recorded is the first song notated, a *dhrupad* in *rāg* Khammāc in *tāl* Chautāl. The song is his own composition.

> *Lāg rahī tū se lagan.* I am longing for you and continuously thinking of you, you, the fulfiller of hopes, the defeater of woe, a friend to those without friends, who gives a hand to the drowning. A savior to the helpless, who have only you for support. You give strength to those whose courage is broken. In sorrow you alone can help. You make those who weep smile; they depend on you alone. The world is your crown jewel, you have dominion over the kings. Joy is lasting only in your care; Inayat is your devotee.[38]

One used to the slow pace of present day Hindustani music will be startled at the fast speed of this *dhrupad* song heard on the recording. The open timbre of the voice is unexpected, slightly harsh, and the pitch seems to be high.[39] An energy and a facility in rhythm is noticeable in the technique, and the fast passages are precisely executed. Aesthetically, one can only make judgments based on one's own sensibilities. It may be a somewhat puzzling experience to listen to the songs of Inayat Khan. They have a feeling of urgency and drive if not sweetness. One can sense the confidence of the singer and the eagerness to communicate the material.

Placing the recording in the larger context which the *Minqār* provides, one can begin to make a few more observations. The presentation of the song is very systematic, according with the notation almost exactly. Certain notes are sung as graces though notated singly, but this is so consistent that one can soon begin to recognize which notated clusters should be sung as ornaments. Brief extemporizations are added to the composed song in the recording, and these are specific to the *dhrupad* style, effectively illustrating techniques appropriate to *dhrupad.* The variety of songs is a demonstration of a large repertoire and competent technique. Overall,

---

[38] Ibid., 101.

[39] In fact, the tonic is D sharp, about one full step above the typical tonic used by male singers today. In recordings of 'Abd al-Karīm Khān (1864–1937), a senior contemporary of Inayat Khan, the tonic pitch is a tone-and-a-half higher at F. (*Khansahab Abdul Karim Khan*, Odeon MOAE 165, The Gramophone Company of India). Inayat Khan seems to have been aware of the limitations of his voice, praising his brother Maheboob Khan for a voice as excellent as that of Mawlābakhsh (Mahmood Khan, private correspondence, referring to Nekbakht Foundation, *Biography*, s.v. Maheboob Khan).

the collection is consistent with Inayat Khan's intent to educate and communicate through performance. With such observations in mind one can begin to appreciate this and the other songs on the recording.

By far the most notations in the *Minqār* are those of *ghazal*s, the paired rhyming verses so admired in Urdu poetry. The *ghazal* can be recited or sung. As a sung genre it is not considered highly classical. Inayat Khan explains his inclusion of so many *ghazal*s by mentioning that they are of special popular interest. Indeed, Hyderabad was a center for *ghazal* poetry and the Nizam and the Prime Minister were not only patrons but composers themselves. But *ghazal*s are filled with layers of meaning, emotional and mystical, and we might speculate that Inayat Khan chose texts that were particularly meaningful to him at the time.

Inayat Khan gives us forty notations, most with the texts of two *ghazal*s, one in Urdu and one in Persian. We can assume that Inayat Khan himself composed the melodies, which are set in specified *rāg*s and *tāl*s. The texts are of well-known poets, a notable absence being that of the great Ghālib, the most famous of all *ghazal* poets. Perhaps Ghālib was not a favorite in Hyderabad. The collection does include several by the Nizam and the Prime Minister, who were active participants in the *ghazal* scene of Hyderabad.

> [Prime Minister Kishen Pershād] was a patron of the learned and himself sported the pen name Shad (the 'happy one') for his poetry. His palace became renowned for its mushairas (Urdu poetic gatherings) and the best poets of India recited their compositions there. His were the only poetic assemblies in which poems composed by the Nizam could be recited. The mushairas used to open with the 'auspicious' poem of the ruler recited by a messenger and every line of it was so vociferously lauded as if the poet himself was present. Kishen Pershad used to receive the poems by touching them with his forehead and eyes and then give it to the messenger to recite. People still remember the elaborate ritual and grand scale of those events.[40]

[40] Narendra Luther, *Hyderabad: Memories of a City* (London: Sangam Books, 1995), 224.

Many photographs show Inayat holding the Karnatak *vīṇā* and other instruments. We know that he played instruments and it is a pity that no instrumental pieces are among his Calcutta recordings. A sizeable section of the *Minqār* deals with instrumental music. Inayat Khan begins with a list and brief descriptions of some thirty six instruments followed by notations of compositions for the instruments most popular and accessible to the amateur—the *sitār*, the harmonium, and the *tablā*. The largest number of notations is for the *sitār*. A set of special notational marks denoting ten *gamaks*—techniques and ornaments—is particularly interesting for the history of *sitār* technique.[41] The fifteen short compositions (*gat*) in a variety of *rāgs* are very playable, and in comparison to other books of the time represent a relatively high-quality repertoire. It is clear that Inayat Khan was well trained in instrumental as well as vocal music.

The harmonium most well known today in India is the "portable harmonium" imported from England in the mid-nineteenth century. In the early twentieth century it fast became one of North India's most popular instruments. In earlier periods, however, many harmoniums were large, table-sized instruments pumped with the feet, and it is this harmonium that Inayat Khan describes in the *Minqār*. A member of the elite that would have had one of these in the drawing room was the audience for his book. The aspiring player is directed to practice a set of simple exercises and, when ready, to play the *ghazal* melodies as one sings them.

The *tablā* receives detailed and informative treatment next. The mnemonic syllables that express 14 different sounds on the *tablā* are described with exact instructions on how to produce them with the hands and fingers. The *ṭhekā*, syllabic patterns that represent a *tāl* as played on the *tablā*, are given for eighteen different *tāl*s.

The final chapter of the *Minqār-i mūsīqār* deals with dance. Female dancers attached to service in temples by lineage or adoption, a practice dating as far back as the temples themselves, as well as dancers in the service of courts and wealthy patrons, had been coming under attack from social reformers since the nineteenth

---

[41] The chart for sitār gamaks describes the following techniques for each of which two names are given: tān (āroh), palṭā (avaroh), sūnth (ḍālu), zamzama (sphurat), mūrki (sphurat), gitkiri (sphurat), larzā (kampat), gamak (āhat), ghasīt (pratyāhat), masak, mīnd (āndolan).

century. Many lineage dancers gave up the profession. In the 1920s and 30s a revival would create new contexts and respectability for reconstituted forms of North and South Indian dance. Upper class women, supported by intellectuals and nationalists, began to debut in concert performances. Inayat Khan does not mention the environment of condemnation or revival, and seems very respectful to the tradition of dance in his treatment. In this part of the book he seems to be encouraging amateur women to try dance. One wonders at the size and makeup of this constituency in Hyderabad in 1907. The lively spirit of Inayat Khan's writing comes through particularly here in his expressions of admiration for human nature and its infinite potential:

> What a work of magic is the human being, what grace, that all of creation shines in every hair. He has joy and excitement (*zawq, shawq*), and a voice capable of singing music (*rāg*); and dance is another aspect of the very same capability...[42]

He notes the respectability that dance enjoys in European society and seems to yearn for a similar progressive attitude in India:

> In Europe dance is pursued with great enthusiasm, and there are even special schools for it. People reap the benefits of physical exercise and spiritual renewal from this art. There, everyone, rich and poor, takes part in dances called balls, in which men and women dance together, and they take so much pleasure in this that they are freed of all manner of worries.[43]

Conclusion

The *Minqār* reveals a good deal about the young Inayat Khan during the peak of his early career, especially when read in the context of his family background and the early twentieth century musical milieu. Apparent here are the ecstatic spirituality, scientific realism, eclectic interest in human behavior, ambition, and talent at communicating his ideas which characterized the work he did in his later public life. One also senses the frustration or dissatisfaction that he felt at the circumstances, musical and other, in which he

[42] Inayat Khan, *Minqār-i mūsīqār*, 279.
[43] Ibid.

lived in India. And here is expressed his curiosity about, and admiration of, the West. He would soon seize the opportunity to travel to the U.S. But it was in Hyderabad where his sense of music, self, and the divine had really begun to come together in the powerful combination that would inspire his later work. Some of the final verses in the book express the larger issue that was driving this extraordinary man:

> Inayat, whether every phrase falters or not,
> the divine melody will resound until the Day of Resurrection.
>
> What form can be more beautiful than ours?
> Still, with all our delicate beauty, we mingle with dust in the end.
>
> As many dances as the stars and the peacocks have,
> all of these movements are just ringings of the Truth.[44]

---

[44] Ibid., 301.

Glossary of foreign musical terms

ālāp – a non-composed section in a classical music performance.

bīn – colloquial for *vīṇā*, also called the *rudra vīṇā*, the prestigious solo instrument of *dhrupad* music.

bhajan – devotional song

cok varṇam – a South Indian song genre used in dance performance

dādrā – a semi-classical song genre related to *ṭhumrī*, named after the six-beat rhythmic cycle (*tāla*) in which it is sung.

ḍhol – a small barrel drum of North India, used primarily in light and folk musics

dhrupad – the premier art music genre of the North Indian courts, flourished 15th-18th centuries

dhrupad rabāb – fretless short-necked lute, a prestigious instrument of courtly dhrupad music.

garbā – a folk/devotional song and dance of Gujarat.

gharānā – lit. "household," a musical lineage based on family line and style

ghazal – a type of Urdu poetry consisting of series of rhymed couplets; also a song genre.

gīt – song

Hindī gīt – Hindī-language song

horī – a song genre contemporaneous with dhrupad; its lyrics celebrate the spring Holi festival

kaharvā – an eight-beat rhythmic cycle (*tāla*) used for semi-classical, light and folk musics

khyāl – the premier vocal genre of North Indian classical music; it developed into its modern form in the 19th century

komal - a flat note

lāvanī – a folk song genre of Maharastra

marsiyā – a song in honor of a deceased person, elegy

mātrā – a count or beat in a rhythmic cycle

nāda – tonal sound, or cosmic original sound in Sanskrit philosophical and musicological texts

naqārā – a two-piece drum of North India, usually played with sticks

pad – lit. "foot," a line of a classical song or subsection of a poem

---

The editor thanks Allyn Miner for compilation of this glossary, which consists of foreign musical terms used in the preceding two articles.

Panjābī – named after the region of Panjāb

qasīda – a poem similar in form but longer than a ghazal

rāga – the melodies of classical Indian music, used in performing both compositions and improvisations

riyāzī tarāz – a style displaying difficult musical technique

saṅgīt – music, traditionally including vocal and instrumental music and dance

sāraṅgī – North Indian fiddle, a bowed lute, formerly known primarily as an accompaniment instrument to dance

sarod – short-necked fretless lute of North India; became a premier classical concert instrument in the 19th and 20th centuries

śikṣak – teacher

sitār – long-necked fretted lute of North Indian music; became a premier classical concert instrument in the 19th and 20th centuries

sursingār – a large *sitār*-like instrument used in the 19th century to emulate the *bīn*

tablā – the two-piece drum of North Indian classical music, played by hand

tāla – rhythmic cycles in Indian classical music

tān – a passage of improvised melody in classical music

ṭappā – a North Indian song genre originally from the Panjāb region

tarānā – a type of classical song usually sung in fast speed, uses non-meaningful syllables as text

ṭhumrī – a North Indian song genre with romantic lyrics cultivated particularly by courtesan singers in the 19th and early 20th centuries

tirvaṭ – a North Indian song genre in which *tablā* syllables are used as text

tīvra – a sharp note

vīṇā – originally a Sanskrit term denoting all stringed instruments, later designated specific instruments; the *rudra vīṇā* (colloquial, *bīn*) of North India, a fretted stick zither, was a premier instrument of dhrupad music

Hazrat Inayat Khan, circa 1921

Sufism

Shaykh Ṣan'ān and the Christian girl

The Downward Path to Wisdom: Gender and Archetype in Persian Sufi Poetry

JEROME W. CLINTON

Introduction

For anyone familiar with the history of Sufism and Sufi orders the decision of Hazrat Inayat Khan to elevate women Sufis to the rank of Murshida in the Sufi Order in the West, and the steady advancement of women teachers at all levels of the Order under the leadership of his son, Pir Vilayat Inayat Khan, are hallmarks of a revolution as astonishing as it is welcome.[1] Historically, as Annemarie Schimmel has observed, while Sufism was generally more favorable to women than other branches of Islam, its attitude was essentially ambivalent—at times in conflict with the prevailing orthodoxy's dim view of the sex, and at times in harmony with it.[2] This ambivalence is reflected in Sufi literature. The portrayal of the great Sufi saint Rābi'a, who appears in many tales, is unambiguously positive. But Rābi'a stands almost alone, and women more often appear as snares in the path of the (male) believer. At the same time Sufism, somewhat paradoxically, has a deep and positive

[1] Hazrat Inayat Khan's romantically idealist yet spirited assessment of women is expressed in his book, *Rasa Shastra* ("the science of emotions," in *The Sufi Message* collected-works series, vol. 3), in earlier articles, and in his discussion of "East and West" in *Biography* (Nekbakht Foundation, ed.). In the latter he writes: "There is no line of work or study which woman in the West does not undertake and does not accomplish as well as man. Even in social and political activities, in religion, in spiritual ideas, she excels man. ... I can see as clear as daylight that the hour is coming when woman will lead humanity to a higher evolution" (242–43).

[2] Annemarie Schimmel, *Mystical Dimensions of Islam* (Chapel Hill: University of North Carolina Press, 1975) 426–8, and "Women in Mystical Islam," in *Women and Islam*, ed. Azizah Al-Hibri (Oxford: Pergamon Press, 1982), 46. Quoted in Leila Ahmed, *Women and Gender is Islam* (New Haven, CT: Yale University Press, 1992), 98, n. 37.

connection with qualities of heart and mind such as patient and enduring love and a deep inner spirituality that we think of as feminine. In the essay that follows, I examine the tension between the Sufi attitude toward women on the one hand and the feminine on the other in the famous tale of "Shaykh Ṣan'ān" from Farīd al-Dīn 'Aṭṭār's *Conference of the Birds*.[3]

A few preliminary comments are in order. While we know there was poetry and prose in the languages of Persia for centuries before the Arab invasion of Iran in the mid-seventh century, little of this work now survives. What we now know as Persian literature grew up in Iran roughly two centuries after this invasion, and was written in the Arabic alphabet. This literature, which was predominantly poetry and drew on the long history of pre-Islamic Iranian literature to nourish its growth, quickly developed a variety of genres—epic, romantic, lyric—and a rich inventory of themes. Sufism began to penetrate Persian poetry and prose in the eleventh century, and by the time of Rūmī in the thirteenth century, it had become a dominant voice, particularly in poetry. Sufism did not stimulate the creation of new genres in Persian poetry, but rather the transformation of existing ones, adding a transcendent dimension to the erotic language of both the lyric and the romance, and giving a characteristically Sufi flavor to didactic tales and stories.

One should also keep in mind that throughout the classical period, and, indeed, down virtually to the present day, Persian poetry has been exclusively a male preserve. The poets, both major and minor, were men, as were their audiences and the rulers and powerful courtiers who supported them. In the first two centuries of its new existence (late ninth to early eleventh centuries), when the dominant forms were the courtly, panegyric *qaṣīda*, and the epic, it was also a literature in which women characters were generally ignored or relegated to minor, supporting roles, and in which little or no scope

[3] The standard edition of 'Aṭṭār's poem is that of Ṣādiq Gawharīn, *Manṭiq al-ṭayr* (Tehran: BTNK, 1978). A brilliant English translation of the whole poem, based on Gawharīn's edition, is available in paperback: Farid al-Din 'Attar, *Conference of the Birds*, translated with an introduction by Afkham Darbandi and Dick Davis (London and New York: Penguin, 1987).

was given to the feminine. The eleventh century saw the growing importance of the romance, and, consequently, of tales which focus upon personal concerns of individual men and women. By the end of the twelfth century the erotic lyric and the romance moved to center stage, and, in the latter genre especially, female characters and the feminine play leading roles.[4]

The Story of Shaykh Ṣan'ān[5]

Shaykh Farīd al-Dīn 'Aṭṭār was born in 1145–46 in Nishapur in northeastern Iran near present day Meshed. We know very little about his life, but that is true for most medieval writers. His name, 'Aṭṭār, tells us that he was a pharmacist, a profession that was like that of a physician in his time, and he refers in his poetry to attending to many patients in his shop. He seems to have lived a relatively quiet life, and was not especially well known as a poet to his contemporaries. Scholars generally place the year of his death as 1221, the year the Mongol army leveled his home city of Nishapur and slaughtered its entire population.

'Aṭṭār's fame grew rapidly after his death, and he is widely known and respected now as a poet, a theorist of Sufism, and a biographer of Sufi saints. In a famous compliment Rūmī says of his illustrious predecessor, "Aṭṭār traversed all seven of Love's valleys. We are still at the first turning in the road."[6] He is the author of a number of mystical narratives, the most famous of them is the *Conference of the Birds.* Other poets, most notably Sanā'ī (d. ca. 1135), had versified collections of Sufi tales before him, but in these earlier anthologies, such as Sanā'ī's *The Garden of Truth*, the tales and parables had only loose and accidental links to each other. 'Aṭṭār's poem is a new departure in that he embeds his stories in a comprehensive narrative, or frame tale, that gives shape and structure to them. In the *Conference of the Birds* this

[4] On the transition from epic to romance see Julie S. Meisami, *Persian Court Poetry* (Princeton: Princeton University Press, 1987), especially chapter 3.

[5] Some portions of this essay appeared in a preliminary form in Paula Berggren, *Teaching with the Norton Anthology of World Masterpieces Expanded Edition: A Guide for Instructors* (New York: W.W. Norton, 1995), 337–40.

[6] *Haft vādī-yi 'ishqrā gasht 'Aṭṭār. Mā hanūz andar kham-i yak kūcha-īm.*

frame tale concerns, as the title suggests, an assembly of birds. They have come together to seek their king, the Simurgh, a remote and awesome figure whom they know only by name. ʻAṭṭār's choice of birds to be the characters of his poem reflects a long tradition in the Middle East of using animals and birds in works that, like Aesop's fables—which is known in Islam as the fables of Luqmān—have a strong ethical and didactic purpose. A journey to find one's king seems to be a very worldly task, but by making his pilgrims birds ʻAṭṭār announces that it is a spiritual one. The bird was and is a common metaphor for the soul. The remote and unknown king the birds seek is the King of Souls, or God, and they elect the hoopoe as their guide because he is Solomon's messenger (Qur'ān 27.20), and so is more experienced in the ways of kings and courts than they are. His responsibilities as guide are, first, to strengthen their resolve and prepare them for their coming journey, and second, to guide them through the perils of the seven valleys they must cross to reach their destination.

The first task takes up most of the poem. The birds are reluctant to begin the journey, and they express their reluctance in terms of specific human failings—a love of wealth or ease, or fear of the unknown, or a greed that won't let them leave their wealth behind. The hoopoe overcomes each objection by first showing the falseness of the bird's reasoning, and then telling a story to illustrate his argument.

When at last the birds decide to commit themselves to the quest, they ask the hoopoe what their first step should be. He tells them that they must abandon their egos (here called the Self), transcend the claims of the body, and give up all attachments—even to faith. He warns them that their way will pass through pain, poverty, and humiliation, and they must be ready to confront these challenges with unquestioning submission to the pains and dangers of the journey.

> Heart's blood and bitter pain belong to love,
> And tales of problems no one can remove;
> Cupbearer, fill the bowl with blood, not wine—
> And if you lack the heart's rich blood take mine.

Love thrives on inextinguishable pain,
Which tears the soul, then knits the threads again.[7]

He then tells the story of Shaykh Ṣan'ān as a powerful illustration of the depths to which this submission may take them. It is also a story in which the perils that the pilgrim confronts are cast in terms of an irresistible and destructive sexuality. The Shaykh's tale is the longest in the *Conference*, and also one of the most widely known and admired.

Shaykh Ṣan'ān is the most pious of Muslims. He has passed the whole of his life in Mecca, the most sacred spot in Islam, and has performed the pilgrimage virtually every year of his life. For ordinary Muslims to visit Mecca even once is the fulfilment of a lifetime aspiration. He is a master of Islamic law and theology, and has gathered about him a vast army of four hundred disciples. He continually breathes the air of asceticism and piety, and would seem to be secure against any temptation. Then one night he has a dream in which he sees his world turned upside down. Rome (by which we should understand Constantinople, the capital of the eastern Roman empire and the Byzantine Church) has replaced Mecca as the focus of his faith. In a word, he has become a Christian. He dwells in a church not a mosque, and worships idols.

The vision terrifies him, yet he reads it as a sign from God that he must journey to Byzantium to meet his fate. He travels there with his disciples and journeys widely for a year until at last he comes upon a young Christian maid whose beauty is more radiant than the sun's. The aged Shaykh falls hopelessly in love with her.

The Christian girl at first does not notice him. When she does she is more inclined to mock him than take his passion seriously. At last she agrees to return his love if he will do four things that will separate him from his faith and seal him in her own: burn the Qur'ān, drink wine, close his eyes to the True Faith (Islam), and worship idols. To these she later adds the indignity of tending swine. These are all shocking acts to a Muslim. The Qur'ān is more than revelation, it is the uncreated word of God. To burn it is

[7] Attar, trans. Darbandi and Davis, *Conference*, 57, lines 1172–4.

sacrilegious, and for Muslims apostasy is a mortal sin. Worshipping idols is expressly forbidden in the Qur'ān. One of Muḥammad's first acts on entering Mecca as its conqueror was to destroy the pagan idols that filled the Ka'ba. The Qur'ān also discourages wine drinking as leading to impiety, and this stricture is made even more emphatic in the traditions of the Prophet.

The Shaykh at first is reluctant to accept these terrible conditions, but eventually he fulfils all of them. His disciples are understandably horrified at the apostasy of their Shaykh, but are unable to dissuade him. Eventually, they despair of rescuing him, and, not wishing to witness his further disgrace, they return to Arabia.

In Mecca a disciple who did not accompany them on their journey hears their story. He upbraids them for abandoning their guide and teacher, and at his insistence they return to Rome to pray for the Shaykh's deliverance. After forty days and nights of fasting and prayer, an agent of God appears to their leader in a dream and grants their wish. The Shaykh's faith is restored, and the obsessive passion that has bedeviled him vanishes from his mind like a dream.

His faith restored, Shaykh Ṣan'ān sets out with his disciples for Mecca. At the same moment the Christian maid suddenly realizes the error of her ways, repents her sins against the Shaykh, and sets out across the desert to join him. The way is too hard for her, and she falls to the ground unable to move further. The Shaykh is guided back to her just as she is on the point of death. He is able to revive her long enough to instruct her in the elements of Islam, and she dies in ecstasy.

Within the context of the frame tale, the story fulfils its admonitory function. The birds are both challenged and buoyed up by the story of Shaykh Ṣan'ān's fall and rise, and continue their journey, eventually making their way across all the seven perilous valleys that stand between them and the court of their king.

There are, however, other messages to be read from the story that are more complex than a simple admonition to persevere in adversity. In form it resembles a romance, but a strange and dark one. The lovers are virtual opposites—a venerable, pious, Muslim male on the one hand, a nubile, seductive, Christian maiden on the other—and so antagonistic are their differences that each threatens the existence of the other. There is no common ground where they can meet, and their passion is not a refuge from adversity, but the cause of it. He can only become her lover by annihilating all that he has been, and she loses both her religion and her life when she belatedly discovers a love for him. And yet by some strange alchemy, both are enriched in spiritual terms by their experience of each other.

Her gain, in Muslim eyes, is greater and more obvious than his. By her conversion she loses her life but gains paradise and immortality. At first, what the Shaykh gains seems no more than to be rescued from a disastrous misadventure, and to regain his life as it was before God sent His terrible, portentous dream to disrupt his life. But ʻAṭṭār means him, and us, to learn a deeper and more subtle lesson than this. Late in the story, as the Shaykh is busy tending swine, he comments,

> This reverend Shaykh kept swine—but who does not
> Keep something swinish in his nature's plot?
> Do not imagine only he could fall;
> This hidden danger lurks within us all,
> Rearing its bestial head when we begin
> To tread salvation's path—...[8]

There has been nothing in the poem before this to suggest that the Shaykh harbored the ethical equivalents of untended swine in his soul, but the nature of his lover/adversary suggests what these might be. The agent of Shaykh Ṣanʻān's spiritual humiliation is an explicitly sexual one. It is not Christianity that seduces him from Islam, but his lust for a young, exquisitely beautiful Christian woman. The Shaykh appears as an innocent victim here because when a seduction takes place the convention in Islam is to blame the seducer, however innocent. Women are obliged to veil their beauty in order not to arouse lustful thoughts in men, but there is no parallel injunction for men to avert their eyes.[9] But in a more important sense, the Christian maid is free of responsibility here

---

[8] Attar, trans. Darbandi and Davis, *Conference*, 68, lines 1420–3.

[9] The roles are sometimes reversed, as when Zulaykha's attempt to seduce Yūsuf is excused by his angelic beauty (Qur'ān 12.31–2), but in general it is the woman who appears as the seducer. *Ed.*

since her fateful encounter with the Shaykh was stage managed by God. She has not sought him out, but simply appeared on her balcony at the right moment. I shall return to this point in a moment.

The Shaykh's failing is that he makes the Christian maid his idol and worships her instead of God. In this narrative lust itself takes on a taint since it is opposed to faith. Since Islam, unlike Christianity, does not condemn sexual desire and opposes celibacy, the young woman's Christian faith is present here as a necessary screen to allow the poet to make sexual desire the villain without at the same time advocating celibacy. The young woman's death at the conclusion of the story, which seems as abrupt and unexpected as her conversion, conveniently eliminates the necessity of dealing with how she, and her obvious sexuality, might be included in the Shaykh's all male spiritual community once they return to Mecca.

Female sexuality is a commonplace metaphor for the snares of the world, so that what she embodies for the Shaykh is not just lust or sexual license, but all those longings for worldly pleasures and distractions that tempted him as a young man, but which he had to repress in order to become the learned, pious divine that he is. What he denied in this way didn't vanish. It lay hidden in his psyche like a landmine waiting to explode. In his journey to Byzantium he has had to confront all that he refused to live as a young man. The confrontation is harsh and terrible, but he survives it by yielding to it completely. 'Aṭṭār does not say this specifically, but the tale implies strongly that the Shaykh has been strengthened by his journey, and that had he not confronted what he would call his baser nature—the swine he tended in Byzantium—he would not have been able to proceed further in the journey of his soul.

In considering more closely how gender and sexuality function in the tale, two points emerge. The first is that the dominant sensibility is feminine even though the protagonist is male, and second that the negative aspects of the feminine appear in the female character, while the more positive aspects are given to the male. Shaykh Ṣan'ān is the hero of the poem, but his is a strangely un-masculine kind of heroism. From *Gilgamesh* to *Beowulf*, poets portray their heroes as men of action who accomplish feats of strength and daring against terrible odds. The Shaykh, however, does not conquer the unconquerable. What characterizes his actions throughout is a patient, long-suffering acceptance of whatever tribulations God has set in his path. Such patient endurance is archetypally feminine. His journey contains distant but surprising echoes of the descent of Ishtar, the holy priestess and Queen of Heaven, into the underworld. At each stage of her journey she was divested of crown, jewelry and clothes, until at the nadir she died and was hung from a hook on the wall, a piece of rotting meat—a state not unlike Shaykh Ṣan'ān's passage as a swineherd. Like the Shaykh, she was revived and allowed to ascend once more to the upper world not by her own actions, but by the intervention of the wise god. As she returns to her own world, she re-acquires, as does the Shaykh, the symbols of her authority and status in the world.[10]

The only character who behaves in a characteristically masculine fashion in the poem is the unnamed student who has stayed behind in Mecca. It is he who insists that they all return to Byzantium and undertake a regimen of fasting and prayer to liberate their teacher.

The Christian maid, as I have already suggested, embodies a negative femininity—a seductiveness that is no less disruptive for being innocent. Her apparent cruelty is harder to parse. Women often fulfil the role of ethical or spiritual guide for their beloved in Persian romances, and there is a good deal of variation in how this role is enacted. The young Christian girl leads the Shaykh on to wisdom, but by a downward path, and, at least initially, she is not his lover but his antagonist. Like Zulaykha, she plays a role that is essential to the drama, but in which she appears as a villain. While both male and female characters are shown to have failings—"something swinish in their natures"—in this story the man is the protagonist, and it is the progress of his spiritual journey to which 'Aṭṭār draws our attention. The woman is only a means to

---

[10] James B. Pritchard, ed., "The Descent of Ishtar in the Nether World," in *The Ancient Near East* (Princeton: Princeton University Press, 1950), 1:80–5. A modern recasting of the tale is give as "The Descent of Innana," in Diane Wolkstein and Samuel Noah Kramer, *Innana: Queen of Heaven and Earth, Her Stories and Hymns from Sumer* (New York: Harper and Row, 1983), 51–90.

that progress. 'Aṭṭār rewards her in the end, but almost as an afterthought.

In apportioning qualities, he gives the positive feminine to the Shaykh, a man, the negative to the Christian maid, a woman. This pattern recurs frequently in Sufi poetry as well as in classical Persian poetry and Islamic literature more generally. That 'Aṭṭār should treat his women characters as secondary is hardly surprising, although it is surely not a welcome discovery to modern readers. His representation of women conforms in general terms to the norms of medieval patriarchy both East and West. Perhaps what one should note is that 'Aṭṭār's poem, and classical Persian poetry more largely, is free of the misogynistic diatribes that were commonplace in the medieval literature of Europe.[11]

That the feminine should be so essential to the character of the Shaykh is, perhaps, more surprising, but it shouldn't be. A very feminine yearning for a distant and unresponsive lover is at the heart of much of Sufi poetry. Persian romantic lyrics in their pre-Sufi phase are almost invariably laments in which the poet/lover complains of his beloved's cruelty and indifference. Such lover's complaints have a remarkable pre-adaptive fit with mystical lyrics, since in the universe of the Sufi, the Beloved is all too often beyond the poet/lover's reach. His helplessness and utter dependence on the Beloved means that he occupies what we traditionally describe as the feminine position in the love relationship. He longs to be overwhelmed by the Beloved and filled with Him. The poets of such poems are invariably men, but they speak with a very feminine voice.

Consider, by way of example, these quatrains of Rūmī:

I can't take back my heart from you, not now.
It's better that I give it up to you.
And if I don't, what use is it to me?
The reason that I have a heart is you.

---

[11] See, for instance, R. Howard Bloch, *Medieval Misogyny and the Invention of Western Romantic Love* (Chicago: University of Chicago Press, 1991). Feminist studies of Islamic literature are still a relative novelty, but Fedwa Malti-Douglas, *Woman's Body, Woman's World: Gender and Discourse in Arabo-Islamic Writing* (Princeton: Princeton University Press, 1991), provides a useful beginning. On the place of women in classical Islam see Leila Ahmed, note 1 above.

Or, again,

> Longing has drawn so many sighs from me
> I've driven you away. It's so unfair.
> It's your neglect that's given me this wound.
> I'm left in pain. And you? You hardly care.[12]

This is not the only way in which Rūmī evokes his relations with the Divine. Like all lovers, he experiences a wide range of emotions, but that of the suffering lover is surely among the commonest both in his poetry and in that of other Sufi poets. And, to return to Shaykh Ṣan'ān for a moment, it is his willingness to obey without question the divine but perplexing guidance that comes to him in a dream, and to endure the terrible consequences of this obedience that ultimately leads him to the next stage in his journey.

[12] Mawlānā Jalāl al-Dīn Rūmī, *Dīvān-i kabīr*, ed. M. Furūzānfar (Tehran: Publications of the University of Tehran, 1345), vol. 8, nos. 1089 and 1482. The translations are my own.

'Ayn al-Quźāt Hamadānī

The Sufi Path of Love in Iran and India

SEYYED OMID SAFI

I have loved in life and I have been loved.
I have drunk the bowl of poison from the hands of love as nectar, and have been raised above life's joy and sorrow.
My heart, aflame in love, set afire every heart that came in touch with it.
My heart hath been rent and joined again;
My heart hath been broken and again made whole;
My heart hath been wounded and healed again;
A thousand deaths my heart hath died, and thanks be to Love, it liveth yet.
I went through Hell and saw there love's raging fire, and I entered Heaven illumined with the light of love.
I wept in love and made all weep with me;
I mourned in love and pierced the hearts of men;
And when my fiery glance fell on the rocks, the rocks burst forth as volcanoes;
The whole world sank in the flood caused by my one tear;
With my deep sigh the earth trembled, and when I cried aloud the name of my beloved, I shook the throne of God in Heaven.
I bowed my head low in humility, and on my knees I begged of Love:
"Disclose to me, I pray thee, O Love, thy secret."
She took me gently by my arms and lifted me above the earth, and spoke softly in my ear:
"My dear one, thou thyself art love, art lover, and thyself art the beloved whom thou hast adored."[1]

—Hazrat Inayat Khan

Hazrat Inayat Khan's description of the shattering and healing power of love resonates in the hearts of emotionally experienced readers. Many may not be aware, however, of the long history of the ideas he utilizes. The tri-unity of love, lover and beloved, for example, has been discussed by a series of Sufi thinkers for over a thousand years. Bāyazīd Bisṭāmī (d. 874), Aḥmad Ghazālī (d.

[1] Inayat Khan, *The Divine Symphony or Vadan* (London/Southampton: The Sufi Movement, 1931), 12–14.

1126)[2] and Mu'īn al-Dīn Chishtī[3] are each reported to have spoken about the ultimate oneness of love, lover, and beloved in the "realm of unity" (*'ālam-i tawḥīd*).[4] These and other loosely associated Sufis, who called themselves followers of the "Path of Love" (*mazhab-i 'ishq*), meticulously explored the nuances of passionate love, human and Divine. The aim of this essay is to establish this Persian, and Indo-Persian, Path of Love as an important pre-modern context for Hazrat Inayat Khan's work, tracing its teachings through the Chishtī Order, whose doctrinal and methodological repertory Hazrat Inayat Khan transmitted to the West.

The sources of Hazrat Inayat Khan

Some contemporary scholars consider it futile to look for the "sources" of a Sufi master, arguing that inspiration tends to be heavenly rather than earthly, or "vertical" rather than "horizontal."[5] But even if this is the case in the spiritual *experiences* of Sufi mystics, surely it can be admitted that their discursive expressions build on the statements of earlier Sufis. Taking this approach, our aim here is to demonstrate that Hazrat Inayat Khan's discourse on "love, harmony, and beauty" is firmly rooted in a millenium-old Sufi tradition—albeit brilliantly interpreted for a new audience.

The task of tracing Hazrat Inayat Khan's spiritual-intellectual heritage is not a simple one. The Pir-o-Murshid's familiarity with the teachings of the Path of Love seems to have been only secondarily a matter of exposure to the doctrinal canon of Sufism.[6] Still more central to his education were the Sufi-influenced Persian and Urdu poetry that saturated the atmosphere of his early life and

---

[2] See *Majmū'a-yi āsār-i fārsī-yi Aḥmad Ghazālī*, ed. Aḥmad Mujāhid (Tehran: Intishārāt-i Dānishgāh-i Tihrān, 1358/1979), 552. Mujāhid cites Massignon, although I have not been able to verify the citation.

[3] Sayyid Muḥammad Mubārak al-'Alawī al-Kirmānī (Amīr Khwurd), *Siyar al-awliyā'*, (Delhi: Maṭba'-i Muḥibb-i Hind, 1302/1884–85), 45.

[4] Farīd al-Dīn 'Aṭṭār, *Tazkirat al-awliyā'*, ed. Muḥammad Isti'lāmī, (Tehran: Intishārāt-i Zavvār, 1347/1968; reprint, 1372/1993), 189. An alternate reading is somewhat more modest, stating merely the identity of the lover and the beloved.

[5] See, for example, Seyyed Hossein Nasr, *Three Muslim Sages* (Delmar, N.Y.: Caravan Books, 1976), 100.

[6] Hazrat Inayat Khan's formal Sufi training is described in Regina M. Bloch, *The Confessions of Inayat Khan* (London: The Sufi Publishing Society, 1915), 40: "I studied the Koran, Hadis, and the literature of the Persian mystics."

the oral discourses of his master, Sayyid Abū Ḥāshim Madanī. To complicate matters further, while Hazrat Inayat Khan had only one master, the transmission he received included in addition to the Chishtiyya several other lineages (among which the Suhrawardiyya, Qādiriyya, and Naqshbandiyya were given special attention), each having its own method and orientation.

Moreover, Hazrat Inayat Khan's voluminous corpus of teachings in English is relatively opaque, in terms of its sources, in comparison for example with his Urdu writings (which focus on musicology, and are hence of limited interest for present purposes). In addressing Westerners, Hazrat Inayat Khan had to build on the foundations laid by Western spiritual movements, of which the Theosophical Society was the most prominent.[7] While he frequently reoriented the terms of contemporary discourse to accommodate the Sufi tradition he represented, he refrained from invoking litanies of unfamiliar Persian and Arabic authors and titles.

These problematics notwithstanding, there are nonetheless many cases in which the Sufi genealogy of the themes and symbols used by Hazrat Inayat Khan can be easily traced. The already mentioned tri-unity of love, lover and beloved is only one such example. A similarly illustrative example is the exchange between moth and flame which figures as a "Tana" in Hazrat Inayat Khan's *Vadan*:

> Moth: "I gave you my life."
> Flame: "I allowed you to kiss me."[8]

The deadly embrace of moth and flame, which has recently become a familiar trope in anglophone popular culture (occuring in the lyrics of Madonna), pervades the premodern literature of Persian and Urdu. Its origins can be traced to Manṣūr Ḥallāj (d. 922), whose theory of annihilation in love deeply informed the later Path of Love.[9]

---

[7] A notable recent treatment of the Theosophical Society is K. Paul Johnson, *Initiates of Theosophical Masters*, (Albany: State University of New York Press, 1995).

[8] Inayat Khan, *Complete Works of Pir-o-Murshid Inayat Khan, Sayings I*, ed. Munira van Voorst van Beest (London/The Hague: East-West Publications, 1989), 346.

[9] Louis Massignon, *The Passion of al-Hallaj*, trans. Herbert Mason (Princeton: Princeton University Press, 1982), 3:289.

Aḥmad Ghazālī, a figure we will soon approach, deployed the same metaphor.[10] Indeed one can trace a line of transmission from Ḥallāj to Hazrat Inayat Khan through the medium of generations of Persian and Indian mystics and poets. This is a good example of how Sufi symbols have lives of their own: moth and flame inconspicuously carry the cumulative weight of centuries of connotation.

The Sufis of the Path of Love

The Path of Love is quite unlike the many Sufi *ṭarīqas* (orders) deriving from eponymous founders. In its amorphousness, it might be said to resemble the Akbarian tradition traced to Ibn al-ʻArabī, or the Ishrāqī tradition traced to Suhrawardī. It is not held together by initiatic or even doctrinal connections, but rather an aesthetic, a "mood": the immediate intuitive experience—or "taste" (Ar. *dhawq*, P. *zawq*)—of love:

> Of love one can only speak with lovers. Only a lover knows the true value of love. One who has not experienced it considers it all a legend. For such a person, even the claim of love, even the name of love, are forbidden![11]

The Path of Love may be described as a loosely affiliated group of Sufi mystics and poets who throughout the centuries have propagated a highly nuanced teaching focused on passionate love (*ʻishq*). Some scholars have attempted to identify its prominent members and chart its genealogy. Nasrollah Pourjavady, perhaps the foremost scholar today working on the Sufis of the Path of Love, has delineated a "School of Aḥmad Ghazālī" which includes in addition to its namesake, Farīd al-Dīn ʻAṭṭār, Najm al-Dīn Rāzī, ʻIzz al-Dīn Maḥmūd Kāshānī, Fakhr al-Dīn ʻIrāqī, Jalāl al-Dīn Rūmī, and Saʻīd al-Dīn Farghānī. Pourjavady also includes such antecedents of Aḥmad Ghazālī as Bāyazīd Bisṭāmī, Manṣūr Ḥallāj, Abū al-Ḥasan Kharaqānī and Abu Saʻīd ibn Abī al-Khayr. In his opinion "the most exquisite and sublime expressions" of Aḥmad's School are the odes of Ḥāfiẓ.[12]

---

[10] Mujāhid, *Majmūʻa*, 320: "Your fair face is a candle. And I? The moth."

[11] ʻAyn al-Quḍāt Hamadānī, *Tamhīdāt*, ed. ʻAfīf ʻUsayrān, (Tehran: Kitābkhāna-yi Manūchihrī, 1373/1994), 111.

[12] Nasrollah Pourjavady, Introduction to *Sawanih: Inspirations from the World of*

Another definition is offered by Peter Lamborn Wilson, who likewise regards the Path of Love as a distinct movement: "Sufism often expresses itself through love poems, and there exists (particularly in the Persian tradition) a type of sufism which explains itself solely in such terms and which has been called 'The School of Love'."[13]

Building on the work of Wilson and Pourjavady, this essay will seek greater specificity than the terms outlined by Wilson, while tracing a somewhat different trajectory than that indicated by Pourjavady. Whereas Pourjavady's interest is mainly in Persian (and primarily Khurasanian) Sufism, our project here is to trace the Path of Love from Saljūq Iran to the Indo-Persian milieu of the Chishtī Sufis, and finally to Hazrat Inayat Khan. Our genealogy includes then, in addition to Aḥmad Ghazālī, 'Ayn al-Qużāt Hamadānī and Rūmī, such South Asian Chishtī masters as Niẓām al-Dīn Awliyā', Naṣīr al-Dīn Chirāgh-i Dihlī, Mas'ūd Bakk, Gīsū Darāz, Muḥammad Chishtī, and Shāh Kalīm Allāh.

Mazhab and *'ishq*

> The spiritual community of love is apart from all faiths. The lovers' community and path (*mazhab*) is God.[14]
> —Rūmī

The term *mazhab* (Ar., *madhhab*) has multiple connotations in Islamic thought. It has been variously translated as "school," "sect," "creed," and "religion." Accordingly, *mazhab-i 'ishq* has often been rendered as the "School of Love," or "Religion of Love." These renderings can be misleading, however, as the mystics we are concerned with here made no attempt to start a new religion, or contribute yet another school of thought to the already crowded intellectual milieu of Islam. In using the term *mazhab,* they were invoking its etymology: as with several other technical terms current in Sufism (viz., *sharī'at* and *ṭarīqat*), the root meaning of the word *mazhab* is "a trodden path."

Pure Spirit (London: KPI, 1986), 8–10.

[13] Peter Lamborn Wilson, *Scandal: Essays in Islamic Heresy*, (Brooklyn, NY: Autonomedia, 1988), 94.

[14] Mawlānā Jalāl al-Dīn Rūmī, *Masnavī*, ed. Muḥammad Isti'lāmī (Tehran: Kitābfurūshī-yi Zavvār, 1362/1983), 2:82, line 1774.

Perhaps the most common usage of the term *mazhab* is in reference to the various Islamic theological and legal schools, which are generally named after founding figures: Ḥanafī, Ḥanbalī, Malikī, Shāfi'ī etc. The Sufis of the Path of Love no doubt delighted in the irony of belonging to a school-less school, whose eponyms were love and God! Their claim was as radical as it was simple:

> God-willing, I shall expound upon the lover and the beloved ...
>
> I mentioned the *mazhab* (path) and community of the lovers of God. They follow the path and community of God; not that of Shāfi'ī, Abū Ḥanifal or others.[15] The lovers of God follow the *mazhab-i 'ishq* (path of love) and *mazhab-i khudā* (God's path).[16]
>
> They asked Ḥusayn Manṣūr [Ḥallāj]: "Which path are you on?" He said: "I am on God's path." *(anā 'alā madhhab rabbī).*[17]

In appropriating the term *mazhab*, these Sufis did not mean to abrogate the established theological and legal schools, or dismiss their relevance. In fact, many of the Sufis to be discussed were important members of these formal schools as well.[18] And yet the Path of Love Sufis insisted that scholars who limited themselves to externals and denied the primacy of love were, in the words of 'Ayn al-Qużāt, "highway robbers and immature children!" The aim of these Sufis was to reinvigorate religion by uprooting sectarianism and blind imitation (*taqlīd*) and planting the seeds of the actual realization (*taḥqīq*) of God through love.

Rūmī, quoting Sanā'ī,[19] writes:

> Love is nothing,
> Save felicity and grace (*'ināyat*).
> Love is nothing,
> Save heart-opening and guidance.

---

[15] Shāfi'ī (d. 820) was the founder of a major legal school (*mazhab*). The Ḥanafī *mazhab* traces itself to Abū Ḥanīfa (d. 767).

[16] Hamadānī, *Tamhīdāt*, 115–6.

[17] Ibid., 22.

[18] For example, 'Ayn al-Qużāt and Aḥmad Ghazālī followed the Shāfi'ī *mazhab*; Rūmī was a Ḥanafī; 'Abd al-Qādir Gīlānī and Khwāja 'Abd Allāh Anṣārī were Ḥanbalīs. Likewise, there were other Sufis who followed the Malikī and Ja'farī *mazhabs*.

[19] Ḥakīm Sanā'ī, *Dīvān-i Ḥakīm Abū al-Majd Majdūd ibn Adām Sanā'ī Ghaznav*, ed. Mudarris Rażavī, (Tehran: Intishārāt-i Sanā'ī, n.d.), 827.

Abū Ḥanīfa
Did not teach about love.
Shāfi'ī
Has nothing to say about it.[20]

'Ayn al-Qużāt writes:

> O precious one ... If Shāfi'ī and Abū Ḥanīfa, who were leaders of the community, were alive in this age, praise be to God they would find many benefits, Divine sciences, and traces of spiritual words; they would all turn to these words ... and would utter nothing but this![21]

A brief examination of the second term, *'ishq*, is also in order. The words for "love" used by the Path of Love Sufis—*maḥabba*, *'ishq*, etc.—were not new, but acquired an unprecedented centrality in their discourse. Pride of place went to *'ishq* (passionate love). Balking at the idea of describing the human-Divine relationship in erotically charged terms, many earlier Sufis had favored the use of the Qur'ānic word *maḥabba* (lovingkindness). The manual-writer Abū Bakr al-Kalābādhī (d. 385/995), for example, groups statements on love from seminal Sufis like al-Junayd ("Love is the inclination of the heart") and Abū 'Abd Allāh al-Nibājī ("Love for creatures is a pleasure; love for the Creator is an annihilation") under the heading of *maḥabba*.[22] In his celebrated *Risāla*, al-Qushayrī (d. 1072) tries to neutralize the erotic connotations of *maḥabba*, relatively moderate as they are, in order to defend its use against theological criticisms—criticisms that would apply all the more forcefully to *'ishq*: "When the scholars use the term *maḥabba*, they mean 'desire' (*irāda*). But the Folk (i.e., the Sufis) mean something other than desire when they use this term. Desire can not be said to belong to the Ancient One (God)."[23] He further quotes Abū 'Alī al-

[20] Jalāl al-Dīn Rūmī, *Kulliyāt-i Shams (Dīvān-i Shams-i Tabrīz)*, ed. Badī' al-Zamān Furūzānfar (Tehran: Dānishgāh-i Tihrān, 1336/1957; reprint 1363/1984), 1:289. Another manuscript adds the names of the other two founders of Sunnī schools of legal thought: "Ḥanbalī has no tradition dealing with love. Malikī does not narrate about it."

[21] Hamadānī, *Tamhīdāt*, 198–199.

[22] Abū Bakr al-Kalābādhī, *al-Ta'arruf li-madhhab ahl al-taṣawwuf*, ed. Maḥmūd Amīn al-Nawawī (Cairo: al-Maktaba al-Azhariyya, 1412 A.H./1992), 128. The first quote is taken from A.J. Arberry's masterful translation of this text, *The Doctrine of the Sufis* (Cambridge: Cambridge University Press, 1935), 102.

[23] Qushayrī, *al-Risālat al-qushayriyya*, ed. 'Abd al-Ḥalīm Maḥmūd (Cairo: Dār al-

Daqqāq to the effect that *'ishq*—defined as "exceeding all limits in *maḥabba*"—cannot be applied to God since "He cannot be characterized as possessing passionate love for anything."[24]

Yet the resonance of *'ishq* was such that, once opened, the floodgates could not be closed. Successive centuries saw the unabated proliferation of discursive expressions of passionate spiritual love. The first treatise on *'ishq* written in Persian was the *Sawāniḥ* of Aḥmad Ghazālī. It is to this founding figure of the Path of Love that we now turn.

Extant writings of Aḥmad Ghazālī

Abū Ḥāmid Muḥammad al-Ghazālī (d. 505/1111) has for decades exercised the fascination of scholars working on the political and religious institutions of Islam. His younger brother Aḥmad (d. 520/1126), meanwhile, enjoys the attention of a more select group: aficionados of Sufi love mysticism. If his only contribution to Sufism had been authoring the marvelous treatise *Sawāniḥ* it would be enough to count him among the greatest commentators on love, not merely in the Islamic tradition, but indeed in the entire history of human spirituality. The *Sawāniḥ* is a deceivingly simple and brief work. The Persian text printed in Iran covers just over a hundred pages (and, in fact, notes on variant readings take up more than two thirds of the space).[25] Nasrollah Pourjavady's English translation occupies a scant sixty-seven pages.[26] Yet despite its concision, Pourjavady avers that perhaps no work has left a greater impression on Persian Sufism.

Aḥmad Ghazālī was quite prolific, and fortunately many of his works have survived.[27] His Persian writings have been edited by Aḥmad Mujāhid, and published in *Majmū'a-yi āsār-i fārsī-yi*

Kutūb, 1972), 2:611. For a partial English rendering of this text see *Principles of Sufism*, trans. Barbara Von Schlegell (Berkeley: Mizan Press, 1990), 326.

[24] Qushayrī, *Principles*, 330–1.

[25] Aḥmad Ghazālī, *Sawāniḥ*, ed. Helmut Ritter (Tehran: Markaz-i Nashr-i Dānishgāhī, 1368/1989).

[26] Ghazālī, *Sawāniḥ*, trans. Pourjavady, op. cit. This translation contains a useful commentary and glossary of technical terms.

[27] This list is not meant to be exhaustive. There is a full list available in Mujāhid, *Majmū'a*, 538–9. Some of these texts are no longer extant, and there are debates about the authorship of some texts.

Aḥmad-i Ghazālī.[28] The editor has provided a very thorough introduction to Ghazali's life and treatment in later sources.

Another recently edited and noteworthy text is the collected sermons (*majālis*) for which Aḥmad Ghazālī was so well known in the medieval world.[29] Even his detractors admitted that Ghazali's preaching was unusually sweet and effective in finding its way into the hearts of listeners.

An equally important extant source is the series of letters (*maktūbāt*) exchanged between Aḥmad Ghazālī and his junior contemporary 'Ayn al-Qużāt Hamadānī, a portion of which have been edited by Nasrollah Pourjavdy.[30] Another series of correspondence between these two great masters, collected in a treatise entitled *Risāla 'ayniyya*, is distinguished by the approbation of the famous Sufi poet and hagiographer 'Abd al-Rahman Jāmī: "In elegance, eloquence, fluidity and facility, the *Risāla 'ayniyya* is peerless."[31]

In addition to the already mentioned *Majālis*, another Arabic work of Aḥmad Ghazālī also deserves notice: namely, *Al-Tajrīd fī kalīmāt al-tawḥīd.*[32] This is a simple but elegant rendering of classic Sufi themes.

As with many pre-modern Sufis, there are several cases of questionable attribution. The *Bawāriq al-'ilma*, translated by James Robson in *Tracts on Listening to Music,* is no longer accepted as a genuine work of Aḥmad Ghazālī.[33] There also exist texts sometimes attributed to Aḥmad Ghazālī and sometimes to his more famous brother; the most significant among them being the *Risālat al-ṭayr*, the suspected prototype of Farīd al-Din 'Aṭṭār's celebrated *Manṭiq*

---

[28] Mujāhid, *Majmū'a*, op. cit.

[29] Aḥmad Ghazālī, *Majālis*, ed. Aḥmad Mujāhid (Tehran: Intishārāt-i Dānishgāh-i Tihrān, 1376/1997).

[30] Aḥmad Ghazālī, *Makātib-i Khwaja Aḥmad Ghazālī bi 'Ayn al-Qużāt Hamadānī,* ed. Nasrollah Pourjavady (Tehran: Khaniqāh-i Ni'mat Allāhī, 1977).

[31] 'Abd al-Raḥmān Jāmī, *Nafaḥāt al-uns min ḥażārat al-quds*, ed. Mahdī Tawḥīdīpūr (Tehran: Intishārāt-i Kitābfurūshī-yi Maḥmūdī, 1337/1958), 418.

[32] Aḥmad Ghazālī, *al-Tajrīd fī kalīmāt al-tawḥīd* (Cairo: Sharīkat Maktabāt wa Matba'āt Muṣṭafā al-Bābī al-Ḥalabī, 1967); German translation: *Der reine Gottesglaube: das Wort des Einheitsbekenntnisses: Ahmad Al-Gazzalis Schrift At-Tagrid fi kalimat at-tawhid*, trans. Richard Gramlich (Wiesbaden: F. Steiner, 1983).

[33] *Tracts on listening to music, being Dhamm al-malahi, by Ibn abi 'l-Dunya, and Bawariq al-ilma', by Majd al-Din al-Tusi al-Ghazali*, ed. and trans. James Robson (London: The Royal Asiatic Society, 1938).

al-ṭayr ("Conference of the Birds").[34] Similarly unresolved is the authorship of *Baḥr al-maḥabba* ("Ocean of Love").[35]

Somewhat surprisingly, nothing of substance has been written in English—or indeed any European language—on Aḥmad Ghazālī and his legacy. The two useful resources are both in Persian: Nasrollah Pourjavady's *Sulṭān-i ṭarīqat* ("The King of the Spiritual Path")[36] and Aḥmad Mujāhid's extended introduction to the life and works of Aḥmad Ghazālī in his *Majmū'a-yi āsār-i fārsi.*

Aḥmad Ghazālī's life

Aḥmad Ghazālī was born in Khurasan (present-day northeastern Iran) between the years 451-454/1059–1062. Hagiographers are fond of juxtaposing Aḥmad with his more sober elder brother. Ibn Mullaqān even traces their differences back before the birth of either of them, narrating how in the company of jurists their father had prayed for a son who would become a distinguished jurist, and among preachers had prayed for a son who would become a great orator. Not wishing to disappoint him, Ibn Mullaqān explains, God granted him Muḥammad and Aḥmad in turn.[37]

The biographer Subkī states that as a youth in Tus, Aḥmad trained under the supervision of Aḥmad Rūdakānī. He underwent spiritual retreats until he reached the point that his speech became that of travellers on the mystical path. When he went to Iraq, "people's hearts became inclined towards him, and they fell in love with him."[38] Before long he became a saint of the kind whose company he had so eagerly sought in his youth. Concurrent with successive periods of intense spiritual retreat and esoteric study with Sufi masters, including Abū Bakr Nassāj Ṭūsī (d. 487/1094),

---

[34] In Mujāhid's opinion the style of the *Risālat al-ṭayr* is more consistent with the work of Aḥmad. Peter Avery includes the *Risālat al-Ṭayr* as an appendix to his translation of Farīd al-Dīn 'Aṭṭār's *Manṭiq al-Ṭayr: Speech of the Birds* (Cambridge: Islamic Texts Society, 1998).

[35] Published as Abū Ḥāmid Muḥammad Ghazālī, *Kitāb Asrār-i 'ishq yā daryā-yi maḥabbat, tarjuma-yi baḥr al-maḥabba fī asrār al-muwadda*, (Tehran: Chāpkhāna-yi 'Alī, 1325/1956).

[36] Nasrollah Pourjavady, *Sulṭān-i ṭarīqat*, (Tehran: Intishārāt-i Nigāh, 1358/1979).

[37] Ibn Mullaqān's story is cited in Mujāhid, *Majmū'a*, 16, n. 2. A very similar account is provided in Subkī's *Ṭabaqāt al-shāfi'iyya*, 3:53 (Cairo: 'Īsā al-Bābī al-Ḥalabī, 1964).

[38] Mujāhid, *Majmū'a*, 16.

Aḥmad acquired knowledge of the Islamic sciences. His erudition attained such a level that when his brother Abū Ḥāmid felt compelled to leave his distinguished post at the Niẓāmiyya *madrasa* (Islamic seminary), he turned to his younger sibling to take his place. Most sources report that Aḥmad held this post, the most prestigious lectureship in all of pre-modern Islamdom, from 488/1095 to 498/1104-5.[39] This is in itself incontrovertible testimony to the breadth and depth of his learning. Indeed, contemporary sources emphasize his credentials not only as a Sufi, but also as a preacher (*wā'iẓ*), a religious scholar (*'ālim*), a gnostic sage (*'ārif*), and a doctor of law (*faqīh*).[40]

In most of the comparisons of the Ghazālī brothers found in hagiographical and biographical compendia Abū Ḥāmid comes across as a masterful but rather dry scholar who studies what his spiritually more gifted brother Aḥmad experiences first-hand. Such observations are often supported with illustrative anecdotes. One source tells of how Aḥmad, finding Abū Ḥāmid preaching piety to a congregation, rebuked him with a poem:

> You aided them when they were weak;
> When they gained speed [on the path],
> Your aspiration became weak.
> You guide others, and remain unguided yourself.[41]

Later sources, including Rāfi'ī and Jāmī, elaborate this theme in delightful ways. They both relate the story of a Sufi traveler from Qazvin who visited Abū Ḥamid Ghazālī in Tus. Abū Ḥāmid asked the traveler about his younger brother's wellbeing, and inquired whether he had with him any of his sayings. The traveler responded in the affirmative, and produced a small tract. After reflecting on it for some time, Abū Ḥāmid declared: "Glory be to God! That which I have searched for, Aḥmad has found!"[42] Further on we will see how similar stories were remembered in Chishtī circles. To this day,

---

[39] There is some disagreement among the various sources as to the exact length of this period. During this time, Abū Ḥāmid traveled to Syria, Jerusalem, and Mecca.

[40] Among the sources which refer to this are Subkī (*Ṭabaqāt*), Ibn Khallikān (*Wafāyat al-a'yān*), and Yafi'ī (*Rawḍ al-riyāhīn*).

[41] Zābidī, *Sharḥ iḥyā' 'ulūm*, cited in Mujāhid, *Majmū'a*, 27, n. 1.

[42] Jāmī, *Nafaḥāt al-uns*, 380. Mujāhid, *Majmū'a*, 73, also attributes the statement to Rafi'ī's *al-Tadwīn*.

the urge to compare the two brothers often proves irresistible; Henry Corbin quotes a remark of his erstwhile mentor, Louis Massignon: "Aḥmad did not succeed in communicating to him [Abū Ḥāmid Ghazālī] that passion of pure love, of inconsolable desire, which fires his own writings."[43]

Anecdotes of Aḥmad Ghazālī

There are a number of enchanting stories about Aḥmad Ghazālī which poignantly illustrate important aspects of the Path of Love. Often Aḥmad's subtlety in working with the delicate spiritual states of people in vulnerable positions is attested. Abū Ḥafṣ 'Umar Suhrawardī offers a wonderful narrative on the authority of his uncle, Abū Najīb Suhrawardī, a disciple of Aḥmad Ghazālī. A "child of the world" (i.e. "materialistic person") came to Shaykh Aḥmad, and asked for a *khirqa* (cloak of spiritual investiture). Aḥmad told the man to go first to Shaykh Abū Najīb and learn from him about the *khirqa.* Listening to Abū Najīb describe the responsibilities and etiquette involved in wearing the cloak, the man lost his resolve. When the news of this got to Aḥmad Ghazālī, he asked for Abū Najīb, and chastised him:

> I sent that man to you so that you would speak with him and cause his desire and yearning for wearing the *khirqa* to be increased. But you spoke in a way that turned him off to it. What you said to him *is* an accurate account of the responsibilities involved in wearing the *khirqa*. [However] if we hold a novice to these responsibilities, he will never be able to meet them, and will turn away from the path. It is imperative that we clothe him in the spiritual cloak, and bring him into the path of spiritual poverty (*faqr*), so that he comes to resemble the *faqīrs* (*lit.* poor ones; Sufis). This way, he will become more inclined to attend their gatherings and sessions. Through the *baraka* of mixing with them, he will continue to progress on the path until he reaches their station (*maqām*).[44]

In this story, Aḥmad Ghazālī prioritizes experience over detailed theoretical knowledge: what is meaningful to the novice, he understands, is the experience of the path, not the enumeration of its

[43] Henry Corbin, *History of Islamic Philosophy*, trans. Liadain Sherrard (London: Kegan Paul International, 1993), 201.

[44] Suhrawardī, *'Awārif al-ma'ārif*; cited in Mujāhid, *Majmū'a*, 32–33.

duties at each stage and station. Aḥmad Ghazālī's pedagogical style accords with the Prophetic maxim: "Speak to people at their level of understanding."

Another touching story is provided by Zakariyā Qazvīnī, in *Āsār al-bilād:*

> It is said that a man wanted to bring a woman of ill repute to his house, paying her a fixed sum. [Aḥmad] Ghazālī offered her a larger sum and took her to his house. He sat in a corner, and occupied himself with prayers until the morning. In the morning, he offered her the sum. He told her: "Rise, and go wherever you wish." His intention from this was to prevent the man and woman from fornicating. May God's mercy and supreme pleasure be upon him.[45]

Here Aḥmad Ghazālī puts the wellbeing of a woman of ill repute and a promiscuous man above concern for his own social standing. Ghazālī lived in a society in which appearances were subject to constant scrutiny and gossip—complimentary and otherwise. For a Sufi master to take a prostitute into his own house was potentially scandal of a very high order. Yet we are told Ghazālī put himself in this situation to prevent the woman and her solicitor from committing a grave sin. This was, in Ghazālī's own terminology, an act of *malāmat*: intentionally incurring disrepute while remaining blameless in God's eyes.

Aḥmad Ghazālī's teachings on love

Nasrollah Pourjavady has called Aḥmad Ghazālī's *Sawāniḥ* the "scripture" of the Path of Love. Its salient features certainly deserve our attention here. The themes to be described served as points of departure for countless later Sufis. As we will ultimately see, many of these themes can be traced forward to the teachings of Hazrat Inayat Khan.

The words chosen to express love are not the same as its reality, the Sufis are at pains to remind us. Words of love reveal their full meaning only to those who directly experience what is described. The beautiful metaphor used by Aḥmad Ghazālī in the prologue of his work is this: "ideas of love are like virgins, and the

---

[45] Zakariyā Qazvīnī, *Āsār al-bilād*, cited in Mujāhid, *Majmū'a*, 33.

hand of words can not reach the hem of their skirt." Continuing in this erotic vein, Ghazālī suggests that one who intends to write about love needs to "marry" the "men of words" to the "virgins of ideas" in the "private chambers of speech."[46]

Ghazālī explains to the reader that his treatise is not confined to any specific modality of love. In treating love in and of itself, irrespective of attribution to either Creator (*khāliq*) or creature (*makhlūq*), he bypasses the much discussed categories of "Real Love" (*'ishq-i ḥaqīqī*) and "Metaphorical Love" (*'ishq-i majāzī*). According to proponents of this dichotomy, only God is worthy of Real love, while loves experienced in the terrestrial realm can be called love only in a metaphorical sense. Ghazālī circumvents all such considerations, saying: "the difference between the objects to which love turns is accidental."[47]

Interestingly, while Aḥmad Ghazālī's outlook is often worlds apart from the intricate metaphysical cosmology of Ibn 'Arabī, the two Sufis are in agreement on this point. Ibn 'Arabī shares the view that rather than "binding" oneself to a fixed understanding of God—making an idol of the Real, in effect—one's approach should be one of "perpetual transformation" *(taqallub)*—a dynamic and integrative process that can take place only in the heart (*qalb*).[48] Aḥmad Ghazālī and Ibn 'Arabi agree that, rather than limiting one's understanding to static notions of "human love" and "divine love," one must allow one's perspective to undergo continual mutation.

Ghazālī opens his book with the Qur'anic verse which may be legitimately described as the ocean into which for centuries the Sufis of the Path of Love have dived in search of pearls: "God Almighty has said: 'He loves them, and they love Him (*yuḥibbuhum wa yuḥibbūnahu*)'."[49]

It is no accident that God's love for humanity is mentioned first—Aḥmad Ghazālī speaks of the precedence of "He loves them" as humanity's "special privilege."[50] And humanity's response to God's

---

[46] Ghazālī, *Sawāniḥ*, trans. Pourjavady, 15

[47] Ibid.

[48] For a brilliant presentation of this teaching, see Michael Sells, "Ibn 'Arabi's Garden Among the Flames", *Mystical Language of Unsaying* (Chicago: University of Chicago Press, 1994), 90–92

[49] Qur'ān 5.54.

[50] Ghazālī, *Sawāniḥ*, trans. Pourjavady, 29.

love can be nothing but love itself. In a subtle language Ghazālī describes the interrelation:

> The root of love grows out of the infinite pre-existence. The diacritical dot of [the letter] "b" (ب) of *yuḥibbuhum* (He, i.e., God, loves them) was cast as a seed on the soil of *yuḥibbūnahu* (they love Him); nay, that dot was on *hum* (them) until *yuḥibbūnahu* (they love Him) grew out. When the narcissus of love grew out, the seed was of the same nature as the fruit and the fruit had the same nature as the seed.[51]

Affliction-in-love

The theme of the lover's affliction reaches back to the Pre-Islamic poetic trope of lamenting the departed caravan.[52] Junayd and other early Sufis explored this theme in the context of mystical experience.[53] The Sufis of the Path of Love took it further. Commenting on the Qur'ānic verse "When kings enter a village, they decimate it" (27.34), Aḥmad Ghazālī's disciple 'Ayn al-Qużāt interprets the decimation of a village as the divinely appointed affliction that wracks a servant's heart to the point that he becomes the affliction.[54] 'Ayn al-Qużāt maintains that no prophet ever suffered affliction in the way that Muḥammad (ص) did. The difference between "suffering" (*miḥnat*: محنت) and "love" (*maḥabbat*: محبت) is—orthographically speaking—merely in the placement of a dot.[55]

'Ayn al-Qużāt's observations have their basis in the love theory of the *Sawāniḥ*:

> Love, in its true nature, is but an affliction (*balā'*), and intimacy (*uns*) and ease are something alien to it and are provisionally borrowed. This is because separation in love is indeed duality while union is indeed oneness. Everything short of this is a delusion of union, not its true reality. This is why it is said:

---

[51] Ibid., 68–9.

[52] These themes have been well explored by the "Chicago school" of scholars of Arabic literature, including Suzanne P. Stetkevych, Jaroslav Stetkevych, Michael Sells, Th. Emil Homerin, etc.

[53] *The Life, Personality and Writings of al-Junayd*, ed. and trans. Ali Hassan Abdel-Kader (London: Gibb Memorial Trust, 1976), 152–159.

[54] Hamadānī, *Tamhīdāt*, 244.

[55] Ibid., 245.

> Love is an affliction and I am not about to abstain from affliction,
> [In fact] when love falls asleep I turn to it and raise it.
> My friends tell me to abstain from affliction
> Affliction is the heart, how can I abstain from the heart?[56]

Following his master's lead, 'Ayn al-Qużāt elevates the theme of affliction to hauntingly sublime heights: "whoever distinguishes between grace and wrath, is still in love with grace, or with wrath—but he is not yet a lover of the beloved!"[57] Rather than merely a necessary trial, affliction (*balā'*) is "the jewel of God's treasury":

> Take heed ... You think that they give affliction to just anyone? What do you know of affliction? Remain [on this path] till you get to the point where you will buy God's affliction [at the price] of your life-soul. It was from this same perspective that Shiblī said: "O God! Everyone seeks you for grace and ease, and I seek you for affliction." We do not destine anyone for affliction until we list him amongst the saints. This affliction is the jewel of our treasury. We do not bestow jewels to just any unrefined soul.[58]

The early Chishtī master Shaykh Niẓām al-Dīn Awliyā', an admirer of Aḥmad Ghazālī and 'Ayn al-Qużāt, as we shall see, recites:

> Even though He says He'll kill me,
> That He says it can't but thrill me![59]

The sophisticated mystical psychology of the Sufis of the Path of Love represents a profound understanding of the emotions of the soul. Emotions, whether positive or negative, joyous or painful, are not dismissed as illusory; rather, their reality is fully acknowledged. Recognizing the transmundane origin of emotions, the mystic's way is to utilize their power, sublimating desire through remembrance of the beloved.

Eye of the beholder

A "great secret" revealed by Aḥmad Ghazālī is the insight that each beloved's eye is blind to her own beauty. It is only through a lover that beauty can be witnessed: "Beauty necessitates a lover so

---

[56] Ghazālī, *Sawāniḥ*, trans. Pourjavady, 36.
[57] Hamadānī, *Tamhīdāt*, 179.
[58] Ibid, 243–3.
[59] *Nizam ad-Din Awliya: Morals for the Heart*, trans. Bruce Lawrence (New York: Paulist Press, 1992), 63.

that the beloved can take nutriment from her own beauty in the mirror of the lover's love and quest."[60]

In this vision of love, the hierarchical principle that characterizes master-disciple and lord-servant relationships is recast as a subtle dance of reciprocity. For all her coquetry (*nāz*) and charming claims of self-sufficiency, the beloved *needs* the lover. That the lover is utterly dependent (*niyāz*) on the beloved has been obvious all along; but now the beloved is exposed for being similarly obliged. The beauty of the beloved as herself is not the same as the beauty she has when a lover treats her as beautiful:

> The glance of loveliness (*kirishma-yi ḥusn*) is one thing and the [amorous] glance of belovedness (*kirishma-yi ma'shūqī*) is something else. The glance of loveliness has no "face" turned towards anything "other" [than love itself] and has no connection with anything outside [of love]. But as to the glance of belovedness and the amorous gestures, coquetry, and alluring self-glorification (*nāz*), they are all sustained by the lover, and without him they will have no effect. Therefore, this is why the beloved is in need of the lover. Loveliness is one thing and belovedness is something else.[61]

This distinction between "loveliness" and "belovedness" has important theological implications. Whereas in His Essence (*dhāt*) God is invariably regarded as completely transcendent and independent of all creation, the Divine Attributes (*ṣifāt*) may be seen as reflective of God's relationship with Creation. The Attributes of Mercy and Compassion, for example, are meaningful insofar as they have a recipient. And "The Lord" is only lordly in relation to a servant. From this perspective it can be said that creation is *needed* for God to realize the potential of his Attributes.[62]

Thus in the theology of the Path of Love, as in its psychology, the cosmos is appreciated as an inherently positive phenomenon. This view of the purposefulness of Creation is far from the gloomy gnosticism that repudiates *dunyā* (the world) as a veil or distraction. Its locus classicus is the sacred *ḥadīth*: "I was a Hidden Treasure,

---

[60] Ghazālī, *Sawāniḥ*, trans. Pourjavady, 33.

[61] Ibid., 31.

[62] See Henry Corbin, *Creative Imagination in the Sufism of Ibn 'Arabi*, trans. Ralph Manheim (Princeton: Princeton University Press, 1969), 115: "Thus the divine Names have meaning and full reality only through and for beings who are their epiphanic forms..."

and loved to be known intimately, so I created the Heavens and the Earth, so that they may come to intimately know Me."[63]

The very purpose of creation, these Sufis remind us, is for the Divine to manifest in utter fullness, and for the creation to come into an intimate relationship of knowledge and adoration with the Divine. While a created being can offer nothing of substance to the Creator, it can offer its needfulness, the one quality the Beloved lacks. This point is articulated wonderfully by Shams-i Tabrīzī in his *Maqālāt* (collected discourses):

> What good is it if you take your soul in hand, and present it [to God]? What use is it to take cumin to Kirman?[64] How will this add any value, or price, or cultivation (*lit.* water) to what is there? Since there is such a royal court, He is now without need (*bī-niyāz*), so take your needfulness (*niyāz*) there. Since the one without need likes needfulness. Using that needfulness, you can suddenly leap out of the midst of all these creatures (*ḥawādith*; *lit.* caused beings). Something from the Ancient One [God] will be joined to you, and *that* is love (*'ishq*). The trap of love has been set, and you are wrapped up in it, since "they love Him" (*yuḥibbūnahu*) is the impression of "He loves them" (*yuḥibbuhum*).[65]

'Ayn al-Qużāt Hamadānī

In studying the life and writings of 'Ayn al-Qużāt (492/1098-525/1131), one is overcome with a combination of sincere gratitude and wistful longing: gratitude for the wealth that he left behind, and longing for more. One conjectures that his name would today enjoy fame on par with that of Rūmī and Ibn 'Arabī had his young life not been savagely cut short by execution.

'Ayn al-Qużāt's biography is wrapped up in mythical accretions. In fact, it is precisely the tendency of hagiographers—and even contemporary scholars[66]—to depict 'Ayn al-Qużāt as a

---

[63] Badī' al-Zamān Furūzānfar, *Aḥādis-i masnavī* (Tehran: Amīr Kabīr, 1366/1987), 29.

[64] The city of Kirman was known as the main producer of Cumin (zīra) in Iran.

[65] Shams-i Tabrīz, *Maqālāt-i Shams-i Tabrīzī*, ed. Muḥammad 'Alī Muwaḥḥid (Tehran: Intishārāt-i Khwarazmī, 1369/1990), 69.

[66] Even Arberry falls prey to this tendency, introducing 'Ayn al-Qużāt as the middle member of a trinity of martyrs consisting of Ḥallāj, himself, and Shaykh al-Ishrāq Suhrawardī. A.J. Arberry, trans., *A Sufi Martyr: The Apologia of 'Ain al-Quḍāt al-Hamadhānī* (London: George Allen and Unwin Ltd, 1969), 9.

Ḥallājian martyr that has obscured his real claim to fame, his teachings. The legendary accounts of the end of his life are well known, and need not detain us here.

Suffice it to mention a memorable exchange cited in *Tazkirat al-'urafāt*. A theologian named Badī' resented 'Ayn al-Qużāt, and took exception to the fact that he had referred to God by the Avicennian term "the Necessary Being" (*wājib al-wujūd*), contending that the Divine Names should be limited to those in the Qur'ān and the *ḥadīth*.[67] Undeterred, 'Ayn al-Qużāt responded: "He is my beloved, and I will call him by whatever name I please!"[68]

The historicity of this story may well be doubted, but it does convey something of the defiant brashness of the fiery young love-possessed mystic whom later generations would call the "Sultan of Lovers" (*sulṭān al-'ushshāq*).[69] It is this style, above all else, that characterizes his writings, particularly the *Tamhīdāt*.

'Ayn al-Qużāt's relationship with his spiritual mentor Aḥmad Ghazālī is an important link in the genealogy of the Path of Love. In this profound relationship, hierarchy recedes in importance and each soul becomes for the other a polished mirror in which to contemplate spiritual realities. 'Ayn al-Qużāt's own account of meeting Aḥmad Ghazālī deserves to be quoted at length:

> After I had become disheartened with the conventional forms of learning, I occupied myself with the writings of "The Proof of Islam" [Abū Ḥāmid Ghazālī], and spent four years on them until I achieved that which I had been seeking in them, and achieved Union. I was close to ceasing my quest (*ṭalab*), and to limit myself to that which I had discovered from religious sciences.
>
> I remained in that station for one year, until my lord and master, the Shaykh, the Imām, the Sultan of the spiritual path, Aḥmad ibn Muḥammad ibn Muḥammad ibn Ghazālī, may God have mercy on him, came to my hometown, Hamadān. In twenty days of companionship with him such things became manifest to me that nothing remained of "me", and "my desires", except that which

---

[67] Badī' attributes *wājib al-wujūd* to the lexicon of the *ḥukamā'* ("sages"), a term often used for philosophers and physicians.

[68] Raḥīm Farmānish, *Aḥvāl va āsār-i ʿAyn al-Qużāt*, (Tehran: Chāp-i Āftāb, 1338/1959), 68.

[69] E.g., 'Azīz al-Dīn Nasafī, *Insān al-kāmil* (Tehran: Kitābkhāna-yi Ṭahūrī, 1359/1980), 403.

> God has willed. Nothing occupies me now except a quest of annihilation in *that*.
>
> Even if I attain to Noah's [longevity] in life, and annihilate myself in this quest, it is as if I have done nothing—and that *thing* has taken hold of the whole world. My glance has not fallen upon any thing, without seeing *his face* in it. If any breath does not increase my "drowning" in it/him, may it not be blessed for me![70]

Extant writings of 'Ayn al-Qużāt

During the brief thirty-three years that 'Ayn al-Qużāt lived, he authored a number of works, most of which are sadly lost. His masterpiece, without a doubt, is the *Tamhīdāt.*[71] It may very well be said that the *Tamhīdāt* and the *Sawāniḥ* are the foundational texts of the Path of Love. The two go hand in hand, and it is practically impossible to understand one without the other. The *Tamhīdāt* can be read as an extensive commentary on the subtle points of the *Sawāniḥ*. On its own merits alone the *Tamhīdāt* is one of the most important pre-modern Sufi texts, providing an abundance of information about numerous Sufis whose names and words remain otherwise unknown.

Some of 'Ayn al-Qużāt's other works may also be mentioned. *Zubdat al-ḥaqā'iq* ("The Choicest of Spiritual Realities") is an earlier *kalām* (dialectical theology) work.[72] The three volume *Nāma-hā*, comprising more than a hundred of 'Ayn al-Qużāt's letters to various disciples, marks one of the most impressive extant collections of letters from a Sufi master.[73] 'Ayn al-Qużāt's final

---

[70] Jāmī, *Nafaḥāt al-uns*, 418. Jāmī states that he is quoting (a translation) of 'Ayn al-Qużat Hamadānī's *Zubdat al-ḥaqā'iq*, apparently 6–7.

[71] I am preparing an English translation of this work, which will be published—God willing—in 2002 or 2003. The *Tamhīdāt* is already available in a good French translation: *Les Tentations Metaphysiques*, trans. Christiane Tortel (Paris: Les Deux Oceans, 1992).

[72] This work has been edited by 'Afīf 'Usayrān (Tehran: Intishārāt-i Dānishgāh-i Tihrān, 1961). Dr. Omar Jah, in Malaysia, is working on a soon to be published translation of this text.

[73] 'Ayn al-Qużāt Hamadānī, *Nāma-hā-yi 'Ayn al-Qużāt Hamadānī*, vols. 1 and 2, ed. 'Alī-Naqī Munzavī and 'Afīf 'Usayrān (Tehran: Bunyād-i Farhang-i Irān, 1363/1983); vol. 3, ed. 'Alī-Naqī Munzavī, (Tehran: Intishārāt-i Asāṭīr, 1377/1998). Inexplicably, the third volume features a prolix and theoretically flawed introduction by Munzavī, in which 'Ayn al-Qużāt is classified as an "Isma'ili (or esoteric) gnostic" (*gnūsīst-i bātinī*!) and "nationalistic tension" (*kashākash-hā-yi millī*) between Iranians, Arabs, and Turks is anachronistically read into events of the 12th and 13th centuries (58).

work is *Shakwa al-gharīb,* an apologia penned in prison. It is available in a good English translation.[74]

Among academic studies of 'Ayn al-Qużāt, the most helpful remain those of Raḥīm Farmānish[75] and Nasrollah Pourjavady.[76] The studies of Carl Ernst[77] and Leonard Lewisohn[78] also deserve mention. Perhaps the most ambitious project, yet also the most problematic from the perspective of reading 'Ayn al-Qużāt as a Sufi, is Hamid Dabashi's massive work, *Truth and Narrative: The Untimely Thoughts of 'Ayn al-Quḍāt Hamadānī.*[79]

We may now examine some important passages from the *Tamhīdāt*, which elucidate the salient features of 'Ayn al-Qużāt's teachings on love.

Loving God, loving all

The relationship between love for God and love for created beings was the subject of a major theoretical debate among the Sufis in this period. As we have seen, a number of early Sufis considered it inappropriate to apply the term *'ishq* to the love of God.[80] Others, such as Rūzbihān Baqlī, wished to defend the inclusivity of *'ishq*, and suggested that human love was a "ladder" leading to divine love.[81] Later Sufis, and indeed many contemporary scholars of

---

[74] A. J. Arberry, trans., *A Sufi Martyr*, op. cit.

[75] Farmānish, *Aḥvāl va āsār-i 'Ayn al-Qużāt*, op. cit.

[76] Nasrollah Pourjavady, *'Ayn al-Qużāt va ustādān-i ū* (Tehran: Intishārāt-i Asāṭīr, 1374/1995).

[77] Carl Ernst, "Ayn al-Qudat Hamadānī,"in *Words of Ecstasy in Sufism* (Albany: State University of New York Press, 1985), 73–84.

[78] Leonard Lewisohn, "In Quest of Annihilation: Imaginalization and Mystical Death in the *Tamhīdāt* of 'Ayn al-Quḍāt Hamadhānī," in *Classical Persian Sufism: from its Origins to Rumi*, ed. L. Lewisohn (New York: Khaniqahi Nimatullahi Publications, 1992), 285–336.

[79] Hamid Dabashi, *Truth and Narrative: The Untimely Thoughts of 'Ayn al-Quḍāt Hamadānī* (Richmond, England: Curzon Press, 1999). Dabashi's highly original and erudite book is at the same time one of the most problematic recent intellectual studies of Sufism. One could argue that Dabashi is not, as he claims, "rescuing" 'Ayn al-Qużāt, but merely moving him from one "limiting category" (to use Dabashi's words) to another—from Sufism to post-modernism.

[80] 'Ali B. Uthmān Al-Jullābī Al-Hujwīrī, *The Kashf Al-Maḥjūb*, trans. Reynold A. Nicholson (London: Gibb Memorial Trust, 1976), 310.

[81] Rūzbihān Baqlī, *'Abhar al-'āshiqīn*, ed. Henry Corbin and Muḥammad Mu'īn (Tehran: Intishārāt-i Manūchihrī, 1366/1987), 88: *'ishq al-insān sullam 'ishq al-raḥmān.* As I will suggest later, these divisions are arguably somewhat

Sufism, have preferred to refer to love for God as "real love" (*'ishq-i ḥaqīqī*) and relegate love for created beings to a "metaphorical" or "borrowed" (*majāzī*) status.[82] Without resorting to polemics, the Sufis of the Path of Love distanced themselves from these categories, describing divine love instead as an *'ishq* that enfolds the whole of creation.

'Ayn al-Quẓāt writes:

> Whoever loves God should also love His Messenger, Muḥammad, his own spiritual teacher and his own life. He also loves food and drink which extends his life that he may spend in obedience [to God]. He loves women so that the progeny will not be interrupted. He loves silver and gold so that through them he can attain to food and drink. He loves the cold, and the heat, the snow and the rain since if not for them, wheat would not grow. Like this, he also loves the farmer. He loves the Heaven and the Earth since they are God's handcraft: A lover loves the handwriting and every action of the Beloved. All the creatures are His handcraft and action. Loving them for the sake of following His love is no polytheism.[83]

Love as obligation

'Ayn al-Quẓāt earned his honorific—literally, "source (or essence, spring, eye) of judges"—in his training as an Islamic jurist. From this background he introduces legal terminology into the discourse of love in a refreshingly bold manner. Islamic legal jurisprudence is concerned with classifying actions within the categories of "obligatory," "meritorious," "disapproved" and "forbidden."[84] It is with great subtlety, humor, and irony that 'Ayn al-Quẓāt invokes the juridical category of "religious obligation" (*farż*) to talk about love:

> O precious one! Arriving at God is a religious obligation. To those on the [spiritual] quest, whatever through which one arrives

arbitrary. But even in the writings of Hazrat Inayat Khan, who tends to transcend these conventional divisions, one comes across statements which reinforce the notion of human love as pedagogy, e.g.: "When one has risen above human love, divine love springs forth." (*Complete Works, Sayings I*, 1:371).

[82] William Chittick, *Sufi Path of Love* (Albany: State University of New York Press, 1983), 200–1.

[83] Hamadānī, *Tamhīdāt*, 140.

[84] For these legal classifications, and the distinction between *farż* and *wājib*, refer to Mohammad Hashim Kamali, *Prinicples of Islamic Jurisprudence* (Cambridge: Islamic Texts Society, 1991), 324–7.

> at God is a religious obligation. What delivers the servant to the Divine is Love. In this sense, love has become an obligation (*farż*) on the Path … [85]

One can almost see the smirk on the young mystic's face, as he adjudges passionate love a religious obligation for all on the spiritual path. For some time scholars of the Ḥanbalī and other legal schools had been involved in scrutinizing love from a nomocentric perspective.[86] Here 'Ayn al-Qużāt seems to be returning the favor, bringing the actual experience of love to bear on the language of law.

Sufis like 'Ayn al-Qużāt did not limit their analyses to terrestrial phenomena; some of the most intriguing teachings of the Path of Love contemplate the celestial spheres. One such doctrine is 'Ayn al-Qużāt's concept of a paradise beyond the believer's wildest dreams.

A paradise beyond paradise

Since Rābi'a (d. 801), Sufis have frequently spoken of the value of seeking God for his own sake, without concern for the joys of paradise and the torments of hellfire.[87] 'Ayn al-Qużāt takes this idea further, describing paradise as a "prison for the [spiritual] elite." In support he quotes Yaḥyā Mu'ādh Rāzī: "Paradise is the prison of the gnostics, as the world is the prison of the believers." To the conventional conception 'Ayn al-Qużāt offers a radical alternative—"God's paradise":

> The [spiritual] elite are with God. What do you say? That God Almighty is in paradise? Yes, he is in paradise, but in his own paradise—in that paradise that Shiblī spoke of: "There is not, and will never be, anyone in paradise except God Almighty." If you like, hear it from Muṣṭafā as well: "Verily God has a paradise, in which there are no houris, no palaces, no milk, and no honey." And what is in this "God's own Paradise"? That "which no eyes have seen, no ears have heard, and thought of which has not occurred to people's heart." For one who thinks of *this* as paradise, to seek the paradise of the masses is an error. If this group is dragged to paradise in chains of light and grace, they do not go and do not accept … [88]

[85] Hamadānī, *Tamhīdāt*, 97.
[86] For an examination of these themes, see Joseph Bell, *Love Theory in Later Hanbalite Islam* (Albany: State University of New York Press, 1979).
[87] 'Aṭṭār, *Tazkirat al-awliyā'*, 87.
[88] Hamadānī, *Tamhīdāt*, 136.

What is rejected here is not so much the Qur'ānic imagery of paradise, as the tendency of ordinary believers to fixate on these descriptions to the neglect of the One beyond paradise—the cup-bearer who proffers the wine, in the language of poetry. Concurrent with the trend towards transcending the symbols of salvation, among which paradise is pre-eminent, the Sufis of the Path of Love also sought to overcome attachment to particular means of salvation. It is to the explicit universalism of the Path of Love that we now turn.

Paths as waystations

Sufis have often insisted that Truth (*Ḥaqq*) must be identified with God's very Being, rather than with an intellectual conception or spiritual path. To label a religious tradition—even Islam—as "Truth" is to commit the great sin of "associationism" (*shirk*, "polytheism"), since *al-Ḥaqq* is a Divine Name. A frequently cited Qur'ānic verse declares: "We shall show them our signs (*ayāt*) on the farthest horizons, and inside their own selves until it becomes clear to them that He is *al-Ḥaqq*."[89]

'Ayn al-Qużāt approaches this theme from another angle, appealing to the diversity of faith perspectives. In one sweep he mentions Muslims, Jews, Christians, Zoroastrians, and Idol-worshippers—the entire spectrum of religiosity known to him:

> O friend! If you would see what the Christians see in Jesus, you too would become a Christian! And if you would see what the Jews see in Moses, you too would become a Jew! Even more, if you would see what idol-worshippers see in idol-worship, you too would become an idol-worshipper! The seventy-two paths (*mazhab-hā*) are all way stages on the road to God.[90]

Once again, 'Ayn al-Qużāt's choice of words is profound. He mixes metaphors deliberately, depicting spiritual paths (*mazhab-hā*) as waystations (*manāzil*; sing., *manzil*) on the caravan trail, a traditional Sufi image associated with progressive inner states. The important point about a *manzil*, of course, is that it refers to a temporary lodging, where one merely pauses en route to one's ultimate destination—the Presence of God.

---

[89] Qur'ān 41:53.
[90] Hamadānī, *Tamhīdāt*, 285.

Many of these themes were further developed by the next monumental figure in the Path of Love: Mawlānā Jalāl al-Dīn Balkhī, known in the modern West as Rūmī.

Jalāl al-Dīn Rūmī

While Rūmī recognized the inadequacy of words and concepts, perhaps no Sufi has ever produced a greater abundance of images and metaphors in speaking about love. Some of his verbal portraits of love are hauntingly beautiful; others are hilariously funny. Rūmī's stories and poems continue to circulate from heart to heart the world over.

A great deal has been written about Rūmī, and we need not cover old ground.[91] In any case, Rūmī's imagery of love is far too extensive to be surveyed here. A full study has recently been published on this topic.[92] What need to be emphasized here are the historical connections between Rūmī and the figures under discussion.

The most explicit connections are between Rūmī and Aḥmad Ghazālī. Rūmī's principal biographer Aflākī reports:

> He [Rūmī] also stated: "Imām Muḥammad Ghazālī, may God have mercy on him, has dived into the Ocean of the Universe, attained to a world of dominion, and unfurled the banner of knowledge. The whole world follows him, and he has become the scholar of all the worlds. Still ... If he had had an iota of passionate love like Aḥmad Ghazālī, it would have been better, and he would have made known the secret of the Muḥammadan intimacy (*sirr-i qurbat-i Muḥammadī*) the way Aḥmad did. In the whole world, there is no teacher, no spiritual guide, and no unifier like love."[93]

A still more direct connection can also be established through the spiritual chain of transmission (*silsila*) provided by Aflākī, in

---

[91] The classic works on Rumi are Annemarie Schimmel, *I am Wind, You are Fire* (Boston: Shambhala, 1992); idem, *The Triumphal Sun* (London: Fine Books, 1978); William Chittick, *The Sufi Path of Love*, op. cit. To these must now be added Frank Lewis, *Rumi: Past and Present, East and West* (Oxford: Oneworld, 2000), a meticulous piece of scholarship work that has set the new standard for Rumi studies.

[92] A.G. Ravan-Farhadi, *Ma'nī-yi 'ishq nazd-i Mawlānā* (Tehran: Intishārāt-i Asāṭīr, 1372/1993).

[93] Aflākī, *Manāqib al-'ārifīn*, ed. Tahsin Yazici (Tehran: Dunyā-yi Kitāb, 1362/1983), 1:219.

which Aḥmad Ghazālī figures as a predecessor of Rūmī.[94] From a historical perspective, there are some good reasons to doubt the veracity of this *silsila*. Nonetheless, it is evidence of the fact that the spiritual community descended from Rūmī placed a premium on the legacy of Aḥmad Ghazālī.

Rūmī also makes repeated use of the terminology of the Path of Love. Aflākī's *Manāqib al-'ārifin* contains a story in which Rūmī describes the *ṣadr* (head) of a gathering of those who follow the "path of lovers" (*mazhab-i 'āshiqān*) as being any place that is next to the beloved.[95] The same language is frequently found in his poetry. He declares, for instance, "In the path of lovers, to be away from the friend's alley even for an instant is forbidden (*ḥarām*)!"[96] Like 'Ayn al-Qużāt, here is another Sufi judge using Islamic legal terminology to characterize the Path of Love.

Reading Rūmī's poetry in the context of the Path of Love

Rūmī's voluminous works were not read in isolation, but in a context informed by the Qur'ān, Prophetic traditions, and the Sufi literary canon. In Iran, India and Anatolia, later Sufis wove a brilliant tapestry from the writings of Rūmī, 'Ayn al-Qużāt, and Aḥmad Ghazālī, not to mention Jāmī, 'Aṭṭār, Sanā'ī, Niẓāmī and others. The intertextuality of the Path of Love can be documented in the manuscript catalogues of Sufi shrines, such as the *tekkes* of Rūmī's Mevlevi (P., Mawlavī) Order.

The massive collection of manuscripts at the Mevlevi shrine complex in Konya, Turkey, was catalogued by the late Abdulbaki Gulpinarli.[97] The catalogue serves to inform us which texts the pre-modern Mevlevis were reading. Medieval manuscripts of Sufi works were usually not preserved individually, but as part of larger collections (*majmū'a*). Treatises gathered in a single collection would be read together. We can gleam a great deal about the context

[94] Ibid., 2:998. This silsila comprises: the Prophet Muḥammad, 'Alī, Ḥasan Basrī ... Abū Bakr Nassāj, Aḥmad Ghazālī, Aḥmad Khātibī Balkhī, Shams al-A'ima Sarakhsī, Bahā' Walad, Burhān al-Dīn Muḥaqqiq Tirmidhī, and finally, Mawlānā Jalāl [al-Dīn Rūmī].

[95] Ibid., 1:122.

[96] Rūmī, *Dīvān-i Shams-i Tabrīzī*, 1:225, line 4070.

[97] *Mevlânâ Muzesi: Yazmalar Katalogu*, ed. Abdulbaki Gulpinarli (Ankara: Turk Tarih Kurumu, 1967–1972).

in which a particular text was read by noting the texts with which it is grouped.

When the writings of the earlier masters of the Path of Love occur in the Mevlana Muzesi catalogue, it is almost invariably alongside Rūmī's works or commentaries on them. 'Ayn al-Qużāt's *Tamhīdāt*, for instance, was read along with the *Jawāhir al-asrār* ("The Jewels of Secrets") of Husayn Khwarazmī, an important commentary on Rūmī's *Masnavi*.[98] In other words, the Mevlevis read the *Tamhīdāt* as elucidating the commentaries on the *Masnavi*, and vice versa. Another collection contains the Letters (*Nāma-hā*) of 'Ayn al-Qużāt and the *Masnavī* of Rūmī.[99] Here is the ultimate case for the commensurableness, in the eyes of the Mevlevis, of these two Path of Love classics.

The polemics of *shāhid-bāzī*

Rūmī and his community provide us with important information about some of the controversies surrounding the Sufis of the Path of Love. The most frequently discussed controversy, in the literature of the Sufis and their opponents alike, is the debate over *shāhid-bāzī* (*lit.* witness play).

Aḥmad Ghazālī's legacy reflects a consistent fascination with earthly manifestations of divine beauty. Like many Sufis before and after him, Ghazālī would sometimes gaze on the faces of beautiful youths, as a meditative practice. As might be expected, this led many, including some Sufis, to criticize him and those who followed in his footsteps. The contemporary reader, aware of the frequency of abuse under the cover of spirituality, might be taken aback by what seems to be a sensual mode of interaction between spiritual teacher and disciple. It should be noted, however, that there is no suggestion in Ghazālī's writings that his practice involved physical contact. On the contrary, for Ghazālī and many other witness-players consummation was contrary to the nature of the practice. The whole point was to harness the power of anticipation in sublimating desire.[100]

---

[98] Ibid., 2:iv.
[99] Ibid., 3:xvi.
[100] Peter Lamborn Wilson, *Scandal*, 99: "In Tantrik terms one might say that chastity builds up a psychic energy which can be turned towards spiritual

The need for chastity was frequently emphasized by Aḥmad Ghazālī and 'Ayn al-Quḍāt. 'Ayn al-Quḍāt begins his discussion of "the reality and spiritual station of love" in the *Tamhīdāt* with the Prophetic tradition: "Whoever loves passionately, and remains chaste in this love, and hides it, and dies in this love, dies the death of a martyr."[101]

The followers of these masters, however, at times proved far less discriminating, prompting a barrage of criticism. The critics of witness play were usually uninterested in its nuances, and tended to tar all of its practioners with the same brush. One of those who criticized Aḥmad Ghazālī was the influential austere preacher Ibn Jawzī (d. 1200). He provides us with a story about Aḥmad Ghazālī, the endearing quality of which was no doubt lost on him. While one would hesitate to confirm the factuality of material from a polemical source, this vignette is too vivid and sweet to be left untranslated:

> A group of Sufis came to visit Aḥmad Ghazālī. When they entered, they saw that he was sitting alone with a beardless youth. Placed between them was a bouquet of roses. Aḥmad cast his glance now at the roses, now at the youth. When the group of Sufis were seated, one of them said: "Perhaps we are interrupting?" Aḥmad said: "By God, yes!" The whole group screamed in ecstasy ...[102]

Summing up the frustrations of numerous religious scholars, and even some Sufis, Abū Sa'īd al-Sam'anī directed these remarks against Aḥmad Ghazālī:[103]

> This is pure infidelity, which requires the shedding of blood and the destruction of souls. But none of the eminent people of that time approached God for the blood of this sinner.[104]

Nor did all condemnations of witness play come from enemies of Sufism. In fact, the most well-known critique of this practice arose within the Path of Love itself. The most controversial figure

---

ends, 'sublimed' (in alchemical terms) and used in the Transmutation."

[101] Hamadānī, *Tamhīdāt*, 96.

[102] Ibn Jawzī, *Talbīs Iblīs*; cited in Mujahid, *Majmū'a*, 36.

[103] Al-Sam'anī's comments arose in the context Aḥmad Ghazālī's unconventional satanology, but I believe the mood expressed is indicative of a broader rejection of Aḥmad Ghazālī on the part of conservative elements.

[104] Abū Sa'īd al-Sam'anī's comments were recorded by Sibṭ al-Jawzī, which in turn are cited in Farmānish, *Aḥvāl va āsār-i 'Ayn al-Qużat Hamadānī*, 76. I owe this citation to Carl Ernst, *Words of Ecstasy in Sufism*, 162, n. 83.

associated with witness play was Awḥad al-Dīn Kirmānī, whose encounter with Shams-i Tabrīzī is often discussed.[105] Shams, we are told, came upon Kirmānī "gazing at the image of the moon reflected on a body of water." He asked Awḥad al-Dīn why—unless there was something wrong with his neck—did he not look directly at the moon?[106] Shams' remark must be read as a thinly disguised critique of witness play.

Similar denunciations of Kirmānī's indulgence in witness play were evoked from Rūmī. *Manāqib al-'ārifīn* narrates an incident in which some of Rūmī's disciples mentioned Awḥad al-Dīn, saying that while he did engage in witness play, he "played it clean" and did not "do anything." The Mawlānā reportedly responded: "Would that he *had* done something, and then abandoned the whole practice!"[107] In a subsequent section, Rūmī criticizes Awḥad al-Dīn's alleged homosexuality, saying: "Shaykh Awḥad al-Dīn has left a bad legacy behind in this world. He carries that sin, and the sins of all those who engage in that act."[108]

The later Persian poet-saint 'Abd al-Raḥmān Jāmī (d. 1492), whose work represents a synthesis of the Path of Love and the Akbarian tradition, made an attempt to redeem the reputation of the major Sufis who engaged in witness play. He offers this defense:

---

[105] See Peter Lamborn Wilson, "The Witness Game: Imaginal Yoga and Sacred Pedophilia in Persian Sufism", in *Scandal*, 93–121. The deliberately controversial phrase "sacred pedophilia" notwithstanding, the article is an insightful analysis of *shāhid-bāzī*.

[106] Aflākī, *Manāqib al-'ārifīn*, 2:616; Jāmī, *Nafaḥāt al-uns*, 465, 590. It is significant that the other hagiography of Rūmī, written by Sipāhsālār, which is more favorable towards the Akbarian school, does not include this account, but includes Kirmānī in a benign narrative praising Mawlānā. See Sipāhsālār, *Risāla-yi Sipāhsālār*, ed. Sa'īd Nafīsī (Tehran: 1325/1947; reprint, Iqbal Press, 1368/1989), 28.

[107] Aflākī, *Manāqib al-'ārifīn*, 1:439. This account can be independently verified through Jāmī, *Nafaḥāt al-uns*, 590, and also 461, where he is even more explicit: "But he played it clean, and did not engage in any inappropriate (*nā-shāyist*) action." Furthermore, it is significant to note that while Aflākī records a poem of Mawlānā which states: "whoever establishes an ill precedent (*nā-khūsh sunnatī*) is constantly cursed," Jāmī includes the following poem instead: "The reason that I look at the Form through these eyes is because there is a trace of Reality upon the Form. This is a world of Forms, and we are [immersed] in Form; therefore one cannot see Reality except through Form." It is clear that Aflākī's poem affirms the condemnation of Kirmānī, while Jāmī's is intended to soften the critique and extend his own apologetic on behalf of Awḥad al-Dīn.

[108] Aflākī, *Manāqib al-'ārifīn*, 1:440. Significantly, Jāmī does not record this part of the account.

> The best opinion, indeed the truth of the matter, regarding some of the great saints such as Shaykh Aḥmad Ghazālī and Shaykh Awḥad al-Dīn Kirmānī, may God Almighty sanctify their innermost hearts, is this. While they engaged in studying the beauty of external phenomena on the level of forms, utilizing the senses, they contemplated the Absolute Beauty of God in those forms. They were not bound by the form that is perceptible through the senses.
>
> If some of the saints have objected to them [on account of this practice], their intention from this objection is to make sure that others who are veiled would not make this practice a license [to follow their own passions]. [Therefore, those veiled ones] would not make an analogy of their own [lowly, impure] spiritual state with that of the saints, thus avoid being stuck in the basest of disappointments, and the "lowest of low natures" (Qur'ān 95.5).[109]

Clearly the issue is a complex one, the moral ramifications of which are outside the scope of this paper. It is enough to point out the extent to which some Sufis have gone in aestheticizing piety. It is this same trend which, in a rather different trajectory, finds emphatic expression in Hazrat Inayat Khan's work.

Muḥyī al-Dīn Ibn 'Arabī

As we have seen, the Path of Love has a synthetic quality. It is precisely this inclusivity which allowed it to absorb various Sufi theories which were in origin quite distinct from the teachings of Aḥmad Ghazālī and 'Ayn al-Qużāt. One such strand, appropriated by many Sufis of the Path of Love in Iran and India, was the Akbarian tradition traced to Ibn 'Arabī.

It would be a clear mistake to characterize Ibn 'Arabī's teaching as an arid metaphysical system bereft of the tenderness of love. Ibn 'Arabī's well-known poem features the same motifs of universality and love that mark the Path of Love:

---

[109]Jami, *Nafaḥāt al-uns*, 589–591. For a vastly different yet profound reading of this same narrative, see Nasrollah Pourjavady's discussion in *Rū'yat-i māh dar asmān: La vision de Dieu en théologie et en mystique musulmanes* (Tehran: Markaz-i Nashr-i Dānishgāhī, 1375/1996), 27–40, where he analyzes the same narrative not as a pretext for a critique of *shāhid-bāzī*, but as a hermeneutic difference in the mystical problematic of contemplating the Divine Being's reflection on the level of forms.

Wonder,
a garden among the flames!

My heart can take on
any form:
a meadow for gazelles,
a cloister for monks,

For the idols, sacred ground,
Ka'ba for the circling pilgrim,
the tables of the Torah,
the scrolls of the Qur'an.

My creed is love;
wherever its caravan turns along the way,
that is my belief,
my faith.[110]

This poem has its own theoretical context, however.[111] Indeed, scholars such as Pourjavady favor specifically excluding Ibn 'Arabī from the genealogy of the Path of Love. Nonetheless, one has to acknowledge that many later masters of Path of Love Sufism did in fact incorporate Akbarian teachings. How are we to reconcile this contradiction? The best answer seems to be to recall the assimilative nature of the Path of Love. While in the beginning there were some tensions between some of the followers of the Path of Love and the exponents of Akbarian teachings,[112] in time the two came to be more or less harmonized. This was particularly the case in India, the theater to which we now turn.

The transmission of the Path of Love in India

The spiritual, intellectual, and aesthetic universes of Persia and India were much more closely interconnected in the pre-modern era than the contemporary situation might suggest. Persian was the primary language of Sufi discourse in India for long generations (gradually replaced by Urdu in the eighteenth century). Many Sufis

---

[110] Michael Sells, *The Mystical Language of Unsaying*, 90.

[111] Ibid.

[112] For historical connections between Rūmī and Ibn 'Arabī, and the problematic of retrospectively projecting the later synthesis back to the period of Rūmī and Ibn 'Arabī's own time, see my "Did the Two Oceans Meet? Connections and Disconnections between Ibn al-'Arabī and Rūmī," *Journal of the Muhyiddin Ibn 'Arabi Society* xxvi (1999), 55–88.

traveled back and forth between these two lands. The Path of Love, which had taken hold in Persia, was now to flourish in India. Aḥmad Ghazālī, ʻAyn al-Qużāt and Rūmī became well known in India.[113] No less an authority than Annemarie Schimmel observes: "The strongest influence of Rūmī's work in the countries east of Suez is visible in the Indo-Pakistan Sub-continent."[114] Schimmel elsewhere notes the popularity that ʻAyn al-Qużāt's writings enjoyed in fourteenth-century Delhi, citing the contemporary historian Barani.[115]

The masters of the Chishtiyya, perhaps to a greater degree than any other order in India or Persia, developed the themes of the Path of Love with depth and artistry. The remainder of this essay will be devoted to this line of transmission, traced through Niẓām al-Dīn Awliyā', Naṣīr al-Dīn Chirāgh-i Dihlī, Sayyid Muḥammad Gīsū Darāz, Muḥammad Chishtī, Shāh Kalīm Allāh, and finally Hazrat Inayat Khan.

Niẓām al-Dīn Awliyā'

Perhaps the most revealing window into Khwāja Niẓām al-Dīn Awliyā's (d. 1325) lifework is the collection of his conversations (*malfūẓāt*) entitled *Fawā'id al-fu'ād*, translated by Bruce Lawrence as *Morals for the Heart*.[116] This important historical document features several references to ʻAyn al-Qużāt Hamadānī and Aḥmad Ghazālī. Khwāja Niẓām al-Dīn mentions the intimate spiritual connection between them, while, intriguingly, denying that they were master and disciple.[117] In another passage Khwāja Niẓām al-Dīn discusses ʻAyn al-Qużāt's relationship with his father. Further

---

[113] The writings of some of the masters of the Firdawsī Order, such as Sharaf al-Dīn Manerī, also display a profound engagement with the seminal figures of *mazhab-i 'ishq*. Cf. Sharaf ad-Din Maneri, "On the Necessity of Proper Intention," trans. Paul Jackson, in *Windows on the House of Islam: Muslim Sources on Spirituality and Religious Life*, ed. John Renard (Berkeley: University of California Press, 1998), 60.

[114] Annemarie Schimmel, *The Triumphal Sun*, 374. While many passionate lovers of Mawlānā in Turkey and Iran might sigh in disagreement with this characterization, it does offer a valuable estimation of the impact of Rumi on Indo-Persian piety and poetics.

[115] Annemarie Schimmel, *Mystical Dimensions of Islam*, (Chapel Hill: University of North Carolina Press, 1975), 348.

[116] Nizam ad-din Awliya, *Morals for the Heart*, op. cit.

[117] Ibid., 177.

on, the Khwāja relates how Aḥmad Ghazālī invited blame while remaining a model of moral purity.[118] This demonstrates that Niẓām al-Dīn viewed Aḥmad Ghazālī and 'Ayn al-Qużāt as exemplary Sufis worthy of imitation.

An important hagiography written by a disciple of Khwāja Niẓām al-Dīn, *Siyar al-awliyā'* offers an extended account of 'Ayn al-Qużāt's death, which suggests that the Chishtīs were as interested in his legendary martyrdom as they were in the content of his teachings:

> When 'Ayn al-Qużāt Hamadānī experienced a rare illumination (*tajallī*), in the essence of that world, he made a wish that he would be burned while God looked on.
>
> I grieve not that they burn this wretch in your alley—
> What pains me is that they do it on your doorstep.
>
> This thought brought about a charge of heresy against him. Khwāja Aḥmad Ghazālī told him to write something about his beliefs in order to secure his release. He replied that he had prayed that this very day would come. At the time 'Ayn al-Qużāt's age was twenty-five years. He was burned alive. As he was burning he uttered a sigh. People said, "You said you have prayed for this day—why do you now sigh?" He replied, "I do not sigh for being burned, but I sigh that I should burn more quickly." …
>
> They say that a small box appeared in the place where they burned 'Ayn al-Qużāt, upon which was imprinted:
>
> This poor heart of mine:
> A jewel-box holding your hidden secrets.
> What I fear is this:
> That it will fall in the hands of a stranger.
>
> In short, the box was opened and this quatrain was found inside:
>
> I have asked my Lord for a martyr's death
> I have asked for three worthless things.
> If the Friend would do as I ask,
> I have asked for fire, oil, and kindling.[119]

[118] My reading differs slightly, but significantly, from that offered in *Morals for the Heart*, 177. I have relied here on the most recent publication of this text: Khwāja Ḥasan Dihlavī (Amīr Ḥasan Sizjī), *Fawā'id al-fū'ād: malfūẓāt-i Khwāja Niẓām al-Dīn Awliyā'*, ed. Muḥammad Laṭīf Mulk (Tehran: Intishārāt-i Rūzāna, 1377/1997), 104–5.

[119] Among other sources, this apocryphal poem is quoted by Amīn Aḥmad Rāzī, author of *Haft aqlīm*, cited in Ghulām Rižā Afrasiyābī, *Sulṭān al-'ushshāq*, 18. Also see the account in Farmānish, 68, citing *Tazkira-yi 'urafāt*.

> Indeed they had wrapped him in a straw mat, poured naphtha over him, and then burned him.[120]

Naṣīr al-Dīn Chirāgh-i Dihlī

The collected conversations of Niẓām al-Dīn's successor Naṣīr al-Dīn Chirāgh-i Dihlī also include mention of both Aḥmad Ghazālī[121] and 'Ayn al-Qużāt. After citing the tradition "God created Adam in his image," Naṣīr al-Dīn enters into a discussion of the meaning of "his image." This brings him to another tradition, one that he describes as "difficult to express in both the spiritual Way (*ṭarīqat*) and the religious Law (*sharī'at*)." 'Ayn al-Qużāt is the source:

> He said that 'Ayn al-Qużāt Hamadānī, may God have mercy upon him, has recorded (the Messenger of God's) (peace and blessings (of God) be upon him) statement: "I saw my lord in the image of a young man, with long hair." The Khwāja said "this *ḥadīth* is not recorded in the well-known books. If the authenticity of this *ḥadīth* is established, I will take it to have an allegorical meaning."[122]

In describing the *ḥadīth* as difficult to express in both the Law and the Way, Naṣīr al-Din is suggesting that 'Ayn al-Qużāt succeeded in articulating something that can be perceived only through *ḥaqīqat* (spiritual reality), the third echelon of inner experience. This account provides a clear example of Naṣīr al-Dīn's high regard for 'Ayn al-Qużāt's spiritual perception.

Another passage finds Naṣīr al-Din in a spiritual state. In this condition he recalls the sacred tradition, "I am with those whose hearts are broken." On opening his eyes he recites a line of poetry attributed to 'Ayn al-Qużāt: "One must rise above the body and the soul ..."[123] This leads on to commentary, in which Naṣīr al-Dīn identifies a number of physical and psychological factors which can act as chains, keeping one from rising upward.

---

[120] Sayyid Muḥammad Mubārak al-'Alawī al-Kirmānī (Amīr Khwurd), *Siyar al-awliyā'*, (Delhi: Maṭba'-i Muḥibb-i Hind, 1302/1884–85), 475–476. Reference provided by the editor.

[121] Ḥamīd Qalandar, *Khayr al-majālis* (*malfūẓāt* of Shaykh Naṣīr al-Dīn Maḥmūd Chirāgh), ed. K. A. Nizami (Aligarh: Department of History, Aligarh Muslim University, 1959), 62. Reference provided by the editor.

[122] Ibid., 195.

[123] Ibid., 97. I have not been able to trace this poem to any of 'Ayn al-Qużāt's works.

Burhān al-Dīn Gharīb

The legacy of Burhān al-Dīn Gharīb (d.738/1337), another major successor of Khwāja Niẓām al-Dīn, affords further insights into the reception of the Path of Love in India. Carl Ernst's meticulous research in the manuscript library of the tomb complex of Burhān al-Dīn in Khuldabad offers important clues as to how Path of Love texts were read.[124] We learn that Burhān al-Dīn's successor Zayn al-Dīn Shīrāzī (d. 771/1369)—who was apparently well versed in the works of Abū Ḥāmid Ghazālī, Amīr Khusraw, 'Aṭṭār, Niẓāmī, Sa'dī, and Sanā'ī—cautioned his disciples that writings of 'Ayn al-Qużāt Hamadānī such as Tamhīdāt and Maktūbāt (i.e., Nāma-hā) were especially esoteric and inappropriate for novices.[125]

Another disciple of Burhān al-Dīn Gharīb, Rukn al-Dīn Kashānī (d. after 738/1337), authored a treatise entitled Shamā'il al-atqiyā', which relies extensively on 'Ayn al-Qużāt's Tamhīdāt in its discussion of mystical infidelity (kufr).[126] The unique bibliography appended to Shama'il al-atqiyā' includes several important texts from the Path of Love tradition.[127] Sawāniḥ is there, as is the treatise on music attributed to Aḥmad Ghazālī, Bawāriq al-'ilma. Several works ascribed to 'Ayn al-Qużāt Hamadānī appear: Tamhīdāt, Zubdat al-ḥaqā'iq, Tanzīh al-makān, Jāvid-nāma, and Rushd-nāma.

Mas'ūd Bakk

The Path of Love also finds expression in the work of another spiritual heir of Khwāja Niẓām al-Din, the martyred Sufi aristocrat Mas'ūd Bakk. Mas'ūd Bakk modeled his major work, Mir'āt al-'ārifīn on 'Ayn al-Qużāt's Tamhīdāt.[128] In the chapter on "the reality of love" (ḥaqīqat-i maḥabbat), Mas'ūd Bakk emphasizes the interdependence of passionate love ('ishq) and beauty (ḥusn): "The being of beauty is naught save for the

---

[124] Carl Ernst, Eternal Garden: Mysticism, History, and Politics at a South Asian Sufi Center (Albany: State University of New York Press, 1992), 136.

[125] Ibid.

[126] For 'Ayn al-Qużāt's presentation of this perplexing theme, see Hamadānī, Tamhīdāt, 204–254.

[127] Ernst, Eternal Garden, 251–263.

[128] Sayyid Muhammad Bulāq, Rawżat-i aqṭāb (Delhi: Maṭba'-i Muḥibb-i Hind, 1887), 88. Reference provided by the editor.

contemplation of love; and the contemplation of love cannot be save for the being of beauty."[129] One is tempted to read this as prefiguring of Hazrat Inayat Khan's tri-unity of "love, harmony, and beauty." In analyzing the relationship between love and beauty, Mas'ūd Bakk specifically invokes the distinction made by Aḥmad Ghazālī between the "glance of loveliness" and the "glance of belovedness." He concludes that in a higher state of love, these two glances are linked together.[130]

Gīsū Darāz (d. 825/1422)

The importance of Naṣīr al-Dīn Chirāgh-i Dihl's successor Sayyid Muḥammad Ḥusaynī Gīsū Darāz in the continued transmission of the Path of Love in India has been recognized for some time.[131] Gīsū Darāz provides a prime example of the tendency of the Chishtiyya to appropriate, synthesize, and elaborate on the discursive traditions of Arabic- and Persian-medium Sufism. The very extent of Gīsū Darāz's literary output evinces the impressiveness of his intellectual depth and breadth and the dynamism of the tradition to which he belonged. His literary legacy includes poetry, conversations, letters, original doctrinal works, and commentaries on Sufi classics.

In his enigmatic treatise *Asmār al-asrār,* Gīsū Darāz recalls a vision in which he encountered the spirits of the Prophet Muḥammad, 'Alī, and famous Sufis such as Abū Yazīd Bisṭāmī, and Junayd, as well as Aḥmad Ghazālī and 'Ayn al-Qużāt Hamadānī.[132] This *'uwaysī*, or transhistorical, connection contributes an inner dimension to the numerous references to the founders of the Path of Love in Gīsū Darāz's writings.

Gīsū Darāz explicitly compared his major work *Ḥażā'ir al-quds* (or *Risāla-yi 'ishq-i ḥaqīqī,* "The Treatise of Real Love") with the *Sawāniḥ* of Aḥmad Ghazālī, which he describes as "a present for everyone on the path and everyone who has arrived."[133]

---

[129] Mas'ud Bakk, *Mir'āt al-'ārifīn*, 51. Reference provided by the editor.
[130] Ibid., 54.
[131] Corbin, *History of Islamic Philosophy*, 202.
[132] Gīsū Darāz, *Asmār al-asrār*, ed. Sayyid 'Aṭā' Ḥusayn (Hyderabad: A'ẓam Istīm Pres, 1341/1922-3), 142–3. Reference provided by the editor.
[133] Wā'iẓī, Ḥabībī, 65; cited in Syed Shah Khusro Hussaini, *Sayyid Muhammad al-Husayni-i Gisudiraz: On Sufism* (Delhi: Idarah-i Adabiyat-i Delli, 1983), 23.

Gīsū Darāz's engagement with 'Ayn al-Qużāt can be seen even in his literary style, which reflects the Persian of the *Tamhīdāt*.[134] His interest in the *Tamhīdāt* found expression in an important commentary (*sharḥ*).[135] Tellingly, Gīsū Darāz's commentary often shies away from 'Ayn al-Qużāt's more audacious assertions, preferring a more *sharī'at*-friendly mode of expression. His explanations sometimes seem intended to take the edge off the *Tamhīdāt*. When 'Ayn al-Qużāt remarks that if all the spiritual communities would come together and contemplate his teachings they would realize that they are following one religion and belong to one community, Gīsū Darāz states his disagreement in no uncertain terms:

> Muḥammad Ḥusaynī [Gīsū Darāz] says that Qāżī 'Ayn al-Qużāt has imagined, using [nothing other than] his conjecture, that all religions are one, and all spiritual communities are one! *There is no power and no strength except in God!* There are two perspectives here: that which we follow is ours, and that which he follows is his own ... This is his mistake, that he has confused the principles of religion with its branches. This is a most grievous mistake, deviation, and heresy![136]

In his *Ḥażā'ir al-quds*, however, he writes:

> That [love-] crazed judge, 'Ayn al-Qużāt has alluded to a beautiful advice: "[I swear] by my soul and my head, transcend the worship of norms, and see the seventy-two spiritual communities as one."

Elsewhere in his *Sharḥ-i Tamhīdāt* Gīsū Darāz cites 'Ayn al-Qużāt's version of an alleged correspondence between the Sufi Abū Sa'īd ibn Abī al-Khayr and the philosopher Ibn Sīnā (Avicenna), in which the latter describes the Way as "entry into real infidelity (*kufr-i ḥaqīqī*) and exit from metaphorical Islam (*islām-i majāzī*)."[137]

Gīsū Darāz's attitude toward Rūmī is ambiguous. Sometimes he appears relatively positive: "Mawlānā Jalāl [al-Dīn] Rūmī is

---

[134] Hussaini, *Gisudiraz*, 24.

[135] A selection of this *sharḥ* (commentary) was published in Iran as an appendix to Hamadānī, *Tamhīdāt* (355–417). The full commentary has been published in India: Muḥammad Gīsū Darāz Chishtī, *Sharḥ zubdat al-ḥaqā'iq, al-ma'rūf bi sharḥ-i tamhīdāt*, (Hyderabad: Kitābkhāna-yi Gulbarga Sharīf, 1364/1945)

[136] Gīsū Darāz, *Muntakhabat-i sharḥ-i Tamhīdāt*, cited at the end of *Tamhīdāt*, ed. 'Usayrān, 412.

[137] This correspondence is recorded in 'Ayn al-Qużāt Hamadānī, *Tamhīdāt*, 349.

mad! He is a lover who is neither known nor understood."[138] In other places, one detects a note of criticism, as when he says that the verse "deaf, dumb, and blind, they will not return [to the path] (Qur'ān 2.180)" refers to those like Rūmī who are bewildered by love and have lost their way. And then there is the outspoken passage in one of his letters, in which he accuses 'Aṭṭār, Rūmī, and Ibn 'Arabī of being "ornamented and deceitful."[139]

Later figures

Pursuing Hazrat Inayat Khan's *silsila* into its Gujaratī phase (14th–17th C), one finds several notable literary manifestations of the Path of Love. Among the best examples is the *Dīvān* of Jamāl al-Dīn Jamman, a descendent of Naṣīr al-Dīn Chirāgh-i Dihlī's nephew Kamāl al-Dīn 'Allāma. Shaykh Jamāl al-Dīn writes: "The love of beauties and love's infidelity (*kāfirī*); Jamman, this is our religion and faith."[140]

Shaykh Muḥammad Chishtī, the son of Jamāl al-Dīn Jamman's successor, furthered this tradition. His treatise *Marājin al-'ushshāq* is a collection of profound meditations on love, incorporating and building on passages from the *Sawāniḥ*. A number of the metaphors Muḥammad Chishtī uses to describe the relationship of love (*'ishq*) and the soul (*rūḥ*) originate with Aḥmad Ghazālī.[141] Like Ghazālī, Muḥammad Chishtī valorizes the state of separation: "Know that separation is better (*afḍal*) than union, since it comes after the latter in the Prophetic tradition, 'I was a hidden treasure and I loved to be known, so I created the creation that I might be known'."[142]

The Gujarati Chishtī-Naṣīrī lineage is succeeded, in Hazrat Inayat Khan's *silsila*, by Shāh Kalīm Allāh and his successors. In

---

138 This description recalls Fakhr al-Dīn 'Irāqī's lament in Aflākī, *Manāqib al-'ārifin*, 1:399–400: "No one comprehended Mawlānā [Rūmī] as he deserved to be understood: he came into this world a stranger and left it a stranger."

139 Gīsū Darāz, *Maktūbāt*, ed. Sayyid 'Aṭā' Ḥusayn (Hyderabad: Barqī Press, 1362/1943), 22. Reference provided by the editor.

140 Jamāl al-Dīn Jamman, *Dīvān-i Jamman*, 7. Reference provided by the editor.

141 Muḥammad Chishtī, *Arba'ūn Rasā'il*, fols. 122r–123v (Reference provided by the editor); Ghazālī-Pourjavadi, 21

142 Chishtī, *Arba'ūn Rasā'il*, fol. 127r; Cf. "Separation is higher in degree than union, because if there is no union, then there will be no separation." Ghazālī-Pourjavady, 47

this phase the doctrines of Ibn ʻArabī become especially pronounced. Shāh Kalīm Allāh's *Tilka ʻashara kāmila* represents a spirited defence of the school of *waḥdat al-wujūd* (unity of being) against Aḥmad Sirhindī and other detractors. Nonetheless, glimmers of the Indo-Persian Path of Love are detectable. Consider this verse, cited by Shāh Kalīm Allāh toward the end of his *Kashkūl-i Kalīmī*: "Love knows not the infidel nor the faithful; this must be written on the walls of the mosque and the temple."

Hazrat Inayat Khan

While this essay has tended to emphasize the more explicit and specific citations of the Persian Path of Love in the Indian Chishtī tradition, very often the content of the Path of Love was transmitted without reference to its founding figures. Ultimately ideas have always been more important to Sufis than authors. In the work of Hazrat Inayat Khan, although Aḥmad Ghazālī and ʻAyn al-Qużāt are never mentioned, the legacy of the Path of Love is abundantly evident.

Some names do appear. Hazrat Inayat Khan discoursed at length on Rūmī, Sa'dī, Ḥāfiẓ, ʻAṭṭār, and Sanā'ī. These lectures demonstrate a deep familiarity with the poetics of love in the Persian literary tradition.[143] In other lectures, the romances of Shirīn and Farhād, Yūsuf and Zulaykha, and Layla and Majnūn—the legendary heroines and heroes of the Path of Love—are retold with inspired and exquisite commentary.[144]

Although Aḥmad Ghazālī is nowhere mentioned in Hazrat Inayat Khan's writings, it is noteworthy that he does figure in the *silsila* of the Suhrawardiyya, one of the four principal *silsilas* through which Hazrat Inayat Khan's initiatic heritage is traced (Shaykh Ziyā' al-Dīn Abū Najīb was a disciple of Aḥmad Ghazālī).[145] Thus, in lieu of an explicit textual connection, we have a spiritual connection.

And then there is the body of his teaching, in which one encounters the symbols and themes of the Path of Love at every

---

[143] One set of lectures on the Sufi poets can be found, along with poetry of these poets in versions by Coleman Barks, in *The Hand of Poetry: Five Mystic Poets of Persia* (New Lebanon: Omega Publications, 1993).

[144] See especially, Inayat Khan, "Love, Human and Divine," in *The Sufi Message of Hazrat Inayat Khan* (London: Barrie and Rockliff, 1960–67), 5:139–188.

[145] Jāmī, *Nafaḥāt al-uns*, 420.

turn. The word "love" itself occurs more that fifteen hundred times in his recorded lectures. The remainder of this essay will highlight some of the salient features of Hazrat Inayat Khan's mystical philosophy that can be traced to the foundational teachings of the Path of Love.

Seeking God in the heart

We have seen that many Sufis specifically identified themselves with the Path of Love. This is also true of Hazrat Inayat Khan. Summing up his spiritual journey, the Pir-o-Murshid says: "I advanced on the path of Love."[146] In a number of places he describes Sufism as "the religion of the heart" or "the religion of love":

> If anybody asks what Sufism is, what kind of religion is it, the answer is that Sufism is the religion of the heart, the religion in which the thing of primary importance is to seek God in the heart of mankind.[147]

The idea that the human heart is the ideal locus of divine manifestation is, as we have seen, a recurrent theme in Sufism. Its scriptural basis is in the Qur'ānic *āyat* that declares that God will reveal his signs within "the very souls" of humanity.[148] Hazrat Inayat Khan's saying, "The heart of man is Thy sacred shrine,"[149] echoes this perspective, and recalls in particular the sacred tradition, "The Heavens and the Earth could not contain me, but the heart of my believing servant suffices Me."[150]

Hazrat Inayat Khan returns to this theme time and again, from various angles. In one passage, he explains the indwelling of God in terms of the complementarity of *tashbīh* (immanence) and *tanzīh* (transcendence):

> Those who think that God is not outside but only within are as wrong as those who believe that God is not within but only outside. In fact God is both inside and outside, but it is very necessary to begin by believing in the God outside.[151]

---

[146] Khan, *Complete Works, Sayings I*, 1:298.

[147] Khan, *The Sufi Message*, 9:19.

[148] Qur'ān 41.53.

[149] Khan, *Complete Works, Sayings I*, 1:295.

[150] This sacred *ḥadīth*, long a favorite of many Sufis, is cited by both Ghazālī (*Iḥyā' 'ulūm al-dīn*) and Suhrawardī (*'Awārif al-ma'ārif*). See Badī' al-Zamān Furūzānfar, *Aḥādis-i masnavī*, 25–26.

[151] Khan, *The Sufi Message*, 9:98.

While the pedagogical necessity of beginning with belief in the external is underscored, the clear implication—and this is confirmed elsewhere—is that the spiritual path involves progressive internalization. This perspective is resonant with the view expressed by 'Ayn al-Quẓāt in a remarkable passsage in the *Tamhīdāt*:

> Do you know what I am saying? I say that the spiritual seeker has to search after God not in paradise, not in the world, and not in the Hereafter. He has to stop seeking God in everything that he has seen and everything that he has known: the path of the seeker is inside his own self. He has to find the path in himself, as the Qur'ān says: "[We shall show them our signs...] and inside their own selves, do they not reflect [on this]?" ... There is no path to God better than the path of the heart. This is the meaning of "the heart is the house of God."[152]

A popular poem attributed to Rūmī bears quoting here:

> I was in that day when the Names were not,
> Nor any sign of existence endowed with name.
> By me Names and Named were brought to view
> On the day when there were not 'I' and 'We.'
> For a sign, the tip of the Beloved's curl became a
> centre of revelation;
> As yet the tip of that fair curl was not.
> Cross and Christians, from end to end,
> I surveyed; He was not on the Cross.
> I went to the idol-temple, to the ancient pagoda;
> No trace was visible there.
> I went to the mountains of Herāt and Candahār;
> I looked; He was not in that hill-and-dale.
> With set purpose I fared to the summit of Mount Qāf;
> In that place was only the 'Anqā's habitation.
> I bent the reins of search to the Ka'ba;
> He was not in that resort of old and young.
> I questioned Ibn Sīnā of his state;
> He was not in Ibn Sīnā' range.
> I faced toward the scene of "*two bow-lengths' distance*";
> He was not in that exalted court.
> I gazed into my own heart;
> There I saw Him; He was nowhere else.
> Save pure-souled Shamsi Tabrīz
> None ever was drunken and intoxicated and distraught.[153]

---

[152] Hamadānī, *Tamhīdāt*, 23.

[153] R.A. Nicholson, trans., *Selected Poems from the Divani Shamsi Tabriz* (Cambridge: Cambridge University Press, 1977), 70–72.

The theme of ultimately discovering God within one's own heart is expressed similarly in a poem from the *Gayan* of Hazrat Inayat Khan:

> I searched, but I could not find Thee; I called Thee aloud, standing on the minaret; I rang the temple bell with the rising and setting of the sun; I bathed in the Ganges in vain; I came back from Kaaba disappointed;
>
> I looked for Thee on the earth; I searched for Thee in the heaven, my Beloved, but at last I have found Thee hidden as a pearl in the shell of my heart.[154]

Love as the reason for manifestation

Hazrat Inayat Khan shares the teleology of his predecessors in the Path of Love, who identify love as the source and goal of all creation, tirelessly citing the sacred tradition, "I was a Hidden Treasure ...":

> The Sufi says that since the whole of manifestation is the manifestation of love, and since God Himself is love, then it is natural that the same love which comes from the source returns to the source, and that the purpose of life is accomplished by it. Somebody asked a Sufi, "Why did God create the world?" and he said, "In order to break the monotony of loneliness." And how is that monotony broken? It is broken through God loving His creation and through His creatures loving God.[155]

Here it is asserted that *'ishq* is common to both God and man, a point of view that is not taken for granted in Sufism in general, but which is characteristic of the Path of Love. Hazrat Inayat Khan does sometimes distinguish between "human love" and "divine love," as when he says: "Man learns his first lesson of love by loving a human being; but in reality love is due to God alone."[156] Nonetheless, for Hazrat Inayat Khan ultimately love is a single phenomenon:

---

[154] Khan, *Complete Works, Sayings I*, 1:223.

[155] Khan, *The Sufi Message*, 11:164.

[156] Khan, *Complete Works, Sayings I*, 1:66. In another passage, (1:29), he states "The fountain stream of love rises in the love for an individual, but spreads and falls in Universal love."

> We see the same love of God in all things: in the love of a mother for her child, in the love of a friend for his friend, in all the different aspects it is the same love manifesting. Outwardly it may seem human, but inwardly it is all divine.[157]

Love, harmony, and beauty

Recognizing the dynamic tension inherent in triads, Sufi thinkers have often articulated their ideas in the form of tri-unities. Perhaps the earliest is the configuration of *islām, imān,* and *iḥsān,* which the Prophet Muḥammad (ص) refers to in the well-known *ḥadīth* of Gabriel. The generally assented compatability of the Law (*sharī'a*), Way (*ṭarīqa*), and Reality (*ḥaqīqa*) is another example. Bisṭāmī's declaration of the unity of love, lover, and beloved has already been mentioned. Shaykh al-Ishrāq Shihāb al-Dīn Suhrawardī proposed the trinity of "beauty, love, and sadness."[158]

Hazrat Inayat Khan offered his own formula: "love, harmony, and beauty." This trinity occurs dozens of times in the Pir-o-Murshid's recorded lectures, and has pride of place in the inspired prayers that form the liturgy of his Sufi Order, in which God is invoked as "the Perfection of Love, Harmony, and Beauty."[159]

While love and beauty are ubiquitously paired in Sufi discourse, the introduction of the term "harmony" marks a fresh contribution. A possible precedent is the concept of *munāsaba* (affinity), which entered into Islamic philosophy from Neoplatonism, and which was frequently discussed as a precondition to the occurrence of love between lover and beloved.[160] For Hazrat Inayat Khan, however, love itself prefigures the affinity that harmony represents: "love develops into harmony, and of harmony is born beauty."[161] Perhaps the most important context informing the concept of harmony in Hazrat Inayat Khan's teachings is music.

---

157 Khan, *The Sufi Message*, 11:164.

158 Shihabuddin Yahya Suhrawardi, *The Mystical and Visionary Treatises*, trans. W. M. Thackston, Jr., (London: The Octagon Press, 1982), 62–3.

159 Khan, *Complete Works, Sayings I*, 1:200-2, 1:205-7.

160 Bell, *Love Theory*, 74.

161 Khan, *Complete Works, Sayings I*, 1:89.

Aesthetics

As with earlier Sufis of the Path of Love, Hazrat Inayat Khan emphasizes the experiential (*zawqī*) aesthetic of Sufism over mere theoretical knowledge. Nature and art both serve as media for ecstatic contemplation and attunement to the divine.

Hazrat Inayat Khan regards the totality of nature (including human nature) as the theater of divine manifestation (*tajalliyāt*): "I see Thine own image, Lord, in Thy creation."[162] Thus, as with many Sufis of the Path of Love, the Pir-o-Murshid's teaching is unambiguously world-affirming, valorizing rather than denigrating embodiment. This positive appreciation of creation is most evident in his many "nature meditations."[163]

For Hazrat Inayat Khan, nature and art are inextricably related. "True art," he insists, does not take humanity away from nature, but closer to her.[164] But art also adds something to nature:

> Many think that art is something different from nature, but it would be better to say that art is the completion of nature. One may ask how man can improve upon nature, which is made by God, but the fact is that God Himself, through man, finishes His creation in art. As all the different elements are God's vehicles, as all the trees and plants are His instruments through which He creates, so art is the medium of God through which God Himself completes His creation.[165]

Not surprisingly, Hazrat Inayat Khan deemed music the highest form of art. The collection of his lectures that has been published under the title *The Mysticism of Sound and Music* has to be considered among the most profound Sufi commentaries on music ever recorded.[166]

Universalism

One of the best known and most beloved—and, for certain critics, most objectionable—aspects of Hazrat Inayat Khan's

---

[162] Ibid., 85.
[163] Ibid., 74–77.
[164] Ibid., 36.
[165] Khan, *The Sufi Message*, 10:159.
[166] Khan, *The Mysticism of Sound and Music* (Boston: Shambhala Press, 1996).

teaching is its universalist perpective. In keeping with the practice of his predecessors in the Chishtiyya, Hazrat Inayat Khan initiated non-Muslims into Sufism. Moreover, he developed an inclusive ritual, named Universal Worship, in which candles representing each of the major world religions are kindled from a single source (the "God candle") as their respective scriptures are read. The pluralist outlook that informs the Universal Worship is, as we have seen, perfectly consistent with the world-view of earlier Path of Love masters such as ʻAyn al-Qużāt.

"Spiritual liberty," the relativization of dogmas, is a persistent theme in Hazrat Inayat Khan's corpus. The Pir-o-Murshid clearly differentiates the divine reality from our, necessarily limited, conceptions of that reality. We need a "God-Ideal" to focus our aspirations, yet every ideal must be ultimately shattered on the "rock of Truth."[167] Here we find an implicit affirmation of the complementarity of *imān* (faith) and *kufr* (disbelief) taught by ʻAyn al-Qużāt. More explicitly, in Hazrat Inayat Khan's recognition that "we each create our own God,"[168] allusion is made to Ibn ʻArabī's notion of "the ʻgod' created in the beliefs" (*al-ilah makhlūq fī al-iʻtiqādāt*).[169] For Sufis like Ibn ʻArabī and Hazrat Inayat Khan, religious wars have their basis in the rigidity of human beliefs. The first step toward interfaith peace, then, is to recognize our own tendency to make God into a static conception. Only then can we attempt to transcend limitation—not through an intellectual effort, but by expanding the perceptions of the heart.

Conclusion

This essay has endeavored to outline an important context within which the brilliant, multi-faceted, and influential teachings of Hazrat Inayat Khan may be read. It is hoped that this may encourage enthusiasts of Aḥmad Ghazālī, ʻAyn al-Qużāt, Rūmī and Ḥāfiẓ to discover the enfoldment of their vision in Hazrat Inayat Khan, and by the same token, that devotees of Hazrat Inayat Khan may feel moved to explore his predecessors in the Path of Love.

---

[167] Khan, *Complete Works, Sayings I*, 1:371.
[168] Ibid., 1:183
[169] Cited in Henry Corbin, *Creative Imagination*, 303, n. 30. See also, 195–200.

As a tribute to Hazrat Inayat Khan, let us close with these words of ʻAyn al-Qużāt Hamadānī: "O precious one ... the sending down of the Qur'ān, the Messengers and the Apostles was all because of God's *'ināyat*, compassion, mercy, and blessing towards creation."[170]

[170] Hamadānī, *Tamhīdāt*, 180.

The "Silsila-i Sufian": From Khwāja Mu'īn al-Dīn Chishtī to Sayyid Abū Hāshim Madanī

ZIA INAYAT KHAN

Chained with gold chains about the feet of God.
—Tennyson[1]

In a final ceremony before returning to India, on 13 September (Hejirat Day[2]) 1926 Hazrat Inayat Khan laid the cornerstone of the prototype of the Universel, the "temple" he envisioned as the ideal vessel for the universal spirituality of the future.[3] Beneath the granite block was placed a document entitled "Silsila-i Sufian." This was a copy (by the hand of his cousin Muhammad Ali Khan) of his certificate of succession (*khilāfat-nāma*), listing the Pīrs (spiritual masters) of the Chishtī Order from the Prophet Muḥammad to Sayyid Abū Hāshim Madanī, with his own name duly appended at the end.

While Hazrat Inayat Khan's followers have always regarded the ritual interment of the Silsila-i Sufian document as significant, interpretations vary considerably. Did the Pir-o-Murshid intend to firmly establish his traditional Sufi heritage in the soil of the West? Or rather to respectfully enact its termination at the commencement of the new Confraternity of the Message? Perhaps both readings

---

[1] Cited in R. M. Bloch, *The Confessions of Inayat Khan* (London: The Sufi Publishing Society, 1915), 61.

[2] Literally, "The Day of Emigration" (cf. the Islamic *hijra*, the emigration of the Prophet Muḥammad from Mecca to Medina): the commemoration of Hazrat Inayat Khan's embarkation (together with Maheboob Khan and Muhammad Ali Khan) for the West, on 13 September 1910; one of two official annual Festivals celebrated in the Sufi Order he established (*Sufi Order Constitution and Rules* [unpublished], 7–8), the other being Viladat Day (Hazrat Inayat Khan's birthday: July 5th)—to which was later added, unofficially, a third: Visalat Day (Hazrat Inayat Khan's death anniversary, or *'urs*: February 5th).

[3] Hazrat Inayat Khan's vision of the Universel is outlined in "Our Efforts in Constructing," Message Paper dated 21 July 1925 (privately circulated).

are simultaneously, if relatively, true: in Hazrat Inayat Khan's act we seem to have not a simple sign, but an overdetermined and multivocal symbol.

The names on the list represent one of the pieces in the puzzle. Who were these figures, most of them unmentioned in the Pir-o-Murshid's recorded lectures? In the variously interpreted—in fact, often hotly debated—interplay of tradition and inspiration in Hazrat Inayat Khan's lifework, their stories, preserved mostly in musty, worm-eaten manuscripts and lithographs, remain unexamined evidence. The present essay endeavors to redress this critical dearth of information.

The Prophet Muḥammad's spiritual magnetism (*baraka*) did not come to an end with his death, Sufis maintain, but rather devolved upon those in whom his profound attunement found resonance. Thus the torch passed from prophethood (*risāla*) to sainthood (*wilāya*).[4] Muhammadan sainthood gradually crystallized in history as an initiatic tradition offering guidance in the esoteric Way (*ṭarīqa*). Proceeding "from heart to heart," link by link, it took the shape of a chain (*silsila*), while unlike the political Caliphate it accommodated multiple successors at each juncture and hence branched out like a tree (*shajara*).[5]

Every authorized representative (*khalīfa*) of organized Sufism is able to trace his or her initiatic pedigree through one or more branches of this spiritual family tree. This was indeed true of Hazrat Inayat Khan. In his first book written in the West, entitled *A Sufi Message of Spiritual Liberty* (1914), Hazrat Inayat Khan introduced his interpretation of the traditional Sufi concept of initiatic transmission:

---

[4] For a good discussion of Ibn al-'Arabī's influential theorization of *risāla* and *wilāya* see Michel Chodkiewicz, *Seal of the Saints: Prophethood and Sainthood in the Doctrine of Ibn 'Arabi*, trans. Liadain Sherrard (Cambridge: The Islamic Texts Society, 1993). Hazrat Inayat Khan presents his views in *A Sufi Message of Spiritual Liberty* (London: The Theosophical Publishing Society, 1914), 33–35, *The Way of Illumination* (Southampton: The Sufi Movement, 1922), 75–80, and *The Unity of Religious Ideals* (Southampton: The Sufi Movement, 1928), 121–158.

[5] Perhaps the most appropriate botanical analogy would be the fig tree, with its latticework structure.

> ... A Mystic Order called the Sahaba-e-Safa, Knights of Purity, was regularly organized by the Prophet, and afterwards, was carried on by Alli and Siddikh ... This Order was carried on by their successors (who were called *Piro Murshid, Shaikh*, etc.), one after another, duly connected as links in a chain. The spiritual bond between them is a miraculous force of divine illumination, and is experienced by worthy initiates of the Sufic Order; just as the electric current runs through all connected lamps and lights them. By this means the higher development is attained through nominal efforts.[6]

As a disciple and successor of Sayyid Abū Hāshim Madanī of Hyderabad, Hazrat Inayat Khan traced his lineage primarily through the Chishtī Order.[7] In the By-laws of the Sufi Order (Suresnes, undated) he wrote, "The later development of the Sufi Order, which was called Chishtia, culminated in the present Order of Sufis, which is established in the West ..."

The Chishtiyya derives its name from the town of Chisht, situated along the Harīrūd River some 95 miles east of Herat in present-day Afghanistan. Sufism was brought to Chisht by Shaykh Abū Ishāq Shāmī ("the Syrian") (d. A.H. 329/A.D. 941), a disciple of Shaykh Mumshād 'Ulū Dīnwarī of Baghdad (d. 299/911).[8] Before returning to the Levant, where he lies buried in Acre, Shaykh Abū Ishāq initiated and trained the son of the local Amīr, Khwāja Abū Aḥmad Abdāl ibn Sulṭān Farasnāfa (d. 355/966), who became the first of a long line of hereditary Pīrs. Later tradition remembers these figures above all as outspoken advocates and enthusiastic practitioners of *samā'* (ritual audition and ecstatic dance), a practice noticeably redolent of Central Asian shamanism.[9] Khwāja Abū Aḥmad Abdāl's grandson Khwāja Yūsuf Chishtī (d. 459/1067) is quoted as remarking, "My friend, there are discoveries in *samā'* not to be found in a hundred years of

---

[6] Inayat Khan, *Spiritual Liberty*, 35–6.

[7] Alongside the Chishtiyya, Hazrat Inayat Khan received the transmission of several other Orders, among which special emphasis was placed on the Suhrawardiyya, Qādiriyya, and Naqshbandiyya.

[8] Nūr al-Dīn 'Abd al-Raḥmān Jāmī, *Nafaḥāt al-uns min ḥażarāt al-quds*, ed. Mahmūd 'Ābidī (Tehran: Intishārāt-i Iṭṭilā'āt, 1373/1953–54), 328.

[9] On the distinctive Central Asian heritage of the Chishtiyya, see Thierry Zarcone, "Central Asian Influence on the Early Development of the Chishtiyya Sufi Order in India," in *The Making of Indo-Persian Culture*, ed. Muzaffar Alam, Françoise Delvoye and Marc Gaborieau (New Delhi: Manohar, 2000), 99–116.

canonical worship (*'ibāda*)."[10] Under Khwāja Yūsuf's son Khwāja Quṭb al-Dīn Mawdūd (d. 567/1172) the *khānqāh* (Sufi hospice) reached the apogee of its influence. Among his senior representatives was the chain-clad "Pole of the Ascetics" Hājjī Sharīf Zindanī (d. 612/1215), whose successor in turn was Khwāja 'Usmān (d. 617/1220) of Harvan, near Nishapur. It was through this sub-lineage that the Chishtī transmission reached Khwāja Mu'īn al-Dīn Chishtī (d. 633/1236), our point of departure.

What follows is largely a compilation of the contents of several Persian and Urdu sacred-biographical compendia (*tazkira*, pl. *tazkirāt*). As a genre of hagiography the *tazkira* is principally concerned with constructing the sanctity of its subjects, the Sufi Shaykhs. This is done by representing the Shaykhs as personifying, to an exemplary degree, paradigms of piety recognized by the readership—in the present case, South Asian Muslim elites in the pre-modern and modern eras.[11] While this agenda is common to all *tazkira* writing, narrative styles vary considerably, ranging from matter-of-fact empirical description to unrestrained appeals to the miraculous.

While the following is more an exercise in translation than interpretation, it is nonetheless true that the process of selecting, paraphrasing, and combining texts necessarily involves choices, which in turn reflect pre-commitments. Positivist historians—sticklers for "hard facts"—tend to treat *tazkiras* with extreme skepticism, and often end in confessing their inability to reconstruct anything worthwhile from them. The opposite extreme is to take all source material at face value and ignore questions of rhetorical construction. In the spirit of *epoché*, the suspension of both belief and disbelief, a middle course has been pursued here. Every effort has been made to use the sources nearest in time and space to the figures portrayed. But the miraculous content of these sources has been respected as an integral aspect of the genre.

---

[10] Allāhdiya Chishtī, *Siyar al-aqṭāb* (Lucknow: Naval Kishūr, 1889), 75.

[11] On the typology of Indo-Muslim sainthood, see Bruce B. Lawrence, "The Chishtīya of Sultanate India: A Case of Biographical Complexities in South Asian Islam," in *Charisma and Sacred Biography*, ed. M.A. Williams (Chico, CA: Scholars Press, 1981), 47–67.

More than seven centuries divide Khwāja Mu'īn al-Dīn Chishtī and Hazrat Inayat Khan. Within this span, some periods are better documented than are others. Our guide to the early period (13th-14th C) is *Siyar al-awliyā'*, written by Sayyid Muḥammad bin Mubārak Kirmānī, known as Amīr Khwurd.[12] As the son of a disciple of Khwāja Farīd al-Dīn, and himself a disciple of Khwāja Niẓām al-Dīn, Amīr Khwurd was well placed to record and reconstruct the lives and teachings of the founders of the Indian Chishtiyya. Although Amīr Khwurd's treatment of the more obscure figures, including Khwāja Mu'īn al-Dīn Chishtī, sometimes draws on the "retrospective" *malfūẓāt* (recorded conversations) literature that was then insinuating itself into the tradition, *Siyar al-awliyā'* is a work of rigor and insight, setting the standard for all subsequent *tazkira* writing.

Little is available on the five successive lineage-holders following Khwāja Naṣīr al-Dīn (d. 757/1356). The civil war that enflamed Ahmadabad in 1572, destroying the library of the Chishtī-Naṣīrī *khānqāh*, accounts in part for this lacuna. Most of our information concerning these figures comes from the conversations of the Shaykh who witnessed the devastation, Shaykh Ḥasan Muḥammad Chishtī (d. 982/1575): *Majālis-i Ḥasaniyya.*[13]

The lives of Shaykh Ḥasan Muḥammad, his son Shaykh Muḥammad (d. 1041/1631) and great grandson Shaykh Yaḥyā (d. 1101/1689) were attentively reconstructed, with supporting chains of narrative transmission, in a *tazkira* compiled by the latter's grandson Shaykh Ḥusām al-Dīn Farrukh (d. 1175/1762), entitled *Farādīs-i Farrukhshāhī*. This book seems to be no longer extant, but is quoted extensively by the author's prolific grandson Shaykh Rashīd al-Dīn Mawdūd Lālā (d. 1242/1827) in his sprawling hagiographic tour de force *Mukhbīr al-awliyā'*.[14] The sections of

---

[12] Sayyid Muḥammad Mubārak al-'Alawī al-Kirmānī (Amīr Khwurd), *Siyar al-awliyā'*, (Delhi: Maṭba'-i Muḥibb-i Hind, 1302/1884–85).

[13] Thanks are due to Khwaja Ruknuddin Mohammed Farrukh Chishty, Sajjada-nishin, and the late Prof. Abdul-Haqq Munshi for providing copies of two manuscripts of this rare work, the former transcribed by Farrūkh Rukn al-Dīn 'Abd al-Rashīd ibn Sirāj al-Dīn ibn Shaykh Muḥammad in A.H. 1161 (hereafter, respectively, Shahibagh MS and Munshi MS).

[14] Again thanks are due to Khwaja Ruknuddin Farrukh Chishty, for granting access to the only complete manuscript of *Mukhbīr al-awliyā'* in existence, an autograph (hereafter, Shahibagh MS); Also to Prof. Mahmud Husain Shaikh

Mukhbīr al-awliyā' treating the Chishtī *Sajjāda-nishīns* ("ones who sit on the [founder's] prayer-carpet," i.e., principal successors) of Ahmadabad are paraphrased in Urdu and supplemented with subsequent biographies in *Shajarat al-Maḥmūd*, a product of the late nineteenth century.[15]

We have in the collected letters (*maktūbāt*) of Shaykh Yaḥyā's successor Shāh Kalīm Allāh Jahānābādī (d. 1142/1729) a fascinating historical document, deserving much more scholarly attention than it has received.[16] A convenient if relatively late source, used extensively here, both for Shāh Kalīm Allāh and his successor Shāh Niẓām al-Dīn (d. 1142/1730), is *Takmila-i siyar al-awliyā'* ("The Supplement to *Siyar al-awliya*").[17] Its author, Gul Muḥammad Aḥmadpūrī (d. 1243/1827), was a successor of Qāżi Muḥammad 'Āqil (d. 1229/1814), who was in turn a successor of Shāh Niẓām al-Dīn's son Mawlānā Fakhr al-Dīn (d. 1199/1785).

The first Nizam of Hyderabad, Āṣaf Jāh I (d. 1748), wrote a biography of Shāh Niẓām al-Dīn Awrangābādī, entitled *Rashk-i gulistān-i Iram*, that has not been traced. But a 349-page *masnavī* in praise of Shaykh Yaḥyā, Shāh Kalīm Allāh, Shāh Niẓām al-Dīn and Mawlānā Fakhr al-Dīn, composed by a grandson of the Nizam, the Mughal Vazīr and kingmaker 'Imād al-Mulk Ghāzī al-Dīn Khān Firūz Jang III, survives at the Aurangabad *dargāh*.[18] Of still greater historical value is Ghāzī al-Dīn Khān's prose hagiography of his spiritual master Mawlānā Fakhr al-Dīn, *Manāqib-i Fakhriyya*.[19]

Despite continuing, indeed deepening, connections between *khānqāh* and court, nothing of the kind is available for Mawlānā Fakhr al-Dīn's son Mawlānā Quṭb al-Dīn or grandson Mawlānā

---

for providing a copy of a second manuscript (original in the collection of the Royal Asiatic Society, Bombay; hereafter R.A.S. MS).

[15] Ḥāfiẓ Muḥammad Munīr al-Dīn Maḥmūdī, *Shajarat al-Maḥmūd*, (Hyderabad: Maṭba'-i Gulzār, 1304/1886–87).

[16] Shāh Kalīm Allāh Jahānābādī, *Maktūbāt-i Kalīmī* (Delhi: Maṭba'-i Mujtabā'ī, 1315/1897–98).

[17] Gul Muḥammad Aḥmadpūrī, *Takmila-yi siyar al-awliyā'*, MS K.A. Nizami. Thanks are due to Prof. Carl W. Ernst.

[18] Prof. Hasan Nizami kindly drew our attention to this manuscript. Thanks are due to Mohammed Miyan Sahib, Sajjada-nishin, and Nayyar Jehan Begum, Mutawalliya, for granting access to it.

[19] Ghāzī al-Dīn Khān, *Manāqib-i Fakhriyya* (Delhi: n.p., 1315/1897–98); thanks to Prof. Carl W. Ernst. On Ghāzī al-Dīn Khān, see Jadunath Sarkar, *Fall of the Mughal Empire* (New Delhi: Orient Longman Ltd., 1988), vols. 1–2, passim.

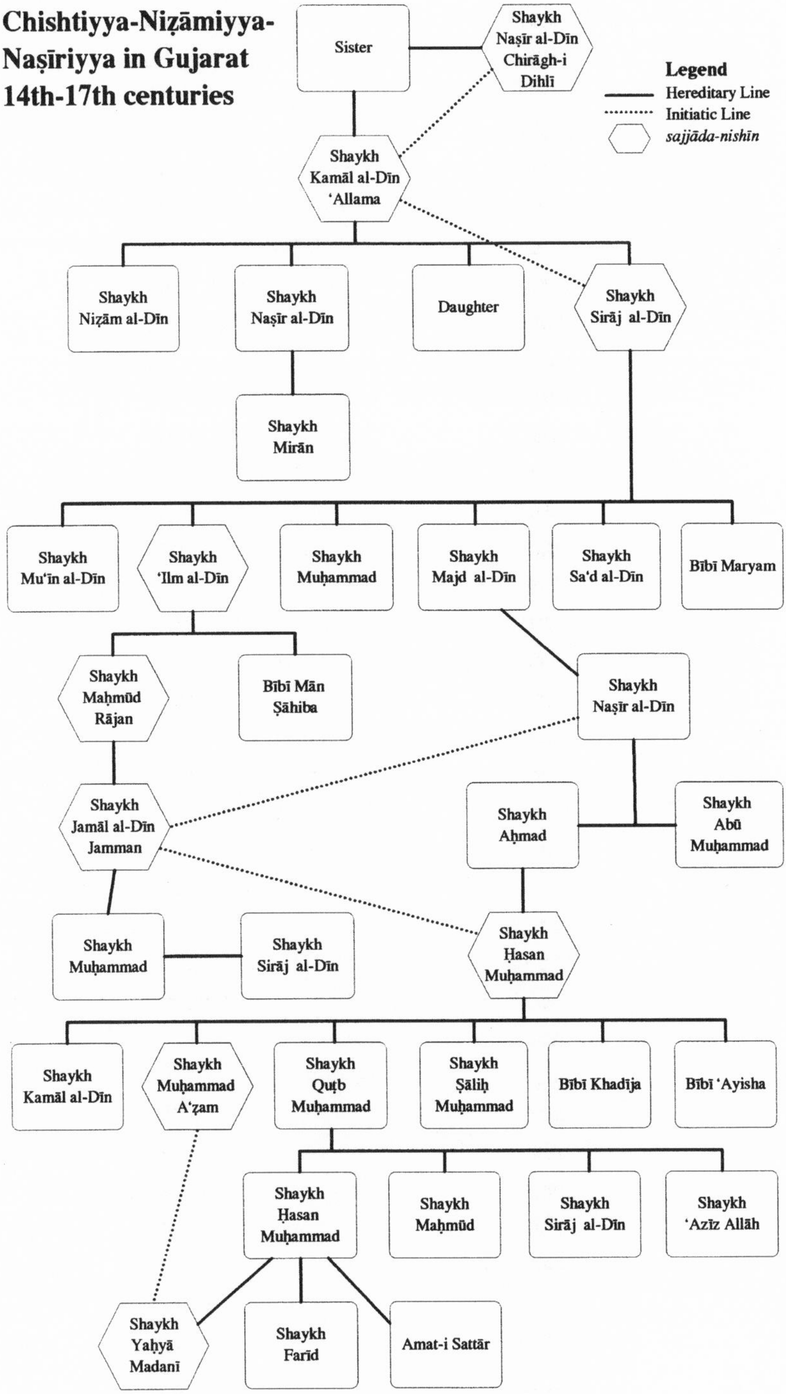
Chishtiyya-Niẓāmiyya-Naṣīriyya in Gujarat
14th-17th centuries
Sister
Shaykh Naṣīr al-Dīn Chirāgh-i Dihlī
Legend
Hereditary Line
Initiatic Line
sajjāda-nishīn
Shaykh Kamāl al-Dīn 'Allama
Shaykh Niẓām al-Dīn
Shaykh Naṣīr al-Dīn
Daughter
Shaykh Sirāj al-Dīn
Shaykh Mirān
Shaykh Mu'īn al-Dīn
Shaykh 'Ilm al-Dīn
Shaykh Muḥammad
Shaykh Majd al-Dīn
Shaykh Sa'd al-Dīn
Bībī Maryam
Shaykh Maḥmūd Rājan
Bībī Mān Ṣāhiba
Shaykh Naṣīr al-Dīn
Shaykh Jamāl al-Dīn Jamman
Shaykh Aḥmad
Shaykh Abū Muḥammad
Shaykh Muḥammad
Shaykh Sirāj al-Dīn
Shaykh Ḥasan Muḥammad
Shaykh Kamāl al-Dīn
Shaykh Muḥammad A'ẓam
Shaykh Quṭb Muḥammad
Shaykh Ṣāliḥ Muḥammad
Bībī Khadīja
Bībī 'Ayisha
Shaykh Ḥasan Muḥammad
Shaykh Maḥmūd
Shaykh Sirāj al-Dīn
Shaykh 'Azīz Allāh
Shaykh Yaḥyā Madanī
Shaykh Farīd
Amat-i Sattār

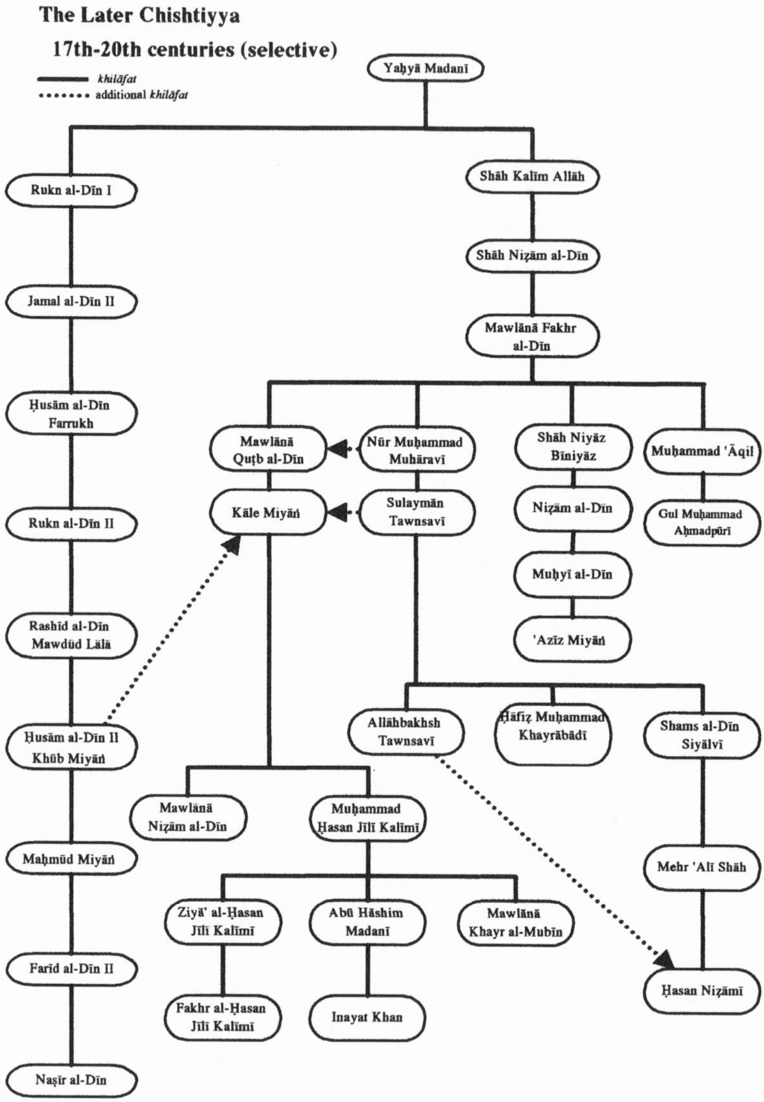
The Later Chishtiyya
17th-20th centuries (selective)
khilāfat
additional khilāfat
Yaḥyā Madanī
Rukn al-Dīn I
Shāh Kalīm Allāh
Shāh Niẓām al-Dīn
Jamal al-Dīn II
Mawlānā Fakhr al-Dīn
Ḥusām al-Dīn Farrukh
Mawlānā Quṭb al-Dīn
Nūr Muḥammad Muhāravī
Shāh Niyāz Bīniyāz
Muḥammad 'Āqil
Kāle Miyāṅ
Sulaymān Tawnsavī
Niẓām al-Dīn
Gul Muḥammad Aḥmadpūrī
Rukn al-Dīn II
Muḥyī al-Dīn
Rashīd al-Dīn Mawdūd Lālā
'Azīz Miyāṅ
Allāhbakhsh Tawnsavī
Ḥāfiẓ Muḥammad Khayrābādī
Shams al-Dīn Siyālvī
Ḥusām al-Dīn II Khūb Miyāṅ
Mawlānā Niẓām al-Dīn
Muḥammad Ḥasan Jīlī Kalīmī
Maḥmūd Miyāṅ
Mehr 'Alī Shāh
Ziyā' al-Ḥasan Jīlī Kalīmī
Abū Hāshim Madanī
Mawlānā Khayr al-Mubīn
Farīd al-Dīn II
Ḥasan Niẓāmī
Fakhr al-Ḥasan Jīlī Kalīmī
Inayat Khan
Naṣīr al-Dīn

Naṣīr al-Dīn. What is more, Mawlānā Quṭb al-Dīn's mention is all but missing in the *tazkiras* arising from the other lines of succession from Mawlānā Fakhr al-Dīn, which tend to evince, not uncharacteristically, a spirit of competition. Nor have later descendents of Mawlānā Fakhr al-Dīn or their spiritual heirs endeavored to fill the gaps. Most of the little information we have comes from non- or semi-Sufi sources, like Sir Sayyid Aḥmad Khān's *Asār al-ṣanādīd*.

Surprisingly perhaps, the two most recent figures in the lineage are the least well documented. Our account of Shaykh Muḥammad Ḥasan Jīlī Kalīmī (d. 1308/1890) is almost entirely dependant on oral traditions: specifically, the recollections of his grandson Syed Mohammed Fakrul Hasan Jeeliul Kaleemi (d. 1391/1971) (as narrated to Pir Vilayat Inayat Khan) and great grandson Syed Mohammed Rasheedul Hasan Jeeliul Kaleemi.[20] Similarly, we are apprised of Shaykh Muḥammad Ḥasan's *khalīfa* Sayyid Abū Hāshim Madanī (d. 1325/1907) almost exclusively through the scattered references to him in Hazrat Inayat Khan's lectures.

Ḥażrat Khwāja Mu'īn al-Dīn Chishtī

Khwāja Mu'īn al-Dīn Ḥasan Chishtī Ajmirī was born in the Central Asian region of Sijistan in the mid-twelfth century. In the course of travels he became the disciple of the itinerant Chishtī dervish Khwāja 'Usmān Hārvanī. For twenty years he continuously attended his master, carrying his bedroll and luggage. Only then, when he had fully realized the condition of selfless devotion, did Khwāja 'Usmān ennoble him with his spiritual blessings.[21]

Late in his life Khwāja Mu'īn al-Dīn made the decision that would immortalize him in the memory of posterity. Leaving behind the familiarity and security of Islamdom, he ventured to the "seventh climate," the Indian Subcontinent. The city in which he chose to settle, Ajmer in Rajputana (Rajasthan), had been until recently—or, as most accounts (including *Siyar al-awliyā'*[22]) have

[20] Letter dated 2 June 1999 (5 pages).
[21] Al-Kirmānī, *Siyar al-awliyā'*, 45.
[22] Ibid., 46.

it, still was—the capital of the Hindu Chauhān dynasty. It is not known precisely what Khwāja Mu‘īn al-Dīn did in Ajmer, but in retrospect it may be said that he succeeded in laying the foundations of Indian Sufism.

Khwāja Mu‘īn al-Dīn is remembered as "Gharīb-nawāz," the succor of the dispossessed. The few plausibly authentic sayings that come down to us evoke, among more conventional esoteric themes, a strong commitment to the service of humanity:

> The mark of knowing God is to shun publicity and keep silence in wisdom.
>
> When like a snake I shed my skin and looked, I saw lover, beloved, and love as one; in the world of unification all is one.
>
> Hajj-goers circumambulate the Ka‘ba with their bodies, but the mystics circumambulate the Throne of God and the Veil of Majesty with their hearts, desirous of a tryst with the Divine.
>
> There was a time when I circumambulated the Ka‘ba, but now the Ka‘ba circumambulates me.
>
> The seeker is entitled to be counted among the poor when he or she attains endurance in the world of transience. [When is this state established?] When the angel who records sins has had nothing to write for twenty years.
>
> The mark of lovers is to be submissive and not to fear being cast out. The mark of wretchedness is to sin and expect to be accepted.
>
> On the Day of Resurrection God will command the angels to extract Hell from the mouths of snakes. Then will flare up such hellfire that in an instant the whole world will be roiled in smoke. Whoever would be safe from the torment of that day should perform the service regarded by God as the ultimate service. [Which service is that?] To answer the cries of the oppressed, to fulfil the needs of the needy, and to fill the stomachs of the hungry.
>
> Know him or her to be dear to God in whom these three qualities are found: First, generosity like a river; second, affection like the sun; and third, humility like the earth.
>
> The one who finds grace finds it through generosity. The one who attains eminence attains it through purity.
>
> In truth, the one who is reliant on God is the one who disposes of people's pain and suffering.

> In this way, there are two things that bring about tranquility: one is servitude and the other is the glorification of God.[23]

Khwāja Mu'īn al-Dīn expired on 6 Rajab 633/1236.[24] His tombstone was inscribed, "A lover of God, he died in the love of God."[25] Today, hundreds of thousands of pilgrims flock to his *dargāh* for the annual *'urs* (death anniversary) festival.[26]

Ḥażrat Khwāja Quṭb al-Dīn Bakhtiyār Kākī

A native of Awsh in Transoxiana (present-day Kirgistan), Khwāja Quṭb al-Dīn Bakhtiyār Kākī came into the light of sacred history under the dome of the Abū al-Layth Samarqandī mosque in Baghdad, when in the presence of Shaykh Shihāb al-Dīn Suhrawardī,[27] Shaykh Awḥad al-Dīn Kirmānī[28] and other spiritual luminaries, he received initiation at the hands of Khwāja Mu'īn al-Dīn Chishtī.[29]

Khwāja Quṭb al-Dīn did not accompany his *murshid* (spiritual master) to India, but arrived in the region several years later and established himself in Delhi, the capital of the nascent Turkish sultanate. Sulṭān Shams al-Dīn Iltutmish (1211–36) treated him with great respect and visited his *khānqāh* regularly. But the atmosphere in Delhi became difficult when the government-appointed chief cleric (Shaykh al-Islām), who was apparently jealous of Khwāja Quṭb al-Dīn's charisma and influence, began fulminating against

---

[23] Ibid., 45–6.

[24] Chishtī, *Siyar al-aqṭāb*, 141.

[25] Al-Kirmānī, *Siyar al-awliyā'*, 48.

[26] On the history of the Ajmer shrine, see P.M. Currie, *The Shrine and Cult of Mu'in al-Dīn Chishti of Ajmer* (Delhi: Oxford University Press, 1989); also S.A.I. Tirmizi, "Mughal Documents Relating to the Dargah of Khwaja Mu'inuddin Chishti," in *Muslim Shrines in India*, ed. Christian W. Troll (Delhi: Oxford University Press, 1989), 48–60. For an insider's account of practices at the shrine, see "Rituals and Customary Practices at the Dargah of Ajmer," in *Muslim Shrines*, 60–76.

[27] Shaykh Shihāb al-Dīn Abū Ḥafṣ 'Umar Suhrawardī (490/1097–632/1234) was the founder of the Suhrawardī Order and author of the influential Sufi manual *'Awārif al-ma'ārif.*

[28] Shaykh Awḥad al-Dīn Ḥamīd ibn Abī al-Fakhr Kirmānī (d. 635/1238) was a prominent Sufi teacher, a friend of Ibn al-'Arabī, and the author of a celebrated *dīvān*. His *rubā'iyyāt* are translated in *Heart's Witness: The Sufi Quatrains of Awḥāduddīn Kirmānī*, B. M. Weischer and P. L. Wilson, trans. (Tehran: Imperial Iranian Academy of Philosophy, 1978).

[29] Al-Kirmānī, *Siyar al-awliyā'*, 48.

him. Distressed by this state of affairs, Khwāja Mu'īn al-Dīn resolved to bring his *khalīfa* to Ajmer. But as the two Shaykhs set out from Delhi, the whole city burst into tears and a grief-stricken mob pursued them. Khwāja Mu'īn al-Dīn's heart was so moved by this display of love that he changed his mind and allowed Khwāja Quṭb al-Dīn to stay.[30]

Khwāja Quṭb al-Dīn's path was one of severe asceticism. He hardly slept, fearing that even light sleep would "pose a problem." The greater part of his day was spent in prayer and meditation. His absorption in divine remembrance was so total he failed to notice when his young son fell gravely ill. When his wife's wailing woke him from his reverie and a *khalīfa* informed him that his son had died, he expressed deep remorse, saying, "Why did I not ask God for the preservation of his life? Had I only asked my wish would certainly have been granted."[31]

In the end, Khwāja Quṭb al-Dīn died as he had lived—lost in ecstasy. It happened in this way. The Khwāja was present at a mystical soiree (*maḥfil-i samā'*)[32] at the *khānqāh* of Shaykh 'Alī Sikzī. At a decisive moment, the *qawwāl* (ritual singer) sang a verse from the *Dīvān* of Shaykh Aḥmad-i Jām: "All those by the knife of submission killed; Each moment from God with new life are filled."[33] Hearing these words, Khwāja Quṭb al-Dīn was transported. Rapture so overwhelmed him that others had to carry him home, escorted by the musicians, who continuously recited the verse at his bidding. For four days and four nights he remained in a state of intoxication, and on the fifth night—14 Rabī' I 633/1235—he "embarked on his journey." He was buried in a meadow outside of Delhi (now long since urbanized) where he had once paused and remarked, "This earth has the fragrance of hearts."[34]

---

[30] Ibid., 54–55.

[31] Ibid., 49.

[32] On *samā'*, see Bruce B. Lawrence, "The Early Chishtī Approach to Samā'," in *Islamic Society and Culture: Essays in Honour of Professor Aziz Ahmad*, ed. Milton Israel and N.K. Wagle (Delhi: Manohar, 1983), and Regula Burckhardt Qureshi, *Sufi Music of India and Pakistan: Sound, Context and Meaning in Qawwali* (Chicago: University of Chicago Press, 1995).

[33] Amīr Ḥasan Sijzī, *Morals for the Heart*, trans. Bruce Lawrence (Mahwah, N.J.: Paulist Press, 1992), 246.

[34] Al-Kirmānī, *Siyar al-awliyā'*, 55.

Ḥażrat Khwāja Farīd al-Dīn Mas'ūd Ganj-i Shakkar

Khwāja Farīd al-Dīn Mas'ūd—Ganj-i Shakkar ("Treasure of Sugar") as he came to be known—was born in Kahtwal, in the district of Multan (present-day southeast Pakistan).[35] His grandfather Qażī Shu'ayb, a jurist from the house of Farrukh Shāh "the Just" (whose lineage is traced through Sulṭān Ibrāhīm ibn Adham to 'Umar al-Farūq[36]), had left his native Kabul after it was swallowed up by the Ghaznavid Empire.[37]

After completing his education in Kahtwal, for higher studies Farīd al-Dīn proceeded to the city of Multan, which was then an important center of Islamic learning. In Multan, Farīd al-Dīn lodged at a mosque, where he busied himself with books. One day as he was reading, Khwāja Quṭb al-Dīn Bakhtiyār Kākī appeared in the mosque. Farīd al-Dīn recognized at once that this was no ordinary man. As Khwāja Quṭb al-Dīn prayed his *namāz*, Farīd al-Dīn meekly seated himself nearby. When the Khwāja was finished, he addressed him: "Mas'ūd, what are you reading?" Farīd al-Dīn answered, "I am reading *Nāfi'* (a legal text, the title of which means 'useful')." "And do you find it useful?" Farīd al-Dīn confessed, "What is useful to me is the alchemy of your glance." Overcome with emotion, he kissed Khwāja Quṭb al-Dīn's feet.[38]

Farīd al-Dīn accompanied Khwāja Quṭb al-Dīn to Delhi, where amidst an august assembly of Chishtī and Suhrawardī dervishes, Khwāja Quṭb al-Dīn gave him his hand in initiation (*bay'at*).[39]

As an initiate Farīd al-Dīn followed the example of his *murshid* in fasting continuously and practicing the most rigorous spiritual disciplines—undertaking even the daunting *chilla ma'kūs* ("inverted retreat"): forty nights of *zikr* ("remembrance," invocation) while suspended upside-down in a well.[40] One day when Khwāja Mu'īn al-Dīn Chishtī, Khwāja Quṭb al-Dīn Bakhtiyār Kākī, and Farīd al-Dīn were sitting together, Khwāja Mu'īn al-Dīn said to

---

[35] For a full study of Khwāja Farīd al-Dīn Ganj-i Shakkar, see K. A. Nizami, *The Life and Times of Shaikh Farid-ud-din Ganj-i-Shakar* (Delhi: Idarah-i Adabiyat-i Delli, 1973).

[36] Imām al-Dīn Aḥmad Gulshanābādī, *Tazkīrat al-ansāb*, 20 (Bombay: n.p., n.d.).

[37] Al-Kirmānī, *Siyar al-awliyā'*, 58–59.

[38] Ibid., 60–61.

[39] Ibid., 61.

[40] Ibid., 68–70.

Khwāja Quṭb al-Dīn: "How long will you scorch this youth with spiritual exertions? Show him some kindness." Khwāja Quṭb al-Dīn assented, and both Shaykhs rose and together gave Farīd al-Dīn the blessing of a glance of kindness.[41]

After completing his training and receiving the honor of *khilāfat*, Khwāja Farīd al-Dīn asked his master's permission to withdraw to the cantonment town of Hansi, where he hoped to maintain a low profile. With tears in his eyes, Khwāja Quṭb al-Dīn said, "Mawlānā Farīd al-Dīn, I know you will go. Go. It is destined that you will not be present at the time of my death." Bidding those in attendance to recite Sūra Fātiḥa and Sūra Ikhlāṣ, he conferred on him his prayer carpet and staff, and uttered his final testament, "My place is yours."[42]

In Hansi one night Khwāja Farīd al-Dīn saw his master in a dream, beckoning him. In the morning he left for Delhi. On the road he learned that Khwāja Quṭb al-Dīn had passed away that very night. On his arrival in Delhi Qażī Ḥamīd al-Dīn Nāgawrī presented him with the remaining mystical insignia (*tabarrukāt*) of Khwāja Quṭb al-Dīn—a robe, turban, and pair of wooden sandals—and Khwāja Farīd al-Dīn took his seat in his master's house.[43]

Before long Khwāja Farīd al-Dīn again grew tired of the fast-paced life of the imperial capital and resolved to return to Hansi. His disciples and admirers protested that Khwāja Quṭb al-Dīn had entrusted Delhi to him—why should he go elsewhere? Khwāja Farīd al-Dīn simply replied, "My *pīr's* blessings will remain with me in equal measure whether I am in the city or the desert."[44] After some time in Hansi, Khwāja Farīd al-Dīn moved on to Kahtwal, and then finally settled in the lonely town of Ajhudan (now Pak Pattan, in the Pakistani Punjab).

In Ajhudan Khwāja Farīd al-Dīn lived with his family—two or three wives and five children—in a thatched hut near the village

---

[41] Ibid., 72.

[42] Ibid., 73.

[43] The transmission of mystical insignia and authority among the early Chishtīs is analyzed in Simon Dibgy, "*Tabarrukāt* and Succession among the Great Chishtī Shaykhs," in *Delhi Through the Ages: Essays in Urban History, Culture and Society*, ed. R.E. Frykenberg (Delhi: Oxford University Press, 1986), 63–103.

[44] Al-Kirmānī, *Siyar al-Awliyā'*, 148.

mosque. There was no *khānqāh* to speak of, but a *jamā'at-khāna*, or communal hall, was erected to house the dervishes who attended him. In accordance with the principle of *tawakkul* (reliance on God) Khwāja Farīd al-Dīn's family and disciples refused all offers of fixed income. Often they went hungry. At other times they received large donations in the way of *futūḥ* (serendipity), which they promptly disposed of.

Hindu yogis were known to visit the *jamā'at-khāna*. Khwāja Farīd al-Dīn himself practiced and taught a Hindavī *zikr*.[45] He also wrote poetry in the regional dialect, some of which survives in the Sikh scripture *Gurū Granth Ṣāḥib*. In these *slokas* (couplets) the Khwāja evokes imagery that is quintessentially Indian; koils, crows, cranes, and swans replace the moths and nightingales of the Persian poetic imagination. Faithful to indigenous conventions, he assumes the voice of a woman pining for her beloved husband.[46]

Like his predecessors, Khwāja Farīd al-Dīn wrote no books, but a number of his sayings were recorded by his disciples and incorporated in *Siyar al-awliyā'*. These are among them:

> God feels shame in denying the request of a worshipper whose hands are raised in supplication.
>
> If you have something, there is no reason to be sad. If not, there is still no reason to be sad.
>
> For a "true man", a day of contentment is like the night of the Prophet's Ascension (*mi'rāj*).
>
> One should not be dissuaded from one's work by the hotness or coldness of others.
>
> The Sufi is one who elucidates everything and is roiled by nothing.

---

[45] Sayyid Muḥammad Gīsū Darāz, *"Risāla azkār-i Chishtiyya,"* in *Majmū'a Yāzda Rasā'il* (Hyderabad: Intiẓāmī Pres, n.d.), 11–13; Shaykh Muḥammad Chishtī, *Majālis-i Ḥasaniyya* (Shahibagh MS.), 7; Shāh Kalīm Allāh Jahānābādī, *Kashkūl-i Kalīmī* (Delhi: Maṭba'-i Mujtabā'ī, 1308/1890–91), 65; Shāh Niẓām al-Dīn Awrangābādī, *Niẓām al-qulūb* (Delhi: Maṭba'-i Mujtabā'ī, 1309/1891–92), 32.

[46] *Sri Guru Granth Sahib*, trans. Dr. Gopal Singh (Chandigarh, India: World Sikh University Press, 1978), 4:1309–1315. The authenticity of the verses attributed to Khwāja Farīd al-Dīn is supported by K.A. Nizami in *The Life and Times of Shaikh Farid-ud-din Ganj-i-Shakar* (Delhi: Idarah-i-Adabiyyat-i-Delli, 1987), 121–22, and further reinforced by Carl W. Ernst in *Eternal Garden: Mysticism, History, and Politics at a South Asian Sufi Center* (Albany: State University of New York Press, 1992), 166–68.

> When a dervish dons new clothes it should be known that he dons his shroud.
>
> The prophets are alive even in their graves.
>
> A single experience of divine attraction (*jazba*) is better than the combined piety of both worlds.
>
> We are content with our portion: for us, knowledge; for the ignorant, wealth.
>
> Disaster comes with contrivance; peace comes with submission to the Divine will.
>
> A *faqīr* ("poor one") among the *'ulamā'* (religious scholars) is like the full moon among the stars.[47]

Khwāja Farīd al-Dīn would often lie in prayerful prostration (*sijda*) for hours on end, reciting, "I die for You; I live for You."[48] Having reached his ninety-third year, on the evening of 5 Muḥarram 664/1265, the Shaykh breathed his last. As he expired he uttered, "Yā Ḥayy, Yā Qayyūm" (O Living, O Eternal).[49]

Khwāja Farīd al-Dīn's tomb in Pak Pattan, originally built with unbaked bricks pried from his hut, is today a major pilgrimage center, attracting tens of thousands of devotees each year.

Ḥażrat Khwāja Niẓām al-Dīn Awliyā'

Khwāja Muḥammad Niẓām al-Dīn was born in the city of Bada'un in the Gangetic plain, where his grandfathers had taken refuge from the havoc wrought on their native Bukhara by the army of Ghengis Khan.[50] Early in Niẓām al-Dīn's childhood his father died, leaving his mother Bībī Zulaykha in straitened circumstances. The family often went hungry, but Bībī Zulaykha's forbearance and unshakable faith morally nourished her two children. At death's door she took Niẓām al-Dīn's hand

---

47 Al-Kirmānī, *Siyar al-awliyā'*, 150–3.

48 Ḥamīd Qalandar, *Khayr al-majālis* (*malfūẓāt* of Shaykh Naṣīr al-Dīn Maḥmūd Chirāgh), ed. K. A. Nizami (Aligarh: Department of History, Aligarh Muslim University, 1959), 224–225.

49 Al-Kirmānī, *Siyar al-awliyā'*, 174.

50 For a full study of Khwāja Niẓām al-Dīn Awliyā', see K. A. Nizami, *The Life and Times of Shaikh Nizamuddin Auliya* (Delhi: Idarah-i Adabyat-i Delli, 1991).

and said, "O Lord, I entrust him to you": words he always counted more precious than jewels.[51]

Niẓām al-Dīn devoted his youth to the acquisition of knowledge. Having completed his basic education in Qur'ān, *ḥadīth* (prophetic traditions) and *fiqh* (jurisprudence) he moved on to Delhi, where he enrolled with Khwāja Shams al-Mulk and Mawlānā Kamāl al-Dīn Zāhid. Within a few years his erudition was an established fact, marked by his nicknames *bahhās* (the debator) and *maḥfil-shikān* (the assembly-breaker).[52] He hoped to be appointed *qażī* (judge), and once asked his pious neighbor Shaykh Najīb al-Dīn al-Mutawakkil, the younger brother of Khwāja Farīd al-Dīn Ganj-i Shakkar, to pray for this outcome. Shaykh Najīb al-Dīn replied only, "Don't be a *qażī*. Be something else."[53]

Shaykh Farīd al-Dīn's reputation had reached Niẓām al-Dīn's ears in Bada'un. The inexplicable attraction he already felt deepened with his acquaintance with Shaykh Najīb al-Dīn. Desire eventually overwhelmed him. Mawlānā Jāmī relates that the turning point came when he experienced an epiphany on hearing a *mu'azzin* (caller to prayer) recite: "Has not the time arrived for the believers that their hearts in all humility should engage on the remembrance of God" (Qur'ān 57.16).[54] At once he set out for Ajhudan.[55]

The octogenarian Shaykh greeted him with a Persian couplet: "The fire of your absence has roasted the flesh of our hearts; the flood of desire for you has devastated our souls." Finding the visitor dumbstruck, he reassured him, "Every newcomer is nervous." The same day Khwāja Niẓām al-Dīn offered his allegiance.[56]

Resolutely shearing his long curls, Niẓām al-Dīn joined the sodality of the communal hall, where he shared in the chores and received the Shaykh's teachings. This was the first of three lengthy stays in Ajudhan during the three years that remained of Khwāja Farīd al-Dīn's life. The Shaykh described himself as a "dresser of brides": one who prepares souls for union with God. He encouraged

---

[51] Al-Kirmānī, *Siyar al-awliyā'*, 152.
[52] Ibid., 101.
[53] Ibid., 168.
[54] *The Holy Quran*, trans. A. Yusuf Ali (Lahore: Sh. Muhammad Ashraf, 1973), 2:1501.
[55] Jāmī, *Nafaḥāt al-uns*, 505.
[56] Al-Kirmānī, *Siyar al-awliyā'*, 106–7.

Niẓām al-Dīn to continue his academic studies, saying, "A certain amount of knowledge is also necessary for a dervish."[57] But when he witnessed a trace of intellectual arrogance in his disciple he rebuked him severely, sending him weeping into the desert. The ordeal came to an end with the Shaykh pardoning him and draping his shoulders with a robe.[58]

On several occasions Khwāja Farīd al-Dīn conferred special blessings on Niẓām al-Dīn. In the month of Ramaẓān, 1265, he granted him a *khilāfat-nāma* and announced, "You will be a tree in whose shade the world finds rest."[59] The Shaykh foresaw that Niẓām al-Dīn would not be present at his death. While Niẓām al-Dīn was in Delhi Khwāja Farīd al-Dīn's fragile health collapsed. Brushing past the Shaykh's sons who jealously guarded the door, Sayyid Muḥammad Kirmānī (Amīr Khwurd's father) entered his chamber and fell at his feet. When the name of Niẓām al-Dīn came up amid the affectionate words that passed between them, Khwāja Farīd al-Dīn produced his mystical insignia—prayer carpet, robe, and staff—and asked the Sayyid to convey them to his *khalīfa*, to the great consternation of his sons.[60]

Khwāja Niẓām al-Dīn's years at the "locus of Shaykhdom" of the Chishtī Order coincided with the most energetic phase of Turkish imperial expansion and consolidation in the subcontinent. Under the Khaljī dynasty[61] (1290–1320) the writ of the Sultan of Delhi ran from the Indus in the North to the Kaveri in the South. Khwāja Farīd al-Dīn had blessed Niẓām al-Dīn with the words, "Both the spiritual and temporal (*dīn ū dunyā*) have been given to you; go and take the empire of Hindustan!"[62] As Khwāja Niẓām al-Dīn's career progressed, he increasingly became the "King of Shaykhs" (*Sulṭān al-mashā'ikh*), a saint whose stature at once mirrored and challenged the absolute sovereignty of the temporal ruler.

---

[57] Ibid.
[58] Amīr Ḥasan Sijzī, *Fawā'id al-fū'ād* (*malfūẓāt* of Shaykh Niẓām al-Dīn Awliyā') (Lucknow: Naval Kishūr, 1326), 26–27.
[59] Al-Kirmānī, *Siyar al-awliyā'*, 117.
[60] Ibid., 122.
[61] On the Khaljī dynasty, see Kishori Saran Lal, *History of the Khaljis, A.D. 1290–1320* (Bombay and New York: Asia Publishing House, 1967).
[62] Ibid., 123.

Khwāja Niẓām al-Dīn's *khānqāh* beside the Jamuna fulfilled multiple functions: economic, cultural and spiritual. It was a welfare agency where donors with varied motivations deposited gifts in cash and kind (*futūḥ*) which were, as a rule, promptly distributed among the disadvantaged. It was an egalitarian enclave in a highly stratified society, effervescent with the best qualities of mind and heart. And it was a school of Sufism, where advanced disciples instructed novices in mystical theory and practice under the watchful supervision of the Shaykh.

Remembered as "the Beloved of God" (*maḥbūb-i ilāhi*), Khwāja Niẓām al-Dīn emphasized the service of humanity and the love of God over formal religious observance. Punctilious as he was in his own prayers and devotions, he taught that warmth of heart and openness of hand were more meaningful than mere obedience to the Law. Ardent love (*'ishq*) he regarded as an end in itself. But it called for nothing short of total self-sacrifice: "to live for God alone." On this the Shaykh was uncompromising:

> Sulṭān al-Mashā'ikh *God sanctify his precious secret* said, "*Maḥabbat* (affection) is the first stage of *'ishq* (ardent love) and *'ishq* is the last stage of *maḥabbat*. The word *'ishq* derives from *'ashiqa*, which is a kind of vine that grows in gardens. First it secures its roots in the earth beneath a tree, then climbs up its branches and twists itself around the tree. It does this until it has completely enfolded the tree, choking it until no sap remains in its veins. Whatever sources of air or water reach the tree it plunders, until the tree withers. '*Beauty plundered my life's sovereign sphere. The heart once mine is no more.*'" And he said, "When *'ishq* twists itself around a person, he cannot extricate himself unless he transcends his human nature. Just as the *'ashiqa* twists itself around a tree, causing it to wither, *'ishq* does the same to a person. As one of the saints said: '*Love, forbearance, and death: What a triumph over gratification and long life!*'"[63]

[63] Ibid., 466–467. Shaykh Niẓām al-Dīn's words bear the mark of a very similar passage in Shaykh al-Ishrāq Shihāb al-Dīn Suhrawardī's *Risāla fī haqīqat al-'ishq*: *Majmū'a-yi maṣannafāt-i Shaykh-i Ishrāq*, vol. 3, ed. S.H. Nasr (Tehran: Pazhūhishgāh-i 'Ulūm-i Insānī va Muṭāla'āt-i Farhangī,1373/1953–54), 287; English translation: *The Mystical and Visionary Treatises of Suhrawardi*, trans. W.M. Thackston Jr. (London, Octogon, 1982). The notion of an Ishraqī imprint in early Chishtī literature is an intriguing one, already tentatively suggested by Bruce B. Lawrence: *Notes from a Distant Flute* (Tehran: Imperial Iranian Academy of Philosophy, 1978), 48.

Under the direction of Shaykh Niẓām al-Dīn, the Chishtī Order sent tendrils into the provinces of Hariyana, Malwa, Gujarat, Deccan and Bengal, inextricably entwining Islamicate South Asia with its message of divine love. Muḥammad Ghawsī Shaṭṭārī speaks—suggestively if highly implausibly—of seven hundred *khalīfas* spread out across the Subcontinent.[64]

In his eighty-second year, as his health deteriorated, Shaykh Niẓām al-Dīn dreamed that the Prophet was eagerly awaiting him.[65] On 18 Rabīʿ II 725/1325 he "attained union" and was buried in a favorite garden near his *khānqāh.* A dome was later constructed by Sulṭān Muḥammad bin Tughluq, and successive centuries have seen the shrine's continuous embellishment.[66] In death as in life the saint is a source of solace for the dispossessed, who flock to the village that has sprung up around the shrine—now a bustling neighborhood within the urban sprawl of New Delhi.[67]

Ḥażrat Khwāja Naṣīr al-Dīn Maḥmūd Chirāgh

Khwāja Naṣīr al-Dīn Maḥmūd—Chirāgh-i Dihlī ("The Lamp of Delhi") as he became known—was born in Awadh (in present-day Uttar Pradesh), the son of a prosperous wool merchant of Khurasani descent.[68] He was just nine years old when his father died, but his pious and virtuous mother saw that he received an excellent education. By the age of twelve he had memorized the Qur'ān. He later studied *fiqh* with Mawlānā ʿAbd al-Karīm Shirvānī and Mawlānā Iftikhār al-Dīn Gilānī.

In his mid-twenties, disturbed by the desires flaring up in his body, Naṣīr al-Dīn turned pensive. Forsaking the pleasures of Awadh society he roamed the wilderness, praying in the company of sylvan dervishes by day and keeping lonely vigils by night. For

---

[64] Muḥammad Ghawsī Shaṭṭārī Mandvī, *Gulzār-i abrār*, trans. (Urdu) Fażl Aḥmad Jīvrī (Lahore: Islamic Book Foundation, 1326/1908–09), 84–84.

[65] Al-Kirmānī, *Siyar al-awliyā'*, 141.

[66] Ibid., 152.

[67] Contemporary practices at the Niẓām al-Dīn shrine are desribed in Desiderio Pinto, *Piri-Muridi Relationship: A Study of the Nizamuddin Dargah* (New Delhi: Manohar, 1995).

[68] For a full study of Khwāja Naṣīir al-Dīn Chirāgh-i Dihlī, see K. A. Nizami, *The Life and Times of Shaikh Nasiruddin Chiragh* (Delhi: Idarah-i Adabyat-i Delli, 1991).

nourishment he relied on lemon juice and the leaves of the *sambhālū* (chaste-tree)—both recognized in *yunānī* medicine as suppressants of lust.

It was in a diurnal vision that Naṣīr al-Dīn first encountered the saint who would become his master. Entering a mosque to perform the mid-morning supererogatory prayer (*chāsht*) he found himself facing "a man in green from head to foot, with large blood-shot eyes, a long beard, and a massive turban." The man began a cycle of prayer, but when his palms touched the floor in prostration he disappeared into thin air. Naṣīr al-Dīn knew in his heart that he had seen Khwāja Niẓām al-Dīn.[69]

At the age of forty-three, already a seasoned theologian and ascetic, Naṣīr al-Dīn joined the discipline of Khwāja Niẓām al-Dīn. Khwāja Niẓām al-Dīn had only to put the final touches on his personality. When he requested permission to retire in solitude, the Khwāja replied, "You must live in society and bear its blows, offering kindness and generosity in return."[70] Admonitions of this kind served to redirect Naṣīr al-Dīn's energies from self-mortification to the service of humanity.

As Khwāja Niẓām al-Dīn's life approached its term he authorized Naṣīr al-Dīn and a number of other senior disciples as *khalīfas*. A few months later, on his deathbed Khwāja Niẓām al-Dīn called Khwāja Naṣīr al-Dīn to his side and bequeathed to him the sacred insignia of the lineage—patchwork robe, rod, prayer-carpet, rosary and beggar's bowl—thereby confirming him as his principal successor.

Commenting on the death of Khwāja Niẓām al-Dīn, the historian 'Iṣāmī writes, "as soon as that holy man of virtue departed from Delhi to the other world, the country in general and the city in particular fell into turmoil and were subjected to ruin and destruction."[71] 'Iṣāmī's dim view of the reign of Muḥammad bin Tughluq (r. 1325–1349) was clearly shared by Khwāja Naṣīr al-Dīn, who regarded as a divinely decreed ordeal the harassment he

[69] Sayyid Akbar Ḥusaynī, *Jawāmi' al-kalim* (*malfūẓāt* of Sayyid Muḥammad Gīsū Darāz) (Kanpur: Intiẓāmī Press, 1356/1937–38), 71.

[70] Al-Kirmānī, *Siyar al-awliyā'*, 237.

[71] 'Iṣāmī, *Futūḥ as-salāṭīn* (English), trans. Agha Mahdi Husain (Aligarh: Department of History, Aligarh Muslim University, 1967), 3:689.

suffered for rebuffing the ambitious Sultan's efforts to conscribe him in the service of the state. The relief that Khwāja Naṣīr al-Dīn must have felt when Muḥammad bin Tughluq succumbed to an illness while campaigning in 1349 is evinced by his uncharacteristic participation in the coronation of Firūz Shāh Tughluq.

In an era when Ibn Taymiyya's (d. 1328) call for religious reform was finding echoes, Khwāja Naṣīr al-Dīn sought to defend Sufism by regulating it. He discontinued the practice of prostration before the spiritual master despite the fact that his predecessors had explicitly allowed it. While firmly rejecting the arguments of the *'ulamā'* against the legality of *samā'*, he forbade the use of musical instruments in his gatherings (a stricture his successors in Gujarat applied only to public *samā'* sessions—privately, instruments of every kind and even the voices of female singers were enjoyed).

Khwāja Naṣīr al-Dīn's reputation for legalism is no doubt deserved.[72] But an ecstatic streak was also known to exist in him. Sayyid Muḥammad Gīsū Darāz,[73] Khwāja Naṣīr al-Dīn's *khalīfa*, narrates an episode in which considerations of pious propriety fail to stifle the Shaykh's mystical emotion. On a certain day, in the *khānqāh*, Khwāja Naṣīr al-Dīn was deeply moved on hearing the verse:

> You promised not to oppress your lovers, but you did.
> You promised not to scratch out the names of your hopeless adorers, but you did.

Mawlānā Mughīs, who had been in attendance, drafted a tract repudiating as blashpemous the suggestion that God is capable of oppression. Presented with the tract, Khwāja Naṣīr al-Dīn summoned the Mawlānā and honored him with a turban. The following day, the Shaykh danced wildly on hearing the couplets:

---

[72] Cf. Carl Ernst, *Eternal Garden: Mysticism, History, and Politics at a South Asian Sufi Center* (Albany: State University of New York Press, 1992), 125.

[73] On "Banda-nawāz" Sayyid Muḥammad Gīsū Darāz (d. 825/1422), the prolific Chishtī master whose legacy dominates Deccani Sufism, see Syed Shah Khusro Hussaini, *Sayyid Muḥammad al-Husaynī-i Gīsūdirāz: On Sufism* (Delhi: Idarah-i Adabiyat-i Delli, 1983).

How fearlessly we beat the Magian drum last night
and hoisted his proud flag heavenward.
For the sake of a single drunken Mage-boy
We threw down a hundred times the skullcap of repentence.

Afterward, sitting on the roof, Khwāja Naṣīr al-Dīn called Mawlānā Mughīs and said "Yes Māwlāna, write about the actions you have seen here!"[74]

Khwāja Naṣīr al-Dīn explained the nature of ecstasy in one of his conversations, recorded by his disciple Ḥamīd Qalandar:

> I attained the pleasure of kissing his feet. First he said, "I have just come from paying respects at the tomb of Shaykh al-Islām Khwāja Quṭb al-Dīn Bakhtiyār Kākī, *God sanctify his precious secret.*" His words expressed utter delight. Then he remained in meditation for a time, awaiting the inspiration to speak. Meanwhile an intimate of the circle asked, "Where does the *ḥāl* (ecstatic state) experienced by dervishes come from, and what is it?" The Khwāja answered, "*Ḥāl* results from the integrity of one's actions, and actions are of two types. There is the action of the limbs, which is well known. Secondly, there is the action of the heart, which is called meditation (*murāqaba*). 'Meditation is what instills in your heart the knowledge that God is gazing on you.'" Then he said, "The lights of heaven first descended on the spirits. Their traces then manifested in the hearts, and afterward in the limbs. The limbs follow the heart. When the heart is in motion, the limbs likewise move."[75]

On the morning of 18 Ramażān 757/1356, at the age of eighty-two, Khwāja Naṣīr al-Dīn expired. In Medina, the funeral prayer of the "Lamp of Delhi" was offered in absentia by the Shaykh of Medina himself, 'Abd Allāh Muṭrī.[76] Khwāja Naṣīr al-Dīn was buried in his own house. Eighteen years later Firūz Shāh Tughluq constructed a suitable dome. In accordance with the Shaykh's directions, the sacred insignia of the lineage were intered with him. Thus ended—or so later Chishtī authorities

---

[74] Ḥusaynī, *Jawāmi' al-kalim*, 337.
[75] Qalandar, *Khayr al-majālis*, 57.
[76] Sayyid 'Alī bin Sa'd, *Jāmi' al-'ulūm* (*malfūẓāt* of Sayyid Jalāl al-Dīn Ḥusayn Bukhārī, "Makhdūm-i Jahāniyān"), ed. Qazi Sajjad Husain (New Delhi: Indian Council of Historical Research, 1987), 89.

maintain—the cycle of the twenty-two Khwājas. The cycle of Shaykh al-Mashā'ikhs was now to begin.[77]

Ḥażrat Shaykh Kamāl al-Dīn 'Allāma

Shaykh Kamāl al-Dīn was the son of Khwāja Naṣīr al-Dīn's sister. His father, Shaykh 'Abd al-Raḥmān, was a descendent of Farrukh Shāh of Kabul.[78] Having no children of his own, as a celibate like his own master, Khwāja Naṣīr al-Dīn treated Kamāl al-Dīn as his own son—even jesting with the boy's mother, "He's mine, not yours." When Kamāl al-Dīn was older Khwāja Naṣīr al-Dīn always stood up to greet him when he caught a glimpse of his turban.[79]

Kamāl al-Dīn attained such mastery of the exoteric and esoteric sciences he was accorded the prestigious title *'allāma* ("very learned"). Having completed his studies, he asked Khwāja Niẓām al-Dīn Awliyā's leave to go on *ḥajj*. Khwāja Niẓām al-Dīn blessed him, dressed him in his own robe, and deputized him as a *khalīfa*. He was also given *khilāfat* by Khwāja Naṣīr al-Dīn.[80]

Leaving India, Shaykh Kamāl al-Dīn performed the *ḥajj* not once but seven times. Finally he circled back through Khurasan. Everywhere he went Sultans and Amīrs honored him with gifts. By the time he reached Delhi he had accumulated thirteen camel-loads of gold, silver, and miscellaneous goods. Aghast at the spectacle, Khwāja Naṣīr al-Dīn exclaimed, "Shaykh Kamāl al-Dīn, how much of the world you have piled up!" Shaykh Kamāl al-Dīn explained that his intention was to give everything away. Blackening the coins, he distributed them among the *'ulamā'*, the pious and the poor, saying, "It is darkness, accept it." This done, he went into seclusion.[81]

Shaykh Kamāl al-Dīn 'Allāma passed away on 27 Dhū al-Qa'da 756/1355. His tomb is beside the shrine of Khwāja Naṣīr al-Dīn Chirāgh.

---

[77] Gul Muḥammad Aḥmadpūrī, *Takmila-yi siyar al-awliyā'*, folio 12b.
[78] Gulshanābādī, *Tazkīrat al-ansāb*, 21.
[79] Chishtī, *Majālis-i Ḥasaniyya* (Shahibagh MS), fol. 23r.
[80] Ibid.
[81] Ibid., fols. 23v–24r.

Ḥażrat Shaykh Sirāj al-Dīn

On his return from *ḥajj*, Khwāja Naṣir al-Dīn Chirāgh urged Shaykh Kamāl al-Dīn to marry, predicting he would produce a long line of saintly descendents. Shaykh Kamāl al-Dīn acquiesced, and fruit of his marriage was Shaykh Sirāj al-Dīn, popularly known as Sirāj al-Awliyā' ("Lamp of the Saints")—the first of a line of Gujarati Chishtī-Naṣīrī Pīrs that, true enough, continues to this day.[82] Shaykh Naṣīr al-Dīn looked on the boy with great favor and arrayed him with a robe of succession at the tender age of four years. When he reached adulthood, his father gave him his own *khirqa*.[83]

For forty years Shaykh Sirāj al-Dīn devoted himself to the acquisition of religious knowledge. In his father's absence he studied under three of his father's most distinguished students: Mawlānā 'Allāma Aḥmad T'hānisarī, Mawlānā Aḥmad Panīpatī, and Mawlānā 'Ālim Sangrīza Multānī. In piety (*taqwā*) the Shaykh was considered peerless, and the Sultan of Delhi accordingly designated him Shaykh al-Islām.[84]

As a denizen of Delhi in the latter half of the fourteenth century, Shaykh Sirāj al-Dīn was witness to the gradual unraveling of the sultanate. In all likelihood it was the news, in 1398, of the immanent arrival of Tamerlane's Mongol horde that convinced the Shaykh to abandon the moribund metropolis. Firūz Shāh Bahmanī (r. 1397–1422) offered him a generous sum to settle in his Deccan kingdom—similar to an offer he extended to Sayyid Gīsū Darāz[85]—but we are told the Shaykh's conscience revolted at the idea of chasing silver *tankas*. Instead he established himself in Patan, the capital of the newly founded independent sultanate of Gujarat.[86]

Muẓaffar Shāh,[87] the Sultan of Gujarat, held Shaykh Sirāj al-Dīn in high esteem. This is the backdrop to an interesting story.

---

[82] The current Sajjāda-nishīn of this hereditary line is Khwaja Ruknuddin Mohammed Farrukh Chishty.

[83] Lālā, *Mukhbīr al-awliyā'* (R.A.S. MS), fols. 231r–v.

[84] Ibid., fol. 231v.

[85] Richard M. Eaton, *Sufis of Bijapur 1300–1700: Social Roles of Sufis in Medieval India* (Princeton: Princeton University Press, 1978), 52.

[86] Lālā, *Mukhbīr al-awliyā'* (R.A.S. MS), fol. 231v.

[87] On Muẓaffar Shāh and the early Muẓaffarids, see Satish C. Misra, *The Rise of Muslim Power in Gujarat: A History of Gujarat 1298–1442* (New York: Asia

There was a man who attended Shaykh Sirāj al-Dīn for a year, during which time the Shaykh showed him every kindness. One day the man requested the Shaykh's recommendation to the court. Shaykh Sirāj al-Dīn asked him his name. The man was astonished: "For a year I have been in your service and you have instructed me with utmost affection—how can you not know my name?" The Shaykh simply replied, "Until now I had no need to ask your name. Now I do."[88]

Shaykh Sirāj al-Dīn composed four treatises and a *divān* of poetry, all of which were later lost. Just one couplet has come down to posterity: "O Sirāj, I've said it before and again I say; Only toward the face of my beloved do I pray." The "beloved" whom the poet invokes as his *qibla* (prayer niche) is Khwāja Naṣīr al-Dīn Chirāgh-i Dihlī.[89]

During his last illness, Shaykh Sirāj al-Dīn told his son Shaykh 'Ilm al-Dīn that angels had recently come to look into his affairs. He told them, "I am a Muslim. My sins are accidental. I have repented. Accidents are not important." Then he said, "Decree the unveiling of the paradisial delights my Lord has granted me and recite, 'Ah me! Would that my people knew (what I know)! —For that my Lord has granted me forgiveness and that has enrolled me among those held in honor'" (Qur'ān 36.26–27).[90]

Shaykh Sirāj al-Dīn "strove toward the abode of rest" on the evening of Thursday, 21 Jumāda 817/1414.[91] He was buried in Patan, in the grounds of the old fort, hence known as Pirpur.

Ḥaẓrat Shaykh 'Ilm al-Dīn

Shaykh 'Ilm al-Dīn was the second son of Shaykh Sirāj al-Dīn. His mother, Bībī Ṣafīya, a granddaughter of the saint Makhdūm Laṭīf al-Dīn "The Ocean-Drinker," was a soulful woman possessed of unique powers of insight.[92]

Publishing House, 1963).

[88] Lālā, *Mukhbīr al-awliyā'* (R.A.S. MS), fol. 232r.

[89] Ibid.

[90] *The Holy Quran*, trans. A. Yusuf Ali, 2:1176.

[91] Chishtī, *Majālis-i Ḥasaniyya* (Shahibagh MS), fols. 21r–v.

[92] Ibid., 15v–16r.

Shaykh ‘Ilm al-Dīn eventually succeeded his father on the prayer-carpet of Shaykhdom. He also received certification from Sayyid Muḥammad Gīsū Darāz.[93]

Shaykh ‘Ilm al-Dīn is remembered as an accomplished scholar and teacher of religious sciences. When his father died, he took up the instruction of his father's students, each from the place he had reached. Once he became engaged in a learned discussion with Mawlānā Badr al-Dīn Mālikī, a highly reputed authority on *ḥadīth*. By the end of the discussion the *muḥaddith* was so impressed he declared, "You are a lion and the son of a lion!"[94]

Shaykh ‘Ilm al-Dīn died on 26 Ṣafar—the year is uncertain.[95] He was buried under the dome of his father's mausoleum in Patan.

Ḥażrat Shaykh Maḥmūd Rājan

Shaykh Maḥmūd, known as Rājan (from *rāja*; "king"), was the son and principal successor of Shaykh ‘Ilm al-Dīn. He also received *khilāfat* from several other Shaykhs, significantly widening the purview of his lineage. Qażī Qāzan of Sindh granted him *khilāfat* in the Suhrawardiyya[96] as well as in a parallel branch of the Chishtiyya deriving from Khwāja Quṭb al-Dīn Mawdūd.[97] Another, nearer Chishtī transmission reached him through Shaykh Abū al-Fath Qurayshī (d. 1464), son of Mawlānā

---

[93] Lālā, *Mukhbīr al-awliyā'* (R.A.S. MS), fol. 345r.

[94] Ibid.

[95] In the writer's copy of *Mukhbīr al-awliyā'* (R.A.S. MS), the date is illegible (fol. 345r); *Shajarat al-Maḥmūd* (91) gives two alternatives, 809/1406 (also given by *Tazkirat al-ansāb*) and 901/1495, but the truth would seem to lie somewhere in-between.

[96] *Silsila*: ...Ibrāhīm Ad'hamī, Shaqīq Balkhī, Ḥātim-i Aṣamm, Abū Turāb Nakhshabī, Abū ‘Umar Iṣṭakhrī, Abū Muḥammad Ja'far Kharrāz, Abū ‘Abd Allāh ibn Khafīf, Abū al-‘Abbās Nahāwandī, Akhī Farrukh Zanjānī, Muḥammad ibn ‘Abd Allāh, Wajīh al-Dīn Abū Ḥafṣ Suhrawardī, Ziyā' al-Dīn Suhrawardī, Shihāb al-Dīn Suhrawardī, Lāl Shāhbāz Qalandar, Jalāl al-Dīn, Bahā' al-Dīn Zakariyyā, Ṣadr al-Dīn Muḥammad, Rukn al-Dīn Abū al-Fatḥ, Makhdūm-i Jahāniyān, Ṣadr al-Dīn Rājū Qattāl, ‘Ilm al-Dīn Shātibi, Qāzan.

[97] *Silsila*: ...Quṭb al-Dīn Mawdūd, Abū Aḥmad ibn Muḥammad, Najīb Lālā Samarqandī, Jamāl al-Dīn Makhdūm Jahāniyān, Ṣadr al-Dīn Rājū Qattāl, ‘Ilm al-Dīn Shātibi, Qāzan.

'Ala al-Dīn Gwaliyarī, Sayyid Gīsū Darāz's leading *khalīfa*.[98] Makhdūm 'Azīz Allāh al-Mutawakkil (d. 912/1506) deputized him in yet another branch of the Chishtiyya (a hereditary branch, traced from Khwāja Quṭb al-Dīn Mawdūd to Shaykh Zāhid), and also gave him his daughter's hand in marriage. Shaykh Aḥmad of Khattu[99] (d. 1445), one of the four eponymous founding fathers of Ahmadabad, initiated him as *khalīfa* of the Maghribī Order.[100]

Shaykh Maḥmūd Rājan authored a book entitled *Fawā'id al-Maḥmūdiyya*, which has been lost. Some of its contents, however, have been preserved in the work of Shaykh Muḥammad Chishtī. Shaykh Maḥmūd, we learn, delineated three degrees of *tawḥīd* ("affirmation of unity"). The first, the "common *tawḥīd*," entails the performance of religious observances. The second, the "elite *tawḥīd*," further entails the practice of superogatory spiritual practices. The third, the "ultra-elite *tawḥīd*," entails the upliftment of the downtrodden. The paragon of this degree is Muḥammad, the true *quṭb* ("pole") and *ghaws* ("protector").[101]

Shaykh Maḥmūd Rajan expired at the break of dawn on 22 Ṣafar 900/1494. He was initially buried in Ahmadabad, the new headquarters of his lineage, but five months later his son Shaykh Jamāl al-Dīn decided to have his remains moved to Patan, to the *dargāh* of Shaykh Sirāj al-Dīn and Shaykh 'Ilm al-Dīn. When his grave was opened, his descendents recount, his blessed body was found resting in the soil perfectly intact.[102]

---

[98] On Mawlānā 'Alā' al-Dīn Gwaliyarī and Shaykh Abū al-Fatḥ Qurayshī, see Muhammad Suleman Siddiqi, *The Bahmani Sufi Orders* (Delhi: Idarah-i Adabiyat-i Delli, 1989), 51–55.

[99] On Shaykh Aḥmad-i Khaṭṭū, see Z. A. Desai, *Malfuz Literature as a Source of Political, Social and Cultural History of Gujarat and Rajasthan* (Patna, India: Khuda Bakhsh Oriental Public Library, 1991).

[100] *Silsila*: Muḥammad, 'Alī, Ḥasan al-Basrī, Ḥabīb 'Ajamī, Ma'rūf Kharkī, Sarī Saqaṭī, Junayd Baghdādī, Aḥmad Rūdhbārī, Abū 'Ali Khatīb, Abū 'Uthmān Maghribī, Abū al-Qāsim Gurgānī, Abū Bakr Nassāj, Aḥmad Ghazālī, Muḥammad ibn Ḥasan Baghdādī, Yamanī ibn Sakhar, Abū al-Fidā' Mas'ūd Andalusī, Abū Madyan Shu'ayb, Abū Ṣāliḥ Khiqrī, Abū al-'Abbās Aḥmad, Muḥammad Maghribī, Abū Isḥāq ibn Muḥammad, Aḥmad-i Khaṭṭū. Lālā, *Mukhbīr al-awliyā'* (R.A.S. MS), fol. 369v.

[101] Shaykh Muḥammad Chishtī, *Risāla al-tawḥīd* in *Arba'ūn rasā'il* (Hazrat Pirmohammedshah Library, MS 1480), fols. 71r–73v. Thanks are due to Dr. M.G. Bombaywalla and the Trustees of the Hazrat Pirmohammedshah Dargah Sharif Trust.

[102] Chishtī, *Majālis-i Ḥasaniyya* (Shahibagh MS), fol. 15r.

Ḥażrat Shaykh Jamāl al-Dīn Jamman

Shaykh Jamāl al-Ḥaqq wa al-Dīn, known as Jamman, was the son and successor of Shaykh Maḥmūd Rājan. His mother was Mālik Bībī, daughter of Shaykh 'Azīz Allāh al-Mutawakkil. As a young man he enjoyed the joint tutelage of his father and his father's cousin Shaykh Naṣīr al-Dīn II, who also made him his *khalīfa.*

Little has come down to us of his life and teachings. He is said to have written several works, including a certain *Risāla-yi muzākira* ("Treatise of the Reminder"), but all seem to have been lost but one, his collected poems, or *Dīvān*. But even on its own the *Dīvān* speaks volumes.

In the best traditions of Persian Sufi poetry, *Dīvān-i Jamman* mellifluously reconciles a sweet and refined piety with the hot sanguinity of a free spirit. Many of the *ghazals* contemplate the omnipresence of God, conceived (as in Plato's *Phaedrus*) as "the ocean of eternal beauty." Others intone the praises of the Prophet Muḥammad or Shaykh Maḥmūd Rājan. Often the poet indulges in the rhetoric of the "infidelity of love" (*kufr-i 'ishq*), using scandal-tainted imagery to celebrate "the love of beauties" and lambaste heartless legalistic ritualism. This is the message of a choice *ghazal* that toys with taboos with a Hafiz-esque playfulness:[103]

> Last night as I roamed the Magian quarter aching for the comely face of a certain wineseller,
> The beloved came out demanding, "What are you doing here dazed and reeling?"
> "My heart and soul and faith are yours," I said, "In my passion for you sense and reason are gone."
> "Tear down the shop of supplication," she told me, "burn your prayer carpet, rip up your pious robe, and drink wine.
> Then I'll show you the path to peace. Give ear to this advice: Make nothing of yourself."
> Leaving being in my wake I reached a place booming with commotion.
> Drunk without wine, reveling friends delighted in unsung music.
> I felt myself waxing poetic, but when I raised my voice they all said, "Hush!"

[103] *Muntakhaba-yi dīvān-i Jamman* (Hyderabad: Maṭba'-i 'Azīz, n.d.), 21–2.

"This is not the Ka'aba that you can visit without decent attire.
It's not a mosque that you can just wander in like an animal.
This is the winehouse of love, our folk are of the heart, eternally drunk in lust of the Truth!"
If the comely face of an idol compels you, like Jamman, go sell this world and the next for a gulp of wine.

Shaykh Jamāl al-Dīn Jamman died on 20 Dhū al-Ḥijja 940/1534, and was buried in Ahmadabad.[104]

Ḥażrat Shaykh Ḥasan Muḥammad

The son of Shaykh Aḥmad Miyānjīv, a second cousin of Shaykh Jamāl al-Dīn Jamman, Shaykh Ḥasan Muḥammad Abū Sāliḥ was born in Ahmadabad. His mother, Bībī Khadīja, was from the saintly lineage of Shaykh Laṭīf al-Dīn "the Ocean Drinker."

When Shaykh Ḥasan Muḥammad was a small child, the Qādirī-Nūrbakhshī master Shaykh Muḥammad ibn 'Alī Nūrbakhsh visited his father's *khānqāh*. Seeing greatness in the child, he taught him Sūra Takāthur and told his father, "this son of yours, Ḥasan Muḥammad, will take on the qualities of God."[105] When Shaykh Ḥasan Muḥammad reached his fifth or sixth year, Shaykh Jamāl al-Dīn Jamman initiated him as both a *murīd* (disciple) and a *khalīfa*, saying, "O Ḥasan Muḥammad, I have given you my own outer and inner *jamāl* (beauty)."[106] Later, on returning from *ḥajj*, Shaykh Muḥammad ibn 'Alī Nūrbakhsh deputized him in the Qādirī,[107] Nūrbakhshī, and Tayfūrī Orders.[108]

Succeeding Shaykh Jamāl al-Dīn Jamman and Shaykh Aḥmad Miyānjīv, Shaykh Ḥasan Muḥammad attained great eminence. His

---

[104] Maḥmūdī, *Shajarat al-Maḥmūd*, 95.

[105] Lālā, *Mukhbīr al-awliyā'* (Shahibagh MS.), fol. 568v.

[106] Mawlānā Raḥīmbakhsh Fakhrī, *Shajarat al-anwār* (MS 22/31, Habib Ganj Collection, Maulana Azad Library, Aligarh Muslim University), fol. 364r; Thanks are due to the late Prof. K.A. Nizami and Prof. Nur al-Hasan.

[107] *Silsila*: ...Ḥabīb 'Ajamī, Dā'ūd Ṭā'ī, Ma'rūf Karkhī, Sarī Saqaṭī, Junayd Baghdādī, Abū Bakr Shiblī, 'Abd al-'Azīz Tamīmī, Abū al-Faraj Tartūsī, Abū al-Ḥasan 'Alī Hankārī, Abū Sa'īd Makhzūmī, 'Abd al-Qādir Jīlānī, Żiya' al-Dīn Suhrawardī, Najm al-Dīn Kubrā, Majd al-Dīn Baghdādī, Rażi al-Dīn 'Alī Lālā, Jamāl al-Dīn Jūrfānī, Nūr al-Dīn Isfarā'inī, 'Alā' al-Dawla Simnānī, Sharaf al-Dīn Maḥmūd, Sayyid 'Alī Hamadānī, Isḥāq Khuttalānī, Muḥammad Nūrbakhsh, Muḥammad 'Alī Nūrbakhsh, Muḥammad Ghiyās Nūrbakhsh.

[108] Lālā, *Mukhbīr al-awliyā'* (Shahibagh MS), fol. 569r.

fine character and saintly credentials won him the devotion of Sulṭān Maḥmūd III (r. 1537–1553), who granted him the annual income of four villages—a very considerable sum! The Shaykh spent this money on Sufi festivals (*a'rās*), replete with lavish banquets at which all were welcome. When he went on pilgrimage to the tombs of saints he traveled with such heaps of luggage that people took him for a wealthy Amīr, but all that he brought was for the poor.[109]

Shaykh Ḥasan Muḥammad spent one hundred thousand rupees building a magnificent stone mosque near Shahpur Gate in Ahmadabad.[110] With its intricately carved ornamentation in the Gujarati Jain style, the mosque took eight years to build, but in the last stage of construction civil war broke out and it was never quite finished.[111] The chaotic death throes of the Muẓaffarid dynasty brought the Shaykh's prosperity to an end. Amid the pillage and plunder, not even his library could be saved; important writings of Shaykh Sirāj al-Dīn, Shaykh Maḥmūd Rājan, and Shaykh Jamāl al-Dīn Jamman are now lost forever.[112]

Fortunately, Shaykh Ḥasan Muḥammad's commentary on the Qur'ān, entitled *Tafsīr-i Muḥammadī*, has survived the ravages of time. His teachings have also come down to us in the form of a collection of his conversations (*malfūẓāt*) recorded by his son Shaykh Muḥammad. *Majālis-i Ḥasaniyya*, as it is titled, is a highly readable melange of stories, Sufi sayings, family memories, and prescriptions for *zikr* and prayer. In the penultimate *majlis* (assembly), Shaykh Ḥasan Muḥammad recounts a powerful inner experience of spiritual turmoil allayed by divine grace:

> Friday, Dhū al-Qa'da 20 … I paid my respects (to Shaykh Ḥasan Muḥammad) and he said: "Last night as I was drinking water that had been boiled with rock salt a voice came, saying, 'Whenever

[109] Ibid., fol. 569v.

[110] See photograph included in the color plates following page 304.

[111] Lālā, *Mukhbīr al-awliyā'* (Shahibagh MS), fol. 469v; 'Alī Muḥammad Khān Bahādur, *Khātima-yi mirāt-i Aḥmadī*, ed. Sayyid Nawāb 'Alī (Baroda: Oriental Institute, 1930), 65; thanks are due to Prof. Nanavati and the Trustees of the Oriental Institute.

[112] Maḥmūdī, *Shajarat al-Maḥmūd*, 86.

> you drink water a fever will come over you. Do not drink.' I drank. The fever came, accompanied by an indescribable heat. Then the voice said, 'Drink water from a small cup instead of a bowl and the fever will leave you.' I drank water from a cup and at once the fever left. Afterward I felt a tinge of sadness. I then saw Quṭb al-Aqṭāb (the Pole of Poles) Ḥażrat Shaykh Naṣīr al-Ḥaqq wa al-Dīn Maḥmūd come and seat himself on a throne. He said, 'You are my flesh and blood. Where does your gargling stand in relation to this? You will travel to Ḥażrat Dihlī, 'the City of Men', and *inshā'allāh* God will make you like me—no, He will raise you higher still than I!' This slave replied, 'It will be enough for me if He will forgive my sins, great and small. These disturbances that afflict me are the fault of my avarice.' Quṭb al-Aqṭāb said, 'I will request of the Messenger Ḥażrat Muḥammad the Chosen—peace and blessings be upon him—that your sins be pardoned.'" ... Then [Shaykh Ḥasan Muḥammad] said, "I felt in my heart that Ḥażrat Makhdūm Quṭb al-Aqṭāb was invoking the Qur'ānic *āyat*: '[If they had only, when they were unjust to themselves, come unto thee] and asked Allāh's forgiveness and the Messenger had asked forgiveness for them, they would have found Allāh indeed Oft-Returning, Most Merciful'" (4.64).[113] Tears welled up in his eyes. [114]

The Shaykh explained to his son that all of this had occurred during a state of wakefulness, but with eyes closed. Hearing the account Shaykh Muḥammad became distressed, remembering Shaykh Niẓām al-Dīn Awliyā's observation that a taciturn saint only reveals his extraordinary experiences when death is near.

Shaykh Ḥasan Muḥammad lived to the age of fifty-nine. At the stroke of noon on 28 Dhū al-Qa'da 982/1575, he called Shaykh Muḥammad to his side and prayed in Arabic, "O Creator of the heavens and the earth, You are the Master of this world and the next; Keep me safe, and unite me with the good." Then he chanted *la ilāha illā Allāh* and *la ilāha illā Allāh Muḥammad rasūl Allāh*. Finally he uttered the name of Shaykh Naṣīr al-Dīn Chirāgh-i Dihlī, smiled, and "slipped into paradise."[115]

---

[113] *The Holy Quran*, trans. A. Yusuf Ali, 1.199.

[114] Chishtī, *Majālis-i Ḥasaniyya* (Shahibagh MS), fols. 29v–30v; (Munshi MS), fols. 45v–46r.

[115] Chishtī, *Majālis-i Ḥasaniyya* (Shahibagh MS), fol. 31r.

Ḥażrat Shaykh Muḥammad Chishtī

Shaykh Muḥammad Abū al-Ḥasan Shams al-Ḥaqq wa al-Dīn was the second son of Shaykh Ḥasan Muḥammad. His mother, Bībī Amat al-Ghanī, was a descendent of the itinerant Chishtī saint Shaykh 'Azīz Allāh al-Mutawakkil (d. 1447). As a young man, Shaykh Muḥammad received thorough training in the exoteric and esoteric sciences from his father, whose guidance is said to have continued to reach him even after his death.[116]

Shaykh Muḥammad succeeded his father soon after the 1572 conquest of Gujarat by Akbar, the ascendant Mughal Pādshāh. The deeds the Muẓaffarid Sultans had issued for the expenses of the Chishtī-Naṣīrī lineage were now null and void. Accustomed to a spectacularly wealthy *khānqāh*, Shaykh Ḥasan Muḥammad's disciples urged Shaykh Muḥammad to allow them to petition Akbar for their renewal. But in deference to hallowed Chishtī tradition, which permitted only unsolicited donations (*futūḥ*), the Shaykh refused, saying, "What need have dervishes to ask favors of metaphorical kings? The true King—who is the Sustainer of His slaves—is sufficient." When further pressure was applied, Shaykh Muḥammad rubbed out the documents and threw them into the reservoir. Finding himself surrounded by resentment he retired to his father's mosque, where he lived in seclusion, returning to the *khānqāh* only for weekly communal prayers. It was several years before the overwhelming evidence of his saintliness compelled the *murīds* to welcome him back.[117]

Shaykh Muḥammad's life was, by all accounts, riddled with "breaches of the ordinary." In the year 1020/1611, an invisible presence conferred on him *quṭbiyyat* (*lit.* polehood; centrality in the spiritual hierarchy; glossed by Shaykh Rashīd al-Dīn Mawdūd Lālā as "having the inner identity of Muḥammad"), and the Shaykh fell into an intoxicated trance. When he returned to his senses three days later, everyone greeted him as Quṭb.[118] Hence he is known to posterity as Quṭb al-Aqṭāb (Pole of Poles; a title also accorded to

[116] Lālā, *Mukhbīr al-awliyā'* (Shahibagh MS), fol. 474v.
[117] Ibid., fol. 475v; Bahādur, *Khātima-yi mirāt-i Aḥmadī*, 66–7.
[118] Lālā, *Mukhbīr al-awliyā'* (Shahibagh MS), fol. 477v; Bahādur, *Khātima-yi mirāt-i Aḥmadī*, 67.

Khwāja Naṣīr al-Dīn). Twelve years later, during a musical soiree, a still more sublime initiation was bestowed on him from above: *maḥbūbiyyat* (*lit.* belovedhood; the privilege of God's special affection; the station previously attained by Ḥażrat Niẓām al-Dīn Awliyā'[119]).[120] Shaykh Muḥammad's exceptional sanctity is believed to have been miraculously confirmed when, as he paid respects at the shrine of his ancestor Khwāja Naṣīr al-Dīn Maḥmūd Chirāgh-i Dihlī, the marble sarcophagus split open and he descended into the grave. Two hours later the tomb-sweepers reportedly watched in amazement as he reemerged, his face beaming—carrying, according to some accounts, the *tabarrukāt* buried with Khwāja Naṣīr al-Dīn.[121]

Shaykh Muḥammad was wont to pore over books late into the night in a room lit only by the sidereal light pouring out from under his turban.[122] The Shaykh's writings certainly reflect a vast erudition. Following the example of his father, Shaykh Muḥammad composed a commentary on the Qur'ān, which he dedicated to his father: *Tafsīr-i Ḥasanī*. His most celebrated work, *Baḥr al-asrār* ("Ocean of Secrets"), is a heavy tome in three parts treating the Way (*ṭarīqat*) and the Truth (*ḥaqīqat*). The Shaykh's shorter works are collected in a compendium entitled *Arba'ūn rasā'il* ("The Forty Treatises"). Also to his credit are several commentaries on Sufi classics, including the *Risāla* of Qushayrī[123] (d. 1072), the *Lama'āt* of 'Irāqī[124] (d. 1289), and the *Asmār al-asrār* of Gīsū Darāz.[125] In the following passage, excerpted from his *Sharḥ-i lama'āt*, Shaykh Muḥammad explains a famous *ḥadīth qudsī* (sacred tradition):[126]

> The question is: How did the inner qualities of the lover and the outer qualities of the beloved become known? The answer is: God

---

[119] Sayyid Nūr al-Dīn Ḥusayni Fakhrī, *Fakhr al-ṭālibīn* (*malfūẓāt* of Mawlānā Fakhr al-Dīn Dihlavī) (Delhi: Maṭba'-i Mujtabā'ī, 1315) 32.

[120] Lālā, *Mukhbīr al-awliyā'* (Shahibagh MS), fol. 479v.

[121] Ibid., fol. 481v; Bahādur, *Khātima-yi mirāt-i Aḥmadī*, 67.

[122] Lālā, *Mukhbīr al-awliyā'* (Shahibagh MS), fol. 479v.

[123] For a partial English translation of the *Risāla*, see *Principles of Sufism by al-Qushayri*, trans. B.R. von Schlegell (Berkeley: Mizan Press, 1992).

[124] For an English translation of the *Lama'āt*, see *Fakhruddin 'Iraqi: Divine Flashes*, trans. William Chittick and Peter Lamborn Wilson (Ramsey, N.J.: Paulist Press, 1982).

[125] Lālā, *Mukhbīr al-awliyā'* (Shahibagh MS), fols. 485r–v.

[126] Shaykh Muḥammad Chishtī, *Sharḥ-i lama'āt*, fols. 57r–v; copy graciously provided by Khwaja Ruknuddin Farrukh Chishty.

> has said, "I was a hidden treasure and I desired to be known so I created the creation." That is to say, what I was was unknown, with all of my qualities I was a hidden treasure, and I desired to know and manifest My qualities, so I created manifestations of my unknown qualities. It is the nature of the divine power (*jalāl*) to be lover and the nature of the divine beauty (*jamāl*) to be beloved. Thus it is clear that passion, ardor and love are properties of inner power. Indeed, all that finds manifestation comes about through power. But the abiding of these phenomena comes about through beauty. God wished His belovedness to be manifest and revealed to Himself; thus His act of becoming lover is actually His own belovedness. Whatever exists within Him is thus an impression of beauty. He said, "My mercy precedes My wrath." And His saying, "He hath inscribed for Himself mercy that He will gather you together for the Day of Judgement" (6.12) is of the same meaning. For existence is a product of mercy, of beauty. Non-being is a product of wrath, of power. Everything in existence is a manifestation of the impression of beauty. His beauty, which is the beloved, is contained within his power, which is the lover—abiding eternally with respect to its original principle. The impressions of the qualities that are manifest were originally unmanifest, as 'I was a hidden treasure' indicates, and the impressions of the qualities that are unmanifest are of the essence. Thus is established the fact that God plays the game of love with Himself. He himself is His own lover and He Himself is His own beloved. He is not occupied with anyone else, for there *is* no one else.

Shaykh Muḥammad "gave up his life in the path of the Eternal Lord" on Sunday 29 Rabīʿ I 1040/1630.[127] He was buried beside his father in Ahmadabad.

Ḥażrat Shaykh Yaḥyā Madanī

Shaykh Muḥammad Yaḥyā Abū Yūsuf Muḥy al-Dīn was born in 1602 to Shaykh Maḥmūd Chishtī, the second and most beloved son of Shaykh Muḥammad Chishtī, and Bībī Rābiʿa, the daughter of an aristocrat named Shaykh Tāj Muḥammad.[128] Shaykh Yaḥyā grew up under the tutelage of his paternal grandfather. By the age of twenty he had memorized the whole of the Qur'ān, and completed his studies in the exoteric and esoteric sciences. While

---

[127] Lālā, *Mukhbīr al-awliyā'* (Shahibagh MS), fol. 484v.
[128] Ibid., fol. 654r.

his grandfather lived, he accepted military service, but kept aloof from the immoral practices of the soldiery. On one occasion, his integrity brought him to the attention of the smaragdine immortal Khwāja Khiżr.[129]

The death of Shaykh Muḥammad in 1630 brought gloom over the family. The Shaykh's eldest son, Shaykh Ḥasan Muḥammad, could not endure life without his father, and died two days later. His second son Shaykh Maḥmūd, Shaykh Yaḥyā's father, soon followed. Shaykh Muḥammad's disciples expected his seniormost surviving heir, Shaykh Sirāj al-Dīn, to assume the succession. But Shaykh Sirāj al-Dīn insisted that his father had instructed him in the event of his passing to array Shaykh Yaḥyā with the sacred relics and install him to the office.[130]

For many years Shaykh Yaḥyā oversaw the *khānqāh* in Ahmadabad. During this time his fame reached the ear of the Mughal prince Awrangzīb, who was then Viceroy of Gujarat. Awrangzīb desired to have his blessing, but Shaykh Yaḥyā refused to wait on him at the palace, so the prince came to the Sufi's cell. Awrangzīb asked for words of guidance. The Shaykh replied with an *āyat* from the Qur'ān: "O you who believe, remember God often" (33.41). Awrangzīb asked, "which *zikr* shall I practice?" The Shaykh replied, "The best *zikr* is 'there is no god but God'" (*ḥadīth*: *Afḍal al-dhikr lā ilāha illā allāh*). "When shall I practice it?" "… And glorify Him morning and evening" (33.42). "In what posture?" "Those who remember God standing and sitting and lying down…" (3.191). The Shaykh then granted the prince his blessing—a boon that Shaykh Yaḥyā's followers believe spiritually preordained Awrangzīb's accession to the Peacock Throne.[131]

When, as Pādshāh of Hindustan, Awrangzīb later ordered the *muḥtasib* (enforcer of the Law) of Ahmadabad to prohibit sessions of *samā'*, Shaykh Yaḥyā and his dervishes performed the ritual with swords in hand. On receiving letters of protest from the Shaykh, Awrangzīb retracted the order and apologized in writing.[132]

---

[129] Ibid., fol. 656v.
[130] Ibid., fol. 657v.
[131] Maḥmūdī, *Shajarat al-Maḥmūd*, 115–16.
[132] Lālā, *Mukhbīr al-awliyā'* (Shahibagh MS) fols. 664v–668v.

One evening during the month of Ramażān, after presiding over a *maḥfil-i samā'*, Shaykh Yaḥyā paid his respects at the tombs of Shaykh Ḥasan Muḥammad and Shaykh Muḥammad. Muṣṭafā, the *qawwāl* who accompanied him, watched as he raised his hands and quietly uttered a soulful prayer. From the Shaykh's wistful expression Muṣṭafā understood that he longed for the tomb of the Prophet in Medina. So he sang a devotional *ghazal* of Mawlānā Jāmī, which begins, "How it would be, O Lord, to turn toward Yathrib and Batiha; to sojourn for a time in Mecca, then to dwell in Medina." The Shaykh stroked his beard and said, "I am deeply moved by this *ghazal*."

On another occasion, a few days later perhaps, during a *samā'* session, this same *ghazal* was sung. All at once, with tremendous intensity, Shaykh Yaḥyā declared, "*Inshā'allāh*, not today or tomorrow, but *right now* I will go!" Upon performing ablutions, he immediately set out for the Holy Cities.[133]

Shaykh Yaḥyā's disciple Shāh Kalīm Allāh narrates in his recorded conversations that before leaving Ahmadabad the Shaykh asked his mother's permission to embark on his pilgrimage and promised he would return. But after spending some time in Medina he developed such a strong attachment to the tomb of the Prophet that he could not bring himself to leave. He thought often of his promise to his mother, but was hindered from returning by his intimate love for the Prophet's tomb.[134]

Shaykh al-Ḥaramayn ("The Shaykh of the Two Shrines"), as he became known, "attained union" in the city of Medina on 27 Ṣafar 1101/1689 and was buried beside the tomb of Ḥaḍrat 'Uthmān.[135]

Ḥażrat Shaykh Shāh Kalīm Allāh Jahānābādī

Shāh Kalīm Allāh was born into the famous family of architects whose genius gave shape to such immortal monuments as the Taj Mahal in Agra and the Lāl Qil'a (Red Fort) and Jāmi' Masjid (Congregational Mosque) in Shahjahanabad ("Old Delhi"). His

---

[133] Maḥmūdī, *Shajarat al-Maḥmūd*, 117.

[134] Muḥammad Kāmgār Khān, *Majālis-i Kalīmī* (*malfūẓāt* of Shāh Kalīm Allāh Jahānābādī) (Hyderabad: Maṭba'-i Burhāniyya, 1328/1910), 6.

[135] Lālā, *Mukhbīr al-awliyā'* (Shahibagh MS), fols. 678v–679r.

family saw that he received a comprehensive education under the leading lights of Delhi.

As a young scholar, an affaire de coeur changed the course of Shāh Kalīm Allāh's life. He was going about his business one day when his gaze fell upon a young maid and he was instantly smitten by her charms. Her heart, however, was unmoved. Disconsolate in his longing, he remembered the local *majzūb* (intoxicated dervish), who was known to fulfil the desires of those who brought him sweets. Sweets in hand, Shāh Kalīm Allāh paid a visit to the *majzūb*. When the following day he returned to the object of his affection, this time with great warmth of feeling she seated him by her side. But now that he was cheek by jowl with her, he found that his heart was elsewhere—it was with the *majzūb*. So he got up and hurried back to the *majzūb*, and became his companion.

One day the *majzūb* went to sleep on Shāh Kalīm Allāh's knee and then suddenly awoke in a fit of divine intoxication. As the *majzūb* danced and called out, Shāh Kalīm Allāh made a bid to extricate himself from the spectacle. When it was over, the *majzūb* called him over and said, "If you want fire like this, I have plenty. But Shaykh Yaḥyā Madanī has water. Go to him." Hearing this, without so much as asking his mother's leave Shāh Kalīm Allāh set out for Medina.[136]

In Medina, Shaykh Yaḥyā accepted Shāh Kalīm Allāh as a disciple and a deep inner connection soon developed between them. Before long Shaykh Yaḥyā granted Shāh Kalīm Allāh a robe of succession and sent him back to the Mughal capital to do the work of the Chishtī Order.

On returning to Delhi, Shāh Kalīm Allāh leased the *ḥavelī* he had inherited from his family and occupied a more modest house in Bāzār-i Khānum, the busiest marketplace in Shahjahanabad, situated directly between the Lāl Qil'a, the city's "head," and the Jāmi' Masjid, its "heart." This house became his home, *khānqāh*, and *madrasa* (Islamic seminary) in one, and people of all kinds streamed through its doors seeking spiritual upliftment and theological instruction.

[136] Aḥmadpūrī, *Takmila-yi siyar al-awliyā'*, fols. 70r–v.

Above:
Dargāh of Ḥażrat Khwāja Mu'īn al-Dīn Chishtī, Ajmer

Below:
Dargāh of Ḥażrat Khwāja Quṭb al-Dīn Bakhtiyār Kākī, Mehrauli

Above:
Ḥażrat Khwāja Farīd al-Dīn Mas'ūd Ganj-i Shakkar: popular religious art from Ajmer (anonymous)
Below:
Dargāh of Ḥażrat Khwāja Farīd al-Dīn Mas'ūd Ganj-i Shakkar, Pak Pattan

Above:
Dargāh of Ḥażrat Khwāja Niẓām al-Dīn Awliyā', Basti Hazrat Nizamuddin, New Delhi

Below:
Khānqāh of Ḥażrat Khwāja Niẓām al-Dīn Awliyā', New Delhi

Above:
Dargāh of Khwāja Naṣīr al-Dīn Maḥmūd Chirāgh-i Dihlī, Chiragh Delhi, New Delhi

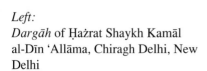

Left:
Dargāh of Ḥażrat Shaykh Kamāl al-Dīn ʻAllāma, Chiragh Delhi, New Delhi

Right:
Dargāh of Ḥażrat Shaykh Sirāj al-Dīn, Ḥażrat Shaykh ʻIlm al-Dīn, and Ḥażrat Shaykh Maḥmūd Rājan, Patan

Above:
Dargāh of Ḥażrat Shaykh Jamāl al-Dīn Jamman, Naurangpura, Ahmedabad

Right:
Dargāh of Ḥażrat Shaykh Ḥasan Muḥammad and Ḥażrat Shaykh Muḥammad Chishtī, Shahpur, Ahmedabad

Below:
Masjid of Ḥażrat Shaykh Ḥasan Muḥammad, Shahpur, Ahmedabad

Top of page:
Dargāh of Ḥażrat Shaykh Shāh Kalīm Allāh Jahānābādī, Old Delhi

Above:
Dargāh of Ḥażrat Shaykh Shāh Niẓām al-Dīn Awrangābādī, Aurangabad

Right:
Dargāh of Ḥażrat Shaykh Mawlānā Fakhr al-Dīn, Mehrauli

Above:
Dargāh of Ḥażrat Shaykh Ghulām Quṭb al-Dīn, Mehrauli

Right:
Dargāh of Ḥażrat Shaykh Ghulām Naṣīr al-Dīn Kāle Miyāṅ, Mehrauli

Below:
Dargāh of Ḥażrat Shaykh Muḥammad Ḥasan Jīlī Kalīmī, Toli Chowki, Hyderabad

Right:
Dargāh of Ḥażrat Shaykh Abū Hāshim Madanī, Purana Pul, Hyderabad

Below:
Dargāh of Hazrat Pir-o-Murshid Inayat Khan, Hazrat Nizamud-din Basti, New Delhi

Shāh Kalīm Allāh initiated numerous disciples; women as well as men. In the spirit of "universal peace" (*ṣulḥ-i kull*; a term appropriated from Abū al-Fażl, Prime Minister to Akbar), Hindus were not excluded from the fold, as was the case in most other orders.[137] Disciples who proved especially capable and committed were deputized as *khalīfa*s and entrusted with a region of mystical jurisdiction (*vilāyat*). Shāh Kalīm Allāh sent his foremost *khalīfa*, Shāh Niẓām al-Dīn, to the Deccan, where Awrangzīb was leading the Mughal army in an interminable campaign. Since the majority of officers were of Tūrānī (i.e., Turkic) descent, Shāh Kalīm Allāh urged Shāh Niẓām al-Dīn to make special use of the transmission of the Central Asian Naqshbandī *silsila*, which he had received from Mīr Muḥtarim Allāh of Lahore and in turn passed on to his *khalīfa*s.[138]

Many of Shāh Kalīm Allāh's letters to his *khalīfa*s survive in a collection that has been lithographed under the title *Maktūbāt-i Kalīmī*. The Shāh's other writings include treatises on astronomy and medicine (*Risāla sharḥ tashrīḥ al-aflāk 'āmilī maḥshī bi al-fārīsa*, *Sharḥ al-Qānūn*), an Arabic commentary on the Qur'ān (*Qirān al-Qur'ān bi al-bayān*), and several works on various aspects of the theory and practice of Sufism (*'Ashara kāmila*, *Siwā' al-sabīl*, *Kashkūl*, *Muraqqa'*, *Tasnīm*, *Ilhāmāt*). Among these, *Kashkūl* and *Muraqqa'* have earned unparalleled distinction in the literary canon of the Chishtiyya, to such an extent that manuscript copies are often treated as equivalent to robes of succession. *Muraqqa'* ("The Patchwork Robe") is a manual of supererogatory acts of worship. Its companion volume, *Kashkūl* ("The Alms Bowl"), is a manual of esoteric discipline, detailing various methods of *zikr*, *fikr* (contemplation), and *murāqaba* (meditation).

The introduction to *Kashkūl* serves as a concise summary of Shāh Kalīm Allāh's mystical philosophy:

---

137 Jahānābādī, *Maktūbāt-i Kalīmī*, 74.

138 *Silsila*: ... Abū Bakr, Salmān Fārsī, Qāsim ibn Muḥammad, Ja'far Ṣādiq, Abū Yazīd Bisṭāmī, Abū al-Ḥasan Kharāqānī, Abū al-Qāsim Gurgānī, 'Alī Fārmadī, Yūsuf Hamadānī, 'Abd al-Khāliq Ghijduwānī, 'Ārif Rivkirab, Ashhar Faghnawī, 'Alī Rāmtīnī, Muḥammad Bābā, Amīr Kulāl, Bahā' al-Dīn Naqshband, Khwāja Ya'qūb, Khwāja Aḥrār, Muḥammad Qāżī, Khwājagī Amkunagī, Khwāja Kalān, Muḥammad Hāshim, Muḥammad Miskīn, Mīr Muḥtarim Allāh. Ahmadpuri, *Takmila-yi siyar al-awliya'*, fols. 75v–82r.

> O seeker of God, may God cause you to reach the highest station of the gnostics. Know that before its association with shadowy phenomenal being, the limitless being was hidden. There was no trace from the traceless. By the necessity of its own love for itself, the limitless being descended through a procession of divine and phenomenal emanations. In every creature, by virtue of the constraint of limitation it appears as "lover", and by virtue of transcending limitation it reveals itself as "beloved". The perfection of every creature is in its return to freedom from limitation, its return to the pristine state (*bīrangī*) from which it has emerged. I speak in particular of the human being, the comprehensive epiphany of Essence and Attributes, distinguished above all other creatures through upholding the Covenant. The perfection of the human being is in passing away in God (*fanā fī Allah*) and living on in God (*baqā bi Allah*). The first journey is the journey toward God, while the second is the journey in God. The first has an end, while the second has none.[139]

In his old age Shāh Kalīm Allāh suffered from gout. He passed away on 24 Rabī‘ I 1142/1729, and was buried in the precincts of his *khānqāh*, which remained a flourishing Sufi center until it was demolished during the Revolt of 1857.[140]

Ḥażrat Shāh Niẓām al-Dīn Awrangābādī

A descendent of the great Persian saint Shaykh Shihāb al-Dīn Suhrawardī, Shāh Niẓām al-Dīn was born in Purab, the region outlying Lucknow. After completing his basic education in his hometown, Shāh Niẓām al-Dīn came to Shahjahanabad for further studies. Hearing of Shāh Kalīm Allāh's impressive reputation, he decided to visit him at his *khānqāh*. As it happened, he arrived at the Shaykh's door at a time when *samā‘* was in session. Despite the circumstances, Shāh Kalīm Allāh sent someone to ask his name, and then called him in. When some of the dervishes in attendance protested that the entrance of a stranger was a breach of the rules of *samā‘*, Shāh Kalīm Allāh silenced them, saying, "This gentleman is no stranger."[141]

Shāh Niẓām al-Dīn requested the Shaykh's permission to frequent his circle, and in due time became a devoted student. As

---

[139] Jahānābādī, *Kashkūl-i Kalīmī*, 3.
[140] Fakhrī, *Shajarat al-anwār*, fol. 383v.
[141] Aḥmadpūrī, *Takmila-yi siyar al-awliyā'*, fols. 83r–v.

days passed, Shāh Kalīm Allāh's magnetism and its affect on others increasingly fascinated him. On one occasion a disciple of Shaykh Yaḥyā came to Shahjahanabad from Medina and, seeing Shāh Kalīm Allāh, fell into a swoon of ecstasy. Amazed by what he had witnessed, Shāh Niẓām al-Dīn asked the Shaykh for an explanation. Shāh Kalīm Allāh simply replied, "This is one of the sciences I will teach you." The promise filled Shāh Niẓām al-Dīn with anticipation, and eventually he could not keep himself from asking, "Has this slave become worthy of a lesson in that science?"[142]

One day as Shāh Kalīm Allāh rose from a gathering Shāh Niẓām al-Dīn placed his sandals before him. The Shaykh was touched by this gesture of devotion, and said, "In the acquisition of esoteric sciences, *tawajjuḥ* (concentration on the teacher) is first and foremost." Shāh Niẓām al-Dīn replied with a couplet, "I have entrusted my very essence to you; you know the accounting, whether more or less." Shāh Kalīm Allāh suddenly remembered a prophecy that had been uttered by Shaykh Yaḥyā, that the one destined to become the next "master of the lineage" (*mālik-i nisbat*) would recite this verse. At once he initiated Shāh Niẓām al-Dīn, imparted an abundance of blessings, and gave him permission to teach.[143]

Shāh Kalīm Allāh soon sent Shāh Niẓām al-Dīn to the Deccan. After some time in the Mughal camp offering spiritual guidance to the soldiery, Shāh Niẓām al-Dīn settled in Aurangabad, where he established a *khānqāh*. The Shaykh's popularity in the Deccan grew rapidly. When he lead *zikr* in the mosque—a practice Shāh Kalīm Allāh asked him to discontinue because of the risk of controversy—two or three hundred people joined in.[144] It is said that his disciples numbered over one hundred thousand.[145] Among them was Niẓām al-Mulk Āṣaf Jāh, the first Nizam of Hyderabad.[146]

---

[142] Ibid., fol. 84v.
[143] Ibid., fol. 84r.
[144] Jahānābādī, *Maktūbāt-i Kalīmī*, 78.
[145] Khān, *Manāqib-i Fakhriyya*, 4.
[146] On Āṣaf Jāh I, see Yusuf Husain, *The First Nizām: The Life and Times of Nizāmu'l-Mulk Āsaf Jāh* (Bombay: Asia Publishing House, 1963).

Unlike his prolific predecessor, Shāh Niẓām al-Dīn composed only one book, a manual of esoteric discipline entitled *Niẓām al-qulūb* ("The Harmony of Hearts"). Building on the work of Sayyid Muḥammad Gīsū Darāz (*Risāla-i murāqaba* and *Risāla-i adhkār-i Chishtiyya*) and Shāh Kalīm Allāh (*Kashkūl*), *Niẓām al-qulūb* catalogs various types of *zikr*—mostly in Arabic formulae, but some couched in Persian or Hindavī (e.g., "the *azkār* of the yogis"). This is a sample of Shāh Niẓām al-Dīn's writing, excerpted from the charmingly original chapter "On the *Zikr* of Animals":

> Ḥażrat Bandagī Sayyid Maḥmūd (may God sanctify his secret) lived in the wilderness of Pilas Khwaja. His father used to beat him for the sake of his education. But he could not tolerate the sting, so one day he left his parents and struck out into the desert. There he found himself without any access to knowledge, meditation, divine remembrance (*zikr*), or wisdom, and became disheartened. He went and sat under a tree. After the third day a sugar-eater perched on the tree and started chirping, "tū'ī tū'ī tū'ī" (which means in Persian, 'you are, you are, you are'). The Sayyid liked that sound very much, and began to chirp in the same way. After a year he had a revelation. Thereafter he would sit still watching his breath for twenty counts and then rapidly recite "tū'ī, tū'ī" until he became exhausted. Once exhausted, he would start over again.

Shāh Niẓām al-Dīn "attained union" on 12 Dhū al-Qa'da 1142/1730, just months after the death of Shāh Kalīm Allāh.[147]

Ḥażrat Shaykh Mawlānā Fakhr al-Dīn

In 1717 the second son of Shāh Niẓām al-Dīn was born to the first of his two wifes, Sayyid Bigum, a descendant of Sayyid Muḥammad Gīsū Darāz. On hearing the news of his birth, in high spirits Shāh Kalīm Allāh christened him Fakhr al-Dīn and declared him his own honorary son.[148]

In Aurangabad Mawlānā Fakhr al-Dīn received an exceptional education. In addition to his learned father, with whom he read Qur'ān commentaries and Jāmī's *Nafaḥāt al-uns*, his teachers included the doctor of law Mawlānā 'Abd al-Ḥakīm, the traditionist

---

[147] Aḥmadpūrī, *Takmila-yi siyar al-awliyā'*, fol. 92r.
[148] Khān, *Manāqib-i Fakhriyya*, 4–5.

Ḥāfiẓ As'ad al-Anṣārī, and Miyāṅ Muḥammad Jān, an interpreter of Ibn al-'Arabī's doctrine of "Unity of Being."[149]

Mawlānā Fakhr al-Dīn was sixteen when his father died. On the completion of his formal studies three years later, he immersed himself in the practice of rigorous ascetic and esoteric disciples. Serving in the miltary as an officer under Niẓām al-Dawla Naṣīr Jang, the son of Niẓām al-Mulk Āṣaf Jāh, he spent his days exercising his swordsmanship and his nights secretly meditating in a small tent.[150]

After some years he found that military service no longer provided an effective screen for his inner life and resigned. On assuming his father's place at the *khānqāh* in Aurangabad, he was soon inundated with petitioners. He felt the desire to go elsewhere but filial piety held him back. In the throes of indecision, while at prayer a message came to him: "Break your chains, be free my son!" A sign from the spirit of Khwāja Mu'īn al-Dīn Chishtī further confirmed that he should go to Delhi.[151]

In 1165/1752 the Mawlānā left Aurangabad for Delhi, where he assumed the leadership of the *khānqāh* of Shāh Kalīm Allāh, taking up residence first at Katra Phulel and later at a *madrasa* built by Ghāzī al-Dīn Khān near the Ajmeri Gate.[152] The mood in Delhi in the years following Nādir Shāh's invasion (1739) was bleak, as the satires of Saudā' (d. 1780) grimly attest. As rival polities struggled for power the central institutions of the Mughal Empire decayed and the demoralized citizens of its capital fell prey to relentless waves of depredation and invasion.

Mawlānā Fakhr al-Dīn won the devotion of Shāh 'Ālam[153] (r. 1759-1806) and many of his courtiers—the Shī'ī Amīr al-Umarā' Mīrzā Najaf Khān being a notable exception—but remained aloof from the effete luxury of the court. He is reported to have appealed to the Emperor to assert his prerogatives for the sake of social order: "If the incumbent Sultan does not bother to take the trouble to

[149] Aḥmadpūrī, *Takmila-yi siyar al-awliyā'*, fols. 94v–95r.
[150] Khān, *Manāqib-i Fakhriyya*, 6.
[151] Ibid., 8–9.
[152] Ghāzī al-Dīn Khān, *Masnavī*, fol. 132r.
[153] On Shāh 'Ālam, see Michael Edwardes, *King of the World: The Life of the Last Great Moghul Emperor* (New York: Taplinger Publishing Co., 1971).

personally concern himself with the control and management of the kingdom, matters will never be put right."[154]

An avid traditionist, Mawlānā Fakhr al-Dīn assembled a voluminous library and authored three learned works: *Niẓām al-'aqā'id*, *Risāla-i Murjiyya*, and *Fakhr al-Ḥasan*. The latter work is a refutation of Shāh Walī Allāh's[155] (d. 1762) argument (in *Intibāh fī silāsil awliyā' Allāh*) against the historicity of Ḥasan al-Baṣri's initiation from 'Alī ibn Abī Ṭālib, implying discontinuity in the *silsila* of the Chishtiyya. The Mawlānā's conversations are recorded in *Fakhr al-ṭālibīn*, which includes this discourse on the nature of ecstasy:

> One day he was in the vestibule of the *khanqah* and I attained the boon of an encounter. A discussion transpired on states of ecstasy and audition. Ḥażrat Mawlānā said: "The ecstatic state of a Sufi is exactly like the intoxication of wine. If someone is silent at the outset of intoxication he will maintain silence as long as the intoxication lasts. And if he is speaking in the beginning, he will raise hue and cry until the end, when he will most likely lose consciousness. In this same way, if someone shows control in his ecstatic state, the experience will be an agreeable one. But if he begins with speaking, he will speak until his last breath, and will lose all reason and discrimination. Whatever is on his tongue comes out, duly followed by something else. He loses control and the time of others is wasted. As is well known, a heart is needed to speak in such a state, but it is necessary for the Sufi to be attentive at such times and to speak faithfully what is in his heart. But how will the listeners comprehend him? For from where do his words come? Sometimes that which comes out is unacceptable even to himself, and other times he speaks with utmost knowledge."[156]

Mawlānā Fakhr al-Dīn trained dozens of *khalīfa*s and dispatched them "throughout the seven climates." Among them Shāh Nūr Muḥammad Muhāravī and Shāh Niyāz Aḥmād, who founded

---

[154] Khān, *Manāqib-i Fakhriyya*, 18.

[155] On the influential Naqshbandī theologian and reformer Shāh Walī Allāh, see S.A.A. Rizvi, *Shāh Wāli-Allāh and His Times* (Canberra, Australia: Ma'rifat Publishing House, 1980). Shāh Walī Allāh's magnum opus, *Ḥujjat Allāh al-bāligha*, has been translated into English by Marcia Hermansen: *The Conclusive Argument from God: Shah Walī Allāh of Delhi's Ḥujjat Allāh al-bāligha* (Leiden: E.J. Brill, 1996).

[156] Fakhrī, *Fakhr al-ṭālibīn*, 40.

khānqāhs in Muhar (Punjab) and Bareilly (U.P.) respectively, attained great prominence. The success of Mawlānā Fakhr al-Dīn's organizational work was such that Khwāja Ḥasan Niẓāmī, a spiritual heir of Shāh Nūr Muḥammad, described him as the *mujaddid* or "reviver" of the Niẓāmi *silsila.*[157]

The death of Mawlānā Fakhr al-Dīn, "the Beloved of the Prophet" (*muḥibb al-nabī*) as he was known, occurred on the night of 27 Jumāda II 1199/1785. He was buried opposite the inner gate to the tomb of Khwāja Quṭb al-Dīn Bakhtiyār Kākī in Mehrauli.[158]

Ḥażrat Shaykh Ghulām Quṭb al-Dīn

When Mawlānā Fakhr al-Dīn shifted to Delhi he left behind a son, Ghulām Quṭb al-Dīn. After memorizing the Qur'ān and completing his formal studies, Mawlānā Ghulām Quṭb al-Dīn felt a strong desire to see his father. Journeying to Delhi, he fell at his father's feet. Mawlānā Fakhr al-Dīn imparted inner and outer blessings to his son, arrayed him in a robe, and sent him back to Aurangabad.[159]

After the death of Mawlānā Fakhr al-Dīn, Mawlānā Ghulām Quṭb al-Dīn returned to Delhi, and was installed as his father's *sajjāda-nishīn*. In time he appointed sixty *khalīfas*, from all walks of life. The Mughal Emperor Muḥammad Akbar II[160] (r. 1806–1837) became his *murīd*, as did many of the princes and courtiers.[161]

Mawlānā Ghulām Quṭb al-Dīn's saintly career is overshadowed by the fame of his "*pīr*-brothers" (i.e., fellow *khalīfas*) Khwāja Nūr Muḥammad Muhāravī and Shāh Niyāz Aḥmad. The Mawlānā is reported to have spent time in Muhar and received *khilāfat* there from Khwāja Nūr Muḥammad.[162]

---

157 Khwāja Ḥasan Niẓāmī, *Niẓāmī Bansurī* (New Delhi: Khwāja Awlād Kitābghar, 1984), 500.

158 Hajjī Najm al-Dīn Sulaymānī, *Manāqib al-maḥbūbayn* (Urdu), trans. Prof. Ikhtiyār Aḥmad Chishtī (Lahore: Islamic Book Foundation, 1979), 90; thanks are due to Prof. Marcia Hermansen for kindly providing this.

159 Fakhrī, *Shajarat al-anwār*, fol. 579v.

160 On Akbar Shāh, and his son Bahādur Shāh, see Percival Spear, *Twilight of the Mughals* (Cambridge: Cambridge University Press, 1951).

161 Fakhrī, *Shajarat al-anwār*, fol. 580r.

162 Sulaymānī, *Manāqib al-maḥbūbayn*, 92; Aḥmadpūrī, *Takmila-yi siyar al-awliyā'*, fol. 107r.

Like so much of his biography, Mawlānā Ghulām Quṭb al-Dīn's death-date is open to question. Sir Sayyid Aḥmad has 17 Muḥarram 1212/1797.[163] Another source has 18 Muḥarram 1233/1817.[164] What is known for certain is that his mortal remains are havened in an inconspicuous corner of the Khwāja Quṭb al-Dīn tomb complex.

Ḥażrat Shaykh Ghulām Naṣīr al-Dīn Maḥmūd Kāle Miyāṅ

Mawlānā Ghulām Quṭb al-Dīn's son and successor Mawlānā Ghulām Naṣīr al-Dīn Maḥmūd was born in Delhi at the turn of the eighteenth century. For reasons now forgotten, he is popularly known as Kāle Miyāṅ, "The Black Master," and poetically styled "The Black Ocean of Truth."

In midlife Kāle Miyāṅ performed a pilgrimage to Mecca and Medina. On the journey home he visited the Chishtī centers of Gujarat, Rajasthan, and Punjab. In Ahmadabad he was the guest of Khūb Miyāṅ Ṣāḥib (d.1257/1841), from whom he received the honor of *khilāfat*.[165] In Taunsa he was "in the service of" Shāh Sulaymān Tawnsavī—thereby, reportedly, giving the Punjabi Pīr great pride—and received *khilāfat* once again.[166]

In the absence of a literary legacy, and due in part to the termination of his patrilineal succession (in Aurangabad), Kāle Miyāṅ's memory has faded in contemporary Chishtī circles. His name is nonetheless familiar to old Delhiwalas,[167] who remember him for his associations with celebrated contemporaries Bahādur Shāh Ẓafar, Mīrzā Ghālib, and Sir Sayyid Aḥmad Khān.

Bahādur Shāh Ẓafar followed Akbar II on the throne of an almost purely ceremonial Mughal Empire in 1837. Just as his father had submitted to the discipline of Mawlānā Quṭb al-Dīn, Bahādur Shāh became the *murīd* and *khalīfa* of Kāle Miyāṅ. This was a role

---

[163] Sir Sayyid Aḥmad Khān, *Asār alṣanādīd*, ed. Khalīq Anjum (New Delhi: Urdu Academy, 1990), 2:29.

[164] Gulshanābādī, *Tazkirat al-ansāb*, 12.

[165] Maḥmūdī, *Shajarat al-Maḥmūd*, 181–183: (*silsila*: Yaḥyā Madanī, Rukn al-Dīn Aḥmad, Jamāl al-Dīn II, Husām al-Dīn Farrukh, Rukn al-Dīn II, Rashīd al-Dīn Mawdūd Lālā, Khūb Miyāṅ).

[166] Sulaymānī, *Manāqib al-maḥbūbayn*, 92; Khān, *Asār-i ṣanādīd*, 29.

[167] Not to mention viewers of the popular Indian television miniseries "Mirza Ghalib" (distributed on videocassette), in which he is portrayed by the late Qadir Khan.

he put into active practice, duly initiating and instructing *murīds* of his own.[168] Coming to terms with the complete loss of its temporal authority to the British East India Company, the Timurid dynasty seems to have seriously considered reinventing itself as a charismatic Chishtī hierocracy, an experiment cut short by Bahādur Shāh's banishment to Rangoon in 1858.

It was Kāle Miyāṅ who introduced Mīrzā Asad Allāh Khān Ghālib (d. 1869)—today the most frequently recited Urdu poet—to the court, where he would later succeed Ibrāhīm Zawq (d. 1271/1855) as the Emperor's *ustād* (ghazal corrector). Ghālib was then living in a wing of Kāle Miyāṅ's house, the Pīr having taken him in after his release from prison on gambling charges. He once joked, "Who has been released from prison? Then I was in the prison of the *gore* (white) and now I am in the prison of the *kāle* (black)."[169] But there is no doubt about his respect for Kāle Miyāṅ. In his unfinished history of the Mughal dynasty, *Mihr-i nīmrūz*, Ghālib writes:

> The melody of Manṣūr has no admittance to his Truth-hearing ears, and what business could Bayazīd's murmuring have with his Truth-telling lips? Others may drink wine, but this Khwāja drinks the tavern dry. Other people's casks are his cups. He lives in the midst of the world, but he is far above it. As long as I am his neighbor the celestial spheres are in my shadow, and as long as I sit in the dust of his door the angels envy my station.[170]

Similarly outspoken in his praise of Kāle Miyāṅ is Sir Sayyid Aḥmad Khān (d. 1898), the influential modernist reformer who founded Aligarh Muslim University. In his survey of Delhi's great monuments and personalities, *Asār al-ṣanādīd*, Sir Sayyid has this to say:

> Due praise for him is beyond the scope of words. His manner cannot be described, his spiritual poverty is impossible to illustrate. His state is extremely fine and his deeds are exceptionally beautiful. He is never for a moment unoccupied

[168] Spear, *Twilight of the Mughals*, 24.
[169] Alṭāf Ḥusayn Ḥālī, *Yādgār-i Ghālib* (English), trans. K.H. Qadiri (Delhi: Idarah-i Adabiyat-i Delli, 1990) 40.
[170] Mīrzā Asād Allāh Khān Ghālib, *Kulliyat-i nashr-i Ghālib* (Kanpur: Naval Kishūr, 1875), 268.

> with spiritual practice. Conversation is difficult for him. When someone asks a question he responds only out of necessity. If it seems that his tongue is disinclined to work it is because his heart is busy with God. In this era there is no more distinguished Shaykh. His Majesty and all the princes and high aristocracy are deeply devoted to him. Whenever he enters an assembly everyone scurries about excitedly, falling at his feet and considering himself eternally fortunate. Divine passion overtakes him quickly, and his heart aspires to the inspiration of his grandfather. This inspiration has indeed reached him, 'heart to heart', through his distinguished father, but his passion and its spiritual rewards are such that his seeking never desists. As much as is given, that much more is desired.[171]

The date of Kāle Miyāṅ's "union" is given as 15 Ṣafar 1262 (12 February 1846), but this cannot be correct.[172] A grim possibility presents itself. Referring to the devastation of the 1857 Revolt, Ghālib wrote to a correspondent in 1862: "Mīr Naṣīr al-Dīn descended on his father's side from a line of Pīrs and on his mothers' from a line of nobles, was unjustly put to death." The editor of Ghālib's collected letters has identified this "Mīr Naṣīr al-Dīn" as Kāle Miyāṅ, as have Ghālib's English biographers.[173]

Kāle Miyāṅ's simple stone grave adjoins his father's in the Khwāja Quṭb Ṣāḥib complex. His family dispersed after the Revolt; Ghālib observes of the devastation they suffered, "The cow ate all this up, and the butcher killed the cow, and the butcher died on the road."[174] But the archway over his *ḥavelī* in Qāsim Jān, in the heart of Old Delhi, still bears a plaque reading: *Aḥāta Kāle Ṣāḥib* (Premises of Kāle Ṣāḥib).

---

[171] Khān, *Asār al-ṣanādīd*, 69.

[172] Gulshanābādī, *Tazkirat al-ansāb*, 12; Mīrzā Aḥmad Akhtar Dihlavī, *Tazkira-yi awliyā'-i Hind ū Pākistān* (Lahore: Mālik Sirāj al-Dīn and Sons, 1972), 320. This death date is questionable in light of the following facts: In *Athār al-ṣanādīd* (first edition 1846, second revised edition 1852) Sir Sayyid Aḥmad Khān writes about Kāle Miyāṅ as if he were alive (*Athār al-ṣanādīd*, 2:29). In *Yādgār-i Ghālib* Ḥālī recounts how Kāle Miyāṅ offered Ghālib lodging after the latter's imprisonment. Ghālib was released from prison in 1847 (*Yādgār-i Ghālib*, 40). In *Mihr-i nīmrūz*, composed in 1850, Ghālib writes about Kāle Miyāṅ as if he were alive (*Kulliyat-i nashr-i Ghālib*, 268).

[173] *Khuṭūṭ-i Ghālib*, ed. Ghulām Rasūl Mihr (Lahore: Shaykh Ghulām 'Alī, 1957), 266; R. Russell and K. Islam, *Ghalib: Life and Letters* (Cambridge: Harvard University Press, 1969), 269.

[174] Russell and Islam, *Ghalib*, 291.

Ḥażrat Shaykh Muḥammad Ḥasan Jīlī Kalīmī

Sayyid Muḥammad Ḥasan Jīlī Kalīmī—popularly known as "Ṣāḥibzāda Ṣāḥib" (approximately: Sir, son of Sir)—was born in Baghdad in the year 1223/1808.[175] Among his paternal ancestors he counted the legendary saint 'Abd al-Qādir al-Jīlānī (hence the patronymic Jīlī). Ṣāḥibzāda Ṣāḥib's parents moved to Delhi during his childhood. It was there, in the turbulent twilight of the Mughal Empire, that he grew up.

When Kāle Miyāṅ first encountered Ṣāḥibzāda Ṣāḥib he immediately recognized him as his divinely appointed *murīd*-to-be. Ṣāḥibzāda Ṣāḥib, however, declined his offer of *bay'at*, citing his connection with the Qādiriyya in Baghdad. That night he experienced a dream-vision in which Ḥażrat 'Abd al-Qādir appeared to him in all his glory and instructed him to follow Kāle Miyāṅ. The next day he met Kāle Miyāṅ, but stopped short of accepting initiation. Kāle Miyāṅ asked, "Have you forgotten your dream?" Awestruck, Ṣāḥibzāda Ṣāḥib acquiesced.[176]

In time Ṣāḥibzāda Ṣāḥib became the leading disciple and *khalīfa* of Kāle Miyāṅ.

The story is told that the great saint of Khayrabad, Ḥāfiẓ Muḥammad 'Alī Khayrābādī,[177] expressed the wish of meeting Ṣāḥibzade Ṣāḥib, and Kāle Miyāṅ urged his *khalīfa* to visit the elder Pīr.[178] When he arrived at Ḥażrat Ḥāfiẓ Khayrābādī's *khānqāh*, he found him on his deathbed. Greeting Ṣāḥibzāda Ṣāḥib from his cot, Ḥāfiẓ Ṣāḥib pulled the sheet that covered his body over his face. Suddenly the veil between the worlds was lifted and Ṣāḥibzāda Ṣāḥib gazed into the hereafter. In this way Ḥāfiẓ Ṣāḥib enabled his visitor to fulfil the mystical injunction *mūtū qabla an tamūtū* ("Die before you die"). Afterward, Ḥāfiẓ Ṣāḥib's *khalīfa* Mīrzā Sārdār Beg accompanied Ṣāḥibzāda Ṣāḥib

---

[175] Maḥmūdī, *Shajarat al-Maḥmūd*, 124; mentioned alongside Kāle Miyāṅ's sons and Mawlānā Khayr al-Mubīn.

[176] Narrated to Pir Vilayat Inayat Khan by Sayyid Fakhr al-Ḥasan Jīlī Kalīmī.

[177] The life of Ḥāfiẓ Muḥammad 'Alī Khayrābādī (d. 1266 A.H.), a *khalīfa* of Khwāja Sulaymān Tawnsavī, is treated in K.A. Nizami, *Tarīkh-i Mashā'ikh-i Chisht* (Delhi: Nadwat al-Muṣannifīn, 1953), 667–684.

[178] In suggesting that Kāle Miyāṅ was alive in 1266, this oral tradition corroborates the case outlined above (note 172) against the death-date of 1262.

to the edge of town. When he returned to the *khānqāh*, he found that his master had expired.[179]

Ṣāḥibzāda Ṣāḥib married Muḥtarima Potī Begum Ṣāḥiba, daughter of Shāh Pīr 'Usmānī, a descendent of both the Ṣābirī saint Ḥażrat Jalāl al-Dīn Panīpatī and the Niẓāmī saint Shāh Kalīm Allāh (hence Kalīmī). Seven sons were born to them, together with an undisclosed number of daughters. The fifth son, third in line of succession, Sayyid Muḥammad Żiyā' al-Ḥasan Jīlī Kalīmī (d. 1360/1941), attained special prominence, and is buried beside his father.

Ṣāḥibzāda Ṣāḥib's descendents recall how divine guidance saved the family from the tragic events of 1857. A few months before the ill-fated Revolt, Ṣāḥibzāda Ṣāḥib witnessed a dream-vision in which a terrible fire raged around him on all sides, with the exception of the South, which remained cool and tranquil. Heeding the warning, the family moved to the nizamate of Hyderabad, where they were spared the horror and misery that befell Delhi.

In Hyderabad, Ṣāḥibzāda Ṣāḥib's family settled near Toli Chowki, in the village surrounding the *dargāh* of the architect-saint Ḥusayn Shāh Walī (d. 1068/1658), a descendent of Sayyid Muḥammad Gīsū Darāz. There a *khānqāh* was established, and maintained solely on *futūḥ*. Whenever Ṣāḥibzāda Ṣāḥib emerged from his solitary meditations and prayers, devotees thronged to receive his teachings. Nor, apparently, was his fold confined to humankind; shape-shifting djinn are also reported. Once a gigantic cobra slithered into his cell, terrifying those in attendance. Ṣāḥibzāda Ṣāḥib simply smiled and said that his *murīd* had come to see him.

In addition to his sons, Ṣāḥibzāda Ṣāḥib granted *khilāfat* to several other *murīds*, the most outstanding of whom were Sayyid

---

[179] Cf. Hazrat Inayat Khan, Sangatha II (privately circulated): "There is a well known story of the Murshid of Sayyed Shaikh Mohammed Abu-Hashim Madani, of how he heard, in an assembly, a voice calling him by name, and the voice was heard by all present. He sprang up, saying that he was being called by his Murshid. He took the train, and after some hours arrived at the house, where he found his Murshid about to pass from this earthly plane. The Murshid said to him, 'My cup of life in this place is already filled, and the call has come since last night. I have been holding on that I might see you and bless you; and now I am passing on from this mortal plane to the life everlasting.'"

Abū Hāshim Madanī and Mawlānā Khayr al-Mubīn. Ṣāḥibzāda Ṣāḥib breathed his last on 21 Rabīʿ I 1308/1890, at the age of eighty-five years. He was buried in the compound of the Ḥusayn Shāh Walī mosque on the initiative of the Sajjāda-nishīn, who is said to have been directed to provide this accommodation by the spirit of the entombed architect-saint himself.[180]

Ḥażrat Shaykh Sayyid Abū Hāshim Madanī

As his name suggests, Sayyid Abū Hāshim Madanī was of sharifian Arab descent. On the basis of available records, little more can be said about his ancestry or early life. It is as a *murīd* and *khalīfa* of Sayyid Muḥammad Ḥasan Jīlī Kalīmi, a *pīr*-brother of Sayyid Żiyā' al-Ḥasan Jīlī Kalīmi and Mawlānā Khayr al-Mubīn, and the *murshid* of Hazrat Inayat Khan that Sayyid Abū Hāshim is remembered.

This is Hazrat Inayat Khan's account of his first encounter with his *murshid* (in the redaction of R. M. Bloch):

> ... After six months of continuous searching, I chanced to visit an old and revered acquaintance, Moulana Khairulmubeen, to whom I confided my desire of embracing Sufism. While reflecting on the matter, he suddenly received a telepathic message that his friend, a great murshid, was about to come to him. He at once arranged a seat of honor and placing cushions upon it, walked toward the gate in order to bid him welcome. After a time of suspense the Pir-o-Murshid entered, bringing with him a very great sense of light. As all those present greeted him, bowing down in their humility, it seemed to me all at once that I had seen him before, but where, I could not recall. At last, after gazing at him earnestly, I remembered that his was the face which so persistently haunted me during my silence. The proof of this was manifested as soon as his eyes fell on me. He turned to the host, saying, 'O! Moulana, tell me who this young man may be? He appeals intensely to my spirit.' Moulana Khairulmubeen answered: 'Your holiness, this young man is a genius in music, and desires greatly to submit himself to your inspiring guidance.' Then the Master smiled and granted the request, initiating me into Sufism there and then.[181]

---

[180] Except as otherwise noted, this account is based entirely on the family recollections of Syed Mohammed Rasheedul Hasan Jeeliul Kaleemi (letter dated 2 June 1999), to whom thanks are due.

[181] Bloch, *The Confessions of Inayat Khan* (London: The Sufi Publishing Society, 1915), 38–39.

In his lectures Hazrat Inayat Khan frequently recalls Sayyid Abū Hāshim Madanī's pedagogical style. For the first six months of Inayat Khan's muridship Madanī Ṣāḥib never spoke a word of metaphysics, ruminating instead on the most ordinary things. When at last he did, and Inayat Khan eagerly took out his notepad, the Murshid summarily switched subjects. The moral Inayat Khan drew is that words of wisdom are to be inscribed on the tablet of the heart.

Sayyid Abū Hāshim Madanī was certainly not inimical to Sufism's intellectual traditions. Hazrat Inayat Khan mentions that he studied "Koran, Hadis, and the literature of the Persian mystics" under the tutelage of his *murshid.*[182] Sayyid Madanī's erudition may be gauged by his editorship of *Risāla mīzān al-tawḥīd*, a 162-page disquisition of Ibn al-'Arabī's doctrine of "Unity of Being."[183] The title page prominently notes, "with the correction and revision of the mystical savant (*'ālim-i 'ilm-i ladunī*) Mawlānā Murshidanā Mawlvī Sayyid Muḥammad Abū Hāshim al-Madanī.

A number of Sayyid Abū Hāshim Madanī's sayings and verses are preserved in Hazrat Inayat Khan's works. The aphorism most often quoted—albeit in varying versions—is this: "There is only one virtue and one sin for a soul on this path: virtue when he is conscious of God, and sin when he is not."[184] On the subject of the *murshid-murīd* relationship he is reported to have observed: "This friendship, this relationship which is brought about by initiation between two persons, is something that cannot be broken … cannot be separated … cannot be compared with anything else in the world; it belongs to eternity."[185] Asked how to recognize a godly person, he responded: "Judge him not by what he says or what he does; feel his atmosphere."[186]

A poem resonant with the Sufi tradition of *shaṭḥ* (ecstatic utterance) is also credited to him:[187]

---

[182] Bloch, *Confessions*, 40.

[183] Mawlvī Muḥammad Makhdūm Ḥusayn Sāvī al-Qādirī, *Risāla mīzān al-tawḥīd* (Hyderabad: Maṭba'-i Burhāniyya, 1311).

[184] Inayat Khan, *The Sufi Message of Hazrat Inayat Khan* (London: Barrie and Jenkins, 1973), 8:231.

[185] Ibid., 10:84.

[186] Ibid., 11:35.

[187] Inayat Khan, "The Journey to the Goal" in Metaphysics I (privately circulated papers).

> I, the poor, have such a strength,
> That if the eyes had eyes,
> They could not see the rapidity of my steps,
> If the eyes had their utmost power, they could not see the
> Rapidity of my paces. This is the strength of the strong.

Sayyid Madanī's circle of *murīds* was small. Nightly *zikr* sessions took place under the Murshid's own roof, in the Purana Pul quarter of Hyderabad. Among cognoscenti, however, his reputation was well established. Hazrat Inayat Khan informs us that the Nizam himself requested the honor of taking Sayyid Madanī's hand in initiation—a request that was declined.

Hazrat Inayat Khan offers this account of the end of Sayyid Madanī's life (again, in the redaction of R.M. Bloch):

> His death was as saintly as his mortal life had been. Six months before his end, he predicted its coming and wound up all his worldly affairs in order to be free for his future journey. ... He apologized not only to his relatives, friends, and Mureeds, but even to his servants lest there be aught that he had done to their displeasure and hurt. Ere the soul departed from his body, he bade farewell to all his people with loving words. And then, sitting upright and unwavering, he continued *zikar*, and lost in his contemplation of Allah, he, by his own accord freed his soul from the imprisonment of this mortal frame forever. I can never forget the words he spoke, while he placed his hands upon my head in blessing: "fare forth into the world, my child, and harmonize East and West with the harmony of thy music. Spread the wisdom of Sufism abroad, for to this end art thou gifted by Allah, the most Merciful and Compassionate.[188]

Sayyid Muḥammad Abū Hāshim Madanī died on 29 Sha'bān 1325 (7 October 1907) and was buried in his own neighborhood, beside the *dargāh* of the intoxicated Qādiri saint Miyāṅ Paysā (d. 1831).[189]

Perusing this chronicle, a reader acquainted with Hazrat Inayat Khan's lifework will recognize much that is familiar: the rhetorical primacy of love, the ubiquity of music and poetry, egalitarian and pluralist tendencies. Some of the other characteristics

---

[188] Bloch, *Confessions*, 42.

[189] On Miyāṅ Paysā, see *Tazkirat-i awliyā'-i Ḥaydarābād*, Sayyid Murād 'Alī Ṭabi' (Hyderabad: Minar Book Depot, 1972), 3:79–81.

of the pre-modern Chishtiyya will no doubt appear remote. Indeed, Hazrat Inayat Khan's emphasis on universal spirituality has often been deemed sufficiently radical as to require the rethinking of his relationship with the Chishtī tradition. Hazrat Inayat Khan once observed, "The portraits of the different Sheikhs of Khandan-i Chisht all look as if they had been molded in the same mold."[190] The question may be asked: did Hazrat Inayat Khan himself fit this mold?

Tradition is best understood as "a modality of change."[191] The Chishtī tradition (*sunnat-i mashā'ikh-i Chisht*) involves a perpetual negotiation between, in Hazrat Inayat Khan's phraseology, "the same truth which was ever taught in schools of Sufis" and "the consideration of the psychology of the time and the people to whom it is given."[192]

A number of original developments have been documented in the preceding pages. Consider Khwāja Farīd al-Dīn's introduction of a Hindavī *zikr*, Khwāja Naṣīr al-Dīn's prohibition of devotional prostration, Shaykh Maḥmūd Rājan's integration of multiple *silsilas*, Shāh Kalīm Allāh's institutionalization of the inclusion of Hindus. All of these may be evaluated as examples of *tajdīd* (revivification), cases in which the relevance of the tradition is updated. Far from slavishly imitating and deferring to long-dead exemplars, the Chishtī masters insisted on the vitality of their tradition and brooked no dimunition of their prerogatives.[193]

The recognition that the Chishtī tradition has undergone continual transformation over the centuries does not mitigate, however, the bold originality of Hazrat Inayat Khan's contribution to Sufism. The pre-modern Chishtī masters kept apace with historical changes that were quite moderate when compared with the unprecedented acceleration of history that marks modernity. In bringing Sufism to the United States and Europe in the early twentieth century, Hazrat Inayat Khan confronted not only

[190] Sherifa Lucy Goodenough, *Love, Human and Divine*, "Voice of Inayat" Series (London: The Sufi Publishing Society, 1919), 26.

[191] See Marilyn Robinson Waldman, "Tradition as a Modality of Change: Islamic Examples," *History of Religions* 25 (1986): 318–340.

[192] Inayat Khan, "The Message Which has Come in all Ages" in The Message Papers (privately circulated).

[193] Cf. Chishtī, *Majālis-i Ḥasaniyya*, folio 12a.

differences of culture and language, but also a more profound difference of fundamental paradigm. In his response to the new context he indulged in neither complacent conservativism nor uncritical accommodation. What emerged was a creative and farsighted renewal of the Sufi tradition. "I came as I was made to come; I live as life allows me to live; but I will be what I wish to be."[194]

[194] Inayat Khan, *Nirtan or the Dance of the Soul* (London and Southampton: The Sufi Movement,1928), 23.

Khwāja Ḥasan Niẓāmī, 1924

Common Themes, Uncommon Contexts: The Sufi Movements of Hazrat Inayat Khan (1882–1927) and Khwāja Ḥasan Niẓāmī (1878–1955)

MARCIA HERMANSEN

It was the twilight of colonial Delhi in the year 1927 when the Sufi teacher Inayat Khan, who for seventeen years had carried the Chishtī message to the West, met for the first time with Khwāja Ḥasan Niẓāmī.

Niẓāmī had risen from orphanhood and poverty to become a prominent literary figure, political activist, and Sufi guide in the Chishtī Order. Inayat Khan had left behind a career as an accomplished Hindustani-Karnatak musician in order to spread Chishtī spiritual teachings in Europe and America.

As they walked through the environs of the *dargāh* of the fourteenth century Sufi saint Ḥażrat Niẓām al-Dīn 'Awliyā', the important Chishtī shrine of which Niẓāmī was a hereditary custodian, the following exchange is said to have taken place.

> Surveying an abandoned mosque in a landscape studded with the ruins of the tombs of Sufi saints from the watchtower of Pir Hasan Nizami's home, Pir-o-Murshid (Inayat Khan) confided how happy he felt there. The pir (Ḥasan Niẓāmī) responded, "You are welcome to come and stay." "Yes," answered Pir-o-Murshid, "when I come I will stay forever." The pir understood that he meant to be buried there.[1]

This proved to be prophetic and within weeks Inayat Khan passed away. Niẓāmī and the Niẓām al-Dīn *dargāh* area were to remain connected to the mysterious visitor, however, for Niẓāmī provided land that he held near the saint's tomb for the burial place

[1] Pir Vilayat Inayat Khan, *The Message in Our Time* (New York: Harper and Row, 1979), 403.

of Inayat Khan. During the next decades he often received a new kind of pilgrim in Delhi, European and American visitors male and female, who were completing the traditional Sufi practice of *ziyārat* or visitation to their master's tomb. Today the site of Inayat Khan's tomb in Delhi embodies the best of Chishtī spirituality, constituting a tranquil garden oasis, clean and secluded, in the midst of the tremendous congestion and pollution of the Indian capital. It is a living shrine with a thin but constant stream of reverential pilgrims and the weekly celebration of *qawwālī*, the singing of poetic tributes to mystical ecstasy and the legacy of the Sufi saints, including Inayat Khan.

In the following paper I will consider these two Sufi masters of the early twentieth century whose careers display intriguing similarities and connections. They were born within a few years of each other in colonial India near the end of the nineteenth century. They shared the same spiritual lineage although they came to it in different ways.

This comparison will be undertaken in the light of the theme of the present volume, the legacy of Inayat Khan, in order to provide background on the intellectual, political, religious, and cultural milieu of the India which he left behind. At the same time, our consideration of Khwāja Ḥasan Niẓāmī will illuminate how impulses similar to Inayat Khan's existed in contemporary Indian Sufism but clearly could not develop along exactly the same trajectories, given the cultural and historical context in which each figure operated.

I will explore ways in which each individual responded to the new developments of his age, focusing on the themes of: 1) contemporary Indo-Muslim intellectual currents, 2) attitudes to other religions, 3) Chishtī Sufism and Sufi identity, 4) strategies for spreading their teachings and ideas, 5) respectful attitude to women and their spiritual and intellectual capacities, 6) understandings of the West, and 7) political activities.

Hazrat Inayat Khan

Hazrat Inayat Khan was born in Baroda into a family of prominent classical Indian musicians in 1882. As a young man he frequented courtly society and became a Sufi disciple of the

Hyderabadi Chishtī Murshid, Abū Ḥāshim Madanī (d. 1907). His teacher instructed him that his mission lay far to the West and Inayat Khan first embarked on a career bringing classical Hindustani music to America in 1910. In the aftermath of the World Parliament of Religions in Chicago in 1893 and through the activities of groups such as the Theosophical Society, the West was ready to receive Eastern spirituality of a certain type. Inayat Khan is said to have realized that his Western audiences in many cases needed spiritual enlightenment from him more than musical edification. He therefore reoriented his activities and to a great extent sacrificed his music in order to better serve the spiritual needs of the West.[2]

Inayat Khan traveled throughout the U.S., Western Europe and Russia, giving lectures and musical performances after which he would often hold informal talks with potential disciples, conferring formal initiation into the Sufi Order upon all those who requested it.[3] Circles of disciples, or mureeds (*murīds*) as they were called, were well established in England, France, Switzerland and the U.S. In 1915 the Sufi Order of the West was registered in London under the Constitution and Rules of the Sufi Order,[4] and in 1923 the International Headquarters of the Sufi Movement was legally instituted in Geneva.[5]

In the United States, his first disciple, and later head of the American branch of the Sufi Order, was Ada Martin (known as Rabia Martin). Another early American disciple was Samuel Lewis who was to become a seminal figure in the development of Sufism in America during the 1960s. Martin helped establish a center in San Francisco prior to World War I[6] and a center called Kaaba Allah was opened in Fairfax, California in 1925.[7] In 1913 Inayat

---

[2] Inayat Khan, prologue to *The Mysticism of Sound and Music* (Shaftesbury, England: Element, 1991).

[3] James Jervis, "The Sufi Order in the West," in Peter Clark, ed., *New Trends and Developments in the World of Islam* (London: Luzac Oriental Press, 1997), 214–215.

[4] Ibid., 215. Jervis also discusses the problems associated with the exact date of the so-called London constitution (249, n. 33).

[5] Elizabeth de Jong-Keesing, *Inayat Khan* (London and The Hague: East-West Publications and Luzac & Co., 1974), 209.

[6] "Sufi Order" in Gordon J. Melton, *Encyclopedia of American Religions*, 3rd ed. (Detroit: Gale Research, 1989), 835.

[7] Samuel L. Lewis, *Sufi Vision and Initiation*, ed. Neil Douglas-Klotz (San

Khan married an American woman, Ora Ray Baker, who had initially been his student in music.[8]

Inayat Khan's career as a Sufi master was cut short by his death during a return visit to India at the age of forty-four. By the time of his death he had initiated a number of European and American disciples into Sufism and lectured extensively. Most of his published works are based on transcripts of his talks made by disciples. His teachings explored the common spiritual themes of various world religions and he did not require his followers to formally accept Islam or to practice the Islamic *shar'īa.*

In his *Niẓāmī Bansurī*, a biography of Niẓām al-Dīn Awliyā', Khwāja Ḥasan Niẓāmī consecrated a section to subsequent developments of the Niẓāmiyya branch of the Chishtī Order, including a notice about Inayat Khan and his movement.

> Sufi Inayat Khan, may Allah be pleased with him.
>
> In the very same way Sufi Inayat Khan from Baroda, who was a *murīd* in the *silsila* of Mawlānā Fakhr al-Dīn, used to pursue the profession of vocal and instrumental music. In the pursuit of his profession he traveled to Europe where he recast the same lyrics that he sang for the Europeans into their languages in order to present these to them through a process of translation. He then began to initiate Europeans as disciples and established [Sufi] circles in Suresnes France, Rome Italy, San Francisco, U.S.A., Switzerland and other countries where he used to travel in order to provide spiritual instruction to the *murīds*. In this manner in every country he brought innumerable men and women into the Chishtī *silsila.* I used to send him guidance about his work from Delhi. Finally he came to meet me in Delhi where his death occurred. I had his tomb constructed near my house and countless European pilgrims have come to visit it, evidencing a remarkable degree of spiritual development. When they say, "Murshid, Murshid" while speaking, it is with a sense of intoxication and when they reach the tomb they practice meditative concentration (*murāqaba*). They also convene sessions for *zikr* and the performance of spiritual exercises. One female *murīd* of Inayat Khan, Rabia A. Martin, has established a *khanqah* in the famous American city of San Francisco, where she gives the teachings of the Niẓāmiyya *silsila* to Americans. Twice she came to visit me. After the death of Inayat

---

Francisco: Sufi Islamia, 1986), 24. I am indebted to Eric S. Ohlander, "Inayat Khan," unpublished paper, for some material in the previous paragraphs.

[8] De Jong Keesing, *Inayat Khan*, 106–7.

Khan I gave her the permission to initiate disciples and give spiritual instruction and she is in continuous correspondence with me.[9]

Khwāja Ḥasan Niẓāmī

Niẓāmī was born in 1878 into the tight inner circle of families who were hereditary custodians of the shrine of Niẓām al-Dīn Awliyā' in Delhi. Niẓāmī's parents and two sisters died before he was twelve and he was brought up by his older brother. His ancestors were said to have come long before from Bukhara. One of them, Badr al-Dīn Isḥāq,[10] had been a *khalīfa* of Bābā Farīd, and friend of Niẓām al-Dīn Awliyā', so that after his death his two sons were raised by Niẓām al-Dīn Awliyā', who brought the family to Delhi. Niẓāmī was given a traditional education in the Niẓām al-Dīn *bastī* and later at Rashīd Aḥmad's *madrasa* in Gangoh for one and a half years.[11]

When he was eleven his father had made him a *murīd* of Shāh Allāhbakhsh Tawnsavī, then later, at sixteen, his brother made him a *murīd* of Khwāja Ghulām Farīd.[12] At the age of twenty-four, following a spiritual sign, he chose to become a *murīd* of Mihr 'Alī Shāh and eventually was appointed his *khalīfa*. He describes finding this spiritual guide through a dream visitation by Niẓām al-Dīn Awliyā' which convinced him to undertake self-reform as well as a trip on foot (partially) to Pak Pattan in emulation of the saint's trip to find his *murshid*.[13]

Mihr 'Alī Shāh would seem in some ways to be an unusual choice of *murshid* for the young Ḥasan Niẓāmī. Although a Chishtī in the Niẓāmī line, Mihr 'Alī Shāh was not an ecstatic who remained withdrawn from political controversy. He was, rather, an intellectual and literary figure, writing in the fields of Islamic polemic, traditional commentary, and poetry. He was active politically in opposing the Aḥmadiyya, a late nineteenth century movement that claimed the continuity of prophethood in Islam.

---

9 Khwāja Ḥasan Niẓāmī, *Niẓāmī bansurī* (New Delhi: Khwāja Awlād Kutub Ghar, 1990), 505–6.

10 Mullā Wāḥidī, *Savāniḥ 'umrī: Khwāja Ḥasan Niẓāmī* (Delhi: Munādī Khwāja Number, 1957), 18.

11 Ibid., 13. Cf. Khwāja Ḥasan Niẓāmī, *Āp bītī* (Delhi: Khwāja Awlād Kutub Ghar, 1922), 14.

12 Niẓāmī, *Āp bītī*, 6.

13 Ibid., 7.

It seems that some aspects of the murshid were kindled in the disciple, for in his career Niẓāmī was to follow both literary and political pursuits. His greater leeway in tolerating religious and intellectual diversity may come form his situation as a Delhiwala North Indian, as opposed to Mihr 'Alī Shāh's base in Golra, near present day Islamabad in the Pakistani Punjab.

Niẓāmī spent the majority of his career pursuing literary and journalistic activities. He frequented intellectual and Muslim political circles, and also had a great number of disciples. A contemporary critic of Urdu literature, Ali Jawad Zaidi, gives this summary of Niẓāmī's literary activities:

> He was a prolific writer, who wrote in a simple, colloquial style with an intimacy, mystic perception, and light-heartedness that enlivened any subject he touched. He has written over a hundred books and pamphlets including the moving story of the Great Rebellion of 1857 in twelve parts in the form of a romance. ... He also edited a weekly, *Munadi*, which contained his personal diary and other writings. ... His works are replete with outspoken autobiographical references which add to their charm.[14]

Muhammad Sadiq, another critic of Urdu literature, is less enthusiastic about the skills of Khwāja Ḥasan. He ranks him with Rashīd al-Khayrī (1868–1936) as one of those rare Urdu writers who has been able to live off the income from his writings.[15] Sadiq claims that Niẓāmī rose from being an itinerant bookseller to become a millionaire.

> With his long loose cloak and an outlandish conical cap, his beard and long flowing hair, he looked like a patriarch of old, despite his short stature.[16] ... Ḥasan Niẓāmī wrote more than a hundred books and pamphlets, besides editing a number of newspapers, mostly written by himself. Consult the catalogue of any well-equipped library and you will be surprised by his versatility and amazing output. Here was a man who could write on any conceivable subject under the sun. They range from metaphysics, religion, history, philosophy to such items as confectionery. The fact is that he did

---

[14] Ali Jawad Zaidi, *A History of Urdu Literature* (Delhi: Sahitya Academy, 1993), 262.

[15] Muhammad Sadiq, *A History of Urdu Literature* (Delhi: Oxford University Press, 1984), 512.

[16] Niẓāmī's height was considered above average by his contemporaries, and in his autobiography he characterizes himself as "tall." *Āp bītī*, 4.

> not write all these books himself. Some of them, no doubt, are his own; others were written by hacks employed for the purpose. These he corrected and improved and gave out as his own.[17]

In the latter years of his life Khwāja Ḥasan Nizāmī was afflicted with weakening health and loss of eyesight. He lived through the difficult times of partition and in his old age seems to have felt embattled by the political and ideological conflicts raging around him. For example, a small statement entitled, "A Message from My Last Days" is attached to his work on the permissibility of performing prostration before one's spiritual guide.[18]

This text was written in 1951 when Niẓāmī was seventy-five years old. In it he addresses his "lakhs of *murīds*" and "hundreds of *khalīfas*" stating that:

> The time of the Last Days (*qiyāmat*) is approaching, fighting and wars are on the increase all over the world. After the division of Hindustan, in both India and Pakistan, the believers in the saints appear to have lost out to the *mawlvīs* due to the political influence of the latter. Therefore I feel that it is necessary to write this—that those who have the love of Sufism should not become frightened and should remain firm in their belief. The *mawlvīs*, since the beginnings of Islam, have been opponents of the dervishes since they find the dignity of the dervishes to be a threat.[19]

Indo-Muslim intellectual currents

As Indian Muslims born at about the same time, Inayat Khan and Khwāja Ḥasan Niẓāmī both experienced the sense of disenfranchisement and nostalgia for the apogee of Muslim power represented by Mughal rule. The deposition and exile in 1857 of the last Mughal Emperor, Bahādur Shāh Ẓafar, himself a patron of the Chishtī Order, was to cast a pall on Muslim self-confidence, and also had material consequences for many Muslim families. In Niẓāmī's autobiography there is a story relevant to this theme.

> When I was three years old I became ill, to the extent that I was near death. At that time a close relative of the (Mughal) King, Bahādur Shāh, lived as a dervish in the shrine. My mother had me

[17] Ṣadiq, *Urdu Literature*, 514–15.
[18] Niẓāmī, *Murshid-ko sajda-yi ta'ẓim* (Delhi: Khwāja Awlād Kitābghar, ca. 1970), 64.
[19] Ibid. Note here the critique of *mawlvi*-style Islam, which opposed Sufism and stressed exoteric and literal interpretations.

> sent to him and he recited some Qur'ān and then blew on me. He ordered an amulet of silver, and inscribed a talisman on it with his own hand. When this talisman had been fastened around my neck my mother said: "This is a *nād-i 'Alī*[20] and the King of India has made it for you. On saying, "the King of India," tears came into my mother's eyes. I therefore asked, "Mommy, why do you weep?" She replied, "Son, now this King who gave you the *nād-i 'Alī* is no more, and the English have seized his throne." This was the first time that I had ever heard of the King or the English. I believe that the seed of love for the Timurid (Mughal) house, which my mother sowed in my heart, sprang from this incident.[21]

Niẓāmī is said to have studied Urdu as a child with the young Muslim princes of the deposed Mughal house and their tutor, Mawlānā Muḥammad Ismā'īl.[22] This explains his mastery of the finest in Urdu stylistics.

Inayat Khan also felt the effects of colonial rule. His maternal grandmother was said to be from the descendants of the ruler of Mysore, Ṭīpū Sulṭān, who conducted heroic resistance against the British.

> In Inayat Khan's family, the oldest memories [of the British] were the most decidedly negative. The Battle of Seringapatam was silently remembered in the household in which he grew up; for Inayat Khan's grandmother Qāsim Bībī, whom his maternal grandfather Mawlābakhsh (1833–1896) had married in Mysore after being invested with royal honors by the Maharaja in recognition of the eminence of his musical virtuosity, was a daughter of the house of Ṭīpū Sulṭān (1749-1799). The lifelong resistance of the "Tiger of Mysore" against the encroachments of the British East India Company, culminating in his death on the battle-field, cast Ṭīpū Sulṭān as a martyr who, for all his valiant efforts, could not defend the old order against the incursion of the new.[23]

---

[20] A special invocation, "the call of 'Alī".

[21] Niẓāmī, *Āp bītī*, 29.

[22] Wāḥidī, *Savāniḥ*, 28.

[23] Zia Inayat Khan, "Sufism and Modernity: Aspects of the Life and Teachings of Pir-o-Murshid Inayat Khan," *Heart and Wings: the Quarterly Journal of the Sufi Order International* (Winter, 2000): 1. Cf. Nekbakht Foundation, ed., *Biography of Pir-o-Murshid Inayat Khan* (London: East-West Publications, 1979), 22–23; De Jong-Keesing, *Inayat Khan*, 12; Wil van Beek, *Hazrat Inayat Khan* (New York: Vantage Press, 1983), 9–10. The best overall treatment of Ṭīpū Sulṭān is Mohibbul Hasan, *History of Tipu Sultan* (Calcutta: World Press, 1951).

The Chishtī Order had been in favor at the courts of the later Mughal rulers, including the last Mughal, Bahādur Shāh Ẓafar, who was himself a Chishtī *khalīfa*. When this Emperor was deposed by the British and exiled to Burma, Chishtīs were persecuted and viewed with suspicion.

Niẓāmī, unlike Inayat Khan, spent most of his career within the context of Indian Islam. Niẓāmī's family were not the sort to participate in the modernist world of Aligarh Muslim University, a new institution founded to combine the best of modern English and traditional Muslim knowledge. Still, he broke with the expectations of the very insular world of shrine custodians to the extent of attending a Deobandi *madrasa* and by traveling to the Middle East and meeting there with Muslim reformers. The Deobandis, along the spectrum of nineteenth century Muslim intellectual movements, supported intellectual aspects of Sufism while condemning many of the popular practices associated with the cult of the Sufi saints.[24] Niẓāmī himself may be characterized as a reformer of sorts, a Sufi who disassociated himself with many traditional elements of shrine practices, typically those associated with moral laxity such as the presence of dancing girls at *'urs* festivals. In terms of devotional practices and beliefs associated with Sufism, however, his position would be more compatible with the Barelvīs, who retained most aspects of shrine reverence.[25] For example, he wrote a treatise in support of the practice of disciples prostrating out of respect for their spiritual guide,[26] an aspect of Sufi practice condemned by more literalist Muslim groups.

Attitude to other religions

Each of our subjects must have experienced a certain ambivalence of status in the hierarchical world of Muslim society at that time. Inayat Khan as a musician, was able to frequent court society and move across a wide range of social classes. Still, even

---

[24] See Barbara D. Metcalf, *Islamic Revival in British India: Deoband, 1860–1900* (Princeton: Princeton University Press, 1982).

[25] On the Barelvī movement see Usha Sanyal, *Devotional Islam and Politics in British India: Ahmad Riza Khan Barelwi and his Movement, 1870–1920* (Delhi: Oxford University Press, 1996).

[26] Niẓāmī, *Murshid-ko sajda-yi ta'ẓim*, op. cit.

accomplished classical musicians would be considered beyond the social pale by more traditionally bourgeois Muslims. At the same time, musicians could move across Hindu-Muslim lines more easily than many others due to the shared love of the artistic fusion represented by Hindustani music and the dynamics of court patronage by the rulers of both Muslim and Hindu princely states.

Chishtī Sufism provided another area of Hindu-Muslim encounter. Traditionally the Chishtīs have been associated with Indian identity. They were the Sufi order that permitted the audition of music, where *qawwālīs* were often sung in the vernacular languages along with classical Persian and Arabic. Their shrines were frequented by both Hindus and Muslims while Chishtīs such as Niẓām al-Dīn Awliyā' had notable Hindu disciples of whom conversion was not required. Khwāja Ḥasan Niẓāmī is said to have studied with Hindu yogis; Hazrat Inayat Khan had contacts with them throughout his years of study and travel in India as well as in Nepal.

Khwāja Ḥasan Niẓāmī took an interest in other religions, studying Hinduism and visiting the Hindu holy places as a young man to study with saddhus,[27] and publishing a biography of Kṛṣna.[28] He wrote favorably about the Sikhs[29] and Bahā'Allāh, founder of the Baha'i faith.[30] His autobiography intimates that his discussions of pilgrimage to the Hindu sites and praise for the methods of the yogis were so strong as to be unpublishable at that time.[31] Some of his later works sympathetic to Hinduism such as the reverential biographies of Kṛṣna and Rāma[32] led less ecumenically minded Muslims to brand him an infidel idol-worshipper.[33]

Niẓāmī, writing within the context of India, urged accommodation to diversity, i.e., the perspectives of non-Muslims. For example, he

---

[27] Wāḥidi, *Savāniḥ*, 39.

[28] Khwāja Ḥasan Niẓāmī, *Kirshin kathā*, 5th ed. (Delhi: Anṣārī Press, 1941).

[29] Khwāja Ḥasan Niẓāmī, *Bīvī kī ta'līm* (Delhi: Ḥalqa-i Mashā'ikh Book Depot, 1924), 172 ff.; *Sikh qawm* (Batala, India: Khwāja Press, n.d.).

[30] Niẓāmī, *Irānī dārvīsh* features a translation of Bahā' Allāh's *Kitāb al-asrār* and is advertised in *Fransisī dārvīsh ke malfūẓāt* (Delhi: Muḥammad Ṣādiq, 1915), 33. This work is also mentioned in *Āp bītī*, 79. He met with the Baha'i leader 'Abd al-Bahā' while in Egypt. Wāḥidī, *Savāniḥ*, 90.

[31] Niẓāmī, *Āp bītī*, 60.

[32] *Rām apdīsha* is mentioned in other works but I have thus far been unable to locate a copy.

[33] Niẓāmī, *Āp bītī*, 60.

is the author of a tract against cow slaughter.[34] In *Niẓāmī Bansurī*, Niẓāmī makes extensive use of a text, *Chār Roza*, which is supposed to have been written by a contemporary Hindu, Har Dev. This account often portrays the Hindu as the sympathetic one, for example, in a story in which a coarse Muslim shopkeeper claims that the Hindu is a *zimmī*[35] and thus under his protection. The Muslim saint later corrects the shopkeeper saying that rather all are under the protection of God.[36] Still, Niẓāmī opposed Muslim assimilation to Hinduism or the apostasy of Indian Muslims and more than once articulated his purpose as being the propagation of Islam.[37]

Niẓāmī presented the broader Muslim world to the Indian Muslims through some of his travel accounts and through translations that he made from Arabic into Urdu. These translations included major Islamic sources such as the Qur'ān and *ḥadith*. It should be noted that in his writings he cites Western sources such as the *Encyclopedia of Islam*[38] and he speaks approvingly about the Sufī mission of Hazrat Inayat Khan to the West.[39]

A strikingly innovative aspect of Inayat Khan's mission to the West was that the object was not formal conversion to Islam. Inayat Khan's non-proselytizing approach is clearly stated in *The Unity of Religious Ideals*:

> The Sufi Movement is constituted of those who have the same ideals of service to God and to humanity, and who have the ideal of devoting a part or the whole of their life to the service of humanity in the path of truth. This Movement has its groups, the members of which belong to all the different religions, for all are welcome, Christians, Buddhists, Parsis, Muslims. No one's faith or belief is questioned; each can follow his own church, religion, creed; no one need believe in any special creed or dogma. There is freedom of thought. At the same time personal guidance is given on the path, in the problems of both outer life and inner life.[40]

---

[34] Niẓāmī, *Tark-i gā'o-kushī* (Delhi: Thakur Das and Sons, 1920).
[35] A non-Muslim subject under Muslim rule, literally "a protected responsibility" of the Muslims.
[36] Niẓāmī, *Niẓāmī bansurī*, 39–46.
[37] Wāḥidī, *Savāniḥ*, 175.
[38] Niẓāmī, *Niẓāmī bansurī*, 526.
[39] Ibid., 505–507.
[40] Inayat Khan, *The Unity of Religious Ideals* (London: The Sufi Movement, 1921), 309–10.

Niẓāmī, on the other hand, is often associated in historical memory with a movement that he conducted during the 1920s against the Aryā Samāj, a Hindu revivalist sect. This group had undertaken a campaign known as *shuddhi* (purification) to reintegrate untouchables and recently converted castes of Muslims and Christians into Hinduism.

After an initial period of Hindu Muslim cooperation, epitomized by the support of Gandhi and his followers for the Khilāfat movement,[41] the two religious communities became increasingly polarized. Accompanying rising communal tensions, the 1920s represent the most intensive period of Ḥasan Niẓāmī's *tablīgh* campaign to preserve the Indian Muslims in their faith by providing them material and political support as well as basic Islamic education.

The very period in which Inayat Khan made his final visit to India was a heated one for communal relations. During this period Niẓāmī was embroiled in a conflict with some other Muslim leaders, such as Mawlānā Muḥammad 'Alī, who advocated cooperation with the Hindu-dominated Congress. 'Alī tried to discourage Niẓāmī from his opposition to the Aryā Samāj. The chief proponent of the Shuddhi movement, Swāmī Shrāddhānandā of the Aryā Samāj, was assassinated during Inayat Khan's visit. The date of its publication indicates that Niẓāmī must have been compiling his work which collects exchanges of condemnations and criticisms between himself and Muḥammad 'Alī at this very time of Inayat Khan's visit, since the book was published in 1927.[42]

While both Inayat Khan and Ḥasan Niẓāmī were open to the concept of pre-Muḥammadan prophethood, in his work on Kṛṣna Niẓāmī was careful to term Kṛṣna a "guide" (*hādī*) rather than a prophet. Still he was not reluctant to compare aspects of Kṛṣna's mission and miracles to the experiences of Moses and other prophets of the Islamic tradition.[43] Hazrat Inayat Khan went even further in his affirmation of the Hindu tradition as an integral part of his Sufism:

---

[41] A movement among Indian Muslims calling for the restoration of the Caliphate after the deposition of the last Turkish representative of this office in the 1920s. See Gail Minault, *The Khilafat Movement: Religious Symbolism and Political Mobilization in India* (New York: Columbia University Press, 1982).

[42] Khwāja Ḥasan Niẓāmī, *Namūna bi jang-i Ṣiffīn* (Delhi: Ḥalqa-i Mashā'ikh, 1927).

[43] Niẓāmī, *Krishen kathā*, 52.

> The Sufi Message which is now being given in the Western world is the child of that mother who has been known for many years as Sufism. The Sufi Message which is being given to the world just now, therefore, connects the two lines of the prophetic mission, the Hindu line and that of Beni Israel, in order that they may become the medium to unite in God and Truth both parts of the world, East and West. It is the same Truth, the same religion, the same ideal, which the wise of all ages have held. If there is anything different, it is only the difference of the form. The Sufi Message given now has adopted the form suitable for the age. It is a Message without claim; and the group of workers in this Message, and those who follow it, are named the Sufi Movement, whose work it is to tread the spiritual path quietly, unassumingly, and to serve God and humanity, in which is the fulfilment of the Message.[44]

In the Gayatri "Salat," Inayat Khan's prayer addressed to "the Messenger," a number of prophetic exemplars are invoked:

> Allow us to recognize Thee in all Thy holy names and forms; as Rama, as Krishna, as Shiva, as Buddha. Let us know Thee as Abraham, as Solomon, as Zarathustra, as Moses, as Jesus, as Mohammed, and in many other names and forms, known and unknown to the world.[45]

The evocation of the historical lineages of the prophets of Eastern and Western traditions is in the spirit of the Islamic teaching that prophets have been sent to all nations. The "Spirit of Guidance," as Hazrat Inayat Khan termed the prophetic essence, takes us beyond historical limitation. "[Masters] have appeared with different names and forms; but He alone was disguised in them who is the only Master of eternity."[46] As the Spirit of Guidance, "all Masters from the time of Adam till the time of Mohammad have been the one embodiment of the Master-ideal."

Hazrat Inayat Khan then compares the teachings of Jesus and Kṛṣna on this point, concluding by citing the *ḥadīth* of Muḥammad:

---

[44] Khan, *Unity of Religious Ideals*, 159.

[45] Inayat Khan, *Notes from the Unstruck Music from the Gayan of Inayat Khan*, ed. Munira van Voorst van Beest and Munir Graham (New Lebanon, N.Y.: Omega Publications, 1988), 46–7.

[46] Inayat Khan, *The Sufi Message of Hazrat Inayat Khan* (London: Barrie & Rockliff/Jenkins, 1960–67), 1:31.

> "I existed even before this creation and shall remain after its assimilation." In the holy traditions it is said, "We have created thee of Our light and from thy light We have created the universe." This is not said of the external person of Muhammad as known by this name. It refers to the spirit which spoke through all the blessed tongues and yet remained formless, nameless, birthless, and deathless.[47]

Chishtī Sufism

Khwāja Ḥasan Niẓāmī grew up in one of the hereditary lineages of custodians of the major Chishtī institution in India, the Niẓām al-Dīn shrine in Delhi. Breaking with the hereditary role of being a pilgrim guide and professional prayer-sayer (*du'ā gū*), Niẓāmī became one of the more successful Urdu journalists and writers of the early twentieth century, writing principally on Islamic themes and on the past glory of the Mughal Empire.

Niẓāmī's youth was marked by great poverty and sorrow. He was orphaned and for a time made a living selling postcards and holy pictures to pilgrims. He eventually became a self-made man through literary activities such as writing journalistic articles and publishing books and magazines that he practiced alongside being a Sufi teacher.

Through his writings Niẓāmī was fashioning a new intellectual space for Muslims in India. He published in the vibrant popular press of the time and started several publications of his own. Some such as *Pīr Bha'ī* ("*Pīr*-Brother") were ephemeral but others such as the monthly, *Munādī* ("The Caller"), are still current. He would anticipate coming trends and issues and put these concerns into writing. He was forward looking, adaptive, and at times political and controversial.

In terms of Sufi mission Niẓāmī represented himself primarily as an "educator Shaykh" rather than making charismatic claims for himself. At one point in his autobiography, Niẓāmī states that all of the trials and difficulties that he faced early in life enabled him to realize his aim of "presenting Islamic Sufism in a new way and a fresh manner."[48] Perhaps his "new" style in Sufism could

---

[47] Ibid., 1:34.
[48] Niẓāmī, *Āp bītī*, 21.

be characterized as being more egalitarian—for example, the egalitarian *pīr bhā'ī* (*pīr*-brother) idea, and his allowing more participation of women.[49]

An early example of Niẓāmī's reformist approach to Sufism is that in 1908 he formed a group consisting of young shrine custodians (*sajjādas*) and some famous patrons, such as Abū al-Kalām Āzād and Shiblī Nu'mānī, into an organization called the "Ḥalqa-i Mashā'ikh" (Circle of Great Shaykhs), in order to reform *khanqāhs* and *dargāhs* in India and support the authentic teachings of Sufism. The four principles of the organization were:

1) To spread and preserve Sufism
2) To unite the Sufi Shaykhs within one body.
3) To reform customs at *'urs* festivals and *khanqāhs* so as to eliminate practices outside of the *sharī'a* and *ṭarīqa*.
4) To protect the political rights of Sufi Shaykhs[50]

Due to this Niẓāmī faced criticism and opposition from those who feared his reforms of unnecessary customs and corruptions at the shrines. Some declared him to be an enemy of Islam and Sufism and an attempt on his life was made.[51]

The founding of this organization marked a turning point in his career. As his biographer, Wāḥidī observed:

> The Circle of Shaykhs Organization was not only for the reform of the shrine of Niẓām al-Dīn Awliyā' but for the reform of all *dargāhs*. The Pīrzādas from the Niẓām al-Dīn *dargāh* went from shrine to shrine spreading the rumour that Ḥasan Niẓāmī had studied at Gangoh and become a Wahhābī,[52] and that by supporting him all of us would be destroyed.
>
> But while on the one hand opposition was arising from the *dargāhs*, at the same time interest in Khwāja Ṣāḥib was increasing in the colleges.

---

[49] For example, in the preface of Niẓāmī's autobiography, the voice of his wife, Khwāja Bānū, encourages literate women to read the work to illiterate women and to involve them in Sufism. Ibid., 4–5.

[50] Ibid., 21.

[51] Niẓāmī mentions this incident, and the fact that bullet holes can still be seen in the wall, in his *Niẓāmī Bansurī*, 515.

[52] Here the term "Wahhābī" is used perjoritively to indicate a follower of one of the Muslim groups such as the Ahl-i Ḥadith, which opposed Sufism. Since Niẓāmī had attended a Deobandi *madrasa* and supported a certain degree of reform, he was a potentional target for such accusations in the polemically charged exchanges among various Muslim groups.

> Those Muslims who supported English education were not ignoring the religious scholars and Sufi Shaykhs, and were searching for such scholars and Shaykhs who could cooperate with them. In Khwāja Ṣāḥib they found someone worthy and capable. Newspapers also turned their attention to Khwāja Ṣāḥib and gave their prominent support to the objectives of the Ḥalqa-i Niẓām al-Mashā'ikh.[53]

This characterization of Niẓāmī by Mullā Wāḥidī, a close associate and life-long companion, situates him among those who wanted the best of both traditional spirituality and modern progress. In fact, the Indian Muslim social classes supporting Sufism were changing their attitudes. Movements such as the Ahl-i Ḥadīth and Deobandis criticized the expressions of devotion to saints and belief in charismatic spiritual powers on the part of any human being. This undercut many elements of traditional shrine culture and the belief in the real efficacy of spiritual practices.

The contemporary Muslim poet and philosopher, Muhammad Iqbal, reflects the ambivalent attitude of the twentieth century Muslim intellectual to the Sufi heritage. On the one hand, great mystics of the past such as Ḥallāj and Rūmī could provide inspiration, at the same time contemporary South Asian Sufis were portrayed as corrupt impostors who lived by "selling the bones of their ancestors."

Muslim reformers of the nineteenth century considered the claims of some Sufis to be miracle mongering. The hereditary lineages of certain orders had become feudal institutions in which descendents made money off the pilgrims to the tombs of the saints while offering quick spiritual fixes in the forms of amulet writing and various folk cures.

Niẓāmī's efforts were to present Sufi teachings to a mass audience of newly literate Muslims while continuing to operate within the context of traditional Sufi practices such as *pīrī-murīdī* (master-disciple relationship). Many of Ḥasan Niẓāmī's writings deal with the practice of Sufism and he is said to have had more than 100,000 disciples. He is credited as the author of a vast number of works,[54] often pamphlets or articles, in addition to his novels.

---

[53] Wāḥid, *Savāniḥ*, 44.
[54] By some accounts, as many as five hundred. Wāḥidī, *Savāniḥ*, 130.

The family of Inayat Khan was not associated with a specific shrine although Inayat Khan is reputed to have had a Sufi saint in his ancestry (Juma‘ Shāh, Punjab). His connections with the Chishtiyya begin with his *bay‘at* at the hands of Sayyid Abū Hāshim Madanī, and he is said to have had initiations in the other major orders of India. It may be concluded that because Inayat Khan was not anchored to a particular shrine or associated with any one Muslim intellectual faction he had wider scope from which to address the concerns of Western non-Muslims.

Strategies of reaching a mass audience with the Message

In the introduction to his autobiography, Niẓāmī states that the work is written for his disciples whom he terms, "*pīr*-brothers" (*pīr bhā'ī*), since they are on the same level as him in being *murīds* of Allah. Later he mentions that many of his disciples have never met him and have pledged their allegiance by post.[55] By 1919 he was said to have 60,000 disciples.[56]

The increasing importance of print is evidenced in Niẓāmī's writings. An example would be Niẓāmī's giving permission (*ijāzat*) in print[57] to whoever read his book on the subject to perform Sufi practices such as the recitation of *Ḥizb al-baḥr*.[58] Many of his *murīds* apparently never actually met him but corresponded with him by post.[59]

It is noteworthy that Niẓāmī entered the field of journalism just at the time when print culture in South Asia was expanding. As Francis Robinson observes:

> [In Muslim South Asia] when the Ottoman Empire entered its terminal stages from 1911 onwards, the Press boomed as never before. Great newspapers flourished—Abu-l Kalam Azad's *al-Hilāl*, Muhammad Ali's *Comrade*, Zafar Ali Khan's *Zamindar*.[60]

---

[55] Niẓāmī, *Āp bītī*, 8.

[56] Ibid., 24. By 1951 it was said to be hundreds of thousands (lakhs) of disciples.

[57] Niẓāmī, *Amāl-i Ḥizb al-baḥr* (Delhi: Khwāja Kutub Ghar, 1952), last page.

[58] *Ḥizb al-baḥr* is a lengthy invocation said to have been inspired to the Sufi master al-Shādhilī. Normally permission to perform certain practices is given only to qualified followers by Sufi masters in person.

[59] Niẓāmī, *Āp bītī*, 8.

[60] Francis Robinson, "Technology and Religious Change: Islam and the Impact of Print," *Modern Asian Studies* 1, no. 27 (1993): 243.

Overall, Niẓāmī's role, including his approach to Sufi biography, could be categorized as popularizing and humanizing Islamic/Sufi teachings[61]:

> By breaking the stranglehold of 1200 years of oral transmission, by breaking the stranglehold of the madrasa-trained ulema on the interpretation of Islamic knowledge, print helped make possible an era of vigorous religious experimentation. Print came to be the main forum in which religious debate was conducted; it was an era of pamphlet wars and of religiously partisan newspapers and magazines. Scholars, some madrasa-trained, some not, delved with increasing vigour into the resources of both the Islamic tradition and Western civilization, now made so freely available by print, to find answers to contemporary challenges.[62]

Niẓāmī was given the honorific title, "*muṣawwir-i fiṭrat*" (the depictor of creation/nature), probably because of his talent for bringing out human nature and for writing in a more natural and accessible style. As a writer he was an innovative stylist, particularly in the field of biography, autobiography, and diary writing. It is said that his oratorical style and eloquence was shaped by the fact that he went to school with Mughal princes and he certainly associated with the great figures of Urdu, Shiblī Nu'mānī, Abū al-Kalām Āzād, Akbar Allāhabādī,[63] and Iqbal.[64] Niẓāmī also went beyond the book as a form by becoming involved in all kinds of journalistic activities, writing articles for Muslim newspapers as well as starting a number of his own magazines such as *Pīr Bhā'ī*, *Dārvīsh*, and *Munādī*. Printing and publishing was not a centralized activity at that time, and in fact many vernacular language books in India and Pakistan are still self-published in small runs of 500 to 1000 copies.

Therefore Niẓāmī could be seen as a pioneer in "the production of 'Islamic' books [which] set aside the language of

---

[61] Imām Murtażā Naqvī evaluates Niẓāmī's popularization of Sufi teachings in accessible and appealing prose as one of his major contributions. *Khwāja Ḥasan Niẓāmī: Fann awr shakhṣiyat* (Karachi: Urdu Academy Sindh, 1991), 338–9.

[62] Robinson, "Technology and Religious Change," 246.

[63] Wāḥidī, *Savāniḥ*, 136–145.

[64] Iqbal and Niẓāmī met and exchanged letters on a number of topics, occasionally disagreeing.

authoritative discourse by religious scholars in favor of a direct understanding of texts."[65]

Extensive travel, facilitated by new networks of railroads, was part of the experience of both men. It has been traditional for Sufi seekers to go in search of wisdom and Inayat Khan's biographers recount his youthful travels around India, both for the sake of musical performance and patronage and for seeking out spiritual contacts, especially after meeting his *murshid* in Hyderabad. Niẓamī also set out in search of a *murshid* and continued traveling throughout the rest of his career. After partition, due to the disturbances in Delhi, he and his family spent several years residing in Hyderabad.

In 1911 Niẓāmī went to Egypt, Syria and Palestine and the Hijaz under the auspices of his organization, the Ḥalqa-i Mashā'ikh.[66] There he contacted various Sufis and activists including a *khalīfa* of Shaykh Sanūsī.[67] In fact, he took a great interest in the teachings and activities of Sanūsī and wrote about him in a number of contexts as well as translating some of his teachings and other Shadhilī practices.[68]

During his career Khwāja Ḥasan Niẓāmī also traveled extensively within British India, this travel being facilitated by a new network of railroads connecting the major cities and towns and facilitated the role of the Sufi master in contacting his *murīds*.

Inayat Khan's first trip to America in 1910 was highly unusual for the time. His extensive travels and residence in Europe, including Britain, France, the Netherlands, Switzerland, and Russia must have also been extremely unusual in those days. Performance

---

[65] Dale F. Eickelman and Jon W. Anderson, "Print, Islam, and the Prospects for Civil Pluralism: New Religious Writings and Their Audiences" in *Oxford Journal of Islamic Studies* 1 (1997): 49.

[66] He writes about this trip in diary form in his *Roznāmcha bā-taṣvīr: Safar-i-Miṣr va Shām va Ḥijāz* (Meerut, India: Hashimī Press, 1913).

[67] Shaykh Sayyid Aḥmad al-Sanūsī (1873–1933). Third Grand Master of the Libyan Sanūsiyya Order of dervishes who sided with the Ottomans and Germany during WWI.

[68] Khwāja Haṣan Niẓāmī, *Shaykh Sanūsī* (Delhi: Muḥammad Ṣādiq, 1915); *Risāla-yi Shaykh Sanūsī* (Meerut: Hashimī Press, 1914); *Fayżān-i Shaykh Sanūsī* Part 3 (Meerut: Hashimī Press, 1914). In one work all the copies of which were seized by the British police, Niẓāmī translated some prophecies of Sanūsī regarding a "German Khilāfat." Niẓāmī, *Āp bītī*, 81. Wāḥidī, *Savāniḥ*, 112–3.

of music was certainly one way of facilitating contacts and introductions into European society. Reading the biographical accounts one has the impression of Inayat Khan being drawn to contact as many artists, opinion makers, and intellectuals as possible in order to spread his message and perhaps to seek out those with resonant spiritual experiences. One means for reaching a larger audience which was employed by Inayat Khan was the newspaper interview.[69]

The idea of spreading the Sufi message evokes an implicit comparison with another early twentieth century movement, the Aḥmadiyya or Qadiyānīs. This was a sect that emerged in British India based on the teachings of Mirzā Ghulām Aḥmad (d. 1908). These teachings were considered controversial and even heretical in cases where followers accepted that Ghulām Aḥmad was a latter-day prophet, a teaching unacceptable to Orthodox Islam. At the same time the Aḥmadis were among the earliest to send Islamic missions to the West and Khwāja Kamāl al-Dīn, an Indian *mawlvī* who worked in England, seems to have been a prominent and respected figure even outside Aḥmadī circles. For example, Niẓamī credits him with being a Chishtī Sufi.[70]

At one point Niẓāmī make this comparison of missions to the West explicit:

> Once I asked Sufi Inayat Khan about the difference between his way of spreading the message and that of the Qadiyānīs. He replied, "The Qadiyānīs change minds by force of logical proofs, I change hearts through the influence of love."[71]

Attitudes to women

Each figure recognized the intellectual and spiritual stature of females. Khwāja Ḥasan Niẓāmī's work, "The Education of the Wife" is said to have been composed during a forty day spiritual retreat when he realized that his younger and inexperienced wife, if

---

[69] Some of these interviews are preserved in Munira van Voorst van Beest, ed., *Complete Works of Pir-o-Murshid Hazrat Inayat Khan*, 1923 I: January–June (London and The Hague: East-West Publications, 1989), 90–99.

[70] Khwāja Ḥasan Niẓāmī, "*Yūrup meṅ Chishtiyya taḥrīk*" ("The Chishti movement in Europe"), *Roznāmcha* (Jan. 8, 1933): 6. Hazrat Inayat Khan speaks of Khwāja Kamāl al-Dīn in Nekbakht Foundation, *Biography*, 233.

[71] Niẓāmī, "*Yūrup men Chishtiyya taḥrīk*": 7.

she were to be left a widow, would be at a loss concerning how to handle worldly and family affairs. He therefore composed twenty lessons for her, initially treating religious, family and economic matters but ending with topics of contemporary political urgency such as British colonialism, the Indian home rule movement, etc.[72] In terms of his respect for women, he states that he believed that what he had learned in twenty years, she could learn in twenty days. After each of his lessons, his wife replies within the text, commenting on and critiquing his opinions.

Niẓāmī's wife, Laylā Bānū,[73] is given her own voice in order to respond critically to his advice and she contributed a preface to his autobiography. She was also expected to take an interest in politics and world events. Further evidence of Niẓāmī's interest in women's issues is the fact that in the 1920s and 1930s he published several women's magazines including *Ustānī* (Female Teacher) and *Niswānī dunyā* (Women's World).[74]

It seems that encounters with some of the female disciples of Hazrat Inayat Khan may have led Niẓāmī to rethink traditional strictures against granting the rank of *khalīfa* to women, on the basis of the following passage:

> Although we don't find reports in the biographies of the great ones of the past of them granting *khilāfat* to women,[75] still on investigating the principles and rules of Sufism there does not appear to be any harm in granting females *khilāfat*.
>
> Therefore I gave permission to teach my *silsila* to the daughter of Ḥakīm Alṭaf Ḥusayn, Rashīd al-Nisā Begum, and bestowed on her the name of Malakūt Begum.
>
> Especially in Europe and America it is the women who can contribute to laying the groundwork and bringing to conclusion the work of spreading the message (*tablīgh*).

---

[72] Niẓāmī, *Bīvī kī ta'līm*, op. cit.

[73] Niẓāmī remarried in 1916, after the death of his first wife and three of their four children in 1908. Hazrat Inayat Khan had been twice married in India before coming to the West and had in both cases experienced the tragedy of the sudden loss of a young spouse.

[74] Gail Minault, *Secluded Scholars: Women's Education and Muslim Social Reform in Colonial India* (Delhi: Oxford, 1998), 153.

[75] In fact, at least some biographies of Mu'īn al-Dīn Chishtī, who brought the lineage to India, mention that he granted *khilāfat* to one of his daughters, Bībī Ḥāfiẓa Jamāl. Peter M. Currie, *The Shrine and Cult of Mu'in al-din Chishti of Ajmer* (Delhi: Oxford University Press, 1989), 83.

> Today it is due to the efforts of these very women that Sufi Inayat Khan's thousands of disciples are increasing in Europe and America, in whom feelings of spiritual purity, moral goodness, worship of God, love, and empathy are to be found to a much greater extent than in others.[76]

Niẓāmī commented elsewhere that it is women who have always been the first to recognize and respond to new prophetic messages, citing as examples Āsiya wife of Pharaoh, Khadīja wife of Muḥammad, and Jasudhā, foster-mother to Kṛṣna.[77]

Hazrat Inayat Khan went even further in recognizing women, giving female disciples the highest initiations and leadership roles in his organization. In fact, of the four persons initiated by Inayat Khan to the level of Murshid[a], all were women: Murshida Rabia Martin, Murshida Sophia Green, Murshida Sherifa Goodenough, and Murshida Fazal Mai Egeling. The fact that Inayat Khan worked in the West is no doubt significant, but recall that even in Europe and America at that time women were restricted from many public roles, especially those of religious leadership, as well as in many expressions of religion.

Inayat Khan clearly had a deep respect for the spiritual dignity of women, but at the same time he did not advocate the abandonment of gender distinctions: "Woman, whom destiny has made to be man's superior, by trying to become his equal, falls beneath his estimation."[78]

Attitudes to the West

A theme of Niẓāmī's activities is both modernizing and popularizing, not simply Sufism, but general attitudes to knowledge. I understand this from his style and subjects of composition.

Although he claimed not to have known English, Niẓāmī took a strong interest in the West and supported "English" education for

---

[76] Niẓāmī, "*Yūrup men Chishtiyya taḥrīk*": 8.

[77] Niẓāmī, *Krishen kathā*, 56.

[78] Munira van Voorst van Beest, ed, *The Complete Works of Pir-o-Murshid Hazrat Inayat Khan*, Sayings I (London and The Hague: East-West Publications, 1989), 489. Inayat Khan's views on gender and sexuality are elaborated in *Rasa Shastra: The Science of Life's Creative Forces* (Deventer, Holland: Kluwer, 1938).

boys and girls.[79] Niẓāmī's relationships with Westerners were also non-traditional and ambivalent. For example his disciples included an English army officer, Major Dixon. He was under suspicion for anti-British activism and at the same time he wrote a book on the sights of Delhi that he dedicated to the British governor. While in the Middle East he met with Pan-Islamic activist circles and thus he became the subject of intense surveillance and harassment on the part of the British authorities. Meetings of his organization became impossible and it was only in 1917 that this surveillance was lifted by the commissioner of Delhi, William Hailey. Niẓāmī's guidebook to Delhi is dedicated to Hailey and seems to be designed to assuage British suspicions as to his loyalty.[80]

Shortly after the abdication of King Edward, Niẓāmī composed an imaginary diary portraying the Prince's inner struggle as a Sufi fable but also critiquing British understandings of the Indian situation.[81] Another early work, "The French Dervish," excerpts anecdotes from a life of Napoleon Bonaparte that had been translated into Urdu, treating them as Sufi *malfūẓāt* and proof of Napoleon's spiritual wisdom and insights.[82]

Hazrat Inayat Khan's attitudes to the West changed over time, but remained consistent in certain essentials. On the one hand, Inayat Khan, like other Indians at that time, would have regretted British imperial domination of India. The inventiveness and progress represented by the West had a strong appeal, however, and during his early career in India Inayat Khan often wore Western suits and ties, in contrast to his habit of wearing Eastern robes during his later career in America and the West.

Inayat Khan sometimes found himself cast as an apologist for the East in the face of Western stereotypes, but was careful not to

---

[79] Niẓāmī, *Bīvī kī ta'līm*, 16–19.

[80] *Rāhnumā-i sayr-i Dihli.* Niẓāmī, *Āp bītī*, 85. William Malcolm Hailey (1872–1969) went on to become "the most distinguished member of the Indian Civil Service in the twentieth century and one of the few raised to the peerage". On his career see John W. Cell, *Hailey: A Study in British Imperialism (1872–1969)* (Cambridge: Cambridge University Press, 1992).

[81] Khwāja Ḥasan Niẓāmī, *A Modern Gulistan for Modern Man: Ex-King Edward's Diary, "The Sufi's Secret of Real Happiness"*, trans. M. Fażl al-Ḥaqq (Delhi: Munādī, 1937).

[82] Khwāja Ḥasan Niẓāmī, *Fransisī darvīsh ke malfūẓāt* (Delhi: Muḥammad Ṣādiq, 1915).

confine the understanding of Sufism to something exotic and alien. He said:

> People often wonder if it (the Sufi Order) is a mission from the East. I answer that neither is it from the East or from the West, it is from Above. It is for the work of God and the service of humanity, in which people of the East and the West, of the North and the South, have all joined together in their sacred task. The word Sufi is eastern as well as western; it comes from the Greek word *Sophia*, and in the Persian language is *Sufia*, so the word should be acceptable both in the East and in the West [83]

In a lecture entitled "East and West" delivered in Brussels in 1923, and later included (in an edited form) in the book *The Problem of the Day*, Inayat Khan emphasized harmony between East and West as a desideratum valuable beyond the power of words to describe. He likened East and West to two eyes, which must unite in purpose for the vision of the world to be complete. In the unity of East and West in wisdom was there hope for real peace.[84]

Political activities

A discussion of the experience of Indians in the early part of the twentieth century has to take into account the impact of the broader forces of colonialism, nationalism, and a rising identification with religious communalism that defined this period. Although the Chishtī Order was marked by the principle of *bu'd al-salaṭīn* or "remaining aloof from political rulers," India at this period was chafing under the yoke of British rule. The issues that home rule or Indian independence entailed, however, included the complex nature of any future Indian nation. What role should

---

[83] Van Voorst van Beest, *Complete Works*, 1923 I, 69. When pressed by the interviewer on the question of home rule for India he replied, "The situation in India as it concerns the natives and Great Britain? I have nothing to do with that. I am not a disciple of strife, or a disseminator of violent propaganda …" In another interview the same week, Inayat Khan explained, "I am not concerned with politics at all. I am interested in the humanitarian side of the world. If the general attitude develops, humanity will think and act better, and the effect will be seen in politics as well as education, social relations, and religion." Ibid., 95, 90.

[84] Munira van Voorst van Beest, ed., *The Complete Works of Pir-o-Murshid Hazrat Inayat Khan*, 1923 II: July–December (London and The Hague: East-West Publications, 1988), 901–908; Cf., Khan, *The Sufi Message*, 10:258–261.

religion play in such a diverse environment? While dreams of communal harmony and shared Indian nationhood were cherished by early activists, Muslims and Hindus soon found that their interests were not always the same. For Khwāja Ḥasan Niẓāmī the specter of Hindu movements attempting to turn Muslims back to Hinduism was a force that had to be opposed, and thus he appeared during one phase of his career to be a political opponent of Hindus. In the 1920s he conducted a campaign against the Aryā Samāj's Shuddhi (purification) movement, which was attempting to get Indian Muslims and Christians to convert back to Hinduism.[85] As part of this he published a number of pamphlets[86] on basic Islamic teachings and sponsored activities such as the tour from Delhi to Lahore of a "Muslim Mahārānā."[87] He was later to categorize these activities of *tablīgh* as one of the least important aspects of his career.

A study of his numerous writings illustrates that his political positions modified during the years of his major literary production, approximately 1915–1940. Some of the political themes treated in his works are Pan-Islamism,[88] Khilāfat,[89] home rule,[90] opposition to the 'Alī brothers,[91] and accommodation to other religious communities.[92] His initial support for Gandhi[93]

---

85 On his activities in this regard see Wāḥidī, *Savāniḥ*, 148–159. On the Shuddhi movement see R. K. Ghai, *The Shuddhi Movement in India* (New Delhi: Commonwealth Press, 1990).

86 Advertised as "*insidād-i irtādd kī kitāben*" or "books designed to block the flow of apostasy."

87 Khwāja Ḥasan Niẓāmī, *Tazkira-i Musulmān Māhārāna* (Delhi: Ḥalqa-i Mashā'ikh, 1927).

88 There are many examples of this. For example in his memoirs of a journey to the Middle East in 1911: "The nation of Christ not only demands to rule but they have also seized civilization, good manners, and virtues from us." Wāḥidī, *Savāniḥ*, 108.

89 In his work *Government awr khilāfat* (Batala, India: Niẓāmiyya Book Depot, 1920), 12, Niẓāmī takes the rather odd strategy of inviting the Prince and the British generally to accept Islam and establish their own Caliphate: "I am quite certain that if Britain becomes Muslim, then in a short while the Muslims will accept its Caliphate and the center of the Caliphate will be transferred from Constantinople to London."

90 There is some discussion of this in Naqvī, *Khwāja Ḥasan Niẓāmī*, 139–141.

91 Niẓāmī, *Namūna bi jang-i Siffīn*, op. cit.

92 For example, works on Hinduism, Sikhism and the Baha'is, as well as a life of Jesus, *Ta'rīkh-i Masīḥ* (Delhi: Mashā'ikh Book Depot, 1927).

93 For this see Wāḥidī, *Savāniḥ*, 162–187 passim.

changed to some disappointment with the latter, and support of Nehru:

> Mr. Gandhi's ambition is more to become a mahātma—a big religious leader—than a political leader of the Hindus. But his genius is on the ebb, his popularity is on the wane, and his political leadership has failed. Mr. Gandhi has no sympathy with the aspirations of the Indian Muslims and he is definitely hostile to their Urdu language and culture because he wants to make an end of their political power by destroying the last shreds of their national solidarity.[94]

Inayat Khan had left India for the West just before the major communal rifts became intensified. His musings on common spiritual themes idealize the shared spiritual repertoire of Hinduism and Islam. His Sufi Movement was officially apolitical, although in private classes matters of political ideology were occasionally and elliptically discussed.[95] Hazrat Inayat Khan associated with Indian freedom fighters but was careful to avoid any appearance of anti-colonial rhetoric in his public persona.

His final visit to India was clearly a strain since rising communal tensions could not be ignored. Intriguingly, his biographer suggests than Inayat Khan met with Swāmī Shrāddhānandā as a Hindu spiritual leader and was dismayed at his assassination a few days later in 1926.[96] This is the same Swāmī whom Niẓāmī saw as an enemy of Muslims. A possible explanation for their different appreciations of the Swāmī lies in the complexity of inter-communal relations during this period. Swāmī Shrāddhānandā had even been invited by Muslims to speak in the Jāmiʿ Masjid in Delhi in 1919.[97] "As fraternization of Hindus with Muslims reached its peak the Swami was taken to speak from the elevated pulpit of the Jama masjid to thousands who assembled in

---

[94] Niẓāmī, *Ex-King Edward's Diary*, 92–93.

[95] E.g., Inayat Khan, *The Soul Whence and Whither*, ed. Elise Guillaume Schamhart (Hounslow, England: East-West Publications, 1984), 44: "The socialist point of view that all property is theft is an extreme attitude. Those who say this do not know that, if there was not this 'theft' as an inner impulse behind this manifestation, the souls would not have come on earth. . . ."

[96] Kismet Stam, *Rays*, (The Hague: East-West Publications, 1970).

[97] G. R. Thursby, *Hindu-Muslims Relations in British India: A Study of Controversy, Conflict, and Communal Movements in North India 1923–28* (Leiden: E. J. Brill, 1975), 148.

the courtyard of the great Mosque."[98] The Swāmī split from the Congress, however, by late 1922, and began the work of converting untouchables and others back to Hinduism. As tensions rose polemics produced on both sides became increasingly nasty. This was the very period in which a number of works were issued depicting the Prophet Muḥammad in a most negative light, and rioting and assassinations were provoked by such tactics.[99]

Some of the statements in Kismet Stam's short book *Rays* suggest that while back in India Inayat Khan became interested and involved in social and political causes. She records a rather mysterious but suggestive remark, "If I took up the work for India, I should have to leave everything, everything." [100]

Conclusions

In summary, both Hazrat Inayat Khan and Khwāja Ḥasan Niẓāmī can be seen as renewers of Chishtī spirituality in the twentieth century, although the arena of their respective activities differed and consequently so did many aspects of their approach.

Both were sensitive to the requirements of a new era, marked increasingly by global connections and the potential of universal brotherhood. The spiritual needs of individuals in both the West and India were changing in fundamental ways. Westerners longed for practices that would develop them spiritually and put them personally in touch with refined spiritual states. Inayat Khan seems to have revived the role of being an individual "teaching" Shaykh who developed intense personal relationships in order to transform an inner circle of disciples. At the same time he also was an organization builder who delegated authority and sought out dedicated and evolved persons to transmit his message over vast distances and networks of people. The artistic language of Hazrat Inayat Khan was music and in his struggle to translate the total experience of Sufi spirituality to a receptive but naive audience in the West he needed to distill the essence of the "love, harmony, and beauty" that he was striving to communicate.

---

[98] Ibid.
[99] On these publications see Thursby, *Hindu-Muslims Relations*, 40–62.
[100] Stam, *Rays*, 115.

In the early twentieth century many Indian Muslims were no longer part of the traditional networks of clientship and authority that obviated the search for religious answers on an individual basis. In general, nineteenth and twentieth century Indian Sufism had become characterized by the prevalence of the "mediator Shaykh," a style of guidance featuring a devotional approach stressing loyalty and submission to the Sufi Shaykh as representative of the Prophet, rather than training individual disciples to attain enlightenment on their own.[101]

As a Sufi Shaykh, Niẓāmī may be said to have been on a campaign to promote individual liberation rather than mediation based on his own charisma as a teacher, and for this reason he never seemed interested in setting up an authoritarian hierarchy of succession. He was more of a one-man show, remaining within most of the cultural expectations of *pīrī-murīdī* while availing himself of new possibilities of mass communication in order to reach many disciples through his writings, if not in person. In fact, as a self-made and successful writer, he became somewhat removed from the networks of shrine custodians from which his ancestors came, although he continued to live in the shrine area and participate in some aspects of the culture and maintenance of its traditions.

The India of Niẓāmī's lifetime was fraught with ideological tensions among Muslims. Massive political and social change strained the relationships among India's religious communities and often erupted into terrible violence. Against this background, Khwāja Ḥasan Niẓāmī's efforts to revive Chishtī teachings, preserve inter-religious harmony, and remain receptive to new trends appear to be even more remarkable.

There is a touch of nostalgia or even sadness in the reflections of the two Sufis. The world of the Indian princely states and *sharīf* culture[102] was passing away during the lifetime of Niẓāmī and Inayat

---

[101] Arthur Buehler, *Sufi Heirs of the Prophet: The Indian Naqshbandiyya and the Rise of the Mediating Sufi Shaykh* (Columbia, S.C.: University of South Carolina, 1998).

[102] On the *sharīf* (noble and refined) culture of the Indo-Muslim elites see David Lelyveld, *Aligarh's First Generation* (Princeton: Princeton University Press, 1978), 28, 35ff.

Khan.[103] Materialism and a loss of sensitivity and refinement came with the advent of modernity and mass culture. Niẓāmī's lament at the domination of Islam by the *mawlvīs* that was supplanting the dignity of the dervishes evokes Hazrat Inayat Khan's reminiscences on the dervishes of Ajmer who greeted each other as kings and sultans although they were dressed in rags.[104]

Some six years after the passing of Inayat Khan, Niẓāmī mentioned him in his diary, *Roznāmcha*, in the course of describing the expansion of the Chishtī *silsila*:

> Professor Inayat Khan
>
> He was the disciple of a Chishtī dervish. His musical artistry was much appreciated in Europe and America and in this context he began giving lectures on Sufism. That is, he took the subjects about which his songs were speaking and let people understand the ideas in English, which for the people of Europe and America were very touching and amazing.
>
> Once he found that the reception for Sufi ideas was becoming broader he established a society by the name of the Sufi Order according to the taste of Europe and America. It issues a monthly magazine and he began to send me his books and the magazine.
>
> He got married in France and thousands of men and women became his disciples. In the large cities he established study circles where at appointed times men and women would hold joint *zikr* sessions and they would also perform the *zikr* out loud.
>
> Sufi Inayat Khan did not attempt to change anyone's religion nor did he teach changing one's faith. His mureeds remained in their own ethnic and religious milieu while performing the Chishtī *zikr* and practices.
>
> In about 1920 one of the lady disciples of Ṣūfī Ṣāḥib visited India and at the order of her *murshid* came to see me. I arranged a lecture for her at the Sangham Theatre which was attended by approximately 1000 Hindus and Muslims. My well-known friend, Shaykh Muḥammad Iḥsān al-Ḥaqq of Meerut, was especially impressed by her and he established a "Circle of Unity and Love" to spread the mission and distribute his books.

---

[103] Stam, *Rays*, 125, 127, 128.

[104] Regina Miriam Bloch, *The Confessions of Inayat Khan* (London: The Sufi Publishing Society, 1915), 29–30.

The Coming of Ṣūfī Ṣāḥib

One day he was sitting in a room of the Arabic Wing of my house drinking tea. Looking out of the small window he remarked, "This house and this place draw me, and my heart feels love and intimacy here."

I answered, "You could stay here; I could have this place vacated for your occupancy." He was silent upon hearing this and he merely thanked me.

He spoke very little and for this reason I did not want to interfere with his silence; then he departed for Delhi.

After fifteen days his traveling companion, a European lady disciple, sent a servant to inform me that Ṣūfī Ṣāḥib had passed away with pneumonia and had left last instructions that I should be informed.

I went with brother Shaykh Iḥsān al-Ḥaqq, whom I have already mentioned, to Tilak Lodge and had Ṣūfī Ṣāḥib's body brought back to my house with me, and I had a grave prepared for him at the very place which he had liked while drinking tea and he was buried there.

His traveling companion, the lady disciple, kept her *burqa* on so I never saw her face.

Two years later his wife and four children together with his brother and uncle came from Europe and had his tomb permanently constructed.

His relatives had come from France where Ṣūfī Ṣāḥib had many disciples. They requested that since so many European and American disciples had asked that Ṣūfī Ṣāḥib's remains be brought and buried there, they wanted to put his corpse in a casket and take it to Europe.

After reflecting on this request I agreed because I felt that there would be a lot of spiritual benefit for Europe and America through it.

Thus after two years we opened the tomb and while I lifted the filling stone with my own hands I saw that Ṣūfī Ṣāḥib's corpse, even after two years, had not decayed at all and was in the same condition. The hair of his head and beard, as well as the skin of his face and chest had not decayed.

We placed the body in a solid wooden casket with scent and replaced the casket in the same grave until the body could be transported to France on obtaining permission from the French government. But after that no instructions came from Ṣūfī Ṣāḥib's relatives, so the casket still remains buried where it was originally.[105]

---

[105] Niẓāmī, "*Yūrup meṅ Chishtiyya taḥrīk*": 7.

Hazrat Inayat Khan, Suresnes, 1926

Hazrat Pir-o-Murshid Inayat Khan's Message for Our Time

PIR VILAYAT INAYAT KHAN

In the course of last century, a voice was heard opening new perspectives for the spirituality of the future. It was that of a great pioneer, Hazrat Pir-o-Murshid Inayat Khan, who called it the message of spiritual liberty. It meets the trend in the soul-searchings of many in our day and age for a reexamination of the belief systems of the world religions, encompassing them in the light of the common ground of spiritual experience. While we are enriched by the wisdom, know-how and attunement that these religious traditions have bequeathed to us, we are also called upon to explore new paradigms for the spirituality of the coming Millennium. And we grapple with our concern about our own role as participants in the social and psychological problems that beset our challenging civilization.

Precariously poised as we are at the threshold between the last century and the next Millennium, as we ponder upon the hazards that afflict our planet and humanity, the urgency of meeting the terrifying scourge—the cruelty of wars decimating our beautiful planet persisting in our day and age, of concentration camps, of the torture of prisoners of conscience—twitches our hearts in despair. Clearly, many of these are motivated by religious bigotry.

Jalāl al-dīn Rūmī warned:

> The blind religious are in a dilemma, for the champions on either side stand firm: each party is delighted with its own path. Love alone can end their quarrel, Love alone comes to the rescue when you cry for help against their arguments.[1]

[1] Reynold A. Nicholson, *Rūmī: Poet and Mystic* (London: George Allen & Unwin Ltd., 1964), 173.

Against the background of intolerance and hatred, culminating in cruelty and atrocities, in feuds and wars fuelled by a lack of understanding and appreciation of differences in religion and races, the message of our time awakens respect, friendship, kindness—ultimately touching upon the core of religion: spiritual realization, attunement and experience.

Warning of coming dangers, Hazrat Inayat Khan called for the urgency of a meeting of religious leaders to explore their common denominator while respecting their differences. "Unity is not uniformity" was a judicious motto of his. Such was the message of Hazrat Inayat Khan for our time, calling upon the need to affirm the human spirit in its quest for freedom from the imposition of misconstrued dogmas perpetrated by what he called the "followers of the followers." They often misinterpreted the words of the Prophets, either by ignorance of what the Prophets really said or meant, or, in some cases, to gain ascendancy over the masses in securing positions of authority.

Hazrat Inayat Khan observed that the faithful of different religions know God according to the form in which they conceive Him, not in the form in which another religion conceives Him. The message of our time collects all forms in one universal form, an idea to which people are not accustomed, so that the followers of all religions may worship at the same time.

There is a *ḥadīth* (an adage) ascribed to Prophet Muḥammad:

> The Prophet (*Peace be upon him*) said that on the day of resurrection God will manifest Himself to the creatures in the forms that they themselves refuted, announcing "I am your Lord." In the face of this unfamiliar apparition, they will seek refuge in their own representation of God. Then God will appear in that representation, and then they will believe that, indeed, it is Him.[2]

Hazrat Inayat Khan described the aim of the all-encompassing perspective he promoted:

> The message of the Sufi movement is a call to humanity in general to unite in a world brotherhood beyond the boundaries of

---

[2] See Sahih Al-Bukhari Hadith, 1.770, 8.577, 6.105, 9.532A, 9.532B. This *ḥadīth* is also discussed in Henry Corbin, *Creative Imagination in the Sufism of Ibn 'Arabī* (London: Routledge and Kegan Paul, 1970), 199.

> caste, creed, race, nation, or religion.[3] The whole of humanity is one single body, and all nations, communities, and races are the different organs. The happiness and well-being of each of them is the happiness and well-being of the whole body.[4]

It is the answer to the cry of the whole humanity. Sufism respects all religions and their prophets, saints and masters, encouraging people to value the gift of their religion by discovering its deeper meaning.

Hazrat Inayat Khan founded an inter-religious ceremony called the Universal Worship, in which the scriptures of the world religions are read from the same altar, starting with the invocation:

> Toward the One, The Perfection of Love, Harmony and Beauty, The Only Being. United with all the Illuminated Souls, Who form the embodiment of the Master, the Spirit of Guidance.

And in this ceremony all the prophets, masters and saints of the great world religions are recognized as manifestations of the "Spirit of Guidance":

> Allow us to recognize Thee in all Thy holy names and forms: as Rama, as Krishna, as Shiva, as Buddha. Let us know Thee as Abraham, as Solomon, as Zarathustra, as Moses, as Jesus, as Muhammad, and in many other names and forms, known and unknown to the world.[5]

Already in the 16th century Emperor Akbar had convened what certainly may be considered one of the first Congresses of religions. In the last century, Mahatma Gandhi included several religions in a form of worship. A memorable meeting was convened at Assisi by the Pope, in which the priests of a great number of world religions participated. Even the United Nations, aware of the role of religious intolerance in obstructing world peace, convoked a mammoth jamboree of religious world leaders.

Ibn al-'Arabī:

> My heart is capable of every form,
> a cloister of the monk, a temple for idols,

---

[3] Inayat Khan, Hazrat, *Gathekas* (privately circulated), number 24.
[4] Ibid., number 29.
[5] Excerpt is from the prayer *Salat* composed by Hazrat Inayat Khan. This and other prayers have been published in Hazrat Inayat Khan, *Complete Sayings* (New Lebanon: Omega Publications, 1978) 54–58, 139–141.

a pasture for gazelles, the votary's Ka'aba,
the tables of the Torah, the Qur'ān.
Love is the creed I hold.[6]

Jesus is given a special place in the Qur'ān:

> We gave Jesus son of Mary the clear signs, and confirmed him with the Holy Spirit.[7]

Reconciling the large variety of beliefs amongst the adepts of the different religions, Hazrat Inayat Khan observed:

> Christ has said: I am the Alpha and the Omega. This means that He is first and last and thus is ever there, not that He is absent in between times. The prophecy of Muḥammad was: Now that the world has received a Message through a man who is subject to all limitations and conditions of human life, the Message will in the future be given without the claim.[8] Muhammad, ... the seal of the prophets, ... gave the final statement of divine wisdom: "None exists but Allah." This message fulfilled the aim of prophetic mission.[9]

The New Paradigms

Hazrat Inayat Khan pioneered perspectives for people seeking a spiritual dimension while living in our day and age, faced with the challenges that have arisen through the rat race for material gain. He pointed the way to finding that ideal called God in oneself rather than in the belief of God as "other".

> The central theme of the Sufi Message is ... to bring about in the world the realization of the divinity of the human soul.[10] The purpose of the soul is that for which the whole of creation has been striving, and it is the fulfilment of that purpose which is called God-consciousness.[11]

Where are you to find God if not in the God-conscious?

---

[6] As quoted in Annemarie Schimmel, *Mystical Dimensions of Islam* (Chapel Hill: University of North Carolina Press, 1978), 271.
[7] *Qur'an*, 2.253 cf. Arthur Arberry's translation (*Koran Interpreted*, New York: Simon & Schuster, reprinted 1996) and 'Abdullah Yusuf 'Ali (*Meaning of the Holy Qur'an*, Maryland: Amana Publications, 1989).
[8] Inayat Khan, *The Message Papers* (privately circulated).
[9] Inayat Khan, *The Sufi Message*, 5:20.
[10] Inayat Khan, *Addresses to Cherags* (privately circulated).
[11] Inayat Khan, *Complete Sayings* (New Lebanon: Omega Publications, 1978), 217.

> Some say: "If all is God, then God is not a person, for 'all' is not a person. ..." This question can be answered that, though the seed does not show the flower in it, yet the seed culminates in a flower, and therefore the flower has already existed in the seed.[12]

Hazrat Inayat Khan does not dismiss belief.

> Believing is a process. By this process the God within is awakened and made living.[13] In order to attain to God-consciousness the first condition is to make God a reality, so that He is no longer an imagination.[14] Man can reach God only as far as his imagination can take him.[15] By making God great, we ourselves arrive at a certain greatness.[16]

In the words of Ibn al-'Arabī:

> To Him we attribute no quality without ourselves having that quality.[17]

Upon reflection, prayer avers itself to be the most creative act; to worship what one imagines as God, one projects a representation featuring qualities which one posits to be perfect. In so doing, one is arousing the exemplars of those archetypes in one's psyche. For the Sufis, one's idiosyncrasies are the means by which God is revealing Himself to one in a tangible way, just as an archetype comes through its exemplar. What is more, here we stumble upon the crucial paradox facing our understanding: What do we mean by God? In orthodox religious belief, God is envisioned as "up there"; whereas, what others have only believed in, mystics of all religions discover unfurling within their own being.

'Abd al-Karīm al-Jīlī:

> O Thou who art absent there, we have found Thee here. Thou art non-existent in Thy Essence, existent in Thy person.[18]

---

[12] Inayat Khan, *Unity of Religious Ideals* (New Lebanon: Sufi Order Publications, 1979), 95.
[13] Ibid., 106.
[14] Inayat Khan, *The Sufi Message,* 1:145.
[15] Inayat Khan, *Religious Gathekas* (privately circulated).
[16] Inayat Khan, *The Sufi Message*, 6:214.
[17] Muhyiuddin Ibn 'Arabi, *The Wisdom of the Prophets [Fusus al-Hikam]*, trans.from Arabic to French with notes by Titus Burckhardt; trans. from French by Angela Culme-Seymour (Aldsworth: Beshara Publications, 1975), 16.
[18] 'Abd al-Karīm al-Jīlī, *Universal Man*, trans. with comm.. by Titus Burckhardt into French, trans. from French by Angela Culme-Seymour (Sherborne: Beshara Publications, 1983), 5.

One's representation of what one means by God depends upon one's state of consciousness. We turn again to the words of al-Jīlī:

> All these changes or evolutions in forms, and elsewhere, in all that is in relation or connection, they arise only from the modes according to which God reveals Himself to us.[19]

And Ḥusayn ibn Manṣūr Ḥallāj considers:

> Is it Thee? Is it me? That would be adding another essence inside the Essence. Far from Thee the affirmation of duality.[20] It suffices for the contemplative if the Only Being stands witness in him.[21]

Meister Eckhart saw divinity as a dimension of one's being, saying, in essence, that there is something in me that is uncreated (*increatus*) and not subject to being created (*increabile*).[22]

When Ibn al-'Arabī is elevated to the level where he sees unity, he says:

> Thou art not thou: thou art He, without thou; not He entering into thee, nor thou entering into Him. ... Thou never wast nor wilt be, whether by thyself or through Him or in Him or along with Him. ... Then if thou knowest thine existence thus, then thou knowest God; and if not, then not.[23]

But when back in the perspective of existential consciousness, he says:

> Acknowledge then ... by what thou art God and by what thou art "world" or "the other".[24]

Hazrat Inayat Khan reconciles these complementary viewpoints:

---

[19] Ibid., 32.

[20] Louis Massignon, La Passion de Ḥusayn Ibn Manṣūr Ḥallaj: martyr mystique de l'Islam, execute a Bagdad le 26 mars 922 (Paris: Editions Gallimard, 1975) vol. 3, 55.

[21] Louis Gardet, *Experience mystique en terre non-chretienne* (Paris: Alsatia, 1954), 141.

[22] Cf. Meister Eckhart, *Deutsche Predigten und Traktate*, herausgegeben und ubersetzt von Josef Quint (Munchen: Carl Hanser Verlag, 1955), 294, 454.

[23] Muhyiuddin Ibn 'Arabi, "*Whoso Knoweth Himself ...*" from *The Treatise on Being (Risale-t-ul-wujudiyyah)*, trans. T.H. Weir (London: Beshara Publications, 1976), 4–5.

[24] Ibn al-'Arabī, *Wisdom of the Prophets*, 64.

> The soul may be considered to be a condition of God.[25] The creator is hidden in His creation.[26] The aim is to find God within ourselves, to dive deep into ourselves, so that we may touch the unity of the whole Being.[27] God is beneath all, beyond all, within all, and without all things, covering all, surrounding all that is in Heaven and earth. God is the sum-total of all that exists and which is knowable and also of the existence which is beyond man's knowledge.[28] By making a concept of someone who is beyond conception, we only make Him limited.[29]

This is complementarity; in an encompassing view, one sees the two poles of the same thing. Abū Saʿīd Aḥmad al-Kharrāz declares:

> God can only be known by the synthesis of antinomic affirmations [30]

Christian mystics also had adopted this vision. St Augustine called it *coniunctio oppositorum*, the conjunction of opposites. Hazrat Inayat Khan honored this paradoxical dichotomy, pointing out that the Sufis differ among themselves as to their concepts of God. This conception varies according to their attunement, and therefore can be considered as complementary rather than contradictory. The same reality can look different according to the vantage point from which you look at it.[31]

As a consequence Hazrat Inayat Khan advocated integrating two forms of knowledge, allowing wisdom to be born out of the meeting of the knowledge of the heavens and the knowledge of the earth:

> Knowledge can be divided into two aspects: one aspect is the knowledge which we call learning; the other aspect is knowing.[32] Not all the knowledge learnt from books and from experiences in the world and collected in the mind as learning is wisdom. When the light from within is thrown upon this knowledge, then the knowledge from outer life and the light coming from within make a perfect wisdom.[33]

---

[25] Inayat Khan, *The Sufi Message,* 1:162.
[26] Inayat Khan, *Complete Sayings*, 33.
[27] Inayat Khan, *The Sufi Message* 10:80.
[28] Inayat Khan, *Sangitha I* (privately circulated).
[29] Inayat Khan, *The Sufi Message* 12:31.
[30] Ibn al-'Arab¥, Wisdom of the Prophets, 36
[31] See, for example, Inayat Khan, *The Sufi Message*, 6:213; and *Unity of Religious Ideals*, 89-94.
[32] Inayat Khan, *The Sufi Message*, 1:199.
[33] Inayat Khan, *The Sufi Message,* 4:228.

'Abd al-Jabbār al-Niffarī:

> When thou perceivest, thou seest limitation openly, and thou seest Me at the back of the unseen. When thou art with Me, thou seest the opposites.[34]

Actuating this antinomy—instead of observing ourselves from our personal vantage point and alienating our creative will from its cosmic ground—will make all the difference. The whole universe has contributed to the way humanity thinks today.

> The experience of every soul becomes the experience of the divine mind.[35]

Hazrat Inayat Khan applies this audacious, all-integrating view to working with our self, pointing out how we can use our mind as an extension of the divine mind rather than being encapsulated in our personal vantage point, while enlisting our personal incentive. Some of the perspectives opened up by Hazrat Inayat Khan are totally surprising and challenging in regard to the traditional view: God (as the ultimate potentiality) becomes a reality as us! In the Sufi parlance he now uses the word "divinity" (*ulūhīya*):

> The divine mind becomes completed after manifestation. ... The creator's mind is made of His own creation.[36] It is in man that divinity is awakened, that God is awakened, that God can be seen.[37] Make God a reality.[38]

Divinity resides in humanity; it is also the outcome of humanity:

> Spiritual attainment is to become conscious of the Perfect One, who is formed in the heart.[39] The same aspiration which works through all aspects of life and has brought forth such varying fruits culminates in humanity, and prepares through humanity a path that reaches up to the height called divinity, which is the perfection of beauty.[40] Manifestation has taken place so that every being here may rise from imperfection towards perfection. That is

---

[34] 'Abd al-Jabbār al-Niffarī, *The Mawāqif and Mukhāṭabāt of Muḥammad Ibn ʿAbdi'l-Jabbār al-Niffarī*, ed. and trans. Arthur J. Arberry (London: Luzac & Co, 1935), 50.

[35] Inayat Khan, The Unity of Religious Ideals, 153.

[36] Ibid.,153.

[37] Inayat Khan, *The Sufi Message*, 10:16.

[38] Inayat Khan, *Complete Sayings*, 6, 210, 238, 256.

[39] Ibid., 61.

[40] Inayat Khan, *The Sufi Message* 3:161.

> the object and joy of life and for that this world was created.[41] Divinity is human perfection and humanity is divine limitation.[42]

Such all-encompassing views have frequently shocked the orthodoxy, but they have been incubated through the centuries in the course of the advancing realizations of the more progressive Sufi dervishes. Their pronouncements are further elaborated and masterfully processed by Hazrat Inayat Khan into guidelines for mureeds (disciples) in their work with themselves, and represent the spiritual dimension of psychotherapy—which is becoming increasingly relevant in our time.

By underscoring the importance of the individual, and hence personal incentive, Hazrat Inayat Khan corroborates a surprising view of Ibn al-'Arabī:

> When God sent Himself down to the waystation of His servants, their properties exercised their influence over Him. Hence He only determines their properties through them.[43]

As Hazrat Inayat Khan says:

> The soul of every individual is God, but man has a mind and a body which contain God according to the accommodation.[44]

The Concept of God

Admittedly, the word God embodies anthropomorphic projections. Owing to the widespread influence of Buddhism in our time, the word universe, often used by Hazrat Inayat Khan, is more acceptable to some. However, as he points out,

> There is no way of getting proof of God's existence except by becoming acquainted with oneself, by experiencing the phenomena which are within one.[45] Very often, many who are ready to accept the God-Ideal, question the personality of God.[46] No doubt it would be a great mistake to call God a personality, but it is a still greater mistake when man denies the Personality of

---

[41] Inayat Khan, *The Sufi Message*, 4:102.
[42] Inayat Khan, *Complete Sayings*, 19.
[43] William C. Chittick, *The Sufi Path of Knowledge: Ibn al-'Arabī's Metaphysics of Imagination* (Albany: State University of New York Press, 1989), 299.
[44] Inayat Khan, *Complete Sayings*, 195.
[45] Inayat Khan, *The Sufi Message*, 4:265.
[46] Inayat Khan, Unity of Religious Ideals, 95.

> God. ... God is the seed from which comes the personality.[47] He has no personality until He manifests Himself to Himself.[48] No doubt at this stage the God of the believer is the form made by Him, the form of a human being. God is behind that form, and He answers His worshiper through that form.[49]

Although he points to the aspect of God actuated in existence and, by the same token, in ourselves, Hazrat Inayat Khan does not limit God to that dimension:

> It is owing to our limitation that we cannot see the whole Being of God, but all that we love in color, line and form, or personality—all that is beloved by us—belongs to the real Beauty who is the Beloved of all.[50]

A *ḥadīth* (saying) of the Prophet says:

> I was a hidden treasure and loved to be known.[51]

And in the Qur'ān one finds:

> There is not a thing but its treasures are with Us.[52]

According to the Sufis, we cannot grasp this ultimate value (the divine code sparked by the divine intention) by our own endeavor; it is revealed to us in the measure of our capacity. And therefore it eludes our grasp while being imparted through clues. Events, and also our idiosyncrasies, are clues to that which transpires through that which appears.

Mawlānā Jāmī, Iran's renowned poet, exclaims:

> Glory be to Him who hides Himself by the manifestations of His light and manifests Himself by drawing a veil over His face.[53]

And Ibn al-'Arabī expresses the paradox in these words:

---

[47] Ibid., 76.
[48] Inayat Khan, *The Sufi Message* 7:12.
[49] Inayat Khan, Unity of Religious Ideals, 73.
[50] Inayat Khan, *The Sufi* Message, 2:73.
[51] See Schimmel, *Mystical Dimensions of Islam*, 189; see also Chittick, *Sufi Path of Knowledge*, 66, 126, 204, 391.
[52] Qur'ān, 15.21.
[53] Nuruddin 'Abdurrahman Jāmī, *Lawa'ih: A Treatise on Sufism*, trans. E.H. Whinfield and Mirza Muḥammad Kazvini (London: Royal Asiatic Society, 1914), 15.

> How can I know Thee since Thou art hidden, unknown to me; how could I fail to know Thee since Thou art that which appears and all things make Thee knowable to me?[54]

At first glance, one might infer that the signs that are ephemeral convey clues leading to the divine code, which is considered to be eternal.

In a first step, we may envision ourselves as exemplars that convey clues to the archetype of these qualities, which the Sufis call the divine attributes and represent as perfect. Indeed, this is the first step as articulated in the *āya* of the Qur'ān showing God revealing the clues to His being in our very qualities (41.53).

A *ḥadīth* says :

> He who knows himself knows his Lord.[55]

And Ibn al-'Arabī indicates He is known by ourselves:

> Since the ephemeral being manifests the form of the eternal, it is by the contemplation of the ephemeral that God communicates to us the knowledge of Himself.[56]

But there is a second step. Could the reciprocal not also be true? If you include the antipodal point of view—that is, the divine point of view—in your point of view, is it by the contemplation of the eternal that we make sense of the ephemeral?

Ibn al-'Arabī indeed sees the reciprocal:

> The ephemeral is not conceivable as such, that is, in its ephemeral and relative nature, except in relation to a principle from which it derives its possibility.[57]

These are two steps. This explains why Hazrat Inayat Khan says, on one hand, there is no way of knowing God except by knowing yourself.[58] And the converse:

---

[54] Cf. *Etudes traditionelles. Publication exclusivement consacree aux doctrines metaphysiques et esoteriques d'Orient et d'Occident.* trans. from Arabic into French Michel Valsan, (Paris: Chacornac/Editions Traditionelles, 9/1949), 255.

[55] See Schimmel, *Mystical Dimensions*, 189; also Ibn al-'Arabī, *Wisdom of the Prophets*, 41.

[56] Ibn al-'Arabī, *Wisdom of the Prophets*, 15

[57] Ibid.

[58] See above, note 45.

> It is not by self-realization that man realizes God, it is by God-realization that man realizes self.[59]

However, as Ibn al-'Arabī says:

> [Man] is incapable of appropriating the divine knowledge which is applied to those archetypes in their state of non-existence...The essence only reveals itself in the "form" of the predisposition of the individual who receives this revelation.[60]

A yet richer outlook is gained by extrapolating between these two converse points of view: the personal and the transpersonal (ascribed to God). Just ponder upon the marvel that we are experiencing and in which we participate:

> Man may be called the seed of the whole existence. As the seed comes last, after the life of trunk, branch, fruit and flower. And, as the seed is sufficient in itself and capable of producing another plant, such as that of which it was but a small product, so man is the product of all the planes, spiritual and material, a being small in comparison with the mountains and rivers and seas, or even in comparison with many beasts and birds, and yet in him alone that shines forth which caused the whole—that primal intelligence, the seed of existence—God. Therefore is man termed Ashraf-ul-Makhluqat, the Ideal of the Universe.[61]

The intelligence of the universe has become intelligent beings: intelligent beings are a condition of the originating intelligence!

Avicenna confirms this:

> He began with the noblest of substances, Intelligence, and He concluded with the noblest of beings, the Intelligent.[62]

Hazrat Inayat Khan adds:

> Consciousness must always be conscious of something. When consciousness is not conscious of anything, it is pure intelligence.[63]

Awakening

Hazrat Pir-o-Murshid Inayat Khan touches the souls of people by alerting us to a nostalgia in the depth of our being which we often dismiss because we are too busy or find it difficult to reverse

---

59 Inayat Khan, *The Sufi Message,* 8:211.
60 Ibn al-'Arabī, *Wisdom of the Prophets*, 23.
61 Inayat Khan, *Sangatha I* (privately circulated).
62 Cf. Arthur J. Arberry, *Avicenna on Theology* (London: John Murray, 1951), 17.
63 Inayat Khan, *The Sufi Message* 11:69.

the attunement aroused by our worldly pursuits. It meets an imperative need that we have to make sense of our life, and is decisive in our self-esteem—since we suffer from a sense of frustration at our ignorance of our purpose and our failure to attain a full satisfaction in the life-style of our day and age. This longing for meaningfulness is the very definition of what one means by spirituality: the insatiable quest for awakening.

> Every atom, every object, every condition and every living being has a time of awakening. Sometimes this is a gradual awakening and sometimes it is sudden.[64]

One might define awakening as downplaying the commonplace perspective and highlighting another perspective which surfaces when zooming on a loftier dimension of one's being and, by the same token, the universe. Since it relentlessly lures us beyond our reach, in infinite regress, we can never claim to have attained it. Therefore Hazrat Inayat Khan calls it the unattainable:

> There is a time in life when a passion is awakened in the soul which gives the soul a longing for the unattainable, and if the soul does not take that direction, then it certainly misses something in life for which is its innate longing and in which lies its ultimate satisfaction.[65] This craving for the attainment of what is unattainable, gives the soul a longing to reach life's utmost heights.[66]

One may reach a point in one's life journey when one sees this longing for the unattainable as the purpose of one's life, and also that one's effectiveness in recreating one's personality is a function of one's degree of awakening.

> True exaltation of the spirit resides in the fact that it has come to earth and has realized there its spiritual existence.[67] Perfect realization can only be gained by passing through all the stages between man, the manifestation, and God, the only Being; knowing and realizing ourselves from the lowest to the highest point of existence, and so accomplishing the heavenly journey.[68]

---

[64] Inayat Khan, *The Sufi Message*, 8:318.
[65] Inayat Khan, Unity of Religious Ideals, 88.
[66] Ibid., 86.
[67] Inayat Khan, *The Sufi Message*, 6:242.
[68] Inayat Khan, *The Sufi Message*, 5:17.

If one does not know what this means, it is encouraging to hear it described by one talking from personal experience. Hazrat Inayat Khan intimates to his disciples what it feels like.

> When the soul is awakened ... its condition is then as that of a person sitting in the midst of the night among hundreds and thousands of people who are fast asleep.[69] The sign of this awakening is that the awakened person throws a light, the light of his soul, upon every creature and every object, and sees that object, person, or condition in that light. It is his own soul that becomes a torch in his hand; it is his own light that illuminates his path. It is just like directing a searchlight into dark corners which one could not see before, and the corners become clear and illuminated; it is like throwing light upon problems that one did not understand before, like seeing through people with x-rays when they were a riddle before.[70] One whose every glance, wherever it is cast, breaks through every object and discovers its depth and its secret.[71] Wherever his glance falls, on nature, on characters, he reads their history, he sees their future. Every person he meets, before he has spoken one word with him he begins to communicate with his soul. Before he has asked any question, the soul begins to tell its own history. Every person and every object stand before him as an open book.[72] The will power works through the glance.[73] And when this light is thrown within oneself, then the self will be revealed to a person; he will become enlightened as to his own nature and his own character.[74] One's consciousness has become so light and so liberated and free that it can raise itself and dive and touch the depths of one's being.[75]

> In spiritual awakening the first thing that comes to man is a lifting of the veil, and that means the lifting of an apparent condition. Then a person no longer sees every condition as it appears to be, but behind every condition he sees its deeper meaning. ... When ... the veil of immediate reason is lifted, then one reaches the cause, then one is not awakened to the surface but to what is behind the surface. Then there comes another step in awakening. In this man does not even see the cause, but he comes to the

---

[69] Inayat Khan, *The Sufi Message*, 8:304.
[70] Ibid., 303
[71] Inayat Khan, *The Sufi Message*, 1:79.
[72] Inayat Khan, *The Sufi Message*, 4:214.
[73] Inayat Khan, The Sufi Message of Hazrat Inayat Khan, Volume Thirteen: Sacred Readings, The Gathas (Katwijk: Servire, 1982), 110.
[74] Inayat Khan, *The Sufi Message*, 2:194.
[75] Inayat Khan, *The Sufi Message*, 4:203.

> realization of the adjustment of things: how every activity of life, whether it appears to be wrong or right, adjusts itself.[76]

Ibn al-'Arabī:

> He may see the Real from "behind" the veil of the things.[77] The things are like curtains over the Real. When they are raised, unveiling takes place.[78] Knowledge is a veil covering the known.[79]

Hazrat Inayat Khan distinguishes between awakening beyond the existential plane and awakening in the world. The first is lifting one's consciousness into the divine intention behind the programming of the world. The next, looking at the way manifestation would appear from the divine point of view when the dream comes true.

> God lost in the manifestation is the state which we call waking. The manifestation lost in God is realization. In my language I would call the latter awakening and the former a dream.[80]

> The pure consciousness has, so to speak, gradually limited itself more and more by entering into the external vehicles, such as the mind and the body, in order to be conscious of something.[81]

The caution spelled by the Hindu theory of *maya* only points out that things are not what they seem:

> There comes a time when all that he had accepted in his mind, all that he believed in, now appears to be quite the contrary to what it seemed before.[82]

However, the Sufis draw attention to the complementary view: that situations, events, interactions with other people serve as clues to what is enacted behind the facts.

Mawlānā Jāmī:

> The world is an illusion but eternally Reality manifests through it.[83]

---

[76] Inayat Khan, *The Sufi Message*, 8:320–321.
[77] Chittick, Sufi Path of Knowledge, 228.
[78] Ibid., 225.
[79] Ibn al-'Arabī, *La parure des abdal (Hilyatu-l-Abdal)*, trans. and annotated by Michel Valsan (Paris: Arche/Edidit, 1992), 21.
[80] Inayat Khan, *Supplementary Papers: Psychology* (privately circulated).
[81] Inayat Khan, *The Sufi Message*, 5:89.
[82] Inayat Khan, *The Sufi Message*, 8:313.
[83] Nuroddin 'Abdorrahman b. Aúmad Jāmī, *Les jaillissements de lumière. Lavayeh,*

This is based upon a verse in the Qur'ān, which may be rendered:

> God reveals Himself through signs (*ayāt*) in the physical world and also in your nature (psyche).[84]

Paradoxically, to grasp these tenuous revelations, one needs to reverse the overt orientation of one's consciousness and turn within. One begins to think

> there are some realities of which I am vaguely aware, and yet, compared with them, all I have studied and done seems to be of no account.[85]

Consequently, rather than reckoning upon your assessment of your problems, turn within to detect how your problems are related to qualities or defects or incongruities in your own being.

You are yourself the object of your realization. Awakening cannot be limited to zooming a new perspective on the physical or psychological environment (the object), but a shift in the notion of the subject. To paraphrase a key tenet in the teaching of Najm al-Dīn Kubrā: You thought that you were the spectator, the witness of what you experience, but the real witness in you is your angelic counterpart: the witness in the heavens.[86]

'Abd al-Jabbār al-Niffarī:

> The least of the sciences of My nearness is, that thou shouldst see the effects of My regard in everything, and that it should prevail in thee over thy gnosis of it.[87]

Limitation and Perfection

One would of course like to know how to trigger off awakening. Hazrat Inayat Khan gives two essential tips: First, he draws our attention to the dichotomy between our middle-range self image which is flawed by limitation, and our total being, in which the whole universe (God) is latent and is perfect. In fact, this is one

---

edit. Yann Richard (Paris: Les Deux Oceans, 1982), 125.

[84] Cf. Qur'ān 41.53 and 51.20 and Schimmel, *Mystical Dimensions of Islam*, 25.

[85] Inayat Khan, *The Sufi Message*, 12:65.

[86] Cf. Henry Corbin, *The Man of Light in Iranian Sufism*, trans. Nancy Pearson (New Lebanon: Omega Publications, Reprinted 1994), 61–97.

[87] al-Niffarī, *The Mawāqif and Mukhāṭabāt*, 28

of the leitmotifs in Hazrat Inayat Khan's teaching: reconciling limitation with perfection. How is higher consciousness attained?

> By closing our eyes to our limited self and by opening our heart to God, ... who is all-perfection.[88] The soul's unfoldment comes from its own power, which ends in its breaking through the ties of the lower planes.[89]

The soul's unveiling is reached by closing your eyes to your limited self and rising above your earthly conditions at the command of your will, and realizing your immortal self—which is God within.

The second clue deals with our body identity, and shifting your attention to your subtle bodies in order to discover these. Hazrat Inayat Khan points out that awakening incurs becoming aware of levels of your being beyond the commonplace—which one represents sometimes as celestial spheres, or higher levels of consciousness, or transcendent levels of one's being—without losing touch with the physical world.

> Mankind is clothed in the garb of an angel, of a jinn, and of a human being; but when he only sees himself in the garb of a human being without seeing the other garbs, he believes he is nothing but a human being.[90] We live in the world to which we are awakened, and to the world to which we are not awakened we are asleep. We are asleep to that part of life which we do not know.[91] The soul in its manifestation on earth is not at all disconnected from the higher spheres. It lives in all spheres, though it is generally conscious only on one plane.[92]

Jalāl al-Dīn Rūmī:

> We are bound for heaven: who has a mind to sight-seeing?
> We have been in heaven, we have been friends of the angels;
> Thither, sire, let us return, for that is our country.[93]

---

[88] Inayat Khan, *Sangatha III* (privately circulated).
[89] Inayat Khan, *The Sufi Message*, 5:237.
[90] Ibid., 91-92.
[91] Inayat Khan, *The Sufi Message*, 8:309.
[92] Inayat Khan, *Complete Sayings*, 218.
[93] Jalāl al-dīn Rūmī, *Divani Shamsi Tabriz*, ed. Reynold A. Nicholson (San Francisco: Rainbow Bridge, 1973), 33.

The Way of the Ascetic Versus the Way of the Knight

At a time when the industrial revolution had wetted appetites for material domination and, on the other hand, the seekers for a spiritual dimension were intrigued by the exploits of anchorites in exploring uncharted reaches of the mind in *samādhī* (beyond the existential state), Hazrat Inayat Khan came to the West pioneering the new spirituality: the validation of the bounty of life instead of asceticism; awakening in life rather than evasion; arousing the qualities of the cosmos lying in wait in one's being so as to become a more bountiful personality; mastery through achievement; and building a beautiful world by becoming beautiful people.

In the vicinity of the home of Hazrat Inayat Khan's grandfather, Mawlābakhsh, was a Sufi *dargāh* (shrine) where *saddhus* and dervishes used to commune in their spiritual attunement. As a youth, Hazrat Inayat Khan joined in, which left an indelible influence on his inter-religious ecumenistic vision. The difference in the outlook of these dervishes was striking:

> When walking in a district where dervishes lived in solitude I found ten or twelve dervishes together, sitting under the shade of a tree in their ragged clothes, talking to one another. As I was curious to hear and see people of different thoughts and ideas, I stood there watching this assembly to see what was going on. These dervishes, sitting on the ground without a carpet, at first gave an impression of poverty and helplessness, sitting there in disappointment, probably entirely without possessions. But as they began to speak to each other that impression did not remain, for when they addressed one another they said, "O, King of kings, O, Emperor of emperors". At first I was taken aback on hearing these words, but after giving some thought to it I asked myself: what is an emperor, what is a king? Is the real king and emperor within or without? For he who is the emperor of the outer empire depends on all that is without. The moment he is separated from that environment he is no longer an emperor. But these emperors, sitting on the bare ground, were real emperors. No one could take away their empire, for their empire, their kingdom, was not an illusion, their kingdom was a real kingdom.[94]

[94] Inayat Khan, *The Sufi Message*, 6:142.

There is a tradition in India according to which one needs to leave the world and live as an ascetic to attain illumination, whereas the Sufis seek awakening in life. However, appreciating the value of their input for people living the ordinary life, Inayat Khan says of these ascetics:

> Such people are the ones who make experiments of life by the sacrifice of all the joy and pleasure that the earth can give. By their solitude they experiment, just as a scientist shuts himself up in his laboratory for years and years; and these ascetics who left everything in the world also attained a certain knowledge which they give us.[95]

> The Sufi takes the contrary path; he stands in the midst of the world and sees all the ugliness and beautiful side of it, looks into human nature on its surface, in its depth.[96] Therefore a Sufi considers it necessary to live in the world and at the same time to be not of the world. Where the Yogi lives the life of an adept in the forest or in a mountain cave, the Sufi lives it in the world. For he considers that to awaken one's heart to human sympathy, one must experience oneself the struggles and responsibilities of life in the world, and realize that man lives not for himself alone, but that his greatest joy must be to share every benefit and bliss he has in life with others.[97]

> It is easier to gain mastery in the wilderness, away from all temptations, but the mastery you gain in the world is of much more value; for the former is easily thrown down by a slight stroke, while the latter, achieved in the crowd, will last for ever.[98]

One does not have to leave the world.

> Solitude in the crowd … means when you are in the midst of the crowd, even then you can hold your tranquility, your peace; you are not disturbed by the environment. It is this which enables one to live in the midst of the world and yet progress spiritually. It takes away that necessity which compelled many souls in ancient times to go to the wilderness in order to develop spiritually.[99]

One may find peace in one's own room.

---

[95] Inayat Khan, *The Sufi Message*, 4:129.
[96] Inayat Khan, *Sangatha II*, (privately circulated).
[97] Inayat Khan, *The Sufi Message*, 5:191.
[98] Inayat Khan, *The Sufi Message*, revised edition (Dorset: Element Books, 1991), 8:32.
[99] Ibid., 37.

> Closing the door of one's room, sitting in solitude, closing the eyes, being oneself once again, and trying to put one's mind within, seeking the source within, getting the knowledge which can be gotten only from within.[100] You may see by the experience of your own life what solitude does. If you try to go out all day to talk with acquaintances and friends, you will find that each day so much is gone from your speech. ... When people come—people whom you like or undesirable people—the impression of their words and actions falls upon you and your peace of mind is broken. A part of your time should be given to solitude. The more you cultivate solitude, the more you will like it. ... I think that it is most desirable to be well-balanced: to spend so much time with others, and so much time in solitude.[101] One may be more spiritual in a cave in the mountains, in silence and in solitude, but there one will never be able to test one's spirituality: whether it is strong enough to bear the contact of a contrary environment.[102]

Indeed, one is pulled between two needs: to accomplish something of value or service, to contribute to the advance of evolution: to build a better world. And, on the other hand, the need to free oneself, not just from dependence upon circumstances, but from one's conditioning, the constraint of one's self image, the limited range of the perspective of one's ordinary consciousness and middle-range thinking.

> Indifference gives great power. But interest also gives great power. The whole of manifestation is a phenomenon of interest. All that we see in this world of art and science, the new inventions, the beautiful houses, all this world that man has made, where has it come from? It has come from the power of interest. ... The whole creation and all that is in it is the product of the Creator's interest. ... It is motive that gives man the power to accomplish things. But at the same time the power of indifference is a greater one still ... because although motive has a power, at the same time motive limits power.[103]

Hazrat Inayat Khan shows how one can fulfil one's purpose in life while honoring one's need for freedom.

---

[100] Inayat Khan, unpublished lecture for mureeds and friends, December 17, 1923.
[101] Inayat Khan, *The Sufi Message*, revised edition, 8:20.
[102] Ibid., 31–32.
[103] Inayat Khan, *The Sufi Message*, 6:176–177.

> Man seeks freedom and pursues captivity.[104] All that produces longing in the heart deprives it of its freedom.[105] The real proof of one's progress in the spiritual path can be realized by testing in every situation in life how indifferent one is.[106] If you will not rise above the things of this world, they will rise above you.[107]

As a result, one develops spiritual power to fulfil one's task. Shaykh 'Abd al-Qadr Gilānī bears witness to the power gained by an extreme case of retreat in the wilderness: to prepare you, God alienates you from humans so that you may acquire faith in isolated places. Then things come to you. In the solitude you acquire spiritual power.[108]

Rather than personal power, the Sufis call it divine power. To awaken the conscience rather than the consciousness one needs to substitute the divine "I Am" to the power of the ego. Then miracles happen. Things come to the one who has committed himself to service, when he or she does not hanker after things.

On the other hand, Hazrat Inayat Khan says,

> The man conscious of his duties and obligations to his friends is more righteous than he who sits alone in solitude.[109] The Sufi makes no restrictions and has no principles of renunciation, nor does he teach renunciation. He believes that to sacrifice anything in life which one does not wish to sacrifice is of no use, but that renunciation is a natural thing, and grows in one with one's evolution. A child which cries for its toy at one stage of its childhood, comes to an age when it is quite willing to give away the toy it once cried for.[110]
>
> The way of those who renounce is to know all things, to admire all things, to get all things, but give all things, and to think that nothing belongs to them and that they own nothing.[111] So long as you have a longing to obtain any particular object, you cannot go further than that object.[112] Be obstinate in the path of success.

---

[104] Inayat Khan, *Complete Sayings*, 172.
[105] Ibid., 24.
[106] Inayat Khan, *Sangitha I* (privately circulated).
[107] Inayat Khan, *Complete Sayings*, 115.
[108] Cf. Shaykh Abd al-Qādir al-Jīlānī, *Utterances (Malfūzāt)* trans. Muhtar Holland (Houston: Al-Baz, 1992), 94–96.
[109] Inayat Khan, *Complete Sayings*, 206.
[110] Inayat Khan, *The Sufi Message*, 3:255.
[111] Ibid., 262.
[112] Inayat Khan, *Complete Sayings*, 242.

> Nothing should keep you back from your effort when your resolution is once taken. Renounce your object of attainment only when you have reached it and you have a better one in view. But when you have attained the object and you cling to it, then you hinder your own progress, for the object is greater than yourself. You are greater than the object when you are able to renounce it after attaining it.[113] All things one possesses in life one has attracted to oneself; ... and if one can renounce them before that power of attraction is lost, one rises above them.[114] Renounce the world before it renounces you.[115]

Working Creatively with the Personality

While traditional spiritual transmissions from the East in pursuit of *samādhi* have often led to what psychotherapists have coined the "spiritual bypass," overlooking one's own idiosyncrasies, Hazrat Inayat Khan defines the spirituality of the future: rather than a belief in God, making God a reality by incorporating more and more of the bounty of the universe in that wonderful work of art that is the personality. This requires one, while working with the personality, to continually be aware of the action of the universe (God) upon one's person, rather than slipping back into one's personal identity.

> The art of personality is ... the purpose for which man was created.[116] Other arts cannot be compared with the art of personality.[117] One may ask: If we have a personality, why must we develop it? But even a diamond must be cut! It has light in it, yet cutting is required to awaken it. It cannot show its glow and brilliance before it has been cut.[118]

Hazrat Inayat Khan prescribes three steps: first, ask yourself how all one sees affects one, and how one reacts to it. How does one's spirit react to the objects or the conditions one encounters, to the sounds one hears, to the words people speak to one? Second, see what effect one has upon conditions, and upon others when one

---

[113] Inayat Khan, *Githa I* (privately circulated).
[114] Inayat Khan, *The Sufi Message*, 3:255.
[115] Inayat Khan, *Complete Sayings*, 129.
[116] Inayat Khan, Creating the Person: A Practical Guide to the Development of Self (New Lebanon: Omega Publications, 1995), 57.
[117] Inayat Khan, *The Sufi Message*, 10:166.
[118] Inayat Khan, *The Sufi Message: revised edition*. 8:139.

comes in contact with them. Third, one should learn one's condition: the condition of one's spirit, of one's mind, of one's body, of one's situation in life, and of one's relationship with others.[119]

Furthermore, no sooner does one unmask the hoax of one's self-image, then the awareness of one's true being begins to strike one.

> The soul changes its own identity with the change of its constantly changing vision.[120] A person needs to analyze himself and see "where does 'I' stand?" Does it stand as a remote exclusive being?[121] What is meant by concentration is the change of identification of the soul, so that it may lose the false conception of identification and identify itself with the true self instead of the false self.[122] When the soul goes further in the path of knowledge it begins to find ... there is a feeling of 'I'-ness, but at the same time all that the soul identifies itself with is not itself.[123] One finds a kind of universe in oneself, and by the study of the self one comes to that spiritual knowledge for which one's soul hungers.[124] As God comprehends the whole universe within Himself, being one, so man contains within himself the whole universe as His miniature.[125] One finds that all is in oneself, and that one can cultivate in oneself what one wishes.[126]

Hazrat Inayat Khan points to the limitation incurred by our ignorance of who we are.

> Man is born in this world ignorant of the kingdom which is within himself.[127]

Further, he draws our attention to the fact that what we think we are is a faulty representation of ourselves, which we erroneously call the ego.

> The false ego is ... what that ego has wrongly conceived to be its own being.[128] It is not that the false ego is our ego and the true ego

---

[119] See Inayat Khan, *The Sufi Message*, 11:205–209; also, 10:172–175.
[120] Inayat Khan, *The Sufi Message*, 5:237.
[121] Inayat Khan, *The Sufi Message*, 2:248.
[122] Inayat Khan, *The Sufi Message*, 6:167.
[123] Inayat Khan, *The Sufi Message*, 2:247.
[124] Inayat Khan, *Mastery* (New Lebanon: Omega Publications, revised 1985), 75.
[125] Inayat Khan, *The Sufi Message*, 5:131.
[126] Inayat Khan, *The Sufi Message*, 11:199.
[127] Inayat Khan, *The Sufi Message*, 10:245.
[128] Inayat Khan, *The Sufi Message*, 2:248.

> is the ego of God; it is that the true ego, which is the ego of the Lord, has become a false ego in us.[129]

> When the soul is absorbed in God, one loses the false sense of being and finds the true reality. Then one finally experiences what is termed Baqa-i-Fana, where the false ego is annihilated and merged into the true personality, which is really God expressing Himself in some wondrous ways.[130]

By identifying ourselves with the personal dimension of our being, we fail to realize the bounty of our potentials, and ascribe this to God as "other". This teaching calls for a complete re-examination of our concept of God as "up there," and encourages us to strongly and realistically discover God in ourselves as a potentiality that becomes an actuality as us.

The Sufis stalk the secret of creativity; it is by reversing one's consciousness to its antipodal pole (that is, the divine consciousness) and imagining God, dynamic rather than static, becoming a personality as us. To arouse the potentials lying in wait in the seed of our personality, we need to learn the skill of contemplating our personality from the antipodal vantage point—what the Sufis call the divine point of view. The realization arrived at by making this shift in perspective contrasts with the knowledge acquired by the personal vantage point (acquired knowledge); it is revealed when, having seen that one's personal vantage point is limited, one invites the thinking of the universe (which, albeit, adumbrates one's thinking) to take over from one's personal thinking.

Immortality

If we clearly see that we exist at several levels, then we can envision ourselves as a pendulum whose base is moving in space-time and whose point of suspense remains unchanged.

> Immortality is not to be sought in the hereafter; if it is ever gained, it is gained in one's lifetime.[131] Once the soul realizes itself by becoming independent of the body that surrounds it, then

---

[129] Inayat Khan, *The Sufi Message*, 11:201.
[130] Inayat Khan, *Githa II* (privately circulated).
[131] Inayat Khan, *The Sufi Message*, 8:220.

> the soul naturally begins to see in itself the being of the spirit.[132] Once ... the realization is no longer in one's imagination but has become a conviction, then one rises above the fear of death. This knowledge is gained fully when an adept is able to detach his soul from his body.[133] The Sufi ... practices the process by which he is able to touch that part of life in himself which is not subject to death.[134]

One does not need to leave behind one's body, one can also become aware of one's higher bodies. One needs to downplay one's body identity while highlighting one's magnetic fields, one's celestial body or aura. The method advocated by Hazrat Inayat Khan is to sublimate body functions by the impact of consciousness. In one's spiritual practices, in a stage of deep concentration, one can awaken dormant faculties that one does not usually use.

How does one achieve this?

> Man has become motionless, stagnant, by attaching himself to this world into which he is born and in which he has become interested. If he makes his soul more subtle in order to turn away from this world he can experience all that has been said of the different worlds, of the different planes of consciousness. He will find the whole mystery within himself only by being able to make his soul so subtle that it can turn and move.[135]

> There is a gradual awakening of matter to become conscious and through the awakening to consciousness matter becomes fully intelligent in man.[136]

In matter, according to Hazrat Inayat Khan, life unfolds, discovers and realizes the consciousness that has been, so to speak, buried in it for thousands of years.[137] By the practice of the *zikr* (remembrance of God), the Sufis arouse certain centers which control the way in which the mind affects the body that otherwise would remain dormant. The secret lies in arousing consciousness in the endocrine glands and the neurotransmitters in the autonomic and

---

[132] Inayat Khan, *The Sufi Message*, 11:69.
[133] Inayat Khan, *The Sufi Message*, 13:31.
[134] Inayat Khan, *The Sufi Message*, 6:272.
[135] Inayat Khan, *The Sufi Message*, 8:321.
[136] Ibid., 316.
[137] Inayat Khan, *The Sufi Message*, 14:115.

central nervous system where the connection between mind and body is triggered off.

> We pass to the higher planes of existence in the lift by means of the breath, and hold on to the rope, the physical body, and come back to the first floor, the earth, again.[138]

Hazrat Inayat Khan is now pointing to the next clue: the notion of space changes as one rises in *samādhī.* As one identifies oneself with a body of energy instead of matter, instead of space appearing as three-dimensional, it is a vortex (without a boundary) where everything intercepts everything else. Then, as one's identity is transmuted further, one reaches beyond the perspective of imagination so that space looses its meaning altogether. However, one must not lose touch with the world of forms that can serve as a ladder on which one can climb.

> The man who has not made any steps no sooner loses touch with the objective world than he is lost in space. ... The mystic finds steps already made in space to help him in his climb upward.[139]

Ibn al-'Arabī:

> Imagination ... embodies meanings and subtilizes the sensory thing. It transforms the entity of every object of knowledge in the viewer's eye.[140] Imagination causes archetypal notions to descend into perceptible forms.[141] The dreamer operates a transposition from the form perceived into the reality implied by it.[142] ... He manifested it in tangible form after it had appeared in imaginative form.[143]

Ḥusayn ibn Manṣūr Ḥallāj:

> No one knows Him except the one to whom He makes Himself known.
> No one really affirms that God is One unless He unifies him in Him.
> No one believes in Him unless it is by His grace.
> No one describes Him unless He manifests Himself in his consciousness.[144]

---

138 Inayat Khan, *The Sufi Message*, 5:220.
139 Inayat Khan, *The Sufi Message*, 11:210.
140 Chittick, Sufi Path of Knowledge, 123.
141 Cf. *Études traditionelles*, 7–10, 1961, 248.
142 Cf. Ibn al-ᵉArabī, *Wisdom of the Prophets*, 59.
143 Ibid., 61.
144 Massignon, *La Passion*, 62.

The maze of pathways in the psychological topography of states of consciousness needs to be carefully observed if one deigns to venture beyond well-established (and comfortable) areas of the mind.

> The soul manifests in the world in order that it may experience the different phases of manifestation, and yet not lose its way but regain its original freedom, in addition to the experience and knowledge it has gained in this world.[145]

The secret lies in finding the bridge between the mortal and immortal dimensions of our being:

> In the knowledge of the ego, there is the secret of immortality.[146]

That secret lies in awakening. Hazrat Inayat Khan's last words were:

> When the unreality of life pushes against my heart, its door opens to the reality.[147]

---

[145] Inayat Khan, *Complete Sayings*, 208.
[146] Inayat Khan, *The Sufi Message*, 2:250.
[147] Inayat Khan, *Complete Sayings*, 163.

Hazrat Inayat Khan entering the gate at Fazal Manzil in Suresnes

Memoirs

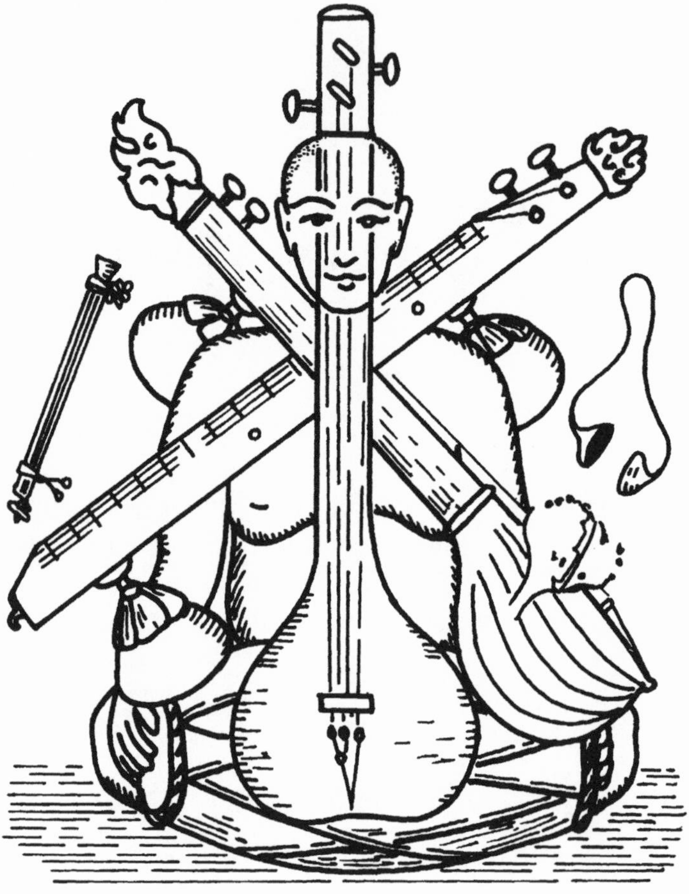

The body as instruments

From "Autobiography"

R.A. Jodjana

One day in London I went to a concert given by Hindu musicians at the Royal Asiatic Society. A great Hindu singer, Hazrat Inayat Khan, was accompanied on string instruments, the *dilruba* and *sitar*, played by Muhammad Ali, his cousin, and Musharaff, his youngest brother. Maheboob Khan played the *tabla*, the Hindu drums.

Hazrat Inayat Khan was sent by his Guru from India to the West, to bring a gentle message of love and humility to Western people. Inayat Khan was a great musician, a singer, a bard. And he was sent to bring the message by song, and by the poetry of the great Sufi Masters.

Many Western people came and listened to the songs sung by Inayat Khan, accompanied on his sacred instrument, the *vina.* Many of them could not understand these songs, not being accustomed to listen to the Creative Presence. And they silenced their Master.

It was in Ladbroke Road in London that I came to Inayat Khan for the first music lesson. I entered the room with a book and pencil. He asked me why I brought that book and pencil. And when I said that I wished to take notes of all he was going to teach me, he seemed amazed and said:

This article has been excerpted and condensed from the chapter titled "Autobiography" in Raden Ayou Jodjana, *A Book os Self Re-Education: The Structure and Functions of the Human Body as an Instrument of Expression* (Essex, England: L.N. Fowler & Co., 1981), 163-176.

> Have you not received the gift of memory? Learn to listen well to all I am going to teach you. Let it enter and impress you. Then you will forget to 'remember'. What will be forever stored in your memory must for some time stay in oblivion, until it can serve you in creative expression at a certain moment. Only what you need to remember in the moment should mount in the consciousness of the brain. Never come to me with a book and pencil. One should not use crutches on the path to Being. When you are with me, dive deep within yourself. Try to become at one with that all-pervading, Infinite Being, that you may live to know the end of separation.

He let me leave the room to put away the book and pencil. Coming back, I sat down prepared to listen as he asked me to do. He sang to me, and opened that wonderful world of silence, which I had entered into for the first time when I heard him sing in the concert he gave at the Royal Asiatic Society in London. This was just before the First World War broke out.

He sang. It must have been for quite a long time. In the world of silence one lives timelessly. When he had finished he said to me: "Now it is your turn." By my vows I was not allowed to put a question, nor to hesitate to obey an order. I became suddenly very uncertain, having to improvise after his singing in the same *rag*, on the same theme and in the same *tal*, or rhythm.

He had not yet taught me the patterns of the *ragas* and *raginis*. Previously, when we lived in Addison Road, he made me sing the prayers I had heard sung by him and his musicians. Now in the lesson starting to improvise in a *rag*, I became conscious of my incapacity to live up to the task.

When I finished there was a long silence. Then he said: "I see that you can still enormously develop the quality of your memory; you may remember that this is 'Pilu'." He did not explain what Pilu meant. A Guru does not give explanations. Knowledge should come from within. Knowledge is born from the depth of being.

Once, discouraged by the lack of results in my lessons, I ceased straining my ears. I just sat listening to my master's sweet voice singing, no longer trying to rivet my attention in order to capture information about the structure of the songs. I just listened to the music and entered the marvelous state of inner silence. Suddenly I recognized an inner atmosphere I had experienced before. And when Inayat Khan asked me: "Khurshid, what expresses this song?" I answered: "Pilu." He smiled, and I knew that at last I had learned to listen, to listen with the whole body. One hears with the ear!

From then on I began to know the *ragas* and *raginis*, to know how to sing and to improvise. I became able to absorb sound and rhythm at the same time. I began to feel and follow, deep down in my body, the pulsation of time. I could follow the melodic line of the songs against the background of the accompaniment by the string instruments—*vina*, *dilruba*, and *sitar*; or the soft humming of the musicians, feeling the pulsation in time in the sound pictures.

This formed a basis for the number of measured moments of the *tal*, the rhythm. I then started to work with Maheboob who played the *tabla*, the two Hindu drums.

Inayat Khan initiated me when we lived in Addison Road before there was a Sufi Order. His brothers, his cousin and his wife were then the only mureeds. Later, in Ladbroke Road he asked me not to join the Sufi Order. He ordered me to teach Western music to his musicians, thus enabling Muhammad Ali to become a very wonderful singer, and also, later, to prepare concerts in the Lecture Hall of the Sufi Centre in Ladbroke Road. He wrote plays to be performed by us. He sang duets with me, and presented me at the Queen's Hall, to the English public.

In this way, Inayat Khan stayed true to his own vow—by singing in his unique sweet way, opening, for those who could listen, the path into the inner world to meet the Divine Presence within, and so to learn to serve the Presence silently in full acceptance of one's destiny, meeting all beings as expressions of the same Presence.

In meditation I learned to enter within inner space, into inner silence, and began to become aware of the inner interrogative state. I started to know how to serve, what to do, and how to obey without the mind interfering, questioning or discussing. Just the clear inner awareness of what to do in the moment.

It was not easy, as I had never learnt before to accept with the whole body, mind, and soul this inner guidance. Never before had I known that the body can and should become wholly receptive. Therefore I had to teach the body to open to all sides its nervous system, the brain included, and to relax the whole muscular structure. The mind then stays receptive. The centers of attention absorb impressions and let them descend to the source of life.

Inayat Khan did not tell and explain all this to me, and no questions were allowed. But the questions were there, and the mind had to be silenced. Downwards the questions went, and created, by and by, the inner interrogative state. Taking the habit of listening towards within, at last one discovers that the inner questions receive their true answer, awakening awareness of what to do or not to do, of what to say or not to say, in the moment.

From the center of gravity, from the center of balance and being, inspirations and ideas, inner awareness and intuition will be born and create intentions to act and to speak, or not to move and keep silent. In this way Inayat Khan was directing me to the deepest consciousness of life. But I struggled a long time in utter darkness. It brought me to the last choice, leading me on the inner path, backward-downward, never again to change direction.

In this way one learns that there is only one way to go for our attention. And its direction we should know—backward-downward.

I witnessed different people beginning to frequent Inayat Khan's house, not in search of a Sufi message, but eager to introduce into their lives something very attractive by its beauty, and by its unique artistic expression. They tried to create a closed circle of people under the gentle guidance of a great artist, beginning to be known in Europe for his art. Inayat Khan was the head of a family group stranded in London when the First World War broke out, without any means of a livelihood. The group of adepts in London began to lay down restraining rules for those becoming members of their circle. They fixed a contribution, imposing the responsibility of paying for housing the Centre, sheltering Inayat Khan's family and assuring their livelihood.

Inayat Khan never created the Sufi Order in London. He accepted the offer of the group of people who made the proposal. He was then told by the board of the circle to give lectures and lessons, as they wished to know more about the still unknown secrets of Hindu Yoga. They wanted him to teach by word and explain clearly what it was all about.

Shortly before leaving Addison Road, the family and I began to listen to Inayat Khan during the services of music in the evenings, when he started to explain many truths not previously taught in the English language. Later, in Ladbroke Road, I was often astonished and sometimes shocked how people reacted when Inayat began his first teaching by word. This made him come to the conclusion that Western people could never be pupils or adepts, as they always knew better! There were a few exceptions, like Miss Goodenough, whom Inayat always saw in private.

I think she helped the family to live. She must have taken the vow of silence. She never mixed with the family, nor did she speak with the other mureeds. Inayat Khan seemed to trust her more than anybody else outside the family. I saw her frequently and liked her. She was discreet, and treated me as a member of Inayat's family.

In the intimate circle of Inayat Khan's family in Addison Road, we formed the first group in England of initiated adepts. Begum, his young wife, and I were the only women in this circle. Inayat Khan taught us all to master emotional states causing reactions in conduct and expression. He submitted all of us to severe tests. Maheboob was the most advanced mureed. He showed me the way to listen towards within for the answer to the problems we met in daily life. Muhammad Ali, a man of deep passions, was very severe with himself and with others. Musharaff never arrived at mastering his emotions. Inayat was very severe with him. I knew Musharaff to the very last, always reacting in an emotional way, crying and sobbing and causing painful scenes, having no inner understanding of Western people, not even of his own people in their reactions to Western adepts. He came to the West too young, and was never able to cope with the experience of intimate contact with a people so different from his own.

After moving to Ladbroke Road, we stopped leading a family life. The whole family lost their original happy attitude towards the outside world. They were kind but aloof in their contacts with people. Thus our group in Ladbroke Road became isolated. Miss Goodenough, in silence, was ever present although never entered the family circle, nor any other part of the house then reserved for members of the Sufi Order.

Even Miss Williams, the secretary living in the same house, did not join us in private life. She, though meaning to be humble, could not master her emotional reactions. She suffered much, being neither appreciated by members of the Sufi Order, who made her life hard, nor by the family, silently witnessing her sufferings and her reactions. I understood her well.

Bound by vows, living in the cave of my body, suffering stayed subdued. So I lived, silently united with Miss Goodenough and Miss Williams. The other mureeds, giving me little attentions, treated me as the servant of the family. Inayat Khan often left the house in order to avoid meeting the always-intruding mureeds. He made me answer the door. I trained myself to meet them, understanding their Western outlook and conduct.

In Ladbroke Road no one ever came to the top floor where the family wished its privacy to be respected. Inayat lived in the front room with his wife and child. The three "boys" stayed in the back room with a view on the garden. I had to clean the rooms, took out the child, as Begum no longer went out in the world. She started to live in purdah. The "boys" never entered the front room. I was the only person to serve Inayat and his wife in their room. There was often a sad atmosphere.

Begum, whom I had known young and smiling in Addison Road, changed entirely living in the center of the Sufi Order. She lost her radiance, and avoided contact with the Western adepts. It was in Holland, in the house of Mrs. van Goens-van Beyma, whose daughter Maheboob was to later marry, that I saw Begum leading a family life again, just as in Addison Road.

In Ladbroke Road, the midday meal was taken by Inayat Khan, Maheboob, and Muhammad Ali in the basement, where I used to join them. Inayat begged me not to become a member of the Sufi Order. He wished to lead me, according to the wish of his Guru, in the path of the Sufi way of life. I am most indebted to him.

As Inayat Khan asked me not to join the Sufi Order, but desired to lead me according to the wish of his Guru in the path of the Sufi way of life, where no explanations were given, no questions were allowed. Discussion, according to Inayat Khan, was postponement of application. I had to take the vow of immediate obedience. I was directed towards within by transcendental meditation. I had to live in space inside the body, in the dark. This was necessary to awake, accept and create the inner interrogative state. Later, joining my husband in the circle of Javanese Sufis, the esoteric "Wayang" play of "Bhimo" gave clear insight into Inayat Khan's own initiation by his Guru, and the teaching he gave to me.

Within the family circle of Inayat Khan there was no "talk." Silence was a very expressive and necessary state in order to listen towards within, and to cultivate inner silence.

All sound expression was in music. Inayat Khan asked me to help to keep sound-expression in music alive in Ladbroke Road. As soon as the Sufi Order was established there, very disturbing talk was heard. It was then that Inayat Khan began to write plays, and the "boys" and I performed in them. Inayat Khan checked my inner progress severely, purposely causing distressing, unforeseen and very trying situations. I will give an example.

Once I was offered a unique chance, and invited to make my London debut at Leighton House in Holland Park, a European concert-hall of great repute. I had introduced Inayat Khan into the circle of great artists who managed the hall. Inayat ordered the "boys" to accompany me in the performance. The day before the performance I went to Ladbroke Road for a last rehearsal. I did not know that Inayat had told the boys to play the accompaniment out of tune, and to upset the rhythmic structure of the songs. I made tremendous efforts and spent hours trying to adjust myself to accept the strain. Going home I became very distressed, not knowing how they would play in the performance. They played marvelously well in the twilight concert the next day. The performance was a great success.

Another time Inayat Khan was presenting me at the Queen's Hall to the English public. He was singing duets with me. Suddenly, during the performance, he began to sing my small solo part. My knees started to tremble. I tried to save the situation by repeating words and melody in a humble, questioning expression, as if I asked him: "Do you now wish me to sing this? Do I sing it in the way it should be sung?" This was, so to say, a true interpretation of the situation. In moments of utter distraction, Inayat Khan, seeing my efforts to master the situation, laughed heartily, as if he enjoyed exposing me to public shame.

In a quite incomprehensible way, I always felt an astounding inner help in these vexing moments. And these experiences formed the basis of a rare joy, when once, after singing a *khyāl*, I saw him very moved. He said: "You will go far on this long Path."

THE LAST SONG OF INAYAT KHAN

Before you judge my actions
Lord, I pray you will forgive.
Before my heart has broken,
Will you help my soul to live?
Before my eyes are covered,

Will you let me see your face?
Before my feet are tired,
May I reach your dwelling place?
Before I wake from slumber,
You will watch me, Lord, I hold.
Before I throw my mantle
Will you take me in your fold?
Before my work is over,
You, my Lord, will right the wrong.
Before you play your music,
Will you let me sing my song?

above: Murshid Samuel L. Lewis, 1962
below: Kaaba Allah, Fairfax, California (prior to fire of 1949)

A Sunrise in the West: Hazrat Inayat Khan's Legacy in California

MURSHID WALI ALI MEYER

When Hazrat Inayat Khan left India he sailed initially to America, and he was to return several times. The unique grace that was infused in his being left a palpable legacy here. This can be traced in the impact he had on certain key individuals in California. This account begins with his meeting of Rabia Ada Martin and, in a sense, culminates with the unique career, life and influences of Samuel L. Lewis (Sufi Ahmed Murad Chishti). Rabia Martin became his first mureed and his senior Murshida. Samuel Lewis later became called "the proof of Inayat" because of his tremendous influence in spreading the message of our time. There are many other people important to the understanding of Hazrat Inayat Khan's legacy that deserve mention along with these two, not the least of whom is the Zen teacher Nyogen Senzaki, whose account of his meeting with Inayat is unparalleled in its clarity and brilliance.

In 1911 a married woman in her mid-thirties, Ada Martin, attended a concert of Indian music performed by Hazrat Inayat Khan and his brothers as the opening of the program of the American dancer Ruth St. Denis. Mrs. Martin was so impressed by the being of Inayat that she was taken into a spiritual state that night and in the ensuing days. It was described as a visitation of the Prophet Muhammad and she felt impelled to follow Inayat to his next concert, which was a very long distance away. Her husband borrowed the money for her to go and later was a source of support for her many Sufi activities. When she reached Inayat he immediately recognized her state and initiated her, and thus a very seminal relationship was begun.

Hazrat Inayat Khan continued to instruct her frequently in letters addressed to her as "Dear Mother." In a letter dated 18 December 1911 from New York City, he tells her that she is "developing more rapidly than I expected," and requests her presence for about forty days for spiritual practices and training. He writes:

> I want somebody to undertake my mission as my successor in America before I would leave, and you know that my presence is very necessary in India to save Hindu music from its downfall. I find you the most suited among my mureeds because I see in you a great faith and devotion besides very good heartful of love and affection together with illuminated intellect. Also you are possessing all the attributes of humanity that is the most important thing for a spiritual guide. Now in your spiritual development I see a great improvement and every hope for the future. All this shows that God almighty and all Murshids in Chain have selected you to bestow upon you this honour but before I give you a written diploma of Khilafat in Sufic order, I must teach you the work of training mureeds of different dispositions. You are trained by quite an exceptional method. It was no training, it was just a divine blessing. But this could not be the case with others. Mureed is a patient and Murshid is supposed to be the doctor. Now the spiritual doctor should first see the disease of the patient and then should prescribe him the medicine especially beneficial to him. In case he's not better with one he should prescribe another medicine and so on until he finds that the mureed has developed to the right state of mind. Now for this training is wanted for about 40 days at least but I am not sure whether I will go to San Francisco and also I cannot ask you to come over here so far leaving all your works aside. It is very expensive too. So now I leave it to you to decide it.

It is signed, "with my heartiest blessings, yours in the Infinite, Inayat Khan."

This is a persistent theme—wishing to get together but being separated by great distances and the pressure of events—that recurs many times over the years. We know that Murshida Martin pursued her Sufi studies and began classes in San Francisco and elsewhere. Her difficulties in setting up a school were met with kindness and sympathy by her teacher. He writes:

> I am extremely sorry for your new school not being well patronized but I think the time of trial was very short. I am working here (London) day and night at the sacrifice of my musical profession and after three years continuous effort of us all it is not yet self-supporting and besides my family responsibility

> and spiritual attainment, I am still striving hard. All things great cost greatly in their accomplishment. You are my mureed so naturally hardship comes as a mureed's share. Was it easy for Christ or Moses or Mohammed or Krishna or Buddha to work for the spiritual cause? If it was not how can we expect our path to be easy? It is always been most difficult and always will be. Virtue has its own rewards. We are the swimmers of Allah's sea. Our destiny is the port of spiritual absorption, but in order to smooth our path Allah will not hold the tides which undoubtedly is the most difficult task but it is for us.

He then continues in a very practical vein:

> If you think it is materially impossible to keep the place after this term, I think it is advisable to work in a place which will suit the purpose and not be heavy in support ... have courage and patience and in time it will all be well. I will take my first opportunity to come and help you in America after these trying times have passed.

He then goes on to speak about her spiritual practices.

On other occasions in the years between visits to the U.S., Hazrat Inayat Khan continued to emphasize Rabia Martin's special responsibilities and the importance of her efforts. In a letter dated 17 December 1914, he writes:

> Sorry to give you this trouble but you are always chosen to work on my behalf. When I will go for the life of absolute retirement you will have to attend to all my affairs in the West also sometimes in the East. I don't know if circumstances will permit me to come the World's Faire as it is much expense to take such a trip but I will try to see what can be done. My little daughter sends you her love and wants your blessings and also my wife and my brothers. How is Etta[1]? My blessings to her and all in the Order and my heartiest wishes for you to have strength and courage to resist all hindrances on your way.

One more letter from this period bears quoting here. It was written by Inayat on a lecture tour while in Dundee, Scotland and postmarked 19 November 1918. As always it begins, "My Dear Mother":

> I received your kind letter some time ago and today I am writing to you as soon as I have got some time. My work and

---

[1] Rabia Martin's daughter.

> responsibilities are grown with my age and if will see me you will perhaps not recognize me. I am not the same Murshid in my appearance as you saw before. I look much older. I wonder how your work is prospering in America. I am anxious to know of its success. Do you receive lessons regularly by our correspondance department? Since I have heard you were going to take seclusion I have been praying for your success in it. There is no necessity of fasting but a vegetable food is advisable …

He proceeds with further spiritual instructions and concludes by saying,

> I, myself, and all the sincere members of our Order are indeed proud of you. Your photograph is placed in 'Khankah' and the members point out to the notice of the visitors and strangers that this is Murshid's first mureed in the Western World and first Murshida in the West and everyone of them know and admire how you have striven in your life and are striving hard to bring our blessed Order to a great glory in your land. My only wish and prayer is to be with you once again. With my blessing to yourself, Etta, your husband and our beloved helpers and members in the Order, Murshid.

From an early paper of Samuel Lewis, "In Quest of the Super-miraculous," we have a very brief account of his first meeting with Murshida Martin in November of 1919 and also his first meeting with Hazrat Inayat Khan in June of 1923. Scene I of this paper takes place at the World's Fair, San Francisco, 1915:

> Youth comes to the Palace of Education. "Lord I know nothing, show me." He places his hands on his forehead, moving each in the opposite direction as if to empty his mind and walks in. He walks in as if a Socrates and asks and asks and asks. Then he meets the Theosophists. "All religions are right. They differ on the outside when taken exoterically, they agree on the inside if taken esoterically. All religions are from God. There are seven planes of existence, the lower ones experienced in life after life, the higher ones only by sages and the illumined." The youth is satisfied. He thinks he has found The Way.
>
> Scene II. November 1919. This way has proven only intellectual.
>
> He is on Sutter Street in San Francisco looking at a display of books. He is unaware, but soon he is upstairs facing a little dark-haired lady. She is Jewish. "You can explain the Kaballah?"
> "Yes, and all religions."

> "What is Sufism?"
> "Sufism is the essence of all religions. It has been brought to the West by Hazrat Inayat Khan."

Scene III shifts to June of 1923 and reports a dream Samuel Lewis had at that time, the night before he would meet Inayat:

> It is night. It is morning. Hazrat Inayat Khan is coming. The youth is in a hurry. The train draws closer. Inayat Khan sticks his head through the smokestack. Youth jumps out of his body. Inayat Khan jumps into his heart. The two hearts rush and blend and become the Infinite Whole.

> Scene IV. The next day:

> It is noon. The Summer Solstice. Youth enters the Clift Hotel. He is summoned to see Pir-o-Murshid Inayat Khan. There is nobody there, only a tremendous light. "Come don't be afraid." Youth walks on and sees a man and experiences joy. The quest of the Super-Miraculous becomes real.

Pir-o-Murshid Inayat Khan had indeed returned to the U.S. and California to bring his light to the work of Murshida Martin and others over those many years. She had by this time with her husband's help and that of some early mureeds purchased some land in Fairfax in Marin County north of San Francisco. She had ridden horseback on those hills, picked out the property and developed it from scratch. As the years went along, buildings were financed and this became the basis for what came to be called Kaaba Allah, the first Sufi khanqah in America. The most noteworthy geographical feature of the land was a stone faced into the mountain, which was large and ideal for sitting in meditation. When Inayat Khan returned again in the spring of 1926, he named this rock Pir Dahan, "the Mouth of the Pir," and said that it had the highest spiritual vibration in America that he had experienced. He also named Kaaba Allah at that time. This rock was later the scene of much spiritual practice by groups and individuals, and some noteworthy experiences.[2]

The man who had driven Inayat Khan to Fairfax and who routinely drove him around in California was Paul Reps, who was given the spiritual name Saladin. Reps is widely known for his work

---

[2] See "Baraka (Blessing) – Direct Experience at the Rock Pir Dahan," in Samuel L. Lewis, *Sufi Vision and Initiation*, ed. Neil Douglas-Klotz (San Francisco and Novato, CA: Sufi Islamia / Prophecy Publications, 1986), pp. 53–54. *Ed.*

on Nyogen Senzaki's famous *Zen Flesh, Zen Bones* and for other poetry, writings, and ink drawings. He had been introduced to Senzaki by Samuel Lewis and both of these men studied Buddhism under Senzaki as well as being initiated on the Sufi path by Pir-o-Murshid Inayat Khan. In the spirit of universality and as a natural outgrowth of his experience with Senzaki, Samuel Lewis arranged for a meeting between what can now be seen as two legendary individuals in the spiritual history of America. What is perhaps equally remarkable is the fact that an illuminated teacher from Buddhism writes an open account of his experience with an illuminated teacher from another path. Thus we get a contemporary view of Inayat Khan from someone who can perhaps see his essence most clearly.

Senzaki Sensei wrote an account of his meeting that was published in Japan in a collection called *On Zen Meditation* in 1936 by the Rinzai priest Nanshin Okamoto. It included the clipping from the article Senzaki had written for the Japanese American shortly after the time of the meeting and titled, "Mohammedan Zen: Sufism in America." I will quote extensively from this charming and revealing account.

> Zen is not confined to Buddhism. In Christianity there is an element of Zen. Mohammedanism is supposed to be monotheistic but its offspring which calls itself Sufism encourages introspection among its students so as to realize Allah or God within one's innerself. If the thoughts of Saint Bernard and of Meister Eckhart can be called Zen then the ideas of Jalaludin Rumi of Persia as well as those of Kabir may also be called Mohammedan Zen.
>
> I've been told that there is only one Sufi teacher in America, a woman residing in San Francisco, though there are several teachers of both sexes in Europe. The Sufi teachings I understand also have some influence in India. The teacher in San Francisco is Mrs. Martin, a Hebrew scholar, whom her students call Murshida, the Persian feminine form for the word Murshid which means teacher.
>
> Inayat Khan is known to his followers as Pir-o-Murshid and they consider him to be the greatest teacher of this age. Since the latter part of March he's been at the Sufi Temple, 153 Kearny Street of this city, engaged in lectures and the personal guidance of his students.

Senzaki then gives a brief description of Inayat Khan's background concluding with, "he is also a poet and a musician in addition to his other accomplishments and he is now lecturing on Sufism under the auspices Paul Elder, the book dealer, while the intellectual groups of San Francisco crowd around him." He continues:

> Mrs. Martin invited me to her home to meet her teacher and as I had benefitted very much by the use of her library over a period of several years, I did not hesitate in accepting her kind invitation. On my way there I happened to meet Dr. Hayes, an old friend of mine and a psychologist. "Where are you going," he asked. "I am going to meet Inayat Khan," I replied. "Oh that Sufi teacher," said the doctor, "I attended his lecture this morning at the Sufi Temple. It was such a tiresome ceremony—the lighting of candles, much bowing and all that. The lecture bristled with too much about God and Love. There was nothing new in it and I had to pay $1 for admission. I believe I will go along with you to meet him." "If you do not feel like going," I replied, "you need not come with me. I'm not asking you to do so." "Well," he said, "they may not charge anything for an interview. I will come with you."
>
> Thus it was that the two of us went to the home of Mrs. Martin, the only Murshida in America. When we arrived we were ushered into the meditation room. It was dimly lighted by a lamp covered with green silk cloth while fragrant Persian incense filled the atmosphere. After Mrs. Martin introduced us and after shaking hands in the American custom with the Murshid, we were seated at a square table, Mrs. Martin facing Dr. Hayes and the teacher facing me. My friend the psychologist began talking to the teacher by asking him how he liked America and its people, meanwhile selecting a cigar from his pocket, which however he hesitated to light at such a meeting.
>
> Inayat Khan smiled at me and asked, "Mr. Senzaki will you tell me what the significance of Zen is?" I remained silent for a little while and then smiled at him. He smiled back at me. Our dialogue was over.
>
> The psychologist not having recognized what had happened said, "You see Mr. Khan, Zen is Japanized from Sanskrit. Its original meaning was Dhyana which means meditation, and ... At this point Inayat waved his right hand gracefully and stopped the psychologist's conversation. Mrs. Martin then interposed, "I will get a book which describes Zen very well. It is an English translation from the Japanese of the twelve sects of Buddhism. I will get it for you." Before she could rise from her seat, Inayat

> Khan again waved with his left hand gracefully stopping the Murshida. Then he glanced at me. His eyes were full of water—not the tears of the world, but water from The Great Ocean—calm and transparent. I recited an old Zen poem not with my mouth, not in thought, but with a blink like a flash. It reads,
>
> No living soul comes near that water—
> a vast sheet of water as blue as indigo.
> The abyss has a depth of ten thousand feet.
> When all is quiet and calm at midnight,
> only the moonlight penetrates through the waves,
> reaching the bottom easily and freely.
>
> "Murshid," said I, "I see a Zen in you." "Mr. Senzaki, I see a Sufism in you," he replied. Both of us then smiled at each other. Mrs. Martin again interposed, "Mr. Senzaki, you should practice your English. Why don't you talk more about Zen." At this both the Murshid and I laughed loudly in which the Murshida and the psychologist both joined without knowing why. The happy interview was over. I should have gone home at this time but the psychologist seemed to wish to talk further with the Murshid and interpose his whys and becauses, while the Murshida, our Hebrew scholar, must show us her collection of books and documents. So we remained there the whole evening while we discussed Life, Death, Humanity and the Universe.
>
> I noticed that the Murshid uses the Nyaya system of logic in making affirmations and this made me feel very much at home with him as we Buddhists use the same system. The Murshid told us his ideal of a universal brotherhood which he believes will be established, and which he thinks will transcend all racial considerations, as well as harmonize all religions to the extent that they will work together in harmony for the uplifting of humanity, and for the advancement of the spiritual world.

Senzaki proceeds to speak about this possibility in specific terms relating to the existing religions and focusing on Buddhism with its own problems of working together harmoniously and concluding with, "Inayat Khan now has adherents in London, Paris and Geneva. May his brotherhood become stronger year after year—let us sincerely hope for it." Senzaki then describes his last meeting with Inayat Khan:

> One day Inayat Khan expressed the wish to attend a Japanese concert. I could not find any that were billed for that week, so I went to Madam Nakamura,who teaches the koto in her home, and

> asked her to invite him to hear her play. She consented gladly and I went to the Sufi temple to tell Inayat Khan about this arrangement. It was about 2 o'clock in the afternoon and the Murshid asked me to meditate with him in a secluded room where his pupils received personal guidance. We sat down to meditate together, but before even one stick of incense was consumed, both of us must have entered into Samadhi, for Mrs. Martin suddenly called us stating that it was already dark, time for us to go home for our respective dinners. We looked at each other with surprise, but nodded a knowing assent to each other. The incense had been completely consumed so long that no fragrance remained in the room. Both Sufism and Zen had become, after all, only yesterday's dream.
>
> It was in this evening of 1923, that we, Mrs. Martin accompanied by Inayat and me, went to Mrs. Nakamura's studio. The simplicity of Inayat Khan's manners and conduct on the way reminded me of the time when a certain Japanese high priest came to America, accompanied by a flock of attending priests, with a great show of pomp and ceremonials–he could not even move a hand without the assistance of his two chief attendants (the chief and his vice-chief). This high priest was the abbot of a certain Japanese sect, but with all his pomp and glory his influence in America never reached an inch beyond the Japanese immigrants, and his appearances here went entirely unnoticed by Americans.
>
> On the other hand, Inayat Khan's influence was widely spread among intellectual groups both in Europe and America. He could have put on a 'big show' of himself alone if [he] wished to do so but he was not that kind of teacher. Wearing a Turkish hat and a long black mantle and carrying a cane, the Murshid modestly rode in the streetcars instead of in a flock of honking automobiles.

Senzaki goes on to report on the concert at Madam Nakamura's and that it was a success. He concludes:

> After definite expression through keen attention and breathless silence of his appreciation of the performance, Inayat Khan warmly praised Madam Nakamura saying that she was music itself, not only with her koto but also even in drinking tea or in walking around the room. Madam Nakamura should appreciate this commendation very much, as the Murshid is a poet and a musician who is not given to flattery.
>
> Having been served with tea and cakes, and having been presented with pictures of other performances given by Madam Nakamura, Inayat Khan left the studio saying that he would tell

> European musicians about the deep impression the music had made upon him.
>
> At the corner of the street where I was about to bid the Murshid good-bye I remarked, "All sounds return to one, and where does that one go?" Inayat Khan stopped walking, and shaking hands with me, responded,"Good night Mr. Senzaki."

Murshid Samuel Lewis, who passed through the Rinzai training in *koans* under Senzaki and others, as well as the Sufi training, would often speak of this last encounter between his two teachers saying that Senzaki affirmed the vision of Sufism in speaking of the glorious unity of the realm of all sound, light and vibration, while Inayat with his words affirmed the great Void associated with Zen realization. In an innocent and transcendent egolessness, they had become each other.

Senzaki's article ends with these words, "Now bodhisattvas I have translated my old clipping. What do you think of Inayat Khan? If you wish to meet him today, just open the door and face the lovely shrubbery in front of this meditation hall."

If one imagines that Senzaki's experience of other gurus coming from the East was as equally full of respect as his account of his meetings with Inayat Khan, one should hear the following story reported by Murshid Samuel Lewis on a number of occasions and included in his commentaries. Senzaki at the time had a *zendo* in Los Angeles and attended a lecture by a very famous Swami entitled "Being equal-minded in pleasure and pain." According to Murshid Sam, Senzaki reported that he was impressed by the lecture and wished to pay his respects to the Swami afterwards. Senzaki was made to wait for a very long time in an outer office while the Swami went about his business. There was an expensive vase on the table opposite where Senzaki was waiting and dozing off. Finally, the Swami came out and Senzaki rose to greet him. As he did so, he knocked over the vase and broke it. The Swami reacted by screaming, "You clumsy idiot! Don't you know that vase was worth five hundred dollars?" Senzaki, who at that time had money, though his appearance was unassuming, took five hundred dollars from his wallet and gave it to the Swami with a big smile saying, "Thank you very much, now I know what it means to be equal-minded in pleasure and pain!"

This Zen teaching of being totally in the perfection of the moment gives us an opportunity to more properly evaluate the actual effects of extraordinary individuals beyond the usual conceptual categories. It is in these terms that we can best understand the people being featured in this brief historical account.

The writer interviewed Paul Reps in 1972 about a year after the passing of Murshid Samuel Lewis.[3] Naturally he was asked to speak about Hazrat Inayat Khan, Rabia Martin, and Samuel Lewis. His words strongly show the influence of Inayat Khan:

> Inayat Khan brought his message of Sufism to the western world and he previously had been a very much respected musician in India. He gave up his music in order to teach his message, which he called the Sufi Message. It was certainly from his heart, and he couldn't call it Islamic because the western world was antithetical towards Islam and yet it seemed to have traces of Islam in it as it did of the ancient Hebrews. So he delivered this message through speeches. And instead of music, which he had already played, he began to teach or deliver the Sufi Message. Now this message was from his soul, and he was the most remarkable man I ever met, and so it was as if one's soul were speaking all the time.
>
> He was completely humble and completely at peace and completely relaxed and completely concentrated at the same time. His eyes were concentrated to one point which was outside his body a few feet, but he looked right through your forehead all the time when he talked to you. And yet at the same time he was utterly at ease and said nothing for himself. He was always letting you do the talking and drawing you out. But he was certainly practicing what we might now call Sufism, or the mind on the breath, or however you want to interpret it. And this kind of a presence with this great gentility and king-like bearing and rather tall body and complete modesty simply overcame those who had never seen anything like it. They were much impressed and extremely touched by his sympathy for them and everyone felt here at last is the one person who understands me thoroughly.

Reps then reported how this very quality might help lead to problems organizationally and with various egos. He went on to say:

---

[3] As Murshid Samuel Lewis' esoteric secretary I endeavored to secure interviews with everyone who had played an important role in his life, and particularly people who could provide first hand historical accounts. Many of these interviews were carried out throughout the years of 1972 and 1973, and provide material used in this paper.

> And feeling that way, with such love from Inayat, why they felt, "Now I am really right. You see? Now I am really right." And this contact and the Sufi Message dug so deep in their heart that they felt, "I am really right but the other people might be wrong." And so all of these various appointees and representatives of Sufism in the different countries began to have that kind of feeling and they began to get at odds with each other.

In March of 1925, Samuel L. Lewis left his family home in San Francisco to go to Kaaba Allah, the Sufi Retreat near Fairfax, California. He was not in good health and was a sensitive and introverted person with a grim family upbringing. It was with difficulty that he mounted the steps in Fairfax and he reports that he actually fell down when he reached Kaaba Allah. He then began an extended spiritual retreat concentrating on meditation and Sufi practices. The powerful spiritual experiences of this retreat became the basis of his first interview with Hazrat Inayat Khan in the Beverly Hills Hotel in the year 1926. What follows is an extended quotation from Murshid Samuel Lewis account, "Six Interviews with Hazrat Inayat Khan":

> In the year 1925, one had come to the end of one's tether and had gone into the wilderness to die, he thought. Instead, he was completely resurrected ... Briefly, there were encounters with Khwaja Khizr at the beginning, and with the Mursaleen (Chain of Prophets) at the end Lord Mohammed appearing in double capacity, the other Messengers singly, and one was vested with a special Robe. ... Pir-o-Murshid listened to this report and told me to write.

Hazrat Inayat Khan had accepted Samuel's spiritual report and seen in him the prodigious powers of mind, and of devotion that were certainly outstanding characteristics. On Hazrat Inayat Khan's previous visit to America, he had given mureeds a concentration on the heavenly spheres—that they feel an accommodation there for the harmony of all religious faith. In what was to prove characteristic of his lifetime, Samuel Lewis was amazed to find that he was the only one who had continued with this concentration in the intervening years. Inayat Khan had asked him to return for follow-up interviews and much to the consternation of his secretary who was trying to coordinate a busy schedule, he saw Samuel five additional times. During some of those meetings Saladin Reps was outside the door and was, on one occasion, called inside to join them.

The second interview was by far the most dramatic and significant. When Samuel entered, Inayat Khan initiated him as a Sufi. We will pick up Murshid Sam's account at this point:

> Before we sat down, Inayat Khan said to me, "Samuel I am going to ask you a favor. I want to speak to you as man to man. I am not Murshid; you are not mureed. We are just men. If we cannot act as men it will not help me. Can you act to me as man to man? If so let us shake hands and then we can sit down and talk as man to man." We did so and sat down.
>
> "How many loyal mureeds do you think I have?" he asked.
>
> "Oh, I guess about a hundred."
>
> "I wish I had a hundred. But how many do you think, at the least, loyal mureeds I have?"
>
> "Well," I said, "I don't believe it but just to give an answer I'd say twenty."
>
> "I wish I had twenty! I wish I had ten!"
>
> Then he arose in full majesty and yelled at me out loud. "I wish I had ten!" Then he lifted his right hand and using the index finger of his left hand pointed to the middle of it and yelled, "I wish I had five loyal mureeds. Samuel can you believe it? I have not as many loyal mureeds as I have fingers on one hand."
>
> By that time the chair in which I had been sitting toppled over like in a Hollywood movie and I was sitting on the floor totally amazed, but by this action and by his loud speech I received the full magnetism of his baraka or blessing and I believe I still have it.

Murshid Samuel Lewis would make reference to having received the *tawajjuh* (spiritual attention) of Pir-o-Murshid Inayat Khan in this unusual *jalali* state throughout his whole life. Later when he was accepted far and wide as a spiritual teacher and had scores of disciples who were loyal to him he would constantly give all the credit to Inayat. He knew that the great strength and fearlessness and boundless magnetism that he radiated was a grace and he traced it to that moment of receptivity, man to man, to his teacher's cry in that hotel room in 1926.

During the course of this and subsequent interviews Hazrat Inayat Khan spoke to Samuel Lewis basically on two subjects: the first on succession, the second on the nature of the Sufi Order. According to Samuel Lewis's account:

> He began telling me some things which were also told to Pir-o-Murshid Hasan Nizami on his (Hazrat Inayat Khan's) deathbed. ... I was told over and over again: Pir-o-Murshid Inayat Khan intended that Murshida Martin be his successor. ... I was to stand by her and protect her but see to it that she never defended herself. ... He went over that again and again. ... She was never to defend herself on any occasion and positively never in public. She was to divest herself of all right to handle funds. ... He said he expected trouble and that in case of any difficulty I was to write to a Mr. E. DeCruzat Zanetti in Geneva. ... This was the history. The aftermath was terrible.

Saladin Reps was called into the room during the sixth interview and the two were together asked to promise Hazrat Inayat Khan that they would stand as defenders and protectors of Murshida Martin. They both agreed to do so. Samuel Lewis was to write as part of his account:

> It is to one's great regret that Murshida Martin always insisted on defending her nafs (ego) in public, and this led to her downfall. ... It must have been this spirit which was felt in Europe where the vast majority of disciples refused to accept Murshida Martin as successor to Pir-o-Murshid Inayat Khan.

He also reports that shortly after the death of Hazrat Inayat Khan he was removed from the Board of Trustees, which handled the funds. He therefore was not able to do what Hazrat Inayat Khan had requested of him. Nevertheless he honored that promise to his teacher by always remaining loyal to Rabia Martin until her death some twenty years later.

Reps in his interview spoke of his own relationship to that solemn promise:

> And as far as I'm concerned he only told me to *help* Murshida Martin. So I was glad to do that, but she was beyond help because she was always having her own opinion and her own viewpoint. So she stormed into Europe expecting them to receive her as the real Murshida and they didn't go for that at all. And she initiated Sam Lewis as her Khalifa but later on she had differences with

> Sam Lewis and before she passed away she gave her materials to Mrs. Duce. So what a mess it was. It was impossible for me to help her anyway. So I simply kept out of it because I felt if there was to be so much assertion and quarreling that this was beautiful Sufism turned into anti-Sufism. So I just lived a simple life in my own way. And as the years went on Samuel was living in his own way too. Sam had a very hard life himself in his family. So I felt very deeply in sympathy with him for that reason. Then later he always said he was not on the Murshid line at all, not on the teacher's line at all, but the young people of America turned him into a Murshid. So he got converted into a teacher instead of the line that he always thought he was on, which was maybe a defense of the Message or something.

A short vignette from the Reps interview will give a bit of context to the subject of Murshida Martin's personality:

> Once when I was driving from San Francisco to Los Angeles with Murshida Martin in the backseat and Murshid in the front seat she scolded so much about the woman Los Angeles representative that he couldn't bear it anymore. So he said, "Now I make Reps in charge of Los Angeles." So I turned around to Murshida Martin immediately and said, "Now you must stop talking."

Samuel Lewis had noted in the paper "Six Interviews":

> Murshida Martin was then under attack by several people. She had had the *fana-fi-rassul* with Mohammed soon after she met Hazrat Inayat Khan. She had had a long training in European Occultism and in Comparative Religion. But during the years I knew her, although she was a Murshida, I know of only one or two experiences on her part in *fana-fi-rassul* and one in *fana-fi-lillah*. This was much more than others experienced. I was not initiated into *fana-fi-sheikh* until 1930 when Hazrat Inayat Khan began to appear to me from the other side.[4]

We will return later to the aftermath of the rejection of Murshida Martin's claims to successorship by the Sufis of Europe. The other theme of Samuel Lewis' interviews with Inayat Khan deserves discussion at this point because it shows again the tremendous influence of his teacher on his subsequent life's work. Hazrat Inayat Khan had regarded him as having a great intellectual

---

[4] The successive stages of *fana fi shaykh*, *fana fi rasul*, and *fana fi 'llah* are outlined in Inayat Khan, *The Sufi Message of Hazrat Inayat Khan* (London: Barrie and Rockliff/Jenkins, 1960–67), 1:42; 5:33, 186–7; 12:73. *Ed.*

gift and the ability to interpret mystical teachings in the intellectual arena:

> He directed me toward the integration of the mystical and the intellectual. He went into exact details and told me to work with Miss Sakina Furnee in Suresnes, France, but if anything happened to her I was to take over the Brotherhood work. ... It has been very difficult, although times are changing, to present in the Western world a picture based on mystical attainment which transcends all religious separatism. Still one has gone on trying to bridge the gap between mysticism and general culture, and the last few weeks[5] show that if one persists for forty years he will surely succeed.

Samuel Lewis's concentration in this sphere ultimately produced one of the most substantial literary outpourings of this or any time. In following up his *murshid's* suggestions, when he discussed the provisions of the various Sufi constitutions that had been made, he proceeded, for example, to write voluminous commentaries on all the Gathas and Githas of Hazrat Inayat Khan, as well as commentaries on a great many of the writings published for the general public. As his understanding grew through the years, he rewrote these commentaries and finished the third rewriting of them during the last years of his life. But this is just a small fraction of the spiritual writings, prose and poetry, which were written as a result of this assignment. Moreover, he began a correspondence with university professors of oriental philosophy and the like, trying to bring out a greater awareness of the real mystical teachings of those whose knowledge was "based on experience not on premises."

During her years at Kaaba Allah with Samuel Lewis, Rabia Martin came to rely more and more on Samuel's inspired writings and transmissions. She also used Samuel as a foil to continually put forward her claims to successorship in a hopeless situation that was increasingly difficult for both of them. She had felt crushed by her rejection in Europe and was known to have believed it was because she was a woman, an American, and Jewish. She became hardened and embittered in her pain and this impression never left her. One bright spot for her that did occur was when she traveled to India and was recognized by the Sufi teacher who had been with Hazrat Inayat

---

[5] This account was written in 1968.

Khan during the period preceding his death. Hasan Nizami allowed her to address an audience of hundreds in Delhi, though she was required to speak from behind a protective screen.

A certificate was issued at that time. It was written in Urdu with the English translation below it. It reads:

> All praise be to almighty Allah and His Prophet Mohammed and all His Sahabaas and Auliya-e-Ummat. I, Hasan Nizami, as a grandmaster of the Chishtia Nizamia Order authorize Sister in Silsila, Rabia A. Martin to disseminate the blessed teachings of my Sufi Chishtia Nizamia Order among the people of all religions in the Western World and for this purpose to build Khanqahs wherever necessary and to adopt all means for spreading and teaching practical Tasawwuf (Sufism). I give this letter of authority because Sufi Inayat Khan, Pir-o-Murshid of Rabia Martin told me in 1927 seven days before his death, when he came from the West to visit me in Delhi, that he found Rabia Martin most capable of teaching Sufism in the highest degree and that he had allowed Rabia Martin to give the Spiritual education in the Western World and that she was his Khalifa (Spiritual Successor). Sufi Inayat Khan passed away on the 5th of February, 1927, and was buried near my house. According to his will and wish, I give this Letter of Authority to Rabia Martin to disseminate the teachings of the Chishtis for which I have every authority, being the Grand Master of the Chishtia Order, recognising her as the true Spiritual Successor of Pir-o-Murshid Inayat Khan. In the end I pray to God that Rabia Martin be successful in spreading the Chishti message of love, harmony, and contentment of heart.

It should be noted that this document of permission from Hasan Nizami to Rabia Martin contains both the Urdu writing of Hasan Nizami as well as the English translation given above. In the course of writing this article, the Urdu version alone was conveyed to Prof. Marcia Hermansen for an independent translation. The differences between the two versions are so striking that it seems advisable to reproduce the latter one here in its entirety:

> Certificate of Authorization (*ijazat*) of the Chishtiyya -Nizamiyya Sufi Lineage (*silsila*)
>
> All praise to Allah and peace and blessings upon Muhammad the messenger of Allah and on his family and companions and the saints of his community. *Amin.*

> I, Hasan Nizami, in my capacity as head (*qa'im maqam*) of the Chistiyya-Nizamiyya silsila, give permission (*ijazat*) to my spiritual sister, Rabia A. Martin, to propagate Chistiyya-Nizamiyya spiritual teaching of my Sufi lineage (*silsila*), the Chishtiyya-Nizamiyya, in the entire United States, and to spread the benefits of the Chistiyya silsila to the inhabitants of America of all religions. As part of this work she may also establish *khanqahs* wherever she deems judicious for spreading Sufism in this country.
>
> This certificate of permission (*ijazat nama*) is given on the basis that Rabia Martin's *murshid*, Sufi Inayat Khan, came from Europe and America to meet with me in Delhi in 1927, and seven days before his death he had told me about Rabia Martin. He informed me that he had found Rabia Martin capable of being given every type of spiritual teaching and that for this reason he had given Rabia Martin permission to give spiritual instruction.
>
> Sufi Inayat Khan passed away on 5 February 1927 and was buried in front of my house. Thus I also, in accordance with the last wishes (*wasiyya*) of Rabia Martin's *murshid*, give Rabia Martin permission to spread the Chishtiyya-Nizamiyya teachings in the United States of America. This I have full right to do in my capacity as head of the Chishti silsila.
>
> In conclusion, I pray God to make Rabia Martin succeed in establishing the Chishti teachings that spread love and contentment in the heart. I was given spiritual inspiration that the American nation possesses more capacity for genuine spiritual development that brings people to (realization of) God than any other people. The human being can see and understand things that materialists using the latest scientific means cannot perceive or understand. Therefore in the coming age America alone will become the spiritual exemplar for the whole world in the same manner that it is currently the most developed from the material standpoint. Listen Rabia! Give my message to America and prepare America for this coming age.

We can only speculate as to the reasons for the differences between what was included on the document and what the original actually stated. It seems evident to this writer that Rabia Martin wished to use Hasan Nizami to fortify in writing her claim to being the true spiritual successor of Inayat Khan and that Hasan Nizami, seeing a great spiritual future for America, wished to use Rabia Martin as a representative of his own order in the new world. Since

Hasan Nizami knew little English and Rabia Martin knew little or no Urdu, we are left to speculate about the person of the original translator and how the process of translation took place. Was the phrase "spiritual successor" added solely at Rabia Martin's suggestion? Or was it a clarification of what Hasan Nizami understood to be Hazrat Inayat Khan's intention? Why was the last paragraph totally omitted? Was it due to considerations of space and tone or some other reason?

In any case, Murshid Samuel Lewis, who also spoke no Urdu, was unaware of any of these nuances when he commented in the "Six Interviews" manuscript:

> True, when she visited Pir-o-Murshid Hasan Nizami in New Delhi, he proclaimed her as successor to Hazrat Inayat Khan. There were deliberations and newspaper notices and she was accepted or at least respected, in the undivided India. But none of this had the slightest effect in Europe. Still, if we have to see life from the standpoint of another as well as of ourselves, the outlook is that there is nothing that can be called exactly right or exactly wrong. Later on in life, much later than the above events, when an outsider came along and insisted that Rabia give up public self-defense and control over funds, she did so without a whimper. She could not do that at the dying request of her own Pir-o-Murshid but for an outsider she did that. Her death was a tragedy.

Murshid Samuel Lewis is referring here to what occurred at the end of Rabia Martin's life, when, sick and discouraged with the fruits of her work, she decided to turn her organization over to Ivy Duce, a prospective devotee of the supposed Avatar Meher Baba. But before we look into this period we should examine life at the first Sufi *khanqah* in America, Kaaba Allah.

The best account that we have of those days was given by Vera Zahn, who had been initiated by Samuel Lewis and come to Kaaba Allah as a young married woman in her early twenties. She remained in the order for years and was later made a Sheikha by Murshida Martin. She departed from the organization at the time of the Meher Baba episode, but returned to be amazed at what Murshid Sam was doing with his young disciples in the late '60s. Samuel Lewis had referred to her in his paper on the experiences of psychics and others at Pir Dahan. Later, as Murshida Vera, Zahn became known for her work in early childhood education based on the teachings of Hazrat Inayat Khan.

These remembrances are drawn from an interview the writer did with Sheikha Vera in February of 1972. She had had early psychic experiences with Pir-o-Murshid Inayat Khan as a very young child, five years of age, and though she had never seen him in the flesh, or knew that he lived in the flesh, when she saw pictures of him in the home of Hazel Armstrong in 1936, her interest immediately turned to Sufi literature and Sufi work.

She was prepared for initiation and a time was set for her to meet Samuel Lewis at the Sufi headquarters on Sutter Street, San Francisco. She says:

> I came in not knowing what to expect. I hadn't any idea. No one had told me a thing about Samuel, who he was or what he was or anything, so it was a great surprise. But the minute I saw him we recognized each other immediately and went towards each other and enfolded each other in our arms, and both of us were overwhelmed with emotion. It was as though we had been separated for centuries and all at once we again met. And neither one of us could put it into words or explain it. He initiated me immediately following this without any speech or explanations. ...
>
> Every weekend all the Sufis, on Friday evenings, got on the Ferry boat and we went over to Fairfax and we met in what was called the lower house on the property, in the biggest room on the property second to the chapel. The room was kept bare in the center. It had a large fireplace. It had a dining alcove and a large kitchen led off this room also. We all sat in a circle and Samuel led us in practices. ... Murshida Martin did not live at Kaaba Allah at this time.[6] She had lived at Kaaba Allah in the early days.

Vera's perspective on this period was that of a member of the younger generation. While in her twenties and married to Arjuna, she and her husband visited Kaaba Allah often, staying as many as four days in the week, but were primarily a part of a generation of people who were the children of mureeds and who were being given their Sufi and religious education by Samuel Lewis. Her accounts of life there do, however, include periods when Murshida Martin was present, up until the advent of World

---

[6] I.e., 1937.

War II and the dispersal of people. The scope of this paper allows for but a few glimpses from Vera's account:

> We've all come in now, wandered in. Some of us on Friday night. As soon as we can get away from work we hie it down to the Ferry boat and over to Kaaba Allah. ... We had a big gong on the front of that building which was always struck by Hazel Armstrong, and when you heard that gong you got yourself in your robe and came down to dinner. ... Everyone had a robe. Some of the girls wore the Japanese kimonos. The young girls—thirteen, fourteen year old kids—seem to like those. Apricot was the great Sufi color used during Inayat Khan's days at Suresnes and we all copied that. If Murshida Martin had given the robes to you, they had openings down the front, and all those that she brought from India and from the great holy places of the Sufi poets which she visited in her lifetime had a great deal of Sufi *wazifas* in Arabic or Urdu stamped or painted down the shoulders, over the breast and down to the knees.
>
> But anyhow all the robes would be hung on this big bannister. When you came in and came to the table, you stood much as you do at the Catholic and Anglican retreat houses. You did not sit for the blessing. You stood behind your chair until the Murshid entered. If it was Murshida Martin, she entered first and then Samuel entered. He was a Khalif then. He sat at the foot of the table and she sat at the head. They were long refectory tables with straight-backed chairs and you stood behind your chair until the blessing was given. And a quotation was also given for that day, which was usually a reprimand it seemed to us, the young ones – that wherever we'd gotten off too wildly we were given a quotation to cool us down. When we sat down, Samuel would soften this with his own talk and interpretation, which might be about what the Chinese were doing this week in Chinatown in San Francisco, or anything under the sun. And when the silent time came and people were eating you'd be trying to mull over in your mind, "What was he thinking, what was he talking about?" And then, bing! You had it. It was always something for the younger generation, you know. But it had been hidden in this jumble, that the older generation never knew what he was talking about, and we felt very wise, you know, and it sort of encouraged us.
>
> At ten or eleven on Sunday morning, all the young people would gather together with Samuel and we would visit a church of his choice in Fairfax. Sometimes it would be Methodist, Baptist, Pentecostal, Catholic—we visited every parish in that area and we were taught a Sufi enters any church of God, any house of God,

> and behaves as that denomination behaves. He honors God in that manner. And when we went to the synagogue we honored God in that manner and we sat separately and we learned by experiencing these different congregations. When we came back to Kaaba Allah, Samuel would give us the heart of that message in that religion's own texts. And then he would swing back and immediately quote from Inayat Khan, so that you would see that Inayat Khan's was the same universal message.

According to Vera's account there were really three distinct groups at Kaaba Allah in those years: the young adults, the group in their twenties of which she was a member, and the older mureeds. Practice was extremely formal and modeled on what were thought to be Hazrat Inayat Khan's practices in Suresnes. Samuel Lewis was a Khalif and would present *zikr* or other Sufi practices. When Murshida Martin was not involved in her world travels and was in residence she would give talks, and Samuel would always lead the practices thereafter.

Vera reported on one memorable day at Kaaba Allah:

> When Murshida Martin came back from South America I had been up at four in the morning with all the young ones and we sat on the front porch of the lower house and we made garlands. And these garlands were just draped over every entranceway and we had tons and tons of marigolds, a beautiful orange color, you know, with all the greens. And they were on everything along with the Sufi ribbons with sayings in Urdu. And the bushes had been adorned with *wazifas*, every bush leading out to the rock because I had thought something was needed to welcome Murshida when she first went out to the rock where Samuel was trying to build a chapel, a little round pergola with a pointed roof. But the morning that Murshida Martin came and walked out there —and I had been so worried that she not have anything to welcome her on this path—as she walked out, all of the bushes bowed and everyone saw it! I felt it was one of the highest spiritual moments I had ever seen her in.... When she later returned to teach at the lower house, Samuel and I sat at her feet.

As the chief gardener, Samuel Lewis would constantly work the grounds of Kaaba Allah. He received the enthusiastic help of the young men, especially when he devised projects of moving massive stones using the power of breath. The upper house at Kaaba Allah was referred to as the Khankah and was the house that the older mureeds lived in. According to Sheikha Vera, "this group of white-haired women lived up until the time of the advent of Meher Baba on the scene and then they seemed to die one after the other and are buried in a Sufi plot in a cemetery in San Rafael.

To continue with Vera's account:

> When Samuel opened the books to me in preparation to my becoming a Sheikha, he took me into a hall between the front and the back part of the upper house. And this room had all of the files, locked files with the entire Sufi papers—everything that Inayat Khan had written—and most precious materials, all of which later burned in the fire which destroyed entirely the upper house. A large Sufi library, which took in all four walls, was there, and this was a place that the older mureeds loved to read and work in. Every afternoon at three o'clock they opened their bedroom doors, which led off a long hall from this library, and each one sat in their room with their Sufi book and each one read aloud from the Sufi book—whatever they were currently on. The droning here was like a hive of bees. Each one doing their own work on a different level.

In addition to all of his other duties at Kaaba Allah, Samuel Lewis wrote incessantly. Once again to refer to Sheikha Vera's account:

> Samuel, in those early days, at the time when he was gardener and second Murshid, Khalif, and manager of Kaaba Allah during Murshida Martin's many travels, was very much receiving on the spiritual plane. His messages, his commentaries, the work which he gave to us was all dictated from the spirit. And he was down in the little apartment down below and you'd hear that typewriter going faster than anyone could ever type and reams of material were coming out to every level, to every age and to every interest. Such breadth of view that you could not imagine that a human being could do it.

Toward the end of her life, Rabia Martin became somewhat estranged from Samuel Lewis. Vera reports a number of interviews where she was questioned by Murshida Martin as to her interpretations of materials that Samuel had written for Rabia as she pressured him for some transmissions from Hazrat Inayat Khan pertinent to her organizational difficulties. She had been secretly training Ivy Duce in Berkeley in the Sufi teachings. Mrs. Duce did not wish to be publicly known as a Sufi and never came to Kaaba Allah. Murshida Martin was also struggling with the cancer in her shoulders that would eventually take her life. She made it known that she was making Mrs. Duce her spiritual successor rather than Khalif Samuel Lewis, which had been generally assumed. It came as quite a surprise and shock to all.

In January of 1948, just months after being named as Rabia's successor, Murshida Duce traveled with her daughter to India, where she met Meher Baba and turned the whole Sufi organization over to him to re-orient according to his teachings.

Murshida Duce finally agreed to an interview with this writer in December of 1976. Murshida Duce at first refused to see me and expressed the opinion that, as a close disciple of Samuel Lewis, I could hardly accept what she might have to say. When I reminded her that Hazrat Inayat Khan had said that a Sufi was one who could see from the point of view of another as well as himself, she agreed to see me, but would allow only note-taking and no tape recording. Later, after a courteous meeting, she had sent to me a few copies of Hazrat Inayat Khan's voluminous correspondence with Rabia Martin, most of which were filled with spiritual instructions, as well as a copy of the document from Hasan Nizami, which we have already discussed. Mrs. Duce told me in the interview:

> Rabia Martin, at Murshid's request, did traveling abroad. She stayed a year or more in South America. She was very successful in Brazil and Australia. Toward the end of her life, when she traveled, she asked me to take over her students while she was gone. I saw her in New York. She said she was convinced Meher Baba was the Qutb and she planned to go see him. Murshida Martin got ill and was never able to go. I was horrified when I was told that I was to take over. I felt unprepared. I thought it was a shame that the work would fail. I decided to go meet Baba. My daughter and I went to India. I told Baba, "I understand you're the Qutb and I've come for help." He said, "It's your destiny to do this work and I'll help you."
>
> In 1952, when Meher Baba came over to America, he felt Sufi teachings were uniquely suited to the Western World, but he was very anxious that they be pure, so Sufism Reoriented was started. He said many of the things we'd been given properly belonged to Yoga. I told him there was lots of trouble with our symbol. Many felt it was a Mohammedan symbol. He suggested we put a "1" in it replacing the crescent and star. Later, when Musharaff Khan visited our headquarters in San Francisco, this was the thing he most objected to.

Murshid Samuel Lewis reported that he had visited Rabia Martin as she lay dying of cancer in her home in San Francisco in 1946, and had begged her that after she had passed that he finally be released from the vow that he had made to Hazrat Inayat Khan to continue to support her claims. She refused to do so. She had called on what Samuel regarded as his duty over and over again and he had written time and again on her behalf to European headquarters and elsewhere. He wished to be relieved of that burden now that she had named Mrs. Duce her successor, and especially as the work appeared to be taking this new direction in which the personality of the "Avatar" was to be paramount. But what Sheikha Vera and others referred to as his "crucifixion" was to continue for a number of years as he tried to cooperate with Murshida Duce and the new organization. His relations with Murshida Duce grew worse and worse. She informed me during our interview that, "on January 7th, 1949, Samuel Lewis resigned from my Sufi Order." She had asked him to resign his seat on the Board of Directors and he had refused.

Kaaba Allah burned down on New Year's Eve, 1949. Samuel had removed many of his own writings the previous day. Amidst all the calumny that was put upon him over these years and the years following, the innuendo spread among some that he was responsible for burning the place down. Ivy Duce gave me a copy of a letter to Samuel Lewis she had written on 1 February 1950, which concludes:

> I would also advise you not to brag about taking the Sufi School with you when you left. I regret to say that most people do not understand the esoteric meanings you are hinting at and there is already considerable speculation in Marin County as to whether or not you had any part in this holocaust since you were there that day and no one was there that night. I must say here and now that I do not believe this at all. There was no baraka or darshana there except the rock Murshid blest. The backbiting and fights and gossiping and performances of all sorts sent out no baraka. I am sure it was to free the place from just such samskaras that the place burned down and through its purification we have a clean slate for Baba's NEW PHASE and the new era that is soon here.

Looking back from the vantage point of the present, the Meher Baba phase, however it be evaluated for its contribution to spirituality in our times, did not play a significant role in advancing the universal Sufi teachings espoused by Hazrat Inayat Khan.[7] On the other hand, the being of Samuel Lewis manifested in such a remarkable way in subsequent years that a total rebirth of the message of Hazrat Inayat Khan was initiated, and its effects felt more and more with the passage of time. He often said that the saying of Jesus Christ encapsulated his life: "The stone which is rejected has become the cornerstone."

During the culminating period of his life, Murshid Samuel Lewis wrote to an associate, Elizabeth Patterson, at the Meher Baba center in Myrtle Beach, South Carolina, where he had lived briefly in 1947, and, while not allowed to teach, had prepared gardens that exist to this day. Among the many "New Age" young people whom he had met in the late '60s he had recently encountered some devotees of Meher Baba and he reflected a bit on this in the letter, which is dated 25 August 1969:

> The view that these young people have is that Baba came with a universal impersonal message for the world while the stress among leaders here has been that he came with a very personal message for the few. ... Indeed I had to withdraw from the Baba movement because of the questionable ethical standards of personalities presumably high in his entourage. ... The joint inheritance of spiritual music and dancing from Hazrat Inayat Khan and Ruth St. Denis is a continuance of the work they started in 1911. It is remarkable how young people are being attracted, abandoning drugs and artificial stimulants and joining in the joyful praise to God. The experience of ecstasy is proclaimed in the Upanishads ... The Sufi teaching with which Meher Baba seems to have been in substantial accord, is that in the ultimate nothing exists but Allah. I am not going to argue for this nor try to impose it on anybody. This is a New Age, this is an age of the vital young. This is an age in which hearts listen ...
>
> Today, before God I am still operating. Tomorrow, before God, if He so wills I shall still be operating. I do not believe there can be any limitation imposed upon any human being by any church, sect or legal entity. Jesus has said, "Ye shall know the Truth and the Truth shall make you free." One asks nothing from mankind, and

[7] For an account of Sufism Reoriented's history issued by its Board of Directors, see "Sufism Reoriented 1948–1980," in *Sufism Speaks Out: Sufism Reoriented Responds to Attacks from India* (Walnut Creek, CA: Sufism Reoriented, 1981), 7–20. *Ed.*

> one accepts everything coming from God whom I believe exists in the hearts of all, and I mean just that, in the hearts of all.

It is difficult to properly evaluate the being of Murshida Martin. Sheikha Vera, in her interview in 1972, complained that it seemed like she'd been utterly forgotten, but that her dedication to the Sufi Message of Hazrat Inayat Khan had been deeply sincere, and that she had devoted her considerable wealth to financing efforts for decades. This writer asked Paul Reps for his overall evaluation of Murshida Martin:

> I knew her for maybe ten years or more. She was very faithful to Inayat Khan and she was his first representative here in the West. … I think she was formalized. I think she had formalized a method of teaching people and I think in that time there was no other idea of how to teach really … and it might be as some thought that Murshid's practices and the practice of his brothers and his cousin were the things that unfolded their whole inner nature. It may be that, but it may be that we have nothing to do with what unfolds our inner nature, it just unfolds. So at that time there was nothing like there is now. However, there were people who were immensely drawn to Murshid and he would give them the different practices to do, and that rather cemented their connection with him but the connection was already made when they met him … in other words it's more electronic than it is formalistic or verbal.

During this interview, which took place in 1972, Reps did his best to explain how he understood what was meant by "The Message":

> If you feel you should really do something, and there's something speaking through you to do this, whatever it is, that's kind of your message, see. And so Inayat Khan felt deeply, "I must put God first, I must turn to the Only Being, because these Westerners are not doing this and this is what they need." That's what he expressed, and this is what is called his Message, but his Message was his Being, the way he felt about it. … There was a lot of love surrounding him … and it might have been the greatest Message ever, it might have been the Message for the times. It was certainly a most beautiful expression, which, then, people began strangely enough to quarrel over. And now we come to a living expression of the Sufi with you and all these young people of Sam's, and there's no quarrel whatever, you see. So times change and people change and the old folks go, and the old folks went

> still believing each one was the one right one, and now we have, beautifully enough, a more living interpretation of the Sufi Message. Inayat always said, "call me Inayat," but no one dared to call him Inayat because they were overcome by his presence. And the one thing I could never understand was why he organized, so I asked him, and his answer just flowed simply out, "to reach more people."

It seems appropriate now to focus briefly on the career and influence of Samuel Lewis. In 1956 he traveled to the East meeting Zen teachers in Japan, Buddhists in Thailand and Burma, Sufis in East Pakistan, Swamis and Sufis in India and more Sufis in West Pakistan. He had the facility for being immediately accepted in all these vastly different spiritual and cultural situations. He received the recognition and blessings on this and subsequent sojourns in the East that ultimately gave him the inner validation that he felt he needed to renew the work of Hazrat Inayat Khan in America. He was in Egypt in 1960 and Pakistan in 1961, back and forth between India and Pakistan in 1962. The amazing chronicle of his experiences has been in large part included in the book *Sufi Vision and Initiation: Meetings with Remarkable Beings*.[8] In addition to the meetings with the living teachers in all traditions, Samuel Lewis's experiences in the tombs of the Sufi Saints were quite active. He was later to say on many occasions that one distinctive thing that he ultimately would become known for was the demonstration of the stage of *fana fi pir*, in which the departed teacher continues to teach those who become attuned.

We can get a glimpse of him during this period through the eyes of his goddaughter and Khalifa, Saadia Khawar Khan Chishti. She met him in Pakistan in 1961 as a young woman with a Master's degree in home economics living with her aunt in the family home of her grandfather in Lahore. Her life was changed by her meeting and subsequent initiation from the man who was known there as "Sufi Sahib." Her aunt had dragged her reluctantly to a talk by Sufi Sahib, and his light and knowledge had overwhelmed her. Her grandfather, however, was in charge of the house and she knew he was suspicious of spiritual teachers. So she mentioned that there was a visiting soil scientist from America,

---

[8] Lewis, *Sufi Vision*, 101–307.

and her grandfather had them invite him to dinner. There ensued a wonderful conversation on scientific matters related to agriculture. After all, finding the right crops for the right soils in different countries had become one of Samuel Lewis's driving goals, and he had pioneered a program of bringing appropriate seeds to different lands. After this cordial dinner their house was open to him and Saadia became accepted as his goddaughter. She reported on him taking an extended spiritual retreat at the tomb of Shaykh 'Ali Hujwiri, author of *Kashf al-Mahjub*, in Lahore, walking miles in the plus hundred degree temperatures of the summer to do practices there each day, for several weeks. Saadia also reported on his return from the tomb of Khwaja Mu'in al-Din Chishti having received a robe and blessing from the Saint in vision, only to go to a *khanqah* in the wilderness at Salarwala where he received a robe in the flesh.

Murshid Sam continued to train Saadia and wrote exhaustively to her over the years, letters steeped with classical Sufi teachings interpreted always in the light of universality. At the time of the reminiscences quoted here, Saadia was serving as a senior fellow representing Islam at the Harvard University Center for the Study of World Religions. She received her Ph.D. from Cornell University, contriving to come to this country to spend a little more time with her Murshid during his lifetime. Her article "Female Spirituality in Islam" is published in the book *Islamic Spirituality*.[9]

Throughout his career Murshid Samuel Lewis tirelessly pursued the goals he understood to be part of the Brotherhood work. These included efforts to use spiritual knowledge as a means of working towards world peace. He was uniquely gifted in being able not only to pray and worship with all people and be accepted by them on their terms, but even to be seen as a teacher and inspirational figure within many spiritual traditions. His wide knowledge of the philosophies and cultures of different peoples allowed him to show the intrinsic similarities. His practical focus and scientific orientation gave him a vast and fruitful arena in the efforts to solve world food problems. In this area he was primarily

---

[9] Seyyed Hossein Nasr, ed., *Islamic Spirituality I* (New York: Crossroad, 1987).

serving as a Mercury-like figure bringing information from universities to other scientists in other countries. It is impossible for the ordinary person to conceive of the sheer volume of his worldwide correspondence. For most of his life his efforts seemed to fall mostly on deaf ears but this never seemed to slow him down.

A significant portion of his prolific writing was in free verse. He portrayed in poetry the truths of all religions and all prophets, including Jesus Christ, Shiva, Krishna, Buddha and many others. His treatment of Islam in the poem "Saladin" features a whole book said by him to have come directly from *fana fi rasul* in the prophet Muhammad. This poem was later published along with poems honoring the Jewish and Christian traditions in a volume called, *The Jerusalem Trilogy*.[10] Peace in the Middle East had been an inspiration in meditation for him. He worked to combine knowledge of desert reclamation—"Sooner or later the Arabs and Israelis are going to have to drink from the same well"—with respect for the sacred places and practices of all the religions. He sponsored cross-cultural gatherings—"Eat, Dance, and Pray Together"—in which participants, through spiritual practice, experienced the depth of the one God from Whom all their various traditions arose.

It is truly difficult to describe the full scope of all his efforts. He worked so hard in so many areas with little or no response that he was amazed in the mid-1960s when he began to meet acceptance where he had previously met rejection. More and more opportunities existed, any one of which he would have gladly devoted considerable energy to in previous years. In his diaries from this period he describes his experience:

> I feel like a gardener who planted a bunch of seeds and nothing came up; and again the next year and nothing came up, and again the next year more seeds with same result and so on and on and on. And then this year he planted a bunch of seeds not only did they all come up but all the seeds from the previous year came up and all the seeds from the year before and so on. So I've just been frantically running around trying to harvest all the plants until

---

[10] Samuel L. Lewis, *The Jerusalem Trilogy: Song of the Prophets* (Novato: Prophecy Pressworks, 1975).

> Allah came to me and said, “Don’t worry, harvest what you can and leave the rest to Me.”

Just as the seed his teacher Inayat Khan had sowed in him had brought such a return beyond measure, Murshid Samuel Lewis felt confident in those with whom he had left his blessings. His advice to people in the 60s trying to sort out the claims of different teachers was to ignore the rhetoric and to look instead at their disciples.

Let’s go back to the beginning of this period. On many occasions he described a crucial moment. It occurred after a heart attack in 1967. In a letter to Pir Dewwal Shereef dated 17 June 1970 he wrote:

> One was flat on his back in the hospital. The Voice of Allah appeared and said, “I make you Spiritual Teacher of the hippies.” One may surrender to Allah willingly or unwillingly or one may refuse to surrender to Allah but when one is flat on one’s back one has not even a choice. This was followed immediately by a series of visions. Every one of those visions has now come into outward manifestation. ... Now this is in harmony with the predictions or commissions of several Pirs and holy men that one was to get fifty thousand Americans to say and repeat “Allah” and believe in Him. This of itself looked immense, and when one considers in the past that this person was a recluse and an outcast, it looked even more ridiculous but so did the outlook no doubt of Siddiq when he was in The Cave with the Blessed Messenger.

Immediately following this experience in the hospital, Murshid Sam began attracting students and disciples in increasing numbers. From three disciples, in stages, he went up to a hundred. All of a sudden he was accepted on a wide scale as a spiritual teacher. This latter commission of getting fifty thousand Americans to recite the name of “Allah” was easily fulfilled in his lifetime through the Dervish Dances, which he began and which he expanded into the Dances of Universal Peace. They incorporated sacred phrases and movements from many of the world’s religions and spiritual traditions.

This period after he was released from the hospital began a process of acceptance among the young people who were flocking to San Francisco as “flower children” during what became called the psychedelic revolution. The writer’s own experience is illustrative of the time. In June of 1968 I was led to his door. I had previously completed a Ph.D. program at Vanderbilt University in philosophy and theology, with the exception of writing a dissertation. I became derailed by experiences on LSD of an extraordinary intensity. I dropped out of the program, but not before getting a dissertation topic approved on the subject of Cosmic Laughter, an experience I believed I had had on acid. Since the universities seemed to be more about speculation than realization I wandered away and in the summer of 1967 ultimately landed in San Francisco.

One day in June of '68 I was wandering in Golden Gate Park high on LSD. At a certain point Krishna devotees approached me and invited me to come to a love feast at their temple on Stanyan Street. I accepted the invitation. Amidst the chanting and sweet *prasad* and music I floated in my state rather unconcerned. But I was attracted by the appearance of a young man, a street musician, with a long red beard, and decided to open a conversation with him. I said, "I'm writing my dissertation"—though of course I wasn't—"on the laughter of God, and I wonder if you could be of any help." He looked at me for a second and said, "You know, I think I do know somebody that has that quality. But I don't know if he would be interested in helping you with your dissertation. He would be more interested in your spiritual development." That sounded good to me, and he proceeded to write down the dates and times of the public meetings held by Sufi Sam Lewis. There was a meeting that very night and so I set off to his home, the Mentorgarten on Precita Avenue in the Mission district. I got lost on the way there and ended up taking a cab and arriving late to what turned out to be his Dharma night class. On the front door of his house an ink drawing of a tea cup had been stuck up with the words of Paul Reps on it, "Drinking a cup of green tea, I stopped the war." The upstairs room was filled to capacity with young radiant brightly dressed people. I sat down in the entranceway to listen. Sufi Sam shouted at me, "Don't block the doorway." Ever since then I have tried to heed this advice.

That evening, like a whole generation of psychedelic young people, I met someone who not only had the answers to my questions, his very being was the answer. He spoke with an inner knowledge and certainty that I had never encountered before and certainly not in academia. In the course of an evening he read from his poem on Sri Krishna, we chanted Ram Nam, we did meditations from the centering exercises Paul Reps includes in the back of *Zen Flesh, Zen Bones*, and Sam talked on a wide variety of subjects and told many stories. One of the stories was about when his Zen teacher Nyogen Senzaki had called him aside and said, "There are seven known forms of laughter. Come to me when no one else is around and I will show you the eighth form of laughter." Again it was clear I had come to the right place. In the course of his talk that evening, Sam railed out against the teachings of so-called experts on Oriental philosophy who had never studied under a teacher or submitted to any spiritual discipline. He also said that he needed physical help around the house and in the office. I decided to respond to this request but to keep my university background a secret. Subsequently I became his disciple and, in January of 1969, moved in with him to help him full time.

Later I was to learn of his intellectual commission to communicate the truths of mystical experience to academic philosophers and the like. Here again he was becoming pleased that a breakthrough was occurring and a new generation of scholars was beginning to arise. He said that the publication of Philip Kapleau's *The Three Pillars of Zen* marked a new age in this regard because of its objectivity and straightforwardness in speaking of actual experiences undergone during Zen training.

Let me relate another story from this period that I think may give the reader a sense of the unique atmosphere of Murshid Samuel Lewis' role as a teacher of the hippies. I was one of those present at a packed class in the front room of the Mentorgarten where Murshid Sam was giving teachings. In the middle of the class a fellow barged in from the street, very intoxicated in his ego, and in a strange voice shouted at Sam, "God has appointed me to be your spiritual teacher." Without missing a beat, Sam rose up from the chair where he was teaching and stunned the man and everyone else into silence by shouting back, "I accept!" There was a pregnant pause while he continued, "On one condition. You show me one person in this room that God has not appointed to be my spiritual teacher." The man in question sobered up and sat respectfully through the remainder of the class.

It was only a few weeks after I met Murshid Sam when he announced at one of his meetings that the son of his teacher, Inayat Khan, was coming to speak there. Shamcher Bryn Beorse, a contemporary of Murshid and a mureed of Hazrat Inayat Khan, had encouraged this meeting between Pir Vilayat Khan and Murshid Samuel Lewis. He felt that if they met they would be able to find a harmonious relationship, and this proved to be true. Samuel Lewis was later to say that he had only a breath in which to decide whether he would accept Vilayat or not, "And you know why I accepted him? Because I am a romantic."

As someone who was present that evening I recall the young Pir Vilayat wrapped in a heavy wool robe, sweating intensely in the packed room at the Mentorgarten and speaking with great reverence of the dervish, and of the dervish dance, that he had witnessed in Turkey. At the end of his talk someone asked, "Where would one go to actually meet a dervish?" He gestured at Samuel Lewis and said, "You have one right here." This was the kind of acceptance that Samuel had sought. They were later to cooperate in spreading the Sufi teachings. He introduced Vilayat to a whole generation of young people who began to fill up his camps and seminars. Pir Vilayat acknowledged him as a Murshid and as the senior functioning mureed of Hazrat Inayat Khan in America. However, Murshid Sam also insisted on initiating Sheikhs and Khalifs and appointing his own spiritual successor, and thus his line remains a parallel one to this day.

The person Murshid Samuel Lewis appointed as his spiritual successor was his Khalif, Moineddin Jablonski, who from the time of Murshid Sam's passing on 15 January 1971 until his own passing on 27 February 2001 directed the activities of what became known as The Sufi Islamia Ruhaniat Society.[11] During those intervening years as the influence of Murshid Sam's disciples and their disciples spread throughout the world, a profound rapprochement also occurred with Pir Hidayat Khan of the Sufi Movement. And at the

---

[11] The Articles of Incorporation, Bylaws, and Esoteric Rules of the Sufi Islamia Ruhaniat Society were published in *Bismillah* 3, no. 1 (December 1977): 82–94. *Ed.*

time of writing there is more organizational harmony than ever before. Shabda Kahn was named by Pir Moineddin as his successor.

But to return to that seminal meeting with Pir Vilayat Khan at the Mentorgarten, Samuel Lewis was to say that this was the starting point for the Dances of Universal Peace because he had experienced, amidst the Sufi *tariqas* of the Chishtis, Bektashis, Rifa'is and many others, just those states that Pir Vilayat had referred to in his talk. He began having dreams, and the first Dances were born, using the *bismillah* and the *zikr* and certain *wazifas*. I remember the first gatherings where the Dances were done. They occurred in the garage of the Mentorgarten with about twenty people present, but they caught the hearts of people immediately. They were part of his program for the hippies: "joy without drugs." Even then he knew they would become a spiritual phenomenon and spread throughout the world because he was confident that this form, which expressed in action the ideal of celebrating the divine presence in many names and forms, had not come from his own ego.

In a letter to his goddaughter in Pakistan he described this work:

> The next thing is the Dervish dancing. No doubt some of the "muslims" one meets look down on it. They're stuck with words and rituals. Allah is far away. Islam means surrender to Allah. … So we do the dancing and repeat the zikr. Then we use the Sifat-i-Allah, and then we bring in the psychic science by putting the arms in accord with the attribute involved. And yesterday we introduced the Saluk, the Moral Science by deep meditation on the quality involved so we could become vehicles of the Sifat-i-Allah, each one of us. So let people criticize if they will. … My own work especially with wazifas and their repetitions in the dance is on the Glories of Allah not the shortcomings of mankind. Hazrat Inayat Khan also left the keys to the Psychic Sciences. We use the glorious names, their import, their magnetism (baraka) and also now ingest them into human consciousness so the perfections of Allah can be part of human nature.

Along with the Dances, which quickly developed in an ever-broadening way, came the work with the Walks. It was an inspiration which Murshid Samuel Lewis had put into practice even before the first Dances. This use of walk involved what he called third and fourth dimensional manifestation of the Gathas and Githas of Hazrat Inayat Khan. Training in the Walks involved training in breath, rhythm, centering, etc. Years before, he had gone to the American dance pioneer Ruth St. Denis and told her that he was going to start a revolution. When she asked how he said, "I'm going to teach young people how to walk." Miss Ruth jumped up from her chair and shouted, "You've got it!" In this realm as in so many others it was his genius for bringing abstract truths into expression and manifestation that brought success. He credited Ruth St. Denis with the faculty of drawing dances right out of the sphere itself (the ether), and he said that he learned this faculty from her. When he was at the tomb of Salim Chishti at Fatehpur Sikri, the city preserved to chronicle the expression of universal religion at the time of the Emperor Akbar, Murshid Samuel Lewis reported that he was able to draw the Dance of Universal Peace from the atmosphere and perform it.[12]

Murshid Moineddin Jablonski reported "the first Dances were sparked by a living concentration on the prophets, in a practice of *darshan*, which combined Murshid Sam's experience of the Sufi *tawajjuh* (giving blessing through the glance) with *tassawur* (attunement to a teacher)."

Today the Walks and Dances are done all over the world. Murshid Sam's original forty Dances or so have expanded to a repertoire of more than four hundred, and seem destined to become a part of the enduring spiritual landscape of our planet. In 1982, the International Network for the Dances of Universal Peace was organized to further the outreach and application of the Dances and Walks in popular culture. As such, the Dance Network is part of the Sister/Brotherhood work originally envisioned by Pir-o-Murshid Inayat Khan. Saadi Neil Douglas Klotz, a disciple of Murshid Moineddin, was one of those instrumental in this worldwide acceptance of the Dances. Saadi was also able to harvest another seed of Murshid Sam's. Beginning in the mid-1980s a cycle of Dances using the Lord's Prayer and the

---

[12] The Persian phrase *sulh-i kull*, which was the slogan of Akbar's social and religious program, translates as "universal peace." On *sulh-i kull*, see K.A. Nizami, *Akbar and Religion* (Delhi: Idarah-i-Adabiyyat-i-Delli, 1989), 19, 216, 230, 287–88. *Ed.*

Beatitudes of Jesus in Aramaic was inaugurated and its influence has spread as well.

Murshid Sam compared his position to that of Khwaja Mu'in al-Din Chishti in that music and the arts would become vehicles for the transmission of the divine message. We can also witness the growth of the music as a phenomenon that both accompanied the Dances and went on to bring joy in a wider arena. This work became particularly known through the mantric music of the Sufi choir under the direction of Allaudin Mathieu, Murshid Samuel Lewis' mureed. Allaudin who was to compose much of this music recalls it this way:

> For me the story begins in 1969 with a dramatic moment: Murshid [Sam] had devised a way of leading a *zikr* wherein different parts of the chant were polyphonically placed against one another. The music wasn't terribly complicated but the idea was new and sophisticated. Shrewdly, he asked me to lead it one day and encouraged me to be creative. It was as if Inayat Khan through the transmission of Sam Lewis had granted me permission to combine diverse sacred phrases and texts into a new music of phrase. Later we devised the technique of using several attuned musicians as leaders instead of only one. ... What eventually resulted (by the '90s) was an eclectic, powerful and deeply prayerful practice of layered contrapuntal *zikrs*. ...

The Sufi choir would perform far and wide at such venues as Winterland (with the Grateful Dead), Herbst Theatre (with Terry Riley), Masonic Auditorium (with Paul Horn), the Cathedral of Saint John the Divine (as part of the Cosmic Mass), and for such occasions as newly elected Governor Jerry Brown's Prayer Breakfast. The great interpretive dancer Zuleikha began her work as a teenager dancing at choir performances. Early choir pieces also featured chorales using the Sufi poetry of Murshid Sam ("Crescent and Heart"), Kabir, Rumi and others. Allaudin went on to write several books on music including the widely used pedagogical text *The Listening Book.*

Allaudin was asked to assess Hazrat Inayat Khan's influence on music in the West:

> Historically, since the beginning of the industrial revolution, the mind of Western music has become increasingly disjoined from its heart, its spiritual center. Romantic music was emotion-laden

> but not spiritually centered; late romantic music often celebrated the grotesque—a premonition of the gradual revealing of the unconscious mind. As the impressionists yielded to the atonalists, the bridge between zealous intellect and spiritual center became alarming in both concept and actual sound. By the mid-twentieth century, perhaps as an anesthetic for the pain of the two World Wars, Western art music tried to find a haven in multi-dimensional schemes.
>
> During this blizzard of academic self-righteousness Inayat Khan's philosophy of music became increasingly well known, presenting musicians of the Western World with a language and a regimen for the reconnection of their heads to their hearts. Throughout the globe, Volume II (*The Mysticism of Sound and Music*) has become, in fact, a kind of musician's bible. ... Inayat Khan was a high musician and he thought musically. His effect on musicians has been so pronounced, not so much because his music was heard by us, but because his syntax proceeded and connected, bobbed and weaved like music. We have a special resonance with him because his thought went like music goes. By reminding us in myriad ways that music is the face of the beloved, he led us from seeming perdition back to our own hearts.
>
> In the present generation there has been a terrific swing in the art music of the west away from mind trips and narrow, doctrinaire scholasticism toward conscious spiritual reawakening and eclectic seeking, all-inclusive, open-minded and open-ended, toward a unity of musical ideals. Was all this due to Inayat Khan? No. Was it to a substantial degree? Well, waves make waves; Inayat Khan's influence among twentieth century composers and performers is subtle and diffuse—transformed, as a measure of its efficacy, entirely into music itself, and on into pure spirit. But I would say also that the influence of Inayat Khan on the musical atmosphere of the West has been pervasive. And since his name is not so well recognized as the resuscitating atmosphere he has nourished, he has become, to borrow words from his own prayer, a master both known and unknown to the world.

Another part of the music story deserves to be mentioned. Several years after Murshid Samuel Lewis' passing a few of his disciples were inspired to follow in Hazrat Inayat Khan's footsteps and go in search of a teacher on the path of classical Indian music. The search led them to the North Indian vocalist

Pandit Pran Nath, who like Hazrat Inayat Khan, devoted himself to music as a path and was sent to the West to carry the lineage of love, harmony, and beauty through music. In 1980, Pran Nath authorized Shabda Kahn, a mureed of Murshid Sam, to start teaching raga under the name "Chishti-Sabiri School of Music." One of the activities of this school has been an annual pilgrimage to India for music intensives. During one of these journeys the sacred musical journey begun by Inayat completed a full circle when Terry Riley and Shabda Kahn gave a concert at the *'urs* of Hazrat Inayat Khan and later at the Music Department of Delhi University.

It is impossible to properly catalog all of the work done carrying on Murshid Samuel Lewis' transmissions by his students. And I offer my sincere apologies to those who no doubt should have been given mention in a properly full account. Saul Barodofsky received his commentaries on Inayat Khan's Healing Service and re-instituted this activity on a large scale. This work has included healing rituals for the planet at sites of great suffering such as the concentration camp at Bergen Belsen and elsewhere. Work in ecology, organic gardening, the development of spiritual communities should also be mentioned, as well as other concentrations, but one begins to run out of space, and one trusts that the phenomenon of an ever spreading legacy of blessings has been sufficiently documented.

In 1970, Murshid Sam attended the conference of The Temple of Understanding in Geneva. As a lifelong student of comparative religion and as a mystic who was well aware of his own teacher's goal of a temple for all religions, he supported this work and dedicated the Dances of Universal Peace to this end. Like so many things for which he had strived for so many years he saw success here as well. He wrote about the conference in Geneva in April of 1970:

> It was the top intellectuals themselves who labored to see that love and devotion, not exhortation and emotion dominated. And it was so. The dominant figure was our very good friend, Swami Ranganathananda of the Ramakrishna Mission. Sam has always

> called him the Vivekananda of the age. He has immersed his whole life in Vivekananda, but now he has functioned as Vivekananda. He was probably without peer. He was so recognized chiefly by Dr. Seyyed Hossein Nasr of Tehran, Iran who represented spiritual Islam (and so Sufism). When the supreme personalities of different religions meet in amity and devotion a certain goal has been reached. ...
>
> I put on a little show that I was an incarnation of Lessing's fictional character 'Nathan the Wise'. Nathan the Wise was a grand hero during the rise of Hitlerism but today nobody refers to him. I've written three epic poems, the themes of which are respectively the Jewish, Christian and Islamic divine aspects of Palestine. They were shunned by the different religionists, but recently have evoked such wonderful response that I can see that today there are persons and forces who are really concerned with peace.

Murshid Samuel Lewis had the words from the *hadith* of the Prophet Muhammad inscribed on his gravestone at Lama Foundation, the universal community in the mountains near Taos, New Mexico where he was invited to teach a number of times at the end of his life. Thousands of visitors have come to his *maqbara* there. These words expressed his personal happiness at the fulfilment of his work as a Westerner who had fully received the blessing of God and lived to see a vision of these blessings dawning in the land of his birth. "On that day the sun shall rise in the West and all people seeing will believe."

Ultimately, any account of the influences of an illuminated being becomes completely interwoven with the fullness of life itself. Perhaps that is why the Zen teacher Nyogen Senzaki asked his students to reflect on the being of Inayat Khan by considering the beautiful shrubbery outside his *zendo*. As Samuel Lewis wrote in October of 1967:

> It is a mistake to assume there is any "teacher." The teacher is the positive pole of the cell and as the pupil or pupils—the negative pole—show more aptitude, the electromagnetic field of the cell increases and knowledge comes through the teacher which would have otherwise been impossible. ... In the real samadhi, one has not only union-with-God but with all humanity; when one is helping others he is helping himself and when one is really helping himself he is helping others. ... The

Sufi not only prays to God, he represents God. By this I mean that he not only asks for Love and Wisdom and Joy and Peace, he does everything possible to awaken Love and Light and Wisdom and Joy and Peace in others. … The essential of all knowledge, wisdom and morality is God. As Inayat Khan said, God is the only teacher.

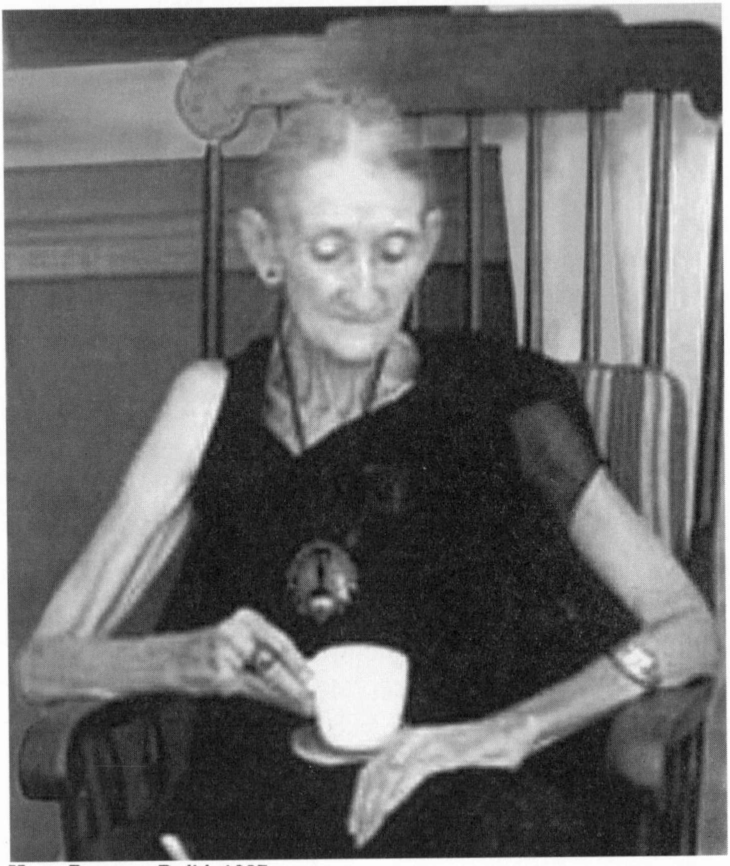

Hayat Bouman, Delhi, 1987

Chishti Reminiscence

PETER LAMBORN WILSON

In the early 1960s there existed a paradise on Earth in New York City, around Union Square (which still had a "Speakers Corner" in those days) and surrounding blocks of Broadway and Fourth Avenue. It was the used book district: sixteen or seventeen huge bookstores, many of them much bigger than the only modern survivor of that era, the Strand, which now (1999) boasts of being "the biggest used bookshop in the world."

Among those heavenly precincts one establishment stood out as particularly celestial: Samuel Weiser's, four storeys of used books, plus the Basement, which was New York's best source for occultism and oriental religions.[1] The late Harry Smith, American surrealist filmmaker and occultist, had a theory that used books migrate according to mysterious patterns and waves, and that at certain periods of history they all pass through certain geographical areas. Well, in the 60s they were all passing through New York, and Weiser's Basement was the very eye of the pattern. Brokenback couches and hotel-style ashtrays were scattered through the stacks, and if the family recognized you as a regular you could sit and read for hours undisturbed.

I had just been turned on to Sufism by a friend, 350-lb. White jazz musician and poet Warren Tartaglia, or Walid al-Taha, who also inducted me into the Moorish Orthodox Church,[2] who later died of an overdose at age twenty-one. He gave me Ghazali's *Confessions* and a book on the Assassins and I was swept away.

---

[1] There were others, especially Orientalia, and Mason's Astrological Books (on the Upper East Side). Weiser's still survives but has long since abandoned the City for rural Maine.

[2] Founded in 1957 in Baltimore by adherents of the Moorish Science Temple, the first "Black Islamic" sect in America, which in turn had been founded in Newark in 1913 by Noble Drew Ali (Timothy Drew), a son of ex-slaves, murdered by Chicago police in 1929. See my *Sacred Drift* (San Francisco: City Lights, 1993), chapter 1.

My friends and I wondered if this marvelous thing called Sufism had died out in the long-ago or if it still existed in the modern world. The early 60s was a period of (re)discoveries: a generation of Americans reared on the educational pabulum and early-TV pap of the 1950s, suddenly confronted with (for example) Gordon Wasson's 1959 *Life Magazine* article on magic mushrooms in Mexico—or Zen, or Ceremonial Magick, or Dada—or Sufism. What did it all mean? Surely the answers lay hidden somewhere in Weiser's Basement.

In our ignorance we failed to locate any living Sufi authors; not that there *were* many. Not even Idries Shah had yet appeared. But at least we discovered one recently-deceased Sufi, beautifully bearded author of many orange books, Hazrat Inayat Khan. We were enchanted, especially by his treatise on music. We adopted him as a spiritual hero of the Moorish Orthodox Church, and began to use his symbol—winged heart with star and crescent—as our own device or Lodge seal and banner. We wrote to Geneva, to the publisher of the orange books, but (as I recall) all we got back was a book-list; —no mysterious beckonings eastward, no faint whiff of distant roses. Anyway, other more pressing events were demanding our attention. Our yogi friend Bill Haines had suddenly moved his Sri Ram Ashram from Monroe to Millbrook, and become part of the greatest of all scenes, Tim Leary's unbelievable LSD "commune" on the estate of millionaire Billy Hitchcock.[3]

Nowadays they say that "anyone who claims to remember the Sixties *wasn't there*"—so perhaps it would serve to protect my *bona fides* if I gently skipped over the next few years. In any case, it wasn't till 1968 that the question of "living Sufism" became urgent for me again. For the previous few years I had become very political—refused to go to Vietnam, served as a Conscientious Objector (1966–68), and got involved in several conspiracies for peace. But then in May and June of '68 the Revolution happened ... and failed. I left my C.O. hospital job the day of Martin Luther King's funeral. America was finished and I was planning to exile myself from it permanently. While I was at it, I would go on a mission for the Moors, to send back reports about whether Sufism

---

[3] The best memoirs of this period are *Millbrook* by Art Krebs, Chief BooHoo of the Neo-American Church, and Leary's own *Flashbacks*.

still existed or not. I raised some extremely dubious money and flew to Lebanon. Didn't come back for twelve years.[4]

"Once Sufism was a reality without a name; now, it is a name without a reality"—or so said some Sufi long ago. In India one could scarcely help noticing real dervishes, authentic in appearance as one could wish, like illustrations from old books, complete with patched cloaks, begging bowls, tangled locks, blithe spirits, and fuming *chillams* of ganja. What was not clear to me, however, was whether these seeming survivors of vanished times could be considered anything more than colorful beggars. To be sure, India had more than its share of beggars, including religious beggars—Hindu *saddhus* in the millions—an embarrassment of choice! Moreover there was a language problem. Although nearly everyone seemed to speak a few words of English, the dervishes generally had no "Western" education and often proved an exception to this rule. And everywhere I went people spoke yet another new language; —the Indian one rupee note had "One Rupee" printed in fifteen different alphabets! The Sufi question got lost in a sea of incredible distractions, ranging from exquisite unheard-of sensations to agonies of "Delhi belly" and culture shock. In Benares I fell under the spell of Shiva and Shakti and the cult of Tantra, and began a pilgrimage devoted to this new fascination that took me to Darjeeling, where I met my Tantrik *gurus* Ganesh Baba, elephantine *saddhu* and champion of the *chillam*, and Mr. K. Biswas, mild-mannered government clerk and former member of the Bengali Terrorist Party. I went to Kamkhya in Assam (without a travel permit) for the great sacrificial festival of the sacred *yoni*: hundreds of naked *saddhus* ecstatic on tiger skins, thousands of sacrificed goats, the gutters foaming with blood.

After about six densely packed months of adventures and diseases I was "resting" in Kathmandu (old India hands will know what I mean by this) during the monsoon season of 1969, when I

---

4 I did return briefly in 1975 at the invitation of British Theater director Peter Brook. When that gig was over I quickly became disgusted by the USA again (New York City had just declared bankruptcy!) and fled for another five years.

met a friendly American musician, on vacation from his *tabla* lessons in Benares, who seemed to know something about Sufism. His conversation inspired me to renew the neglected quest. I can't remember his name I'm sorry to say. I wish I'd kept a diary—but then I would've lost it somewhere (probably when I left Tehran just before the Revolution in 1979). All this was so long ago.

I made my way back to Delhi; it took a long time; more adventures and disease. It was spring when I arrived: all the old ruins were writhing with flowers: I began to have dreams about an earlier incarnation as an impoverished Mughal nobleman with a taste for classical music (probably based on Satyajit Ray's masterpiece *The Music Room*[5]). My spirits revived and I set out to find the Sufi whose address I'd been given in Kathmandu. I took a rickshaw-cum-scooter to the tomb of Gandhi in New Delhi and found the nearby garden-villa of Raihana Tayabji.

She was an elderly woman, of noble Muslim Rajasthani descent I believe, who had been a close disciple of Gandhi and now maintained some sort of cult about the tomb. She had visions of Krishna, and had written a little book about them called *The Heart of a Gopi*.[6] This kind of syncretism is common enough in India—but I never met a more exalted example of it than Raihana Behin. Although her English was perfect she seemed more like a character from my Mughal dream than anyone I'd met so far;—perhaps a very intellectual mystical princess at the court of Akbar or Bahadur Shah. She was extremely gracious. After a cup of tea she told me, "If you're interested in Sufism, you have a rare opportunity. You mentioned Hazrat Inayat Khan. His son, Pir Vilayat, is in Delhi, staying at Nizamuddin. You should meet him." What an amazing coincidence! (Later I learned that "amazing coincidences" are merely par for the course in these matters.) Early the next day I took a "taxi" (a Harley-Davidson three-wheeler with four tiny seats behind and one burly Sikh before) and headed for the suburb/necropolis

---

[5] I later met Ray at a film festival in Tehran, where I had the pleasure of introducing him to local Sufis. Everyone loved him; I suspect he may have been some sort of saint.

[6] At least I think that was the title. I lost it of course. A *gopi* is a woman who enjoys the love of Krishna, a "cowherd maiden."

where one of the great Shaykhs of the Chishtiyya—Nizam al-Din Awliya'—still rules like a living presence.

Over the years I went back to Nizamuddin many times; I don't remember what I saw of it that first visit. The old section consists of a living village squeezed in amongst a most beautiful chaos of tombs, mosques, tanks, shrines, khanqahs, kitchens, flower-sellers and picturesque dervishes on pilgrimage or in residence at the great saint's mausoleum. The new section has western-style villas and bungalows and gardens in a steamy riot of tropical blooms, sleepy avenues of former colonial suburban decency. Here I found the house of Hayat Bouman, an old Dutch lady who had been a disciple of Hazrat Inayat Khan, had settled near his tomb, and who became one of my best friends in India: —a bit of a fussbudget, a fanatic for anything mystical, a loving heart. And here was Pir Vilayat: — gorgeously dressed in Moroccan robes, trying to look less young and handsome but not succeeding, and charismatic as the dickens.

The first thing they noticed was my lapel pin. One of the New York Moors, a jeweler, had made silver flying hearts for all of us, and I was wearing mine. I explained our devotion to Hazrat Inayat Khan and of course they were pleased; Pir Vilayat gave retroactive permission for our appropriation.[7] After tea we set out to make a *ziyarat* to the tomb of Hazrat himself, in a small enclosure, lost in a tiny back lane outside the village. I remarked on the fact that no one was there—a rare occurrence in India!—and that the gate was locked. Pir Vilayat explained his reason for being in Delhi. After Hazrat's death his followers had split in two factions, the Sufi Movement and the Sufi Order. One was headed by Pir Vilayat and the other by his nephew Fazal Inayat Khan, whose group published the orange books. These schisms in Sufism are so common as to be unremarkable, and sad to say they are never peaceful. In this case Fazal was suing Pir Vilayat for control of the Founder's Tomb. When the two happened to meet at the gravesite the quarrel had almost descended to scandalous blows. While the suit was in process the enclosure was locked; if I hadn't been with Pir Vilayat I

---

[7] Oddly, another branch of our movement, the Noble Order of Moorish Sufis in Baltimore, unknown to us at the time, had also applied for and received permission to use the flying heart from a representative of Fazal Inayat Khan—of whom more anon.

would never have succeeded in paying my respects and laying blossoms on the tomb. (I don't remember ever hearing the result of this case; I seem to recall the place stayed locked up and I never saw it again on any subsequent visit.)

After several long friendly and interesting talks Pir Vilayat and I agreed mutually that we were not cut out for each other as *murshid* and *murid*. He seemed to feel I should pursue my search in Iran, where he had recently made several Sufi acquaintances, and he gladly gave me their addresses. In India, he said (and I later found this to be true for the most part) Sufism has declined into a family business. The Shaykhs are often no more than those who "sit on the prayer-carpet" (*sajjada-nishin*) of the departed grandfather saint. In Iran, however, succession only remains in a family if the family provides new saints—otherwise new blood is introduced. Pir Vilayat believed I was an intellectual and that the "bhaktic" Sufism of India wouldn't suit me. We parted friends; he flew off on his global rounds, and we never met again.

I followed Pir Vilayat's advice, and those addresses he gave me ended by keeping me occupied for another seven years. But this is not the story of my life, I'm relieved to say, and I need not pursue my career in Iran except to add that while I lived there I re-visited India countless times and that most of those visits involved the Chishti Order in some way.

The first trip from India to Iran took maybe another year. I lingered along the way for all the usual reasons: another New York Moor, Bro. James Irsay, flew out to join me and we went to Rishikesh to live in a yogi's cave; to an elephant sanctuary; back to Benares, where we met the Aghoris or cannibal *saddhus* and slept in their garden.[8] We overstayed our visas and got in trouble; finally made it to Pakistan and the City of Saints, Lahore. There I decided to find a bookseller/publisher with whose books I had become very familiar, even back in Weiser's Basement: Shaikh Mohammed Ashraf.

[8] See Robert Svoboda, *Aghora: At the Left Hand of God* (Albuquerque, NM: Brotherhood of Life, 1986), the best and most authentic book on modern Tantra I've ever read.

The bookshop was in a very old section of the walled city near the Golden Mosque. As soon as I inquired about Sufism the super-polite clerks in their crisp white pajamas whisked me upstairs to the Presence. There, seated at an ancient roll-top desk under the slow propeller of a ceiling fan, sat a tall neat cadaverous old gentleman with a distinct resemblance to Boris Karloff as Ardis Bey in the original "Mummy"—fez and all. But the Shaykh was graciousness itself. At his gentle command the crisp disciples plied me with tea and biscuits, and soon a heap of cheap badly-printed books on Sufism (including several Chishti subjects) piled up before me. As he was the only person I'd ever seen in the Subcontinent wearing an Ottoman fez, I made bold to inquire. I learned for the first time of the Caliphate Movement, in which many Indian Hanafis took part, to restore the Ottoman Caliph as ceremonial head of a pan-Islamic revival. The cause had long since vanished into history, but the Shaykh kept it alive on his head. After a long delightful afternoon the Shaykh gave me the heap of books at a ruinously generous discount (I lost them all when I left Iran), and I went my way.

More adventures and diseases. Finally I made it to Tehran, where I actually got a job. I was art critic for the *Tehran Journal*; I was studying Sufism and working on my first book (*Kings of Love*, a collaboration with N. Pourjavady, a "poetic history" of the Ni'mat Allahi Order); but I could not get a residence permit for Iran. Every three months I had to leave the country and apply for a new visa. As often as finance permitted I would extend these trips all the way back to India, and stay with Hayat Bouman. My partners in these trips included at various times the Hon. James George, genial gurdjieffian Canadian Ambassador to the Imperial Court of Persia, who had a Range Rover and no noticeable official duties; Mitchell Crites, a descendant of Jesse James, archeologist and art historian, who lived in one tiny room next to the very *dargah* of Nizam al-Din Awliya'; Terry Graham, Vietnam vet and convert to Shi'ism, a fellow reporter on *The Journal*. I think of these visits to India as Chishti trips, if only because so many of them began or ended at Nizamuddin. But on several occasions I made deliberate expeditions to Chishti shrines and festivals, as I had a great thirst for Chishti music and the rose-scented devotionalism of the Order's milieu—if only as a counterbalance to the more austere and *'irfani* ("gnostic") brand of Sufism I was experiencing in Iran.

According to some Sufis, visiting the tombs of the saints is not merely a devotional practice. Initiatic dreams can be "incubated" at such shrines; non-ordinary events, psychic unveilings and "coincidences" are easier to access there. Moreover, each of the really major shrines has its own distinct personality or flavor, which is taken to reflect the special presence of the saint.

At Madhu Lal Husayn in Lahore, for example, the twin tomb of an antinomian dervish and his lover, a beautiful Hindu youth, the atmosphere is ecstatic and intoxicated, and the entertainments none too orthodox. At Nizam al-Din Awliya' there is a more sober air, dignified and rather aristocratic, but suffused with music and love. Mu'in al-Din Chishti in Ajmer is royal, rich and hieratic; a visit to the solid silver catafalque is said to equal one-seventh of a *hajj* to Mecca. In India the proper time to visit the tomb is the *'urs*, the "wedding day," that is, the death-day anniversary of the saint. Huge amounts of food are given away, *qawwali* music is played, *baraka* is guaranteed. Whenever possible I would attend an *'urs*, but one way or another I eventually visited most of the major Chishti shrines in northern India. I used to write up these trips for the *Tehran Journal*, which had such an insatiable need for copy it would print anything I produced. Naturally I lost all the files in 1979. I'll have to reconstruct some of the highlights from memory. I could go to the library and then pretend to remember all sorts of things I never even noticed at the time. I used to be arrogant enough to believe that if anything were important I would certainly remember it. Actually the few shards that survive seem quite precious compared to the distressing gaps that surround them.

Before Independence in 1947 some of the major shrines like Ajmer used to provide *qawwali* music every day. When India and Pakistan split the musicians were stuck or had to choose between them; as a result there were fewer gigs for everyone, and the circuit declined. *Qawwali* music had already suffered artistically when the squeezebox harmonium replaced the much more subtle stringed *sarangi* sometime around the turn of the century. The present ensemble (usually a family group) consists of a lead singer, two or three back-up singers and drums. All the songs are religious, although the effect is very different than that of, say, the Protestant Hymnal. Poems in honor of the buried saint, the Prophet, famous Sufis and the like are interspersed with classical mystical love poems, usually in Urdu. The singers face the tomb; the lead singer addresses the saints as if present and alive, gesturing with his hand as if imploring or praising a king. The master of the art was Nusrat Fateh Ali Khan, a mountainous babyfaced genius who combined the *qawwal's* emotional delivery with superb classical training. I saw him perform at the *'urs* of Data Ganj Bakhsh in Lahore in (I think) 1976, before he became famous in the West. Terry and I, as the only Euro's present in a vast sea of locals, were swept graciously on a wave of people up to the front row, where we watched Nusrat up close, shining and gesticulating like a delicate dancer with fat butterfly fingers as he threw the crowd into literal transports of ecstasy (men flipping into *hal*, leaping up and twirling in their seats like kites in an updraft); a steady stream of enthusiasts rushed forward and half buried the musicians in rupee notes. (Nusrat had an interesting career after that. He went West, added some horrid electric guitars to the group, and played in concert halls where guards were hired to throw out anyone who slipped into *hal*. At last he was persuaded to return to his earlier purer style, but shortly thereafter died of a heart attack.)

The Chishti Order rather specializes in *qawwali* music and always has. Supposedly the early Chishti masters "allowed" music in order to convert the music-loving Hindus to Sufism—but the truth is that most pre-modern orders indulged in the *sama'* or "spiritual audition." Hyper-Islamic reform in the nineteenth century and modernism in the twentieth have badly eroded the role of the arts in Sufism. In the days of Nizam al-Din Awliya' the dervishes organized musical and poetical soirees, whirled in their long-sleeved gowns, and sometimes invited handsome youths to attend. In more heterodox orders hashish or even wine might be consumed, but on such matters the Chishtiyya are quite strict. In modern times the gatherings have been opened to the public and become more like concerts, and I believe the music must have changed as well. At some point *qawwali* must have been more like Persian music: more sedate, slower, not so insistently rhythmic. Probably the Persian "high" tradition brought to India by the early Chishtiyya melded with Indian folk music and has been changing gradually ever since. The latest developments—the squeezebox and electronic amplification—can only be viewed as degradations, although the result still has plenty of vitality and genuine popularity.

Music and poetry seem to play an even more important role in Chishti Sufism than in other orders. Not that anything extra-canonical or "non-Islamic" has been added[9]—but a certain distinct flavor or "taste" is discernable. *Dhawq*, "taste" in Arabic (*rasa* in Sanskritic languages), implies not only an aesthetic category but also an act, that of "direct tasting" or spiritual intuition. Chishti Sufism is not different from other kinds except in this subtle aestheticism, and in its great emphasis on love and devotion. On a social level the Chishti "personality" seems very close to that Mughal essence I felt so strongly in Delhi—despite the fact that everyone else felt it to be in decay or even lost beyond recall. Every time I returned there, however, I usually met some new character from my dream; usually through Hayat, but sometimes through other connections. I remember Prof. S.A. Ali of the Institute of Islamic Studies, for example, or the directors of the Hamdard Institute[10] (who served the best and most subtly-spiced Indian banquet I ever tasted); I remember the earnest young homeopathic doctor at Nizamuddin,[11] curing the poor for free (or with donations from Hayat); and the family of Tibetan Sufis who had taken refuge in the village. Somehow I associate all this sweetness and light with the Chishti "style."

The one big exception to this style amongst the early major Shaykhs of the order was a Sufi named Sabir Chishti. Although he permitted *sama'* he was apparently in other respects something of a bear, a crosspatch, and a sobersided hermit. Nevertheless I have a particular fondness for him because of his *'urs*, which was one of the most interesting Sufi occasions I ever attended.

Unlike most saints, whose tombs are near some town or village, Sabir Chishti was buried where he lived—out in the middle

[9] Islam does not "ban" music in the same way it prohibits certain kinds of imagery. The question for Islam remains the *purpose* of any art. What does it serve, and how?

[10] Practitioners of *Yunani* or Greco-Islamic medicine as handed down from Avicenna and the alchemists. They ran a free clinic in Old Delhi, and a factory, and a school as well.

[11] Dr. Mohammed Qasim. *Ed.*

of nowhere (about 50 or 100 miles north of Delhi as I recall) in a forest. No village ever grew up around the *dargah*, which I suppose reflects the rather inhospitable or somber aspect of Sabir's path: — he'd make an uncomfortable neighbor. As a result of this isolation his *'urs* fails to attract the hordes of gawking pilgrims who usually frequent such events. Instead only the truly serious attend, and the old traditions are more strictly observed. Most of the people there were practicing dervishes or devotees—including some Muslim versions of the kind of Hindu fakirs who earn a living by spectacular feats of asceticism (such as wearing chains, or lying under a 500-lb. rock). I saw a drum there like none other in India, as big as one of those Japanese monsters, played with élan by a toothless ecstatic—and of course I fell in with dervishes of the lowest sort, who were abusing the sober hospitality of Sabir by puffing away at giant *chillams*.

In India the sensation of slipping backward in time is not a rare one. At a Vedic sacrifice in Rishikesh one might have plunged back 3500 years. In hill stations like Darjeeling or Ootacamund the spectral presence of the British Raj was still palpable enough to haunt the streets in daylight. At Sabir Chishti I began to have the eerie sensation that I'd become displaced back into the very period I often dreamed about: the late Mughal era, say around 1850. Although I had a camera and there were a few lightbulbs and wristwatches to be seen, these were the only threads holding one to the twentieth century—or so it seemed.

Around sundown the main event got started—audition of *qawwalis*—when suddenly there appeared a whole regiment of Shaykhs out of nowhere to sit and listen. Never—before or since—and nowhere else—have I ever seen such people. They were dressed not at all like modern Muslims but like Sufis out of a Mughal miniature. Even the size of their turbans was unprecedented and archaic. Their beards were longer than long, their faces ecstatic but serene. After the music they filed out and I never saw them again. This sounds absurd I know. Did they change costume and mingle with the crowd? At the time I really suspected they'd vanished into the *'alam-i mithal*, the World of Imagination—or back into the mid-nineteenth century—or even earlier. I couldn't get any coherent explanation out of the stoned dervishes. I've lost all the photographs needless to say. No proof.

I never joined the Chishti Order. To tell the truth my current interests lie more with antinomian sects such as the Qalandariyya, the "free spirits" and "madmen," lawless beggars, ritual transvestites,[12] and devotees of *bhang*.[13] But I always considered that evening at Sabir Chishti as a kind of "initiation of blessing." Sufis are allowed to accept these secondary or informal initiations from any Shaykh they admire. Some Sufis, like the famous traveler Ibn Battuta, seem to have collected them like Masonic degrees.

In any case the attractiveness of the Chishti path for me has a lot to do with my strange "Mughal" dreams. If I believed in reincarnation I would say that these dreams are not "my" dreams but those of somebody else—of an other. Once or twice around Delhi I experienced strong déjà vu feelings in connection with some late Mughal ruin. I heard the sound of a *surbahar* (a bass sitar) playing a midnight monsoon *raga* on a porch overlooking a dense green garden, like the background of a Rajasthani miniature.

"I" was never there. It was the other. And the other, I believe, *was* a Chishti.

---

[12]A photo of one whirling at Madhu Lal Husayn is reproduced in my *Scandal; Essays on Islamic Heresy* (Brooklyn, NY, 1988).

[13]*Bhang* is a liquid preparation of cannabis. According to legend cannabis was "discovered" by a Khorasani Sufi, Shaykh Haydar, in the fourteenth century. But in India the dervishes learned how to make bhang from the devotees of Shiva, for whom it is quasi-sacramental. The method of preparation is exactly that described in the Rig Veda for the preparation of Soma, the sacred hallucinogen. In many a Sufi *bhang-nama* or treatise on hemp, *bhang* is praised as the "green parrot" of spiritual eloquence. (See my "Note on Hemp, Opium and Wine," in *Scandal*.)

Acknowledgements

The publisher wishes to thank each of the following for their assistance and courtesy in allowing us to reproduce images in this book.

In the color plate section following page 48: for the images of Mawlabākhsh and Hazrat Inayat Khan playing the *vīṇā*, our thanks to the Indian Petrochemicals Corporation, Baroda. We thank Mawlabākhsh House for the image of 'Ala al-Dīn Khān and Chānd Bī, and that of Allāhdād Khān and Mehr al-Nisā'. The *zanāna* photograph was taken by 'Usmān Khān in 1896, and appears courtesy of the Pir-o-Murshid Musharaff Khan Museum Foundation. Courtesy of this same Foundation are the photographs of Murtażā Khān; Murtażā Khān with his wife, Sardār Bī; Prof. Inayat Khan Rahmat Khan Pathan; and of the brothers, Maheboob, Musharaff, and Muhammad Ali Khan. The colored portrait of Hazrat Inayat Khan was painted by M.H. Thurburn in Paris, 1913. The prints of Ḥaydar 'Alī and Ṭīpū Sulṭān belong to the editor.

In the color section which follows page 304: all of the photographs are the editor's with the exception of the *dargāh* of Mu'in al-Dīn Chishtī, and the *dargāh* of Khwāja Farīd al-Dīn Mas'ūd Ganj-i Shakkar; these appear courtesy of Sultani Photographers, New Delhi.

The photograph of the Nizam of Hyderabad (Maḥbūb 'Ali Pāshā, Āṣaf Jāh IV) is reproduced courtesy of Raja Deen Dayal & Sons, Secunderabad. The painting *Shaykh Ṣan'ān and the Christian Girl* is found in S.J. Falk, *Qajar Paintings* published by Faber and Faber Ltd., London; it is attributed to Muḥammad Ḥasan, Iranian, circa 1810–1820. The line drawings of Shaykh Aḥmad Ghazālī and 'Ayn al-Qużāt Hamadānī are reprinted from *Majālis al-'ushshāq* (Lucknow: Naval Kishūr, 1293/1876). The photograph of Khwāja Ḥasan Niẓāmī appears as the frontispiece in his 1924 book *Roznāmcha*. The line drawing *Body as Instruments* is taken from Minappa Vyankappa Kelyad (a South Indian Braḥman student of Mawlabākhsh), *Ganacaryamala Mūladar*, and is provided to us thanks to Prof. R.C. Mehta. The photograph of Murshid Samuel Lewis appears courtesy of Sufi Islamia/Prophecy Pressworks, and the photograph of Hayat Bouman was taken shortly before her death in 1987 by Nur Richard Gale, and is used with his permission.

We have tried to credit and acknowledge all whose work has been included in this book. Despite our efforts, in a work of this size and complexity many persons play a role at various stages throughout the process. To all of them our sincere appreciation and gratitude. If we are notified of any omissions in credit due we will be pleased to include notice in future printings, and offer our apologies for the oversight.

Bibliography

Abdel-Kader, Ali Hassan, ed. *The Life, Personality and Writings of al-Junayd*. London: Gibb Memorial Trust, 1976.

Aflākī. *Manāqib al-'ārifīn*. Edited by Tahsin Yazici. Tehran: Dunyā-yi Kitāb, 1362/1983.

Afrāsīyābī, Ghulām-Riḍā. *Sulṭān al-'ushshāq*. Shiraz: Intishārāt-i Dānishgāh-i Shīrāz, 1372/1993.

Aḥmadpūrī, Gul Muḥammad. *Takmila-i siyar al-awliyā'*. MS K.A. Nizami.

Ahmed, Leila. *Women and Gender is Islam*. New Haven: Yale University Press, 1992.

'Alī bin Sa'd, Sayyid. *Jāmi' al-'ulūm (malfūẓāt of Sayyid Jalāl al-Dīn Ḥusayn Bukhārī, "Makhdūm-i Jahāniyān.")* Edited by Qazi Sajjad Husain. New Delhi: Indian Council of Historical Research, 1987.

Arberry, Arthur J. *The Doctrine of the Sufis*. Cambridge: Cambridge University Press, 1935.

———. *Avicenna on Theology*. London: John Murray, 1951.

———. *A Sufi Martyr: The Apologia of 'Ain al-Quḍāt al-Hamaḍhānī*. London: George Allen and Unwin, 1969.

———. *Koran Interpreted*. New York: Simon & Schuster, 1996.

'Attar, Farid al-Din. *Conference of the Birds*. Translated by Afkham Darbandi and Dick Davis. London and New York: Penguin, 1987.

———. *Tazkirat al-awliyā'*. Edited by Muḥammad Isti'lāmī. Tehran: Intishārāt-i Zavvār, 1347/1968; reprint, 1372/1993.

———. *Manṭiq al-ṭayr*. Edited by Ṣādiq Gawharīn. Tehran: BTNK, 1978.

———. *Manṭiq al-Ṭayr: Speech of the Birds*. Translated by Peter Avery. Cambridge: Islamic Texts Society, 1998.

Awrangābādī, Shāh Niẓām al-Dīn. *Niẓām al-qulūb*. Delhi: Maṭba'-i Mujtabā'ī, 1309/1891-92.

Bahādur, 'Alī Muḥammad Khān. *Khātima-yi mirāt-i Aḥmadī*. Edited by Sayyid Nawāb 'Alī. Baroda: Oriental Institute, 1930.

Baqlī, Rūzbihān. *'Abhar al-'āshiqīn*. Edited by Henry Corbin and Muḥammad Mu'īn. Tehran: Intishārāt-i Manūchihrī, 1366/1987.

Barks, Coleman, and Hazrat Inayat Khan. *The Hand of Poetry: Five Mystic Poets of Persia*. New Lebanon: Omega Publications, 1993.

Beek, Wil van. *Hazrat Inayat Khan: Master of Life, Modern Sufi Mystic*. New York: Vantage Press, 1983.

Bell, Joseph. *Love Theory in Later Hanbalite Islam*. Albany: State

University of New York Press, 1979.

Bhāṭkhaṇḍe, Viṣṇu Nārāyaṇ. *Bhāṭkhaṇḍe saṅgītśāstra Part 1*. Hathras, Saṅgīt Kārlaya 1964.

Bloch, Regina Miriam. *The Confessions of Inayat Khan*. London: The Sufi Publishing Society, 1915.

Bloch, R. Howard. *Medieval Misogyny and the Invention of Western Romantic Love*. Chicago: University of Chicago Press, 1991.

Bor, Joep, and Phillipe Brugiere. *Masters of Raga*. Berlin: Haus der Culturen der Welt, n.d.

Buehler, Arthur. *Sufi Heirs of the Prophet: The Indian Naqshbandiyya and the Rise of the Mediating Sufi Shaykh*. Columbia: University of South Carolina, 1998.

Bulāq, Sayyid Muhammad. *Rawżat-i aqṭāb*. Delhi: Maṭba'-i Muḥibb-i Hind, 1887.

Burckhardt, Carl. *Kultur der Renaissance in Italien*. Edited by Kaegi. Bern: Hallwag, n.d. [1944].

Cell, John W. *Hailey: A Study in British Imperialism (1872–1969)*. Cambridge: Cambridge University Press, 1992.

Chishtī, Allāhdiya. *Siyar al-aqṭāb*. Lucknow: Naval Kishūr, 1889.

Chishtī, Shaykh Ḥasan Muḥammad. *Majālis-i Ḥasaniyya*: Shahibagh MS.

Chishtī, Shaykh Muḥammad. "*Risāla al-tawḥīd*." In *Arba'ūn rasā'il*. MS 1480: Hazrat Pirmohammedshah Library.

Chittick, William C. *Sufi Path of Love*. Albany: State University of New York Press, 1983.

———. *The Sufi Path of Knowledge: Ibn al-'Arabī's Metaphysics of Imagination*. Albany: State University of New York Press, 1989.

Chodkiewicz, Michel. *Seal of the Saints: Prophethood and Sainthood in the Doctrine of Ibn 'Arabi*. Translated by Liadain Sherrard. Cambridge: Islamic Texts Society, 1993.

Corbin, Henry. *Creative Imagination in the Sufism of Ibn 'Arabī*. Translated by Ralph Manheim. London: Routledge and Kegan Paul, 1970.

———. *History of Islamic Philosophy*. Translated by Liadain Sherrard. London: Kegan Paul International, 1993.

———. *The Man of Light in Iranian Sufism*. Translated by Nancy Pearson. New Lebanon: Omega Publications, 1994.

Currie, Peter M. *The Shrine and Cult of Mu'in al-din Chishti of Ajmer*. Delhi: Oxford University Press, 1989.

Dabashi, Hamid. *Truth and Narrative: The Untimely Thoughts of 'Ayn al-Quḍāt Hamadānī*. Richmond, England: Curzon Press, 1999.

Day, C.R. *Music and Musical Instruments of Southern India and the*

Deccan. Delhi: Manohar, reprinted 1996.

Desai, Vibhukumar. *Uttar Hindustani-na Saṅgīt-no Itihās*. Baroda: Pustakalaya Sahayak Sahakari Mandal, 1928.

Desai, Z.A. *Malfuz Literature as a Source of Political, Social and Cultural History of Gujarat and Rajasthan*. Patna, India: Khuda Bakhsh Oriental Public Library, 1991.

Dibgy, Simon. "*Tabarrukāt* and Succession among the Great Chishtī Shaykhs." In *Delhi Through the Ages: Essays in Urban History, Culture and Society*, edited by R.E. Frykenberg. Delhi: Oxford University Press, 1986.

Dihlavī, Mīrzā Aḥmad Akhtar. *Tazkira-yi awliyā'-i Hind ū Pākistān*. Lahore: Mālik Sirāj al-Dīn and Sons, 1972.

Dihlavī, Khwāja Ḥasan, (Amīr Ḥasan Sizjī). *Fawā'id al-fū'ād: malfūẓāt-i Khwāja Niẓām al-Dīn Awliyā'*. Edited by Muḥammad Laṭīf Mulk. Tehran: Intishārāt-i Rūzāna, 1377/1997.

Eaton, Richard M. *Sufis of Bijapur 1300-1700: Social Roles of Sufis in Medieval India*. Princeton: Princeton University Press, 1978.

Eckhart, Meister. *Deutsche Predigten und Traktate*. Edited by Josef Quint. Munich: Carl Hanser Verlag, 1955.

Edwardes, Michael. *King of the World: The Life of the Last Great Moghul Emperor*. New York: Taplinger Publishing, 1971.

Eickelman, Dale F., and Jon W. Anderson. "Print, Islam, and the Prospects for Civil Pluralism: New Religious Writings and Their Audiences." In *Oxford Journal of Islamic Studies* 1 (1997).

Ernst, Carl. *Words of Ecstasy in Sufism*. Albany: State University of New York Press, 1985.

———. *Eternal Garden: Mysticism, History, and Politics at a South Asian Sufi Center*. Albany: State University of New York Press, 1992.

Fakhrī, Mawlānā Raḥīmbakhsh. *Shajarat al-anwār*. MS 22/31, Habib Ganj Collection. Maulana Azad Library: Aligarh Muslim University.

Fakhrī, Sayyid Nūr al-Dīn Ḥusayni. *Fakhr al-ṭālibīn* (*malfūẓāt of Mawlānā Fakhr al-Dīn Dihlavī)*. Delhi: Maṭba'-i Mujtabā'ī, 1315.

Farmānish, Raḥīm. *Aḥvāl va āsār-i 'Ayn al-Qużāt*. Tehran: Chāp-i Āftāb, 1338/1959.

Figl, Johann. *Die Mitte der Religionen: Idee und Praxis universalreligioser Bewegungen*. Darmstadt: Wissenschaftliche Buchgesellschaft, 1993.

Fuller, Jean Overton. *Madeleine*. London: Gollancz, 1952; revised edition, *Born for Sacrifice* (London: Pan Books, 1957); revised edition, *Noor-un-Nisa Inayat Khan* (Rotterdam and London, East-West Publications and Barrie & Jenkins, 1971).

Furūzānfar, Badī' al-Zamān. *Aḥādis-i masnavī*. Tehran: Amīr Kabīr, 1366/1987.

Gardet, Louis. *Experience mystique en terre non-chretienne*. Paris: Alsatia, 1954.

Ghai, R. K. *The Shuddhi Movement in India*. New Delhi: Commonwealth Press, 1990.

Ghālib, Mīrzā Asād Allāh Khān. *Kulliyat-i nashr-i Ghālib*. Kanpur: Naval Kishūr, 1875.

Ghawsī Shaṭṭārī Mandvī, Muḥammad. *Gulzār-i abrār*. Translated by Faẓl Aḥmad Jīvrī. Lahore: Islamic Book Foundation, 1326/1908–09.

Ghazālī, Abū Ḥāmid Muḥammad. *Kitāb Asrār-i 'ishq yā daryā-yi maḥabbat, tarjuma-yi baḥr al-maḥabba fī asrār al-muwadda*. Tehran: Chāpkhāna-yi 'Alī, 1325/1956.

Ghazālī, Aḥmad. *Sawāniḥ*. Edited by Helmut Ritter. Tehran: Markaz-i Nashr-i Dānishgāhī, 1368/1989.

———. *Majālis*. Edited by Aḥmad Mujāhid. Tehran: Intishārāt-i Dānishgāh-i Tihrān, 1376/1997.

———. *al-Tajrīd fī kalīmāt al-tawḥīd*. Cairo: Sharīkat Maktabāt wa Matba'āt Muṣṭafā al-Bābī al-Ḥalabī, 1967. German edition: *Der reine Gottesglaube: das Wort des Einheitsbekenntnisses: Ahmad Al-Gazzalis Schrift At-Tagrid fi kalimat at-tawhid*. Translated by Richard Gramlich. Wiesbaden: F. Steiner, 1983.

———. *Makātib-i Khwaja Aḥmad Ghazālī bi 'Ayn al-Qużāt Hamadānī*. Edited by Nasrollah Pourjavady. Tehran: Khaniqāh-i Ni'mat Allāhī, 1977.

———. *Sawanih: Inspirations from the World of Pure Spirit*. Translated by Nasrollah Pourjavady. London: KPI, 1986.

Gīsū Darāz, Sayyid Muḥammad. *Asmār al-asrār*. Edited by Sayyid 'Aṭā' Ḥusayn. Hyderabad: A'ẓam Istim Pres, 1341/1922–23.

———. *Maktubat*. Edited by Sayyid 'Aṭa' Ḥusayn. Hyderabad: Barqi Press, 1362/1943.

———. "*Risāla azkār-i Chishtiyya*." In *Majmū'a Yāzda Rasā'il*. Hyderabad: Intiẓāmī Pres, n.d.

———. *Sharḥ zubdat al-ḥaqā'iq, al-ma'rūf bi sharḥ-i tamhīdāt*. Hyderabad: Kitābkhāna-yi Gulbarga Sharīf, 1364/1945.

Goodenough, Sherifa Lucy. *Love, Human and Divine*, Voice of Inayat. London: The Sufi Publishing Society, 1919.

Graham, Sharif, ed. *The Sufi Message: Index to Volumes I–XIII*. Delhi: Motilal Banarsidass, 1990.

Gulpinarli, Abdulbaki. *Mevlânâ Muzesi: Yazmalar Katalogu*. Ankara: Turk Tarih Kurumu, 1967–1972.

Gulshanābādī, Imām al-Dīn Aḥmad. *Tazkīrat al-ansāb*. Bombay: n.p., n.d.

Ḥali, Alṭāf Ḥusayn. *Yādgār-i Ghālib*. Translated by K.H. Qadiri. Delhi: Idarah-i Adabiyat-i Delli, 1990.

Hamadānī, 'Ayn al-Qużāt. *Tamhīdāt*. Edited by 'Afīf 'Usayrān. Tehran:

Kitābkhāna-yi Manūchihrī, 1373/1994. French edition: *Les Tentations Metaphysiques*. Translated by Christiane Tortel. Paris: Les Deux Oceans, 1992.

———. *Nāma-hā-yi 'Ayn al-Qużāt Hamadānī, vols. 1 and 2*. Edited by 'Alī-Naqī Munzavī and 'Afīf 'Usayrān. Tehran: Bunyād-i Farhang-i Irān, 1363/1983.

———. *Nāma-hā-yi 'Ayn al-Qużāt Hamadānī, vol. 3*. Edited by 'Alī-Naqī Munzavī. Tehran: Intishārāt-i Asāṭīr, 1377/1998.

———. *Zubdat al-ḥaqā'iq*. Edited by 'Afīf 'Usayrān. Tehran: Intishārāt-i Dānishgāh-i Tihrān, 1961.

Hasan, Mohibbul. *History of Tipu Sultan*. Calcutta: World Press, 1951.

Hermansen, Marcia. *The Conclusive Argument from God: Shah Walī Allāh of Delhi's Ḥujjat Allāh al-bāligha*. Leiden: E.J. Brill, 1996.

Hoorn, Theo van. *Herinneringen aan Inayat Khan en het Westers Sufisme (Memoirs of Inayat Khan and Western Sufism)*. The Hague: East-West Publications, 1981.

Hoyack, Louis. *Die Botschaft von Inayat Khan*. Zurich: Bollman, n.d.; Dutch original: *De Boodschap van Inayat Khan*, Deventer: Kluwer, n.d. 1947?

al-Hujwīrī, 'Ali B. Uthmān al-Jullābī. *The Kashf Al-Maḥjūb*. Translated by Reynold A. Nicholson. London: Gibb Memorial Trust, 1976; reprinted as *Revelation of the Mystery*, Accord, NY: Pir Publications, 1999.

Husain, Yusuf. *The First Nizām: The Life and Times of Nizāmu'l-Mulk Āsaf Jāh*. Bombay: Asia Publishing House, 1963.

Ḥusaynī, Sayyid Akbar. *Jawāmi' al-kalim* (*malfūẓāt* of Sayyid Muḥammad Gīsū Darāz). Kanpur: Intiẓāmī Press, 1356/1937–38.

Hussaini, Syed Shah Khusro. *Sayyid Muḥammad al-Husaynī-i Gīsūdirāz: On Sufism*. Delhi: Idarah-i Adabiyat-i Delli, 1983.

Ibn al-'Arabi, Muhyiuddin. *The Wisdom of the Prophets [Fusus al-Hikam]*. Translated by Titus Burckhardt and Angela Culme-Seymour. Aldsworth: Beshara Publications, 1975.

———. *Whoso Knoweth Himself, from the Treatise on Being (Risale-t-ul-wujudiyyah)*. Translated by T.H. Weir. London: Beshara Publications, 1976.

———. *La parure des abdal (Hilyatu-l-Abdal)*. Translated by Michel Valsan. Paris: Arche/Edidit, 1992.

Inayat Khan, Hazrat (Prof. 'Ināyat-khān Raḥmat-khān Paṭhān). *Ināyat gīt ratnāvalī*. Baroda and Mumbai: The Auspices of the Government of Sayājīrāo Mahārājā Gaekwaṛ, 1903.

———. *Inayat hārmoniyam śikṣak pustak pahalā*. Baroda and Mumbai: The

Auspices of the Government of Sayājīrāo Mahārājā Gāekwāṛ, 1903.
———. *Inayat phiḍal̤ śikṣak.* Baroda and Mumbai: The Auspices of the Government of Sayājīrāo Mahārājā Gāekwāṛ, 1903.
———. *Minqār-i mūsīqār.* Allahabad: Indian Press, 1912. English translation by Allyn Miner forthcoming.
———. *A Sufi Message of Spiritual Liberty.* London: The Theosophical Publishing Society, 1914.
———. *Songs of India.* London: The Sufi Publishing Society, 1915.
———. "Moula Bux." *The Sufi Quarterly* 1, no. 3, 1915.
———. "The Music of India." *The Sufi Quarterly* 2, April 1916.
———. *Hindustani Lyrics.* London: The Sufi Publishing Society, 1919.
———. "Pir-o-Murshid's Address." *The Sufi Quarterly*, January, 1920.
———. *The Unity of Religious Ideals.* London: The Sufi Movement, 1921.
———. *Nirtan or the Dance of the Soul.* London: The Sufi Movement, 1928.
———. *The Divine Symphony or Vadan.* London/Southampton: The Sufi Movement, 1931.
———. *Rasa Shastra: The Science of Life's Creative Forces.* Deventer: Kluwer, 1938.
———.*The Sufi Message of Hazrat Inayat Khan.* 12 vols. London: Barrie and Rockliff/Jenkins, 1960–67; revised edition, 13 vols., 1973–1982; new revised series in process under title *A Sufi Message of Spiritual Liberty*, 14 vols., various publishers, 1991– .

The Way of Illumination. Vol. 1. (also known as *Inner Life*)
The Mysticism of Sound. Vol. 2.
The Art of Personality. Vol. 3.
Health. Vol. 4. (also known as *Healing and the Mind World*)
Spiritual Liberty. Vol. 5.
The Alchemy of Happiness. Vol. 6.
In an Eastern Rose Garden. Vol. 7.
Sufi Teachings. Vol. 8.
Unity of Religious Ideals. Vol. 9.
Sufi Mysticism. Vol. 10. (also known as *Path of Initiation*)
Philosophy, Psychology, Mysticism. Vol. 11.
The Vision of God and Man, Vol. 12.
Sacred Readings, The Gathas. Vol. 13; revised 2000, as *Wisdom of Sufism: The Gathas.*
The Smiling Forehead. Vol. 14.

———. *Complete Sayings.* New Lebanon: Sufi Order Publications, 1978.
———. *Unity of Religious Ideals.* New Lebanon: Sufi Order Publications, 1979.
———. *Mastery (Through Accomplishment).* New Lebanon: Sufi Order Publications, 1979; revised 1985, Omega Publications.
———. *The Music of Life.* New Lebanon: Omega Publications, 1983.
———. *The Soul Whence and Whither.* Edited by Elise Guillaume Schamhart. Hounslow: East-West Publications, 1984.

———. *The Complete Works of Pir-o-Murshid Hazrat Inayat Khan.* London: East-West Publications, 1988–90; New Lebanon, NY: Omega Publications, 1996–

1923 II: July–December. Edited by Munira van Voorst van Beest.

1923 I: January–June. Edited by Munira van Voorst van Beest.

Sayings I. Edited by Munira van Voorst van Beest, 1989.

Sayings II. Edited by ed. Munira van Voorst van Beest.

1922 I. Edited by Munira van Voorst van Beest and Donald Sharif Graham.

1922 II. Edited by Munira van Voorst van Beest and Donald Sharif Graham.

———. *Notes from the Unstruck Music from the Gayan of Inayat Khan.* Edited by Munira van Voorst van Beest and Sharif Graham. New Lebanon: Omega Publications, 1988.

———. *The Complete Recordings of 1909.* Calcutta: The Gramophone Company of India NF 1 50129-30, 1994. Stereo double CD set.

———. *Creating the Person: A Practical Guide to the Development of Self.* New Lebanon: Omega Publications, 1995.

———. *The Mysticism of Sound and Music.* Boston: Shambhala Publications, 1996.

Inayat Khan, Pir Vilayat. *The Message in Our Time.* New York: Harper and Row, 1979.

Inayat Khan, Zia. "Sufism and Modernity: Aspects of the Life and Teachings of Pir-o-Murshid Inayat Khan." *Heart and Wings: the Quarterly Journal of the Sufi Order International* Winter, 2000.

'Iraqi, Fakhruddin. *Fakhruddin 'Iraqi: Divine Flashes.* Translated by William Chittick and Peter Lamborn Wilson. Ramsey, N.J.: Paulist Press, 1982.

'Iṣāmī. *Futūḥ as-salāṭīn.* Translated by Agha Mahdi Husain. Aligarh: Department of History, Aligarh Muslim University, 1967.

Jahānābādī, Shāh Kalīm Allāh. *Kashkūl-i Kalīmī.* Delhi: Maṭba'-i Mujtabā'ī, 1308/1890–91.

———. *Maktūbāt-i Kalīmī.* Delhi: Maṭba'-i Mujtabā'ī, 1315/1897–98.

Jairazbhoy, Nazir. *The Rags of North Indian Music: Their Structure and Evolution.* London: Faber & Faber, 1971.

Jāmī, Nūr al-Dīn 'Abd al-Raḥmān. *Nafaḥāt al-uns min hażarāt al-quds.* Edited by Mahmūd 'Ābidī. Tehran: Intishārāt-i Iṭṭilā'āt, 1373/1953–54.

———. *Nafaḥāt al-uns min ḥazārat al-quds.* Edited by Mahdī Tawḥīdīpūr. Tehran: Intishārāt-i Kitābfurūshī-yi Maḥmūdī, 1337/1958.

———. *Lawa'ih: A Treatise on Sufism.* Translated by E.H. Whinfield and Mirza Muḥammad Kazvini. London: Royal Asiatic Society, 1914.

———. *Les jaillissements de lumière. Lavayeh.* Edited by Yann Richard. Paris: Les Deux Oceans, 1982.

Jamman, Shaykh Jamāl al-Dīn. *Muntakhaba-yi dīvān-i Jamman*. Hyderabad: Maṭba'-i 'Azīz, n.d.

Jervis, James. "The Sufi Order in the West." In *New Trends and Developments in the World of Islam*, edited by Peter Clark. London: Luzac Oriental Press, 1997.

al-Jīlānī, Shaykh Abd al-Qādir. *Utterances (Malfūzāt)*. Translated by Muhtar Holland. Houston: Al-Baz, 1992.

al-Jīlī, 'Abd al-Karīm. *Universal Man*. Translated by Titus Burckhardt and Angela Culme-Seymour. Sherborne: Beshara Publications, 1983.

Jironet, K. "The Image of Spiritual Liberty." Ph.D. dissertation, University of Amsterdam, 1998.

Johnson, K. Paul. *Initiates of Theosophical Masters*. Albany: State University of New York Press, 1995.

Jodjana, Raden Ayou. *A Book of Self Re-education*. Essex: L. N. Fowler, 1981.

al-Kalābādhī, Abū Bakr. *al-Ta'arruf li-madhhab ahl al-taṣawwuf*. Edited by Maḥmūd Amīn al-Nawawī. Cairo: al-Maktaba al-Azhariyya, 1412 /1992.

Kamali, Mohammad Hashim. *Prinicples of Islamic Jurisprudence*. Cambridge: Islamic Texts Society, 1991.

Kapileśvari, Bālakṛṣnabua. *Abdul Karīm Khān: Yanche Jīvan Charitra* Bombay: B. Kapileśvari, 1972.

Kaufmann, Walter. *The Ragas of North India*. Bloomington: Indiana University Press, 1974.

———. *The Ragas of South India*. Calcutta/Bombay and New Delhi: Oxford University Press and IBH, 1976.

Keesing, Elisabeth de Jong-. *Inayat Khan: a biography*. The Hague: East-West Publications, 1974; revised edition New Delhi: Munshiram Publishers, 1981. Second revised edition forthcoming 2001.

———. *Inayat Answers*. London: Fine Books and East-West Publications, 1977; reprinted as *A Sufi Master Answers*, Delhi: Motilal Barnarsidass, 1997.

Khān, Ghāzī al-Dīn. *Manāqib-i Fakhriyya*. Delhi: n.p., 1315/1897–98.

Khān, Muḥammad Kāmgār. *Majālis-i Kalīmī (malfūẓāt of Shāh Kalīm Allāh Jahānābādī)*. Hyderabad: Maṭba'-i Burhāniyya, 1328/1910.

Khān, Sir Sayyid Aḥmad. *Asār al-ṣanādīd*. Edited by Khalīq Anjum. New Delhi: Urdu Academy, 1990.

Khān, Vilayat Husain. "*Fan mūsīqī ke kuc baḍe fankār*." In *Ajkal, mūsīqī ank*. N.p., n.p., 1957.

Kirmānī, Awḥāduddīn Ḥamīd ibn Abī'l-Fakhr. *Heart's Witness: The Sufi Quatrains of Awḥāduddīn Kirmānī*. Translated by B.M. Weischer and P.L. Wilson. Tehran: Imperial Iranian Academy of Philosophy, 1978.

al-Kirmānī, Sayyid Muḥammad Mubārak al-'Alawī (Amīr Khwurd). *Siyar*

Siyar al-awliyā'. Delhi: Maṭba'-i Muḥibb-i Hind, 1302/1884–85.

Lal, Kishori Saran. *History of the Khaljis, A.D. 1290–1320*. Bombay: Asia Publishing House, 1967.

Lālā, Shaykh Rashīd al-Dīn Mawdūd. *Mukhbīr al-awliyā'*. MS, Royal Asiatic Society, Bombay.

Lawrence, Bruce B. *Notes from a Distant Flute*. Tehran: Imperial Iranian Academy of Philosophy, 1978.

———. "The Chishtīya of Sultanate India: A Case of Biographical Complexities in South Asian Islam." In *Charisma and Sacred Biography*, edited by M.A. Williams. Chico, CA: Scholars Press, 1981.

———. "The Early Chishtī Approach to Samā'." In *Islamic Society and Culture: Essays in Honour of Professor Aziz Ahmad*, edited by Milton Israel and N.K. Wagle. Delhi: Manohar, 1983.

———, translated by. *Nizam ad-din Awliya: Morals for the Heart*. Mahwah, N.J.: Paulist Press, 1992.

Lelyveld, David. *Aligarh's First Generation*. Princeton: Princeton University Press, 1978.

Lewis, Samuel L. *The Jerusalem Trilogy: Song of the Prophets*. Novato: Prophecy Pressworks, 1975.

———. *Sufi Vision and Initiation*. San Francisco and Novato: Sufi Islamia/Prophecy Publications, 1986.

Lewis, Franklin. *Rumi: Past and Present, East and West*. Oxford: Oneworld, 2000.

Lewisohn, Leonard. "In Quest of Annihilation: Imaginalization and Mystical Death in the *Tamhīdāt* of 'Ayn al-Quḍāt Hamadhānī." In *Classical Persian Sufism: from its Origins to Rumi*, edited by L. Lewisohn. New York: Khaniqahi Nimatullahi Publications, 1992.

Luther, Narendra. *Hyderabad: Memories of a City*. London: Sangam Books, 1995.

Maḥmūdī, Ḥāfiẓ Muḥammad Munīr al-Dīn. *Shajarat al-Maḥmūd*. Hyderabad: Maṭba'-i Gulzār, 1304/1886–87.

Mahmood Khan, Shaikh al-Mashaik. "Music and the Mystic." *Caravanserai* 7, Dec 1992.

Malti-Douglas, Fedwa. *Woman's Body, Woman's World: Gender and Discourse in Arabo-Islamic Writing*. Princeton: Princeton University Press, 1991.

Maneri, Sharaf ad-Din. "On the Necessity of Proper Intention." In *Windows on the House of Islam: Muslim Sources on Spirituality and Religious Life*, edited by John Renard. Berkeley: University of California Press, 1998.

Massignon, Louis. *La Passion de Ḥusayn Ibn Manṣūr Ḥallaj: martyr mystique de l'Islam, execute a Bagdad le 26 mars 922*. Paris: Editions Gallimard, 1975. English edition: *The Passion of al-Hallaj*. Translated by Herbert Mason. Princeton: Princeton University Press, 1982.

Meisami, Julie S. *Persian Court Poetry*. Princeton: Princeton University Press, 1987.

Melton, Gordon J. "Sufi Order." In *Encyclopedia of American Religions*. Detroit: Gale Research, 1989.

Metcalf, Barbara D. *Islamic Revival in British India: Deoband, 1860–1900*. Princeton: Princeton University Press, 1982.

Mihr, Ghulām Rasūl, ed. *Khuṭūṭ-i Ghālib*. Lahore: Shaykh Ghulām 'Alī, 1957.

Minault, Gail. *The Khilafat Movement: Religious Symbolism and Political Mobilization in India*. New York: Columbia University Press, 1982.

———. *Secluded Scholars: Women's Education and Muslim Social Reform in Colonial India*. Delhi: Oxford, 1998.

Miner, Allyn. *Sitar and Sarod in the 18th and 19th Centuries*. Delhi: Motilal Banarsidass, 1997.

Misra, Satish C. *The Rise of Muslim Power in Gujarat: A History of Gujarat 1298-1442*. New York: Asia Publishing House, 1963.

Monna, M.C. *Short Dictionary of the Foreign Words in Hazrat Inayat Khan's Teachings*. Alkmaar, The Netherlands: Stichting Bewustzijn, 1991.

Mourik Broekman, M.C. van. *Geestelijke Stromingen in het Christelijk cultuurbeeld*. Amsterdam: Meulenhoff, 1949.

Mujāhid, Aḥmad, ed. *Majmū'a-yi āsār-i fārsī-yi Aḥmad Ghazālī*. Tehran: Intishārāt-i Dānishgāh-i Tihrān, 1358/1979.

Musharaff M. Khan. *Pages in the Life of a Sufi*. London: Rider, 1932, reprint, Wassenaar: Mirananda, 1982.

Naqvī, Imām Murtazā. *Khwāja Ḥasan Niẓāmī: Fann awr shakhṣiyat*. Karachi: Urdu Academy Sindh, 1991.

Nasafī, 'Azīz al-Dīn. *Insān al-kāmil*. Tehran: Kitābkhāna-yi Ṭahūrī, 1359/1980.

Nasr, Seyyed Hossein. *Three Muslim Sages*. Delmar: Caravan Books, 1976.

———. *Islamic Spirituality I*. New York: Crossroad, 1987.

Nawn, Munira. "An Old Mureed Remembers." In *Forty years of Sufism, 1910–1950*. Deventer: Nic. Kluwer, 1950.

Nekbakht Foundation, ed. *The Biography of Pir-o-Murshid Inayat Khan*. London/The Hague: East-West Publications, 1979.

Nicholson, Reynold A. *Rūmī: Poet and Mystic*. London: George Allen and

Unwin Ltd, 1964.

———. *Selected Poems from the Divani Shamsi Tabriz*. Cambridge: Cambridge University Press, 1977.

al-Niffarī, 'Abd al-Jabbār. *The Mawāqif and Mukhāṭabāt of Muḥammad Ibn 'Abdi'l-Jabbār al-Niffarī*. Translated by Arthur J. Arberry. London: Luzac, 1935.

Niẓām al-Dīn Awliyā', *see* Sijzī, Amīr Ḥasan.

Nizami, K.A. *Tarīkh-i Mashā'ikh-i Chisht*. Delhi: Nadwat al-Muṣannifīn, 1953.

———. *The Life and Times of Shaikh Farid-ud-din Ganj-i-Shakar*. Delhi: Idarah-i Adabiyat-i Delli, 1973, reprinted 1987.

———. *Akbar and Religion*. Delhi: Idarah-i-Adabiyyat-i-Delli, 1989.

———. *The Life and Times of Shaikh Nizamuddin Auliya*. Delhi: Idarah-i Adabyat-i Delli, 1991.

———. *The Life and Times of Shaikh Nasiruddin Chiragh*. Delhi: Idarah-i Adabyat-i Delli, 1991.

Niẓāmī, Khwāja Ḥasan. *Roznāmcha bā-taṣvīr: Safar-i-Miṣr va Shām va Ḥijāz*. Meerut, India: Hashimī Press, 1913.

———. *Sikh qawm*. Batala: Khwāja Press, n.d.

———. *Risāla-yi Shaykh Sanūsī*. Meerut: Hashimī Press, 1914.

———. *Fayzān-i Shaykh Sanūsī Part 3*. Meerut: Hashimī Press, 1914.

———. *Shaykh Sanūsī*. Delhi: Muḥammad Ṣādiq, 1915.

———. *Fransisī darvīsh ke malfūẓāt*. Delhi: Muḥammad Ṣādiq, 1915.

———. *Tark-i gā'o-kushī*. Delhi: Thakur Das and Sons, 1920.

———. *Government awr khilāfat*. Batala: Niẓāmiyya Book Depot, 1920.

———. *Āp bītī*. Delhi: Khwāja Awlād Kutub Ghar, 1922.

———. *Bīvī kī ta'līm*. Delhi: Ḥalqa-i Mashā'ikh Book Depot, 1924.

———. *Ta'rīkh-i Masīḥ*. Delhi: Mashā'ikh Book Depot, 1927.

———. *Namūna bi jang-i Ṣiffīn*. Delhi: Ḥalqa-i Mashā'ikh, 1927.

———. *Tazkira-i Musulmān Māhārāna*. Delhi: Ḥalqa-i Mashā'ikh, 1927.

———. "*Yūrup meṅ Chishtiyya taḥrīk* (The Chishti movement in Europe)." *Roznāmcha*, Jan. 8, 1933.

———. *A Modern Gulistan for Modern Man: Ex-King Edward's Diary, "The Sufi's Secret of Real Happiness"*. Translated by M. Fazl al-Ḥaqq. Delhi: Munādī, 1937.

———. *Kirshin kathā*. 5 ed. Delhi: Anṣārī Press, 1941.

———. *Amāl-i Ḥizb al-baḥr*. Delhi: Khwāja Kutub Ghar, 1952.

———. *Murshid-ko sajda-yi ta'ẓim*. Delhi: Khwāja Awlād Kitābghar, ca. 1970.

———. *Niẓāmī Bansurī*. New Delhi: Khwāja Awlād Kitābghar, 1984, reprinted 1990.

Pallandt, Floris baron van. "Hazrat Inayat Khan's Life and Work." In *The Sufi Message and the Sufi Movement*. London: Barrie and Rockliff, 1964.

Pinto, Desiderio. *Piri-Muridi Relationship: A Study of the Nizamuddin*

Dargah. New Delhi: Manohar, 1995.

Pourjavady, Nasrollah. *Sulṭān-i ṭarīqat*. Tehran: Intishārāt-i Nigāh, 1358/1979.

———. *'Ayn al-Qużāt va ustādān-i ū*. Tehran: Intishārāt-i Asāṭīr, 1374/1995.

———. *Rū'yat-i māh dar asmān: La vision de Dieu en théologie et en mystique musulmanes*. Tehran: Markaz-i Nashr-i Dānishgāhī, 1375/1996.

Pritchard, James B. "The Descent of Ishtar in the Nether World." In *The Ancient Near East*. Princeton: Princeton University Press, 1950.

Qalandar, Ḥamīd. *Khayr al-majālis (malfūẓāt of Shaykh Naṣīr al-Dīn Maḥmūd Chirāgh)*. Edited by K. A. Nizami. Aligarh: Department of History, Aligarh Muslim University, 1959.

Qureshi, Regula Burckhardt. *Sufi Music of India and Pakistan: Sound, Context and Meaning in Qawwali*. Chicago: University of Chicago Press, 1995.

Qushayrī. *al-Risālat al-qushayriyya*. Edited by 'Abd al-Ḥalīm Maḥmūd. Cairo: Dār al-Kutūb, 1972.

———. *Principles of Sufism*. Translated by Barbara von Schlegell. Berkeley: Mizan Press, 1990.

Ravan-Farhadi, A.G. *Ma'nī-yi 'ishq nazd-i Mawlānā*. Tehran: Intishārāt-i Asāṭīr, 1372/1993.

Rawlinson, Andrew. *The Book of Enlightened Masters*. Chicago: Open Court, 1998.

Rizvi, S.A.A. *Shāh Wāli-Allāh and His Times*. Canberra, Australia: Ma'rifat Publishing House, 1980.

Robinson, Francis. "Technology and Religious Change: Islam and the Impact of Print." *Modern Asian Studies* 1, no. 27 (1993).

Robson, James. *Tracts on Listening to Music*. London: The Royal Asiatic Society, 1938.

Rosse, Michael. "The Movement for the Revitalization of 'Hindu' Music in Northern India, 1860–1930: The Role of Associations and Institutions." Ph.D. dissertation, University of Pennsylvania, 1995.

Russell, R., and K. Islam. *Ghalib: Life and Letters*. Cambridge: Harvard University Press, 1969.

Rūmī, Jalāl al-Dīn. *Kulliyāt-i Shams (Dīvān-i Shams-i Tabrīzī)*. Edited by Badī' al-Zamān Furūzānfar. Tehran: Dānishgāh-i Tihrān, 1336/1957; reprint 1363/1984.

———. *Divan-i kabir*. Edited by M. Furūzānfar. Tehran: Publications of the University of Tehran, 1345.

———. *Masnavī*. Edited by Muḥammad Isti'lāmī. Tehran: Kitābfurūshī-yi Zavvār, 1362/1983.

———. *Divani Shamsi Tabriz*. Translated by Reynold A. Nicholson. San Francisco: Rainbow Bridge, 1973.

Sadiq, Muhammad. *A History of Urdu Literature*. Delhi: Oxford University Press, 1984.

Safi, Omid. "Did the Two Oceans Meet? Connections and Disconnections between Ibn al-'Arabī and Rūmī." *Journal of the Muhyiddin Ibn 'Arabi Society*, xxvi (1999).

Saintsbury-Green, Sophia. *The Wings of the World or The Sufi Message as I See It*. Deventer: E. Kluwer, 1934.

Sanā'ī, Ḥakīm. *Dīvān-i Ḥakīm Abū al-Majd Majdūd ibn Adām Sanā'ī Ghaznavī*. Edited by Mudarris Razavī. Tehran: Intishārāt-i Sanā'ī, n.d.

Sanyal, Usha. *Devotional Islam and Politics in British India: Ahmad Riza Khan Barelwi and his Movement, 1870–1920*. Delhi: Oxford University Press, 1996.

Sarkar, Jadunath. *Fall of the Mughal Empire*. New Delhi: Orient Longman, 1988.

Sāvī al-Qādirī, Mawlvī Muḥammad Makhdūm Ḥusayn. *Risāla mīzān al-tawḥīd*. Hyderabad: Maṭba'-i Burhāniyya, 1311.

Schimmel, Annemarie. *Mystical Dimensions of Islam*. Chapel Hill: University of North Carolina Press, 1975; reprinted, 1978.

———. *The Triumphal Sun*. London: Fine Books, 1978.

———. "Women in Mystical Islam." In *Women and Islam*, edited by Azizah Al-Hibri. Oxford: Pergamon Press, 1982.

———. *I am Wind, You are Fire*. Boston: Shambhala, 1992.

Sells, Michael. *Mystical Language of Unsaying*. Chicago: University of Chicago Press, 1994.

Shams-i Tabrīzī. *Maqālāt-i Shams-i Tabrīzī*. Edited by Muḥammad 'Alī Muwaḥḥid. Tehran: Intishārāt-i Khwarazmī, 1369/1990.

Siddiqi, Muhammad Suleman. *The Bahmani Sufi Orders*. Delhi: Idarah-i Adabiyat-i Delli, 1989.

Sijzī, Amīr Ḥasan. *Fawā'id al-fū'ād (malfūẓāt of Shaykh Niẓām al-Dīn Awliyā')*. Lucknow: Naval Kishūr, 1326.

———. *Nizam ad-din Awliya: Morals for the Heart*. Translated by Bruce Lawrence. Mahwah, N.J.: Paulist Press, 1992.

Singh, Gopal. *Sri Guru Granth Sahib*. Chandigarh: World Sikh University Press, 1978.

Sipāhsālār. *Risāla-yi Sipāhsālār*. Edited by Sa'īd Nafīsī. Tehran, 1325/1947, reprint, Iqbal Press, 1368/1989.

Spear, Percival. *Twilight of the Mughals*. Cambridge: Cambridge University Press, 1951.

Stam, Kismet. *Rays*. The Hague: East-West Publications, 1970.

Stolk, Sirkar van, and Daphne Dunlop. *Memories of a Sufi Sage*. Wassenaar: East-West Publications, 1967.

Subkī. *Ṭabaqāt al-shāfi'iyya*. Cairo: 'Īsā al-Bābī al-Ḥalabī, 1964.

Sufism Reoriented. "Sufism Reoriented 1948–1980." In *Sufism Speaks Out: Sufism Reoriented Responds to Attacks from India*. Walnut Creek: Sufism Reoriented, 1981.

Suhrawardī, Shaykh al-Ishrāq Shihāb al-Dīn. *Risāla fī haqīqat al-'ishq: Majmū'a-yi maṣannafāt-i Shaykh-i Ishrāq*. Edited by S.H. Nasr. Vol. 3. Tehran: Pazhūhishgāh-i 'Ulūm-i Insānī va Muṭāla'āt-i Farhangī, 1373/1953–54.

———. *The Mystical and Visionary Treatises*. Translated by W.M. Thackston, Jr. London: Octagon Press, 1982.

Sulaymānī, Hajjī Najm al-Dīn. *Manāqib al-maḥbūbayn*. Translated (Urdu) by Prof. Ikhtiyār Aḥmad Chishtī. Lahore: Islamic Book Foundation, 1979.

T'Serclaes de Kessel, Ryckloff-Michael Cunningham baron de. "Biography of the Author." In *A Sufi Message of Spiritual Liberty*. London: Theosophical Publishing Society, 1914.

Ṭābi', Sayyid Murād 'Alī. *Tazkirat-i awliyā'-i Ḥaydarābād*. Hyderabad: Minar Book Depot, 1972.

Tagore, Sourindro Mohun. *Universal History of Music*. Varanasi: Chowkhamba Sanskrit Series Office, 1963.

———. *Hindu Music from Various Authors*. Varanasi: Chowkhamba Sanskrit Series Office, 1965.

Thursby, G. R. *Hindu-Muslims Relations in British India: A Study of Controversy, Conflict, and Communal Movements in North India 1923–28*. Leiden: E.J. Brill, 1975.

Tirmizi, S.A.I. "Mughal Documents Relating to the Dargah of Khwaja Mu'inuddin Chishti." In *Muslim Shrines in India*, edited by Christian W. Troll. Delhi: Oxford University Press, 1989.

Valsan, Michel. "*Etudes traditionelles: Publication exclusivement consacree aux doctrines metaphysiques et esoteriques d'Orient et d'Occident.*" *Editions Traditionelles*, no. 9 (1949).

Waldman, Marilyn Robinson. "Tradition as a Modality of Change: Islamic Examples." In *History of Religions*, vol. 25, 1986.

Widdess, Richard. *The Rāgas of Early Indian Music: Modes, Melodies and Musical Notations from the Gupta Period to c.1250*. Oxford: Clarendon Press, 1995.

Wilson, Peter Lamborn. *Scandal: Essays on Islamic Heresy*. Brooklyn: Autonomedia, 1988.

———. *Sacred Drift*. San Francisco: City Lights, 1993.

Witteveen, Dr. H. J. *Universal Sufism*. Shaftesbury: Element Books, 1997.

Wolkstein, Diane, and Samuel Noah Kramer. *Innana: Queen of Heaven and Earth, Her Stories and Hymns from Sumer*. New York: Harper and Row, 1983.

Wāḥidī, Mullā. *Savāniḥ 'umrī: Khwāja Ḥasan Niẓāmī*. Delhi: Munādī Khwāja Number, 1957.

Yusuf 'Ali, 'Abdullah. *The Holy Qur'an*. Lahore: Sh. Muhammad Ashraf, 1973.

———. *Meaning of the Holy Qur'an*. Maryland: Amana Publications, 1989.

Zaidi, Ali Jawad. *A History of Urdu Literature*. Delhi: Sahitya Academy, 1993.

Zarcone, Thierry. "Central Asian Influence on the Early Development of the Chishtiyya Sufi Order in India." In *The Making of Indo-Persian Culture*, edited by Muzaffar Alam, Françoise Delvoye and Marc Gaborieau. New Delhi: Manohar, 2000.

Contributors

Jerome W. "Aziz" Clinton began his academic training in English, receiving degrees from Stanford (A.B. 1959) and the University of Pennsylvania (M.A. 1962). After spending two years with the Peace Corps in Iran (1962–64) he switched fields and went on to earn M.A. and Ph.D. degrees in Persian and Arabic literature from the University of Michigan (1972). As part of his graduate training he spent two years in Tehran as a Fulbright-Hayes scholar. He returned to the U.S. in 1970 to teach at the University of Minnesota (1970–72). From Minnesota he returned to Iran to serve as director of the Tehran Center of the American Institute of Iranian Studies. In 1974 he joined Princeton's Department of Near Eastern Studies where he has remained ever since. At Princeton he has taught all levels of Persian as well as courses in Islamic Culture, Persian literature in translation, and seminars on various literary topics—most recently: "The Theme of the Martyred Hero in Classical and Modern Literature," and "Women and the Feminine in Classical Literature." He has supervised dissertations on topics from Firdawsi to Gulshiri. Aziz Clinton's chief professional interests have been language teaching, translation, and, most importantly, literary criticism. He has published studies of a number of classical poets including Manuchihri Damghani, Khaqani Sharvani, Abu al-Qasim Firdawsi, Jalal al-Din Rumi and Shaykh Sa'di, and the modern writers Jalal Al-i Ahmad, Simin Danishvar and Ghulamhusayn Sa'idi. He has a number of translations to his credit as well. The most notable of these are verse translations of two stories from the *Shahnama*. The first of these, *The Tragedy of Sohrab and Rostam*, was published by the University of Washington Press in 1987 and reissued in 1998. The second, *In the Dragon's Claws: the Story of Rostam and Esfandiyar*, was published by Mage Books in the summer of 1999. He is co-author (with Donald L. Stilo) of a textbook, *Modern Persian: Spoken and Written*.

Donald A. "Sharif" Graham was born in Pasadena, California, in 1942. He was graduated from Yale (B.A. 1963 *magna cum laude*), M. Phil. 1974) and The University of California at Berkeley (M.A. 1965). He taught Comparative Literature and Religion at The University of Arizona and

Pima College in Tucson, Arizona, for thirty years. In 1970 he began an intensive study of Sufism, which soon became his main interest. Since 1982 he has worked each summer in Suresnes, France, on *The Complete Works of Pir-o-Murshid Hazrat Inayat Khan*, a major editorial project of which six of an anticipated twenty volumes have appeared to date. In 1998, he and his family moved to Suresnes to work full-time on this project. He has edited several books of Pir-o-Murshid Inayat Khan and Pir Vilayat Inayat Khan, and has written numerous articles on Sufism in various journals. He often travels, giving seminars on the work of Pir-o-Murshid Inayat Khan.

DR. MARCIA HERMANSEN is Professor of Theology at Loyola University Chicago where she teaches courses in Islamic Studies and World Religions. She received her Ph. D. from the University of Chicago in Arabic and Islamic Studies. In the course of her research and language training she lived for extended periods in Egypt, Jordan, Iran, and Pakistan. Her book, *The Conclusive Argument from God*, a study and translation (from Arabic) of Shah Wali Allah of Delhi's *Hujjat Allah al-Baligha* was published in 1996. Dr. Hermansen has also contributed numerous academic articles in the fields of Islamic Thought, Islam in South Asia, Muslims in America, and Women in Islam. She is an initiate of the Chishti-Nizami line through Hazrat Afzal al-Din Nizami, a *khalifa* of Khwaja Hasan Nizami.

RADEN AYOU JODJANA was born about 1885 in the Netherlands. She studied music, and performed as a singer under the name Madame de Ravalieu. Stranded in London during the First World War, through one of her music pupils she met Inayat Khan, and became his mureed. She was given the name Khurshid, teaching and performing as Khurshid de Ravalieu until her marriage to the Javanese dancer Raden Mas Jodjana, whose performances were celebrated all over Europe. Living into her nineties, she continued teaching throughout her life, having many admiring pupils in France, Britain and the Netherlands.

SHAIKH AL-MASHAIK MAHMOOD KHAN (b. 1927), only son of Shaikh-ul-Mashaik Pyaromir Maheboob Khan, head of the Sufi Movement and Order, 1927–1948, studied History and Musicology at Leiden University. Finding himself, on both the paternal and maternal (Dutch-

Friesian and Netherlands-Indian) side, an actual or potential heir to a wholly embarrassing array of nominal and titular designations at a time when feudal and patrician societies were fast disappearing, he at first intended concentrating fully on family affairs, leaving the representation of Sufism to his Inayatide cousins; a position become untenable after the early death of his father in 1948. He subsequently held numerous honorary Sufi appointments, including membership of the Executive Committee from 1948 onwards, but in 1958 declined the Sufi leadership succession when opened to him over the heads of three more senior candidates. As a member of the then Sufi Co-operative Leadership, 1982–1993, in 1988 he again refused an invitation of his fellow joint leaders to function as Head of the Sufi Order, the Movement's central 'Esoteric School Activity'.

Meanwhile he had gradually been abandoning his Subcontinental roots, after the collapse of the Indian 'States and Estates' system; still effecting, however, as incumbent on him under an agreement accompanying his succession as fifth Shaikh al-Mashaik, its complementary full secularization as Shaikh-i Mahashaikhan, in Europe then rendered as 'Archshaikh', etc. In a belated transition from leisure to career, from 1967 onwards he acted as Public Relations Advisor to the Pakistan Embassy at the Hague, then as Policy Staff Officer in the Netherlands Ministry of Foreign Affairs, retiring in 1988. He has since been fully focusing anew on the Sufism of Hazrat Inayat Khan.

PIR VILAYAT INAYAT KHAN is a senior statesman of the world spiritual community, and the author of several well-known books, including *Toward The One; The Message in Our Time; That Which Transpires Behind That Which Appears;* and *Awakening: A Sufi Experience.* He is the head of the Sufi Order International, a learning community that offers a universal approach to spiritual development. Through the depth of his knowledge and the power of his presence, Pir Vilayat introduces an ancient stream of wisdom—present in all religions and humanistic philosophies—into his lectures, seminars and retreats.

Pir Vilayat is the elder son of Hazrat Inayat Khan; he recalls his mother telling him that, upon his birth in June 1916, his father said "my successor is born." He also tells of sitting with his father on the sofa in the Oriental Room of Fazal Manzil, the family home in Suresnes, on the last Sunday of the summer school in 1926, shortly before Hazrat Inayat Khan returned to India. Pir Vilayat describes his father, during their conversation, turning his gaze toward his feet and saying "you will follow in my footsteps."

He pursued the study of music until Murshida Fazal Mai Egeling, whom the children of Inayat Khan considered as a grandmother, advised him that a training in music would not prepare him to take on the responsibility left to him by his father. At this point, Pir Vilayat pledged himself to fulfil his father's mandate. He studied philosophy and psychology at the Sorbonne, and did graduate work in at Oxford. During WWII he served in the British Royal Navy.

In due course he traveled to India several times, visiting sages in the Himalayas, making retreats in caves at the source of the Ganges, and living as a *sanyasin*. He pursued the study of meditation, and made retreats at the *dargahs* of Sufi saints in Ajmer, Shiraz, Hyderabad and at his father's *dargah* in Delhi. For the past half century, Pir Vilayat has honored his pledge through tireless work for the message of spiritual liberty, following in the footsteps of his father.

PIRZADE ZIA INAYAT KHAN is the eldest son of Pir Vilayat Inayat Khan, born in 1971 in Novato, California. He received his B.A. from the London School of Oriental and African Studies and his M.A., in Religious Studies, from Duke University. Since February 2000, he has served as President of the Sufi Order International, North America.

PROF. R.C. MEHTA was born on 31 October 1918, in Surat, Gujarat, India. Until his retirement in 1978, he served as Principal of the College of Indian Music, Dance and Dramatics (formerly the Baroda State Gayan Shala, founded by Prof. Mawlabakhsh), a constituent of the Maharaja Sayajirao University of Baroda. Musician and academician, Prof. Mehta has served the cause of music education in India, having affiliation with several music faculties in India. As a vocalist, he is the follower of the Kirana style of music of the late Chishti-Sabiri Sufi musician, Ustad 'Abd al-Wahid Khan. Author and editor of a number of books on Indian music, Prof. Mehta is the founder and secretary of the Indian Musicological Society, established in 1970. Presently his research interests include the music and philosophy of Mawlabakhsh and Inayat Khan. He is one of the managing trustees of the Sangeetratna Maulabakhsh and Sufi Hazrat Inayat

Khan Memorial Trust, established in Baroda in 1999. He is based in Baroda.

MURSHID WALI ALI MEYER was born in Starkville, MS, in 1942. He was college newspaper editor of the year in 1962 for editorials at the University of Alabama supporting integration and human rights. Elected to Phi Beta Kappa, he received a graduate fellowship in philosophy to Vanderbilt University, where he received an M.A. in philosophy. In 1968 he became the disciple of Murshid Samuel L. Lewis. He later became his personal factotum, poetry secretary and esoteric secretary. In 1970 he was initiated as a Sheikh by Murshid S.A.M., and two years later founded Khankah Sufi Ahmed Murad Chishti in San Francisco. He edited for publication a number of Samuel Lewis' writings, including *The Jerusalem Trilogy*. For eight years he was Chairman of the Humanities Department at The Tandem School. He now travels extensively, teaching Sufism at seminars and camps around the world.

ALLYN MINER has a Ph.D. in Musicology from Banaras Hindu University and a Ph.D. in Sanskrit from the University of Pennsylvania, where she teaches courses on literature and performing arts in the Department of South Asia Regional Studies. Her research and publications focus on Sanskrit, Hindi, and Urdu sources on the history of music in North India. She is also a performer on the *sitar* and is a disciple of Ustad Ali Akbar Khan.

SEYYED OMID SAFI is Assistant Professor of Islamic Studies and Comparative Religion at Colgate University in Hamilton, NY. He received his Ph.D. in Islamic Studies from Duke University. He teaches classes on Islamic mysticism, theories for the study of religion, Iran, and comparative mysticism. His research specialty is 11th to 13th century Persian Sufism, focusing on figures such as 'Ayn al-Qużāt Hamadānī, Aḥmad Ghazālī, and Mawlana Jalāl al-Dīn Rūmī. He is presently preparing a translation of 'Ayn al-Qużāt's *Tamhidat* for publication.

PETER LAMBORN WILSON'S latest works related to Islamic esotericism include *Shower of Stars: Dream and Book: Initiatic Dreaming in Sufism and Taoism* (Autonomedia: Brooklyn, 1996) and *Sacred Drift: Essays on the Margins of Islam* (City Lights: San Francisco, 1993). Omega

Publications has recently (1999) republished his co-translation (with Nasrollah Pourjavady) of *Drunken Universe: An Anthology of Persian Sufi Poetry*. His latest book is *Ploughing the Clouds: The Search for Irish Soma* (City Lights, 1999). He is the Metropolitan Governor of the Moorish Orthodox Church, Manhattan Lodge, al-Taha Temple #2.

Index

A

S